THE NEW
INDIVIDUALISTS

THE NEW INDIVIDUALISTS

The Generation After The Organization Man

Paul Leinberger
Bruce Tucker

HarperCollins*Publishers*

FIRST EDITION

Designed by Alma Orenstein

Library of Congress Cataloging-in-Publication Data

Leinberger, Paul, 1947–
    The new individualists : the generation after *The organization man* / Paul Leinberger and Bruce Tucker.—1st ed.
        p.   cm.
    Includes index.
    ISBN 0-06-016591-X
    1. United States—Social conditions—1945– 2. Whyte, William. Organization man. 3. Individualism—United States. 4. Baby boom generation—United States. 5. Organizational behavior—United States. 6. Social ethics. I. Tucker, Bruce, 1948– . II. Title.
HN65.L365 1991
306'.0973—dc20   90-55932

91 92 93 94 95 AC/HC 10 9 8 7 6 5 4 3 2 1

In memory of

Hugo Leinberger
(1918–71)

and

Randy Tucker
(1916–60)

reluctant organization men

Contents

Acknowledgments

The authors wish to thank, above all, William H. Whyte, Jr., whose *The Organization Man* has remained the most compelling portrait of middle-class Americans at midcentury and the starting point for all subsequent investigations of their legacy. His generosity with his original files, note-books, and interview materials made the present book possible. Most helpful of all were his encouragement and, early on, his advice to "follow your own trails."

We also could not have done without the gracious cooperation of the hundreds of interview subjects who let us into their offices, their homes, and their lives. We are especially grateful to the Myerses and the Harrisons, two extraordinary families who bore with good humor and understanding our incessant poking into every corner of their histories.

At HarperCollins, William Shinker has been a valued supporter. Hugh Van Dusen guided the project with skill and tact—it is an honor to have him as an editor. Copy editor Wendy Almeleh cast a sharp eye on the final manuscript. We are also deeply grateful to Harriet Rubin, who oversaw the book's initial stages and whose astute suggestions spared us many blind alleys. Carol Mann, who engineered the authors' collaboration, has, as always, been the perfect combination of agent and friend.

A grant from the Chicago Resource Center, a private foundation, supported early research. For help in tracking down some of Whyte's original subjects and conducting initial interviews with them, we are grateful to William G. Livingston and Julie Milburn. Among the many people who offered advice, criticism, intellectual sustenance, and other, less easily characterized forms of support are Albert Anderson, Peter Brown, Mary Bannon Burt, Royal Foote, John Hindle, Mitzi Zilka McCauley, Charles R. Morgan, Barry Phegan, Nevitt Sanford, and Charles P. Wolff.

Paul Leinberger wishes to thank Susan Harris Leinberger for her constant support, good-humored patience, and love, and Harper Jess Leinberger for refraining from being born until the book was completed. In addition, Ralph and Barbara Whitehead, on constant call throughout the project, provided invaluable insights and much gentle advice. And Richard Dennis, founder of the Chicago Resource Center, was an early believer.

Bruce Tucker wishes to thank his wife, Harriet Davidson, whose unpretentious mastery of contemporary theory, in her conversation and her writing, helped unlock some of the central ideas in the book. Katie Tucker, age five, provided insights of an altogether different, though no less helpful, kind.

A collaboration is an organization of sorts, and, as with any organization, individual contributions are hard to trace. Paul Leinberger originated the project, enlisted Whyte's cooperation, and directed the initial research. He is primarily responsible for the material in Chapters 1, 8, and 9. Bruce Tucker is primarily responsible for the material in the introduction and in Chapters 2, 3, 5, 6, 7, and 10, and for the final rewriting of the entire manuscript with an eye toward unity of style and argument. For Chapters 4 and 11, the authors bear roughly equal responsibility.

Finally, the dedication of the book to the memory of our fathers, as so often happens where organization men are concerned, unintentionally slights the wives who loved them—in this case, Ruth M. Leinberger and Ouida Tucker. This book is also for them.

INTRODUCTION

The New Individualists: Authentic Selves and Artificial Persons

An unprecedented transfer of power is about to take place in American life. In corporations, universities, foundations, government, and virtually every other kind of private and public enterprise, the organization men, born between 1915 and 1929, will soon give way to the baby boomers, male and female, born between 1946 and 1964. This passing of the torch will, in effect, skip over the generation born during the Great Depression and World War II, when birthrates were at a historic low. Never before in our history has power jumped a generation in this manner. Never before have the generation relinquishing power and the generation assuming power seemed so unlike.

Generation gaps are not new. To his farmer-father the midcentury organization man explained with difficulty the abstractions of management, the lure of the suburbs, the value of groupthink. The farmer-father explained to *his* father with difficulty why it was necessary to leave the safety of the eastern seaboard for the Great Plains or the old country for the new one. The fact that every generation has surpassed the previous one in wealth and, in the course of doing so, has profoundly altered and been altered by the social structure has always produced differences of values and outlook. In America, to follow in your father's footsteps is to stride far beyond them. The perverse twist in the present story is that the 75 million members of the baby-boom generation, including many of

1

the 19 million offspring of organization men, will likely be the first generation in American history that will not do better economically than its parents.

Nowhere do the differences between the organization man and his children appear more clearly than in their encounters with that acutely American struggle of the individual to come to terms with the group. The generation soon to retire enjoyed a relatively untroubled experience of the problem. From New Deal cooperation to overcome the Great Depression to mobilization for World War II to the fantastically successful collectivities of postwar corporate and suburban life, they found large-scale organizations and group identification effective and rewarding. By contrast, the generation on whom power will soon devolve has been known successively as the Woodstock Generation, the Me Generation, and Yuppies, reductive epithets that only begin to suggest the generation's enormously complex and troubled encounter with the age-old dilemma of the one and the many.

The classic study of the older generation's character appeared in 1956, when its exemplars were energetic junior executives and suburban housewives just beginning to believe that the postwar boom was real. Written by William H. Whyte, Jr., then a young editor at *Fortune* magazine, *The Organization Man* not only went on to become a landmark best-seller of its day but has remained the most widely read book on organizational life for more than thirty years. Indeed, the expression *organization man* has passed into everyday usage.

That expression, Whyte explained, was necessarily vague because the people he was talking about—neither hourly workers nor white-collar clerks—were found in every sort of enterprise. "The corporation man is the most conspicuous example," wrote Whyte, "but he is only one, for the collectivization so visible in the corporation has affected almost every field of work. Blood brother to the business trainee off to join Du Pont is the seminary student who will end up in the church hierarchy, the doctor headed for the corporate clinic, the physics Ph.D. in a government laboratory, the intellectual on the foundation-sponsored team project, the engineering graduate in the huge drafting room at Lockheed, the young apprentice in a Wall Street law factory."

Into their workplaces and their homes, their schools and their neighborhoods, their churches and their civic groups, Whyte followed this new breed of American employee. He talked with their wives, he observed their children, and he examined in detail one of their many new middle-class suburban developments—Park Forest, Illinois.

One of the Park Forest homes Whyte visited most frequently in the early 1950s belonged to Hugo Leinberger, the former U.S. Navy chaplain who founded the community's nondenominational Protestant church and, incidentally, fathered one of the authors of the present book. When that son, some thirty years later, began to wonder what had happened to organization men, their wives, and their children, the present project was born and, in concert with his coauthor, brought to completion.

With Whyte's cooperation and encouragement, the authors and a small team of researchers have tracked down and interviewed more than 175 of the organization men of his original study. We extended his work by seeking out their children and similar organization families, bringing to more than 300 the number of people we interviewed and in many cases reinterviewed. In addition, we devoted detailed attention to two representative organization families, who became the touchstones for much that we have to say here and whose stories took some dramatic turns as we continued to follow them during the seven years of the project.

During those seven years, the direction of the project itself took a dramatic turn. We began by wanting to know what paths the lives of the organization men had taken since Whyte had captured them as junior executives. We wanted to find out what had become of their careers and their marriages and how they felt now about the pact they had made with the organization so many years before. Had the organization, with its implied promise of lifelong employment in exchange for loyalty, held up its end of the bargain? Were the organization man and his wife satisfied by the affluent suburban life, much maligned by social critics, that their devotion to the organization had brought them? In a word, was it worth it? We did pursue those questions and we report our findings here.

But we also wanted to explore what kinds of lives were being pursued by the approximately 19 million adult children of the organization men. As we began to do so, we soon arrived at a crossroads. Were we going to study these organization offspring (as we shall henceforth call the now-adult children who grew up in families where the father toiled for a single, large organization for most of his working life), or were we going to study baby boomers now working in organizations? Obviously, not all organization offspring followed their fathers into large organizations, and just as obviously, not all baby boomers who currently work in organizations grew up in families of organization men. Depending on which road we took, we might arrive at vastly different destinations.

Others have preceded us on the road. Every five years or so, it seems, someone asks in print whether the organization man is dead. To find the answer, they have almost invariably looked only at people who are currently working in large organizations. And if they look at companies that are traditionally organization-man companies—Du Pont, for example—the organization man (and now also woman) turns out to be alive and well. If, on the other hand, they look at certain other companies—Apple, for example—the organization man appears to be extinct. But looking exclusively at organizations *of any kind* at a fixed point in time can be misleading. While such a strategy may produce a composite portrait of current employees, it ignores distinctions of age, social origins, and historical experience that may divide people far more than the fact of common employment unites them. And it leaves out of account their similarities with people outside the organization, people with whom many employees may have more in common than they do with the colleague—or the boss—in the next office.

Our early interviews confirmed this. The now-adult sons and daughters of the organization men—both inside and outside large organizations—resemble no one on Earth so much as they do each other. All these baby-boomer organization offspring—the middle manager chafing at the slow progress up the promotional ladder, the forest ranger dreaming of writing novels, the aging hippie getting by on marginal jobs, the gypsy scholar in today's brutal academic job market, the entrepreneur starting a software company, the corporate star rising rapidly, and the free-lance consultant seeking autonomy—are cut from the same cloth, though they may not realize it themselves. They have an identifiable style of personal relations; they engage in distinctive consumption practices, and they share similar views of organizations and of individualism.

Their striking similarities arise from their organization-family childhoods, their subsequent historical experience, and the consequences of being members of the largest generation in American history in an economy that has been sour for almost two decades. Though individual members of the generation may behave differently from each other—one may act like a so-called Yuppie, another may bash Yuppies unmercifully—we soon realized that their underlying motives, philosophical outlook, and values are identical. (One of the great ironies here, as we will see, is that all of them are stout individualists—*each in exactly the same way*.) In short, they form a unique and, as we also soon discovered, a radically changing social character.

Social character refers to that nexus in which individual personalities meet culture and social structure. By examining that encounter, it is possible to extract the general characteristics that predominate in a given group of people. In the past, such studies were sometimes glibly extrapolated to cover entire nations, suggesting a homogeneity that does not exist, especially in countries as multicultural and multiethnic as America. Many such studies also focused almost exclusively on collective social phenomena, such as rituals and institutions, at the expense of actual individuals, suggesting that societies merely produce appropriate social characters. But to arrive at a really useful notion of social character—what form it takes among a given group and how it came to be that way—it is necessary to look at real individuals *and* at the culture and society in which they are formed. Only then can we arrive at the really interesting question: What are the consequences of a particular form of social character for individuals and for the society?

Social character, far from merely "reflecting" society, can be wildly out of sync with it. For example, when industrialism forced many farmers and craftsmen into factory hierarchies, the characteristic independence of these groups often became obstinacy and obstructionism. Characteristics that had always served them well and had been rewarded by the society had become, almost overnight, out of phase with the social order, leading to wrenching dislocations for the workers and the society. In modern technological civilization, changes in the social order take place with even more dizzying rapidity, producing disjunctions between social structure and social character with increasing frequency.

This continual leapfrogging of social character and social structure is not a process that, in the long run, averages out or unfolds in a uniform and predictable way. Rather, different historical circumstances may produce various kinds of situations, conflicts, and crises. Moreover, different kinds of social character, produced by differences in group and generational experiences, may coexist at any one time. For example, as is currently happening with the organization man, far-reaching changes in the economic structure may render the society's dominant social character obsolete, though members of that group remain in power. The result may be institutional paralysis, loss of economic vigor, and failure of leadership. Or, as is currently happening with some of the organization offspring vis-à-vis the silent generation immediately above them, new social conditions may unexpectedly elevate people with one set of characteristics over those whose social character has been differently formed.

It should be obvious as well that it is not necessarily desirable that social structure and social character be in sync. A smoothly functioning social order—which makes the trains run on time—is hardly the highest mark of virtue in a society or in the individuals who make it up. And in thoroughly repellent social structures like that of South Africa, participation in a maladaptive social character becomes a badge of honor.

It should be equally obvious that social character is a framework for understanding the general characteristics of a group, not a calculus for predicting the specific behavior of individuals. It cannot foretell who will become the Yuppie, who the Yuppie basher; who the consultant, who the choreographer; who the entrepreneur, who the corporate soldier. But the notion of social character can make intelligible the behavior of all these seemingly disparate individuals; it can reveal the broad orientation out of which they operate, and it can provide clues about what is likely to happen to such people under particular social regimes.

Our direction, then, was clear: to pursue the social character of this coherent group of organization offspring, however they might live and wherever they might work, a pursuit that ultimately could be more rewarding than yet another ephemeral look at a cross section of corporate employees. Though the picture of their social character at which we arrived is intended to apply only to them—and certainly not to be extrapolated to all Americans—it is at least plausible that it may have wide application, because to focus on the offspring of the managerial class is tantamount to focusing on the American middle and upper-middle classes, the people who, historically, have run the technocracy and whose ideology has dominated American life for at least 150 years. Given the social location and sheer numbers of the organization offspring—in and out of organizations—they are, for better or for worse, likely to be decisive for the shape of American life to come.

In addition to concentrating on a particular social class, our view of social character also entails important assumptions about generations, dividing them according to a principle we believe to be crucial: their relative size. Recent work in many fields—demographics, the sociology of age, and relative income theory in economics—points to the overwhelming significance of the size of generations for what may be broadly called life chances: in housing, employment, education, marriage, family size, and just about every other aspect of social existence.

The interpretive method this scheme implies resembles some other familiar explanations of generational differences, but it should not be confused with them. One popular explanation, amounting almost to a folk belief, sees the differences between the organization man and his baby-boomer children solely in terms of their sharply contrasting childhood experiences. Many organization men themselves resort to this explanation. The hard times of the Great Depression, so the story goes, imbued the organization man with dedication to hard work, a craving for security, and a willingness to submerge his individuality in large organizations. Conversely, the good times of the 1950s are said to have imbued his children with indifference toward work, ignorance of economic reality, and an insistence on having their own way in all things.

Like many such folk stories, this one contains a good bit of truth. As we shall see, the Great Depression did leave an indelible mark on the organization man, just as the affluence of the fifties and sixties would leave an indelible mark on his children. But the folk formulation, often underpinned by popularizations of psychoanalysis, reductively assumes that adult life consists of merely living out the consequences of character acquired in childhood.

Another popular explanation for generational difference can be found in life-cycle theory. Based on the theoretical work of Erik Erikson and the empirical work of psychologist Daniel Levinson, the concept of the life cycle achieved widespread currency through Gail Sheehy's 1976 book *Passages*. Different age levels, the theory goes, are universally marked by different psychological characteristics and developmental tasks. Generational differences are therefore inevitable, though predictable and uniform. Unlike the folk story, life-cycle theory admits psychic change after childhood, but it discounts the substance of historical experience. According to simplifications of the theory, no matter what one's specific experiences may be, they will be filtered through the immutably fixed psychological stages associated with one's chronological age. Affluence or no, Great Depression or no, the forty year old, for example, is bound to have a midlife crisis.

In the midseventies, when Sheehy was popularizing Levinson's work, which was confined entirely to men, there were plenty of fortyish males experiencing profound unease. These were men of the silent generation who, having rarely experienced any kind of economic difficulty or competition for careers, suddenly found the expansive progress of their lives stalled by the economic problems of the time, precisely at a point in their careers when they should have been poised to make great leaps forward in prestige and power. They also found themselves squeezed between the large and undeniably accomplished generation of organization men above them and the baby boomers below (male and, for the first time, female) whose enormous numbers had assured that those who had survived were ferociously competitive and often prodigiously talented. No wonder that members of the silent generation suffered a "midlife crisis." But it was not an inevitable crisis of age forty; it was a historical crisis of the 1970s and early 1980s. There is no reason to suppose that in the future people will experience in large numbers any such forty-caused crisis or that they did so in any large numbers in the past. (For evidence, one need look no further than literature, from which midlife crises are strikingly absent before the 1970s.) Similarly, the youthful "identity crisis" owes more to industrialism's historical extension of adolescence upward than it does to chronological age. (Literature often portrays youthful identity crises, but only rarely before 1800, when the complexity of roles demanded by advanced industrial societies began to push back the time at which one entered fully into adult roles.)

Undeniably, psychological development continues throughout the life span, and the biological process from birth through maturity to death has a kind of shape. But the mechanistic life-cycle model ignores the role that social change plays in determining the life *course* and, therefore, the psychological "tasks" for any given age group. Because the varying rhythms of social change are unconnected to biological rhythms, people born at different times follow different life courses. *They age differently.* And at a higher level of generality, the same may be said of generations. Because of changing historical circumstances, various milestones of the life course—age at marriage, at entry into the work force, at birth of the first child, at birth of the last child, and at retirement—have all been subject to wide fluctuations down through the centuries, producing widely varying life courses in different epochs.

Rigid popular conceptions of a normal life course may bear little resemblance to the actual practice of large numbers of people. The life courses of organization offspring differ markedly from those of their parents, yet we cling to the notion that there is a normal life course from which all departures are seen as more or less deviant. Only when the reality of new practices becomes widely understood and accepted does a new conception of the normal life course emerge. Such recognition is slow to come and is usually preceded by hysterical warnings of social disorganization, the decline of the family, and the decay of morality. Today it is still the life course of the organization man and his wife that is seen as normal: As soon as you complete your education, you marry; enter the work force if you are male, take up homemaking if you are female; and have your first child almost simultaneously. By your midthirties, at the latest, you have the last of your two or more children. At age sixty-five men retire and women continue homemaking. By contrast, many baby boomers are said to have "prolonged" their adolescence by staying in school well into their twenties and even their thirties, to have married "late," and to have "delayed" childbearing. Such rhetoric often implies abnormal psychological or social development, though it should be obvious that this is the normal life course for this generation.

But what induces millions of people to make private decisions that, in the aggregate, constitute new norms for the life course? The answer—circular, of course—is social change. Changing conditions of work, leisure, economics, politics, and family life influence even the most intimate choices of life, and those choices precipitate further social change, which becomes the background for further personal decisions. None of this process is orderly or even particularly rational. Millions of private decisions, evoked by the social structure, backed with ideology, and channeled by cultural forms, lead to many complicated consequences, intended and unintended.

In fact, the organization man himself did not really follow the "normal" pattern. Obviously, World War II drastically altered the life course for millions of young Americans, affecting the timing of key life-course events like entry into the work force, marriage, and birth of the first child. Many women, who might otherwise not have done so, went to work. But so strong is the pull of the stereotype that we tend to regard the war as an aberration, an interruption of the "normal" life course by a rare cataclysmic event. We think of the postwar period as a time for reestablishing the norm, but it was no such thing. The organization man's life course was distinctly of its time and place; it was never seen before, and we are not likely to see it again.

The example of World War II points to two crucial factors—the nature of a historical event and where one is in one's life course when the event occurs. A war obviously affects people differently than does a famine or a period of great abundance. Somewhat less obviously, the same social, economic, or political event has, as we have said, differential effects for different age groups. A war, for example, affects the life course of young people differently from that of children or the elderly. One could say it has a different *meaning* for them. The Great Depression was, in the long run, far more devastating to males who were just about to enter the work force in 1929 than it was to males born that year, whom it could almost be said to have helped. Moreover, effects of social change differ not only with age but according to social class and gender. The Great Depression, as we will see, affected the organization man's wife-to-be far differently than it did him, and it affected working-class men and women differently from middle-class men and women. Similarly, the long-term slide of the American economy that began in 1973 has had vastly different meanings for the generations and for the gender and class divisions within them.

To do justice to all these complications and to throw into relief the different life courses of the two generations and the different social characters they produced within a single (and highly influential) social class, we began with the family. A consideration of the "organization family," as the phrase suggests, encompasses not only the kind of middle-class family in which our subjects grew up, but the social and economic order—the world of large organizations—in which that family was situated. Through the lens of the organization family, we are afforded a look not merely at occupations and incomes, but at a whole way of life. Thus, as the children moved to center stage in our work, it was easy to see why they form a coherent group. And by following the offspring of that way of life through their unique generational experience of subsequent American history—that is, through the *way* in which they aged—we arrived at the portrait of their social character presented in these pages.

In exceeding our original intentions, we were, in fact, returning to Whyte. For *The Organization Man* was nothing less than a sweeping portrait of American social character at midcentury, as it had been forming for fifty years. In Whyte's hands, the term *organization man* stood for far more than a kind of statistical average of current employees. It encompassed an entire way of life—its social forms, its historical and economic development, and its ideological justifications.

Whyte's original findings disturbed him. The organization man, he argued, was enthusiastically producing in American life a major shift from the Protestant ethic of the nineteenth century to what Whyte called the "social ethic" of the twentieth, a retreat from traditional American individualism he regarded with alarm.

In a real sense, the success of the Protestant ethic had helped destroy it. Secularized, its promise of individual salvation through hard work, thrift, and competitive struggle justified greed and the amassing of great wealth, which, paradoxically, produced a world of huge corporations that required complex bureaucracies, cooperative effort, and a culture of consumption for their growth and maintenance. The corporation gave the lie to the individual dream of success. The manager, hardly a self-reliant individualist, replaced the entrepreneur as the dominant reality of economic life. Though these organization men often spoke the language of individualism, they actually adhered to a set of beliefs that were more in harmony with their dependence on the organization. Contradicted by the reality of the organization, the Protestant ethic withered away.

There occurred also, said Whyte, an intellectual assault on the Protestant ethic carried out by pragmatist philosophers, muckrakers, and numerous reformers, all of whom emphasized the social and the practical. A fascination with the environmental pressure on the individual, of which Freud's theories are an early example, led at first to disillusionment. But American optimism, reluctantly relinquishing the idea of the perfectibility of the individual, soon turned to the perfectibility of society. In time there evolved a pervasive social ethic, by which Whyte meant the "contemporary body of thought which makes morally legitimate the pressures of society against the individual." Based on social science's dream of a unified, exact science of man and inspired by the work of the human-relations school of managerial theorists, the major propositions of the social ethic are "a belief in the group as the source of creativity; a belief in 'belongingness' as the ultimate need of the individual; and a belief in the application of science to achieve the belongingness." Thus was ushered in the era of the team player and the good guy, of family togetherness and the airtight security risk, of the well-rounded personality and the yes-man, of the happy homemaker and the well-adjusted child.

Whyte's book, like David Riesman's *The Lonely Crowd*, was widely misunderstood as another cry against superficial conformity. But Whyte was not ridiculing gray flannel suits, ranch wagons, or split-level houses. Nor was he calling for a petulant, quasi-bohemian revolt against the outward forms of social intercourse or organization. The social ethic, he said, draws its power not from expediency, but from the real moral imperative it embodies, the essentially utopian faith that there need be no conflict between the individual's aspirations and the group's wishes. The danger, he warned, lay not in the fact of organization itself, but "in our worship of it." And he reiterated Tocqueville's prophecy: "If America ever destroyed its genius it would be by intensifying the social virtues at the expense of others, by making the individual come to regard himself as a hostage to prevailing opinion, by creating, in sum, a tyranny of the majority."

As we pursued the story of the organization offspring, we continually asked ourselves whether Whyte's—and Tocqueville's—prophecy had come true. The answer is far from a simple yes or no, for it is not a simple question. While it would be pleasingly authoritative to report in ringing tones that individualism lives or to note mournfully its passing, either conclusion would be false to the complicated historical experience of the organization offspring. For the concept and reality of individualism have changed dramatically since Whyte, and certainly since Tocqueville, wrote; so have the concept and reality of organizations.

Continually evolving in meaning since the term was first coined during Tocqueville's time, *individualism* for Whyte was simply the antidote to the imprisoning brotherhood of the organization. By individualism, Whyte meant a principled opposition *within the organization* to the pressures of the social ethic. For the organization offspring, however, individualism became synonymous with individuality and with the cultivation of the private self. In effect, they took individualism, which had previously had a political and social component, and redefined it in entirely psychological terms. Though often regarding their parents (however affectionately) as repressed conformists, the organization offspring initially acquired their obsession with the self in the purely expressive arena of the homes created by those parents, who were largely unaware of what was taking place. These formative experiences were reinforced by the schools, the suburbs, the media, and suburban religiosity, all of which projected the self as the ultimate ground of value. As the organization offspring came of age in the sixties and seventies, they were exhorted to find themselves or create themselves. They undertook the task with fervor, as self-expression, self-fulfillment, self-assertion, self-actualization, self-understanding, self-acceptance, and any number of other *self* compounds found their way into everyday language and life. Eventually, all these experiences solidified into what can only be called the self ethic, which has ruled the lives of the organization offspring as thoroughly as the social ethic ruled the lives of their parents. Many people mistakenly regarded this development as narcissism, egoism, or pure selfishness. But the self ethic, like the social ethic it displaced, was based on a genuine moral imperative—the *duty* to express the authentic self.

As the foregoing sketch suggests, individualism is not only an idea that collides with the material circumstances of organization; it is a set of material circumstances. Conversely, organization is not only a set of material circumstances, it is also an idea. Whether we realize it or not, we carry around with us a philosophy of organization formed, like our individualism, from our cultural experiences. But while we have the term *individualism* to denote our philosophy of the individual, there is no comparable term to cover our philosophy of organizations. For now, the term *organizationalism* will have to serve. An ungraceful neologism, organizationalism is nonetheless useful in clarifying the issues. For although each term—*individualism* and *organizationalism*—must take the other into account, they are not identical. The former foregrounds the individual, and though it may move to a consideration of the group, including the special case of the organization, its fundamental unit is the individuals who compose groups. The latter foregrounds the organization, and though it may involve substantial assumptions about the nature of the individual, it also encompasses issues of authority and legitimacy, efficiency and responsibility, and process and purposes that may fall outside the purview of individualism.

To complicate matters further, Americans have, for more than a century, personified organizations. This habit of regarding the organization as if it were an individual is deeply embedded in American life. Recognized in law as "artificial persons," corporations are entitled to all the rights and privileges enjoyed by individual human beings. On the other hand, a single individual can incorporate himself or herself. These two metaphors, enshrined in law—corporation as person and person as corporation—only begin to suggest the contradictions that bedevil American thinking about organizations and about individuals.

The confusion has its roots in the late nineteenth century, when large corporations—railroads; telegraph companies; and, later, manufacturers and petroleum companies—began to dominate American life. Americans looked on the emerging corporate giants with a combination of fear and admiration. The plundering of the Erie railroad by the robber barons in the 1860s led Charles Francis Adams to warn that modern society had "created a class of artificial beings who bid fair soon to be the

masters of their creator. . . . Everywhere . . . they illustrate the truth of
the old maxim of the common law, that corporations have no souls." For
their part, the corporations, to justify themselves, adopted the rhetoric of
individualism, asserting that they were merely pursuing happiness, guaranteeing the sanctity of property rights, and making the most of equality
of opportunity. In 1886, the Supreme Court ratified the confusion, declaring corporations to be persons covered by the due-process clause of
the Fourteenth Amendment, which, ironically, had been designed originally to protect newly emancipated slaves from unfair treatment.

James Oliver Robertson, who has most thoroughly sorted through
the systematic confusion that governs our views of corporations, observes
that large corporations were often envisioned as vast machines or predatory animals. But, he adds, they were also seen to be operated by a
single individual intelligence—a John D. Rockefeller, J. P. Morgan, or
Henry Ford, men who took on heroic proportions and whose creations are
seen today as the immortal extensions of their individuality. Such confusion, however, serves an important psychological purpose:

> It is precisely the overlapping and confusion of the mythology of the
> corporation with the mythology of the individual—the incorporation
> of individualism—which continues to explain and justify great cor-
> porations to Americans. Throughout the twentieth century, Ameri-
> cans have feared for the independence—and the very survival—of
> the individual in the face of the onslaught of corporate bigness and
> its bureaucratic anonymity. The tension generated by the identifi-
> cation of individualism with corporations, by the admiration *and* fear
> of corporate efficiency, power, wealth, size, is exceedingly strong in
> American society today—but the myths of corporate individualism,
> of individualism incorporated, remain the explanations and continue
> to supply the logic Americans use to justify corporations.

As with other myths and metaphors we examine in these pages, the
notion of organizations as individuals represents an *imaginary* solution to
real contradictions. In this case, the contradictions are organized power
versus democratic values, bureaucratic domination versus personal freedom, authority versus legitimacy. They are, perhaps, finally irresolvable.
But imaginary solutions have real consequences both for individuals and
for organizations, for real persons and for artificial ones.

For one thing, each of the terms of a metaphor alters the others. To
think of corporations as individuals not only changes our concept of
organizations, it changes the way we think about individuals. An understanding of how these terms have been altered in our time and how they
alter each other in the metaphor of incorporated individualism should

take us a long way toward understanding the new social character now emerging in America. To anticipate a bit: We have not only individualized bureaucracies, we have bureaucratized individuals; our corporations have become psychic projections and our psyches corporate reflections. They—we—are all artificial persons now.

Furthermore, just as the terms of a metaphor alter each other, so does history alter the terms. Though the metaphor of incorporated individualism has remained in use for more than a century, the history of organizations and of individualism during that period has changed our concept of both. Large organizations arose, grew, and changed, creating and responding to the events that determined their particular character. That history, especially the portion of it the members of each generation experience in their unique life courses, conditions that generation's thinking about organizations. As we will see, the rising generation thinks about organizations in a radically different way from that of their parents. Similarly with individualism: Its character and the way we think about it change under the pressure of specific historical circumstances.

The thoroughly psychologized individualism of this generation is a historically unique development, with historically unique consequences. It is one thing to personify, say, the Ford Motor Company as an extension of an inventive and ambitious capitalist; it is quite another to endow that personification with a self. And yet that is what a significant portion of the organization offspring would come to do and continue to do. Their expressive individualism, first formed in the organization-man family and in the suburbs, schools, and churches of postwar affluence and eventually refined in the ideal of the authentic self, encountered the artificial person that is the organization. This encounter would produce two dominant strains of the generation's personified and psychologized organizationalism: the humanist and the egoist.

Like Charles Francis Adams, they would charge that corporations have no souls, that as artificial persons, organizations are inauthentic. But after initially turning in disgust from such organizations, some members of the generation would eventually demand that these artificial persons become more like real persons—more caring; more soulful; in short, more authentic. This forms the humanist strain of their organizationalism. But other members of the generation, though equally prone to conflate individuals and organizations, drew a radically different conclusion. If organizations have no souls, they reasoned, why should we? This forms the egoist pole of the generation's organizationalism. How this generation arrived at both these strains of organizationalism and their bearing on issues of authority and legitimacy make up a significant part of our story.

As we examined the collision—and intermingling—of the authentic self with the artificial person, we soon uncovered another means whereby the organization offspring, in a far more concrete way, attempt to bridge the gulf between the private world of the expressive self and the public world of work. In addition to placing creativity and self-expression at the center of their systems of value, nearly all the organization offspring we interviewed harbor artistic aspirations. This characteristic was something we neither expected to find nor looked for. In the beginning, we dismissed this constantly recurring theme as merely part of our time's reflexive cant about creativity. But our interviewees repeatedly expressed highly specific artistic hopes: They want to be musicians, filmmakers, screenwriters, actors, poets, novelists, dancers, or visual artists or to work in related fields. We were further surprised to find that this phenomenon is not confined to a few dreamers or dropouts, but is virtually universal among our subjects. It animates middle managers as well as entrepreneurs, youthful Yuppies as well as aging hippies, practicing artists as well as procrastinating pretenders. It makes no difference whether these ambitions will ever be realized; it is the dream that counts. Realistic or not, the artist figures as their *occupational ideal*. As such, it remains central to their conceptions of themselves, providing an imaginary solution to the lived contradictions of personal identity versus public roles, desire versus duty, happiness versus success, individual authenticity versus social artificiality. And like the psychologizing of organizations, the artist ideal represents an attempt to fuse the expressive values acquired at home in childhood with the instrumental values found at work in adulthood.

In pursuing the ideal of the authentic self, the offspring produced the most radical version of the American individual in history—totally psychologized and isolated, who has difficulty "communicating" and "making commitments," never mind achieving community. But by clinging to the artist ideal, the organization offspring try to escape the authentic self and simultaneously to maintain it as the ultimate value. It is a delicate balancing act to which many of them have been brought by the search for self-fulfillment, but it is a position that they are finding increasingly hard to maintain.

As our story will show, there are signs that the search for self-fulfillment is drawing to a close and with it, the era of the authentic self and its accompanying self ethic. The ideal of the authentic self is everywhere in retreat. It has been undermined from within; it has been attacked from all sides; and, in many ways, it simply has been rendered obsolete by history:

□ Self-fulfillment has proved to be unfulfilling, since the exclusive focus on the self has left many people feeling anxious and alone.

□ The inevitable economic problems experienced by large generations, coupled with the long-term souring of the American economy, have introduced many members of the generation, even the most privileged among them, to limits in all areas of life, including limits on the self.

□ Alternative and more inclusive conceptions of the self, especially those introduced into organizations by the influx of women, now challenge almost daily the more traditionally male conception of unfettered self-sufficiency.

□ The macroeconomic issues of takeovers, buyouts, and restructurings that have dominated organizations for the past five years have left little room for psychological concerns in the workplace.

□ The rise of a genuinely competitive global marketplace linked by instantaneous communications has accelerated the diffusive processes of modernity, further destabilizing the self.

□ The centuries-old philosophical bedrock on which all our conceptions of individualism have rested, including the highly psychologized individualism embodied in the authentic self, is being swept away.

□ Similarly, the most important developments in contemporary art *and popular entertainment* are subverting the conception of the artist on which the integrity of personalities who use the artist ideal to solve problems of identity depends.

□ The rise of postmetropolitan suburbs, which are neither center nor periphery, and the emergence of organizational networks, which replace older hierarchical structures, have thrust the new generation into concrete ways of life to which the authentic self is increasingly extrinsic.

Out of this slow and agonizing death of the authentic self, there is arising a new social character: the artificial person. This new social character is already discernible among a vanguard of the organization offspring and is now emerging among the remainder; it is likely to spread eventually throughout the middle class and, as often happens, attract the lower class and surround the upper.

It cannot be emphasized enough that the designation *artificial person* does not mean these people are becoming phony or insincere. Rather, it refers to a changing conception of what constitutes an individual and indeed *makes* someone individual. In the recent past, the organization offspring believed that individuality consists of a pristine, transcendant, authentic self residing below or beyond all the particular accidents of history, culture, language, and society and all the other "artificial" systems of collective life. But for all the reasons we have cited and many more besides, that proposition and the way of life it has entailed have become untenable. More and more the organization offspring are coming to see that the attributes they previously dismissed as *merely* artificial are what make people individuals—artificial, to be sure, but nonetheless persons, characterized by their particular mix of these ever-shifting combinations of social artificiality of every variety. Starting from this fundamental, and often unconscious, shift of perspective, they are evolving an individualism that is "artificial" but particular, as opposed to one that is authentic but empty. It is an individualism predicated not on the *self*, but on the *person*: while *self* connotes a phenomenon that is inner, nonphysical, and isolated, *person* suggests an entity that is external, physically present, and already connected to the world. In effect, it is the realization that *authentic self* is more of an oxymoron than is *artificial person*.

The way for this momentous change in the organization offspring's individualism has been prepared, in part, by their organizationalism. Their habit of personifying and psychologizing the organization as an artificial person takes in the many contending forces, elements, and people that make up the organization and envisions them as a single, albeit complex, individual. Now the organization offspring are beginning to import this feature of their organizationalism into their individualism, but they are reversing the image: Whereas the artificial person of their organizationalism allows them to see the many as one, the artificial person of their individualism allows them to see the one as many.

To help dissect this emerging social character, we have resurrected the three historical character types identified by David Riesman in *The Lonely Crowd*, a book roughly contemporaneous with *The Organization Man* and equally influential as a reading of American social character at midcentury. According to Riesman and company, the tradition-directed character type predominated in traditional societies, the inner-directed type predominated in nineteenth-century America, and the other-directed type had come to dominate by the time Riesman was writing. The differences among the types could be seen in the different emotional controls that kept each type on course in the world. Shame guided tradition-directed individuals, ensuring that they would follow the timeless traditions of their culture. Guilt, implanted early by parents, guided inner-directed individuals, ensuring that they would behave as their parents might. Anxiety guided other-directed individuals, ensuring that they would behave as their peers behaved.

Many readers mistakenly took Riesman to be saying that the inner-directed type was a rugged individualist, in contrast to the obsequious other-directed conformist. In fact, each of these character types represents a *mode of conformity* that dominated under specific historical conditions. "Inner" and "outer" referred only to the apparent source of the emotional sanctions. Inner direction originated internally as conscience or, in effect, the parentlike superego. Other direction originated externally as peer pressure and public opinion. But between the guilt-ridden inner-directed type and the anxiety-ridden other-directed type there was little to prefer. For Riesman the question is not *whether* individuals conform, but *how*.

To these three historical modes of conformity, we add a fourth: the subject-directed character type. For reasons we will unfold in the pages that follow, the emotional control in this emerging character type is mourning (originating, in part, from the "death" of the authentic self). The source of the sanction of mourning is simultaneously the artificial systems to which the person is *subjected* and the person's particular *subjectivity* in which those systems intersect in unique ways. Thus, the source of mourning is neither "inner" nor "outer," neither "self" nor "other," but arises as part of a more inclusive world in which such simple oppositions have little meaning. As we shall see, the subject-directed character type is remarkably, even alarmingly, open ended—like the culture he or she inhabits.

Despite this talk of mourning, subject direction echoes familiar themes of American optimism. Insofar as the sanction of mourning succeeds, it restores the mourner to the world. Far from appearing glum, such a character type appears to participate purposively, even optimistically, in the play of artificial cultural systems—the worlds of love, work, personal relations, and community. But such behavior, tempered by a simultaneously chastened and expanded sense of identity—one that is both *subjected* and *subjective*—resembles neither the mindless optimism of the booster nor the smug self-congratulation of authenticity. Like subject direction itself, the behavior in which it is manifest is ambiguous—having one foot in mourning and the other in great expectation.

Out of this unquantifiable mix of mourning and optimism, there is growing an accompanying enterprise ethic. Supplanting the self ethic but by no means harking back to the social ethic of the organization man, the enterprise ethic embodies the marching orders for this new social character. It is best understood by reference to the etymology of *enterprise*, which yields *undertaking*, a word having entrepreneurial as well as funereal connotations. In conjunction with mourning, enterprise then suggests something far more complicated than the largely illusory trumpeting of rugged individualism and entrepreneurship to which we were treated in the eighties.

Under the sway of the enterprise ethic, many of the organization offspring certainly appear to take bold risks; they change jobs and even careers with startling frequency, choose where they want to live and only then look for work, desert orthodox career paths in favor of fashioning their own situations, and prize personal freedom over job security and creativity over productivity. But the origins of these seemingly bold attributes may lie equally in the feeling of entitlement the organization offspring acquired in affluent childhoods—the sense that nothing can go wrong—and in the feeling of utter contingency acquired in adulthoods of constricted promise—the sense that there is nothing to lose. In their personal and professional lives, inside and outside organizations, their behavior will be marked by this contradictory temper—outwardly optimistic but based on a gnawing pessimism to which the work of mourning addresses itself.

To trace the evolution of this emerging social character and to do justice to changing historical circumstances and their differential effects on the generations, we have found it helpful to tell the story of the organization man and his offspring more or less simultaneously. For example, the story of the organization man's work life in the 1950s and 1960s is also the story of his children's early psychological development and their perceptions of affluence, suburbia, and their parents' lives. The story of the offspring coming to maturity in the eighties is also the story of the organization man in or nearing retirement.

Through extensive interviews, research, and our own perspectives on American social character and history, we arrived at the portrait presented here. But surveys and research instruments, social theory and history, though valuable, fail to capture the texture of lived experience. So, when possible, we have tried to let people speak for themselves and in some highly typical cases we have traced their stories in great detail.

Part 1 tells the story of two representative organization families: the Myerses and the Harrisons. Former residents of Park Forest and among Whyte's original subjects, Ray and Bee Myers, captured here at the end of the organization-man era, present a striking contrast to their three now-adult sons (one of whom declined to participate in our study) pursuing their lives in the perilous economy of the seventies and eighties. In the story of the other family, that of Dave and Helen Harrison and their four children, we look more closely at the crucible of suburban family life, where the expressive values, artistic longings, and great expectations that eventually issued in the self ethic were first forged. The story of the Harrison offspring, three of whom are female and all of whom departed from their parents' life courses, offers additional perspectives on the transmission of values, the experience of geographic and social mobility, and the effects of upbringing and the rupture of the sixties on choices of career and life-style. The Harrisons also introduce questions of gender and the organization that were simply unthinkable in the organization man's day.

These six organization offspring—two of the Myers boys and the three Harrison girls and one boy—are a diverse lot. Occupationally, they run the gamut from entrepreneur to consultant to middle manager to artist to college professor. Personally, they have experienced their share of marriages, children, divorces, and various economic circumstances and degrees of success. Individually, one might be characterized as a Yuppie, another as a counterculturalist, another as a feminist, another as an aesthete, another as a romantic—some of them earning more than one of these designations. They fall also at different points along the evolutionary line we are tracing from authentic self to artificial person. But like all organization offspring, their similarities unite them more than their differences separate them, and we think that readers who grew up in organization families will see themselves in some or all of these individuals.

Part 2 takes the issues raised in the family narratives of Part One and breaks them into their various components. Using the people presented in the two chapters of Part 1 as touchstones, we address these issues through a combination of exposition, summaries of our findings, and illustrative narratives from other interview subjects to trace the development of the organization offspring from authentic selves to artificial persons.

In Chapter 3, with which Part 2 begins, we explore how the life course of the older generation—from Great Depression to postwar affluence—intersected with the developmental experiences of their children to produce far-reaching consequences for family life, attitudes toward work, sex roles, and ultimately for the conception of the self. Chapters 4 and 5 form a diptych of what we have called this generation's organizationalism, formed when the authentic self of the individual met the artificial person of the organization. Chapter 4, "The Nervous System: From Cybernetics to Psytopia," explores the humanist strain of their organizationalism, ostensibly rooted in the sixties critique of "big business," but having much deeper and more tangled roots in the human-relations movement about which Whyte worried so famously. Chapter 5, "The I of the Beholder: Organizations as Egos," explores the egoist strain of organizationalism that first appeared in the stampede to business careers in the stagnant economy of the seventies and the destabilizing of organizations in the eighties.

By contrast, Chapters 6 and 7 form a diptych of the generation's individualism. Chapter 6, "Personal Artifice: From the Self-Made Man to the Man-Made Self," traces the development of the self ethic, the nature and dynamics of the authentic self, and the artist ideal through which members of the generation attempt to resolve the contradictions of their middle-class identities. Chapter 7, "The End of Authenticity," charts the personal experiences of the organization offspring, as well as developments in the larger culture that are conspiring to bring the reign of the self ethic to an end.

In Chapter 8, "Nobody Home, Nobody Gone: The New 'New' Suburbia," we explore a striking physical manifestation of the new world inhabited by artificial persons: the postmetropolitan suburbs now appearing across the American landscape. Chapter 9, "Networks and Niches: Emerging Organizational Life," treats another material reality now hastening the transformation of authentic selves into artificial persons: the new forms of organization that are developing in response to global competition, instantaneous communications, and a drastically changed business environment in which the chief factor of production is information. Taken together, these conditions support the continual creation of new organizational arrangements and processes—in short, permanent "adhocracy" that further destabilizes any sense of a substantial, acultural self.

Chapter 10, "Artificial Persons: The Rise of the Enterprise Ethic," describes the new American social character emerging with these far-reaching social changes. Though knowledge of the dominant social character and its accompanying ethic cannot predict the behavior of particular individuals, such knowledge can make that behavior intelligible. As we have said, social character is a framework, not a calculus. Nevertheless, we can speculate on what these momentous changes portend in large areas of life for the organization offspring:

□ The myth of personal artistry having died along with the authentic self, the organization offspring will construct their personal identities around the notion of the artists they are not, paradoxically turning their attention from an abstract sense of "creativity" to a concern with concrete creations.

□ In personal relations the impossible ideal of "honest" communication between authentic selves buried under layers of social artificiality will give way to the possibility of understanding between persons whose artificiality makes engagement possible in the first place.

□ In the occupational world, the children, utterly lacking their fathers' loyalty to a specific organization but under no illusions about how the world's work gets done, will be antiorganization but not antiorganizational, more inclined to join many ever-shifting networks than to seek a niche in one immortal hierarchy.

□ In social life, having abandoned the illusory search for the authentic self, they will seek fulfillment in conjunction with other people, but they will not seek the kind of community to which innumerable social commentators have exhorted them to return.

□ In their ethical and spiritual life, they will move beyond the purely self-absorbed morality of the self ethic, but they will not make up a significant part of the resurgence of organized religion so manifest in recent years.

Finally, we conclude with Chapter 11, "In the Spirit of the Enterprise Ethic: Organizational Life Reconsidered," in which we ask what the advent of this new individualism and these new individualists will mean for organizational life in the future. How will this paradoxical form of individualism transform the humanist and egoist strains of the generation's organizationalism? And how will it affect issues of authority and legitimacy in organizations? Given the rising generation's characteristics and a vastly changed economic environment, we explore whether the people just coming to power will be up to the job. That is the intriguing question Chapter 11, weaving together the psychological, social, and economic story we have told, attempts to answer in an even broader sense: whether the enterprise ethic will prove to be the right ideology at the right time or a disastrous mismatch of social structure and social character.

PART ONE

Two Families

1

The Myerses: The Passing
of Organization Man

"I plan everything."

Ray Myers didn't like the sound of it. Roger E. Anderson, the chairman
of the Continental Illinois National Bank and Trust Company, was not in
the habit of calling unscheduled meetings in the middle of the afternoon.

When the call came, the affable, energetic sixty-two-year-old general counsel of the bank was sitting at his desk making plans. "I plan
everything," Myers is fond of saying. "I plan my work, I plan my days,
I plan my life. And then I execute those plans."

But at this moment his mind was not on his legal responsibilities for
Continental; he was thinking instead of the new home he was having
built on the crest of a ridge overlooking the third hole of the Bobby
Jones–designed golf course in the resort community of Keystone, Colorado. In fewer than four weeks, on July 31, 1982, he planned to take early
retirement, to walk for the last time through the massive doors of Continental's Corinthian-style limestone, granite, and marble headquarters
in the heart of Chicago's financial district, to leave behind forever the
organization in which he had spent more than thirty-four years. He had
come to the end of a career that had taken him from a management
training position in the trust department to the very heights of one of the
premier banking institutions in the country. Now he was looking forward
to the pleasures of retirement—to long lazy afternoons lingering over a
good book, to days spent tinkering in his workshop, to chasing golf balls
around the country's most challenging courses. But most of all, he was
looking forward to "grand adventures" with his lovely and exuberant
wife, Bee.

Myers knew from the tone of the chairman's voice on the phone that something out of the ordinary had occurred. Roger Anderson, as Myers had come to know, was not given to melodrama. Anderson and Myers were contemporaries. Both had served in the navy during World War II and both had spent their entire corporate careers with the bank. They had known each other since the early fifties, when Myers, fresh out of Harvard Law School, had joined Continental. Over the years, as each had followed different paths up the corporate hierarchy, Myers had come to respect Anderson's considerable managerial talent. The Anderson style was conservative, unemotional, cautious—qualities to be expected in the head of the nation's eighth-largest bank.

But after taking the helm of the bank in 1976, Anderson had called a press conference to announce that the bank, intent on becoming one of the nation's top three lending institutions, would begin pursuing a newly aggressive loan policy. No longer content to play it safe by lending primarily to staid and stable Fortune 500 companies, the bank would now be making loans to the corporate middle market. Both the potential profits and the potential risks would increase dramatically. Initially, many observers wondered whether such a sober, prudent institution could pull it off. But if a levelheaded guy like Roger Anderson was willing to try, it was a move worth watching. Under Anderson's leadership, Continental's assets swelled from $23 billion in 1977 to $45 billion in 1981.

Stepping off the elevator near the second-floor conference room, Myers found a disturbing scene. Grim faced and murmuring, representatives of four of the country's largest banks stood waiting in the anteroom. Finally, Anderson called the meeting to order. "Gentlemen," he said, "we are here to discuss recent developments pertaining to suspected problems at Penn Square Bank."

The Federal Deposit Insurance Corporation (FDIC) had just dispatched a team of examiners to Oklahoma to investigate the wobbly financial condition of Penn Square, a small suburban bank in Oklahoma City. Over the preceding few years, a number of banks had been buying up portions of Penn Square's loan portfolio. Principal among them were Continental and the other four big banks represented at the meeting—Chase Manhattan, Northern Trust Company of Chicago, Michigan National Bank of Lansing, and Seattle First National Bank. Whatever financial virus was afflicting the smaller bank could thus spread to the larger ones. Continental's exposure was the greatest—a staggering $1 billion.

Myers was aware that Continental and the other four banks had been doing business with Penn Square, but he did not know the magnitude of the loan participations or the nature of the problems that had brought all these men to Continental's boardroom on that hot, humid July afternoon. The meeting was scheduled to take two hours. It lasted the entire weekend.

Then, on July 5, the comptroller of the currency declared Penn Square insolvent. According to the comptroller, the Oklahoma bank owned a portfolio of uncollectible loans whose face value exceeded the bank's capital. The FDIC moved in immediately to settle the bank's affairs. With the fate of Continental's participations in doubt and a quarterly report to stockholders fast approaching, Anderson asked Myers to postpone his retirement, to help put the situation in order.

The loyal and dedicated Myers agreed. Having already sold the family home, he and his wife moved into an apartment near Continental's headquarters. Myers spent the next two months working with the chairman and keeping board members apprised of developments.

When Myers finally retired, it appeared that Continental might come through relatively unscathed. Bank analysts and regulators were saying that the Penn Square failure was an isolated event for the industry and the banks involved. Myers said his good-byes and retired to the Colorado mountains.

But the analysts and regulators were wrong. Continental Illinois did not escape. In the months that followed, rumors swirled about the bank's condition. Inaccurate press reports triggered a run on its deposits. Through a massive infusion of credit and capital, the FDIC and a consortium of banks attempted to stop the hemorrhaging. The attempt failed. On July 26, 1984, the regulatory agencies announced a historic $4.5 billion rescue package. In a move widely viewed as de facto nationalization, the plan called for the FDIC to assume an 80 percent ownership stake in the bank, reducing shareholder ownership to 20 percent. In return, the FDIC pumped $1 billion in new capital into the bank to compensate for a $1.1 billion loss in the second quarter, the largest ever reported by an American bank. Anderson was replaced. Federal investigations uncovered examples of alleged mismanagement, recklessness, and business improprieties in the operation of the bank. Ray Myers, watching in retirement, was devastated.

"It was depressing," Myers says today in a carefully measured voice. "Terribly depressing. If someone asked me what I did, I would find myself saying, 'I was an attorney.' Where were you? 'I was in Chicago.' What kind of attorney? 'Well, I was general counsel for one of the major banks.' Instead of saying I was the general counsel for the Continental Bank of Chicago."

After all those years in the role of the organization man, Ray Myers suddenly found himself in a different role: the organization man betrayed.

Former colleagues believe his contention that he was unaware of Continental's problems until that July meeting in 1982. Says Richard S. Brennan, the current counsel: "To the extent that there was anything funny—and I'm not saying there was—the general counsel would be deliberately left out of the chain."

"Continental Bank to me was one of the great organizations," says Ray Myers. "It was rapidly moving toward being one of the largest banks in the country. Our competition, as far as we were concerned, was Morgan Guaranty, Citibank, Bank of America, and Chemical. We thought we were the cream of the crop, and then to have it all suddenly disintegrate. . . ." He trails off, shaking his head sadly.

"My goal was to give credit to somebody else."

Ray Myers, like most of the organization men William H. Whyte, Jr., originally studied, was a child of the Great Depression. The son of a school principal in Council Bluffs, Iowa, Myers was just nine years old when the stock market crashed in 1929. On Sunday mornings, he remembers, he often accompanied his father, a lay minister, as he made the rounds of nearby churches, preaching for ten dollars per sermon.

Times were hard, but not so hard that the son of a middle-class man whom the depression had not thrown out of work could not aspire to college. Hoping to follow in his father's footsteps, Myers enrolled in DePauw University, studying school administration. After graduation, he won a scholarship to Harvard University to pursue his master's degree. But the Japanese attack on Pearl Harbor changed his plans. Myers enlisted in the navy and spent the next four years breaking Japanese codes at the Office of Naval Intelligence in Washington, D.C.

It was an exciting time for the country's fifteen million new recruits. After years of drift during the depression, many servicemen suddenly found themselves with a secure job, steady pay, and, most important, a feeling of belonging. They found a home in the armed forces. And they found something else, as well: a chance to learn the ways of the biggest, most bureaucratic organization ever known. Young officers without a day's worth of supervisory experience found themselves in charge of hundreds of enlisted men. Men fresh out of boot camp found themselves responsible for millions of dollars worth of military hardware. They learned about teamwork and commitment, authority and obedience, many of them under fire. When the fighting ended and the veterans returned, many changed their career plans dramatically; Myers was one of them.

"After leaving the military," he says, "I knew that I wanted to go back to Harvard, but not to the school of education." He enrolled, instead, in Harvard Law School. As he neared the end of his program—accelerated for veterans who were impatient to get on with their lives—his career plans shifted again.

"I had learned from my experience in the service that I had some ability to organize and some ability to relate to other people," he says. "So as I began to think about getting a job, I decided that rather than using law as such, I was going to try and capitalize on those abilities."

It was not only democracy that had triumphed in the war; it was American management. Veterans, like Myers, came home eager to put into practice the organizational principles they had learned and confident of their ability to do it. But first they had to deal with the possibility of another depression, then being widely predicted by many economists. Housing was scarce, and wartime shortages persisted; millions of men were pouring back into the job market. The recession of 1949 intensified the anxiety.

The safest course, many veterans reasoned, was to sign up with large organizations, companies that could not be hurt in the event of a prolonged economic downturn. And so by the hundreds of thousands, American men exchanged their uniforms for gray flannel suits.

Upon graduation, Myers traveled to Chicago for an interview with Continental. A big firm in a big city was precisely what he was after, a firm that could provide both security and opportunity for advancement. He was offered what the bank called a "business development" position in the trust department. In effect, he would be a salesman, convincing wealthy prospects to do their estate planning with Continental.

"That was extremely interesting and exciting work," he says. "It was exciting because in sales you start out each year wondering how in the world you are going to make as many sales as you had last year. It was interesting because the people you were dealing with were people of means. They were interesting to me not because of the money they had but because of the success they'd had, the opportunities to travel and do things I couldn't do. I lived vicariously through hearing about their latest cruise or latest hunting trip or whatever. In those days I thought I would have been quite content to do that for the rest of my life—it was that stimulating."

Meanwhile, the gloom-and-doom forecasters were proving to have been dead wrong about the economy. They had somehow forgotten the savings Americans had been putting away during the war years. Liquid assets in savings accounts had increased from $50 billion to $140 billion. Americans were ready to devour as many consumer products as American industry could turn out. Between 1945 and 1960, the number of cars increased 133 percent. In 1954 alone, Americans bought 1.5 million new homes. That same year they purchased 1.4 million power lawn mowers, one of the hottest new consumer items on the market.

What America needed was professional managers who could handle massive growth. The issue was not quality, but quantity—turning out enough sewing machines; washing machines; dryers; television sets; electric irons; barbeque grills; tricycles; and, above all, automobiles to meet the demands of millions of young couples who were moving to the suburbs and having children in profusion. The population grew by 30 million in the 1950s, and for a time the rate of population growth approached that of India. In 1957 the fertility rate peaked at 123 and the birthrate at 25 per 100,000 (compared to a prewar fertility rate of 80 and a birthrate of 19 per 100,000). Between 1950 and 1960, 13 million homes were built in the United States, 11 million of them in the suburbs. During the 1950s, more Americans moved to suburbia each year than came to our shores during the height of the great European migration.

Ray Myers and his family led the pack. In early 1950, they were among the first families to move to Park Forest, Illinois. They had heard about a "model city" being built expressly for returning veterans and their brides on the outskirts of Chicago. It was on the Illinois Central commuter line, so Myers could take the train to his new job in the financial district, and the community was being planned with children in mind, so he and Bee could have the family they wanted. In 1951, *Pageant* magazine named Park Forest Community of the Year and wrote: "It was built . . . for young, white-collar families with a middling income and *kids*. The more kids the merrier. . . . The town has the look, feel and sound of youth. Youngsters make up forty per cent of the populace. Rental homes cluster about a parking circle and on a warm summer's night you're likely to find a neighborhood party in full swing. Everyone brings his own supper, and no one has to worry about baby sitters, for the children are within easy hearing." The magazine closed the article by proclaiming: "Here's to bigger and better Park Forests, stretched across the U.S.A.!"

Pageant got its wish. Park Forest and Levittown became models of the new prosperity and a new and distinctive way of life. Millions of young executives and their wives flocked to suburbia in search of a place where they could own their own homes, allow their children to run free, and enjoy relaxed and informal social relationships.

It was a unique time because in the early days of Park Forest everyone was about the same age and had the same problems and needs. Most of the men were veterans; a majority were just beginning their professional careers in large organizations. Most had no experience of organizational life, save what they had gained in the military, and the move to suburbia was the biggest move of their young married lives. The excitement, as well as the anxiety, of the times drew them together. The swarms of children created a continuous frenzy of activity. Young families joined to transport their children to piano lessons, Little League practice, and Brownie and Scout meetings. Young wives formed baby-sitting clubs to look after each other's kids and organized car pools to get their husbands back and forth to the commuter station. For many, the togetherness of suburban life was an extension of their experience in the military or their memories of fraternity or sorority life. Leisure was a series of kaffeeklatsches, bridge games, children's birthday parties in the "tot lot," potluck suppers, and barbecue and beer parties for the gang.

The Myerses fondly recall life in Park Forest's courts, as the clusters of homes were called. "We had extremely close friendships in the courts," Bee recalls. "There were ten or twelve couples who interacted constantly. Friendships grew out of the fact that you had children the same age with the same interests and so on."

Says Ray: "We never had any baby-sitting problems because our social lives revolved around the court. You'd be playing bridge with someone two doors away, and you'd just go home and check on the kids every now and then."

In its Easter 1954 issue, *McCall's* proclaimed all this "togetherness" as a new and highly desirable social trend. But many critics looked on with scorn and dismay. What they saw in suburbia was conformity, rootlessness, and blatant and vulgar materialism. Suburbia, they said, was creating an uncritical and unquestioning citizenry—a "cult of consensus." Historian Arthur Schlesinger, Jr., warned that America was in danger of becoming "one great and genuinely benevolent company town—the bland leading the bland."

Perhaps the most devastating critique would not come until 1963, when Betty Friedan's courageous book *The Feminine Mystique* assailed togetherness as a bad-faith substitute for women's equality. Moreover, the move to suburbia further racially segregated an already dangerously segregated society. The Levitt company, developers of the famous Levittowns, publicly refused to sell to blacks until 1960. In fact, rental contracts for Levitt homes specified that the "tenant agrees not to permit the premises to be used or occupied by any person other than members of the Caucasian race." Many suburban developments also institutionalized religious bigotry as well, excluding Jews or, in some cases, observing a quota system.

But while the critics wailed, the organization man and his family went about their business, attempting to make the most of the rising economic tide. For most Park Foresters, the early and midfifties remain a cherished period in their lives. They see them as golden days, filled with memories of their children growing up; close friendships; and, for the men, significant professional growth. "I never agreed with the social critics who called us 'other directed' and the 'new barbarians,' " says one former Park Forester. "But, then, none of those intellectuals ever lived in suburbia, did they?"

But the critics *had* raised a significant issue—the frightening willingness with which that generation of Americans subordinated themselves to the collective values demanded by large organizations. On the other hand, the critics had largely missed the real achievements of suburban life. The zealous cooperative spirit and volunteerism of suburban residents provided the means to create a sense of community where none had existed. Suburbanites created local governments, developed excellent school systems, and involved themselves in the life of their communities. In building institutional structures, they forged bonds of emotional support and solidarity that helped them to face successfully a world of strangers and change that might otherwise have overwhelmed them. The suburbia the critics warned America against did not possess the virtues of the small town, but neither was it the "split-level trap" of caricature.

While Bee stayed home with the children and involved herself in the life of Park Forest, Ray, like many organization men, was free to pursue his career as ambitiously as he wished. He turned out to be a banker's banker. With his carefully combed brown hair and his custom-tailored suits, he was the picture of comity. "Ray," says a former colleague, "was the kind of guy you hoped your daughter would marry. He had a ton of integrity."

And a ton of enthusiasm. His passion for work soon paid off. He was asked to take over the corporate trust division, though he had had no experience in the area. Overnight, his staff went from two to three hundred.

"I went into it knowing nothing about the work," he says. "But I saw it as an opportunity to head a department and to try out any abilities I had at working through other people."

For the next six years he ran the division, giving it all his considerable talent and dedication. He loved his work and, except for his wife and three sons, there was nothing he cared more about.

During the long economic honeymoon of the fifties, Continental was led by Walter Cummings, who had assumed the chairmanship during the depths of the depression. Cummings's goal was to move Continental, through careful management and prudent lending practices, into the top ten among commercial banks. At the end of 1955, Continental reported earnings of $17.5 million on an asset base of $2.7 billion, which made it the nation's seventh-ranked bank in earnings and ninth overall. (By comparison, the country's largest bank at the time, Bank of America, reported earnings of $66 million on an asset base of $9.7 billion.) Cummings had succeeded in turning Continental into a world-class bank, known for its sound, trustworthy policies.

Ray Myers thrived in the sober yet energetic atmosphere of the Cummings-led bank. Myers's sales ability, intelligence, and a management style that brought out the best in the people under his direction all worked to make him a star among the legion of vice presidents. The kind of prudent manager-banker into which he had evolved fit perfectly the economic environment of the fifties and early sixties.

By the midsixties, the winds of change blowing through America's largest corporations began to have an impact on the banking industry. In 1967, First National Citibank, one of the nation's top three commercial banks, commissioned a wide-ranging study of its organizational structure and managerial practices. In 1968, following a study by the management consulting firm of McKinsey and Company, Citibank reorganized on a market-concept basis, or what was known as "decentralization by market segment." Instead of serving the public through full-service branches, as they had done in the past, Citibank decided to specialize at various locations. For example, one branch would take charge of corporate business, with professionals in corporate banking running it. Professional management had finally come to the banking world.

Continental also recognized the need to take a hard look at its range of products and services and to expand the scope of its thinking about the future. In January 1967, chairman David Kennedy (who was to become secretary of the treasury of the United States) asked Myers to set up a long-range-planning division. Kennedy understood that Myers had the kind of understated panache necessary to bring strategic planning, and its unfamiliar ways of thinking, into the bank. Myers would be able to effect change without drawing battle lines between old-timers and new managers. His style of quiet leadership made it possible for all sides to be heard, all factions to participate.

"My goal, always," he says, "was to try and do things that would give the credit to somebody else. At some point in my life I read the statement that 'there is no end to how successful a person can be as long as they give credit to somebody else.' I adopted that as my credo."

It was a trait that served Myers well, but William H. Whyte, Jr., found such a denial of individualism disturbing. "In studying an organization," he wrote, "one of the most difficult things is to trace a program or innovation back to its roots." Even the person who first conceived the plan "is apt to deny—except to his wife—that his contribution was really that important."

Two years after bringing strategic planning into the bank, Myers returned to head the trust department, the division where, nineteen years earlier, he had begun his career. During his tenure as head, he was elevated to the ranks of the country's most honored bankers when he was elected president of the trust division of the American Bankers Association, the national industry trade group.

Myers ran the 1,200-member trust department for five years. Then, in 1976, two of Myers's contemporaries assumed leadership of the bank. Roger Anderson was elected chairman and John Perkins became president. One of the first actions of the new management team was to commission the New York consulting firm of Booz, Allen & Hamilton to review the bank's organizational structure. Out of that study came the recommendation to create an internal legal department. Once again Continental turned to Myers for leadership.

Although Myers had never practiced law during his career at the bank, he was persuaded to organize the new department. Over the next three years Myers recruited fifty-six lawyers with different specialties to join him in creating a full-fledged corporate legal department. It was to be the capstone of his career, but the demands of building and running a legal department increasingly isolated him from the substance of what was taking place in the bank's affairs.

With the demand for loans at one of its lowest levels since World War II and nonbank financial institutions, such as insurance companies, investment banking houses, and commercial finance companies, challenging the bank's larger corporate business, Anderson and Perkins agreed that Continental needed to pursue a new, more aggressive lending strategy. Continental, they believed, had the resources and the talent to challenge the industry leaders, Bank of America and Citibank, but it would have to change its style to live up to its motto: We'll Find a Way.

As the bank's policies were changing, so were its internal rules and procedures. The company had recently reorganized its lending department, granting less-senior officers greater power to make loans. A ranking executive still had to approve their decisions, but no longer was it necessary for two or three older veteran lenders to ponder and sign a loan agreement together.

Meanwhile, with his fateful news conference, Anderson had propelled Continental into the realm of high-stakes banking. In 1978 Penn Square contacted Continental, wanting to know if the Chicago bank would take on part of a $1.5 million loan to a local oilman. Continental accepted and before long was striking other such deals with Penn Square. When the energy industry began to soften in the early 1980s, so did Penn Square's loan portfolio. And then the whole rickety structure came crashing down and with it, much of the pride and identity of men like Ray Myers.

Ray's wife Bee more than anyone else understood how her husband felt. For thirty-three years she had stood by him, a loyal partner during his climb up the corporate ladder.

"We both felt very sad," she recalls, the pain still evident in her voice. "The reputation of what we had felt was such a superior corporation was just wiped out. It was just terribly, terribly sad."

"Living for a living."

Three thousand feet above Boulder, Colorado, sits the little town of Nederland. The approach from Boulder is dramatic—a constant, steady climb on a winding road that switchbacks over and over beside the churning, tumbling rapids of Boulder Creek. Higher and higher you climb until, suddenly, you reach the summit. And there, stretched out before you, you see it—the past. Except for the state highway that meanders through town, there are no paved roads here, no sidewalks. A few of the old frame buildings have boardwalks in front of them, as in Hollywood westerns, but the walks are not connected and so serve little purpose. Children play in the dirt streets. The houses—shacks, really, with abandoned cars and appliances littering their front yards—are scattered randomly about the town.

Follow the main highway through town and you come to a junction. Turn right and the road will take you to Estes Park, gateway to Rocky Mountain National Park; turn left and the highway takes you to Central City, site of the Colorado gold rush. But get out of your car and wander into the local bar and you will find yourself in the sixties. The men at the bar all have long hair. Some sport ponytails, some have handlebar mustaches. Birkenstocks and overalls are the uniform here, and the sweet, pungent smell of marijuana often fills the air. Time stopped in Nederland back around 1968.

Sometime in the midsixties, young people began migrating up here from Boulder in search of inexpensive housing and a "freer" life-style. Randy Myers, the eldest son of Ray and Bee Myers, remembers those days well.

"Nederland is very much a hippie town," he says. "When I first came here, there were still frequent battles between rednecks, who were the longtime residents of Nederland, and hippies, who were moving in and renting area housing. The battles were literal, not just verbal arguments. There would be fights in the streets. There would be reports of hippies being picked up, mugged, and thrown on the street. It was real heavy for a while. That was the late sixties. Ten years later the hippies owned the town. And the rednecks either liked them or weren't around anymore."

Though Nederland is only two hours by car from Keystone, the resort community where Randy's parents have one of their two retirement homes (the other is in Carmel, California), the two communities are, culturally, light years apart. Keystone is the pot of gold at the end of the organization man's rainbow. As the resort's promotional materials proclaim, Keystone is "renowned throughout the world for both architectural design and environmental care, for opulent accommodations paired with dedicated service. Keystone is a place where . . . you and your partner . . . can simply come to have a grand time of it. Come and live the Keystone experience." The Nederland experience, on the other hand, is a rejection of everything the Keystone experience stands for. How could it be that the eldest son of a senior executive of a major corporation, like so many other such sons and daughters, would choose to live in a place like this long after the sixties and his own period of youthful rebellion had passed?

Randy was born in 1948 on the cusp of the baby boom. True to the idealistic, craft-oriented, back-to-the-land ethos of the sixties, he became a carpenter. In Nederland he runs his own small custom building and remodeling business. He calls it The Prince and the Pauper. He and his wife Debbie have two children, a daughter born in 1981 and a son born in 1984. They live down a gravel road in a house that Randy built.

The house is modern inside, and except for a corner filled with plants hanging from macramé holders and a hodgepodge of new and old furniture, this could be suburban Dallas. Randy has his father's sharp features and chiseled good looks. He is tan, with sun-bleached hair, strong arms, and roughened hands. He used to wear his hair long, but now, in 1986, his hair is not much longer than that of his father. And Randy possesses the same quiet, reflective manner that served his father so well.

The road that brought Randy to Nederland begins at the height of the sixties, when Randy came of age. It was a difficult time, made doubly so by the inevitable struggle of a first-born son seeking to build an identity separate from that of his father.

"When I got out of high school," says Randy, "Vietnam was cooking up hot and heavy. So you had your basic choice of whether you should go to college or go to Vietnam. And, of course, as an organization man's son, college is what you did.

"I grew up with a basic contradiction. I was taught that corporate men were bad guys. And bankers were as bad as anyone you could find. Yet, I loved my dad and do to this day—very, very much. I respect him. He's brilliant, hardworking, scrupulous—you name it—he's got the positive attributes you'd look for in a person. At the same time, I'm being told that these guys are all bad and nasty. They kick little old widows out of their houses.

"I was never against my dad or had any feeling that I was trying to get back at him. I just didn't know what to do. Only one thing was clear: I didn't want to go to Vietnam; that wasn't a good place. So, I went to college. But I dropped out as soon as I could. I remember walking through this room and kind of watching this television show where they were calling out the draft numbers for each day of the year. All of a sudden, I heard my birthday and then my draft number. It was number three thirty-nine. And at the end of that school year I quit. I didn't want to be there. I was wasting a lot of time and I knew I was wasting a lot of money. But the money wasn't of any concern to me. I knew dad would spend twice the amount if he thought he would get a positive end product. That's just the way he does things. But I could see that it wasn't going to happen.

"When I told my parents that I wasn't going back to college, they were greatly disappointed, but also a bit relieved, I think. They knew I wasn't going anywhere in school and I think they thought if I got out for a few years and worked, then I would go back and get that MBA that my dad wanted me to get so badly and become a corporate giant. But I don't think that corporate giantism is in my horoscope."

Randy and his college roommate packed an old car with as many of their belongings as they could jam into it and headed for Colorado. Randy did not know what he wanted to do, but he was quite sure about what he did not want to do: He did not want to live in a city and he did not want to be an organization man.

"What you've got to understand is this," says Randy. "My dad got out of school and he was completely focused on his career. He would go anywhere. If he had been sent to Nome, Alaska, he would have gone there in a second. I, on the other hand, am not interested in living in a crummy place and having a good career. I wanted to live in a nice place and see what I could do to make a living once I was there. That's where he and I differ radically."

Randy is by no means alone among the organization offspring. Many of them, including many who eventually went to work for large organizations, have followed a similar pattern—first choosing where they want to live and only then worrying about what they would do there. Those who as children were moved around with their father's job, sometimes yearly, now find it astonishing that their parents not only put up with it, but embraced it eagerly. Reversing the organization man's credo, which placed the dictates of the organization ahead of almost everything else, many of the offspring have vowed that they would not let it happen to them.

"My dad still cannot understand why I would not go to Philadelphia or New York or Chicago or some other big city, in order to find work," says Randy. " 'Why *Colorado?*' he would ask. 'There's nothing out there, nothing happening.' But for me the most important thing in life was not working, but living. It makes no sense to live for your work."

Though it may seem incredible to his father, Randy believes his attitude grew out of the way he was raised.

"Growing up as the son of an organization man, I felt a little deceived in certain senses. I found that when I got out into the real world, it wasn't as I had imagined it. My dad never discussed finances of any sort with us kids. If we wanted to know how much the bill at the restaurant was, dad would say, 'Sure, you can have this bill, but if you want it you are going to have to pay for it.' Of course, that stopped the conversation quick.

"There was never any sense of what things cost. I never knew how much my father made. If we asked, he would not tell us. He always hid his tax forms. To this day I do not know how much money my father makes. He wouldn't tell us because he was afraid we would think he was rich. Whenever I would say to my father, 'Gee, we're rich,' he would say, 'No, we're comfortable. We are certainly not rich. Rich is a whole different story.'

"I thought four-week vacations were standard, just like you got a paycheck every month. For four weeks each summer we would jump in the car and go someplace. I thought it's what everyone did. So it was pretty shocking to me to have to live on three dollars an hour and have to pay all the bills that mom and dad had always paid. So I felt deceived in that sense.

"However, it wasn't that dad was trying to cheat me in any way. I'm sure that what he had in mind was keeping us from having money on our mind all the time—having it be such a big deal that it ran our lives. It appeared to me that he made money so effortlessly."

That is exactly the way the organization man wanted it to appear, for he and his wife had, over the years, become experts in the fine art of inconspicuous consumption. As Whyte put it, "On the one hand, suburbanites have a strong impulse toward egalitarianism; on the other, however, they have an equally strong impulse to upgrade themselves. Somewhere in the middle lies the good life." Throughout their lives, Ray and Bee Myers have sought the good life for themselves and their children, but without ever flaunting the fact that they were becoming more and more successful.

For the organization man, it was certainly okay to make money, and lots of it, but money was a by-product. What was important was to be part of something, to belong to an organization where you could make a contribution, where you could be proud of the work you were doing. Over time, if you lived by your word and worked hard, opportunities for advancement would present themselves. You believed in the firm because the firm believed in you. You did not have to worry about the future because the future would take care of itself. Hard work, competence, loyalty, and a sense of shared purpose—those were the ingredients of the successful career. The organization man wanted to be known for having done a good job, for personal integrity, for human decency. Take that path, and the money would follow.

The ostentatious show of wealth never appealed to the organization man. He believed a man should be measured by his loyalty and his accomplishments, not by the amount of money he made. And it was such beliefs, not a worship of money, that he hoped to pass on to his children.

For Randy Myers, the lessons continued long after he had left school for Colorado.

"My dad always had a lecture for me," Randy recalls with a pained expression. "There were times after visiting my parents that I would leave with a bad taste in my mouth. He would lecture me on how I wasn't doing anything with my life, how I wasn't getting any further ahead, getting nothing accomplished. He was getting panicky. It was okay for me to be a hippie for five years or so, but 'Randy, you've got to stop and take stock of your life.' "

Debbie, Randy's wife, adds: "At one time Ray thought the only answer was for Randy to go get a job with a big corporation. And even to this day he talks about Randy getting dressed up in a suit and going out and trying to get some sort of corporate job. He has even suggested to Randy that he contact an employment counselor and sit down with him and figure out what kind of job Randy could get, given the kinds of skills and experience he has."

"Within the last year," says Randy, smiling broadly, "my father has given me three of his three-piece suits so I could have them altered in case I wanted to go out there and find myself a corporate job.

"You have to understand," Randy continues, "my father believes that the only way you can be a success in life is to be an organization man. He says: 'Randy, in your job [as an independent contractor] you can't look forward to a raise. You have no retirement, no life insurance; you don't know month to month what your next paycheck is going to be.' He doesn't say it, but what he means is: 'You shouldn't live this way. It's not right and it's not fair to your lovely wife and beautiful children.'

"It was a real deep concern to him about what was going to happen to us, how we were going to pay the bills. He wanted to help, but he didn't know how. I would like to make dad happy, but I'm not willing to sacrifice my entire life to do it."

Ray Myers respects his eldest son's dedication and his entrepreneurial spirit. But he has difficulty squaring it with his own organizational beliefs. Whereas security was a powerful motivator in Ray's career, a sense of control over his own life is uppermost in Randy's mind. Each man abstractly respects the other's point of view, but neither can appreciate the other's perspective on the basis of their personal experiences.

For Randy, there is one additional point that negates all the arguments that might have persuaded him to trade his carpenter's tools for gray flannel and wing tips: the toll the failure of Continental Illinois took on his father.

"Today," says Randy, "when my father meets a stranger and the stranger asks him what he did before he retired, my father will say, 'I was a lawyer.' He will not tell him that he had a distinguished thirty-three-year career at the Continental bank. He will not tell them that he started the long-range-planning division and the corporate legal division and the corporate foundation of the bank. He simply says he was a lawyer.

"Isn't that sad? Isn't that a tragedy? He had this wonderful thirty-three year career, and the last few months of it blemished the whole thing. It's really sad because he was really, really proud to be part of that corporate team and he was really devastated when he could no longer use that as one of his medals, one of his decorations.

"Here is this man who gave his life to this corporation. He is scrupulous, forthright, a true man of his word. He has very strong moral convictions, and I believe to this day that he knew nothing about what was happening before they came to him with the story. Nevertheless, his incredible career was tarnished by the actions of others. It is a tragedy, a true tragedy."

"You were penalized for being entrepreneurial."

Scott Myers, maneuvering his Mazda through traffic and onto the San Tomas Expressway, is smiling. On this damp and cold spring morning, he is not wearing a coat and tie, the mandatory uniform of the organization man he had worn for almost a decade. A polo shirt, a pair of cotton wash pants, and loafers suffice. For the past eight years he has dreamed of this day, and now, in March 1987, he is about to fulfill his wish to be in business for himself. During the short trip up the valley from his home in Cupertino, where he lives with his wife Charity and their two children, he talks about how he arrived at this day.

"I quit college after one year," he says. "I was not into studying at the time. I flunked out of most of my classes. It was a waste of my time and my dad's money. I went to Colorado and messed around the mountains for about nine months. I had a camping trailer and I lived out in the hills and basically did whatever it took to get food. Construction, mostly.

"I was a real dropout. I just hadn't gotten plugged into a useful life. I had given no thought to what I wanted to do. The building of houses was just something I landed in—learned from scratch, no thought to it, making just enough to live on. I went from paycheck to paycheck. But I got tired of getting up at five in the morning and going out in the cold to build houses. So I went back to school."

Born in 1953, Scott is the youngest of Ray and Bee Myers's three sons. Scott understands very well what his father's thirty-three-year commitment to Continental meant, and he intends to make good use of the lessons he learned growing up as the son of an organization man.

He is his father's son through and through. But when he was wandering the Colorado mountains in the early 1970s, the gap between them could not have been wider. Along with many members of his generation at the time, including older brother Randy, he hardly seemed the son of a senior corporate executive. And his parents, like many at the time, must have asked themselves if this could really be the son they had brought up in suburban Park Forest, Illinois, and neighboring Flossmoor.

Scott stopped wandering in the spring of 1972. Not only did he hate working in the predawn cold of the Rockies, he also wanted a student deferment from the draft, so he returned to school at his father's alma mater, DePauw University in Greencastle, Indiana. But a small, liberal arts school in the rolling hills of southern Indiana was not Scott's idea of what education should be.

"I did not like DePauw at all," Scott says. "It was useless. I told my dad that many times. I felt it was too sheltered. It was a place where parents sent their kids so they wouldn't have to deal with reality. You had to live in the dorm, so you couldn't have any of the responsibilities that I wanted at that age. The college cooked your meals and your parents paid your bills. That wasn't the kind of place I was looking for."

He transferred to Indiana University in Bloomington and eventually persuaded his then-girlfriend Charity to join him. Charity provided a stabilizing influence. By the time they were graduated in 1976, he in biology, she in microbiology, they'd decided that graduate school offered the best route to good jobs. His aimless days now far behind him, Scott headed for business school at Northwestern University. Charity enrolled in the Ph.D. program in medical research.

Scott had watched his two older brothers take dramatically different courses in their lives and he thought he could learn from both. Scott loved Randy and remembered fondly the time they had spent together after Scott had first dropped out of DePauw. But Scott also knew that Randy's life was not for him. He wondered what kind of future there was for a construction contractor in the mountains above Boulder, Colorado. Scott's other brother, by contrast, had taken the opposite course from Randy, becoming the model son of the family—graduating from college on time, earning an advanced degree, and going to work for a major corporation.

Scott wanted the freedom and expansiveness he saw in Randy's life, but he wanted more opportunities than he saw coming Randy's way. He also liked the respectability and predictability that characterized his other brother's career, but he was wary of the corporate straitjacket. Scott thought he could have the best of both brothers' lives—and on his own terms.

Scott loops his Mazda onto Great America Parkway and heads west into the heart of Silicon Valley, past such industry giants as Sun and Tandem. The commute has not gone as badly as it might have, and the rain is stopping. He turns south onto El Camino Real and into a district more reminiscent of Guadalajara than of the manicured, muted center of high technology in America. His new company occupies part of the second floor of a plain, brown stucco, commercial building that also houses a florist, a hairdresser, a certified public accountant, and a bureau of the *Korean Times* newspaper. This part of Santa Clara is the kind of multicultural mecca California is becoming famous for—home to many of the immigrant groups who have come to the valley in recent years from the Pacific Rim, Mexico, and Central America. The street signs along El Camino attest to the area's diverse population and diverse appeals: L'Amour Shoppe Contemporary Books, Ultimate Interiors, Korean Books, and Wet Pleasures (a store that sells skin-diving equipment). A Mexican restaurant sits on one corner, a Japanese fast-food place on the other, and a Chinese carryout across the street.

"It's not the high-rent district," says Scott, "but then we could do what we're doing just about anywhere. All we need is space for our computers and a bunch of telephones. We wanted cheap and close to home."

It has been only a few weeks since Scott left Memorex Corporation, where he spent the previous ten years of his professional life. In 1978, while vacationing in California, Scott told his wife Charity that they should move there and never look back. Never having lived outside Indiana, she agreed to take their next summer vacation there, and if they could both find jobs, try it for two years only. On the last day of the vacation, in 1978, they both received job offers—he from Memorex, a high technology company, and she from Syntex, one of the nation's largest drug manufacturers.

Scott joined the finance department in a development position that moved him within the company every six months. The idea was to give him a feel for many parts of the business, move him into the corporate mainstream, and make him into a "Memorex kind of guy." All it did was bore Scott.

"The first job I had was writing debits and credits at the end of each month. I could not believe anyone did that for a living. I remember the shock. I had been there three weeks and been through the desk procedures and I had no idea what it all meant, like: 'You mean I have to write debits and credits—MBAs don't do that!' "

It was perhaps youthful naivete to think he would not have to perform mundane duties, but his response typifies the high expectations many members of his generation have about work, unlike the more modest expectations their fathers had. As Ray Myers, whose first job for Continental Illinois bank had been as a glorified salesman, says, "I would have been quite content to do that for the rest of my life." Not so Scott, or other organization offspring, who, as a matter of course, expect their jobs not only to be stimulating, but to allow them to be recognized for their personal achievements. Nor for Scott is the organization man's credo of seeing to it that others get the credit. He searched frantically for another job in the company.

"I took a job in systems development," he says, "doing financial planning programs for various departments. I would install financial planning systems and then go in and teach people how to use them. I'd do the programming and then do the teaching."

At first he liked it, but not for long.

"Memorex is a funny place. I'd been there only six months when I decided I was going someplace else. I was in the process of leaving ever since then. The reason I stayed had nothing to do with loyalty. It's just that whenever I got to the point where I actually went looking for another job, an opportunity would come along inside and I would take it. I reasoned that I would never get such an opportunity elsewhere because of lack of experience.

"A while back I switched from finance into sales. I had become bored with finance and I knew that if I was going to move up or ever be successful on my own I needed sales experience. I got involved helping a group that was setting up a software company to package and sell to the marketplace. It was a typical Memorex sort of deal—a skunkworks without support. No one on top said: 'No, you can't do it.' But, on the other hand, they gave us little money to do it. Their attitude was if it doesn't work, they don't want their name on it; if it does work, they want it. But they were unwilling to back the effort."

Failure might jeopardize the careers of all the participants in the project. Nevertheless, Scott saw it as an opportunity to learn and to run a small operation. He took the assignment.

Shortly thereafter, Memorex was sold to Burroughs (which, subsequently, was merged with Sperry to become Unisys) and Scott's little in-house software business found itself on the wrong side of a major corporate policy struggle. Burroughs was not interested in Memorex's small businesses; it had bought the company to gain control of Memorex's main product lines—disk drives and tape drives. Out went Scott's fledgling division and project.

The experience convinced Scott that he would never get where he wanted to go as long as he stayed inside a large corporation. He resolved to commit himself only to tasks that would enhance his own career—eventually outside Memorex.

"Had the company been different," he says, "I might have stayed. But there was no reason to. No one really cared what you did. You were penalized for being entrepreneurial. I knew I would get a check whether I sold or not. And no one seemed to share the same goal."

Scott's criticisms resemble those that were being heard in many of the nation's largest corporations at mid-decade. America, according to Peter F. Drucker, was entering an era of innovation. Yet most corporations remained content to manage the past. Try as they might, many venerable American companies had virtually no idea how to solve the multiple problems that were developing. Many no longer understood their marketplace; many seemed incapable of handling the transition to a global, knowledge-based economy; and few understood their own young managers—most of whom were the sons and daughters of organization men.

"That little software division was a different story," says Scott. "We were like a little family. We shared the same goals, shared the same risks, and felt like we were all in this venture together."

Members of the group began to talk about starting their own business.

"One of the technical guys on the Memorex team had left the company and gone out on his own. He was a brilliant technician and the kind of guy who could have done everything, except for the fact that there are only so many hours in a day. I hired him back as a consultant to me, and it was then we started talking. When things started to fall apart at Memorex, I decided to join this group of guys on weekends. We defined a new product, did market research, figured out what the product should be, specced it out, and started rolling.

"For over a year and a half we worked that way," he says. "I spent most of my weekends and some evenings working with them while continuing my job at Memorex."

He admits his frequent absences from home were hard on Charity, who, after the birth of their second child, had decided to stay at home. Much to her surprise—and some dismay—she was left the job of child rearing, mostly alone. She understood, at least intellectually, the pressures Scott was under. Nevertheless, it was not easy, for either of them. Scott, unlike the organization man before him, does not view this as a natural or desirable state of affairs.

"I want to be more involved with my kids," he insists. "What that means is that I don't expect and don't want Charity's role and my role to be as clearly defined as they were when I was growing up. For example, my father never cooked. His job was to bring in the groceries and that was it. All very well defined. I want it to be different. I don't cook, but I do the dishes sometimes and on Sundays I do fifty percent of the housecleaning. I never saw my dad do any of that stuff."

But Scott's good intentions and the reality of holding down a job while trying to build a new company made for a wide gap between vision and reality—and revealed that the gap between him and his father was perhaps narrower than it seemed.

"Having children really tore up our life-style," he says. "I had a real problem with that. I had a hard time with the lack of control over my time. I could no longer do what I wanted to do when I wanted to do it. You do what is necessary for the child at that point. And though I understood that was the right thing to do, I resented it. I was dedicated to my work and having a child made it difficult for me."

The conflict Scott feels between his role as a father and the importance of his work is hardly unique, for his experience bears the marks of powerful social and economic changes transforming the "Leave It to Beaver" family of the organization man and creating the new American family.

In 1987, with Scott working and Charity at home with the children, the Myers were among an ever-dwindling group of American families with men as the sole wage earners. By 1988 only 15 percent of American families fit the male-as-sole-wage-earner profile, falling from as high as 42 percent in 1960. Ironically, "traditional" households are far more common in the high-stress, entrepreneurial world of Silicon Valley than most people would think. Some see it as a coping mechanism—the only way family life can be sustained in such a high-anxiety setting, while others attribute it to the blatant sexism rampant in many fields of engineering.

Though Scott and Charity were among the small group in their generation managing to have a family on one (male) income, their struggle to define appropriate roles and to find time and energy for work, children, and marriage were not so different from those facing their peers in two-earner households. Finding that balance has not been easy.

Perhaps Scott could have easily resolved his dilemma by adopting his father as a role model, in the unlikely event that Charity would have gone along. But Scott wanted to be a different kind of father, with a "less clearly defined role" than his father had. He wanted to share fully the emotional responsibility and the physical care of his children and said, at least, that he wanted to do half the housework.

But such liberation from traditional roles is not easily accomplished—it requires far more than good intentions. He could have chosen to arrange his life so he could spend more time with his family, but instead he chose the demands of starting a company. Feeling driven by his role as provider, he felt his primary responsibility was "to put bread on the table." Yet he wanted to be more involved with his children. Unlike men and women of their parents' generation, who had sharply defined role models to follow, Scott and Charity had no models to guide them through this contemporary dilemma. So, in the final analysis, Scott fell back on, however reluctantly, the organization-man model. Like many middle-class men, then and now, his identity comes from his work—he is what he does. He feels *more* responsible for his work even while wishing to be more involved with home and family.

As sociologist Arlie Hochschild details (with Anne Machung) in *The Second Shift: Working Parents and the Revolution at Home*, many wives find themselves similarly conflicted, but in the opposite direction. "One reason women take a deeper interest than men in the problems of juggling work with family life," she writes, "is that even when husbands happily shared the hours of work, their wives felt more *responsible* for home and children." If the husband puts his work first and his wife puts home and children first, her behavior tends to reinforce his. Under such circumstances, a substantial change in roles does not come easily.

Though the old way of being parents—in the style of the organization man and his wife—grew increasingly difficult to justify, new relationships between husbands and wives evolved little beyond the rhetorical stage. For the organization offspring, reared in the middle-class paradigm of "breadwinners" and "homemakers," the transition to whatever new form the American family will take will undoubtedly be one of the most difficult struggles they will face. For most, like Scott and Charity, it will occupy center stage, its ramifications played out in their lives every day. But for them, at least, the odds of their winning the struggle increased substantially when Scott's high expectations clashed dramatically with corporate reality.

"I want this guy out. Now."

On the evening of Sunday, December 7, 1986, in the first-class cabin of a Detroit-bound jet high above the clouds over the Midwest, W. Michael Blumenthal, then chairman and chief executive officer (CEO) of Unisys and former treasury secretary in the Carter administration, eased back in his seat and settled into a copy of the Sunday *New York Times*. Thumbing through *Business World*, a new magazinelike section of the paper, he landed on a story that caught his eye. He took a sip of his drink and began to read.

On the third page of the article, he came upon a reference to Memorex, a company Unisys had recently acquired. His attention quickened. But what he read he did not like. By the time he finished the story, he was seething with anger, eager to take action. But trapped at thirty-five thousand feet, in the days before air phones, he was forced to wait until the plane touched down at Chicago's O'Hare airport. When it did, he stormed off the plane and headed for a bank of phones. He called his second-in-command, Paul Stern, at home.

"Did you see the Sunday *Times?*" Blumenthal barked. He didn't wait for a response. "There's this guy from Memorex who's quoted in an article. I want you to find out who he is and get rid of him. I want this guy out. *Now.*"

Stern, who had not seen the article, asked why.

"He's quoted as saying, 'I don't have any loyalty to the company; I'm in it for me.' Get rid of him."

Stern immediately called the president of Memorex, who had not seen the article either but knew what had to be done. On Monday morning he called the head of Marketing and Sales, who assured the president he would take immediate action.

Or so the story goes. Whether it is correct in every detail is a matter of speculation, but that is how it moved through the halls of Memorex in late 1986 and early 1987.

That fateful Monday the employee quoted in the article went to work as usual. He vaguely sensed that he might be in a little trouble if upper management had seen the story. Senior managers at Unisys were not known for allowing deviations from the corporate line. Unisys was a long way from the kind of free-form, slightly irreverent high-tech upstarts that had become common in Silicon Valley.

Unisys was, in fact, a classic organization-man company, a merger of two of the most successful technology companies of the fifties and sixties, Burroughs and Sperry. The resulting company was, as John Sculley of Apple Computer might phrase it, a "second-wave" company all the way, a place where "people are fearful of saying what they really think because they don't trust each other . . . [where] people believe their opinions can get them in trouble." At Unisys, managers pledged their loyalty to the company whether or not they genuinely felt such a bond. You knew your place and played by the rules.

Monday came and went with business as usual. Tuesday came and went without a mention of the article. But on Wednesday afternoon, just as the offending employee was beginning to conclude that he had nothing to worry about, he was summoned without explanation to an urgent meeting with his boss.

The Memorex manager heading into the vortex that fading December afternoon was Scott Myers, Ray Myers's youngest son. The quote that enraged CEO Blumenthal had appeared as a caption under a picture of Myers sitting in his Memorex office in Santa Clara. Entitled " 'Organization Man' Revisited," the article was the first published account of what would become the present book.

Scott's offhand comment about loyalty, he realized, had been careless and perhaps unwise—not good corporate politics. Yet, on the other hand, it had been the truth. It was the way he felt.

He walked into his boss's office expecting the worst. But the boss began merely by detailing the bizarre chain of events that had brought them to this meeting. Then he asked for an explanation. Scott attempted to put his remark in context, to explain the circumstances. What he had meant by saying that he was "in it for me" was that he expected his job to offer him real challenges, give him opportunities to learn and apply new skills, and make substantial contributions to getting the job done and, not incidentally, give him some sense of satisfaction and self-esteem. What kind of employees did the corporation want, after all?

Timeservers? Toadies whose chief talent is paying lip service to loyalty until the time comes for them to start collecting their pensions?

But neither Scott's explanation nor the real attitude of his immediate superior mattered. The fact remained that the highest-ranking officer of the corporation wanted the young manager out. Out he would go.

Though Scott did not know it at the time, those traumatic days in December 1986 were fortuitous. It was in the months preceding that fateful December day that he and his friends had been working on the venture that Unisys had abandoned. Meeting on evenings and weekends, they had been painstakingly developing a business plan of their own and moving closer to the time when they could all walk away from one of the world's largest corporations. Their intention was not to beat the company at its own game, but, rather, to show what they could accomplish, to be recognized for their talent and ability, and to control their own destinies. Thus, while Scott Myers's boss moved ever closer to carrying out CEO Blumenthal's orders, Scott's course of action was already laid out for him. Scott quit before the final showdown could occur.

Who was right? From an organization man's perspective, Scott's breezy dismissal of corporate loyalty betrayed, at best, a scepticism detrimental to the best interests of the corporation or, at worst, a cynicism born of serious maladjustment (the inability to adapt to corporate life) or a wanton disrespect for the legitimate authority of the organization. To the organization man, a young manager like Scott Myers should have learned—and come to believe—the "organization man's litany," which Whyte suggested went like this: "Be loyal to the company and the company will be loyal to you. After all, if you do a good job for the organization, it is only good sense for the organization to be good to you, because that will be best for everyone."

Scott Myers revealed that he believed otherwise. His remark violated the essential, if unwritten, contract that had bound the individual to the organization since World War II. Myers had declared that the individual, rather than the organization, should be paramount. In challenging pieties about corporate loyalty, he was questioning the legitimacy of the organization's authority and, perhaps most cogently, the organization man's premise that "the goals of the individual and the goals of the organization will work out to be one and the same."

In Scott Myers's attitude, one begins to glimpse the organization offspring's complex and often contradictory relationship to organizations and organizational life. One begins also to comprehend the dramatic form that individualism has taken for this generation of middle-class Americans and how individualism has changed in the past three decades.

In the reaction of CEO Blumenthal, one sees vividly the striking and emotionally charged differences that have come to separate the views of the generation now running America's largest organizations from those of the vast majority of managers under their command. From the perspective of the organization man, Scott's honesty about his work represented a threat to legitimate authority—a breakdown of the values that have governed organizational life during the postwar period. The organization man asks: What must be done when legitimacy is challenged? How can a CEO ensure that his commands will be followed? What good is a hierarchy, in which one's right to govern and lead is vested in one's position, if young managers do not take it seriously? How can you mandate loyalty? Blumenthal's answer was simple: instill fear. Thus, when he demanded Scott Myers's head, he was sending a message to the entire corporation.

But to a new generation of managers—managers whose loyalty is not to the organization but to doing the job right in the interests of their own self-development—the meaning of the Myers incident was far different from its significance for Blumenthal. And bark and bluster as he might, Blumenthal sent a different message through Unisys than the one he intended.

On the Monday following publication of the *Times* article, Scott began to receive congratulatory calls from co-workers. They said, in effect: "Nice going, Scott. You said what I believe. Like you, I want to work for a company that recognizes my contributions, allows me to determine how my work should be accomplished, and creates an atmosphere in which the emphasis is on knowledge and skill, not on issues of authority and rank." By telling an interviewer how he really felt, Scott Myers articulated what so many in his generation believe almost as a matter of course. And Blumenthal's autocratic and unreasoning action merely confirmed for them the truth of their perspective.

Scott Myers never set out to make waves. He had always been a hardworking and enthusiastic employee. But he could not pretend to be something other than what he was—someone, like so many in his generation, whose relationship to power and authority is governed by a new and much-changed view of organizations and organizational life. At Unisys, the new generation collided with the old, though neither had intended it. And it is far from clear that Unisys won.

Since Scott left Memorex, his life has changed dramatically. He and his partners went on to develop and market a successful software product for mainframe computers. The product was so successful that they were able to negotiate the sale of the product to a major software company in summer 1989.

With the money earned from the sale, Scott's chief partner was able to realize a dream—to live in the high Sierras on the shore of one of the world's most beautiful bodies of water, Lake Tahoe. There he spends much of his time doing what he loves best—writing computer software—and the remainder of his time hiking, skiing, and taking in the grandeur of the lake. The partner continues to work just as hard as he did when he lived in the Bay Area, but now he works on his own terms, not someone else's.

Scott also achieved a long-held goal—to arrange his life so he could spend more time with his wife and now three children. First, he and his chief partner created a new organization consisting of two separate companies. Once again, they identified another area of the computer mainframe market where advanced software can help companies achieve greater efficiency. But this time, in keeping with his often-stated desire to work toward greater integration of his work life and family life, Scott set up shop at home. The new organization is located in the corner of the Myers's master bedroom. From there, with his computers, telephones, a fax machine, and modems, Scott and his new company are prepared to take on a new challenge.

To an organization man, Scott's new life looks like an employment nightmare. He has no job security, no clearly defined career path, no company health insurance or retirement benefits. He must continually juggle temporary employees, consultants, and suppliers. He has none of the prestige that goes with a corporate title, no staff, no company parking space, and no membership in a corporate health club. All he has to look forward to are wild swings in income and the constant anxiety of never knowing where the next client is going to come from.

But Scott has found what he had always been looking for. He has a job he can control; a career path that will change as he changes; an opportunity to be recognized for what he accomplishes, rather than for where he sits in a hierarchy; and a work life that is in balance with the rest of his existence. Michael Blumenthal got his wish: Scott Myers is out. And Scott could not be happier.

"That day is over."

By the time Scott Myers left Memorex in the mideighties, it was already abundantly clear that the unwritten social contract between organizations and managers had lapsed. His father, by contrast, leaving Continental in the early part of the decade, could not have known how fortunate he was to get out when he did. Like other organization men whose careers began soon after the war, he was ready to retire in the early 1980s, before the big economic slide began (or, to be more precise, before the decline became apparent). Ray Myers escaped relatively unscathed from what soon became wave after wave of economic and organizational trauma. By the close of the decade, almost every institution in America found itself severely strained by new economic and global realities. When the smoke began to clear at the end of the decade, the organization man lay critically wounded. Some observers went further—declaring the organization man dead.

For almost three decades the kinds of organizations—and their values—that Whyte identified had worked wonders. American companies became preeminent in such fields as automobiles, aircraft, energy, and electronics. In the process, they gave the United States the highest standard of living ever known. But in the 1980s, in industry after industry, the nation began to fall behind in innovation, productivity, and market share. Many commentators now believe that the very organization-man revolution that helped create America's robust economic health eventually contributed to and perhaps even caused its decline.

"When you grow up in the organization-man tradition," says organizational psychologist Harry Levinson, president of the Levinson Institute, "you are part of a big family. There is no effective performance appraisal even when someone is inadequate or inefficient." Harvard economist John Kenneth Galbraith agrees: "There is a self-perpetuating mediocrity about this process." Organizations, he believes, begin to suffer from an "encrusting obsolescence." The near-collapse of Continental Bank and the Chrysler and Lockheed corporations and even the mismanagement that led to the deadly explosion of the space shuttle Challenger illustrate the dangers of a sclerotic corporate bureaucracy.

By the 1980s, America was, as Steven Schlossstein argues in *The End of the American Century*, a nation under siege. In less than a generation, America had "seen its standard of living decline, its level of industrial dominance threatened by foreign competition, its political system infested by the narrowness (and money) of special interests, its public education systems plagued by low achievement, its families and children seared by the emotional trauma of single parenthood and divorce, its society ripped apart by drugs, its national defense weakened by fraud and mismanagement, and its position of global leadership increasingly open to challenge."

The malaise that swept across corporate America in the 1980s hit the organization man hard. Tens of thousands of executives were laid off, especially in old-line, Rust Belt industries. The rash of mergers and leveraged buyouts took a heavy toll as conquered companies were shrunk by their new owners. "From the beginning of 1980 to the end of 1987, an eight-year period," writes *Wall Street Journal* reporter Amanda Bennett, "Fortune 500 companies dropped 3.1 million jobs, going from 16.2 million people at the end of 1979 to 13.1 million at the end of 1987. The American Management Association reported that in the year ending in June 1987, 45 percent of its surveyed companies had cut staff; in 1988, 35 percent had downsized; in 1989 it was 39 percent. What's more, as the AMA looked ahead, it predicted that as many as 45 percent of American companies would begin the new decade (the 1990s) by sending some of their people home jobless."

Almost no company was exempt from the carnage. Firestone shrank its work force from 110,000 to about 53,000; Xerox cut its American and European manufacturing operations from 18,000 to 9,000; IBM "retired" 10,000 managers and workers (saving about $1 billion); General Electric slashed its employment rolls by a staggering 100,000; and American steel companies closed 444 mills, eliminating approximately 200,000 jobs.

Between 1980 and 1989, there were close to 25,000 mergers and acquisitions, or an average of more than 200 every month during every year of the decade. More than 100 of the companies that appeared on the Fortune 500 list in 1983 were merged, acquired, or had been taken private by the close of the decade. By 1990, over 59 percent of all companies with 50,000 or more employees had instituted early retirement or voluntary staff-reduction plans. Between 1981 and 1990, according to data cited by Amanda Bennett, an estimated 35 percent of all middle-management jobs were eliminated.

Writing in 1990, Bennett declared, "The corporate world is a cold, hostile war zone. Middle managers with decades of seniority are being fired or forced into early retirement. One employee now does the work that five used to perform. Promotions lie stagnant. . . . What began in the auto and the aerospace industries in the seventies soon spread to computer firms, television networks, publishers, drug companies, chemical companies, and virtually every Fortune 500 company." The faith that the organization man placed in the corporation has been stretched past the breaking point. The social contract that for forty years had bound the individual to the organization, and vice versa, had been abrogated, probably forever.

None of this came as any surprise to organization offspring like Randy and Scott Myers. The ruthless behavior of organizations in the 1980s only served to confirm views that they had held long before the malaise hit. Randy had long since rejected such a life out of hand. Scott, though he had spent nearly ten years with a Fortune 500 company, held no brief for the beneficence of such institutions. And by 1990 he, like

Randy, had become a member of America's new "entrepreneurial economy."

At the same time that America's largest corporations were struggling to respond to sweeping technological advances and dramatic changes in the global economic environment, a new world of small, entrepreneurial companies was forming. Between 1980 and 1987, according to David L. Birch, "small companies were the source of more than one hundred percent of all job growth. . . . We find that companies with fewer than one hundred employees are gaining eighty to ninety percent of those jobs." In fact, more than two-thirds of jobs eliminated by Fortune 500 firms were replaced by smaller companies *within* the manufacturing sector. And it was the very smallest firms, like Scott's, that created the most jobs. The Bureau of Labor Statistics reported in 1990 that almost 79 percent of all businesses in California's booming economy had fewer than ten workers.

Randy and Scott Myers were born during a period of unprecedented prosperity; came of age during a time of economic uncertainty; and, as adults, face the long-term prospect of a sour American economy. Distrustful of large institutions, they plan for their own future. Mindful of the unstable nature of organizational life, they do not count on making their careers with one organization. Cynical about the motives of large organizations and the ability of large institutions to change, they would rather rely on themselves. For them, controlling their own destinies and defining the terms of engagement come far ahead of the idea of organizational loyalty.

"The problem with the loyalty of the organization man was that it was one way," says Randy Myers. "It was militaristic. The corporation said: 'You must be loyal to us.' But they didn't have to be loyal in return. 'We don't have to listen to your feelings or your needs. We are the big shots and you are the drones and we will tell you when to move and you must say yes.' Well," Randy says with absolute finality, "that day is over."

Even in the absence of the economic upheavals of the 1980s or the betrayal of many organization men at the end of honorable careers, it is likely that the passing of the organization man as a model for his children would have occurred anyway. Randy Myers, in his invoking of "needs" and "feelings," hints at the reason why: the highly psychologized form individualism would take for his generation. That individualism, running the gamut from selfishness to self-fulfillment and reaching its highest pitch in the ideal of the authentic self, made inevitable the clash of the organization with an entire generation, even with those of its members who, like Scott Myers, appeared to be most enthusiastically pursuing the corporate brass ring, not to mention those who, like Randy, would not go near large organizations in the first place.

Ironically, it was in the home that the organization man and his wife made for their children that the seeds of that individualism were first planted. That individualism would come to full flower in reaction to the offspring's subsequent experiences of organizations, but its roots reached down into the suburban family—nonauthoritarian, expressive, and socially and geographically mobile. To trace in detail how these dynamics of the organization family collided with the unique life course of the offspring to produce their distinctive individualism, we turn now to another organization family, the Harrisons. We take up their story at a historical watershed, at what might be called the beginning of the end of the organization man: the rancorous 1960s. And there we will see that the passing of the organization man was almost guaranteed by what he and his wife—and the organizations he worked for—passed on to the children.

2

The Harrisons:
Displaced Persons

"The data is correct."

The alarm clock woke Joann Harrison from a dead sleep at 4 A.M., Saigon time. From the suburbs came the distant, muffled explosions of Vietcong mortar fire. As an IBM contract worker for the air force, she had been in the country only a few weeks, but already she was learning to sleep through the ceaseless, reverberant din of the war.

She brewed some Vietnamese tea and tuned in Armed Forces Radio to listen to the network's account of the Apollo 11 moon shot. It would be several hours yet before the first human being actually stepped onto the lunar surface, but Joann had more than a casual interest in the event. She had spent the previous five months with IBM working on the project at the Goddard Space Flight Center in Washington, D.C., meticulously checking thousands of lines of computer code that were crucial to the flight's telemetry.

Her husband, Bill, lay asleep while she listened to the broadcast. Also an IBMer, he had been in Vietnam for ten months longer than she—it had taken that long to cajole senior management at the company to send a woman into a war zone. Married only three years, Bill and Joann had not wanted to live apart, but for Bill it was either go to 'Nam with IBM at 175 percent of his salary, tax free, or with the U.S. infantry as a draftee. He chose IBM.

Persuading the company to send Joann to Vietnam had not been easy, and she had not done it diplomatically. Her bosses, citing the Tet

56

offensive, repeatedly turned down her requests for a transfer. They would be damned if they were going to send a woman to die. Joann raised the specter of the recently created federal Equal Employment Opportunity Commission. The problem was kicked upstairs to a senior vice president. Avuncular and sympathetic, he nevertheless smoothly turned her aside. She sought support from two senior women; they encouraged her but did little else. She was warned about jeopardizing her future with the company, but she stood her ground. At last, her superiors relented. She was barely twenty-three years old.

Despite the obstructionism of her bosses, Joann felt, as she listened to the radio broadcast, that IBM was the greatest organization in the world. And NASA wasn't far behind. She was proud to be associated with both. Together they were about to fulfill John Kennedy's pledge to put an American on the moon before the decade of the sixties was out, a pledge that had been made when she was a fourteen-year-old schoolgirl in Dallas. Now, just three years out of Michigan State University, she could say she had helped redeem that pledge. When Neil Armstrong finally stepped on the moon, she cried.

Today, after a career that has taken her all over the world, Joann Harrison recalls the year of Apollo 11 and her time in Vietnam as both the high point and the low point of her organizational life. Sitting in her Russian Hill cooperative in one of the oldest buildings in San Francisco, commanding a view of the bay from the Golden Gate to the Bay Bridge, she still expresses admiration for IBM, though her eventual frustration with it ultimately led her to start her own software company.

"I was extremely impressed by IBM's management of the Apollo project," she says. "I remember these senior managers in their midthirties, young Jack Kennedy types—jackets off, sleeves rolled up, ties loose—saying 'this is a vitally important mission; we're the ones who have the commands that control that spaceship and whether or not it will get safely onto the moon and whether it will ever get up off the moon. If you see anything that doesn't look right, tell your management immediately. No one gets blamed; we're personally responsible for the lives of three men.' I felt it was Joann Harrison helping keep those three men alive. If I did something wrong, they could die."

From her point of view, Armstrong's lapidary "one small step for a man, one giant leap for mankind" unintentionally revealed who really deserved the credit for the mission.

"I knew from the programming the astronauts were just along for the ride," she says. "It wasn't until years later, when I read *The Right Stuff*, that I realized the astronauts were complaining about being treated like monkeys. They were out there doing things in their space suits that we didn't really care about; we were programming how that ship would be controlled. To this day I think it may be most important thing I've done in my career or in my life."

If Apollo 11 was an organizational triumph, Vietnam was a disaster.

"I had the sense that everybody was over there for the good of their careers," she says, "the military officers and the professionals. There was no sense of being a part of anything great at all and there was even a sense of being part of something slightly wrong."

Two days after her arrival she found herself hiding under a bed, clutching a .45 automatic and sipping brandy for courage while Bill investigated a firefight in the compound. When he returned to tell her it was over, she almost shot him. Now she knew at least one of the reasons so many IBMers left before their eighteen-month tours were up.

"One guy went home after four days. Some went home after six months. I don't know if it was the pressure of the incoming one-twenty-twos, the pressure of the fast night life—the pressure on the men to drink and whore around—or what. But it was frightening. Bill and I had some terrible crying sessions. The mortar shells were coming in, and it was just a feeling of powerlessness and loneliness and fear of death."

Living in the relative safety of Saigon, she was under no illusions about who faced the real danger: "Some people had to go out and get shot at every day. And they were kids. I'd see trucks full of them go out in the morning when I'd go to work and I'd see them coming back covered head to toe with red dirt. At the infirmary I'd see stacks of body bags and I'd shiver because many of the boys came back from the daily hunt that way."

Looking for a house to rent proved equally unsettling, in its way. She and Bill wanted to share a place with several other IBMers.

"Standard villas had only one bathroom, but since there was going to be a married couple and two single men, we wanted a place with three bathrooms. The only places that had that many bathrooms were whore-houses. So we went through quite a few whorehouses which were about to close because they couldn't compete with the bar girls on Tu Do Street. I vividly remember one that was very dirty, and the women were emaciated. I was shocked that prostitution was such a nasty business, having seen a more romantic view of it in Hollywood films. In the movies I had not seen exploited women who were underfed and diseased."

She was assigned to the support group for the Seventh Air Force in Saigon, running bomb-damage assessments on IBM 360s at Tonsonhut air base. Each afternoon she would feed the results of the morning's bombing into her 360. The computer drove a huge Calcomp plotter that spent the night producing a six-foot map of the Ho Chi Minh Trail pinpointing where the bombs had fallen. The map came off the plotter at five-thirty each morning. The generals analyzed it, decided on the targets for that day, and soon had the B-52s airborne again. After the smoke cleared, reconnaissance planes photographed the damage and the entire process began again. Morale was low; the computer people could not communicate with the military personnel; the whole operation seemed poorly managed.

"We were being directly supervised by the military," she says. "We didn't have the moral support we had at IBM, where we were always told we were part of something wonderful. That's a management mistake the military made in running the war."

She recalls sitting in strained silence with a three-star general because he did not know how to ask for the kind of data he wanted from the computers and she did not know how to translate computerese into military terms. On another occasion, an officer who was at least her father's age made a drunken pass at her after a barbecue. But her real disillusionment came with an event that went far beyond poor communications or a pathetic sexual advance.

Having learned early at IBM that it paid to master any system for which she was responsible, she spent long hours printing out everything in the bomb-damage-assessment file and analyzing it. The printout identified bombing targets only by map coordinates, but the coordinates could be checked against a coded list of geographic place names. She was glad she had decided to go through the tedious checking procedure because she soon turned up an anomaly: Some of the targets appeared to be in Cambodia. Since America was not supposed to be bombing neutral Cambodia, she assumed she had uncovered an internal programming problem. She took it to her supervising colonel.

"I told him there was something wrong with the data integrity and asked him what we could do to fix it," she says. "He just gave me a little smile like I was really stupid. All he said was: 'the data is correct.' That's all. 'The data is correct.' "

Though she did not fully appreciate the magnitude of her discovery—the illegal bombing would be among the articles of impeachment considered against President Richard M. Nixon by the House Judiciary Committee five years later—she was deeply shocked.

"That was a real turning point in my life, realizing that they were lying. It wasn't just one or two evil people who decided to tell a lie. It was a management decision to plan to deceive people. Up until that time I thought organizations basically worked for the good of humanity. I don't think I ever conceived that an organization would just not care what the public thought the way the armed forces did. It is still a difficult concept for me."

Vietnam, occurring at the prime of the organization man's life and as an expression of the powerful institutions he had created, remains a watershed in the organizationalism of his children, *whatever their politics*. For Joann, who like many, perhaps most, of her peers was neither hawk nor dove, it was the first in a long series of disillusionments she would experience in large organizations. For her more politicized contemporaries, the war would be similarly disillusioning, whether they viewed its prosecution as bureaucratic cowardice or mechanized murder. At the time, Joann exempted IBM from her criticism, preferring instead to lay the blame entirely on the military and the government. Her disenchantment with the company would come later.

Meanwhile, back in the States, the other members of Joann's family were going about their lives. Her younger sister Carolyn, a junior at the University of Texas, was rolling up an impressive scholastic record that would eventually take her to a doctorate and a career in academe and was, incidentally, demonstrating against the war at every opportunity. Her sister Julia and her brother Tom, both still in high school, lived comfortably at home, though home and city changed about every three years and sometimes year to year, depending on where General Motors sent their father, Dave Harrison. Currently, they lived in the same Detroit suburb they had left for Houston five years before, and they were wrestling with reestablishing their identities there. Dave's wife Helen was, for the ninth time in a little over twenty years, trying once again to make a new home for them all. Dave Harrison himself was locked in a struggle of his own—a fight to save his nearly twenty-five-year-old career with General Motors. His antagonist was an up-and-coming young general manager of Chevrolet named John Z. DeLorean. It was an experience that would be fully as eye opening as his daughter's was with the air force.

Glimpsed at the close of the sixties, the Harrisons strikingly reflect the life of the organization family at a crucial moment in American history. In many ways, it was the end of the best of times and the beginning of the worst of times. The massive resources of the government, the military, and aerospace contractors had combined to put an American on the moon; a similar combination applied to Vietnam was shattering the cultural consensus that legitimates all such vast enterprises. American corporations had never been more prosperous or more hegemonic in the world; oil shocks and a deluge of imported goods were about to signal the emergence of a truly global marketplace for which those same corporations were ill prepared. The unprecedented postwar affluence achieved by organization parents and taken for granted by their children would begin to give way to a long, slow economic decline that attracted little notice until the end of the seventies but that nevertheless would influence the course of the baby boomers' lives far more than would assassinations, the threat of nuclear war, or any of the other cataclysms that are ritually invoked to explain how we got from there to here.

As would many organization men in the decade to come, Dave Harrison was receiving the first of several shocks about the corporate bargain he had struck almost twenty-five years before. But his experience only hinted at the coming dissolution of the mystique of organization. Joann, in Vietnam, stood at its fountainhead, though she understood it only imperfectly. Carolyn, on the other hand, absorbing the sixties' youth culture at its zenith, was unceremoniously—and not altogether reflectively—dumping the values of her parents. Julia and Tom, still in high school, were largely missing the political dimension of the sixties, but they would soon leave home and live the decade's aftermath, when counterculture degenerated into life-style and the search for self-fulfillment went forward in an increasingly inhospitable economy.

What Dave Harrison's troubling experience of the organization neither hinted at nor comprehended in 1969 was the striking form that individualism would take among his children and the children of men like him, though that individualism was incubated in the organization family and though the parents and the children share some thirty or forty years of common history. For despite that common history, the two generations, like all generations, have aged differently: The same events have had different meanings for each. Growing up in what they came to regard as a world of unstable organizations, sterile suburbs, and artificial social relations—characterizations that largely mystify their parents—the organization offspring would develop a thoroughly psychologized individualism based on the elusive ideal of the authentic self. Many, including all four of the Harrison children at one time or another, would adopt the artist as their occupational ideal. But such values did not spring into being outside the family; they were first transmitted in the material circumstances that made those families possible. And they were transformed by the historical circumstances through which the children of such families subsequently lived.

Just as generations age differently, so do, more subtly, different age cohorts within a generation. Joann Harrison, born in 1945, represents the leading edge of the baby boom and has much in common with younger members of the so-called silent generation, while sister Carolyn, born in 1949, epitomizes a kind of high-sixties political consciousness. Julia, born in 1951, seems more a product of the early seventies; for her, the political and social realms hardly exist, except as a kind of a delusory screen obscuring the real psychological drama within. Tom, although born in 1953, did not emerge from college and onto the job market until the late seventies and thus more closely resembles those members of the generation for whom the economy has been one long cold shower. Through a detailed look at such a family, we can begin to see the stark differences between the generations, as well as the more fine-grained differences among the organization offspring themselves.

But beyond—or perhaps among—the offspring's differences lie their overwhelming similarities: their concern with the self, their adoption of a personal myth of artistry to make sense of their identities, and their unique combination of private and public experiences that would eventually prod them out of their belief in authenticity and drag them—kicking and screaming—toward the world of social artificiality they have rejected since adolescence. But until that time, organization families like the Harrisons—nomadic, upwardly mobile, and infused with expressive values in an instrumental world dominated by large organizations—would literally and figuratively displace persons with selves.

"They were always around strangers."

The subdivision lies forty-five minutes from San Francisco, beyond the Berkeley hills in the East Bay's booming Contra Costa County. The low California ranch houses, their deceptive exteriors concealing spacious interiors, stretch along the valley and reach into the foothills of nearby Mount Diablo. In 1974, when Dave Harrison bought here, he was promised that the hills behind his house would remain free of development. But several million-dollar structures, replete with soaring glass cathedral fronts and heliport-size decks, have come to perch precariously above him, minor irritants in an otherwise idyllic setting for his retirement.

On this day, a Sunday in March 1987, his driveway is jammed with Chevrolets. Two of them belong to Harrison and his wife Helen, but the remaining three belong to three of their children. It is no surprise that the children drive Chevys—Dave can buy them wholesale—but what is surprising is that Joann, Julia, and Tom have all settled close enough to their parents to drive over for Sunday dinner.

Unlike the Myers family, who remained stationary during Ray's tenure with Continental Illinois, the Harrisons moved twelve times during Dave's thirty-eight years with the Chevrolet Motor Division of General Motors, a common experience for many organization families of his generation. At General Motors informal policy dictated a move at least once every five years. For the most successful men, like Harrison, who won a raise or a promotion every year, the moves came far more often, sometimes yearly.

Inside the Harrison house, where three generations are gathered, good-humored chaos prevails. Joann, the eldest daughter, and Julia, the youngest, help their mother cook while they catch up on things with Carolyn, the middle daughter, who has flown out for a visit during spring break from the East Coast liberal arts college at which she teaches. Carolyn's eighteen-month-old daughter and Tom's two daughters, aged four and six, weave through the forest of adult legs in the kitchen cadging food and affection. Tom, the youngest of the Harrison siblings, keeps one eye cocked on his children while he talks with Paul, Julia's husband of six months. Six years younger than Julia, Paul has left the frustrating world of New York theater for a career in law.

There is much for the family members to catch up on. Joann has recently developed a new software package that could make her company really take off, but she faces stiff competition from a company she suspects of pirating her product. Meanwhile, her cash-flow problems grow more acute while potential customers—all *Fortune* 500 companies—drag out the contract negotiations. It is unlikely that she and her unethical competitor can both survive.

Carolyn brings similar good news/bad news. Among the hordes of recent liberal arts Ph.D.s, she is one of the fortunate few who actually has a job in her vastly overcrowded profession, and she has just had her contract renewed for an additional three years. But, already the author of one book, she must, within that period, publish another, plus several more scholarly articles, to win tenure. If she does not, she will lose her job. The demands of motherhood and a two-career marriage put the outcome much in doubt. In the meantime, she earns the same amount of money as, and has none of the job security of, the Teamsters who collect her garbage.

Julia, who has spent most of her life in dance, has been named artistic director of a well-regarded but financially strapped Bay Area modern dance company. In her five months on the job, she has auditioned and hired a new set of dancers, reorganized the board of directors, and thrown herself wholeheartedly into raising desperately needed funds. She is also choreographing a lengthy new piece for the company's first concert under her direction. Given the group's past history of financial problems, a poor reception of the concert will likely kill the eleven-year-old company.

Like Carolyn, Tom finds himself whipsawed between job and family. Recently divorced and currently involved in a bitter child-custody dispute, he has managed to arrange his life so he can function four days a week as a single parent. A computer repairman, he is dispatched to jobs from his home. Sometimes no calls come, and he can devote himself to the children. And on heavy days, when he cannot get home in time to pick up the children from school or day care, his parents, who live just twenty minutes away, can be pressed into emergency baby-sitting service. Employment requiring travel or relocation would cost him most of the 50 percent custody he has fought so hard to win. However, the company for which he works is in bankruptcy. Should it fail to reorganize successfully, he will be jobless and hard pressed to find other work that allows him such freedom.

All this information emerges in fragmented conversations interrupted by children's squeals, laughter, and attention to the logistics of feeding ten family members and a visitor. Advice, sympathy, and jokes pass easily back and forth. Out on the patio Dave Harrison grills steaks. Tall, his black silver-streaked hair combed back in a presidential pompadour, he wears golf slacks, a knit shirt, and black horn-rimmed bifocals. His vigor, legendary among the family members, seems undiminished at age sixty-nine. A hearty backslapper with a booming voice and a direct manner, he wields a large spatula like a scepter of jovial authority. It is easy to imagine him when he was national sales-promotion director for Chevrolet, thriving among the bluff, expansive men in Detroit who brought private transportation to the masses. Helen, like her husband, appears at ease with herself, though she sometimes humorously feigns consternation at his high spirits. Matronly and brimming with warm-hearted affection, she alternately dotes on the grandchildren for whom she has waited so long and exhibits rapt interest in even the tiniest details of her children's conversation. Proud and fond parents, Dave and Helen nevertheless seem a bit surprised and even faintly bewildered to find themselves with children approaching middle age whose lives are such precarious blends of success and insecurity.

Of Joann's entrepreneurship Dave says candidly, "She's got more guts than what I had. And I'm glad she's doing it. I'm glad somebody's got the guts to step out there and try it, because the rewards can be great. But I worry about her. She's carrying an awfully big debt load and she's had some setbacks and it concerns me."

"I'm real proud of her doing it," says Helen, "but I do worry about her security in the future, what will happen when she's in her sixties. It's just that we're used to having a big corporation behind us."

When Joann fought IBM for assignment to Vietnam, Dave and

Helen discouraged her. "I told her not to buck her manager," says Dave. "I felt if she insisted on fighting them they were going to fire her."

Joann, overhearing, refuses to let this pass. "It was against the law for them to have fired me, Daddy."

"I know it," he says, "but back in those days we just didn't pay that much attention to women's lib law."

She and her mother both laugh at the blithe incontestability of his statement. "IBM told her Vietnam was no place for her," Helen says, then adds with amusement: "*We* had always done what General Motors told us to do."

Tom, tall like his father, but laconic and bearded and given to blue jeans instead of golf slacks, evokes in his parents similar pride and perplexity. Pride over his determination to keep and raise his children and over his deeply nurturing personality that has emerged. Perplexity over the role reversal: their daughters delaying and forgoing child rearing to pursue high-powered careers, their son eschewing a high-powered career to rear children.

"We always looked for our kids to settle down and start raising children, just like we did," says Dave. "They didn't do it and it always concerned us. Helen would say, 'Will I ever be a grandmother?' Well, now she is, but for a long time we didn't think she would be. And we didn't think our youngest child would give us our first grandchild."

Julia's situation appears equally uncertain. Success in modern dance brings neither security for the future nor even much money for the present. Some of the most prestigious dance companies in the country struggle simply to survive from season to season. Dave and Helen, having reluctantly helped support Julia for the long years of her apprenticeship, which stretched into her thirties, cannot understand why she did not also acquire skills that could pay her way and why she does not now seek the safety of a teaching job.

In Carolyn's case they were spared the anxiety they feel about their other children's insecure lives—until they learned when she finally earned her doctorate what an uncertain profession she pursues. "We thought that once you got a doctorate, hell, everybody would be clamoring for you, because we didn't know too many doctors," says Dave. "We didn't know there weren't any jobs for doctors."

Their perplexity grows, in part, from a general unwillingness to put things in any larger perspective. In characteristic American fashion, none of the Harrisons imagines himself or herself caught up in historical, cultural, and economic forces, despite the turbulent history all have witnessed. Most of what has happened to them they see as personal choice, matters of character, and aspects of individuality.

Julia, for example, worries that most of the hot choreographers seem to be in their late twenties, five to six years her junior. Despite all the media attention to the sheer overwhelming number of baby boomers, she is surprised to be told that the most numerous age group in the population is thirty. Similarly, Dave and Helen, worrying over their children's erratic career paths, difficulty affording housing, and delayed childbearing, sometimes wonder if they are somehow at fault as parents. They take no comfort in, indeed seem unaware of, explanations based on demographics, America's economic decline, or the changing social value of children. The characteristic response of Joann and Julia to problems that conceivably have a basis in society is to seek psychotherapy, capitalism's mechanism for converting collective grievances into personal complaints.

Nevertheless, the Harrisons, in their history and their circumstances, strikingly represent the sweep of American life in this century. Dave's and Helen's parents worked in extractive industries, such as farming and oil; Dave left the land and those quintessentially nineteenth-century industries for the more abstract and typically mid-twentieth-century world of the organization; his children toil in knowledge, information, and service jobs typical of the American economy today. Many American families have taken in three generations a similar journey.

As with occupational life, so with personal life. Dave and Helen, like the overwhelming majority of organization couples, have enjoyed a long, stable marriage of forty-four years. By contrast, their children have accumulated four divorces. And all four children have lived at one time or another out of wedlock with a lover. Dave and Helen, as soon as they were married, began having children and did not stop until they had four. Joann, twice divorced, expects neither to remarry nor to have children. Carolyn, once divorced and now remarried, delayed childbearing until age thirty-six and is not sure whether she will have another child. Julia delayed marriage until age thirty-five and has only now begun to think about the implications of having children. Tom, who had his first child at the comparatively young age of twenty-eight, struggles as a single parent.

The divergent marriage and childbearing patterns, like the divergent work experiences, reflect broad generational, as opposed to merely individual, differences. Under the pressure of historical events and economic circumstances, the generations have aged differently, creating distinctive life courses. But it is not merely a difference of the timing of key events in the life course, such as marriage, childbearing, or entry into the work force, but of the *meaning* of those events. Beyond the question of why members of the rising generation delay marriage and childbearing or change jobs and spouses so frequently lies the more important question of what marriage, children, and work now mean to them. For example, part of the meaning of children has changed strikingly, though it is difficult to admit and perhaps shocking to say. As a child, Dave Harrison, working at odd jobs from the time he was ten and contributing his earnings to the family, was an economic asset. His children, born during a period of unprecedented prosperity, came to be seen as "priceless," having no economic function and existing solely as objects of love for their own sake. His children's children, however, are neither economic assets nor priceless, but rather "opportunity costs" in an economy that increasingly demands that both parents work.

It is worth repeating that it is not merely that the generations lived in different times. Even the large portion of history they have shared has impinged on them differentially. The baby boom itself, witnessed by both generations, stands as a clear example of the differential meaning of the same historical event for the generations. For baby boomers, their vast numbers mean bruising competition in every area of life and uncertain prospects for their old age. For their parents who are approaching retirement, it means a vast horde of younger workers paying the social security taxes out of which the benefits of *current* retirees come (which is how social security actually works, notwithstanding the illusion that it consists of individual annuity accounts).

None of the foregoing is meant to suggest that the Harrisons of either generation are at the mercy of irresistible, unknowable forces, merely that they are prone to overlook those larger issues when examining their lives. If they tend to put too much emphasis on individual choice, then it is possible that an observer puts too much emphasis on impersonal constraint. The Harrisons do have unique personalities that act on and react to the experience of family life, organizational life, and social history. Their story is one of a complex interplay among all these elements, each affecting the other in a way that confounds simple causal analysis.

Over dinner, accompanied by a good California cabernet to go with the steaks and the unforced good cheer of the gathering, they talk about an experience in which all those elements of individual, family, and organizational life converge: the nomadic childhood of the children. Though they appear outgoing and socially adept, all the Harrison children believe the frequent moves made them shy. Their parents agree.

"We had moved around all the time," says Dave, "and they never really had a lot of time to be around other people and make friends, except us. They were always around strangers. You'd think that would help them to get over their shyness, but it didn't."

"When I would take Carolyn to Sunday school," says Helen, "she would sit and tremble." To Carolyn, she says, "you were determined to go, but you would sit there and shake the whole time."

From the group there rises a hoot of amused sympathy for Carolyn. Joann says, "I remember going into schools in the middle of the term. I never felt like I fit in. In fact, I didn't feel like a part of my generation until I was thirty-eight years old."

Though the children can laugh about it now, the moves could be devastating to the little world of friends and accomplishments so carefully cultivated in each new location. One move came at the beginning of Carolyn's senior year at a high school in Michigan where she would have been valedictorian. A series of three moves in three years, each in the middle of the fall semester, ended Tom's dogged attempts to play football. In private, later, Joann will confide that she believes the psychological effects of moving around contributed to her two divorces.

"I felt bad about all the moving," says Dave, "but I always felt that I had the opportunity to progress and make more money and that would allow me to give them the things that they wanted. So I rationalized the moves from that standpoint. When we first uprooted them from the schools, Helen and I both were really upset. When we pulled Joann out of Dallas—"

"I was going to run away," she interjects.

"Yes," says Helen, "and when we pulled Julia out of ninth grade in Michigan, where it was junior high, and put her in Houston where the ninth grade was high school, she fainted a couple of times."

Parents and children remember differently the numerous occasions on which Dave would gather the family around and inform them of yet another impending move.

"I don't think we had any scenes," he says. "Our kids were awfully good."

They laugh in contradiction.

"You didn't yell and scream," Dave says, mock-defensively. "You *cried* some." Now they laugh in appreciation. "I just told them the facts of life. I said, 'This is your daddy's job and if I'm going to keep working for the company I've got to go.' If the company said move, you moved. If you said no, you either sat there and never got another promotion or raise the rest of your life or they fired you."

When dinner ends, Dave and Helen take the grandchildren with them and leave the conversation to the children. The subject is raised of their rootlessness in the present and their responses to it, a subject that will come up many times in the coming week. Joann speaks enthusiastically—sometimes in the tortured jargon of pop psychology—of a women's support group she has been involved with for the past five years. The members, all businesswomen like Joann, get together once a month to talk frankly about their business problems and to "develop intimacy."

"For those of us who don't have a husband to go home to at night, you have someone to tell your problems to," she says. "You can have the sympathetic ear of other businesswomen and not have to worry about posturing because as you rise in the business world, you have to continually posture that you're successful."

What does such a group "support"?

"One's morale," she says.

"Your life," says Tom.

"Human beings aren't islands," says Joann. "We all need somebody not only to keep up morale, but to keep up our emotional connectedness to other people."

She variously characterizes her group as a surrogate family and as a means of establishing community. Julia, intrigued by the operation of the group, expresses mild interest in joining. Tom defends it as offering an emotional outlet that ordinary, tension-filled friendship does not. As the evening winds down, there is more desultory conversation about various remedies for deracination, but no one mentions the solution all of them, with the exception of Carolyn, have actually chosen—that of living near each other and their parents.

This is one version of a contradiction to be found among many of the organization offspring, especially those whose families were the most geographically and socially mobile. The family, as the arena in which the self of the priceless child was first formed, propelled the offspring toward a highly psychologized individualism that would leave them as adults feeling anxious and alone, groping for an intimacy that the ideal of the authentic self makes all but impossible. Thus, their families, to which they are linked in ways they do not clearly see, are central to the very selfhood that blinds them.

Later, both Julia and Tom will express a longing for community and offer visions of it much like Joann's—a collection of people roughly the same age, same values, and same social status, who have *chosen* to be together. In short, they quite unself-consciously envision the antithesis of community *and* family, in neither of which does one choose the other members nor enjoy equal status.

Driving back through the wealthy East Bay suburbs toward the evanescent city life of San Francisco, an observer reflects that what seems to be missing from these evocations of community is the sense of *place*, in its geographic and—anathema to egalitarians—hierarchical sense, both of which dominated the nineteenth-century small-town world of the Harrison children's grandparents. As would become increasingly clear, it was a world Dave and Helen Harrison chose to leave forever and that their children not only do not know, but do not know that they do not know.

"To get more money, you had to move."

The small-town world of Dave Harrison was located in Bossier Parish, Louisiana, where his father, who died in 1923 when Dave was five, worked as a carpenter and had a small farm. Dave's mother, to support her seven children after the death of her husband, opened a boardinghouse, catering to the roughnecks who flocked to Louisiana to work in the oil fields. She earned additional income as a seamstress. All the children found part-time work as soon as they were able and contributed their earnings to the family purse. Dave delivered groceries; did odd jobs; and in high school, worked as an usher at the local movie house.

Today, sitting in a back bedroom he has converted into a home office, he talks quietly about the effect of seeing his mother bent over her sewing, working far into the night after having spent the day cooking, cleaning, and looking after her boarders and children.

"It gave me a work ethic that I still have," he says. "I felt like I had to get out and produce as quickly as I could to bring some money into the household. Any one of our family who had a nickel or a dime or a dollar made it available to all the rest of the family."

Though the Great Depression exacerbated the family's already precarious economic condition, they managed to scrape by from week to week and even to breathe a bit more easily as each successive child matured and entered the work force. Nevertheless, living on the edge of poverty made an indelible impression on Harrison.

"I wanted someplace to go to work that would give me security," he says, "so that my family would not have to go through what I went through. When I had the opportunity to go to General Motors, I felt that this was a place where if I worked hard, I could stay all the rest of my life."

On the wall hang family pictures and mementos of that life spent with the company: sales awards; photos taken with various celebrities who endorsed Chevrolet; a framed letter from Bear Bryant congratulating Harrison on his retirement; and a photograph of Harrison with Gene Autry and Richard Nixon, a memento of an evening in Autry's private box at a California Angels' game. Some of his children's diplomas also hang there. For Harrison, college was out of the question. Following high school, he went to work instead in the parts department of the local Chevrolet dealer, fetching parts for the mechanics and enviously watching the parts manager being courted by Chevrolet's traveling parts representatives.

He liked the work and the steady pay, but he soon grew restless. A parts rep, deigning to talk to him one day, mentioned an opening for a parts manager at a dealership in southern Mississippi. Having no idea how to pursue a job in such a distant place and not daring to let his boss know he wanted to leave, Harrison wrote in the third person a laudatory letter about himself, signed it illegibly, and sent it to the dealer. He got the job and soon found himself living hundreds of miles from home, the first of his family to leave the area. Except for visits, he never returned.

He had been as much pushed out of that world by the social currents of the middle third of the century as pulled by his own savvy grasp of the opportunities they presented: "I had no real desire to leave home. I just had to get out where I could make some money, and I saw that to get more money, you had to move because the money is just not there in a small town. I didn't think about it consciously; I just found myself doing it."

As parts manager he worked the service counter for the mechanics and the front counter for customers. He called on independent garages and persuaded them to buy parts from the dealership. On nights and weekends he put up stock and organized the inventory. He worked harder than he ever had before, but now at least the Chevrolet reps called on *him*, took him to lunch, and tried to sell him ideas and systems that would profit the dealership and Chevrolet. Wearing suits and ties and always driving a brand-new car, the reps were emissaries of a world where no one dirtied their hands. Their medium was people, not things.

"This is the first time I saw somebody working primarily by his wits," says Dave. "He didn't have to work as I had to work. He didn't have to lift a part out of a bin and run over and write up a ticket for it. I guessed he might have had to write a report or something back at the home office, but that was a lot better than doing manual labor. I realized that instead of hustling parts maybe I could hustle somebody else."

Before he could explore the possibilities, the war intervened. He enlisted in the army, went to officer candidate school, and wound up in the quartermaster corps because of his automotive experience. During a two-week leave, he returned to his hometown and married Helen, who was in her last semester at Louisiana State University. He had known Helen since high school, where, he says, "she was the prettiest girl in the school." She left college to accompany him to Tampa, thinking he would soon be sent overseas. Instead, he was assigned to run commissaries at a succession of stateside air bases, and she was able to remain with him for the duration. When he was given his first command, the responsibility frightened him, but like many men caught up in the war's vast mobilization of American resources, he soon learned valuable administrative and organizational skills at a relatively young age.

"I had about twenty-five men I was company commander for, and they looked to me to get things done. I lectured to them, outlined their work program for them, and did all the other things necessary to make a company perform. You took the responsibility of the position and gained the respect of the people under you, and your power came from that, rather than just from the raw power that came with the job. By the time I completed my tour of duty and got promoted to captain, I welcomed the responsibility."

As his discharge date approached, he wrote a blind letter to the Chevrolet zone manager in New Orleans asking for a job as a parts rep. He received an encouraging reply, but nothing definite. When he was finally discharged, he took his young wife and new baby daughter to Shreveport and awaited further word. A long-distance call—a rare event in those days—summoned him to New Orleans for an interview. He put on his only suit, made the six-hour drive overnight, and slept in his car until it was time for the interview. The manager did not show up. The following week the same thing happened. On the third try, he was granted his interview. The manager sat in stony silence while Dave, sitting ramrod straight, answered a subordinate's questions. At last, the manager asked his only question.

"Harrison," he said, "do you drink?"

Dave sensed danger, but decided to risk everything on honesty.

"Socially, sir," he said.

They excused him and went to lunch. When they returned, they told him the job was his.

"God, I broke out in smiles and grabbed their hands and shook them. I was elated. I didn't know if jobs were going to be hard to find after the war; I just knew what I wanted."

"There was family and there was everybody else."

Sitting in her office off Market Street in San Francisco's business district, fielding phone calls from clients and inquiries from employees, Joann Harrison projects a remarkable combination of discipline and flex-

ibility. If she can solve a problem quickly, she does; but she has promised to spend several days talking about her life, and though the phone
calls could mean a lot of money to her, she deflects them without sub-
terfuge or regret.

At work she favors designer ensembles over manlike power suits,
exposed brick over glass and steel, tasteful lithographs over seascapes.
Like many achievers of her generation, she looks far younger than she is,
thanks to a ferocious regimen of diet and exercise. Tall like her father,
possessed of robust Teutonic beauty from her mother, she talks without
pretense about her business: It may survive, it may not. If it does not,
she will sell the Russian Hill cooperative and move back into the tiny
condo whose second mortgage is keeping her company afloat. The next
year or so will tell.

"The business has been up and down, up and down," she says,
"but I'm still here after eight years. The failure rate is ninety percent the
first year and then ninety percent of the remaining ten percent within the
next five years. In eight years my company has evolved from a consulting, service-industry business to a product-oriented business, a product
that I created, packaged, and marketed myself and that, more impor-
tantly, I own."

Born in December 1945 on the Georgia army base where her father
was winding up his wartime service, Joann Harrison missed being a baby
boomer by a few days. It was a lucky miss. She never experienced the
overcrowded classrooms, tight job market, fierce competition for housing, and all the other punishing Darwinian struggles in which most of the
generation, especially its younger members, still find themselves engaged. She unwittingly got another jump on them by completing college
in three years.

She also missed living at home during the period of her parents'
greatest affluence. For the first ten years of her life, spent in, respec-
tively, New Orleans, El Paso, and Houston, her father toiled in the lower
reaches of General Motors' vast hierarchy. Though her father loved his
work as a representative, and later as a manager, in parts and accessories,
it was hardly the most glamorous or most remunerative side of the company. Each successive lower-middle-class house was a bit bigger than the
previous one, and the pay was steadily increasing, but even a five-figure,
never mind a six-figure, salary remained only a possibility. In the meantime, Dave had a wife and, by 1953, four children to support.

The Harrisons were by no means poor, but, haunted like most
members of their generation by memories of the depression, they were
extremely frugal. Joann and the next oldest daughter, Carolyn, both

recall luxuries like Coca-Cola appearing only on special occasions—a recollection Julia and Tom, the two younger children, laughingly dismiss as a family myth.

"Cokes and bean dip was our Christmas Eve ritual," says Joann. "I would generally get sick before we drank them because I was so excited, since we had them maybe twice a year. I was looking forward to them more than to Santa Claus.

"But I'd say I had everything that all my peers had. But it wasn't like kids today being aware of designer things and designer clothes. For example, if it was saddle shoes, I didn't care whether they were good or bad saddle shoes as long as they were black and white."

In her earliest years, her father was often gone from Monday until Friday, canvassing the far-flung Chevrolet dealerships in his zone. Every three years or so he was transferred. For Joann and the other kids, the transfers meant saying good-bye to friends, entering a strange school in a strange city, and making new friends knowing that these friends, too, would soon be left behind.

For the parents the transition was eased by the Chevrolet people in the new city, who offered advice about neighborhoods, tips on new homes, introductions to loan officers, and entree to a ready-made social life. Many of the men rose through the ranks together, their career paths crossing and recrossing in various cities along the way. The children enjoyed no such continuity; for them, displacement was absolute.

Three moves took place by the time Joann was age five, though she remembers none of them. Subsequent moves frequently came in the middle of the school year. Like most schoolchildren, Joann marked time in terms of grade level, not age, and those grade levels loom as large in childish consciousness as the adult milestones of marriage, parenthood, promotions, and retirement. Joann was moved after the beginning of kindergarten, in the middle of third grade, in the middle of seventh grade, and in the middle of eleventh grade.

The effect of such frequent disruptions is difficult to gauge. Of similar children who appeared in the schools of Park Forest for a season or two and then moved on, Whyte wrote: "The children . . . have proved to be highly adaptable material, and the teachers who have had experience in traditional communities are quick to note how much more socially responsive the children of transients are than others." Perhaps, but as all the Harrison children attest, such responsiveness might have also concealed an anxious desire to please, masking deep shyness and insecurity. For Joann, arriving in a new place was even more painful than was leaving an old one.

"I remember always being stared at," she says. "Kids tend to dress differently in different schools, particularly from region to region, and I would always dress the way it was cool to dress in the old school. I felt like I was always the odd person out."

Frequent moves accustomed them to living with a high degree of insecurity, but did not necessarily make them more secure. "I think we got a strong dose of what life does to you," she says, "which is very different from the concept that *you* do to life. It was kind of like ants: They're over here and if you scoop up the anthill and take it over there, they continue about their business."

Joann speculates that moving may have played a part in her two failed marriages. As a child she never knew friendships that lasted more than a couple of years. Rather than resolving rifts with friends, she simply moved on. The experience taught her to regard intimacy as the evasion of conflict, not the overcoming of it.

"I never realized that even with people you like a lot there will be periods of distance and that you don't just abandon the relationship. You work on it and get back together." For most of her formative years, her family was the only arena for the sometimes difficult give and take of genuine affection. "There was family, and there was everybody else," she says. "You could yell at them and scream at them and still you often had to sleep in the same bed. There was always that built-in group to come home to at night to get support from and to play with, even though the friends you really wanted were your own age. But I always had these family members who were there, so I never felt alone."

Joann thinks such intimacy by default accounts for the family's enduring affection today, especially the deep friendship of the siblings as adults. But—a veteran of therapy—she thinks it impeded what the psychologists call individuation, which she carefully distinguishes from individualism.

"I never knew that I was supposed to be part of a peer group. I was always individualistic; I never realized that if I dressed like them, I might be accepted more. Yet I was always disappointed that I was not popular. Now I realize that identification with your peer group is a very important part of separating from your parents, of maturing. And I missed that."

Nevertheless, she came up with the same imaginative solution to the problem of identity as did her peers: She decided to become an artist. In her case, the dream was to be a ballerina. "Not just any ballerina," she laughs, "but a *prima* ballerina." For years she and her two sisters took ballet lessons at the ubiquitous, nearly interchangeable dancing schools in whatever suburb the family happened to reside. After several years, when she was the last student in her class to go on point, the dream changed to becoming a concert pianist.

All four Harrison children took piano lessons—Joann reluctantly, at first. But school field trips to children's concerts by the Houston Symphony, with Leopold Stokowski conducting, and a recital by Artur Rubinstein soon changed her mind. No matter where the family moved, the piano remained for Joann the one constant amid frequent change. In Detroit, as a high school student, she twice won citywide contests for a summer scholarship to the National Music Camp at Interlochen, Michigan.

Interlochen was exhilarating. She received intensive instruction, she practiced endlessly, and she met first-rate musicians. Gradually, however, she began to recognize her limitations. Having once been mildly dyslexic, she found memorizing and executing lengthy sonatas nearly impossible. Then, listening one day to the playing of a young man not much older than she who was already pursuing a career on the concert stage, she came to a painful realization: She would never be good enough. Though she went on to major in music (and math) in college, she never again seriously entertained the notion of herself as a concert pianist.

A child's fantasy, given up in adolescence, would bear little attention except that similar artistic fantasies are nearly universal among the now-*adult* children of organization men (and, one suspects, among a large number of baby boomers in general). Some few, like Joann's younger sister Julia, have achieved their ambitions to be artists. Most have not and never will. Nevertheless, they continue to harbor images of themselves as artists of some sort—writers, dancers, actors, musicians, painters, filmmakers—or as engaging in all their activities "creatively." Joann, in giving up her dreams, represents something of an anomaly. But, then, she was still running just slightly ahead of the baby boom.

By the time she left for college at the University of Texas in 1963, her father had been in central office for only two years. The family was living in a modest suburb of Detroit, and Dave was worried about being able to send all four children to college. He urged Joann to work in the summers and save her money. She did, managing to pay most of her college expenses herself.

Returning from college for summer vacations, she was surprised by the way her youngest sister went through new clothes. Joann's clothing had often consisted of hand-me-downs from a cousin in Louisiana. Otherwise, a minimum number of practical outfits filled out her wardrobe right through high school. Later, she noticed other changes in the family's standard of living—more restaurant meals, exotic company-sponsored vacations, and a refrigerator routinely stocked with Cokes. By then, with fewer expectations and greater opportunities than her siblings would have, she was already trying to earn such things herself.

As it happened, the computer field provided an excellent means of getting them. Though she was a math major, she fell into computers by chance. The field had barely advanced beyond the days of UNIVAC and clumsy machines the size of a house endlessly spinning out the value of pi. Except for a handful of visionaries, few people foresaw the computer-dominated society that would soon emerge. And certainly no one thought of steering young people into computer careers.

According to Joann, the University of Texas offered only one computer course at the time. She enrolled in it when her father told her about summer jobs at General Motors for college students who could help convert warranty records to computer storage. She got the job and lived at home for the summer. During the daily one-hour commute to and from the General Motors complex on the western edge of Detroit, she and her father discussed business. He told her about the sales promotion of new cars, into which he had long since moved, and she told him about computers. For the first time she sensed the vast, teeming organization behind the brand-new Chevrolet he brought home each new-model year, an experience her younger siblings would never have. After the dull routine of school, this huge building, "full of men running around in suits," seemed exciting and important. "I didn't so much think 'this is the life for me,' " she says, "as I did 'this is the real world; this is what I will graduate into.' "

She transferred to the University of Michigan to take more computer courses and, more important, to join Bill, another General Motors brat she had met on the summer computer job. She also worked part time as a programmer at the Michigan department of education. By graduation, she and Bill, now married, were able to go into IBM together, an entry-level path that subsequent baby boomers would find increasingly enviable—and increasingly crowded. She has worked ever since.

"I just thought that when you finished college, you went to work," Joann says. "That's what you did. I wasn't aware that I was going to work for the premier company. They met our qualifications, which were travel, being together, and good money."

Posted to Washington to work on NASA's Orbiting Astronomical Observatory project, she was quickly inducted into organizational life.

"I spent six months being hammered into the IBM image by my manager," she says. "First they started working on your punctuality—be at your desk and working by eight, no rolling in a couple of minutes late, no coffee, only a thirty-minute lunch, no personal phone calls. You were productive eight hours a day and you didn't automatically pop up at five. They expected you to work overtime. Then they started working on my dress. This is the way they manufactured IBM people."

Political opinions were checked at the door. She recalls getting off an all-night shift at six one beautiful April morning and driving home by way of the reflecting pool to see the cherry blossoms. Instead, she encountered streets full of soldiers. Smoke from smoldering buildings floated above the city. Martin Luther King had been killed the previous day in Memphis (where her parents then lived), and she had not yet heard. Bill, already in Vietnam, had begun to write her disturbing letters about the nature of the war. At night she was stuffing envelopes for Eugene McCarthy. She had no idea what her co-workers thought about any of this.

"I had been molded into someone who does not discuss anything but business," she says. "They effectively stamped out all personal manifestations. I just thought this is the way the world is and that somehow I had come out of school this kind of sloppy person with all these personal opinions. From then on, I just assumed that during the eight hours you were at work, they controlled what you said and the way you dressed and the time you had. And that was the way it was."

IBM also turned her into a highly capable technician. Company policy dictated the shifting of personnel to a new project every eighteen months. "It kept your mind constantly having to fight to learn new things," Joann says. "It certainly developed me professionally. It made me a quick study, and that's one of the things that has served me well as a consultant. I can walk in and learn a situation real fast and solve it and get out of there."

IBM offered broad scope for her talents and, at that time, a relatively uncongested career ladder. But the advantages she enjoyed ahead of the baby boom were soon eroded by what she saw as discrimination against women. Though she and Bill had identical education and experience, only he received a raise and a promotion almost immediately. Six months elapsed before she got a similar promotion. Men, including her husband, had no trouble winning assignment to Vietnam. She had to fight for ten months to get there. And though she did not know it at the time, she was among an advance guard of managerial women whose impatience with such treatment would do as much as any other historical development to challenge the complacent paternalism of the organization man's institutions.

"Adulthood seemed like death."

Sipping iced tea and basking in the brilliant California sunshine on her parents' patio, Carolyn Harrison looks comfortably at home in the suburban world she has consciously disdained since her teens. Her daughter splashes happily in an inflatable swimming pool nearby. Motherhood, at age thirty-six, altered many of Carolyn's attitudes.

"The mother image was not something I ever had in mind for myself," she says. "I was extremely naive about all of it. I not only rejected it for myself, but also I had absolutely no understanding of what women with children actually do and no idea of how many women with children have to work. I guess I always thought that when I had children, I would just have someone take care of them. I didn't realize how hard it is to find someone to take care of your children and how badly you wish to be with your children and not have them with someone else. The whole experience has really made me understand my mother a lot better, as well as a whole culture that I really rejected."

She currently lives in one of the industrial towns of the Boston metropolitan area in a house she and her husband bought when she became pregnant. Though the house sits on the edge of a high-crime, high-poverty area, it has nearly doubled in value since they bought it, and were they in the market today they could not afford it. Despite the rise in property values, the neighborhood runs no risk of gentrification.

"It is not a house that I ever would have thought I would live in. And it's not a neighborhood I would like my child to grow up in. Two blocks down the street is the center of crack dealing in the community. The schools are worse than bad; they're awful, with a thirty percent dropout rate. Because we have two incomes and my husband has the possibility of building up his public relations consulting business, we might be able to move out at some point, but social mobility is not something I ever thought I'd be wanting, and I feel bad about it. I feel guilty that I'm exhibiting such class-consciousness. I guess I always thought it was something I never cared about, but I never cared about it because it was never an issue before, I suppose. I never thought it would bother me. But it does bother me to live in a poor and violent neighborhood. And I'm sure it bothers all the other people who live there, too."

Though she laughingly says that living in suburbia for too long "makes you stupid," she can at least understand its appeal now. "The culture of suburbia provides a haven for families, and I understand much more why someone would want that. Before, I couldn't imagine why someone would choose such a life. And I feel embarrassed that I couldn't imagine it."

But she is fierce about people who now glorify the fifties or propound conservative theories of contemporary cultural decline. "Life was not better then," she says, "certainly not for women, not for blacks, not for Jews or for anyone else outside the male WASP world. Some people argue that women and blacks are worse off economically today. Even if that's true, it's no reason to roll back civil rights laws and equal employment or to blame the civil rights movement and feminism. In the fifties, male privilege went absolutely unchallenged, and the role models set before young girls were extremely bleak. I don't say this from the hindsight of feminism—I experienced Jayne Mansfield, Sandra Dee, and Annette Funicello as oppressive *at the time*."

She speaks with warmth and intensity about the left-liberal values she absorbed in the sixties and that, in the eighties, find more sophisticated expression in her feminist scholarship and most satisfying expression in teaching.

"When you teach, your values are totally implicated in everything you do, no matter what anybody says to the contrary. Teaching literature is a way to make young people sensitive not just to poetry, but to ways the world can be shaped and the way the world is valued and given value. Teaching is a way to fulfill some of that sense I had in the sixties of wanting to do something meaningful. Most of the time I do find it meaningful. You feel that students are connecting with ways of seeing, and those ways of seeing have broad implications. No matter what you're teaching, you're not just teaching that subject; you're teaching ways of being. I can't imagine many other careers where that's possible."

She had not always wanted to teach. Like Joann, she had first dreamed of becoming a dancer. Later, she took piano, guitar, and art lessons. When she discovered serious books, sometime early in high school, her aspirations turned to poetry. For girls, who were not expected to desire careers—even those girls who, like Carolyn, were headed for college—one avocation seemed as good as another. The only constant in her childhood besides her family was change.

"I had entered the third grade when we moved from Houston to Dallas in the fall of 1957. In school we were doing a project about cotton in groups of several children each. We were cutting things from magazines for this project, and for some reason I had all these things we had cut out. On the last day before I moved away, I walked home and I realized I had all my group's material with me. I didn't know what to do. I was walking home and I was crying and all these things were blowing out of my hands and I was supposed to have left them at school."

Three years later, when her father was promoted to central office, the family moved to the Detroit suburbs. As a junior high school student, she became more aware of her father's job. He took her to visit his office at the huge General Motors complex, with its four towers and huge sign that could be seen for twenty miles on a clear night. The nature of his business—sales promotions of new cars—confused her. "He was involved in a lot of promotions where he would get all these prizes and bring them home, like a big box of a hundred records or a TV or a stereo. I wondered what kind of business this was where you'd get TVs and things.''

At her parents' dinner parties she was further worried by the cynical banter that passed back and forth over the roast beef and Jell-O salads with mandarin oranges. "They would talk about business and people would ask, 'Oh, Dave, how are you profiting from all this?'—that kind of talk. But I always felt my father was honest. I think my concern was connected to Detroit and this sense of urbanness and that there was something about life that wasn't as clear as I thought."

A wan suburban Methodism did little to make it clearer. "When we went to Detroit, we were very involved in the church there, but religion was not in the household except in prayers before dinner. Other than that, it was strictly at the church that you were religious."

Though it is widely assumed that the vacuum left by suburban Protestantism and similar institutions was irreversibly filled, if not caused, by television, Carolyn has little recollection of early television except as the source of disturbing images of women. Though she and her siblings grew up on television, they watch little today and certainly far less than their parents do. More important to Carolyn, as to many of the older members of the baby-boom generation, were other mass media: popular music, general-interest magazines, and books. Indeed, Carolyn was led to "serious books" by the popularizations of existentialism to be found in numerous publications—though not on television—after Jean-Paul Sartre won and refused the Nobel Prize for literature in 1964.

She had always been a voracious reader, but she now immersed herself in Sartre and soon moved on to the works of Nietzsche and James Joyce, none of which was to be found among the *Reader's Digest* condensed books that dominated the bookshelves at home. She began writing poetry—"pretentious awful stuff, highly metaphoric pieces about *life*," she says today. "One of the things I remember very strongly from early adolescence was that I did not want to be an adult. I remember writing poems about that. Adulthood seemed like death. It seemed you just would not be as alive and as aware of things."

She was eager to go away to college where she could "read philosophy and meet people who weren't like everyone I knew." But at the beginning of her senior year in high school, she still had to endure one more wrenching move, the one that cost her the valedictorianship of her Michigan high school. There was talk of her staying behind with a friend's family for the year, but her father wouldn't hear of it. He drew the line at letting the moves break up his family.

The family returned to Houston, but to a wealthier, newer suburb consistent with the increased status from Dave's four promotions in the intervening ten years. Carolyn's anguish over leaving Michigan disappeared when she found herself attending an enormous campuslike high school already in the grip of folk rock, nascent antiwar sentiment, and intimations of the coming counterculture. She quickly made friends with the school's folk crowd, joining them to play guitars, frequent Houston's coffeehouses, and pore over *Life*'s sensational accounts of the culture wars in Haight-Ashbury. She turned down a full scholarship to Rice, reasoning that she would be more likely to meet people like those depicted in the magazine at the much bigger University of Texas.

"Rice was very small and, I thought, conservative. I never regretted not going there, though I think I would have probably gotten a better education—more attention from teachers and things like that. But I would have missed the sixties, which, by that time"—she smiles at the memory of her younger self—"I knew I didn't want to miss."

"Resigning never entered my mind."

At the time Carolyn Harrison was eagerly anticipating the culture wars to come, the American institutions against which much of the hostility of the late sixties would be directed were enjoying their greatest period of prosperity and power. The automobile business, in which Dave Harrison had labored for twenty years, stood at the center of America's postwar economic boom. And at the center of the automobile business stood Chevrolet, symbol of democratic opportunity, populist mobility, and, for the newly self-conscious subculture of teenagers, style. Chevy was all things to all people, and Dave was proud of the part he had played in bringing at least one element of the good life to the vast middle range of Americans.

The automobile had also vastly altered the American landscape, giving rise to new suburbs, shopping centers, motels, and drive-in movies and contributing to the long, slow decline of the central cities. By itself Chevrolet would have been one of the world's largest industrial corporations. In 1965, at the pinnacle of the postwar boom, Chevrolet built 3 million units, the first time anyone had done so and a figure that would not be achieved again until 1971.

But back in 1946, when Harrison first signed on with the company in New Orleans, automobile dealerships were sleepy affairs, still hampered by wartime shortages and unready for the coming, car-driven boom. Having finally won the parts-rep job with Chevrolet he had dreamed of before the war, Harrison was nervous.

"Dealers didn't have money to spend. Coming out of the war, they had no cars. When we first started back into production, they'd get maybe one or two. Everything was strictly allocated, based on what they had sold before the war. They had to make all their money off those cars or their shop. I used to tell them parts are the main source of your income. And I'd go out and sell to independent garages, too. I didn't know whether I could sell somebody something or not. I was scared to death."

In 1947 he traveled to Detroit for the most important event on the company's liturgical calendar—the annual new-car announcement. It was his first trip ever to the automotive mecca. He was awed by the proceedings—the sheer number of fellow communicants, the sophistication of the audiovisual aids, the majesty of the General Motors officials on the dais. After the evening's speeches, a curtain opened on a huge stage to reveal Dinah Shore at one end and Vaughn Monroe and his orchestra at the other, two of the biggest stars of the day and both working for the same company as Harrison. The high point of the evening was the presentation of the new-model Chevrolet.

"They came on with the new car covered up. They'd build it up—show a little bit here, a little bit there, until they'd shown the whole car. And everybody was on their feet screaming, because it was a beautiful thing up there. Then a guy came out and explained the car and I thought, 'God, I'd love to do that.' "

From Detroit the show went on the road to the various dealer organizations around the country. Before long, Harrison was making the presentation to the dealers in Louisiana, though he required a slug of VO to prepare for his first one. A promotion to parts-and-accessories manager for the El Paso zone soon followed. Harrison still traveled frequently over the vast stretches of west Texas, sometimes for as long as ten days. As the children grew, Helen convinced them that his absences were not only necessary, but a source of pride.

"I've always told Dave that I'm really the best salesperson in the family," she says, "because he was gone so much that I was always telling them what an exciting life he was having, how hard he was working. He was always dressed up when he left in the morning. And he held meetings and drove a new car every three thousand miles, and that impresses anybody, not just children. The neighbors all thought he was Mr. Wonderful, too. He had the kind of job that every American wanted in those days."

He was soon made sales-promotion manager for the Houston zone.

It was an unusual promotion—few people moved from parts and accessories to new car sales. He was delighted: new car sales, where he had
always wanted to be, was the glamor end of the business. But there was
more to it than that. One night, as he sat over a quiet dinner with Helen
to celebrate his tenth year with the company, he could feel that he had
at last achieved the security he had been seeking since he had first seen
his mother working far into the night as a seamstress to support seven
children. In a tone of profound relief, he said to Helen, "Now they can't
fire me, unless it's for something really drastic."

Helen was shocked. "I had never dreamed that he thought he could
be fired. But evidently for ten years that had been in the back of his
mind, driving him."

By the midfifties sales promotion (aimed at motivating dealers to
sell more new cars) was becoming increasingly important to the car industry. The pent-up demand from the war had long since been satisfied,
there were more used cars than ever, and the industry's vastly expanded
production capacity was belching out new cars at a rate that threatened to
outstrip the market. Yearly styling changes, injunctions to "keep up with
the Joneses," and the old-fashioned hard sell all played a part in keeping
the business booming, but it was no longer a foregone conclusion that the
automakers could sell anything they could build. Manufacturers of other
consumer goods faced similar problems. Increasingly, advertising, promotion, and public relations became paramount in maintaining the postwar expansion.

As Whyte and other observers noted, the increased emphasis on
communication in the business world helped bring forth a new breed of
men to direct it, men in whom personality took precedence over character, persuasion over production, people over things. Such attributes
brought success not only in the marketplace, but within organizations.
Dave Harrison found he possessed a real talent for motivating people. As
the promotions and moves followed, he began to think long and hard
about the personal qualities that were most likely to win him advancement in the company.

"When I first started, I thought performance was the real skill you
needed, the ability to get out and sell, a number that you could look at
and say 'that's it.' Your figures were what got you in a position to make
talks. Then I found out that your ability to speak and to put on an
interesting meeting would gain you fame within the dealer organization
and within the company, too. And the third thing along that line was the
ability to write. So I tried to develop my speaking ability and my writing
ability so I could make motivational presentations, which I always com-

mitted to memory. And this impressed people. I was out to impress people, very much."

A year after moving into sales promotion in Houston, Harrison was made a regional sales-promotion manager. Joann said good-bye to her ballet classmates; Carolyn's cotton project blew away on the wind; Helen bundled up five-year-old Julia and three-year-old Tom, and they moved to Dallas. Now Dave managed sales promotion for six zones, of approximately two hundred dealers each. The region received orders from central office and then directed the zones in their execution.

After working diligently at the job for four years, he began to hear rumors that he would soon be promoted to central office. He did not want to go. He preferred the rough and tumble of going head to head against Ford (always Chevrolet's direct competitor) to what he had heard were the Byzantine politics of central office. When the summons came, he reluctantly complied, and the family, moving in winter and the middle of the school year, made the most culturally jarring of all their moves. Julia and Tom recall soot-blackened slush on the ground, hardly the winter wonderland their father had promised. Carolyn noticed everywhere the Kennedy for President signs left over from the previous fall's election; in Dallas everyone had talked only of Nixon. Joann, gamely trying to make the best of it, organized a drill team at her new school. After three football games, the principal inexplicably threatened her with expulsion if she did not disband it.

For Dave and Helen, the transition was far easier. Many of their friends from previous locations had also made it into central office. And the atmosphere at work turned out to be surprisingly tolerable. "I found," says Dave, "that the executives everybody complained about were very responsive if you went to them on the right basis. The biggest problems always involved people in other departments who were on the same level as I was."

But what was for him a logical progression up a hierarchy based on his performance was for his children, especially the two younger ones, merely a steadily increasing affluence unconnected to anything other than their own natural aging. And the moves and the affluence would come with increasing rapidity, as he won three promotions in three years: back to Houston, to Memphis, and then back to central office.

In Houston the city's dealers had fallen behind Ford in sales. Within ninety days of his arrival, Harrison restored Chevrolet's dominance. His reward was to be named zone manager in Memphis, the second-largest zone in the nation.

The move came in 1968. Wrapped up in his work, Harrison only occasionally, and then only vaguely, felt the aftershocks from the earth-shaking events taking place in the outside world. One day as he was driving home from work, he found the streets overrun with police cars racing back and forth. When he got home, he learned from Helen that Martin Luther King had been murdered at the Lorraine Motel, not more than a mile from the Chevrolet offices. There followed several nights of rioting in more than 125 cities around the country, resulting in 46 deaths and more than 20,000 arrests.

The year had opened with the capture of the U.S. intelligence ship *Pueblo* by North Korea. A few days later, in Vietnam, the Tet offensive shattered optimistic projections of an early end to the war. In February, George Wallace inaugurated his nakedly racist campaign for the presidency on the American Independent party ticket. In March, President Johnson announced that he would not seek reelection, driven from office by the antiwar movement. Four days later King was assassinated. Little more than two weeks later, students at Columbia University seized five buildings to protest the building of a gym that would encroach on neighboring Harlem and to protest the school's ties to the Pentagon. The spectacle of these privileged students thumbing their noses (and worse) at the society that had given them so much outraged middle America and created rifts among intellectuals that still run through public discourse. In June, Robert Kennedy, after claiming victory in the California primary, was gunned down in a hotel kitchen. In August, Soviet tanks rolled into Czechoslovakia to crush the "Prague Spring" of Alexander Dubček's liberalizing regime. In Chicago at the Democratic convention thousands of demonstrators fought pitched street battles with Mayor Richard Daley's police while Daley and other party bosses inside the convention engineered the presidential nomination of Hubert Humphrey. Millions of people watched on television, including the Harrisons.

Far from seeing the events of 1968 as evidence of a country gone crazy, Dave Harrison and many organization men like him who had lived through the depression and World War II saw them as surface disturbances on the deep-running current of American prosperity. Besides, Lyndon Johnson and Hubert Humphrey were Democrats; Dave and Helen, like so many other organization couples, had shed their previous allegiance to the party of Roosevelt when they first moved to the suburbs.

Though the media made much of the generation gap, it was manifested mostly in public demonstrations and cultural style in music, dress, and sexual practices. Beyond the odd injunction to boys to get a haircut or girls to dress more demurely, generational differences rarely exploded into confrontation in the home.

"I thought all the kids carrying on in Chicago were a bunch of crazy goons," says Dave, "and I just kind of wrote them off in my mind. I think my kids felt very strongly about some the things the hippies were for that I was not. But I don't think we ever argued about it. I just made a rule that I wouldn't. I said, 'I don't like it and if you do that's your business.' "

Like many children of the period, the Harrison kids just quietly and as a matter of course did things that would have horrified their parents. Until he was interviewed for this book, Dave never knew that Carolyn was demonstrating against the war, that she participated in an illegal march on the state capitol in Austin that degenerated into a rock-throwing, tear-gas chaos. By the end of the sixties both Joann and Carolyn, unbeknownst to their parents, would live out of wedlock with men. Julia would soon follow suit. Dave and Helen were equally unaware of the extent to which drugs had penetrated the high schools Julia and Tom attended. They were by no means uncaring or inattentive parents—quite the reverse, according to them and to their children—it was simply a case of the generations going their separate ways.

Overlooked by chroniclers of the period were the gaps *within* the younger generation, even within the relatively privileged group of organization offspring. Dave's promotion to Memphis represented a quantum leap in his career—both in responsibility and in earnings. Relatively low living costs in the South permitted him to buy a home far more spacious and luxurious than any he had ever owned. By this time, Joann and Carolyn, with their memories of Cokes and bean dip as a treat reserved for Christmas, had already left home for good. But for Julia and Tom, the crucial years of their adolescence would be marked by a rapidly increasing standard of living, more disposable income, and houses that got bigger as the number of occupants got smaller. On the other hand, the number and frequency of those houses—three in three years—would render the two younger children even more rootless than the older two.

One year later, the move from Memphis back into central office brought another significant jump in Harrison's status. As national merchandising manager for all Chevrolet, Dave now held a major staff job and enjoyed even greater benefits in the company bonus plan. He participated in major sales, advertising, and promotional decisions and even exerted influence on the product. A man he greatly admired, Pete Estes, was general manager, the Chevrolet Division's chief executive position. But things soon soured when Estes was promoted to a vice presidency in the corporation in February 1969. The new general manager was a wunderkind from Pontiac named John DeLorean. Just as his daughter Joann in Vietnam was discovering her own doubts about organizations she had revered and daughter Carolyn was joining the opposition to those institutions, Harrison was about to have his own faith challenged.

This was long before the evening news programs presented video-tapes of DeLorean buying cocaine from government agents in a Los Angeles airport hotel room; long before the collapse of his Northern Ireland car company cost thousands of poor people, hundreds of rich ones, and two governments hundreds of millions of dollars; long before the DMC-12, the "ethical sports car" he had long promised, turned out to be little more than a shoddy knockoff of the Lotus's chassis and the Bricklin's gull-wing styling.

Born in Detroit in modest circumstances, DeLorean became a su-perb engineer, first with Packard and later with Pontiac, where along with Estes he helped develop the GTO and the LeMans, the immensely successful "muscle cars" of the early sixties. In 1965, at age forty, he was named general manager of Pontiac, the youngest man ever to head one of General Motors' ten main divisions. His elevation at age forty-four to the leadership of Chevrolet, far and away the corporation's largest divi-sion, made him an odds-on favorite to ascend one day to the president's chair. He was the golden boy of the corporation; even his superiors, wary of the day he might be leapfrogged over them in the hierarchy, feared him.

Under the General Motors management system of centralized plan-ning and decentralized operations, pioneered by Alfred Sloan, the gen-eral managers ran their divisions almost as separate companies. DeLorean, when he was not hobnobbing with Hollywood friends like James Aubrey, ran Chevrolet autocratically, sometimes effectively, some-times not, but always for his own aggrandizement.

Harrison's troubles with DeLorean began almost immediately. Shortly before DeLorean had taken over Chevrolet, Harrison had com-pleted a successful sales promotion in which Chevrolet sold to their dealers at cost record albums of contemporary popular songs to be given away with test drives. Six months later DeLorean called Harrison into his office and told him to mount another such promotion.

Harrison recalls the conversation vividly: "I said, 'Naw, we can't do it; we just got through with one.' He said, 'You didn't hear me; I want to do another one.' 'But Mr. DeLorean,' I said, 'the dealers won't buy it.' He really got incensed then. He jumped all over me and said, 'You will sell one.'

"I went back and told one of my staff to develop the record, to have RCA and Columbia and all of them bid on it. One day DeLorean called me and said, 'What are all these people doing bidding on these records?' 'That's the way I do business,' I said. 'I put it out for bids and get it the cheapest way I can and then sell it to the dealers.' He said, 'Well, a fellow named Burt Sugarman is going to come and see you.' I said, 'Well, he's going to have to bid on it.' John said, 'He's already got the low bid.'

"So Burt Sugarman, the Hollywood producer, came in. I told him he'd have to bid on it. He said, 'What's your low bid?' I said, 'I'm not supposed to tell you that. Hell, you go out and put in your own bid.' He left and later came back with a bid of a dollar ten per record.

"DeLorean calls me and asks how many records I'm going to order. I told him two hundred thousand. He said to order a million. I said, 'No way; we can't sell a million.' I'm arguing to beat hell and I go to see the general sales manager. I said, 'Man, you've got to help me. This guy's crazy.' He said, 'I'm not going to help you. You handle it yourself.' The general sales manager was my boss and normally he'd help, but he said, in effect, to hell with you."

Harrison confronted DeLorean.

"Mr. DeLorean," he said, "we just can't do this to our dealer organization.' "

"How many did you sell last time?"

"Six hundred thousand."

"Okay," DeLorean said, "six hundred thousand is your initial order, and you'll order from Burt Sugarman."

"I haven't gotten his bid."

"You'll order from Burt Sugarman. I've got the bid right here. It's the low bid."

"Could I have it?"

"No."

Says Harrison now, "I saw right then I'd lost the goddamn battle, so I just shut up. We ordered the records, and I called the field and said, 'Now, fellas, I want to tell you something. It's not our idea. It's John DeLorean. I've got to sell a million of these things, so you just better get busy.' They all knew the story because it wasn't the first time I'd had a run-in with him, and it had gotten across the field that John and I didn't get along at all. So they took the records and they sold them. They finally got rid of about half a million. I had a hundred thousand left and I got a travel company to buy those. I paid Sugarman something in the area of seven hundred thousand dollars. I saw the money because it came out of my budget. I had gotten the bids from other companies and I think the cheapest was sixty-three cents, so that's a difference of almost fifty cents a record and off six hundred thousand of them, that's three hundred thousand dollars."

About whether some of the money was kicked back to DeLorean, Harrison is understandably circumspect. Less so are authors Ivan Fallon and James Srodes. In *Dream Maker: The Rise and Fall of John Z. DeLorean*, they write: "Throughout 1970 and 1971, DeLorean used Chevrolet's promotion budget as his own privy purse." They also confirm another story Harrison tells.

Jam Handy, a communications company that frequently did work for Harrison's department, had developed a self-contained film and television machine, something like today's videocassette players, for training salesmen and educating customers.

"We had the thing all set up and ready to sell to the dealers for three hundred fifty dollars," says Harrison. "So we invited DeLorean up to see it. John walked in there and just tore me up: 'Worst thing I've ever seen in my life; I'll get somebody in here that can really develop a program for us.' Then he turned around and walked out.

"The next thing I know, a fellow who handled our loaner cars in California is sitting in my office demanding to see the machine. Before John came in, we'd kept about fifty units in service there, but with John we had about four hundred units in service. This guy got forty dollars a month per car for handling them for us. I told him I couldn't show him the machine because it belonged to Jam Handy. So he picked up my phone and called John. John got me on the phone and said, 'Dave, show the damn machine to him and quit giving me trouble.'

"I showed it to him. Later he called a guy in Hollywood who flew in to see it. The next thing I know DeLorean calls me up and says this guy's going to build a machine. I said, 'What? Hell, I've been working with Jam Handy. You can't do that. That's not ethical.' John said, 'Ethical, shit. I don't like the sonuvabitches anyway.' And he hung up."

Ultimately, says Harrison, the machine DeLorean's pals developed was sold to the dealers for $750 each. Fifty-five hundred dealers bought them. The difference in price of approximately $400 per unit times 5,500 works out to a staggering $2.2 million.

Harrison began to keep detailed notes of all his dealings with DeLorean. In the event of a confrontation, he wanted to be prepared. In the meantime, DeLorean had had enough of Harrison. It was rumored that he had sent papers upstairs to have Harrison fired. The papers landed on Pete Estes's desk. Harrison believes that Jam Handy, who owned the communications company that bore his name, interceded with Estes. In any case, Harrison was told that Estes had torn up the papers. Then the word came down that Harrison might revert to zone manager, manifestly a demotion.

A friend at Buick, who knew what he was going through, offered to bring him over there as director of marketing. Harrison drove up to the offices in Flint for a meeting. For several days, Harrison pondered the offer. He had survived thus far and, perhaps, after nearly two years, the worst with DeLorean was over. Finally, he called his friend at Buick. "I'm with Chevrolet and I know what I'm doing," he told him; "I'm not happy and I may be in trouble, but I'm going to stay here."

Incredibly, DeLorean decided to run another record promotion.

"I knew I was on thin ice, but I just didn't want to do it," says Harrison, "so I went to our purchasing department and told them to get me bids from RCA, Columbia, this, that, and the other—and also Burt Sugarman. When the bids came in, I asked them to give them to me. They said they couldn't do that; they could only tell me who was low. I said, 'The hell you can't; you give me the bids.' Well, I couldn't get them. Finally, a girl over there who knew me real well typed them out for me on the back of a new-car announcement. Burt Sugarman had bid $1.25; Columbia had bid 63 cents. So I sat down and wrote a letter to a superior: *I put out bids on these records and I'm attaching a copy of the bids. The purchasing department refused to put it on their letterhead because various people were not happy with the results. But here are the results. It's your responsibility to make the decision as to who will get this bid and advise me.* I never heard from it again. That was it. No record was done. And right after that, I got promoted out."

Through the years it pained Harrison to see credulous reporters make a hero of John DeLorean, even though the slightest digging into the mountain of litigation his business ventures invariably piled up would have unearthed the real operator behind the carefully crafted public image. Instead, the media portrayed him as the maverick antiorganization man devoted to unpopular causes, determined against all odds to produce an "ethical car." Even the videotaped arrest in the multimillion-dollar cocaine deal elicited from the general public an outpouring of sympathy that did nothing to harm DeLorean's successful defense against the charges. For Harrison, the public's reaction was galling.

A conventional organization man resisting a histrionic character like John DeLorean neither makes good copy nor satisfies the American appetite for morality plays, but far from the glare of the media, such piecemeal, ambiguous struggles are often played out in organizations. The public story of DeLorean's fight with the organization was, by contrast, bold, dramatic, inspiring—and largely untrue. Under the cloud of an in-house investigation of his relationships with Chevrolet suppliers, he negotiated a departure from the company that he was able to parlay into his media image as "the man who walked away from General Motors." Harrison, with twenty-five years of service to the company doing work he frankly loved, wanted neither to give in to DeLorean nor to leave. The prosaic truth is that many Americans, when faced with similar circumstances, neither fully acquiesce in such schemes nor resign in protest.

"Resigning never entered my mind," Harrison says. "And I didn't want to get fired, not after spending all that time with the company. All I wanted to do was fight harder. Not only to prove my point, but to prevent an injustice being done to the dealer organization. I felt it was wrong to charge the dealer organization a dollar and a quarter for a record that we could buy for sixty-three cents. We weren't selling the records to make money. We were selling the records to help the dealers to sell cars. And the purpose of the video machines was to help train salesmen to sell cars. Our job was to find the best promotional tool we could and get it to the dealers as cheaply as we could. I was upset because of all the other goddamn money that was being made by making the dealers take these things.

"The course I pursued was the only one for me because I could not have done otherwise," he says matter-of-factly. "I felt loyalty to the company and that the things I was doing were the right things for the company. And I had to do it, whether it affected my job or not."

In *On a Clear Day You Can See General Motors*, a book DeLorean co-wrote with automotive writer J. Patrick Wright and then tried to suppress for fear General Motors would retaliate against his fledgling motor car company, there is a chapter entitled "Loyalty—Team Play—The System." Deriding the values of men like Harrison, DeLorean reductively confuses the usual kowtowing to superiors with genuine loyalty to an institution.

Loyalty—genuine loyalty—was a virtue Harrison could not have easily jettisoned. He had learned it early, from his family during the depression, and he carried it with him thereafter—into the army; into his marriage; into his job; and into his relations with his children, no matter how far they strayed from his notions of propriety. Nevertheless, the repeated refusal of help from his superiors during the frustrating, two-year struggle strained Harrison's loyalty almost to the breaking point. "It really made me mad and it showed me that some of my management didn't have the guts to stand up to him. They would indicate that I was right, but that they weren't going to fight the battle. Their job preservation was more important."

However, Harrison distinguished the cowardly individuals who refused him help from the corporation to which he had given his lifelong allegiance. The eventual ouster of DeLorean, he felt, justified that faith. A decade later he would struggle to maintain a similar distinction between the organization and the individuals who make it up when, just three years short of retirement, with most of his children having settled nearby, he was given the choice of moving clear across the country or taking early retirement.

"I was going to be famous."

Four women and two men, dressed in rehearsal motley, dance through the dreamy midafternoon sunlight filtering through a skylight overhead. Their movements are duplicated in a mirror that runs along the entire back wall. There is no music, no sound except the rhythmic scuff of their bare feet on the floor. They are rehearsing a complicated ensemble passage in a new piece Julia Harrison is choreographing for her reconstituted company's impending make-or-break concert. The extended, multisection piece will also feature her in a solo, the first time she will have danced in public since an ill-advised comeback attempt five years before, while she was still recovering from the cancer that had almost killed her just as she was entering her prime as a dancer.

"You should end up in the four position," she tells the dancers, as they approach the end of the section and freeze in a tableau. A duet follows. "Right now I want to see weight and flow," she calls to the pair, "not rhythm." She does not like what she sees. "I'm going to have to simplify that transition," she mutters.

The entire company runs through the passage again. They are in the earliest stages of rehearsal, and the piece is still very much a work in progress, so there are the usual mishaps. One of the male dancers rolls over the other's back and lands painfully on knees and elbows. He laughs and keeps dancing. The women perform a slow, lissome collapse—a head or two is heard to bump on the floor.

Over and over they rehearse the passage. Occasionally, Julia stops them to correct a movement or to introduce a new one. She indulges in no displays of temperament, no histrionic agonies of creation; patiently, like a good teacher, she describes what she is after. Following a particularly good run-through, she calls a break.

"This is a standard way of working in modern dance," she explains to a visitor. "Young choreographers tend to make up material ahead of time and then come into rehearsal and dictate it to the dancers. Older choreographers create right in the studio. You can't be afraid to create right in front of the dancers. But, sometimes, nothing happens."

After the break, she demonstrates for two of the women a lengthy unison passage. Suddenly, all the casual activity of the afternoon crystallizes in an incomparable kinetic image: she is a magnificent dancer.

The image is succeeded by the rueful thought of her prime dancing years lost to illness.

It is often mistakenly assumed that good choreographers must be brilliant dancers. Julia, it appears, is both. Videotapes of performances and the testimony of former associates will later confirm this impression. Tall, powerfully built, full figured, and strikingly beautiful, she is the antithesis of the tiny, anorexic female ideal of the art form. Women like her are rarely seen in modern dance; they are hard to lift, and male dancers are touchy about taller female partners. Her height has caused her trouble throughout her career.

As the rehearsal proceeds, there is a palpable uptick in intensity. The dancers sweat now. The mistakes diminish. The passage is beginning to come together. After a half dozen more run-throughs, Julia calls a halt for the day. The dancers cool down and unself-consciously change into their street clothes at the edge of the dance floor—there are no dressing rooms—and one by one disperse.

Julia steps into the office of the company's newly hired general manager. A stylishly dressed young woman, the general manager has just returned from a long lunch with a representative of a prominent local corporation. She tells Julia that the corporation will probably provide them with a one-time grant of five thousand dollars. Julia is delighted to have the prestigious corporation as a grantor, but the sum, given her company's needs, is pitifully small. They discuss several other pending grants, offer each other encouragement, and plan to meet the following day to go over the books.

On the drive to her apartment, Julia talks about suddenly finding herself responsible for building a fiscally sound organization, after having spent all her adult life thinking of herself solely as an artist.

"After a New York concert, one of the dancers, who was exhausted, quit. Then, when the artistic director quit, everyone else quit, except the accountant and me—I was the assistant artistic director. We had a fifteen-thousand-dollar debt and we hadn't had a successful season in a while. I think any other board of directors would have given up. But we have a very committed board, and they asked me to take on the job of artistic director.

"The first few months after I assumed the job, there wasn't a manager, so I was having to manage things and having to learn cash flow and budgeting and all of it. I had to deal with all the foundations, all these people who'd always made me feel intimidated before. We've been able to function for the past six months without incurring any new debt. We've been able to pay salaries and we've reduced our old debt by nine thousand dollars. It's given me a great sense of satisfaction to know that

I can deal with this stuff. I feel I'm more in touch with reality or with life the way it is. Before, my whole life has always been in my head or in these ephemeral things called dances."

Regarded through the window of Julia's fifth-floor apartment, San Francisco itself seems to exist in the head. From the sun shimmering on the Bay to the distinctive white glare of the office buildings and the cake-decorator pastels of Victorian townhouses, the city, suspended in tremulous light, looks dreamed and insubstantial.

Though married only six months, Julia and Paul have lived in the one-bedroom apartment for more than a year at a rent of twelve hundred dollars per month. Because the building's new owners are converting it to condominiums and the place is too small for the children Paul and Julia contemplate, they spend every weekend looking at real estate. Finding an adequate and affordable first house in the Bay Area's extremely inflated market will not be easy, even with the salary Paul earns as a lawyer.

Their modest living room contains a comfortable jumble of cast-offs and secondhand furniture each partner brought to the union. There are Mexican ceramics; American Indian artifacts; and on the walls, a mixture of dance posters and original art. Law books and legal briefs litter a small table tucked in a corner. A hardback copy of dancer Gelsey Kirkland's harrowing autobiography lies open on an end table.

Except for dance classes and a few scattered memories of playmates, Julia's earliest recollections are of the family's first move to Michigan, in 1961, when she was ten. For a month, while their new house was being readied, the Harrisons lived in a suite at the Park Shelton hotel in Detroit. Mercilessly self-critical, she dates what she sees as her love of luxury from that time.

"It was a beautiful, classic old hotel," she says. "Everything smelled wonderful—the wood and brass—and we got things served in the suite on silver. I loved it, the quality of it.

"Joann will tell you that we had Cokes only on Christmas Eve, but I don't remember it. I basically grew up in the family when it started being well off. Mom and Dad were going on trips and they would have fancy dinner parties and there was just a whole new level of living going on that I was intrigued with. And I took everything for granted. I've analyzed this a lot because now I've questioned the part of me that just presumes I'm supposed to have all these things. I think I'm really a classically spoiled person in a lot of ways."

She also admits that she never connected all that abundance to what one had to do to get it.

"Unfortunately," she says, "the work ethic was somehow not passed on to me. I think I've understood the relationship of work and money only in the last few years. I just thought I was going to have money—I don't know how. I never felt I was going to have to earn it."

Despite the material comfort of her childhood, she recalls being generally unhappy from about age twelve until she entered college. She longed for popularity; it did not come. She competed with Carolyn for good grades; it was no contest. She doggedly studied ballet; she was too tall. But it is difficult to see how she could have achieved popularity, good grades, or balletic grace because at the beginning of each of her four years of high school, her family moved. Of all these displaced persons, she was perhaps the most displaced. And perhaps even more than the others, she turned to the private self and the dream of art for some sense of identity and individuality.

"Every day after school I'd go take my ballet classes. I wasn't involved in school activities at all. I never went to football games. At some point, I think I got snobby about thinking I was doing something artsy and that I was just a different level of person."

After pursuing ballet throughout high school, sometimes in semi-professional settings, she discovered modern dance in her freshman year at Michigan State University.

"The teacher there was supportive and enthusiastic and she believed that anyone who wants to be an artist has the right to try. Discovering modern dance was like discovering a world. I felt at home there and I was good instantly and was prominent in the dance circle there and was getting parts. From that point on, my memory of Michigan State is dancing, not classes. I turned into a workaholic—taking full academic loads, choreographing two pieces at once, performing in four pieces, teaching at a high school, and on and on. That was also when I began to be constantly exhausted, too."

She also met a musician and composer with whom, unbeknownst to her parents, she was soon living. He also choreographed.

"He wasn't a dancer, so he choreographed from ideas, like Alwin Nikolais. In rehearsal he would say 'okay, get on the floor and grovel' and have us do things like that, and I had spent my whole life in ballet trying to be beautiful. He taught me that there was a whole other aesthetic, another way to be expressive."

A few of the older people in her circle had been involved in campus antiwar activities, but by the time she entered college in fall 1970, most such activity, having peaked following the killings at Kent State University the previous spring, had simply evaporated. She was never involved in it, and her friends turned increasingly to the faddish pursuit of Eastern religions, transcendental meditation, and other forms of "enlightenment." The year 1970 remains a significant break within the baby-boom generation. When compared to many of their brothers and sisters who matriculated before 1970, many members of succeeding college generations, whether they now affect a sentimental liberalism or a macho conservatism, often appear politically illiterate, innocent of history, and bereft of social ideas.

By contrast, Joann Harrison participates actively in the National Organization for Women, contributes money to the most liberal wing of the California Democratic party, and supports a variety of causes and candidates. Carolyn engages the world of politics through scholarship that is heavily feminist and often polemical. (The short answer to the tedious and predictable objection that such matters are merely "academic" is the obvious fact that American foreign policy—to cite only one example—originates in the seminars of Harvard, Georgetown, and other elite universities, no matter which political party is in power.) Julia and Tom, on the other hand, caring little for politics, identify their concerns as more "metaphysical." They, like many of their contemporaries, generalized their concern with the authentic self into a familiar, if attenuated, American transcendentalism under the cover of Eastern religion.

Julia's total dedication to dance soon hurt her grades in other classes. She ignored her parents' objections to dance as an impractical course of study. She spent six weeks during the summer following her freshman year studying at the American Dance Festival at Connecticut College. The festival, since its founding in 1948, has showcased all the major modern dance companies and offered fledgling dancers the opportunity to study with the greats. Julia took master classes with Alwin Nikolais, José Limón, and Paul Taylor (to whose work as a choreographer her own would frequently be compared by reviewers.) She returned to the festival the following summer.

"That's when I decided I needed to go to New York and try to be a professional dancer and forget all this school stuff, even though the school had been incredibly supportive. Going to New York was a really liberating thing because Mom and Dad didn't want me to go. At that time, I was getting egotistical about my abilities. I was naive and young and had that inflated feeling that I can do anything and I'm immortal. I'd found my calling and all that. And I think that's what drove me."

As it would turn out, she had indeed found her calling, unlike so many other organization offspring who still long for something more satisfying than a mere job—or even a career—but, rather, a vocation that grows naturally out of a self felt to be authentic. Though she would eventually achieve what so many others of her generation only dreamed about, she would also find her belief in the authentic and unfettered self, which had led her to pursue the dream in the first place, sorely tested.

She sold her Vega and took off with another dancer for the big city. She had no job lined up and only the vaguest plan. "My first job was in a bar on Broadway frequented by pimps," she says. "I was a cocktail waitress and I didn't know what I was doing. The pimps would come up to me and ask me if I wanted some coke, and I thought they meant Coca-Cola. What I didn't realize was the bar owner, who was probably a pimp himself, was after my ass. I was just so naive. They called me Country Girl."

Though she soon won a scholarship with Alvin Ailey, the New York dance world proved discouraging. "It was very competitive, and I really hadn't had the kind of training I needed. I also felt that there was no room for me to choreograph in New York. I was too intimidated. It became clear to me that I had to be somewhere that I could choreograph. I interviewed with Juilliard, and they said, 'Well, you can't choreograph here until you're ready; we put you in a cage and teach you until we think you're ready.' I hated that, because my first teacher at Michigan State had instilled a different philosophy in me."

After a year of frustration, she was desperate to resume choreographing, which requires rehearsal space, resources, and willing dancers. Her closest friends from Michigan State had gravitated to the renowned program in modern dance at the University of Utah. At their urging, she joined them there.

She went west just in time to help her parents get settled in their new home outside San Francisco. Dave had been made manager of the entire West Coast region, one of only seven in the country. Though he and Helen were once again supporting her and would continue to do so for the next seven years—until she was thirty—they were delighted to have her out of New York and back in school. They were somewhat less delighted when she informed them she was living with a young man she had fallen in love with almost as soon as she arrived on campus.

"They were furious," she recalls. "I was the first one to tell Mom and Dad that I was living with someone I wasn't married to. I remember Dad yelling at me on the phone saying he wasn't ever going to talk to me again and then hanging up. But then they settled down. We talked again, and they never acted on any of their threats."

Their ultimate reaction, when she brought him home with her one Christmas, shocked her. The boyfriend, from a family that controlled a Fortune 500 company, showed up with waist-length hair, a spoiled hippie's irritating manner of spiritual superiority, and an unconcealed contempt for the Harrisons' way of life.

"Mom and Dad had the conversation where Mom asked Dad

whether he shouldn't talk to my boyfriend about marrying me. And Dad said he wasn't going to because he didn't want me to marry him; he'd rather we just lived together."

Back at school Julia enjoyed an unbroken string of successes.

"I was dancing in classes and productions and because of my size I was cast in a lot of solo roles. I was producing my own work—half of a full-length concert my first year there and an entire concert the following year. It was very well received. Everyone thought I was going to go on and become a really well-known choreographer."

Upon graduation, instead of auditioning as a dancer with well-known companies, she decided to start her own company so she could continue to choreograph. She managed to acquire some small grants; someone's parents contributed a thousand dollars, as did Dave Harrison. Joann contributed money and helped the company acquire a tax exemption and set up a board of directors. For three years, the company managed to produce major concerts and recoup expenses through ticket sales. Julia dismisses much of their work, but videotapes clearly show a competent ensemble and a distinctive, almost fully mature, choreographic style. Though she admits the experience was invaluable for her growth as a choreographer, she deeply regrets her refusal to dance in an established company.

The forsaking of standard career paths is a deeply ingrained characteristic of many of the organization offspring and, more than anything else, it sets them off decisively from their parents. Though the offspring's habit of going their own way has, in many cases, like Julia's, retarded their career advancement and hurt them in conventional terms of success, it has also paradoxically prepared them to survive adroitly in the highly volatile and uncertain economy they have inherited. Nevertheless, Julia, with her company on the verge of extinction, sees it as egotism.

"I was very arrogant. I wasn't going to be subservient to anybody else. From the beginning, I wanted to be the choreographer and the director. That was a really big mistake because I don't have on my résumé that I danced with a major company. People don't know how to look at training for choreographers; they only know how to look at training for dancers. They assume if you've had good training as a dancer and been in a good company, you're going to also be a good choreographer. Of course, it doesn't work that way. But that's the way the people who give grants look at résumés. And the fact that I can't list a major company on my résumé is a real problem.

"Now that I look back on it, I think I really didn't want to test myself in the real world. But I didn't think that then. At the time, I was just arrogant. I just thought I was good, I was talented, I didn't need that shit." She pauses and quietly adds, "I was just stupid."

After three years of holding the company together and simultaneously working full time as a waitress, she was growing exhausted. Rejection by her boyfriend brought emotional exhaustion, as well. A subsequent lover married her best friend. Despite almost daily crying jags, she threw herself more ardently into her work. She flew to Tucson to choreograph a production of Peter Shaeffer's *Royal Hunt of the Sun*. On the plane, while rubbing her stiff neck, she discovered a lump. She ignored it.

"I think it was part of my thing that I was immortal," she explains. "I didn't think anything would really happen to me. I had a destiny to fulfill. I was going to be famous."

Six months elapsed. When she attended her brother's wedding, her mother took one look at her neck and got her to a doctor the next day. She returned to Salt Lake City to await the results of the biopsy. A few days later her father called her at the restaurant where she worked. He was vague about what the pathologists had found, but he insisted on flying out to see her. She knew then that she must have cancer.

"Initially, I went through that whole list of things you feel when you think you're dying—denial, anger, depression, all of that. There was a good chance I could die and I was really bitter about it."

Her denial took the form of resisting surgery and seeking holistic cures for a disease that, no matter how it might be related to diet, attitude, and the like, had reached a stage of advancement that no amount of positive thinking or tofu could affect. When her doctor bluntly told her she would die without the surgery, she reluctantly acquiesced. Following the removal of the tumor and her spleen, a biopsy of her liver, and the taking of bone marrow from her hip, she was to undergo radiation treatment every day for six months. Again, she resisted, giving in only after numerous arguments with her doctor and her parents. Her saliva dried up; she felt constant nausea; her hair fell out; her lungs were scorched. Through it all she continued to choreograph and produce a concert. Nevertheless, the grim reality was breaking through.

"I went through a lot psychologically—every day going into the hospital and being around people who were dying, really dying. It was difficult. There was a subtle change in me. I just lost confidence. My ego wasn't the same."

Nevertheless, she accepted an offer from a prestigious Southwestern dance company to choreograph and perform. The results were disastrous.

"I'd just finished my radiation treatments and would not accept the fact that I was physically weak. And I got ill with a bronchitislike condition that I now get chronically because of my scorched lungs. By the time the concert came around, I was so ill I could hardly perform. It was a pretty excruciating experience."

At last, recognizing that her full recovery would take years, she disbanded her company and enrolled in graduate school at another Western school, with vague plans of preparing for a career teaching dance if she failed as a choreographer.

"Going for a master's was a retreat from everything. It was safe. To be a professional, you have to be out there in the professional world, not in school."

She produced a concert almost as soon as she arrived on campus. The petty reaction of her teachers devastated her. They accused her of being too ambitious, of using too many of the department's resources. She fought them fiercely, walking out of classes and eventually transferring to the theater department, but their harsh treatment and her still-incomplete physical recovery finally demoralized her.

"That's when I stopped performing—when it should have been the height of my career. I think it hurt my work as a choreographer because I got outside of it. Before, I had been so egotistical that I had loved being on stage because it was like 'great, look at me.' Now it was like I don't think I'm so great anymore—and I'm frightened."

"The world can do this even to him."

After Dave Harrison's troubles with DeLorean passed and he had spent three successful years as an assistant regional manager for the Great Lakes Region, he heard he was in line for assistant general sales manager back in central office. He put the word out among his friends in Detroit that he wanted to finish his career in the field, as a regional manager, if possible. So he was delighted when he was called to Detroit one day in 1974 and told he had been chosen to head the Pacific Coast region. He was somewhat less delighted when he was instructed to fly there the following day and inform a dozen district managers and department heads that because of the disastrous effects of the Arab oil embargo on the automobile industry their jobs had been eliminated.

Following that rocky start, he turned his attention to trying to reverse some of those effects. In Harrison's view, central office was blind to the threat posed by Japanese imports. He traveled to Detroit to make a dramatic multimedia presentation, which concluded with the lights going dark in the last Chevrolet dealership in Los Angeles. It won him some extra product to distribute, but the company still did not have the right product—cars that got good gas mileage. The imports continued to make serious inroads on the West Coast.

One of the famous Chevrolet engineer-executives visited Seattle for a speech. On the ride back to the airport, the visiting executive said to one of Dave's zone managers, "What are all these small cars?" The manager informed him that the state of Washington, at 51 percent, had the highest percentage of imports in the nation. The executive promised to take action as soon as he returned to Detroit. Dave was elated. The man had been an engineer; he must surely have understood that the problem was the product.

"They ran a full-page newspaper ad," Harrison says incredulously. "That was their response. Then I knew there were some people up there who didn't know their fanny from a hole in the ground. They just didn't know. And I was afraid that they didn't want to know because it would take a hell of a lot of money to develop a car to meet that market."

He soon discovered that the problems of Chevrolet in the region, where they had run second to Ford in car and truck sales for eighteen years, went beyond the gas crisis and the threat from imports.

"The story goes that a lot of our people had had their hands out to the dealer organization in exchange for getting the product to them," he says. "So there was no trust or loyalty between the dealers and Chevrolet. Plus the dealers had the highest gross profit of any dealer organization in the nation. When the rest of the dealers were making five hundred dollars a car, these dealers were making twelve hundred dollars a car. So they didn't care about beating Ford. They could make their money anyway. So I had a hell of a job to tear down this attitude and show the dealers that we were going to be honest with them and try to get them merchandise they needed and get the job done."

Two years later, in 1976, the region overtook Ford in truck sales and the following year surpassed them in passenger car sales. Chevrolet remained in first place in both classes throughout Harrison's tenure.

It was a highly satisfying time in Dave and Helen's life. Dave had once again inherited a difficult sales situation and turned it around. He and Helen loved California and hoped to spend his retirement there. First Joann and then Tom gravitated to the area. Julia was now safely in Salt Lake City, a city in Dave's region he could find frequent pretexts to visit. Carolyn married the man with whom she lived and, in early 1979, Tom married the woman with whom he had been living.

Then the blows began to fall. Dave was picking up hints that he might be transferred. Joann divorced for the second time. Tom began married life by making a terrible real estate deal. And Julia, whom they had supported financially long after college and then abruptly cut off, developed cancer. Presciently, Dave had continued to carry her, alone among his adult children, on his health insurance policy.

"Julia had a good work ethic," says Dave. "She worked as a dancer. But money was never a problem because she would cry a little bit and I'd send her more and she'd spend it. And I used to get so doggoned mad because I'd send the money and she'd buy props for her dance company."

Though Dave and Helen often proudly attended Julia's concerts, they opposed her career as impractical. They were also disturbed by her bohemian life-style. Says Helen, "I thought she was supposed to be earning a living. And I can remember what a shock it was to Julia when I told her that. I think it was after she had gotten her degree. I said, 'You know, it's time for you to be earning your living.' It was like I had slapped her." Nevertheless, they continued to help her until shortly before her illness. "When it became obvious she couldn't earn a living dancing, I thought she should do it some other way—and not waitressing, either. I felt very badly that she had to do that, but we didn't feel it was up to us to keep supporting her."

Helen says the cancer changed everything. "We certainly decided right then we weren't ever going to let her live the way she had been living before—dancing six hours a day and then waitressing eight hours a day. We just decided that we had the money to help her and we were going to do it.

"I told her the only thing for her to do with her dancing was to teach because I never thought she'd ever have enough energy to perform again. So we offered to send her back to get her master's degree.

"I felt really bad that we had not been supporting her right before she got sick, but what do you do? She was grown; she had chosen that life-style. We just felt fortunate that we still were close because we knew people who would not speak to their children for having chosen to live that way. And we weren't going to do that."

Family had always been paramount with the Harrisons, and now they were daring to hope that their children might all somehow wind up near them. Says Dave, "Every time any of the children came to visit they'd say, 'Hey, this is a beautiful part of the country; I'd like to live here.' That's why we wanted to stay here."

Chevrolet's general sales manager, one of Dave's closest friends in the company, began to make noises about moving him to Atlanta to head the Southeast region. Dave emphatically said he was not interested. Eight months later, the general sales manager called and flatly told him he was to be moved. Dave was furious.

"I said, 'I want to be as honest as I can with you: You can take this job and stick it. I'm not going to move.' "

The sales manager suggested early retirement. Dave was sixty-one years old at the time. Were he to retire then, his pension benefits would revert to those due him at age sixty, about half of what he would receive at age sixty-five.

"I told him if they'd let me stay in California until I was sixty-three, I'd retire then, when my benefits would be about three-fourths of what they would be if I retired at sixty-five. But I said if you move me, I'm going to stay until the last damn day."

They told him to move or retire. He moved. The fact that the company declined his offer to retire at sixty-three leads him to believe that the move was not an attempt by the company to reduce its long-term retirement obligations to him.

"I feel I was betrayed by friends, but not by the total company," he says. "The company was still there and still doing things, and I was still a member of it. I don't think it was the company that moved me. I think it was people who moved me, one in particular I'd had a lot of arguments with about distribution. I think it was a vindictive move."

At Helen's insistence, they kept the California house and rented it out, hoping that they would be able to return after Dave retired. It was a smart move. Housing in overbuilt Atlanta was cheap, and had they sold their old home, it is possible they would have been unable to regain their foothold in California's rapidly inflating market.

One of the few personal compensations for the move to Atlanta was the opportunity to live near Carolyn, who was finishing her doctoral work there. In all other respects, the move, regardless of who was responsible for it, had a devastating effect on his morale.

"I no longer had the burning desire to be a leader," he says. "I was going to serve out my time and that was going to be it. I'd go back into meetings in Detroit and I was really passive. I just didn't care any more, but it hurt me to do that."

Carolyn, reestablishing intimacy with her parents for the first time since she had left for college thirteen years before, was shocked at the change in him. "It was appalling because his best friend had turned on him."

Similar scenes were played out in many organization families during the recessions of the late seventies and early eighties and again during the feverish mergers and restructurings of the middle eighties as vast numbers of organization men were forced into early retirement or simply fired. The adult children of such men looked on with a mixture of anger and pity as corporation after corporation abrogated the implicit bargain they had made with the organization man so many years before—the guarantee of virtual lifetime employment in exchange for the employee's unswerving loyalty. Many of the children vowed that they would not let it happen to them: They could always be fired, of course, but they would be damned if they would give their loyalty to such organizations and thereby leave themselves open to the painful sense of betrayal they witnessed in their fathers.

Dave Harrison's disappointment was compounded by what he saw as General Motors' continuing failure, seven years after the 1973 oil embargo, to respond to a vastly changed car market. The company was, in fact, then in the process of developing a $40 billion strategy to redesign every car and overhaul every plant, but the strategy was still in the early planning stages.

"By the time I got to Atlanta, the recession was pretty well started and I could see then that the corporation had not made any plans for a downturn in business, none whatsoever, and I was very upset about it," he says. "They thought they could force the market. The attitude was that if you put the cars in the dealer's stock, he'd get rid of them, even if he had to give them away. That's the first time in all my career with General Motors I felt they weren't invincible."

Neither was he. Within a year he was forced to undergo triple bypass surgery. Like Julia's cancer, it was for the Harrison children another intimation of mortality.

"My mother and I sat in the waiting room all morning with all these other people who were also awaiting possibly disastrous news," says Carolyn. "And while we were there, some of those people learned that their loved ones had died."

"Seeing my father right after surgery was bone chilling. It was not real; it was like seeing someone in a coffin. It was even worse when he was back in his room and recovering. He was in terrible pain—they cut through his breast bone, and his body ached all over and he was just moaning. That's an image I will never get out of my mind."

"I'm sure at some deep level all sorts of significant changes were made in my relationship to him, just realizing that he's human, but also realizing how the world beat you down. That's what really struck me. The world can do this even to him. He was frail and fragile for a long time after that and I never could really express to him how much I loved him and wanted him to be better."

Though he was forced to take it easy, he made good on his threat to stay on the job until he was sixty-five, retiring in spring 1983. He and Helen remained in Atlanta for six months, but they knew Carolyn would soon be leaving them for the itinerant life of the liberal-arts scholar. So, with her help, they packed up and prepared to return to California, where one grandchild awaited them and another was on the way.

"We were thinking of a simple life-style and found out it's not so simple."

As best they can, Tom Harrison's little girls, Melinda and Suzie, help him make the last-minute preparations for Melinda's sixth birthday party. There are crepe-paper streamers, balloons, party favors, an elaborately decorated cake, punch for the children, wine for the adults. As soon as the decorations are complete, all the guests arrive at once— another six year old and her parents, who are friends of Tom's; a little neighborhood girl; Carolyn with her eighteen-month-old girl; and Dave and Helen Harrison. Tom's house, an early sixties ranch-style house with four small bedrooms, is located in a middle-class community just twenty minutes by freeway from his parents' home.

Everyone has come bearing gifts, and it seems pointless to postpone letting Melinda tear into them. In a kind of laid-back version of his father's heartier authority at the family barbecue, Tom manages the ensuing chaos with imperturbable gentleness. Beneath his placid demeanor there is a fierce and late-developing tenacity forged by his wrenching divorce, a bitter custody battle, and the psychologically difficult decision to rent this house his parents own.

Melinda is delighted with the enormous dollhouse Tom has spent most of the previous evening assembling, but, known in the family for his thoughtful gifts, he has also bought a wicker valise and filled it with outlandish items from an antique clothing store on Haight Street. The children, launched into an ecstasy of playing dress up, provide raucous evidence of his sure touch.

In private Helen has talked about how proud she is of Tom making it as a single parent, but she confesses she is surprised by the emergence of her only boy as a highly nurturing parent. She ascribes it to the influence of Dave. "Dave's always wanted to be with the children. When they were little, he would stay with them on Saturday mornings while I went out and did the grocery shopping." She laughs off the suggestion that the other six days a week, in which she cared for them, might be the key to Tom's behavior. And the notion that a widespread social redefinition of sex roles could also be at work is simply foreign to the individualizing and particularizing ideology she, along with most Americans, habitually assumes, even though those social changes provide the warrant for her pride in her son.

Following the party, Melinda and Suzie go to spend the evening with their grandparents. Tom is tired but relaxed. He opens a beer, waves dismissively at the mess, and settles his six-foot four-inch frame into an armchair. Bearded, with longish hair over his ears, wearing faded jeans, he looks very much the Texan he feels himself at heart to be. Whereas Joann is blithely honest, Carolyn analytical, and Julia ruthlessly self-critical, Tom is laconic and self-deprecating. Of the four children, he is the quiet one, a disposition perhaps reinforced by that first traumatic move from Texas to Michigan, when he was in second grade. He arrived in the middle of the semester with a Texas accent and and a slight speech problem.

"People kidded me about that and about my accent," he says. "I wasn't as talkative after that."

In general, however, he remembers those five years in Michigan as a happy time. Born in 1953, he missed most of the period when his father traveled extensively. Like Julia, he grew up amid the trappings of his parents' increasing affluence. Despite his shyness, he enjoyed scouting and sports and never lacked neighborhood friends. Then, just after he entered junior high, came the series of three moves in three years. He struggled to play football—he was already tall for his age and made a formidable lineman—but he was always joining the team in midseason. He gave it up for good in the tenth grade, when the family moved in the fall of 1968 back to the same suburb in Michigan they had left three years before.

Much had changed. The world of gentle folk rock, earnest political discussion, and occasional beer drinking that Carolyn had experienced in her final year in high school had become, by the time Tom reached high school, the flat-out youth culture of acid rock, reflexive political cynicism, and rampant drug use. The Beatles, Rolling Stones, Jimi Hendrix, and the constant psychedelic drone of an underground FM station from Ann Arbor provided the soundtrack for a frenetic adolescent scene fueled by grass; acid; and, as the decade drew to a close, speed. The startling transformation of former friends in just three years unsettled Tom.

"I felt I didn't fit in anywhere," he says. "I hadn't flowed with a group. Some of my former childhood friends were now into drinking and drugs. One was involved in burglaries, dealing dope. I took it all as a matter of course, but I felt alienated by it."

For males, the social world offered a stark choice of roles: Be a jock or be cool. Overcoming his initial alienation, Tom gravitated toward the latter. Not wishing at this late date to pain his parents, he is reluctant to talk for the record about the extent to which he participated in the wild life. He will only say, "I just went out and did it, and they didn't know and it didn't hurt any of us."

Like many of the generation, his activity was not consciously rebellious. He was simply swallowed up in the culture of his peers, a
culture which, by that time, many adults were themselves slavishly im-
itating.

"I never rebelled against my parents," he says. "They were always
nice and kind and generous. If we were talking about politics, we would
argue. But we didn't talk that much about it. Vietnam was something
rock and roll stars I liked sang against. It wasn't important to me. And I
don't know how important it was to them."

When he was graduated from high school, in 1971, he was not sure
where he wanted to continue his education. Dave and Helen had
dreamed of him becoming an engineer—if not an automotive engineer,
then a civil engineer. Dave, with visions of his son following in the
footsteps of the great engineer-executives he admired, urged Tom to
attend General Motors' engineering school in Flint.

Says Dave: "I wanted him to be an engineer and I wanted him to
come out of college and get a job with a big company and find out what
it's all about and succeed in a company. I wanted an engineer in the
world's worst way."

Tom took one look at the school's yearbook and saw all males who
had "very short hair and were very straight looking and nerdy." He
headed instead for the University of Texas, where he knew no one
except Carolyn, who was there only long enough to discourage him from
doing anything as retrograde as going out for fraternity rush. Then she
left for Atlanta with her soon-to-be first husband.

"I had moved again," Tom laughs. "I had gone someplace where
I didn't know anybody. I remember thinking, 'I did this to myself this
time.' "

In partial concession to his parents' wishes, Tom majored in electrical engineering; otherwise he found at Texas a scene that was more or
less similar to the one he had left in high school, but on a much larger
scale. He even participated, albeit halfheartedly, in a demonstration
when President Nixon visited campus for the dedication of the LBJ
library.

"I was just in the crowd chanting 'end the war' or 'Nixon, go to hell'
or something like that," Tom says. "Politically, I wasn't real astute. I
read the papers and listened to things and kind of formed my opinions by
what I heard from people I liked.

"I took a course in the history of modern America from Walt Rostow. I didn't even know who he was until three-fourths of the way
through the class. I overheard somebody complaining about all the time

we were spending on Vietnam and somebody else said, 'That's because Rostow's the sucker who bombed the shit out of them.' "

"The political is a realm that's not as important to me or that just operates on a certain level. College was a real social time, more of a social awakening than a political one. Later, it was more of a religious awakening, as I got into meditation and yoga."

After a year and a half, he dropped electrical engineering. His parents made a special trip to Austin and tried to talk him into sticking with it, to no avail. A semester and a half later, he dropped out of school altogether. His father, nudging Tom toward a career in Chevrolet, secured him a job in a General Motors parts warehouse in Chicago. Tom worked there for the summer, until the ripple effect of the energy crisis resulted in his layoff. With the money he'd saved, he bought a motorcycle and embarked on a *Wanderjahr* around the South and the Gulf Coast. He eventually returned to Austin, reentered school, and flunked out almost immediately.

He drifted down to the seedy resort town of Port Aransas, Texas, where he found a job doing maintenance for a motel. In his spare time, he wrote short stories. Known as an outlaw town, Port Aransas provided a fine backdrop for living out the Hemingway myth. Fishing constituted much of the commercial activity; disputes were frequently settled with knives; and Tom's employer, wanted in several states, was shot by the woman he lived with. Though Tom now describes the short stories he wrote there as self-indulgent, they at least gave him a purpose for returning to college, where he reenrolled as an English major.

"I was writing, and that was the one thing I liked," he says. "I loved to read books and I was sick of math. So I decided to do something I liked to do. I had no real thought of what I was going to do with an English major. I guess I had visions of being a writer, but the idea really was to get the degree."

He had been undergoing other changes as well. Popularizations of Buddhism by D. T. Suzuki and Alan Watts had led him to Zen, yoga, and meditation. Carlos Castaneda's best-selling books purporting to reconstruct the author's mystical experiences with an Indian wise man provided an additional dollop of turbid metaphysics. All these enthusiasms he shared with his sister Julia. Together they visited a week-long camp at a commune in Arizona that offered a smorgasbord of enlightenment: lectures on acupuncture, macrobiotics, holistic medicine, Hopi culture.

Back in Austin he joined a communal house of a dozen other like-minded young men and women. They shared expenses and duties, rarely locked their doors, and adopted a consciously antimaterialistic stance.

"I think a lot of the antimaterialism was just that it seemed a lot easier and more practical than having to work," he laughs. "If you don't have much, you don't have to work much. Living simply and simplifying your needs is more a spiritual ideal than a political or environmental one, though it fits with that." The irony, of course, was that his parents still paid the bills, an irony not lost on him today. "Really, I guess I felt ashamed of having had it so easy at times," he says.

Superficially, such antimaterialism may appear to be a mild rebellion against dependence on one's parents, but not for Tom. "I always loved my parents and I always respected them in a lot of ways," he says. "They had their faults, but they were always very supportive, very hard-working, and very giving. Of affection, and money, too. And I never had a problem with them judging me that much."

Today he recognizes that the values of generosity and affection he sought in the commune were an attempt to re-create, in slightly different terms, the atmosphere his parents created at home. "I think those values are important, and that's what I liked about the commune that made it very comfortable, that made it very much like the values I liked in my parents."

He applied himself to his books; got good grades; continued to do a little fiction writing; and was graduated from college in summer 1977, six years after he first entered. He could not have emerged into the work force in a worse year, except for almost every year thereafter. College degrees had been devalued; the economic decline that had begun in the early seventies was worsening; and there were simply far more baby boomers than even a healthy economy could have absorbed.

An ethic of voluntary simplicity, however disingenuous it may have seemed when espoused by the affluent college students of the late sixties and early seventies, actually proved adaptive when the students finally entered the work force and found there was no place for them. In fact, those who, like Tom, felt genuinely uneasy about what they saw as rampant materialism simply did not see the economic realities. Still living like ascetic students years after they left school, they had no idea how little choice they had in the matter. Short of an outright depression, middle-class Americans simply do not think in structural, economic terms, preferring instead to believe that they have freely chosen their circumstances, however fortunate or unfortunate. Even during the Great Depression, many middle-class Americans who were thrown out of work by the worldwide economic collapse tended to blame themselves for their misfortune.

An inveterate backpacker, Tom gravitated to the natural beauty of California, working in small Bay-area towns at a succession of jobs: motel maintenance, working at a convalescent home, painting houses, repairing tools in a mobile home factory. Along the way he met and moved in with Ann Mays, a woman who shared his desire to live simply. Within a year, at the gentle urging of his parents, they married. At first, the newlyweds investigated several communes, but were discouraged by what they found; one group advocated free love, another insisted that sex could be only for the purposes of procreation, and another proscribed the reading of certain books. Determined to escape city life, Tom sold some oil stock he had inherited from his maternal grandfather and bought for ten thousand dollars an acre of land in rural Oregon, where Ann had a good friend.

"We wanted to get someplace where we could grow some food and have land and own something and eventually build a house on it ourselves," he says. "We didn't want to move to San Francisco; we wanted a rural area that would be clean and fresh. We were thinking of a simple life-style and found out it's not simple."

The complexity lay in their rapid discovery that they could not secede from the economy. There were mortgage payments on the land, property taxes, and higher-than-expected living expenses. Worse, the economy of rural Oregon was severely depressed; there were no jobs. For two months they lived in a tiny trailer on the lot until the brutal cold burst their pipes. They were forced to move to a motel, which Tom helped reroof in exchange for the room. Shortly thereafter, the entire experiment ended when Ann became pregnant.

True to their ethic of natural living, they had done nothing to prevent pregnancy; but they had done nothing to prepare for it, either. So, without health insurance and unable to make the payments on their land, they more or less gave the property away and hurriedly moved to San Francisco, desperate for jobs and a place to live. Housing was at a premium, and the only place they could afford was an apartment in the Western Addition, a depressed, high-crime area far removed from the city's picture-postcard neighborhoods.

Joann hired both of them to work for her fledgling company, providing Ann with part-time secretarial work and Tom with an impressive-sounding reference. Tom applied for technical writing jobs, but, aside from short stories, had no examples of his work to show. With the baby due any day, he finally landed a job repairing Savin copiers at an annual salary of twelve thousand dollars. With dizzying speed, he had gone from living on his own land in Oregon to living in San Francisco, having a child, and working for a giant corporation. The moral support afforded by the proximity of his parents was soon stripped away when his father was transferred across the country.

"It was all quite an experience," Tom says. "It kind of opened my eyes to my own stupidity. I regret wasting that money when I had the opportunity of doing something. What I most regretted was that it put us in a bad position. We had to come to San Francisco, and I ended up getting a corporate job, which I felt the worst about."

The job required frantic driving to make service calls as far away as San Jose, sixty miles to the south. The company pressured Tom to meet a quota of four calls a day. He was suddenly surrounded by people whose obsessive worry was whether they should try to rise in the corporation by the technical or the managerial route. After six months, a move into more challenging word-processor repair made the job barely tolerable.

"I had never really thought about what I was going to do for a career," he says, "and this has always puzzled me. I thought about writing and I've always been good at fixing things, but career orientation is something I've always lacked." He laughs ruefully. "I *still* lack.

"I did six months in copiers and then a year and a half in word processors," he says, "before I burned out. My manager would push me and make me hustle, but when it came to a raise, he would put it off and criticize my dress and do everything he could to minimize the raise. One day, while I was making calls, I had a flat tire. I got out and I was standing beside the freeway kicking this tire and I said, 'Why the hell am I out here?' I'd had enough. I quit."

He fell into a quandary about what he really wished to do. When Ann unexpectedly became pregnant again, he went to work for a typewriter repair company, hoping that a small business would offer a more humane environment than would a large corporation. He soon found that the company's owner required a dozen service calls a day, did not care whether the jobs were done right, and sometimes dealt in stolen machines. Tom moved on to a more ethical typewriter repair company, but with two children to support, he needed the benefits and raises that were available only in a large organization. Ann continued to work part time for Joann, who, in line with her raised feminist consciousness, had always allowed Ann to bring Melinda to work.

Tom learned of a position repairing word processors that allowed him to work out of his home and to enjoy corporate benefits. More important, he might eventually be able to relocate to a city of his choice. He jumped at the job. But by then the enforced residence in a big city, parenthood, the necessity of both parents working, and the thwarting of pastoral and creative ideals were severely straining his marriage.

"Things weren't going real good even when I worked for Savin," he says. "I had been extremely unhappy there, and that didn't help the marriage. It was a hard time on both of us, and we didn't support each other very well.

"As far as a career goes, it has often been more of a question of where I'm going to be than what I'm going to do. That's one of the arguments Ann and I had near the end. For the kids' sake, we had to get out of the very dangerous neighborhood we were living in. I wanted to move out of the Bay Area altogether. We visited Austin, which I had kind of dreamed of moving to, but it had grown unrecognizable, and Ann was against it. She was so negative I knew it wouldn't be any easier there. So we stayed here."

His parents, having returned from Atlanta, were planning to buy another house in the East Bay for tax purposes. They offered to let Tom and Ann help pick it out with an eye to renting it themselves. Tom was reluctant. Like Carolyn, he had always disliked suburbia.

"Living in the suburbs was something I didn't really want to do— live the materialistic life, commute to work, turn out to be just like your parents. Ann didn't feel that way. She saw it as an opportunity to get a better house than we might have."

A house was found, and they moved to the suburbs, escaping the drug dealing, muggings, and occasional knifings of the Western Addition. But they could not escape the pressures weighing on their marriage. Within three months of the move, they separated and soon filed for divorce.

"I've had my turn on center stage."

Because the breakup of Tom's marriage involved grandchildren, it hit Dave and Helen particularly hard. "This just came like a bolt out of the blue," says Helen. "I had no inkling that anything was wrong." And it came at a time when she and Dave were making the momentous adjustment to retirement. Dave frankly says he feared retirement.

"I did not know what was going to happen. I did not know if I was going to have the money to be able to live the way I wanted to. I did not know whether I was doing the right thing by coming back to California, rather than staying in Georgia, where living is a hell of a lot cheaper. But Helen and I talked about it and agreed we could live on the income that we'd have. And we wanted to come back because of our children and grandchildren out here. We even hoped Carolyn might get hired at Berkeley some day.

"I was fearful, too, of what I would do with my time. I found out pretty quickly that Helen didn't want me to run the house. That was her domain. She had run it for forty years and she had no need for me to come in and run it."

His restlessness was assuaged somewhat by calls from dealers who sought his advice. He sometimes interceded with central office for them. When the calls increased in frequency, he set up a consulting business, but found it awkward to charge his dealer friends and soon abandoned it. An advertising executive whom Dave had known for years bought a Chevrolet dealership and persuaded Dave to run it until the executive could retire and run it himself. Like many men who worked for the corporation, Dave had often dreamed of running a dealership. Unlike most, he got the opportunity. The experience provided an interesting coda to his career.

"The thing that was the most eye opening for me," he says, "was the lack of help Chevrolet really gave its dealers. Of course, I had been a regional manager and I knew an awful lot about a dealership, but I had never run one at retail. And Chevrolet doesn't know anything about running a dealership at retail. The district managers came in and wanted to talk about getting the lead in sales, and I'd tell them we need the cars and the right product mix. Distribution was killing us. I was very unhappy with the way Chevrolet treated me and treated all the other dealers because I talked to them about it. They said, 'Dave, you're just getting a taste of what we've been through for years.' And I had to look back and say I was responsible for some of it."

As he'd learned in distribution battles as a regional manager, General Motors was production oriented rather than market oriented. "We could prove to them from the market standpoint that we could sell double the number of vans that they were building. Well, they couldn't get the panels for them. So it got to be a real mess, and even though you sit there in central office and tell the people, you can't get anything done. As a dealer, it was even more frustrating because you didn't even have a chance to tell the people up there."

Harrison was delighted when his friend relieved him of the dealership after a year. He reentered retirement enthusiastically—golfing, socializing with his children, doting on his grandchildren. As he sums up his experiences, clearly preferring the life of the corporate employee to the life of the entrepreneurial dealer, he does so in words that could have been lifted directly from Whyte's *Organization Man*, a book Harrison has never read.

"The corporation offered you a sense of power; it offered you a sense of belonging; it offered you a sense of fellowship; it offered you a sense of being able to do things on a broad basis to assist a large group of dealers. But a dealer is a small individual sitting out there with twenty employees, and that's all the influence he has. He has no fellowship except what he develops on the personal and local level."

In retirement, Harrison has watched with dismay as the difficulties mount for the company to which he gave most of his working life. The $40 billion dollar plan to redesign every car and upgrade or replace every factory, undertaken at the close of the seventies and just beginning to come on line, looked by 1987 to be a colossal failure. The goal was to lower production costs, fight imports, and leave the domestic competition far behind. Instead, General Motors' costs became the industry's highest; the company's domestic market share dropped from 48 percent in 1978 to 36.9 percent in 1987; and in 1986, for the first time since the days of the Model T, Ford was earning more than General Motors. In addition, an ill-advised acquisition of Ross Perot's EDS resulted in a highly publicized feud between new board member Perot and Chairman Roger B. Smith. To get rid of Perot, the corporation bought out his General Motors stock for $742.8 million dollars, well above its market value.

"I'm very sick about it all," Dave says. "I hate to see my company in trouble. I still have a great deal of loyalty to General Motors. I would like to see our corporation get back on its feet because I take a great deal of pride in being a member of the General Motors Corporation. I gave thirty-eight years to it and I don't want to see it fail."

Most painful to Harrison has been the company's drastic restructuring of the sales organization in which he found such fellowship. Despite his criticisms of the superfluous layers of management in the hierarchy, he believes the face-to-face contact with the dealers it afforded was crucial to the company's success.

"To cut costs, they have now erased the regions and fifty percent of the zone offices. They erased all the dealer contacts. Now the district manager comes to the zone office and makes telephone contact with his dealers. They've taken half the district managers into central office and they're going to be calling the zone or calling the dealers from there. It's a telemarketing program. There is no more going out and calling on a dealer, seeing what his problem is, counseling him, holding his hand, trying to get merchandise for him. Now it's just a voice on the phone."

He is aware that his criticisms sound like those of every retiree shunted aside, second-guessing from the sidelines. "When I was in Atlanta, I had several retirees there who were constantly telling me what needed to be done. Well, this is the last thing an active man needs, a retiree telling him how to run the company. So I determined that I was never going to do that, and I haven't.

"When I came back out here, I had an awful lot of friends with the company who invited me to sit in on meetings to make me feel a part of things, which I appreciated very much, and so the transition was very gentle. It wasn't until recently, when all the people finally got moved out, that I am a stranger now in the local office, the branch office as they call it. But I have no resentment because I know that this is the way it has to be. You have to move along and let the younger people take over, and I'm willing to move along. I've had my turn on center stage. I'm satisfied."

PART TWO

Individualism
Old and New

3

The Wealth of Generations

Relative expectations.

As the stories of Ray Myers and Dave Harrison illustrate, Whyte's junior executive of 1956 went on to become extremely successful. Typically, his annual cash compensation at the time of his retirement was in excess of two hundred thousand dollars, excluding fringe benefits and bonuses normally provided to senior executives of his rank. He is now a member of the first affluent generation of Americans to reach retirement age. By the mid-1980s, Americans aged fifty-five to sixty-five enjoyed the highest per capita income in the country, and those aged sixty-five to seventy-five possessed the highest average assets. And the per capita income for households headed by persons aged sixty-five or older outstripped that of households led by people under age fifty. In advertising parlance, people in this age group are charter members of the "New Old," and increasingly marketers and advertising agencies will turn their attention to this group and its disposable income. With mortgages paid off and children no longer dependent, they are spending their money on retirement homes (not to be confused with housing for the elderly), vacations, eating out, and a variety of consumer goods. We tend to think that most of the "New Old" will have economic difficulty when they retire, but that is not the case with the organization man. In fact, the burning question for the organization man at this stage in his life is: After affluence, what?

But for many of his now-adult children, the question is how to achieve the level of affluence they enjoyed when growing up. For despite all the attention paid to Yuppies and youthful investment bankers, many

119

baby boomers, including the sons and daughters of the organization man, are having difficulty matching the economic achievement of their parents and are likely to continue to have trouble until the day they die. Why?

For one thing, there are simply too many of them. In general, large generations encounter problems in almost every area of life, and it is the baby boomers' misfortune to constitute the largest generation in American history. Between 1946 and 1964, 72.4 million babies were born in the United States. From 1954 through 1964, more than 4 million babies were born every year. By 1964, 40 percent of the population was under twenty years of age. Most Americans who are alive today were born after 1950. During the fifties alone, which constitutes only ten years of the eighteen-year baby boom, the population increased by 28 million. By way of comparison, the American population increased by 17 million during the decade of the twenties, by less than 9 million during the thirties (the lowest absolute figure since the 1860s), and by 19 million during the forties.

For baby boomers, their unprecedented number meant over-crowded classrooms, difficulty winning academic distinction or a place on sports teams, and trouble finding a first job or getting into the college of their choice. To accommodate the huge number of college applicants, higher education expanded—especially during the Vietnam War when so many young men sought the safety of a student deferment—but it did so by hiring a generation of professors, many of whom would not be considered for college teaching jobs today. Degrees were devalued, not only because of the poor quality of many of the new and expanded colleges that issued them, but because so many more people had them. According to Landon Y. Jones, by 1969 half the white males of college age were enrolled; by 1975 one-quarter of all people aged twenty-five to twenty-nine had completed four or more years of college, an increase of 50 percent in five years. In the seventies, for the first time in recent history, the relative earnings of college graduates actually declined.

By the time the first wave of college-educated baby boomers began entering the job market in 1967, there was already a plentiful supply of young workers. From 1953 to 1963 the labor force increased at a rate of about 880,000 per year, but from 1964 to 1974, the annual increase ran at about 1,740,000 per year. Thus, those who entered the job market after 1967 had to compete not only with the numerous members of their own graduating classes, but with the millions of baby boomers who had preceded them. Entry-level employment was harder to find; standards were higher and compensation was depressed. Moreover, when the number of younger workers grows relative to the number of older workers, the younger fall farther behind their older contemporaries. A 1970s worker who made more money than his 1950s counterpart (even after adjusting for the rise in the cost of living) still lost ground vis-à-vis his older contemporaries. It is an oversupply that dogs baby boomers at every stage of their working life; it blocked them at entry level, it is stalling them in midcareer, and it threatens their retirement when the number of younger workers will be insufficient to make good on the social security and retirement benefits for what will become a vast legion of the elderly.

From the numbers at least, the future looks problematical for many members of the generation. Moreover, the economic problems engendered by the generation's large size have been exacerbated by the decline of the American economy. Since about 1973, when energy prices quadrupled, younger workers have been losing ground they are unlikely ever to make up. Economists disagree about the precise causes of the American economic decline, but successive oil shocks, falling productivity, ruinous inflation, the soaring national debt, massive trade imbalance, structural unemployment, and the emergence of a genuinely competitive global economy have made the easy affluence of the fifties and sixties appear a long-ago dream.

The consequences for a large generation in a troubled economy show up most clearly in incomes and housing. Between 1949 and 1973, the average income of families with two children doubled, but after 1973, when the baby boomers were beginning their careers, it fell. By 1986, a thirty-year-old man was earning 10 percent less, even after adjusting for inflation, than his father was earning at the time the man left home.

While income was falling, housing prices were rising, driven up, in part, by the sheer number of baby boomers who were competing for the limited housing stock. From 1968, when the first wave of organization offspring had just left college, to 1989, the median price of an existing single-family home rose from $20,100 to $93,200. During roughly the same period, the market value of residential real estate rose from around $600 billion to about $4 *trillion*, and home prices increased about 2 percent per year faster than did the rate of inflation. Rising prices are reflected even more starkly in the requirements for down payments. In the 1980s alone, the average down payment for first-time home buyers climbed more than 50 percent, from $8,600 in 1981 to $13,000 in 1988. According to a 1990 report on the state of the nation's housing from Harvard's Joint Center for Housing Studies, buying a first home has become more difficult than ever; it now takes 28 percent of a young couple's income to do so, a figure that has declined somewhat from a high of 37 percent in 1982, but that is nevertheless much higher than the 10 to 20 percent rates enjoyed by first-time home buyers in the 1960s and 1970s. Moreover, rents have stabilized at record-high levels, making it increasingly difficult for young families to save enough money to make a down payment on a home of their own. Although 40 percent of young renters have enough income to qualify for the mortgage on a median starter home, only 19 percent have enough money for a 20 percent down payment and only 12 percent have enough money for both.

High interest rates, which push up monthly payments, increasingly put home owning out of reach, and home ownership is the major source of the accumulation of wealth for most Americans. In the 1960s, when the average interest rate was 6 percent, the total interest on a thirty-year fixed-rate mortgage of $100,000 was $115,841 with monthly payments of $600. In the 1970s, when the average interest rate was 9 percent, the total interest would have been $188,810 with monthly payments of $802. In the late 1980s, when the prevailing rate was 10.5 percent, the total interest would be $229,306 with monthly payments of $915.

This combination of rising prices, high interest rates, and falling income put home owning out of reach for many baby boomers. In the decade of the 1980s home ownership declined for the first time since World War II—from a postwar peak of almost 66 percent of the population in 1980, when it began falling, to less than 64 percent in 1988. Home ownership fell most dramatically in the youngest age groups. In 1973, 23.4 percent of people under age 25 owned homes; in 1988 the rate was 15.5 percent. For 25- to 29 year olds the rate fell from 43.6 percent in 1973 to just over 36 percent in 1988. For 30- to 34 year olds the rate dropped from 60.2 percent in 1973 to 52.6 in 1988. And in the 35- to 39-year-old bracket, 68.5 percent owned their homes in 1973, while only 63.8 percent did so in 1988. Meanwhile, Americans over age 65 are more likely than ever to own their own homes. Three out of four Americans over 65 and nine out of ten married couples over 65 own their own homes. And they are benefiting from the rising housing prices.

Even those baby boomers who could afford to get into the housing market were forced to pay a larger percentage of their income than ever before for housing. In the 1950s a typical thirty-year-old man needed only 14 percent of his gross monthly pay to make the mortgage payments on an average home, and by 1973 a typical thirty-year-old man (and thus a member of the generation born when birthrates were at a historic low) needed only 21 percent of his gross monthly pay to do so. But by 1984, a thirty-year-old man (and thus a member of the baby-boom generation) needed a whopping 44 percent of his gross pay to make the payments on a median-priced home.

Given that the greatest burdens brought on by falling income and rising housing costs fall on the poor of whatever age, it seems indulgent to concentrate on the relatively mild financial troubles of a group as privileged as the baby-boomer sons and daughters of the middle and upper middle classes. But the point is not to suggest that persons in these classes are somehow deprived, but to determine what kind of dominant middle-class social character is likely to emerge from such experiences, however much or little sympathy these people deserve. And the key to the effects of those experiences lies not in how well members of the generation do relative to each other, but in how well they do relative to their parents.

Intergenerational mobility lies at the heart of the American dream. For the past 150 years, Americans have measured their success against their fathers (and in the future will likely do so against their fathers *and* their mothers). The further one rises above one's father, the more successful one is felt—and feels oneself—to be. A Rockefeller who winds up as president of a small-town bank cannot be said to have achieved very much; a steamfitter's son who does so is accounted a tremendous success. By such standards, Ray Myers, the son of a public-school administrator, and Dave Harrison, the son of a carpenter-farmer, succeeded handsomely. Their children and the children of men like them may not—at least by the time-honored standard, for they are part of the first generation in American history who will probably not do better economically than their parents. Even those who will eventually outstrip their parents are doing it in a far less secure corporate and economic environment and often at great cost to their personal lives. They have deferred marriage and childbearing, borne fewer children, and increasingly had to depend on two incomes merely to assemble the rudiments of the American dream. The price for all this has been phenomenal psychological stress, reflected in the generation's high rates of divorce, substance abuse, and suicide. To understand them, it is necessary to understand how their peculiar historical experience of intergenerational mobility shapes their expectations, their behavior, and their character.

As Richard Easterlin, among others, has argued, the behavior of young adults, as well as their feelings of well-being, involve the interplay of their economic prospects with their material aspirations. For example, a married couple who feel that their economic prospects are good *relative to their material aspirations* will be more likely to have children than will a couple who feel that their aspirations exceed their prospects. A couple who aspired only to month-by-month subsistence in modest circumstances, aspirations that may be easily fulfilled by the husband's job as a clerk at a hardware store, say, may not hesitate to have a child. Another couple, who desired a spacious suburban home, two cars, expensive vacations, and a college education for their child, but whose jobs in uncertain occupations like education or law made them feel pessimistic about their prospects for acquiring those things, would be less inclined to have a child.

Two factors must be taken into consideration: potential earning power and material aspirations. The proportion between the two is what determines judgments on the difficulty of having a child, buying a house, or getting married in the first place. Thus, says Easterlin, "an optimistic outlook may arise from exceptionally high earnings prospects . . . , unusually low material aspirations, or a combination of the two." Conversely, a pessimistic outlook may arise from exceptionally low earnings prospects, unusually high material aspirations, or a combination of the two.

People learn their earnings prospects from many sources, but experience in the labor market over time generally proves to be the ultimate teacher, which is to say during early adulthood. The formation of material aspirations, however, takes place (largely unconsciously) in one's family of origin, which is to say during childhood. Thus, it is possible for one's material aspirations to be widely out of phase with one's earnings prospects.

The organization man formed generally low material aspirations during his depression childhood and enjoyed high earnings prospects as an adult. His children formed exceptionally high material aspirations during the affluent fifties and sixties and faced, if not low, at least relatively diminished, earnings prospects in the seventies and eighties. Thus, it should come as no surprise, for example, that many baby boomers, especially those from comfortable backgrounds like those enjoyed by organization offspring, married later and had fewer children than did their parents. It is not because they are spoiled or they have failed to grow up, as moralists would have it, but because their earnings prospects are lower than their material aspirations, which, having been formed unconsciously, are not easily adjusted downward.

In essence, one of the keys to understanding the striking differences between the two generations lies in these nearly diametrically opposed historical experiences. Baldly stated, the organization man has an ingrained pessimism and an acquired optimism; his children have an ingrained optimism and an acquired pessimism. He craved security; they expected gratification. Fearing the worst, he achieved affluence on an unprecedented scale. Expecting the best, many of his children are finding it increasingly difficult to match, never mind surpass, his achievement.

This formulation is not meant to imply a simple economic determinism. The generations' different historical experiences of affluence merely provide a convenient entry point into the complex interplay of

social institutions, family life, and individual psychology that, taken together, yield the social characters of the generations—their values, their
hopes, their motives, their strengths, and their weaknesses. These social
characters, finally, are the real wealth of generations.

"Things were opening up."

In the fifties, optimism was easy to acquire and easy to ingrain. Per
capita income rose 48 percent, median family income rose from $3,083 to
$5,657, and real wages rose by almost 30 percent. By 1960 there were 10
million more home owners than there had been in 1950, an increase of 50
percent. More Americans owned their homes than rented them. Twenty-
five percent of all homes were fewer than ten years old. Ninety-eight
percent of them had a refrigerator; 90 percent, a television; 18 percent,
a clothes dryer; and 13 percent, an air conditioner. Eighty percent of
American families owned at least one automobile by 1960, and in suburbia 20 percent owned two or more.

Suburban dwellers, like the organization families, enjoyed a then-
astonishing average annual income of $6,500, as against $3,800 for everyone else. During the twenty-five years after World War II, the real
purchasing power of that family income would double. The middle class
rapidly expanded, with nearly 60 percent of American families earning
wages in that bracket. Low inflation made their gains more or less permanent. Even the 55 percent rise in consumer debt between 1952 and
1956 demonstrated optimism, and with vastly expanded hospitalization
insurance and expanded social security benefits, money for a rainy day
seemed less necessary. Many people assumed—incorrectly, as it turned
out—that such abundance would wipe out the age-old problems of poverty, social inequality, and class conflict.

The path to this affluence ran squarely through the large organizations that came to dominate American life following World War II. Increasingly, the new employers were large organizations. As corporate
America expanded, so did the number of white-collar positions. The
number of salaried white-collar workers jumped an astonishing 61 percent between 1947 and 1957. During the same period, clerical workers
increased 23 percent. The greatest growth took place in the professional
and technical occupations, expanding from 2.9 million jobs in 1940 to
over 5.8 million jobs in 1964. The number of scientists jumped 930
percent between 1930 and 1964; the number of engineers increased 370
percent during the same period. The white-collar workforce in the chemical industry, for example, grew by 50 percent between 1947 and 1952,

and General Motors reported 130,000 salaried workers on its payrolls. In 1956, the year *The Organization Man* was published, the number of white-collar workers in middle-class occupations surpassed for the first time in American history the number of blue-collar workers.

But more eloquent than any statistic is the now nearly incredible notion that the organization men, like Ray Myers and Dave Harrison, bought successively larger homes and more expensive cars, raised three or four children, put them through college, and managed to arrange for a handsome retirement, all *on a single income*. What made this miracle possible?

The organization man believes quite naturally that he achieved such unprecedented prosperity through hard work, perseverance, and teamwork of the sort that had won a world war. A hard worker and team player he was. Dave Harrison's first job with Chevrolet following the war, as a parts representative, took in thirty-two dealerships scattered throughout Louisiana's French country. Every morning Harrison climbed into a '46 Chevy, owned by the company, and began his rounds for the week.

"I believed that if a dealer was open, hell, I was supposed to be out there," he says. "I'd leave home at six A.M. on Monday and be out there until Friday night, working my way home calling on dealers. I was home only on weekends. It was rough on the family. My wife complained quite bitterly about it, and understandably so. I just told her, 'This is my job and I have to do it the best I know how.' "

With each new promotion, Harrison's financial situation improved. Harrison joined the General Motors stock program in 1952, when he received his first, largely symbolic, share. The next year he received two shares and his first piece of General Motors' famous, and often criticized, executive bonus program. Through the remainder of the decade, while he climbed the bottom rungs of the organization, he accumulated enough bonuses to make an eight-thousand-dollar down payment on a thirty-thousand-dollar house in 1961. Though his steady rise in the sixties and seventies to near the top of the company would bring him financial rewards he had never dreamed of, it was in the fifties that he, like many of his contemporaries, established a lead in the income race that would remain permanent.

"Things were opening up," he says. "And that's when my financial situation began to improve."

But if the organization man got ahead by dint of hard work, he also benefited greatly from some highly favorable historical circumstances. At the end of World War II, while most of Europe lay in ruins, America, with its productive capacity intact and fully revved up, stood virtually unchallenged for world economic leadership. At home, the pent-up demand for clothing, automobiles, and housing ignited a boom that defied economists, who were direly warning that the overheated wartime economy was bound to collapse in peacetime. A seemingly endless supply of cheap energy made possible a bewildering profusion of labor-saving and luxury consumer items of all descriptions. The baby boom itself, no small measure of optimism, fueled an expanding demand for all manner of products and services and eventually created its own class of new consumers, who spent billions of dollars annually on recordings, clothes, toiletries, food, candy, cars, and entertainment.

In addition to enjoying the general prosperity of the times, the largely white, male, Protestant, suburban-dwelling organization man was the direct beneficiary of a wide variety of governmental subsidies, public policies, and cultural practices. By guaranteeing a relatively inelastic labor supply, the restrictive immigration laws enacted in the 1920s would benefit him for most of his working life, as would racial and religious discrimination, both *de jure* and de facto. The pervasive cultural pressure and outright discrimination that kept women out of the professions following the war protected him from another potential pool of vocational competitors. And it provided him with his wife's cheap domestic labor, freeing him from family obligations so he could pursue his career as zealously as he wished.

Meanwhile, the government's housing policy in effect subsidized his way of life in the suburbs. Federally insured mortgages, which by 1955 accounted for 41 percent of all nonfarm mortgages, not only brought home ownership within the reach of millions of people who otherwise could not have afforded it, but gave preference to single-family, detached houses—the kind that could be built most readily in the wide open spaces. Moreover, the Federal Housing Administration rated neighborhoods on the basis of how much risk it believed lay in insuring a mortgage in them. Entire urban areas were redlined on the agency's maps, so it became almost impossible to obtain a federally insured mortgage to buy an older urban home, a policy that virtually guaranteed the decay of inner cities and the impoverishment of the lives of the people trapped in them by discrimination. Similarly, the freeways on which the organization man fled the central cities each night were built with federal funds; the interstate highway program, begun in 1956, was, up to that time, the most expensive public works project in history.

This combination of happy historical accidents, deliberate policies, and the organization man's own hard work produced for him an adult life marked by increasing prosperity and a genuine sense of accomplishment. Coming as it did after the rigors of the depression and the war, the affluence of his adulthood seemed a worthy goal and an admirable achievement. But for his children, it was merely a given, a starting point that they, like all American generations, expected to exceed handsomely. Not only did the children enjoy the relative comfort and ever-increasing affluence of their parents' homes, but they soon were having their material aspirations further raised by merchandisers who discovered them to be a distinct—and lucrative—market. Easily reachable through the new medium of television, through Top-40 radio, and through specialty magazines like *Seventeen*, the children were exhorted to buy all manner of consumer items, from candy and cereals to cosmetics, clothing, and even furnishings for their bedrooms. In 1959 their annual purchases hit the $10 billion mark and shortly thereafter $25 billion, almost all of it, of course, dad's money. Dad and mom, on the other hand, had formed their material aspirations during the Great Depression.

Hysterical comparisons of subsequent economic downturns with the Great Depression have trivialized the terrible suffering of that period. Terrible it was. Between 1929 and 1933 the gross national product plunged from $104 billion to $41 billion; 5,500 banks failed; stocks listed on the Big Board fell to 11 percent of their pre-Crash value; unemployment climbed to one-third of the work force. It is estimated that the average income of American families dropped nearly 40 percent, from $2,300 in 1929 to $1,500 in 1933. Twenty-eight percent of the nonrural population was without any income. (The rural population was simply left out of account.) Welfare was virtually nonexistent, difficult to qualify for when it did exist, and then only provided pennies a week, which most people were ashamed to take anyway. Millions of young men crisscrossed the country on freight trains, desperately looking for work; millions more simply gave up.

Though financial hardship was the result of structural dislocations in the world economy, people blamed themselves for their plight, often suffering intense guilt and shame at their inability to provide for their families. The writer William Manchester recalls one such incident from his childhood in Springfield, Massachusetts: "One of my most piercing memories is of a man who lived across the street from us. He would put on his business suit and drive to work every day. One day his son and I were wandering around after school. We turned a corner and there was my friend's father on the sidewalk, begging. I will never forget that moment. There was a sense of mutual shock when the father's eyes locked with the son's. They both felt disgraced."

Not everyone suffered equally. Economic hardship varied by region, occupation, social class, race, sex, and residence. Grinding poverty and severe want were confined largely to the urban and rural lower classes. For middle-class people who were unaccustomed to joblessness, underemployment, and a rapidly falling standard of living, life was often an anxious struggle to keep up appearances, rather than a desperate scratching for daily bread. For some people, the loss of income was offset by the decline in the cost of living. Some people even prospered. Thus, it is difficult to generalize about the effects of the Great Depression.

Most of what we think we know about the long-range effects of the depression on individuals comes from retrospective testimony. Books like Studs Terkel's *Hard Times* and our own interviews with organization men like Dave Harrison provide rich reminiscences of the period. But aside from Glenn H. Elder, Jr.'s, *Children of the Great Depression*, few studies have attempted to discover precisely how the period affected the entire life course of those who endured it. Elder analyzed archival data on a group of 167 Oakland schoolchildren who were born in 1920 and 1921. These children were first interviewed in 1932 and then were periodically reinterviewed up through the early 1960s. Though the interviews were originally done for a different purpose by someone else, Elder ingeniously used them to assess the long-range effects of the depression on adult character, while taking into account differences of social class, sex, and degree of economic hardship. Such differences make generalization difficult, but Elder's speculations about those children who experienced decremental deprivation (that is, a gradual constriction of their standard of living, rather than chronic or catastrophic poverty) offer insights into the adult character of many, though certainly not all, organization men and their wives, which most of the subjects in the Oakland group became.

Using Elder's work on depression-reared Americans and extrapolating from it to cover the opposite case of children reared in affluence, we can see how the two generations' sharply contrasting childhood circumstances produced significant differences between them. These two sharply contrasting childhood circumstances—decremental deprivation for many organization men to be and incremental affluence for organization offspring—produced other significant differences between the generations besides those of material aspirations. In both cases, adaptations to economic circumstances produced unforeseen and far-reaching consequences for the experience of family life; work life; group allegiance; sex roles; and, finally, for the very conception of the self.

Apprenticeship versus adolescence.

During the Great Depression, distressed families adopted a number of strategies to cope with the loss of income and status. Many simply reduced expenditures. They found, or were forced to take, less costly housing. They also tried various means of generating supplemental sources of income: They took in boarders, the women took in sewing or did piecework, and the sons sought part-time jobs. Out of necessity many families, especially their female members, developed a more labor-intensive household economy, doing their own canning and dressmaking and growing their own vegetables.

The flush times of the fifties and sixties required no such adaptations of organization families. For them, the "problem" was how to translate their ever-increasing incomes into higher status. Most organization families increased their expenditures year after year. They bought bigger and more costly houses, moved to more prestigious suburbs, and purchased second and third automobiles. Supplemental income, if there was any, came from the organization men's investments, whose means of production remained invisible to the rest of their families anyway. Nor was it necessary or possible for organization children to perform work inside or outside the home that genuinely mattered to their families' economic well-being.

In general, says Elder, the depression extended adulthood downward. Boys working part-time outside the home and girls working inside it were engaged in activities that contributed directly to the economic welfare of their entire families. In effect, many families came to resemble farm families, in which everyone's labor is crucial to survival. In addition, boys who worked were carried out of the immediate orbit of their families, always a significant step toward adulthood. And they were exposed to significant nonfamily adults to whom they had to give allegiance and obedience, another significant step. Though the girls who performed domestic chores experienced no such social independence, their lives nevertheless shared some of the same elements of apprenticeship as did those of the boys.

Conversely, the affluence of the fifties and sixties tended to extend childhood upward. Affluence eradicated the need for meaningful child labor and isolated children from nonfamily adults other than teachers. Those organization children who did hold jobs outside the home did not need to and were, therefore, under no compulsion to subordinate themselves in any important sense to their employers. For the most part, they regarded their jobs as sources of money to be spent on leisure. Their parents regarded such work by their children as vaguely character building. Children's household chores were similarly regarded by parents, whether or not the tasks were performed in exchange for an allowance. But studies of affluent children have shown that contrived household responsibilities have little developmental value.

Affluence not only isolated organization offspring from nonfamily adults, it further isolated them in suburbs far removed from the workaday worlds of farm and city. And, since their parents could afford to send them to college and beyond to graduate and professional school, it expanded the period of their education, generally the most carefree time of life. The upshot of this extension of childhood upward was the sudden discovery of the *teenager*, a word that entered the language only after World War II and that in the sixties gave way simply to *youth*, which encompassed everyone under age thirty.

Historically, the extension of childhood upward, especially among nonfarm families, was already well under way by the time of the depression. Since the coming of the Industrial Revolution, social roles had grown increasingly complex, pushing back the age of entry into adulthood. At the turn of the century, the managerial revolution, and the increasing complexity it entailed, accelerated the process. Simultaneously, powerful ideological currents running since the time of nineteenth-century agitation against child labor were radically altering the social value of children. Instrumental views of children were giving way to sentimental views, replacing the notion of the economically useful child with the ideal of the economically useless, but emotionally priceless, child. Formerly valuable for their monetary contribution to the family, children were now to be valued for their own sake. But the depression temporarily interrupted the expansion of childhood upward and the exaltation of the priceless child by sending millions of young boys to work and millions of young girls into economically useful household labor.

By going to work with serious intent, the boys from distressed families of both classes often gained special skills early in life, committed themselves to a vocation while still in their teens, and began to establish their careers forthwith. Dave Harrison, except for his wartime service, worked in the automobile business from the time he was eighteen years old until he retired. Early commitment to a career did, however, foreclose educational opportunities, but such educational disadvantages were more than offset by the phenomenal postwar expansion of high-status jobs in organizations of all kinds. More abstractly, an early commitment to a career could lead to what psychologists call premature foreclosure of identity.

The organization man's children, enjoying extended adolescence and expanded educational opportunities, felt no need to choose irrevocably a vocation and embark upon it. Nor did they gain any special work skills early in life or benefit from the industrious application of themselves to a task. Instead, they pursued the traditional path to high status—higher education. But by the time they were graduated, their college degrees had been devalued. And educational advantages had been further offset by a declining economy. They did not, however, foreclose their identities. Many still have not.

"She had three baskets of clothes to be ironed."

The nature of family adaptations to the depression and to the father-absent homes of World War II also help explain the kind of family life the organization man and his wife established in the fifties: the husband as sole breadwinner, the wife as full-time mother and homemaker. The organization man's devotion to his family as a youngster had, paradoxically, carried him out of the family and into the world of work, a pattern he would repeat as an adult. Thus, it is possible for organization men, without any consciousness of contradiction, to behave as if work were all that mattered and yet insist that they value family above all.

His wife's behavior is more difficult to understand, though many reasons have been advanced to explain the universal female domesticity of the fifties. Governmental and industrial policymakers urged women to leave the workplace in favor of the returning soldiers. A former Park Forest homemaker recalls: "The propaganda that we were fed when we were of marrying age was, 'It doesn't matter how smart you are, you have to use it in the home.' Magazines carried articles about it. They told you if you had a small family, you were selfish. Why did I have only two children? Large families were more healthy. I got an enormous amount of that. It began before the war was over. I think it was to get women out of the work force. I don't know where the ideas came from, but somehow it got through, and we were inundated with literature about how to be smart and be at home."

In addition, the satisfying of the pent-up demand for children made full-time motherhood necessary in a society that regarded day care for infants as abhorrent, even communistic. Furthermore, universal domesticity occurred, in part, because it was economically possible—a family of five or six could thrive on a single income. But, as Elder speculates, the psychological roots of the high value that organization wives placed on homemaking may lie in views of family life formed much earlier.

In distressed depression families, the economic contributions of wives and daughters to the household economy increased the significance and satisfaction of household labor. Daughters who participated in this important collective enterprise gave their labor and their loyalty. And wives became important economic actors who often shared in crucial decisions about how to allocate scarce family resources. Choices could be cruel: necessities versus status items required to maintain family dignity. Consequently, the wife's power within the marriage increased. And when the husband lost his job, her economic contribution and power increased all the more, as did that of the daughters.

"My father was a traveling salesman for a drug company," recalls a woman who was a child of the depression. "But he didn't travel during the summer of 1932, when I was six. He spent every day with us kids. I remember it so well. My mother did a lot of canning. I never knew she didn't like to do that. In lots of things she did she let her daughters know we could do anything—no restriction because of being female."

Many such daughters, keenly aware of their mothers' power, proud of their own indispensable contributions to their families' welfare, and proficient in domestic tasks, would, as adults, seek fulfillment in family life and domesticity. A similar dynamic would produce similar results in organization wives to be who grew up in the father-absent homes of World War II.

Domesticity during the vastly changed economic conditions of the fifties, however, tended to increase wives' dependence on their husbands, rather than increase their power within the marriage as it had with their mothers. On the other hand, such complete dependence also legitimated husbands' single-minded pursuit of their careers, however difficult for wives to bear otherwise. In the Oakland study, Elder found somewhat paradoxically that women in the 1950s were happiest in marriage to men who were intensely involved in successful careers, that is, to men who were most likely to put work ahead of family. Perhaps, he says, the rewards of the husband's success offset the loss of companionship.

Though numerous studies have shown that housewives in the fifties worked harder than their mothers had, these women were not motivated by dire economic necessity—which is not to say that their labor was without economic value—but by an ideal of service to the family. How much their effort was appreciated is hard to assess, but in the context of relative abundance, it took on a different meaning than did the labor of their mothers and was likely to be regarded differently by husbands and children alike. The ubiquitous and tiresome male jest of the period about the wife "really wearing the pants in the family" generally referred to the husband's acquiescence in matters he considered trivial—choosing home furnishings and the like—and spoke volumes about how little power domestic labor actually conferred within marriage.

Joann Harrison perceived from an early age how demanding her mother's job could be. "She'd have three baskets of clothes to be ironed and she'd start at eight or nine o'clock at night after she had cooked dinner," Joann says with awe. Watching her mother also care for four children, much of the time alone, Joann early on simply could not imagine children in her own future. "I remember I'd come home and complain about the house smelling like dirty diapers and I had had enough of dirty diapers. I remember having responsibility for the younger children, and it was a real drag."

Another daughter of an organization family, recalling her mother endlessly waxing floors, put it even more succinctly: "I thought my mother's job sucked."

We may speculate that this change in the meaning of domestic labor helps account for an impression that we gained from countless interviewees: The daughters of organization families generally failed to identify with their mothers in their roles as homemakers. Many of these daughters either identified with the social role of their fathers, as did Joann Harrison, or with a nonfamily figure—often a peer in their rigidly age-segregated world—who resembled neither parent. They did so despite an oppressive cultural atmosphere in which socially enforced sex roles masqueraded as a natural state of affairs. Subsequent historical experience—especially the decision and often the necessity to enter the work force—would move the daughters (and some of their mothers) even further from the fifties ideal, but the roots of their difference from their mothers may lie in their initial perception of domestic work.

"I gave them a lot of praise."

Historically, the decline in economic value of domestic labor was accompanied by an increase in the spiritual exaltation of domesticity for its own sake. Thus were born notions of the cult of "true womanhood," expert motherhood, and women as the bearers and transmitters of moral values. And the exaltation of domesticity carried a concomitant exaltation of the priceless child. The apotheosis of both, after the interruptions of the Great Depression and World War II, came in the fifties, often reaching absurd proportions, as in the ringing conclusion of an editorial in *Life* magazine's December 24, 1956, special issue on "The American Woman":

> But much as one must praise the diverse accomplishments of saintly women, the inspiration of Jesus' mother is not for saints only and need not lead so far from home. If woman, "the sum and complex of all nature," has one role more important than her others, it is the one

symbolized by Mary as a source of love. Only as women guard the art and guide the quest of love can mankind know all the kinds and heights of love of which they are capable. The art and the quest begin in the family and end at God's feet.

The postwar magnification of domesticity and its accompanying exaltation of the priceless child occurred at precisely the time when children had withdrawn from work, when postwar abundance was creating a mass-consumption society, and when the mass media, especially television, achieved an unprecedented ability to tantalize young consumers with a vast array of goods. In the nineteenth century, the physical removal of the father's place of work from the home to the office had begun the process of ending the urban family's function as a productive unit, a process temporarily interrupted by the depression. The phenomenal affluence following World War II not only completed the process of separating work from home, but transformed the family into a unit of consumption, bombarded constantly with an ideology of leisure and gratification.

Thus, we can begin to see the historical conditions in which the dynamics of the middle-class family, and, preeminently, the organization family, emerged:

□ The father's work, abstract and invisible, nevertheless produced an ever-increasing standard of living.
□ The mother and children were debarred from economically meaningful work and isolated in suburbs.
□ Domesticity was regarded as sacred.
□ Children were seen as emotionally priceless.
□ The family was depicted as a place of emotional and material gratification.

With economic production, education, religion, and care for the sick moved from the site of the home, the family came to exist purely for its emotional rewards—to be an arena for purely expressive values. Those children whose fathers were moved constantly by the corporation were isolated even more completely in this expressive arena. Moreover, in organization families, in which the father zealously pursued his career at the expense of family life, these expressive values tended to be channeled into child rearing, rather than into, say, marital companionship. The result was that in public the organization man may have been an other-directed glad-hander and his wife the proper ornament, but at home they were teaching their children neither the secrets of success nor propriety, but a different set of values, whether they intended to or not.

Formerly, child rearing had been concerned with enforcing the child's conformity to outward social forms, regardless of what the child might feel about them. Such methods were often authoritarian and sometimes cruel, but they focused on the child's behavior, rather than on inner psychological states. The criterion of personal worth was seen to lie in what one *does*, not what one *is*. The self, even when crippled, remained peripheral to maturation.

With the emergence of the family as an arena for purely expressive values and with child rearing the central function of the new domesticity, the emphasis fell increasingly on the individual uniqueness and potential of each child. The first things to go were rigid toilet training and feeding schedules. Helen Harrison, like many postwar mothers, was acquiring her philosophy of child rearing on the fly. Many baby manuals and her first pediatrician had insisted on inviolable feeding times, no matter how much the baby cried. Regretfully, Helen recalls standing in the nursery door watching Joann cry, endlessly it seemed, until the stroke of the hour for feeding time. Often, Helen cried herself. But Dr. Spock and her own misgivings about the way she had been raised soon led her to abandon such fierce regimentation.

Helen decided that the most valuable thing she could give her children was confidence in themselves. "I think I was aware of that from the very beginning," she says. "I gave them a lot of praise and it was all very sincere. I think I grew up in a generation where that was not the thing to do with children. You weren't supposed to tell children that they were pretty or smart. Somehow or other I wanted to do that."

However, such undoubtedly humane practices could produce some unintended and highly problematic consequences. Under such conditions, the child's self-esteem depends purely on expressions of approval and love from parents. As psychologist Jerome Kagan says, such a child of affluence cannot "point to a plowed field or a full woodpile as a sign of his utility." The emphasis is, rather, on what one *is*, not on what one does. It can be difficult and psychologically treacherous ground: One may become overly dependent on such expressions for self-validation, one may starve for them, one may be unconvinced by them, one may be all too convinced by them, or one may bounce wildly among all the possibilities. But no matter how it may play out in individual cases, the central issue for the child becomes the self: the self as the ground of value, as a problem, and as a project.

The organization children have been carrying the problem of the self with them ever since. In the sixties, some of them would attempt to carry into the public realm of politics the expressive values they had internalized in the private realm of the family. The rude awakening they received made the self only more problematic for them and for their more timid brothers and sisters who were looking on. In the seventies, many retreated to the private realm, where they continued their exaltation of the self, only to be rudely awakened again—this time by the economy. In the eighties, some attempted to resolve the problem by assimilating the expressive entirely to the instrumental: They equated self-fulfillment with acquisitiveness. But, as we will see, perhaps the most common contemporary response to the dilemma of self and world, individual and work, the expressive and the instrumental, has been the cultivation of a personal myth of artistry in an attempt to harmonize with the demands of the external world the ultimate value they place on the self.

For better or for worse, the self as a ground of value represents this generation's distinctive version of the ever-evolving nature of American individualism. Thus, it partially explains why the generation has such a troubled relationship to the world of organizations. The expressive realm of the self as a ground of value is frustratingly elusive, difficult to universalize, and possibly nonexistent. It is far more elusive than, say, a notion of individualism that manifests itself as rights embodied in laws or as personal freedom based in private property. And because it is highly problematic in itself, the most recent form of individualism necessarily complicates the other side of the equation—the realm of the group, whether organizations, communities, or polities.

"The best thing about growing up in Park Forest was also part of the worst thing."

What other grounds of value were available? What institutions might have provided countervailing influences? The suburban community? Education? Religion? The mass media? From the self nurtured at the center of the affluent family, we move out in concentric circles to the neighborhood, the schools, the church, and the all-embracing mass media and find that these institutions, too, tended to throw the organization children back on the resources of the isolated and expressive self.

Many reasons have been advanced for the flight to the suburbs, but the most likely explanation is the simplest: People wanted to own their homes, and in the suburbs these homes became readily available. By 1950 suburbs were growing ten times faster than were central cities. For the entire decade—discounting annexation, which arbitrarily redefines suburban areas as urban—suburbs grew forty times as fast as did central cities. In 1950, about 21 million Americans lived in suburbs. By 1960 there were nearly 37 million, equaling the number of people living in cities.

Settling suburbs carved out of the countryside—establishing schools, churches, and local governments—these new suburbanites often thought of themselves in terms that connected them to a venerable American tradition. "We always felt like pioneers," says Helen Harrison, "putting in our forty acres."

For the parents of the organization offspring, the pioneer myth offered an imaginary solution to the real contradiction of the individual and the group. Indeed, it performed the same function for the pioneers themselves, for the frontier—that borderline where civilization meets the wilderness—was not settled by rugged individualists but by federal troops, railroad conglomerates, grain and cattle brokers, cattlemen's associations, the judicial system, and hordes of lawyers. For the organization generation, the pioneer myth both preserves the cherished value of frontier individualism and conceals the extraordinary amount of cooperation and organizational power required to establish a town. It is no accident that Westerns would dominate television programming as the migration to suburbia reached flood tide. In 1958–59 twenty-three Westerns were on network television, eleven of them among the top twenty highest rated programs that season. In 1960, when the population of suburbia achieved parity with that of cities for the first time in American history, twenty-eight Westerns were aired in prime time. Nor is it surprising that America would elect that year a young president who promised a new frontier, the old one having been declared closed as early as 1893.

Where large numbers of people went, social commentators followed. A spate of books accused suburbanites of seeking homogeneity, conformity, and blandness. Titles like *The Crack in the Picture Window* and *The Split-Level Trap* told it all. David Riesman wrote of "The Suburban Sadness." And Whyte's *The Organization Man*, though far more sophisticated than were similar books, presented a generally unflattering portrait of suburbanites who spent their time chewing more than they had bitten off.

But the more sociologists studied suburbia, the more elusive suburbia appeared. Its apparent classlessness proved to be an illusion, its Republicanism more a feature of President Eisenhower's personal popularity than of anything else, its conformity more a feature of American life in general than of anything peculiar to tract housing. One count of the indictment, however, was undeniable: Suburbs remained lily-white. Of the 21 million suburbanites in 1950, fewer than a million were nonwhite. Of the 37 million suburbanites in 1960, 1.7 million were nonwhite. Moreover, most black Americans who were classified as suburban dwellers typically resided in aging, all-black neighborhoods that bore no resemblance to the spanking new postwar developments.

Whatever the ultimate verdict on the myriad charges against the quality of life in postwar suburbs, the organization offspring in our sample have certainly rendered their own interim judgment of guilty. Even those who live in suburbs today remain highly critical of suburban life. No doubt, they absorbed some of their disdain for suburbia from its critics, including Whyte. Nevertheless, their recollections are revealing.

Bob Alekno, a musician and instrument repairman who lives in Berkeley, California, is typical: "A community like Park Forest, starting from the ground up, didn't have any personality, any character to begin with. No different ethnic pockets. You just didn't have a sense of history there. There is a sense of history in New England—people have been living there for generations; there are old buildings, old houses. You didn't feel that around Park Forest. But it never forced anything on me. You could kind of be whatever you were going to be."

Kevin Cole, a writer-producer of film documentaries, expresses similar ambivalence: "The best thing about growing up in Park Forest was also part of the worst thing. The thing that stands out most is a kind of security. It was a safe place, a good place to grow up. One of the things I've thought about a lot since then was just the sheer number of kids around. On our block there were twenty-five kids within a few years' age difference. That kind of atmosphere was good, I think, for the mental health of most people. But the other side of it was that you were just tremendously sheltered. I don't think Park Forest adequately prepared me for a lot of the things that I found out."

Over and over we listened as organization offspring described the communities of their childhood as culturally and emotionally barren, featureless, and lacking in diversity. Many used identical language—the word *neutral* was often heard. Yet, like Bob Alekno and Kevin Cole, they almost invariably tempered their harsh judgments with a kind of gratitude for what they see as such a wan environment's inability to impose an identity upon them.

Of course, it is a delusion to think one's childhood environment leaves no impress. And it is precisely that delusion the suburbs, like the affluent middle-class family, foster: the belief in oneself as an autonomous, self-created being. Because of their isolation (so correctly perceived by the organization offspring) from city, farm, and place of the father's work, the suburbs threw children back ever more decisively into the expressive arena of the family, where the delusion is first and most powerfully formed.

"They dance, they sing, . . . they draw and paint."

Like the family and the suburbs, the schools would also do their part, though far more wittingly, to promote the new psychological dispensation. But at the time Whyte looked at the Park Forest school system, such a development seemed highly unlikely. The schools there were still firmly under the sway of progressive education, which, by the 1940s, had come to dominate American educational thought and practice. And on its face, at least, progressive education seemed merely another facet of the social ethic.

Initially, progressive education had been allied with the larger progressive political and social reform movement that arose in the 1890s. Drawing on the ideas of William James and John Dewey, the movement's educational wing saw the schools as a potentially powerful instrument for producing zealous and thoughtful citizens who would reform society. But following World War I, when the larger progressive political movement withered away, progressive education underwent a sea change. Professionalized and institutionalized in powerful teachers' groups and colleges of education, progressive education gradually reversed its emphasis: Instead of producing individuals who would change society, it aimed to adjust individuals to society.

In part, educators were responding to vastly increased high school enrollments. Beginning in the thirties, when the age of compulsory school attendance was raised, the percentage of high-school-age children who actually attended began to climb. Having traditionally served only those people who desired secondary education, high schools found it difficult to cope with this far more diverse population. They often responded by offering vocational education, home economics, typing, and the like. They began to emphasize concepts like "educating the whole child"; "recognizing individual differences"; and "teaching children, not subjects"—apparently humane pedagogical approaches that in fact concealed a profound contempt for the mental capacities of the newly diverse school population. At the expense of traditional disciplines *and* vocationalism, they designed "life adjustment" curricula devoted to issues of citizenship, health, recreation, and family life. Inspired by a series of educational conferences held throughout the country in the late 1940s and enjoying the full backing of the U.S. Office of Education, life-adjustment education represented the full flowering of thirty years of progressive educational theory and practice. Originally intended for the vast majority of students who fell somewhere between vocational education and college preparatory work, life adjustment was soon being touted as the best possible education for all American students.

It was the inanities of life adjustment that Whyte encountered in the Park Forest schools. In the village's elementary schools, pedagogy focused on the children's experiences: "Everything [the children] learn," crowed a report of a PTA committee, "is related to something they've experienced in their everyday life or through TV, radio, movies, or on the playground." Even though most Park Foresters were college educated and thus their children were highly likely to attend college, the Park Forest high school was designed with a strong emphasis on life adjustment. Only half the seventy subjects offered were in traditional disciplines—a course on family life was the pride of the curriculum. And the high school superintendent complained to Whyte that many benighted colleges still required academic credits for admission.

In addition to embodying a cheerful anti-intellectualism, the curriculum emphasized the moral value of adjustment to group life and offered practical instruction in how to achieve it. "Ours is an age of group action," the high school superintendent told Whyte. Teachers frankly admitted they mobilized the disapproval of the other students against any child who stepped out of line. Parents, queried about the primary job of the high school, said it should teach students how to be good citizens and how to get along with other people. In short, the schools seemed to be reproducing the worst features of the organization man's social ethic.

Whyte need not have worried, however. Criticism of progressive education had been building since John Dewey himself first spoke out against its distortions in 1938. By 1953, when no fewer than four books scathingly attacking it were published within a month of each other, progressive education was on the defensive. In Park Forest itself, as Whyte noted, a vocal minority of parents had begun in 1955 to demand a return to academic substance. In communities throughout the country, there was growing criticism of the educational establishment, and not just from the "know-nothing" Right.

The launching of Sputnik in 1957 delivered the fatal blow. Anguished reappraisals of American education concluded that while little Johnny had been playing at life adjustment, little Ivan had been working at the hard sciences, foreign languages, and all the other academic disciplines that he might one day use to bury us. For a time, education was harnessed to national security and progressive education was in retreat, though many of its features would survive in attenuated form.

Insofar as life-adjustment education succeeded in transmitting the social ethic, it did so not with the postwar baby boomers, but largely with members of the generation born during the Great Depression and World War II, for when Whyte was doing his research in the early fifties, the schools were still largely populated by them. The first wave of baby boomers entered first grade in 1952, did not exclusively populate elementary and secondary schools until 1964, and had not moved through the system entirely until 1982.

Moreover, progressive education had always embraced ideas and aims that ran counter to a purely conformist vision. Partly rooted in romantic and sentimental notions of the nature of children, much progressive educational theory emphasized self-fulfillment, self-expression, and creativity. Diane Ravitch, an astute observer of American educational history, describes the contents of *The Child-Centered School*, an influential work of progressivism first published in 1925:

> The new school was devoted to "self-expression and maximum child growth," a place where children were eager to go to school because "they dance; they sing . . ; they model in clay and sand; they draw and paint, read and write, make up stories and dramatize them; they work in the garden; they churn, and weave, and cook;" its philosophy was "the concept of the Self."

As actually practiced in different school districts throughout the country, progressive education could fall anywhere along a line between individual self-expression and adjustment to group life. Indeed, the mix could differ from teacher to teacher within the same school. No doubt many teachers, unable to get a handle on its ill-defined concepts, paid it lip service while continuing to teach traditional subject matter in traditional ways. In any case, within much progressive theory and practice, expressive values remained fundamentally at odds with the instrumental values of adjustment to the group. Notions like the "well-rounded personality" represented attempts to resolve the paradox, but the ideal of well-roundedness merely put self-expression in the service of group adjustment. The well-rounded personality, so beloved by the corporate personnel officers Whyte interviewed, could be counted on to eschew eccentricity of any kind, to be familiar with many things and devoted to none, and to have no rough edges that would prevent smooth integration into the social machinery.

Even in the absence of Sputnik, the ideal of the well-rounded personality would have been doomed to failure. For in a context of material abundance, consumerist gratification, and isolation from work, the multifarious activities of well-roundedness would inevitably turn from a concern with personality and its emphasis on group adjustment and public behavior to a concern with the self and its emphasis on individual fulfillment and private feelings. There was little need for these relatively privileged children to create marketable personalities, few arenas in which the shoe shine and the smile of their fathers were called for. They were far more likely to be worrying, along with Holden Caulfield, about "phoniness."

Over time it was the expressive values in progressive education that would triumph. These values survived in the "experiential" approaches to learning embodied in the widespread curricular reform following Sputnik; they informed midsixties radical critiques of the schools as soul-killing experiences for black and white students alike; they reemerged with a vengeance in the open-education, free-school, and alternative-school movements of the late sixties; and they underlay the consumer-driven smorgasbord curricula of the seventies.

Depending on when and where they went to school, the organization offspring were subjected, in varying degrees, to these successive waves of educational reform. The constant over time and place, however, remained the expressive values that ran through them all. Even older members of the generation, like Carolyn Harrison, who experienced the schools as repressively authoritarian did so, in part, because the pervasive ideology of the self as the ground of value heightened the dissonance in even the mildest forms of repression. Most of the organization offspring we interviewed, especially the former Park Foresters, remember their education fondly, and what they remember are the classes in art, music, and drama and the extracurricular activities that went with them, where "they danced, they sang, . . . they drew and painted."

"Organized religion doesn't come into the picture."

On the face of it, religion, with its emphasis on the created, rather than on the self-created, nature of God's children would seem to promise a strong countervailing force to the notion of the self as the ground of value. And the phenomenal fifties' boom in *organized* religion would seem, like other organized aspects of the offspring's life, to auger for the continuing production of organization people, specifically, church members. But the suburban religion of the organization man and his wife did neither. In fact, its vague "faith in faith" (as opposed to the content of faith) tended to augment the self as the ground of value and thereby made inevitable the church's devaluation as an institution.

That there was a boom—it cannot be called a revival—of organized religion in the fifties is certain. From 1940 to 1958, church membership rose from 64.5 million to 109.5 million—61.5 million of them Protestants and the bulk of those in just seven denominations. That increase in membership was from 50 percent to 63 percent of the population, an all-time high. (In 1800 only about 10 percent of Americans belonged to a church. In 1900 the figure was 35–40 percent. The figures for 1989 are about 143.8 million members, or about 58.6 percent of the population.) Church attendance also increased, reaching an all-time high of 51 percent in 1957 and tapering off slightly to 47 percent by 1960.

The construction of church buildings, especially in the suburbs, also greatly expanded. The value of such new buildings jumped from $409 billion in 1950 to $868 billion in 1957. For a time in the midfifties, Hugo Leinberger, who established the nonsectarian United Protestant Church in Park Forest, was helping found similar churches in other suburban developments at an average rate of one per week.

Evidence of a general piety abounded. Public opinion polls consistently found that 95 to 98 percent of the American people believed in God. The Bible became more widely available than ever, its distribution increasing 140 percent from 1949 to 1953. Religious songs like "Vaya Con Dios" and "I Believe" climbed to the top of the pop music charts. In 1954 Congress added the phrase "under God" to the pledge of allegiance. President Eisenhower instituted prayer breakfasts and began ostentatiously opening Cabinet meetings with prayer. Billy Graham, immeasurably helped by Henry Luce's decision to promote him in *Time* and *Life*, achieved spectacular success on the revival trail (and, unlike many of his subsequent imitators, urged converts to join their local churches). Bishop Fulton J. Sheen's curiously named television program "Life Is Worth Living" was seen in prime time from 1952 through April 1955; his subsequent program, "Mission to the World," ran from October 1955 until April 1957. Reverend Norman Vincent Peale's *Power of Positive Thinking*, a vulgar mixture of Christianity and self-help published in 1952, rode the best-seller list for 112 consecutive weeks; in 1954 only the Bible outsold it. Though repelled by the likes of Peale, intellectuals of the period struggled with the strenuous theological challenges posed by Paul Tillich, Richard and Reinhold Niebuhr, Martin Buber, Jacques Maritain, and the recently rediscovered work of Kierkegaard.

Many causes converged to produce this apparent religious groundswell. By the 1950s, religions had come to play a central role in conferring social identity, especially for succeeding waves of immigrants and their descendants. In his penetrating look at American religion in the fifties, *Protestant—Catholic—Jew*, Will Herberg observes that when immigrants come to this country, they are expected to change their nationality, language, and culture, but not their religion. By the third generation, it is religion—whether one is, broadly speaking, Protestant, Catholic, or Jew—that differentiates people and is the "context of self-identification and social location." All three of the major faiths are conceived by Americans as expressing fundamental American values: supremacy of God, brotherhood of man, and the worth of each individual human being. By locating themselves in one of these religious categories—as roughly 98 percent of Americans consistently did then—individuals simultaneously tied themselves to their heritage and integrated themselves into American society. Similarly, suburbanites who were uprooted from the small towns and cities of their youth (and many of whom were only two or three generations removed from immigration) also derived much of their social identity from their association with one of the three dominant religions. Churches played an even more crucial social role for the vast number of people Whyte called the transients, the organization families constantly on the move, who looked to the churches for instant community and friendship.

Other currents that favored religion were also running, including an unending stream of unsettling public events. Far from being the placid decade of nostalgic memory, the fifties witnessed the mass hysteria of McCarthyism, the frustration of the Korean War, the terrifying invention of the hydrogen bomb (and its acquisition by the Soviet Union), the "brinkmanship" of John Foster Dulles, American intervention in Lebanon, the sending of federal troops to integrate Little Rock's Central High, a dramatic increase in juvenile crime, the first stirrings of the civil rights movement, the shock of Sputnik, and the disorienting effects of affluence and mobility. The anxiety that resulted fueled a constant search for "peace of mind," often to be attained through the agency of religion. Though sometimes allied with positive thinking, the peace-of-mind movement borrowed ideas more heavily, and not always without sophistication, from psychiatry.

Religion was also enlisted in the Cold War struggle against godless communism. Sheen and Graham, seen by millions of television viewers, played particularly significant roles in this regard, but so did many suburban churches. As a result, according to many commentators, religion grew indistinguishable from the vague set of beliefs known as Americanism or the American Way of Life. We might also speculate that the equation of religion with Americanism might have had the paradoxical effect of loosening the local authority of the church, making religion appear at once more diffuse and pervasive, ubiquitous but remote, like television or the federal government.

Almost no one, other than a few intellectuals, cared overmuch about theology, and many Americans were found to be woefully ignorant of the faith they professed. Despite the phenomenal increase in the distribution of the Bible and the fact that 80 percent of adult Americans said they believed it to be the revealed word of God, numerous surveys of religious knowledge found that most had difficulty naming the three persons of the Trinity or distinguishing the Old Testament from the New Testament or Catholicism from Protestantism. Fifty-three percent of the respondents to a 1951 Gallup poll were unable to name a single one of the Gospels.

A survey of Park Foresters revealed that the decisive factors in choosing a church were, in order, (1) the minister, (2) the Sunday school, (3) the location, (4) the denomination, and (5) the music. Many, after shopping around for a church in a new location, felt no qualms about joining any of the mainstream Protestant denominations that fit the bill. Others joined Hugo Leinberger's United Protestant Church, an ecumenical enterprise designed to relieve the developer of Park Forest from the burden of providing free church land for the numerous denominations clamoring for it.

This is not to say that the organization generation lacked beliefs. Culture, abhorring a vacuum, rushed to fill the theological void not only with Americanism as a kind of civic religion, but with a set of personal beliefs that offered comfort and guidance to individuals who adopted them. The core of this personal religion, and its relation to the larger society, was best expressed by President Eisenhower. "Our government makes no sense," he said, "unless it is founded in a deeply felt religious faith—and I don't care what it is."

Eisenhower, perhaps unwittingly, said it all: The key is not *what* you believe, but *that* you believe. The center of such religion is not faith in God, but faith in faith itself. Herberg summed it up: "The American believes that religion is something very important for the community; he also believes that 'faith,' or what we may call religiosity, is a kind of 'miracle drug' that can cure all the ailments of the spirit. It is not faith in *anything* that is so powerful, just faith, the 'magic of believing.' "

Historically, this American belief in belief has taken many forms, beginning with Christian Science and its secularization in the New Thought movement of the late nineteenth century. In the fifties, as we have noted, it most typically traveled under the names of "peace of mind" and "positive thinking." Today it travels under the name of the New Age.

In its peace-of-mind form, belief in belief promised to deliver the believer from anxiety and guilt, to bring self-acceptance and inner harmony. Joshua Loth Liebman's phenomenally successful *Peace of Mind*, first published in 1946, offered among his "commandments for a new morality" the following:

□ *Thou shalt not be afraid of thy hidden impulses.*
□ *Thou shalt learn to respect thyself and then thou wilt love thy neighbor as thyself.*

□ *Thou shalt transcend inner anxiety, recognizing thy true competence and courage.*

In the form of positive thinking, belief in belief provides the key to success and achievement. By getting rid of negative thoughts, positive thinkers unleash the true power of their personalities and achieve unlimited self-confidence and a happier orientation to all their activities, including—in Peale's crass vision—their financial endeavors.

From its inception, Protestantism has emphasized individual piety, genuineness of religious emotion, and personal encounter with the deity and scripture unmediated by a church hierarchy. But this American development of Protestantism in the fifties reduced that age-old emphasis on the individual believer to a question of psychology. The injunction to have faith came to refer not so much to God as it did to one's own psychological attitude. In short, the ground of value, even in religion, became the self.

Theology, liturgy, and orthodoxy, having historically counted for very little in American Protestantism, counted even less under this psychological dispensation. Moreover, it virtually guaranteed the eventual irrelevance of the church as an institution. In other words, religion of the period, despite its boom, was simply one more feature of the suburban landscape that drove the children back in upon the self. It is no surprise, then, that as adults, no matter what their spiritual beliefs, the organization offspring remain frankly indifferent to religious institutions.

The difference between the generations in church participation is striking—the proportion of young Americans who were born Protestants and later leave their churches has increased from only 6 percent of those people born in the early years of this century to 34 percent of those born since World War II. The scale of these defections began showing up in the midsixties, when the large ecumenical "mainline" religious bodies of the sort in which the organization offspring were reared began reporting net membership losses. The Episcopal Church, the United Presbyterian Church, the United Methodist Church, the Christian Church (Disciples of Christ), and the United Church of Christ all had such losses, some as high as 10 percent per decade. In the seventies the Lutherans and the Reformed Church in America also began reporting net membership losses. Though Catholicism continued to grow, often as a result of immigration, weekly attendance at mass declined from 74 percent of Catholics in 1958 to 51 percent in 1982. (Jews, only about 2 or 3 percent of the population and an even smaller percentage of our sample, are something of a special case; even when religious participation declined, communal and ethnic bonds often remained strong.)

Institutional support faltered along with membership: Religious giving in relation to inflation declined and new church construction slumped. Increasingly, people were more willing to declare themselves "nonaffiliated" to pollsters. And studies showed that these "unchurched" are "disproportionately young, male, white, well educated, nonsouthern, and frequent movers." Moreover, even those affluent, upwardly mobile baby boomers who *joined* mainline churches often did so for reasons of status and therefore had little religious or institutional commitment.

This spurning of organized religion has been obscured by the rise of fundamentalism and the perception among many that during the seventies and eighties it was gaining ground in the suburbs, where many of the organization offspring live. But fundamentalism did not move to the suburbs; fundamentalists did. Frances Fitzgerald, in her revealing look at the congregation of Jerry Falwell's Thomas Road Baptist Church in Lynchburg, Virginia, found that many of the members were first-generation suburbanites who had moved there from rural small towns and had clung to their fundamentalism as an antidote to the anxieties associated with their new-found mobility. This pattern, repeated in numerous middle-class suburbs, especially those in the Sun Belt during the days of its oil and natural-gas boom, created the appearance of a suburban religious revival, when what was actually taking place was a religious *arrival*. The children of such suburban arrivals are no more likely as adults to cling to the faith of their fathers than the organization offspring are to return to the faith of theirs.

Indifference is precisely the word to describe the attitude of the organization offspring. Questioned about their relation to organized religion, the organization offspring we interviewed refrain from petulant rant or tortured theological arguments. Many, like Tom Harrison or his sister Julia, will talk sincerely about their private beliefs in a universe informed by spirit or about their personal sense of the sacred. But whether areligious, engaged in the search for self-fulfillment, or in a private system of belief, the organization offspring simply are not interested in organized religion, church membership, orthodox theology, or communities of believers. Not one of the Harrison children belongs to a church. The story is the same with the overwhelming majority of our other subjects. For example, Tom Howell is a modest, self-effacing vice president of Bank of America. An MBA, he looks and talks like the all-American boy. But ask him the place of religion in his life and he will tell you quietly, "It's pretty nonexistent."

Ask Dale Radcliff, who went from rock musician to banker, and he says, "It hasn't got a place right now."

Bob Cory, raised in Park Forest, was indicted as a young man for refusing induction into the army. When he was first interviewed, he worked at Apple computer while preparing to launch a company of his own. Thoughtful and devoted to the arts, he says, "Organized religion, per se, is not very important." His wife Laura adds, "It's not there at all."

Says Bob Alekno: "Organized religion doesn't really come that much into the picture."

These organization offspring and others like them feel this way as adults not because they rebelled against the religion of their parents, but because they responded to its central concern: the self. The parents did not fail to transmit their values; they succeeded only too well. If they are disturbed by the form their children's spirituality takes, they should not be because it is descended in many ways from their own. And if they are upset by their children's refusal to affiliate with organized religion, they have no one to blame but themselves.

Radio and the return of the repressed.

The only institution apparently more successful in the fifties than organized religion was television. In 1946 only about seven thousand television sets were sold. By 1948, televisions were selling at the rate of two hundred thousand per month. By 1955, 88 percent of American families owned one. Of all the influences that shaped the generation, television has perhaps received the most attention. The sheer volume and often virulence of such commentary, however, has drowned out the real generational story.

The commentary is by now familiar and comes from all points on the political and cultural spectrum. Though occasionally seen as a potential tool for education, television has more often been regarded as the devil's instrument, responsible for everything from juvenile delinquency to shortened attention spans. Formalists, who follow Marshall McLuhan but lack his optimism, claim that television subverts linear thinking and annihilates space and time, changing our very consciousness in the process. Those who analyze television's content see other dangers, depending on their politics: Liberals find it presenting rigid hierarchies of social class, gender, and race; conservatives see it propagandizing for the dismantling of such hierarchies. Marxists, on the other hand, see the apparent relativism of its form and the middle-class values of its content as a smokescreen concealing the operation of capital behind and through the media. This is to say nothing of ordinary concerned citizens who worry about the effects of televised violence on children, of advertising on politics, of mass culture on high culture, of visual culture on literate culture, and of simplistic dramas on people's expectations about real-life problems.

Most organization offspring cannot recall a time in their lives when there was no television. And, not surprisingly, television has often been invoked to account for many of the characteristics of this first television generation. Certainly, television helped raise their expectations as consumers. And network broadcasts—news and shows "from nowhere"—weakened the authority of local institutions like the churches, the schools, and the family, though perhaps no more than those institutions themselves were doing, each with its distinctive privileging of the self. But the influence of television, powerful as it is, is easily overrated. In fact, what would become, and remain, the really meaningful medium for organization offspring and millions of other baby boomers was not television at all. It was popular music.

This is, above all, a generation that defines itself through music, not through television. As adults, the organization offspring may subscribe to cable and they may own a disproportionate percentage of the nation's videocassette recorders, but they are not to be found among the lost souls writing earnest letters of advice to soap-opera characters. They are not mesmerized by tele-evangelists nor tantalized by home shopping networks. They are, however, among the commuters on the freeway who punch up the "classic rock" and "adult contemporary" stations on the car radio. And a surprisingly large number of our interviewees, like Bob Alekno and Dale Radcliff, have pursued careers in popular music at one time or another.

Ironically, television became the unwitting agent for the coming of rock 'n' roll. Having quickly supplanted radio as the center of home and family entertainment, television soon settled into its formula of cozy sitcoms and mythic Westerns, suitable for viewing by all ages. Radio networks withered. To survive, individual radio stations reverted to inexpensive programs of recorded music, in time learning to develop formats aimed at particular kinds of listeners. The result in many organization households resembled a parable of repression. Whatever unspeakable desires television kept at bay in the family room by day emerged at night in the privacy of the children's bedrooms. There the children tuned their radios to stations ruled by bizarre personalities who spun all manner of strange and thrilling music: swaggering electric blues, gritty r & b, smooth urban doo-wop, and hiccuppy hillbilly boogie. Father might know best in his narrowly circumscribed television world, but this phenomenon clearly lay beyond his ken.

Critics may insist that television, as the most formally striking of the media, must necessarily produce the most profound effects, even though, as the most popular medium, it was constrained to be the most vacuous and bland. This view overlooks the fact that Top-40 radio's "content," rock 'n' roll, was itself a medium with compelling formal properties. Rock 'n' roll taps much more directly the oceanic drives of sexuality and desire than the aleatory mosaic of television's form or the rigid hierarchies of its content ever could. Television's highly sanitized lowest common denominator may attract the largest audience, but it also wins the least allegiance. "Great Balls of Fire," on the other hand, is certainly low and maybe common, but the area of experience to which it appeals is renounced only at some psychic risk. Carolyn Harrison put the issue most succinctly: "TV was not what I wanted. I wanted music. It expressed the feelings that TV was trivializing."

Rock 'n' roll, it should be remembered, did not displace Beethoven and Bach, as decline-of-the-West jeremiads imply; it displaced Patti Page, Perry Como, Rosemary Clooney, and any number of other treacly pop singers. Thus, it is hard to sustain the argument that the move from singing along with Mitch to rocking along with sprung-from-the-soil, only-in-America weirdos like Little Richard and Jerry Lee Lewis represents a net decline in culture.

In the beginning, rock 'n' roll celebrated leisure and pleasure and addressed adolescent problems of loneliness, difficult love, and that most pleasurable of emotions, self-pity. And, of course, sex. Many lyrics were delightfully, if sometimes obscurely, salacious. The performers themselves often unleashed considerable libido on stage. Yet insofar as rock 'n' roll did celebrate pleasure and leisure, it remained consonant with an affluent, consumption-oriented society, contributing, like other phenomena of the period, to the ideology of the self as the ground of value, an ideology that later-sixties developments like psychedelia, progressive rock, and the rise of the singer-songwriters would make explicit and programmatic.

Somewhat contradictorily, rock 'n' roll also helped link all the individual selves of its listeners into an ideological community: teenagerdom. Isolated in their rigidly age-segregated world of school and suburb, teenagers discovered themselves to share a state of mind with teenagers all over the country: the dorky kids on "American Bandstand" as well as the juvenile delinquents of sensational journalism. Thus, their earliest notions of social connectedness were modeled on the peer group, nationally and generationally conceived. Thenceforth, successive waves of baby boomers would confuse ideological community, which is a widely shared state of mind, with material community, which is a cooperative way of life. This confusion would achieve its most fatuous expression in the notion of the Woodstock Nation and would survive in adult conceptions of community as consisting of people who share the same age, status, and values.

The birth of rock 'n' roll contained other portents that would have given the organization man pause, had he read them clearly. As an amalgam of rhythm and blues and country music, rock 'n' roll originated from the two most despised cultural groups in the United States: blacks and poor southern whites. Much of its latent significance lay neither in the lyrics nor in the beat, but in the public personae of its performers and the social, cultural, and especially the cross-cultural meanings of their performances. Elvis Presley was a southern white truck driver who sang rockabilly reprises of rhythm-and-blues and country-music standards that led to considerable confusion among early radio listeners as to his race. Chuck Berry was a thirty-year-old black man whose teen anthems expressed perfectly the tenor of white suburban adolescent life. Such performers instinctively manipulated ambiguous images of race, social class, and sexuality, which accounts for the vitality of early rock 'n' roll and for the speed with which that socially dangerous moment passed. The seeds planted then would not bear fruit until nearly ten years later, when, at the apex of the civil rights movement, the British reintroduced young white Americans to the country's indigenous music. In the meantime, rock 'n' roll was assimilated to the egregious teen pop of Frankie Avalon, Fabian, and the like. Nevertheless, it retained its initial emphasis on pleasure and self-gratification, continuing to play its part, along with the family, the suburbs, and the church, in the formation of an entire generation for whom the expressive self would be the ultimate ground of value.

It was this thoroughly psychologized individualism, first formed in childhoods so unlike those of their parents, that the organization offspring would carry into college and the adult world of work. And there the ideality of self would meet the reality of organization, with consequences that would radically alter both. Eventually, this version of individualism would form the basis of the humanist strain of their organizationalism. If the authentic self is the highest value, many members of the generation would reason, why shouldn't the organization have one? Ironically, the way to this humanist position was prepared by the perception that the organization possessed a self all right, but that in most cases that self was deeply irrational—and perhaps insane.

4

The Nervous System:
From Cybernetics to Psytopia

"The system must be first."

Harsh criticism of organizations, whether corporate or governmental, is nothing new. But the contemporary attack differs significantly from that waged by, say, muckrakers on corporations or by anti-New Dealers on bureaucracy. Muckrakers attacked corporations as exploitative, monopolistic, and underhanded; Franklin Delano Roosevelt's critics attacked the "alphabet agencies" as wasteful and protosocialist. But no one ever suggested that Standard Oil was wildly irrational or that the Civilian Conservation Corps behaved as if insane. Beginning in the sixties, however, assaults on organizations began to be based, to a surprising degree, on a widespread perception of their deep irrationality.

The now-classic statement of the irrationality of large organizations appeared in 1961, just as corporations and the government prepared to enter a period of unrivaled growth, influence, and mutual cooperation. Entitled *Catch-22*, a phrase that soon passed into everyday usage, the book was set in World War II, the organization man's most formative experience of organization. Though other artists, most notably Franz Kafka, had captured the sadistic and nightmarish quality of modern bureaucracy, it fell to Joseph Heller to render it with a distinctively American inflection of blithe absurdity. In Heller's prophetic story, pompous and self-aggrandizing bomber-group commanders repeatedly raise to absurd levels the number of required combat missions. Yossarian, a bombardier, discusses with the flight surgeon the possibility of grounding a

153

pilot named Orr, who has flown fifty missions, experienced many close calls, and seems manifestly insane:

> "Sure, I can ground Orr," [said the flight surgeon]. "But first he has to ask me to."
> "And then you can ground him?" Yossarian asked.
> "No. Then I can't ground him."
> "You mean there's a catch?"
> "Sure there's a catch," Doc Daneeka replied. "Catch-22. Anyone who wants to get out of combat duty isn't really crazy."
> There was only one catch and that was Catch-22, which specified that a concern for one's own safety in the face of dangers that were real and immediate was the process of a rational mind. Orr was crazy and could be grounded. All he had to do was ask; and as soon as he did, he would no longer be crazy and would have to fly more missions. Orr would be crazy to fly more missions and sane if he didn't, but if he was sane he had to fly them. If he flew them he was crazy and didn't have to; but if he didn't want to he was sane and had to. Yossarian was moved very deeply by the absolute simplicity of this clause of Catch-22 and let out a respectful whistle.
> "That's some catch, that Catch-22," he observed.
> "It's the best there is," Doc Daneeka agreed.

To challenge the authority of the large organization—whether corporate or governmental—is to challenge the dominant social fact of the twentieth century in industrialized countries. Though organizations—armies, religions, states—have been around for centuries, it was only with the rise of industrialism that corporate/bureaucratic organizations came to dominate virtually every aspect of life, dissolving older patterns of work, authority, community, and family life and leaving us in our uneasy modernity. To challenge specifically the rationality of the organization is to challenge the founding premise of its claim to legitimacy. And to challenge that founding premise is, in effect, to challenge the values of the American middle class and its way of life, both public and private, that has grown up over the past one hundred years.

Between 1870 and 1920, America was transformed from an agrarian society to the most powerful industrial economy in the world. As America's industrial capability increased, the small craft shops and family-run businesses of the nineteenth century gave way to large-scale industrial plants. Such rapid growth over such a short time created a crisis. Trained labor was in short supply; corruption began to creep into the production process, and productivity lagged far behind the demand for production. New technologies and new work arrangements were sought to make the most of large numbers of untrained workers and machines.

The breakthrough came when industrialists discovered that the key lay in simplifying the tasks of individual workers while increasing the power and control of a relatively small number of managers. This simple expedient, carried to its logical extreme by Frederick Winslow Taylor, the father of American "scientific management," proved to be one of the most consequential organizational discoveries of the century.

Taylor advocated dividing all jobs into small, discrete tasks, each one easy to learn and none dependent upon the workers' skills. Workers were to be provided with detailed instructions from which they were forbidden to deviate. Once jobs had been subdivided into their smallest possible components, it would be possible to determine "the one best way" of working. Time and motion studies (undertaken by that soon to be universally satirized figure the "efficiency expert") would determine the optimum way to perform a task. Jobs would be standardized and routinized according to "scientific" principles. It is essential, Taylor told a special Congressional committee looking into Taylorism, to substitute "exact scientific investigation and knowledge for the old individual judgment or opinion, either of the workman or the boss, in all matters relating to the work done in the establishment." Wrote Taylor: "In the past man has been first; in the future, the system must be first."

American business enthusiastically embraced scientific management. Taylor became America's first management guru. In 1914, at the height of his popularity, he spoke to an estimated sixty-nine thousand people attending an efficiency exposition at the Grand Central Palace in New York. Triumphant Taylorism catapulted America into the second stage of the Industrial Revolution—the era of management.

For the first time in the industrial age, the most unpredictable and difficult aspects of production could be quantified and rationalized. The major obstacles standing in the way of expanded production and the increased productivity of workers could be eliminated. Factories could match workers to machines in a predetermined work process that was capable of producing large quantities of standardized products at ever lower per-unit costs.

To monitor this new way of working, control would be centralized and placed in the hands of a new kind of manager who would substitute "objective," measurable work standards and quotas for the subjective judgments and individualized work styles of craftsmen. These new managers would no longer directly supervise factory workers; they would manage the production *process*. They would schedule operations, establish standardized work rules, design complex organizational structures appropriate to the task at hand, and allocate resources. They would plan, implement, monitor, and evaluate all phases of the production process.

As Robert B. Reich puts it: "These specialized thinkers were to be sharply distinguished from the rest of the work force. Planning was to be distinct from execution, brain distinct from brawn, head from hand, white collar from blue collar." Accordingly, the workplace was divided along functional lines. On one side stood the professional managers, who were responsible for developing, implementing, and monitoring the scientific-management principles that governed the production process. On the other side stood the workers, supervisors, and foremen, who were responsible for the day-to-day operation of the plant.

Scientific management promised not only to streamline and rationalize the workplace, but to end the arbitrary and sometimes corrupt practices of authoritarian bosses. Widely viewed as progressive and liberal, scientific management, like civil service reform, promised to take the politics out of work. Organized labor came to see scientific management as a way to prevent employers' capriciousness. Clearly defined work rules, detailed organizational structures and job categories, and regulations setting out lines of authority and grievance procedures were seen by union leaders and rank-and-file members as ways of limiting the control of managers. Scientific management could be a powerful ally in the struggle for better working conditions. To this day, many labor agreements spell out work rules and job classifications in terms that differ little from those of the 1920s.

Over time, this split became institutionalized. Labor unions organized blue-collar workers by industry, instead of along craft lines, and managers began to think of themselves as belonging to a profession that was distinct from production workers and from owners. Between 1900 and 1920, university programs designed to train managers were developed, and by the mid-1920s, the "profession" of management had its own specialized graduate schools, trade journals, and membership societies. Soon, the first management consulting firms appeared. Organizations like Arthur D. Little, Inc., and the Frazer & Torbet spin-off, McKinsey & Company, offered their clients a variety of financial and accounting services, in addition to advice on their production processes.

To achieve ever greater growth and expansion, many family-owned or closely held private companies were taken public. Professional managers found a new role in these publicly held companies; they became agents of the shareholders and professional caretakers of the corporations. Though Taylor had not foreseen this development, it was consistent with scientific management. Who better to mind the store than an elite group of highly trained, rational, objective, full-time professional managers? The federal security laws of 1933 and 1934 formalized this developing relationship between managers and public investors. Corporate control was thereby separated from corporate ownership.

Scientific management swept all before it. The application of its principles—"specialization by simplification, predetermined rules, and detailed management information"—transformed the entire industrial system. Scientific management made mass production possible by conceiving of work—and the worker—as an extension of the machine. And it extended the idea by conceiving of the organization itself and eventually all society as a system of such interlocking machines. In short, its model of rationality—the machine—was astonishingly narrow and all the more powerful for that.

As large organizations, the profession of management, and the middle class evolved together, so did the system of values that was implicit in this view of rationality. In all areas of life, from manufacturing to homemaking, the emphasis began to fall on technique, instrumentalism, efficiency, functionality, and the continuous management of production and social processes. (In 1915 alone two books appeared that applied Taylorism to the home—Christine Frederick's *Household Engineering* and Mary Pattison's *The Principles of Domestic Engineering*, the latter featuring an introduction by Taylor himself.)

Thoroughgoing instrumentalists all, the proponents of scientific management, with their engineering biases, had no use for utopian or organic views of society, no use for history or heredity. Science came to be synonymous with *method*, rather than with a body of results. The old psychology, which saw human personality as consisting of inherent and competing faculties such as intellect, will, and judgment, each producing mental activities, was jettisoned in favor of an emphasis on behavior. In effect, the "inner person" was done away with, clearing the way for modern psychology but also for pervasive attempts to engineer human behavior. For education the new emphasis on behavior meant abandoning the theory of mental discipline in favor of an approach that attempted to harmonize behavior with social needs (the crucial move from rote learning toward life adjustment). In municipal governments, big-city *politics*, based on immigrant voting blocs, was superseded by city *management*—the application of "objective" techniques, the outcome of which always seemed to coincide, as if by magic, with the interests of the growing middle class that advocated them.

Corporations, labor unions, and governmental regulatory agencies, far from being antagonists in any important sense, all came to share this fundamental faith in the continuous management of social process according to ideals of order, regularity, and functionality. Rarely did they stop to ask what they wanted in a substantive way from these processes.

Managing the process became an end in itself—a confusion of means with ends, as Robert Wiebe observed, that endless analogies between society and well-oiled machinery failed to justify.

The practice of management continued to evolve through the Great Depression and World War II, but it was only after the war and the coming of the organization man that management emerged as a full-fledged way of life. The application of management techniques made it possible for postwar America to develop into a "society of organizations," as Peter F. Drucker put it. By 1962, professional managers controlled 169 of the 200 largest nonfinancial companies in America.

Management became a profession as distinctive as law or medicine, but, more important, it became synonymous with a distinctive way of thinking. Taylorist principles of specialization by simplification, predetermined work rules, and detailed monitoring of performance inevitably led to a predominant system of beliefs about how the world works and how to make it work better: Management thinking became analytic thinking. Taylor had advocated a form of understanding based on breaking jobs down to their basic elements. All production problems, he believed, could be solved by measuring the efficiency and effectiveness of each element. Managers developed a preference for solutions based on numbers. Their way of thinking was reinforced in the early 1950s by the development of computers and sophisticated quantitative techniques, such as operations research, game theory, and systems analysis. Modern analytic tools and skills enabled the professional manager to tackle complex production problems and, quite naturally, led him to believe that human problems in the workplace could be solved by the same logic.

The success of analytic methods led to a consensus among business leaders, professional managers, and business-school educators that analytic thinking was good thinking. Business schools put ever more emphasis on the development of sophisticated analytic skills, at the expense of other parts of the curriculum. Potential managers were trained to believe in the efficacy of modern analytic techniques as ends in themselves, a view that was powerfully reinforced by business recruiters. Viewed from an analytic perspective, problems were believed to be context free; therefore, managers did not appear to need a wide range of experience or the wisdom of years to solve important business problems. Thus, young managers, it was believed, were just as likely as were senior managers to perform well.

Though it would be two decades before the heyday of the technomanagerial wizards would arrive, the promise of sophisticated analytic techniques was great enough in the early 1950s to change the face of American organizations forever. Many of the young veterans who were recruited by American corporations in the early 1950s had learned first-hand in the military the potential of analytic tools. They had been bomber pilots and battalion commanders, had served in the Office of Strategic Services breaking Axis codes, and had administered the complex allocation of men and matériel around the world. They had learned the value of analytic techniques and used them to help win the war.

One of the new fields to emerge from the exigencies of the war grew out of work done by Norbert Wiener and his colleagues on automatic predictors for antiaircraft fire. Called cybernetics, from a Greek word meaning steersman or governor, it first involved working out self-correcting loops of information in which the response of an enemy airplane to antiaircraft fire had to be constantly taken into account. It is a more difficult problem than it first appears. The machine must predict where the airplane will be at some point in the future and direct fire at that spot, a relatively simple matter were it not that the plane takes evasive action as a result of the firing; so the machine must correct for the evasive action, which, in turn, changes as a result of the firing correction, which change must be worked into the machine's calculations and so on in an endless cycle. The solution to such problems of military design required the application of a variety of disciplines and techniques: information theory, automation, computer science, and communications research, all involving a related set of interests that had rarely been brought together before.

But such problems were not confined to the military or to purely mechanical systems. Shortly after the war, Wiener, drawing on work in mixed human and mechanical systems of fire control, brought the human element under the broad umbrella of cybernetics. Its dream of self-correcting systems, capable of "learning," was soon extended to cover complex organizations and even the whole society. Thereafter, the cybernetic model, even when it went unacknowledged, would fire the imagination of theorists and technocrats alike with the vision of entire self-correcting organizations in which technology, workers, managers, executives, and information and delivery systems were meshed in a huge automated machine (though not a clockwork machine because its information processing was based on statistical probability, which allows for "learning").

Moreover, an explicit comparison was drawn between such systems and human consciousness. Wrote Wiener, recalling the antiaircraft project: "Thus a field of investigation covering not only such mechanisms, but also their archetype, the brain and the nervous system, came into being." Writing in the *New York Times* in 1966, Jerome B. Wiesner, who had been a colleague of Wiener's at the Massachusetts Institute of

Technology and had served as science adviser to President John F. Kennedy, argued that "a society can be viewed as a giant learning machine, which, in principle, is not too unlike some of the more elaborate electrical systems that have been designed for recognizing patterns or solving mathematical problems. . . . This view—which we at M.I.T. should call a cybernetic view of society . . . points the way to interesting social science research and provides much common sense in the planning of our affairs." Fusing Taylorism, the technomanagerial revolution, and the American habit of individualizing organizations, such ambitious, though as yet unrealized, visions represent the penultimate personification of the system and systemization of the person. (The ultimate such confusion, updated with psychology, would be provided by the organization offspring.)

Such visions were still far in the future, however, when the young World War II veterans returned, eager to use their new skills and to continue their winning ways—this time on the organizational battlefield. It was these junior officers who became the junior executives of Whyte's midcentury portrait. By 1960, when two of their number faced off for the presidency—John F. Kennedy had been a PT boat commander, Richard M. Nixon a lieutenant in the navy—they prepared to ascend to the highest levels of power in American organizational life. Speaking at Yale University's commencement in 1962, President Kennedy expressed perfectly his generation's confident faith in instrumental rationality and the cybernetic dream in which such faith culminated:

> What is at stake in our economic decisions today is not some grand warfare of rival ideologies which will sweep the country with passion, but the practical management of a modern economy. What we need are not labels and cliches but more basic discussion of the sophisticated and technical questions involved in keeping a great economic machinery moving ahead.

The creed of the organization man could not have been stated more concisely. In just two sentences, the young president had proclaimed the end of ideology, welcomed the age of management and the expert, and bolstered his argument by resorting to the machine metaphor for social processes. In short, the system would be first. The historical irony, of course, is that soon thereafter the grand warfare of rival ideologies swept the country with passion, practical management produced the real disasters of Vietnam and inflation, and the great "machinery," along with the machine metaphor itself, broke down.

"When the operation of the machine becomes so odious . . ."

In the early sixties, the system was not only first, but growing bigger and more powerful. Between 1961 and 1966 corporate profits doubled. Bolstered by the 1962 investment tax credit and the 1964 tax cut, total corporate profits increased by an estimated 57 percent in the period 1960–1964, while gross national product was rising less than half as fast, by 24 percent. In contrast, from 1950 to 1955, corporate profits rose by only 14 percent and remained almost flat at 2 percent from 1955 to 1960. But by the end of the 1960s, the 200 largest manufacturing companies would control 60 percent of the nation's manufacturing assets, up from just under 48 percent in 1950. Peter F. Drucker called it "the biggest increase in economic concentration ever recorded in this or any other country."

Government grew at a comparable pace. From 1950 to 1960, the number of employees at all levels of government—federal, state, and local—grew by about 38 percent, while the population, which governments presumably serve, grew by 18.5 percent. But from 1960 to 1970, the number of governmental employees increased by almost 48 percent, while the population increased by only 13.5 percent. To put it another way, in 1950 governmental workers constituted 10 percent of the entire American labor force, a share that had increased to 15 percent by 1970.

Confidence in these ever-expanding institutions and their leaders was high. In 1966, 42 percent of Americans surveyed expressed "a great deal of confidence" in congressional leaders, 41 percent were similarly confident about the president and the cabinet, and 62 percent felt that way about military officers. It was an era of good feeling toward business as well. In 1965, 68 percent of Americans polled by the Opinion Research Corporation (ORC) expressed "very" or "mostly" favorable views of eight key industries: aluminum, automobiles, chemicals, electrical equipment and appliances, food and food products, oil and gasoline, steel, and tire and rubber. Beginning in 1959, the ORC also polled Americans about their attitudes toward twenty-two specific companies, including such giants as Alcoa, AT&T, Dow Chemical, Du Pont, Exxon, Ford, General Motors, IBM, Mobil, Sears, Shell, Texaco, and Union Carbide. Approval of the twenty-two companies stood at 69 percent in 1959, climbed to 70 percent in 1961, and reached an all-time high of 73.5 percent in 1965. It is only a slight exaggeration to say that Americans at mid-decade were, for the first time in their history, nearly unanimous in their faith in business and government.

But historical events and a bewildering variety of oppositional movements soon blasted that faith from all directions. Over the succeeding fifteen years, confidence in all major American institutions would plummet. Approval of the eight key industries in the ORC surveys fell from the 1965 high of 68 percent to less than 36 percent in 1977. In other words, half the people who had been favorably disposed toward those industries in 1965 had lost their confidence in them by 1977. Approval of the twenty-two specific companies in the ORC surveys declined from the 1965 high of almost 74 percent to 50 percent in 1977. Taking into account all such surveys during the period, Seymour Martin Lipset and William Schneider conclude: *"Not a single industry out of twenty-five and not a single firm out of fifty actually improved its public reputation between the late 1960s and the late 1970s."* Moreover, Lipset and Schneider say, the increase in antibusiness feeling between 1967 and 1977 was most pronounced among high-status, college-educated Americans under age thirty—in short, the older organization offspring.

Confidence in government suffered a parallel decline, with Congress, the executive branch, and military leaders all losing about twenty percentage points between 1962 and 1981. Other analysts detected an even steeper decline in public confidence. To a seminar held at Columbia University in 1977, Daniel Yankelovich declared: "Trust in government declined dramatically from almost 80% in the late 1950s to about 33% in 1976. Confidence in business fell from approximately a 70% level in the late 60s to about 15% today. . . . The change is simply massive. Within a ten- to fifteen-year period, trust in institutions has plunged down and down, from an almost consensual majority, two thirds or more, to minority segments of the American public."

The civil rights movement, the antiwar movement, the rise of the so-called counterculture, consumerism, environmentalism, feminism, right-wing neopopulism, and anti-assimilationist ethnic pride all posed significant challenges to business and to government precisely during the period when organization men, in the prime of their lives, were at the pinnacles of their careers. All these movements, attitudes, and ideologies expressed a fundamental hostility to the technocratic system—either to its premises, as in the case of the antiwar movement and feminism, or to its results, as in the case of consumerism.

The sons and daughters of the organization man absorbed the messages of these successive and sometimes overlapping movements—often fragmentarily, unreflectively, and even unconsciously—but absorb them they did. Some few even helped shape and disseminate those messages. Most did not. All, however, were powerfully, if variously, affected by these unrelenting and ubiquitous assaults on organizations and institutions, a fact of great long-range significance that is often obscured by all-or-nothing arguments (either smug or pessimistic, as the case may be) about whether a particular movement "failed" and can therefore be written off as having been ineffectual.

One of the earliest and most profound challenges came from the civil rights movement. Relentlessly exposing glaring racial inequities, the movement called into question the organization man's unlimited faith in social progress. That faith, based on an initial confusion of material abundance with democracy, had been stated most succinctly by, once again, John F. Kennedy: "A rising tide lifts all boats." It was a tantalizing, if morally bankrupt, hope: An unlimited growth economy would defuse the tensions of social inequalities without altering them. Enter Martin Luther King, Jr. Speaking the language of the Bible and the Constitution, King offered a vision of human solidarity rooted not in material abundance but in love. By comparison, the boosterish optimism of the organization man—his vague "faith in faith"—seemed pathetically shallow.

The point is not that the older organization offspring were followers of King, but that King's injection of an expressive value—love—into public discourse would, over time, come to seem more and more appropriate. It would become so familiar that Jimmy Carter would win the presidency in 1976 by echoing King's call for love. (And Carter would lose it in 1980 by making that call indistinguishable from optimism, which, when he came down from *his* mountaintop, he sourly accused the American people of lacking.) A striking measure of King's lasting impact turned up in a 1988 survey of Americans aged eighteen to forty-four conducted by Peter D. Hart for *Rolling Stone* magazine. Hart found that among those he polled, the most admired public figure of the previous twenty years was Martin Luther King, Jr. (King was preferred by 38 percent of the respondents; Robert F. Kennedy was second with 25 percent).

Apart from King's public utterances, one of the most revealing examples of the kind of broad critique the system would soon suffer may be found in a document that was almost contemporaneous with President Kennedy's Yale speech. The "Port Huron Statement," as it came to be called, was drafted in the summer of 1962 during a national convention of the Students for a Democratic Society at a United Auto Workers Center in Port Huron, Michigan. Cautious in tone, restrained in its call for "participatory democracy," it begins: "We are people of this generation, bred in at least modest comfort, housed now in universities, looking uncomfortably to the world we inherit." Thus, in fewer than twenty-five words, it stakes out the generational issue; alludes to the affluence of fifties childhoods; reveals the perhaps unconscious expectation that college, where one is "housed," will be like home; and implies that personal "comfort" in all its senses forms the basis of the detailed complaint that follows.

What made the authors (primarily Tom Hayden) uncomfortable, says the manifesto, is "the depersonalization that reduces human beings to the status of things." The statement goes on to decry "cumbersome academic bureaucracy" and financial arrangements that hold universities hostage to "the value standards of business and the administrative mentality." Against such Taylorism, the statement makes a sweeping case. Borrowing the rhetoric of existentialism, American ego psychology, and progressive education, it makes clear that the grounds of opposition to the system lie in individualism, but of a sort far removed from the Protestant ethic:

> Men have unrealized potential for self-cultivation, self-direction, self-understanding, and creativity.
>
> . . . . .
>
> The goal of man and society should be human independence: a concern not with image of popularity but with finding a meaning in life that is personally authentic. . . .
>
> . . . . .
>
> Loneliness, estrangement, isolation describe the vast distance between man and man today. These dominant tendencies cannot be overcome by better personnel management, nor by improved gadgets, but only when a love of man overcomes the idolatrous worship of things.
>
> . . . . .
>
> Work should . . . be educative, not stultifying; creative, not mechanical; self-directed, not manipulated, encouraging independence, a respect for others, a sense of dignity and a willingness to accept social responsibility.

Again, the point is not that the Port Huron Statement became some sort of scripture for organization offspring. Even those who heard of it probably never read it. But its rhetoric perfectly embodies the nature of the sixties attack on the cultural authority of machinelike organizations and the values of instrumental rationality that undergirded them. "There is a time," said Mario Savio, leader of the Free Speech Movement, which ripped Berkeley apart in 1964, "when the operation of the machine becomes so odious, makes you so sick at heart that you can't take part; you can't even tacitly take part, and you've got to put your bodies upon the levers, upon all the apparatus and you've got to make it stop."

Such rhetoric makes clear, first, that even intensely political thrusts of the period were, from the first, aimed more at organization, rationalization, and technocracy than at capitalism. Second, such thrusts had their origins more in the expressive self as the ground of value than in any political analysis or program. No wonder that in the subsequent schism in "the Movement" the New Left would be overwhelmed by the counter-culture.

In effect, organization offspring left the cozy, democratic, emotionally expressive world of their families and, for the first time, encountered a real world, even one as seemingly benign as the university, with little use for such values. It was as if their parents had forgotten to tell them that such things were not to be taken out of the house or that, once outside, such values enjoyed only limited application. Some of the children felt betrayed, and if they did not blame their parents as individuals, they certainly played out their frustration in ways that suggested wholesale rejection of their parents' public morality.

"The war was certainly a great tragedy."

It is possible, though unlikely, that in the absence of the Vietnam War the kind of critique of American society expressed in the Port Huron Statement would have remained confined to a small number of civil rights activists and New Leftists. Instead, the bitter public debate occasioned by the war also had the effect of spreading such sentiments—albeit sometimes thinly—throughout the younger generation. While politicians continued to engage in traditional, mild policy disagreements about America's longest war, many commentators and critics framed the debate in terms of a much larger crisis of technocracy. Wrote Herbert Marcuse in *One Dimensional Man*, a book whose attempt to synthesize Freud and Marx articulated for many in the antiwar movement the political and psychological dimensions of the critique: "The most advanced areas of industrial society exhibit throughout these two features: a trend toward consummation of technological rationality, and intensive efforts to contain this trend within established institutions. Here is the internal contradiction of this civilization: the irrational element in its rationality."

Perhaps no other figure connected with the war better personified for critics the irrationality of rationalism than Secretary of Defense Robert McNamara. A Harvard MBA, a lieutenant colonel in the air force during World War II, a former president of Ford Motor Company, McNamara came to the Defense Department—the world's largest bureaucracy—as the quintessential organization man, the supreme technocrat. As Charles Morris points out, "virtually all the techniques of management control now routinely used by large businesses—project management, PERT, critical path analysis, matrix management, management by objectives, computerized management information systems—were either invented, developed, or refined in McNamara's Pentagon.'' McNamara's managerial achievements were legendary, diminished only by the fact that such quantitative techniques bore virtually no relevance to the situation on the ground in Vietnam. As David Halberstam details in *The Best and the Brightest*, this superrationalist, with his "body counts" and his percentages of the countryside that had been "pacified," began by misleading the public and ended by deluding himself.

To critics McNamara and his ilk made rationality itself seem mad. The American commander who said he had to destroy a village to save it could have sprung from the pages of *Catch-22*. High-altitude, computer-assisted bombing of civilian populations was seen as a particularly repellent manifestation of bureaucratic murder. The technocratic emphasis on expediency led to official lying so pervasive that the phrase "credibility gap" appeared in the language—a euphemism for the fact that, quite simply, many Americans no longer believed the government of the United States.

Periods of disillusionment with government were nothing new in American history, but previously they had been accompanied by veneration of big business, as in the 1920s. When disillusionment with business set in, the pendulum would swing back in favor of government, as in the 1930s. But in the 1960s business found itself tarred with the same brush as was the government. Lipset and Schneider, examining long-range trends in opinion surveys from 1935 forward, write: "the data reveal a widespread loss of faith in the leadership of business, government, labor, and other private and public institutions at more or less the same time."

Though businessmen in the sixties expressed surprise at being lumped with their traditional adversary, they need not have: The "military-industrial complex" foreseen by President Dwight D. Eisenhower had become a reality. By 1968, more than two thousand high-ranking, retired military officers worked for the one hundred largest defense contractors. Despite the reflexive antigovernment rhetoric of corporations, they had worked in concert with every federal administration since Franklin Roosevelt's, often enjoying federal subsidies, long-term contracts, and the rights to any Pentagon-financed products that turned out to have consumer applications. Through trade associations and close cooperation with governmental agencies that were nominally supposed to regulate them, companies minimized risk, controlled markets, and freed themselves of competition. These arrangements produced technological wonders that neither industry nor the government could have produced alone, but they also exposed the free market as a fiction. As John Kenneth Galbraith, among many others, argued, the

United States had developed into a planned economy coordinated by the government and corporations working together.

To many of the record number of college students who were warehoused on campuses that seemed more and more designed simply to allocate personnel for this vast interlocking system, the corporations appeared no more rational than Robert McNamara's Pentagon. Recruiters for corporations in war-related industries found themselves under siege on many campuses. IBM's headquarters in Armonk, New York, was the site of frequent antiwar protests. At a 1967 symposium of the National Security Industrial Association, a four-hundred-member organization of defense contractors founded in 1944 by James Forrestal to maintain communication between manufacturers and the military, Paul Goodman bluntly told the assembled executives: "Ordinarily I would be ashamed to use such a tone. But you are the manufacturers of napalm, fragmentation bombs, and planes that destroy rice. Your weapons have killed hundreds of thousands in other Vietnams."

For people of all political persuasions, the Vietnam War remains a potent symbol of bureaucratic nightmare. The Vietnam veterans who were interviewed for Myra MacPherson's deeply moving oral history of the war's aftermath, *Long Time Passing*, speak with many voices, but whether hawk or dove or in between, they are nearly unanimous in their condemnation of the political and military bureaucracies that sent them there. Opponents of the war see it as having been a colossally senseless and perhaps immoral enterprise; proponents cannot understand why they were asked to fight but were not allowed to win. A veteran who survived the ghastly siege of Khe Sanh only to see the army then give it up told MacPherson: "We took it, we won it, we died there, and then those fuckers abandoned it. That's what our lives meant to our government."

As MacPherson's book forcefully reminds us and our own interviews confirm, disillusionment as a result of Vietnam came in many varieties and to different people in differing degrees. When Joann Harrison discovered the secret bombing of Cambodia, she was shocked by the deliberate lies of the government, but she saw neither herself nor IBM, her employer, as complicit. By contrast, her younger sister Carolyn, operating from the same mix of existentialism and romanticism found in the Port Huron Statement, accepted a far more sweeping indictment of American society as she marched against the war. For little brother Tom, unaware even of the role that Walt Rostow, his political science teacher at the University of Texas, had played in the war, Vietnam was merely something "rock and roll singers I liked sang against."

Park Forest product Bob Cory refused induction. "I had become heavily politicized at Stanford, active in the antiwar movement," he says.

"I was indicted, fought it for several years on several grounds, including student deferment. But the root was being opposed to the war, and I made that clear."

Another Park Forest alumnus, after dropping in and out of several colleges, sought conscientious-objector status, just as his older brother had. Yet he speaks with little fervor about his motives: "It was just the times as they were. We had been the best and the brightest in high school and saw what we were going into and didn't like it and had no idea what to do about it except to ignore it and avoid it." Nevertheless, he cites with satisfaction the time years later when his father, with whom he had violently disagreed over the war, admitted that his sons had been right.

Only a few of the organization offspring actually served. Tom Howell, after attending college on an ROTC scholarship, was obligated to enter the army. There he found some of the same satisfactions the organization man had found in World War II.

"After some initial training in the States, I went to Germany for eighteen months," he says. "I commanded an artillery battery, which was one of the best experiences I've ever had. I was twenty-three years old, and I had seventy-five men working for me forty-five miles from the Czech border, and we had live nuclear weapons. You don't get that kind of responsibility anywhere. Right in the middle of all the drugs and Vietnam. It was fascinating."

Nevertheless, he says of Vietnam, where he spent nine months flying helicopters: "The war was certainly a great tragedy and the way we fought there was a great tragedy. But I'm not prepared to say we never should have gone."

Even that gentle demurrer reveals the distinctly negative reference point Vietnam became for many members of the generation. Unlike the clear triumph of the organization man's "good war" (World War II), Vietnam, the only war America ever lost, remains a confusing and ambiguous event for many members of the generation—those who went and those who stayed home, those who sincerely opposed it and those who cynically, or merely casually, avoided it. Each approaches it today with his or her own particular mix of frustration, scepticism, guilt, self-righteousness, pride, or forgetfulness—all of which makes sweeping generalizations about the lasting effects of Vietnam on a generation difficult. Yet there is a constant. As a result of the Vietnam experience, most of the older organization offspring, regardless of their politics, carry with them an ineradicable suspicion of institutions—a ready scepticism, considered or not, about the legitimacy; benevolence; and, above all, the rationality of large organizations.

As the political passions of the sixties and early seventies recede, it is easy to forget how thoroughgoing was the attack on the society of organizations. One measure of the virulence of the attack should suffice to make the point: the frequency with which the war and racism, conceived as products of technocratic culture, led many people to compare America with Nazi Germany.

Widespread American interest in the "madness" of the Holocaust had been building since the midfifties. It was heightened by Adolf Eichmann's 1961 trial and Hannah Arendt's memorable coverage of it. As second only to Heinrich Himmler in carrying out the "Final Solution," Eichmann had overseen the application of the factory system to the extermination of human beings. He was the chief organizer of the identification, assembly, and transportation of Jews to death camps like Auschwitz, which had been jointly created by the SS and the industrial giant I. G. Farben. To explain the enigma of Eichmann, an apparently ordinary middle-class citizen who appeared neither insane nor remorseful, Arendt struck a phrase that would resound down the decade of the sixties: "the banality of evil." "The trouble with Eichmann," she wrote, "was precisely that so many were like him, and that the many were neither perverted nor sadistic, that they were, and still are, terribly normal."

Forever after, critics and radicals would revert again and again to Eichmann as the archetype of the insanely rational and murderously efficient bureaucrat, the American version of which was said to be carrying out comparable policies against blacks, native Americans, and Vietnamese. Thus Goodman to the military contractors: "You have disrupted ancient social patterns, debauched . . . cultures, fomented tribal and other wars, and in Vietnam yourselves engaged in genocide."

Allusions to the Nuremberg trials and to Nazi Germany became common. "We have learned lessons from Nazi Germany," proclaimed the Fifth Avenue Peace Parade Committee, "and will not go along with the aggressive war-making policies of any government, even if it happens to be our own." "No doubt there are fine distinctions that can be made between the concentration camp and the strategic hamlet, the gas oven and the thermonuclear missile," wrote Theodore Roszak. "But with how much pride can any of us undertake the exercise in moral pedantry it would require to draw these distinctions?" The "Fourth Reich" was what James Baldwin called America, which many polemicists spelled "Amerika."

Fair or not, the comparison was so ubiquitous as to become a cliché that survived for years in facile ascriptions of fascism to any person or institution even vaguely authoritarian or, indeed, merely in authority. For many who lived through the overheated rhetoric of the times, including those who remain fundamentally apolitical, the notion of the efficient, organizational functionary who claims merely to be following orders will always be tainted by its association with the good burghers who made the trains run on time—straight to Auschwitz.

"I think of myself as a hippie, though I'm not."

A more widespread, though less threatening, challenge to the underlying values of the organization was expressed by the loose collection of attitudes, styles, fantasies, fads, mysticism, hedonism, social experimentation, and Oedipal hostility that came to be known as the counterculture. Though often to be found with the antiwar movement and often confused with it, the counterculture represented a much broader-based reaction to the confusing social currents running at the time. Ill-defined and amorphous, it simultaneously embraced committed communitarians and mildly rebellious middle-class kids, weekend hippies and full-time flower children, addled acid heads and occasional pot smokers, seekers after wisdom and seekers after fun, neo-Luddites and hip capitalists, mendicant dropouts and millionaire rock stars, stylized crazies and serious psychotics.

If there was any defining figure in this crazy-quilt of movements, beliefs, practices, and life-styles, it was a shared hostility to the irrational rationalism of technocracy. In its place, the counterculture elevated virtually every other form of irrationalism in the world, just as long as it was sufficiently removed from the values of the corporate-bureaucratic culture of America. Zen Buddhism, Hinduism, Sufism, the *I Ching*, *The Tibetan Book of the Dead*, tarot, occultism, Hermann Hesse, Amerindian spiritualism, the mysteries of Stonehenge, and even the Hell's Angels all had their acolytes among children of the American middle class. Anything was welcome as long as it was opposed to the values of sacrifice and self-denial.

In hundreds of ways, large and small, the counterculture manifested a deep dissatisfaction with technocracy. The passion for handicrafts implicitly criticized mass-produced products of alienated labor. Practices like home childbirth, midwifery, and folk medicine expressed distrust of arrogant professional elites and the bureaucratic institutions in which they worked. Sexual experimentation, androgyny, open homosexuality, cohabitation, and communal child rearing threatened the traditional nuclear family through which middle-class culture reproduced its values. Voluntary simplicity, the refusal to work, and the cheerful embrace of welfare and food stamps mocked competitive individualism.

Not coincidentally, illegal drugs became widely popular and, indeed, became almost the defining mark of the counterculture. Estimates and surveys of drug use are notoriously inexact, but in 1965 surveys of drug use among college students put the use of marijuana at anywhere from about 4 to 10 percent. By 1969 the figure was almost 32 percent, with some campuses—especially the more prestigious ones—reaching a figure of almost 50 percent. The U.S. Public Health Service estimated that 20 million Americans, most of them young people, had tried pot by the end of the sixties. By the early seventies, the use of marijuana had spread to even the most isolated campuses, invaded the high schools, and filtered down to the elementary schools. By 1975, more than 47 percent of high school seniors reported that they had tried marijuana at least once and 9 percent said they had tried cocaine. By 1979, more than 60 percent of high school seniors had tried marijuana, more than 15 percent had used cocaine, and almost 13 percent had used PCP, the powerful animal anesthetic known popularly as "angel dust."

Drug use undermined the values and authority of the organization man in at least three important respects. First, more than any other cultural phenomenon of the period—clothing styles, rock music, or the sexual revolution—the use of illegal drugs decisively separated the generations: In 1970 less than 1 percent of people over age thirty-five had ever tried marijuana. Second, drug use put the user, no matter how casual, outside the law—and the laws were harsh. Third, drugs induced a state of heightened awareness of the present that was inimical to the future-oriented world of work and self-denial. Above all, drug-induced states were both symptom and cause of the belief that the self is the ultimate ground of value. Just as alcohol lubricated the sociability of the other-directed organization man, drugs enhanced the subjectivity of his inward-looking children.

But the counterculture was not exclusively concerned with subjective individualism. At the same time it valued spontaneity; impulsiveness; the childlike; the mad; and, inevitably, creativity, it was also promoting communitarian ideals. Indeed, it was on the paradox of extreme individualism versus all-embracing community that the more ambitious hopes of the counterculture foundered. In a world where meek flower children stood side by side with that most genuine of all individualists, the true psychotic, the question of social order was often answered by private legislators like Charles Manson or the Hell's Angels. Or, alternatively, the question was resolved in favor of a passive conformism, no less bland for being superficially hip.

To some observers, the counterculture all too quickly became merely another phase of media-manipulated, consumerist hedonism, a perfectly predictable development in an affluent society that had little productive work for millions of self-important young people. Such observers see the counterculture's grandiose social vision as having devolved into trivial matters of life-style that were quickly absorbed by the larger culture. Whatever the justice of that interpretation, many of the counterculture's initial impulses persist today in the attitudes of many of the sons and daughters of the organization man.

"I kind of think of myself as a hippie, though I'm not," says one typical middle manager, who spent a brief time in a commune and was once arrested for possessing pot. "But I am kind of looser, younger, more liberal thinking. The business world today is sick. It's basically run on greed. And I can't believe making all these small companies into one big company makes the world any better."

Contempt for technocratic elites was by no means confined to the antiwar movement or to the counterculture. On the populist right, George Wallace, heading the largest third-party movement in more than a century, was fond of castigating "pointy-headed bureaucrats who couldn't park their bicycles straight" and who were "pussy-footing in Vietnam." (They used limousines, not bicycles, of course, but it has been argued that much of their motivation for escalating the war lay in their deep fear of the effete label implied in Wallace's sly diction.) So-called white ethnics, who made up much of Wallace's following in the North, constituted another significant group of Americans who were disenchanted with the technocratic consensus. By the end of the sixties, after years of assimilationist striving, many white ethnics, following the lead of the African-Americans they so frequently despised, declared their allegiance to their cultures of origin, questioning dominant WASP values of rationalization and quantification. In *The Rise of the Unmeltable Ethnics*, Michael Novak argued that this new ethnic pride represented "disillusionment with the universalist, too thinly rational culture of professional elites." (And it was these voters who, in providing Richard Nixon with his landslide victory in 1972, revealed the antiwar movement and the counterculture themselves to be elites.) The direct impact of white ethnics' disillusionment on the sons and daughters of the organization man was negligible, but the conservative challenge to technocracy that such movements represented found their way into suburbia via the issues of busing and school prayer and constituted another confusing element in the period's pervasive distrust of institutions and their leaders. Far more direct in their impact on the sons and daughters of the organization man were the series of highly organized movements—consumerism, environmentalism, and feminism—that frontally challenged the technocracy.

"That's what the computer does to our minds."

The book, by an obscure lawyer obsessed with automobile safety, first appeared in November 1965. Called *Unsafe at Any Speed*, its subtitle told it all: *The Designed-In Dangers of the American Automobile*. It begins: "For over a half century the automobile has brought death, injury and the most inestimable sorrow and deprivation to millions of Americans." The author, Ralph Nader (at the time an oddly unfamiliar name evoking associations with *nadir* and *radar*), charged that the rear wheels of the 1960–63 Chevrolet Corvair would, with little provocation, tuck under, sending the car into a tailspin nearly impossible to control and often resulting in a rollover. Moreover, he said, General Motors' executives knew of the defects, but to save money did nothing about them. Calling the Corvair "one of the greatest acts of industrial irresponsibility in the present century," Nader was, in effect, charging the company with negligent homicide.

There was more. In subsequent chapters, he examined the lethal features of windshields and dashboards. He detailed General Motors' unwillingness to equip cars with seat belts. He exploded the "nut behind the wheel" theory so dear to auto executives and the National Safety Council as the explanation for traffic fatalities. And he documented the industry's resistance to reducing the harmful engine emissions that made the air nearly unbreathable in some cities.

Few books, before or since, have had a comparable impact on American society. Rachel Carson's *Silent Spring*, published in 1962, alerted the nation to the damage caused to all living things by the widespread use of pesticides. Jessica Mitford's *The American Way of Death*, a best-seller in 1963, revealed the deceptive practices of the funeral industry—even Robert F. Kennedy was guided by it when he chose a coffin for his slain brother. In the first decade of the century, muckrakers (so-called by Teddy Roosevelt) exposed the monopolistic practices of the Standard Oil Trust, the railroads, and the corruption of the cities. And Upton Sinclair's novelistic exposé of the meat industry, *The Jungle* (1906), resulted in the passage of the Pure Food and Drug Act and the Meat Inspection Act.

Nader's book, though destined to achieve similar influence, went largely ignored until early 1966, when General Motors' ham-fisted efforts to discredit its author came to light. The company had hired detectives who interrogated Nader's friends and associates about his sex life, about anti-Semitism (Nader was of Lebanese extraction), and about how he came to be interested in auto safety. Suddenly, Nader also found himself accosted by strange young women; he believed they were prostitutes hired by the company for purposes of blackmail. James Roche, the president of the corporation, was hauled before a Senate subcommittee where, on the advice of former Kennedy speechwriter Ted Sorenson, hired for the occasion as special counsel, he publicly apologized to Nader.

At the time the Harrisons could not believe it. "I thought Nader must have been a madman to say those things about General Motors," says Carolyn; "Chevrolet was the best car in the world to me." Joann, working in Washington for IBM, went out and bought a Corvair "to show people that I wasn't going to believe that kind of crap."

Dave Harrison recalls his response and that of his colleagues as equally emphatic. "We felt Nader was doing a great injustice to us and to the product with that book. And we just did not think it was true. The engineering department felt Nader had exaggerated. We put the car through tests on the proving ground and we couldn't roll it. Of course," Harrison says now with a laugh, "you have to recognize we had trained drivers."

In any case, General Motors had corrected the rear-axle problem before the book appeared, and by 1967 the Corvair had achieved a lower single-car accident rate than that of other cars in its class. Nevertheless, after a decline in Corvair sales of 93 percent, the company stopped production on May 12, 1969.

What angered Dave Harrison more than Nader's charges was Roche's apology. Harrison did not condone the use of detectives or prostitutes, but insofar as the apology applied to Nader's charges about the car, he could not understand it. "I, for one, and I think most of my contemporaries," says Harrison, "never forgave Roche for that."

Harrison's dismay is understandable. He was proud of his association with the largest industrial concern in the world and derived great satisfaction from working with some of General Motors' celebrated engineer-executives like Ed Cole, the designer of the classic 283-cubic-inch engine, which produced 283 horsepower, a one-to-one ratio of which engineers had long dreamed; Semon E. "Bunky" Knudsen, son of the legendary William S. Knudsen and a great engineer in his own right; and Elliot "Pete" Estes, who designed the Olds Rocket 88, the world's first high-compression V-8. It was some of these men—Cole especially—whom Nader impugned by name. After *Unsafe at Any Speed*, the automobile business would never be as uncomplicated, or as much fun, again.

Nader was hardly the first consumer advocate. Since the first Consumers League was founded in New York in 1891, consumerism has flared up fitfully in the United States. In the early days consumerists worried about pure food, unlabeled patent medicines, and unsanitary working conditions for laborers. In the twenties, as industrialism began to flood the market with consumer goods like radios and phonographs, product-testing laboratories appeared. During the Great Depression, when everyone worried about getting the most for his or her severely limited money, consumer groups concentrated on issues of quality and price. In 1936, Consumers Union was chartered to supply consumers with impartial assessments of products. The movement soon gathered momentum from the Elixir Sulfanilamide tragedy of 1937, when nearly a hundred people died from a liquid form of one of the new sulfa wonder drugs that had been rushed to market. The momentum was interrupted, however, by World War II. Though the circulation of *Consumer Reports* grew steadily following the war, consumerism lay dormant through most of the fifties and early sixties, sparked only occasionally by works like Vance Packard's *Hidden Persuaders* (1957), an immensely popular book purporting to expose the hypnotic power of advertising over the American mind, and Carson's *Silent Spring* (1962). Interest quickened when President Kennedy, in a message to Congress, enunciated a "Consumer Bill of Rights" in March 1962. Two months later came the news about thalidomide, a new tranquilizer that had caused eight thousand European women, and a few American women who had been taking it on an experimental basis, to give birth to limbless babies. But the decisive event for the consumer movement came with General Motors' public apology to Nader in 1966.

Nader became a national hero overnight. Sales of his book took off, eventually reaching 450,000 copies in cloth and paper. Nader plowed his royalties back into his consumer crusades and reaped additional money for them from an out-of-court settlement of a $26 million invasion-of-privacy suit he brought against General Motors. In September 1966, President Lyndon Johnson signed the National Traffic and Motor Vehicle Safety Act. Fittingly, Upton Sinclair attended the signing. The bill, written largely by Nader, marks the moment at which the auto industry lost forever the right to be the sole arbiter of automobile safety.

Subsequently, Nader's Raiders undertook investigations of dozens of industries and governmental agencies, uncovering collusion, fraud, deception, and waste everywhere. On college campuses throughout the country, he formed Public Interest Research Groups—PIRGS as they came to be called—to bring similar analysis and pressure to bear on local issues. Legislation sailed through Congress. Poll after poll found that on public issues, Americans regarded Nader to be vastly more credible than the government, corporations, or the media. Millions of people who paid not the slightest attention to the antibusiness diatribes of the peace movement and the counterculture listened attentively to the almost daily revelations that poured forth from consumer activists.

Joann Harrison, shortly after her defiant purchase of a Corvair, found herself powerfully affected by consumerism. "Trying to find the best buy for my money, I started reading *Consumer Reports*," she says. "I was appalled that products were unsafe. Who would make an unsafe product? That was very eye-opening to me that people would not only make unsafe products, but also would make products that weren't any good. I was too idealistic to think that anybody would do something poorly on purpose."

If the counterculture represented the irrationalist response to the technocracy, consumerism, in many ways, represented the rationalist response. Though Nader sometimes spoke as if industrialism itself were the enemy, he behaved essentially like a progressive reformer, proposing familiar rational-technocratic solutions to consumer problems: legislation, regulatory bodies, judicial intervention. Such success as he enjoyed came, in part, from his impressive ability to meet technocrats on their own rationalist ground and to best them.

But Nader's rationalism was and is rationalism with a difference. Unlike the technocrat, Nader's final court of appeal is not instrumental rationality, but substantive rationality: He asks not how we can more efficiently manage social, political, and productive processes but, rather, what we want in a concrete way from them. "We rely on quantification before we make judgments, instead of amplifying it with qualitative judgments," he has said ruefully. "That's what the computer does to our minds, you see. . . . What's being lost is a recognition of certain values as being important." In effect, Nader echoes Marcuse: A limited rationality is irrational.

Inspired by Nader, consumerism moved from evaluating products to evaluating the social costs of producing them, and there it dovetailed with the environmental movement. (As an undergraduate at Princeton, Nader had asked why so many dead birds were to be found on campus after trees were sprayed with insecticide.) A series of celebrated environmental battles over proposals to build a jetport in the Everglades, dam the Grand Canyon, fund the Supersonic Transport, destroy giant redwoods, and stretch an oil pipeline across Alaska brought forth a new brand of ecologically minded activist—young, highly educated, and willing to challenge directly the notion that economic growth was an inherently good idea. Over the years, their case was considerably strengthened by a series of spectacular ecological disasters: a massive oil spill off the coast of Santa Barbara; the discovery that thermal pollution from nuclear power plants was killing fish by the millions; the poisoning of Love Canal; the nuclear near-holocaust at Three Mile Island; the leak at a Union Carbide plant that killed more than 3,500 people in Bhopal, India; the explosion of a nuclear plant in Chernobyl that killed 23 people and necessitated the evacuation of 40,000 more; and the long-term threats posed by acid rain and global warming.

In opposing unlimited growth—the central tenet of the "rising tide lifts all boats" philosophy—environmentalists planted a notion that is only now emerging in all areas of life for the organization offspring: the idea of limits. In a mere decade—from the inauguration of John F. Kennedy to Earth Day—the country went from the expansive promise of new frontiers to the bracing finitude of spaceship Earth (a phrase, incidentally, that demonstrates the hardihood of the machine metaphor). Subsequent oil shortages and economic decline would reinforce the sense of limits, but the lesson would not fully sink in until the country had lurched through one more debauch, the "know no boundaries" period of the mideighties.

Like consumerism, environmentalism is partly rationalist, partly irrationalist. On the one hand, successful environmental activism requires a resort to the techniques and assumptions of the technocracy: quantitative scientific measurements, appeal to experts, technological intervention. On the other hand, environmentalism promotes an organic, biological view of the world that is inimical to the machine metaphor for life and society. Many people were drawn to the movement not only for traditional reasons of reform but for religious or quasi-religious reasons, often of a pantheist character. Like significant numbers of antiwar activists and members of the counterculture, many environmentalists were irrationalists, who consciously called the technocrats crazy.

But of all the movements that challenged the instrumentalist rationality of the organization, the most far reaching was—and is—feminism. For unlike consumerism and environmentalism, which were beating at the walls, feminism would soon be within the gates, directly affecting the internal workings of the organization. Rooted in both an organized movement and in economic necessity, feminism was far more immediately concerned with problems that went to the heart of organizationalism— issues not only of fairness but of the self and identity and the personal. And, perhaps most important, it was based on first-hand, often bitter, experience.

"I couldn't change their thinking."

When Joann Harrison returned from Vietnam, she encountered the same double standard in IBM that she had left. Men returning from

Southeast Asia were reassigned to the city of their choice. Her husband had left the company, and the marriage was dissolving, so she was on her own. A friend in Saigon had convinced her that San Francisco was the most beautiful city in the United States. She requested assignment to the Bay area. Instead, she was sent to New Jersey to work on the Safeguard Anti-Ballistic Missile (ABM) system.

She ran into petty sexism as well. During fights with her manager over the length of her dresses, jocular male co-workers would occasionally whip out a yardstick and make a great show of measuring her thigh from hemline to knee. Today, she is appalled that she tolerated it.

Pants suits were also enjoying their brief moment in style, and the women in the office wanted to wear them. Management said no. The women discussed the rule privately and delegated Joann to challenge it. Joann bought a Bill Blass suit, and one bitterly cold day she wore it to work. Her manager ordered her to go home and change. She refused. There ensued a Marx brothers hall-of-doors routine, with panicked managers running in and out of offices. Eventually, the problem was kicked up to fourth-level management, with the result that she was allowed to stay at work that day, but warned never to wear pants to work again.

The following day two more women wore pants suits. Within days, new rules were promulgated allowing such attire—within limits. In a solemn departmental meeting, a male manager stood and demonstrated on himself how far down the buttocks—he could not or would not say the word, or any of its synonyms—the jacket had to extend. As far as Joann knows, she broke the line against pants suits throughout the company.

The low comedy of the dress code was matched by the high tragedy of the ABM project. Joann's department was working on communication among the four ABM sites in the Dakotas, designing programs to transfer launch responsibilities from one site to another in the event that a site was hit by an enemy missile. After her experiences in Vietnam, she rationalized working on such a project because, technically, the ABMs were a defensive system. But what disturbed her more than the project's morality was that she did not think the project would work.

"I thought the design of the programs was too cumbersome. The programs had to run in seconds, but from what I could see as an analyst it would be fifteen or twenty minutes before they all worked. By that time we'd all be blown off the face of the Earth."

As she was completing her eighteen months in New Jersey, the SALT I treaty of 1972 cut the number of missile sites to two, diminishing the need for intersite communication. Joann was relieved.

"By that time, I had seen a lot of IBMers who were not of the quality I thought everybody was after my first year or two in the space program. After almost seven years with the company, I was more realistic. There are bad apples and there are bad projects and this was a bad project. All I wanted to do was get off it, but I still thought highly of the organization."

From the ABM she moved to the Pentagon, working on several projects for the Joint Chiefs of Staff. When she was finally allowed to manage a project—a complicated conversion of the contingency reporting system from one computer system and language to another—she made the most of the opportunity.

"I had been reading about structured programming, which was the first time programming had ever had a technology applied to the art of programming itself. That and top-down programming and chief programmer teams were all new concepts I had been studying on my own because I loved programming. So my project was one of the first to use all that. And we brought it in on time."

Nevertheless, she felt her days with Big Blue were coming to an end. "IBM was not overt about it," she says, "but I had slower progress than a man with the same capabilities would have. When I first joined IBM, I naively thought that if I show them how smart I am, I'll keep moving up in the ranks the way my dad did in GM. After seven years I realized that in twenty years I probably wouldn't get past third-level manager."

To prepare for her eventual departure, she enrolled in law school at George Washington University, where she attended classes three hours a night, four nights a week, at IBM's expense. She soon discovered that she did not care for law and that women in the profession made even less money than she did with IBM.

"I met some of the key women in Washington politics who were attorneys," she says, "middle-aged women who were talking about how great it was that they were making twenty-five thousand dollars. I was making twenty-six thousand dollars. They were stunned."

She dropped out of law school after one year, but, as she would do throughout her career, she filed away what she had learned until she needed it later. She left IBM for good when George Arnold, a former employee she had been dating, persuaded her to join the international consulting firm for which he worked. The firm specialized in engineering and computer consulting in third world countries and was then heavily involved with the government of Iran. Joann, against the advice of her parents, resigned from IBM and moved to Teheran, where she was soon living with George and working for the shah's planning and budget organization.

The year was 1973. The Arab oil embargo and the dramatic increase in oil prices was soon to bring the shah even more money with which to push the ambitious modernization program he had begun after the CIA restored him to the Peacock Throne in 1953.

"He couldn't spend it fast enough," she says. "A lot of the money went to building new schools and hospitals, to subsidizing child care, to supplying milk to all children under age five. After my first two years there, I had a very positive impression of the shah.

"As he expanded the government with all this oil money, he didn't have enough people to do it. Iran had something like a ninety-five percent illiteracy rate, so most of the people were incapable of working in the government. The five percent of literate people were mostly very wealthy and were away in American schools for ten years playing and didn't want to come home and work. So the shah turned to computers, which were going to take the place of the middle-class bureaucrat and the middle managers. So it was great to work there in computers because the sky was the limit. They wanted everything to be real-time, on-line, data-based technology—the very latest, the very best."

Attracted by the billions in oil money flowing into the country, Iran's wealthy expatriates frolicking at MIT, Harvard, Stanford, and the like began to return home. Though many reasons have been adduced for the shah's fall, Joann thinks that the greed of this class was largely responsible. Over three-hour lunches of frozen vodka and mounds of Beluga caviar at the Imperial Country Club, she listened to their incessant poor-mouthing.

"All of these Iranians who came back from school had maybe a million or two of family money, but they were making low salaries in the government, maybe thirty or forty thousand dollars a year. And you would hear these people in their midthirties and early forties bitching: 'God, all I can do is afford my condo in Gstaad and my co-op in New York and my home here, but the shah has twenty homes.' They felt they deserved to have a hundred million instead of five million. They were jealous of him and they stopped supporting him. And, of course, the mullahs had stopped supporting him long before, when he took their land and took women out of *chador*."

There were other, more disturbing elements of the Iranian situation. Firms like hers walked a tightrope between the Iranian tradition of bribery, called *baksheesh*, and American laws governing overseas activities of U.S. companies. Many American companies put Iranian government ministers on the payroll, paid for their children's education, or arranged lavish vacations for their families. Through rumors, gossip, and thinly veiled anecdotes, Joann also began to realize that the shah's commitment to administrative efficiency carried over into that most representative twentieth-century organization—the secret police.

In her office there worked an Iranian whose function no one could fathom. The man did, however, possess the timeless appearance of the torpedo everywhere—great physical size, a cheap suit that looked like it had been slept in, and a menacing bulge under the breast pocket. Though dimwitted and socially clumsy, he imposed himself on the American employees at every opportunity. After a year had elapsed, when he was certain Joann and her colleagues posed no threat, he admitted that he was an agent for SAVAK, the shah's brutal secret police. He showed George a cache of M-16s in his office, he joked about breaking people's kneecaps; he hinted darkly at torture. In news photographs he was often to be seen standing near the shah. Once when Joann's boyfriend George was out of the country, the agent attempted to procure Joann for a night with the shah. She chose to treat it as another of the agent's lugubrious jokes.

The longer she remained in the country, the more disillusioned she grew with the growing power of SAVAK and the greed of the ruling class. Still, she managed to maintain a distinction between the shah's social programs and his repressive means of social control.

"I was appalled by what he was doing in one area, but I rationalized that he was doing so much good in the other area in terms of bringing his country up to a level of education, nutrition, and child care that was really radical in a third-world country. I closed my eyes to that terrible violence because I could see hospitals and schools being built; they were right there on the street as I drove home, and it seemed good. In Vietnam, I was deeply embarrassed to be involved in an effort I didn't believe in for my own personal gain, but in Iran I believed in the effort. I was proud to be a part of it, but I couldn't reconcile it with the horror. I guess I was saying to myself that 'well, maybe you've got to have some oppression to be able to move ahead at this speed.' "

After two and a half years of such ambivalence, she wanted to marry George and get out of Iran. George refused. And he jolted her burgeoning feminist consciousness further when he announced that he wanted to date other women, yet continue to live with her. Fourteen years older than she and only recently free of a twenty-year marriage, George, according to Joann, felt that he had missed out on the sexual freedom of the sixties. He bombarded her with the rhetoric of "open relationships." She left him.

Exhausted and jobless, she arrived in the United States just before her thirtieth birthday. Realizing that her travels as an adult were merely a repetition, on a worldwide basis, of her nomadic childhood, she, like many of her generation, decided that she would first pick the place where she wished to live and then worry about finding a job there. Fulfilling a dream she had had since her days in Saigon, she chose San Francisco. By coincidence, her father had been promoted to a top job in Chevrolet's western region, but Joann insists that her parents' presence just across the Bay did not influence her decision.

She located a tiny, one-bedroom condominium in Pacific Heights, but could not obtain a mortgage unless she quickly found a job. She put out feelers and accepted the best offer she could get on such short notice—from Ross Perot's EDS. She had heard that EDS was inhospitable to women, but sick of the much more direct brutality she had witnessed in Iran and hopeful that the growing American feminist movement had made inroads during her two-and-a-half-year absence, she took the job.

"When I was hired, I was one of the highest-paid women on the payroll," she says. "In retrospect, I learned they were involved in a class-action suit by women who found out they were being paid half what men were. And I think they hired me at thirty thousand dollars, which was a good salary back in 1976, because they wanted to show they had a woman being paid well. So it was tokenism, and it irritated me."

An uglier feature of the company soon manifested itself.

"Perot would hire people he knew he could manipulate to get a job done for a fixed salary no matter what it took," says Joann. "So he'd bid a job and we'd go out to, say, Raleigh, North Carolina, and work fourteen to sixteen hours a day to make sure the project came in on time and under budget. I'd be on the road for two weeks and I'd have to fight to be able to come home every other weekend and then fly back out on Monday morning.

"Ross Perot came out of IBM, and he structured EDS just like it, only he didn't have the subtlety or delicacy of IBM or their emphasis on human rights. IBM was run by people who were smart enough to realize that their structure had to be tempered by respect for the individual. No matter what trouble I had there, I still felt that they were at bottom looking at respect for the individual. EDS gave a little lip service to it, but the bottom line was the only thing they cared about. They actually talked about the policy of burning people out and letting them resign and then training another group. What they are known for in the industry is the fact that they've stayed in business so long abusing people."

What disturbed her more than the abusive management style and the discrimination against women was the fact that many employees, including herself, were willing to submit to it meekly.

"Sadly enough," she says, "it made me realize how many people want that in their life, how many people have an empty life and turn to their job for structure. And in exchange for that structure they will do almost anything in return for the validation the structure gives them."

She engaged in small gestures of defiance.

"EDS had a policy that you could never reveal your salary and you could be fired if you did," she says. "There was a woman there who had been in the business as long as I had and who was as technically competent, but judging from her life-style, I thought she must be making far less. One day in the rest room I said, 'I don't know how to say this, but I think I make a lot more than you do and I'll be happy to tell you my salary if you'll tell me yours.' She looked at me like I had offered to sell her drugs or something. So I said, 'I'm making thirty thousand dollars a year.' Her mouth fell open. So she told me she was making less than fifteen thousand dollars. She hadn't intended to tell me because she was afraid she would lose her job, and EDS made you feel that if you lost this job you'd never get another one because you weren't good enough. She went to her manager to demand a raise. Within four months, she had left the company. A year later I heard from her, and she was making thirty thousand dollars elsewhere."

According to Joann, she not only felt no loyalty to the company, she refused to adopt its coercive management style. "From day one they knew that was not going to work with me. They realized they had made a mistake when they hired me. They were fooled by my years in Vietnam and Teheran and they assumed that anyone who had been there was CIA or at least definitely promilitary. They had no idea that I was this liberal Democrat. I was not the woman they were looking for, which was a Ross Perot clone they could promote up the line and say, 'See, we don't discriminate.' "

Though she speaks confidently about her contempt for the company now, she was agonizing about what it meant for people to sacrifice their self-respect in exchange for a job. On her rare weekends home, she went to her parents' house for Sunday dinner. The day generally concluded in long conversations with her father about her troubles at EDS.

"I had all this business shit happening that was confusing to me, so I'd talk about it to Dad. He'd give me the standard organization line: 'Well, you've got to do it, Joann; that's the way it has to be.' He seemed to think EDS had a different style than GM, but it was still an organization so it was okay. So I didn't get much support in my outrage. I almost felt it was naive and idealistic of me to expect managers to act differently when people put up with it. Dad would console me, give me advice, and pretty much act like a husband in sending me back to work on Monday morning."

A year passed, and things did not improve. The management responsibilities she had been promised were not forthcoming. The company continued to use her to put out fires on important projects around the country. The magnitude of the assignments flattered her at first, but she soon saw them as a tactic for stalling her advancement. The Sunday conversations with her father grew more emotional.

"Toward the very end I was terribly upset with it all, with my realization of what was going on, with my inability to get any management job or get any respect for anything I felt. And I remember sitting in the living room and I just started crying. And I cried so hard Dad came up to me and I guess I stood up and he held me for a long time. And he had tears in his eyes. And I think he was crying for me because of my disillusionment. It was my total disillusionment with organizations and my realization that I wasn't going to get to the top in any of them, not General Motors, IBM, or EDS. It was the realization that I was not going to help run any organization, because I didn't think the way they did. I didn't want to change my thinking and I couldn't change their thinking. With that long cry, I realized I might as well leave EDS because I had no career there, either. And when I made the decision to leave, Dad supported me."

"My manager saw I was friends with those women."

With historical roots in the suffragette and temperance movements, the contemporary revival of feminism could be said to have begun with the publication of Betty Friedan's *The Feminine Mystique* in 1963. Like the civil rights movement, Friedan's brand of feminism brought expressive values into the public arena. And like the early New Left and the counterculture, it took the expressive self as the ground of value. In the ringing conclusion to her book, Friedan wrote:

> Who knows what women can be when they are finally free to become themselves? Who knows what women's intelligence will contribute when it can be nourished without denying love: Who knows of the possibilities of love when men and women share not only children, home, and garden, not only the fulfillment of their biological roles, but the responsibilities and passions of the work that creates the human future and the full human knowledge of who they are? It has barely begun, the search of women for themselves. But the time is at hand when the voices of the feminine mystique can no longer drown out the inner voice that is driving women on to become complete.

Though feminism did not explode into public consciousness until the early seventies, a number of social and economic trends were preparing the way. In the 1950s married women over age 35 began to enter the work force as service-sector jobs expanded and employers, who were caught in a pinch by the shortage of younger female workers, reached out to older women. Meanwhile, the percentage of working married women with children under age 6 climbed from just under 12 percent in 1950 to almost 19 percent by 1960. By 1965, when the baby boom abruptly ceased, the figure was more than 23 percent; by 1970, it was more than 30 percent.

As children became more of an economic liability, more and more women deferred marriage and childbearing. As inflation grew worse during the years of the Vietnam War and after, more and more women simply had to work, whether they wanted to or not, often in low-paying service jobs. In 1976, the first year such figures were gathered, the percentage of married working women with children *under age one* stood at almost 31 percent. And by 1987 the figure had climbed to 50.8 percent, indicating a social transformation of profound significance: For the first time in American history, more than half the women worked at jobs outside the home *within one year* of giving birth.

Working outside the home for little more than half what men were paid and working inside the home for nothing, women inevitably rebelled. Visible to anyone who cared to look and palpable to employed women—from hourly workers to ambitious careerists—discrimination was real. Of 1,362 senior executives surveyed by Korn/Ferry International in 1985, only 29, which is to say 2 percent, were women, despite the fact that between 1972 and 1983, the number of women managers doubled to 3.5 million and the number of executive women increased by 143 percent. The "glass ceiling," as this nearly impenetrable barrier to corporate promotion for women came to be called, was undeniably real, brutally betraying the optimism with which women had first begun to enter management in the seventies. Like Joann Harrison, stalled at IBM while her identically qualified husband was promoted almost immediately, every woman had her particular horror story. Such firsthand experience, coupled with the organized movement's highly visible agitation, thoroughly discredited for many women any notion of benevolent institutions. For as we have observed, feminism, unlike consumerism and environmentalism, was—and is—within the walls. From the factory floor to the boardroom, the clash of expectations with reality directly affects the internal workings of the organization.

There is a great irony in this situation. Whyte had pointed out that it was the benevolent paternalism of the organization that kept the organization man in happy thrall to the company, in effect, giving the organization its legitimacy. Unable to foresee the day when women would enter management and the professions in large numbers, Whyte could not have foreseen the damage that sex discrimination—an inevitable consequence of paternalism—would do to that legitimacy. Under the pressure of the changing work force, the paternalism Whyte had seen holding the organization together became the very thing that threatened to blow it apart.

Even when paternalism had turned to the autocratic and abusive management policies that came with a souring economy, sex discrimination persisted. And as Carolyn Harrison discovered, sex discrimination and abusive management could be a volatile mix.

Having exhausted her graduate fellowship just as she was about to begin the arduous process of producing a book-length dissertation, Carolyn took a part-time technical-writing job with the Atlanta division of a Pittsburgh-based conglomerate. Within four months, they offered her a full-time job. Given the severely depressed market for academic jobs and with no assurance that she would ever complete her dissertation anyway, she realized she would probably have to switch careers sooner or later. She accepted the job.

She soon found herself immersed in a bewildering variety of intramural battles. On the one hand, there was a power struggle between the older managers, most of whom were originally from the Atlanta area, and the young MBAs whom the Pittsburgh office was sending down to take over. The management style of the MBAs was much like the style that older sister Joann had encountered at EDS.

"They ruled by fear and intimidation," Carolyn says. "They saw their workers as machines. They did not think these people had to go home and live their lives. They treated them like the computers, who could run all night if they had to. And, amazingly, the employees would do it. But in one year I saw the morale of that company disappear. The people who used to do cheerfully these repetitive and mindless tasks became discontented and unhappy. By the time I left, everyone in that company was afraid they were going to lose their jobs. And a lot of them did, good hard-working Southerners who had been there for years and years."

At the same time, a number of women in the company were struggling to win equal pay for equal work. "They were not asking for equal pay for equal *sorts* of work," says Carolyn, "but equal pay for jobs with the same job description."

The women were by no means conscious feminists. Torn between their loyalty to the company and the manifest injustice of their position, they had joined the fight reluctantly. They often turned to Carolyn for confirmation that their feelings were justified.

"I think they turned to me," she says, "because I was an outsider who had not been with the company for years, as they had. I could verify that this was an outrageous situation and that something should be done about it."

Carolyn spent countless hours on the phone with them, joined them in clandestine meetings, and contributed her writing talents to the documentation they were assembling. Their mild activity likely would have come to little, except that at a crucial moment the larger management struggle impinged on the women's struggle. A long-time female employee in the personnel department, angry at what was happening not to the women but to the older, long-term employees who were being forced out by the Pittsburgh managers, fought back with the only means at her disposal: She surreptitiously gave the women copies of the personnel records the company had filed with the federal Equal Employment Opportunity Commission. The records did not tally with the actual employment picture for women in the division. The women were emboldened to continue their fight.

By then, Carolyn had had enough of corporate life. "I partly quit and was partly forced out," she says. "My manager, who was one of the new men from Pittsburgh, saw that I was friends with those women and he wanted me out. I wasn't fired, but I didn't get a raise. In fact, I didn't even get a review, which I now realize would have been further cause for complaint about the company's employment practices. But I was completely emotionally drained from dealing with it every day. I just wanted out."

Like other movements of the period, feminism generated both a rational reform movement and a pitiless critique of rationalism. As reformers, feminists pursued legislative, regulatory, judicial, and constitutional remedies for sex discrimination. As theorists and polemicists, they ripped away the patriarchy's benign mask of rationalism and exposed malign and irrational power arrangements underneath. They challenged everything: the traditional family, conventional sexuality, Freudian psychoanalysis, received history, and the very nature and structure of language. Not even God the Father was exempt, not to mention mortal fathers. Industrialism and technology, the highest creations of instrumental rationality, were seen as specific forms of a generic domination that found its clearest expression in the objectification of women in pornography, sexual harassment, and rape.

Proclaiming that "the personal is the political," feminism in the seventies brought the various tendencies of the sixties full circle: It completed the process of carrying private, domestic values of equality and expressive selfhood into the public realm, and it brought the public, political realm to bear on the most intimate matters of domesticity, sexuality, and psychology. Along with the antiwar movement, the counterculture, and environmentalism, feminism mounted a radical attack on the instrumental rationality of American organizations and institutions—and it carried the attack into the boardroom and the bedroom. The ideality of the self had finally met the reality of organization face to face, and the latter had been found severely wanting.

"Respect was important in itself."

No one who lived through the period's relentless and pervasive denunciation of technocracy could remain unaffected. Though the organization offspring may oppose particular, contemporary political manifestations that grow out of that critique—the antinuclear movement, say, or the Equal Rights Amendment—many of the older members of the generation still share some of the fundamental assumptions of that manifold attack: They disdain machinelike organizations; they harbor doubts about the rationality of the rationalist premises of industrialism; and, above all, they remain devoted to an individualism of the expressive self. It is these attitudes that for them constitute the real legacy of the "failed" sixties. And it is these attitudes that underlie some, though by no means all, contemporary attempts to remake or reconceive organizations.

Joann Harrison, after her frustrating experiences at IBM and EDS, is typical. She wanted the consulting company she founded in 1979 to be different: "I wanted to start a company run on principles I believed in, even though I might not get rich off of them. My goal was to live a life that I could enjoy with values I could be proud of. And perhaps there was a tinge of self-righteousness in not wanting to play the terribly dirty games of intimidation and manipulation I had seen played in other corporations."

Her values included respect from the people for whom she worked and respect for the people who worked for her.

"Respect for myself and for others was important in itself because I never had that. I wanted to provide a better corporate environment than some of the ones I had been in. When I started my company, I felt that I could make the most money if I manipulated and intimidated people the way Perot's company did, where people worked sixteen hours a day for an eight-hour wage. That was an option open to me, that I rejected out of hand."

Proposals to "humanize" the workplace, to create open, participative organizations that are sensitive to the needs of employees and responsible to the surrounding community, have often echoed many of the communal and expressive themes first sounded in the sixties and early seventies. Moreover, some organization men, stung by charges that they were dull, repressed conformists who tolerated inhuman institutions, came more and more to pay lip service, at least, to the notion that people mattered. Newly sensitive managers espoused Theory Y, a participative brand of management that had been first formulated by MIT professor Douglas McGregor in the midfifties.

In *The Human Side of Enterprise* (1960), at one time perhaps the management book most often quoted by managers themselves, McGregor attacked what he called Theory X, the notion that people will work only when coerced and tightly controlled, that they wish to avoid responsibility, that they have little ambition, and that they desire security above all. On the contrary, argued McGregor, borrowing the framework of psychologist Abraham Maslow, people have a hierarchy of needs that begins with the physiological need for food and shelter, ascends through the need for security, and culminates in the need for self-fulfillment— the "capstone" of the hierarchy. "These," he wrote, "are the needs for realizing one's own potentialities, for continued self-development, for being creative in the broadest sense of that term." Instead of organizing for control, organizations should arrange their operations so people can "achieve their own goals *best* by directing their efforts toward the success of the enterprise." (This statement, of course, begs the question of whether the organization's goals are worthy of commitment.) McGregor called this integration of individual and organizational goals Theory Y, and he suggested that it first be developed and refined by application to managers and professionals. To create sensitive managers, many corporations sent their employees to T-groups, encounter sessions supposed to shock them out of their old, authoritarian ways. Many organizations still use T-groups, or their equivalent, today.

Following the spectacular success of Japanese corporations in the world market, Theory Y was supplanted by William Ouchi's Theory Z. Writing in 1981, Ouchi argued that some American corporations had successfully adapted many Japanese management principles—long-term employment, consensual decision making, individual responsibility, informal control, and a holistic concern for the employee—to their own corporate cultures. Like Theory Y, Theory Z was supposed to evoke the commitment of employees to organizational goals by making work meaningful and fulfilling. Numerous impressed executives attempted to order up new corporate cultures overnight. No doubt, many did so in a desperate search for the secret of their foreign competitors' success. But the way for the acceptance of Theory Z among younger managers had been prepared, in part, far earlier by the counterculture's uncritical acceptance of all things Eastern. Similarly, the idea that corporations resemble cultures with shared beliefs, values, and practices was certainly not strange to a generation that at one time was obsessed with the symbolic and ritualistic nature of human groups.

Today, some commentators, carried away by the possibilities of such rosy visions, foresee idyllic, enchanted corporations. Book after book trumpets the coming of humane, egalitarian, fulfilling workplaces where sensitive managers stimulate creativity and caring. These predicted corporate arrangements are often rendered in terms of culture. But the notions that the authors have of culture owe far more to the psychological traditions of motivation theory than they do to anthropology. And the corporate worlds they prescribe are not so much human cultures, properly speaking, as they are psychological utopias—*psytopias*, if you will.

Many organization offspring, reared in a world that taught them to value self-expression above all, are highly receptive to such visions, seeing in them a reflection of their own beliefs and a response to their unique concerns. They are often unaware that the contemporary emphasis on the emotional tone of the workplace has far deeper roots than the sixties and far-from-benign implications. For though many of the themes sounded in recent theory resonate with charming countercultural and pop-psychological motifs, their real provenance lies in the human relations movement, which Whyte analyzed so devastatingly.

In Whyte's view, the human-relations theorists merely extended the logic of scientific management from the realm of machines into the domain of human affairs. Whyte called this utopian leap of faith "scientism," which he defined as "the promise that with the same techniques that have worked in the physical sciences we can eventually create an exact science of man."

Initially, the desire to apply scientific management to the psyche had been more a matter of necessity than of an intellectual shift. Personnel problems had begun to develop on Taylorist production lines. Managers noted behavioral and attitudinal problems among workers that were hampering productivity. But Taylorism, by simplifying tasks and limiting each worker's span of control, was supposed to have eliminated such problems. Workers no longer needed to make decisions; when the possibility of error existed, they needed only to follow orders. Taylor had not realized, however, that in a highly integrated, tightly synchronized production process each task is highly dependent on the timing, accuracy, and efficiency of every other task that precedes it. Inattention or carelessness at any point can jeopardize the production run or, in some instances, the entire operation. Although the simplicity of each task had allowed management to do without workers who possessed special skills, the interdependence of every task made management more concerned than ever with the performance of each worker. Employees' attitudes, then, became crucial to their performance. Technical experience and education counted for less than the worker's state of mind. If a worker came to work with a bad case of the Monday morning blues, she could shut down an entire assembly line.

Searching for ways to prevent such problems, managers turned to scientific management for the solution. Since scientific management had worked so well in solving production-line problems and since workers' attitudes were merely another such problem, why not use the same scientific techniques that had worked so well in the past? Taylor had advocated testing to determine workers' aptitudes, such as manual dexterity, mathematical ability, and hand-eye coordination. From an engineering perspective, it was important to fit workers to the machine, to make sure they could perform the tasks the machine required. Aptitude testing worked well for such purposes. So, the reasoning went, if management could test for visual acuity, why couldn't they develop tests to measure psychological characteristics—maladjustment, potential for loyalty, fear of success, sense of humor, willingness to obey, and almost any other aspect of someone's personality? Soon, managers were using personality tests to screen workers, to find ways to motivate them, and to establish grounds for firing them.

This simple and dramatic transition from engineering to human engineering to social engineering was eased by the pioneering work of Elton Mayo, an industrial psychologist from Harvard. In the late 1920s and early 1930s, Mayo and a team of researchers conducted a series of experiments at a Western Electric plant in Hawthorne, Illinois. The researchers wanted to find out how physical changes in working conditions would affect the productivity of workers. Six telephone assemblers were isolated from their co-workers; the researchers then made changes, one by one, in the conditions of the isolated group. They improved the lighting; increased the rest periods; shortened the hours; and, finally, raised the wage incentives. Productivity increased, as it should have, according to the principles of scientific management. But when the workers were returned to their original ill-lit workbenches to work long days without breaks, productivity increased to levels well above those achieved under the best working conditions. What was happening? After many experiments, the researchers concluded that productivity increased in both situations because the participation of the workers had been sought and their feeling of involvement was more important than were physical conditions. The workers formed an informal social system, the workings of which determined their attitudes toward the job. To Mayo and his fellow researchers, the lesson of the Hawthorne experiments was simple: "Man's desires to be continuously associated in work with his fellows is a strong, if not the strongest, human characteristic."

In the history of industrial psychology and organizational behavior, no other inquiry would have as much impact as these deceptively simple experiments. Their importance, however, rests not so much on the nature of the results, but on their subsequent interpretation and application. For the conclusion industrial psychologists urged on managers was *not* that production workers should be given more responsibility for their work, but that they, the professional managers, should recognize the importance of social intercourse and cooperation among workers and managers. Mayo and his colleagues argued that managers needed to learn how groups work and how to make workers feel like valuable members of the group. Whoever would increase productivity would first satisfy this elemental human craving to belong. But in pursuing such a program, managers failed to distinguish between involving workers more directly in their work and merely manufacturing the appearance of such involvement.

Though ostensibly psychological and therefore cognizant of the irrational, human relations in action was no less a form of instrumental rationality than was Taylorism itself. In essence, it attempted to extend Taylorism from the realm of engineering and operations into the realm of the social. Managers dutifully enrolled in training programs designed to teach them how to talk with their employees and how to dispense a logical impossibility—"nondirective counseling." Few saw the irony of following routine procedures to make workers feel respected and involved. Fewer still worried about the ethical implications of such manipulation.

As Whyte pointed out, workers resisted such manipulation and so, by the 1940s, managers began to turn the techniques of human relations upon themselves. By 1952, Whyte noted, one-third of American corporations were using personality tests to screen potential managers. In 1954 he checked sixty-three corporations and found that about 60 percent were using such tests. Because the increasingly abstract nature of many managerial and professional tasks made it difficult to evaluate individual managers, psychological terms came to figure prominently in assessments of job performance. Many jobs required the ability to motivate, to persuade, or to communicate ("people skills," as they came to be called in a phrase that betrays its manipulative bias). In the interests of increased productivity, managers were encouraged to hone such skills and to practice them on workers and fellow managers alike.

But the human-relations movement stalled, failing to win the universal acceptance Whyte, writing in 1956, thought was imminent. So expansive was the postwar boom that corporations could continue to prosper using the more familiar principles of Taylorism and of "classical" management, such as management by objectives. It was only following the sixties that various refinements of human-relations theory and practice began to win wide acceptance in corporate America, as if in answer to the calls for more humane, less machinelike institutions. The chief beneficiaries of this changed cultural atmosphere were the neo-human-relations approaches of McGregor and of Rensis Likert. In a time of widening cultural reaction against the treatment of human beings as cogs in a vast machine, such theories appeared to be humanistic and democratic alternatives to the cybernetic pretensions of scientific management.

Although the demand to humanize the workplace, growing out of the sixties' irrationalist critique of organizations, is far from identical with the human-relations movement, today the two are almost hopelessly confused and often dangerously conflated. In the face of such widespread confusion, it is worth being clear about the fundamental differences between the two and seeing what happens when those differences are elided.

The early human-relations researchers purported to offer empirical evidence for the collectivist thesis that the individual's most basic desire is for a sense of belonging to the group. In practice the movement drew a straightforward instrumental connection between creating a feeling of belonging, however illusory, and increased productivity. Though its founding premise is nominally psychological (*nominally* because it is merely behaviorist, based on a statistical correlation of stimulus and response), the model for the organization is a social one. And the underlying model for society is the machine.

Contemporary humanizers, however, offer an individualist thesis about self-actualization and self-expression. Because the content of self-expression and self-actualization differs for each person, the task of organizing to encourage their flourishing is much harder. Theoretically, at least, it becomes necessary to manage the entire psychic economy of the organization. Thus, though all organization is, by its nature, social, the organizational model for humanizers becomes a much more nearly psychological one, sanctioned by the ineradicable American habit of personifying organizations. At its most extreme, this model of the organization becomes, in effect, a psychic projection.

Despite basic differences between the two positions, their common psychologism encourages their confusion. One need look no further than the immensely popular *In Search of Excellence* to see this contemporary confusion in action. The authors simultaneously hold up superrationalist Robert MacNamara to ridicule and locate their own irrationalist roots in the work of Elton Mayo, whom they oppose to Taylor and his progeny. But they do no better than any other proponent of the human-relations school at solving the essential paradox of treating people humanely to wring more production from them. Proposing to reveal the secret of long-term success behind innovative big companies as diverse as IBM, McDonald's, 3M, Proctor & Gamble, and Johnson & Johnson, authors Thomas J. Peters and Robert H. Waterman, Jr., assert that "the clear starting point" in understanding the attributes of excellent companies "is the acceptance of the limits of rationality."

Attacking rational models of corporations, Peters and Waterman argue that excellent companies are "value-driven" organizations that emphasize the self-fulfillment of individuals as opposed to emphasizing organization charts, rigid controls, and economies of scale. But here the argument grows slippery as the authors oscillate almost imperceptibly between two potentially incompatible senses of value. Ostensibly, the highest value in excellent companies is the devotion to individual self-fulfillment, autonomy, and achievement. But different companies have different corporate strategies, which dictate attention to more mundane "values," such as service, innovation, quality, or price. (Johnson & Johnson's core value, cited approvingly by the authors, is its determination "to be synonymous with home wound care.") While IBM may compete on service, Hewlett-Packard may compete on innovation, though both companies may believe that humane management practices are more likely to help them achieve their strategic goals. But IBM is not devoted to customer service or Hewlett-Packard to innovation so their employees may achieve self-fulfillment; rather, the companies espouse values like self-fulfillment so that such strategic "values" as market supremacy in, say, customer service may be realized. It is the job of the manager, say the authors, to manage values, which, on inspection, turns out to mean that the manager must find ways to adjust humanistic values to commercial ones. But perhaps the systematic conflation of instrumentalism and "irrationalist" humanism that informs *In Search of Excellence* is best summed up in the authors' assertion that a chief attribute of excellent companies is "productivity through people." It is the old conundrum of human relations: The most effective means is to treat people as ends.

A generation reared in the sixties' hothouse atmosphere of self-expression easily confuses the human-relations position with the sixties humanist critique of organizations. In practice, this confusion allows humanist values to be pressed into the service of the very instrumentalism their basic premises deny. Some purveyors of the humanist position are confessed instrumentalists from the start, at great cost to their intellectual coherence, though not to their consulting fees. Others seem blissfully unaware of their instrumentalist assumptions.

When contemporary efforts to humanize the workplace are assimilated, covertly or overtly, to the instrumentalist goals of the far older human-relations movement, they promise an even more totalizing machine in the form of an even more encompassing personification: the organization as artificial psyche. An early anticipation of the organization as artificial psyche appeared in 1963 in Eric Berne's *The Structure and Dynamics of Organizations and Groups*, which offers "a systematic framework for the therapy of ailing groups and organizations." A full-blown recent view of organizations as psyches may be found in F. R. Kets deVries and Danny Miller's *Unstable at the Top*, which appeared in 1987.

This is, of course, a perverse outcome. Launched from an individualism predicated on the expressive self, the attack on the machinelike nature of the organization plays into the long-standing metaphor of the organization as artificial person, which then results in helping call forth a bigger and better, though "softer," machine. The humanizers agree that the organization is artificial and therefore soulless. But instead of rejecting the entire metaphor, they refine it. What was part legal fiction and part popular conception is updated with psychology: The corporation as an artificial person endowed with all the rights of an individual is now endowed with a psyche. The implication is that the organization is not *enough* of a person, that it wants a little humanizing. But the only way to go about such a thing is through more artifice, more systems of control, however diaphanous or "nondirective." Thus, behind the new dream of psytopia stands the old dream of cybernetics, with the difference that the psytopian dream elevates an indeterminist psychological model of the organization over the more blatantly mechanistic neurophysiological model of cybernetics.

To date, however, these innovations have had little impact on the logic and structure of the workplace. Though "organizational development" grew ever more subtle and sophisticated in the 1970s and 1980s, the distinction between thinkers and doers—that is, management and workers—remained intact. The application of psychological theories to managers themselves remains a set of transparently instrumental techniques, however romanticized and sentimentalized, designed to create the illusion of happiness and collaboration. Moreover, an increasingly unforgiving economy has made it impossible for many large organizations to pursue such practices on the scale implicit in the metaphor.

Nevertheless, the search for psytopias continues to exert a strong attraction for many organization offspring, however intellectually confused or deceived. The important point is that the yearning embodied in this humanistic image of the organization indicates the depth of the dissatisfaction with the machinelike organizations created by the organization man. So strong is the allure of this humanistic image that it is no exaggeration to say that it forms one pole of the rising generation's organizationalism.

But the humanistic image of the organization has had another, unintended consequence. Its psychologizing of the artificial-person metaphor helped prepare the ground for another, competing psychological image: the organization as egoistic. It is this image that stands at the other pole of the generation's organizationalism. For despite the ferocity of the attack on the organization in the late sixties and early seventies, something wholly unexpected was soon to occur: in record numbers and with unseemly haste, the younger members of the generation would attend business school and go to work for large organizations, meanwhile fueling a boom in business publishing and in bombast about the romance of business. If for many of the older members of the generation the self became the measure of the organization, for many of the younger members, it would be the other way around: The organization would become the measure of the self.

5

The I of the Beholder: Organizations as Egos

The reality principle.

The stampede to business began in the midseventies and steadily gained momentum through the eighties. The numbers are staggering. In 1971, American colleges and universities awarded about 115,000 bachelor's degrees in business and management. By 1980 the number was 185,000. By 1985, when the last of the baby boomers were finishing undergraduate work, the figure was 233,000—an increase since 1971 of 100 percent, while the total number of bachelor's degrees awarded had increased by only 17 percent. Put another way, in 1971 only about one in seven of all bachelor's degrees was earned in business and management; by 1985 the figure was almost one in four.

Even those figures understate the magnitude of the shift. Many of the liberal arts and social sciences, trying to stop the hemorrhaging in their enrollments, began to sell themselves to undergraduates as ideal preparation for business careers—English for public relations, psychology for industrial relations, history for public administration. Nonbusiness majors that had always led to work in large organizations—engineering, communications, and computer science—did not have to sell themselves. In engineering, 92 percent more bachelor's degrees were awarded in 1985 than in 1971; for communications, the figure was 290 percent; for computer science, 1500 percent. But in terms of absolute numbers or of percentage of degrees awarded, no other field came close to business and management. Engineering, the nearest competitor, with 96,000 graduates in 1985, garnered only one in ten of all bachelor's degrees awarded that year.

The big loser during the 1971–85 period was education, which awarded only half as many bachelor's degrees in 1985 as in 1971, or fewer than one in ten of all bachelor's degrees in 1985 as against more than one in five in 1971. Of course, the decline in the number of education majors reflected, in part, the narrowing of opportunity in education as the baby boomers passed out of the system. Social science suffered a similar decline, dropping from almost one in five of all bachelor's degrees awarded in 1971 to one in eleven in 1985.

The growth in the number of master's degrees in business—the coveted MBA—was even more spectacular than was the growth in undergraduate business education. In 1960, when the organization man was entering the prime of his working life, only about 5,000 MBAs were awarded. By 1971 that figure had increased to approximately 26,500 and by 1985 to 67,500, an increase of 154 percent, while the total number of all master's degrees increased from 1971 to 1985 by only 24 percent (three-fourths of which increase is accounted for by the increase in MBAs).

Why did so many baby boomers rush to embrace institutions that had so recently seemed thoroughly discredited? Because it was only such institutions that offered at least a chance at the kind of life baby boomers had glimpsed as children—a comfortable house, two or three children, and a secure retirement—the kind of life that had once been possible on one income from almost any kind of middle-class job, including jobs in teaching and social work. But because of the sheer quantity of baby boomers and the long-term stagnation of the American economy, such security grew ever more elusive. In the fifties and sixties, the number of workers aged 25 to 34 ranged from 14 to 17 million; by 1985 the number had skyrocketed to 30 million. Meanwhile, from the end of World War II through 1973, real wages grew at an average of almost 3 percent a year; after 1973 the growth stopped. It was a double whammy that vastly reduced the amount of income a person could expect to earn over a lifetime—a pattern not starkly reflected in any statistic but one that was clearly felt.

Older baby boomers who had vowed voluntary simplicity or had ignored reality found that you could not simply secede from the economy. The more ambitious found a crowded career ladder and experienced a slow but perceptible widening of the gap between their prospects and their expectations. Younger baby boomers, squeezed by the enormous numbers of their older siblings and coming of age in an economy that had been sour longer, felt the impact more directly and more immediately. They swelled the ranks of business majors accordingly.

In many ways it was a hard time for the young—and the younger, the harder. Their liberal arts professors despised them as materialistic, unimaginative, and incurious. Businessmen derided each succeeding graduating class as more uneducated and ill prepared than the last. The media, extrapolating from lives of conspicuous consumption led by young investment bankers in New York, falsely assumed that all young people were affluent, contributing to feelings of inadequacy in the overwhelming majority who were not. (Adjusted for inflation, the proportion of young families with incomes of thirty-five thousand dollars or more was no higher in 1985 than in 1973.) Middle-aged moralists, enjoying hundred-dollar mortgage payments and uncrowded career ladders, simply called them selfish.

Younger members of the generation gave the moralists ample ammunition. For the values of each class of baby boomers arriving at college differed more sharply from those of their older brothers and sisters. According to surveys conducted by the Higher Education Research Institute, 83 percent of incoming freshmen in 1967 had identified "developing a meaningful philosophy of life" as an essential goal. In all but two of the next twenty-one years, the percentage dropped steadily, reaching an all-time low of 39 percent in 1987. Meanwhile, the percentage of freshman who identified "being very well-off financially" as an essential goal climbed steadily from a low of 39 percent in 1970 to an all-time high of 76 percent in 1987.

In the face of such evidence—the increases in business majors and MBAs and the dramatic shift of personal goals—the notion that the seventies and eighties saw a further erosion of the prestige of the organization appears untenable. But that is exactly what happened. For what those thousands upon thousands of freshly minted managers found when they were graduated was organizations that were unstable, unfeeling, and often untrustworthy. Far from providing a haven from the economic uncertainty of the period, large organizations were its seat and center. The same economic forces that had driven so many young people to seek the security of business careers had turned business upside down. As the economy grew more perilous, many organizations lost their stability: They failed; they disappeared into the maw of predatory takeovers, leveraged buyouts, mergers, and calculated bankruptcy. Ever more creative forms of financing produced corporate entities as evanescent as the Perrier bubbles over which they were dreamed up. Furthermore, the status of managers, and even that of chief executive officers (CEOs), declined markedly as investment bankers and corporate raiders wrested control of corporations from managers. Hundreds of thousands of lifelong employees, including many of the offspring's fathers, were summarily fired or forced into early retirement. And many of those offspring, during the 1980s, found themselves treated similarly.

Nevertheless, the cycle continued: The demographic squeeze and stagnant incomes sent ever more baby boomers scurrying for jobs in large organizations, which, despite their instability, remained one of the few avenues leading toward the increasingly elusive American dream. Whereas their fathers had embraced a particular organization, General Motors, say, or Continental Illinois Bank, the offspring embraced organization in the abstract, as a means to an end, but they kept any particular organization at arm's length, withholding their loyalty and their commitment. As a result, the more recent dissolution of the organization's mystique is more difficult to discern—and to credit—than was the sixties' straightforward rejection of large organizations by people who were, for the most part, outside them. To add to the difficulty, the more recent disparagement of the organization differs from the sixties' attack in content, but resembles it in dynamics, in that both involve their own particular blurring of the individual and the organization.

In the prosperous sixties, when the attack was on large, stable organizations, the blurring of individual and organization occurred over the issue of rationality. Measured against the affective values of the expressive self, the limited rationality of organizations was found wanting—was seen, in fact, to be irrational. Moreover, subsequent attempts to rethink and remake the organization—to humanize it—were conceived in psychological terms that were consistent with the original measuring of the organization against the expressive self.

The rocky and highly competitive economy of the seventies and eighties produced its own characteristic blurring of individual and organization. It depended, first, on a revival of all the traditional nineteenth-century rhetoric of corporate individualism, most visibly in the revived romance of the entrepreneur. Used not only to cover a few genuine pioneers but to cloak in the mantle of individualist respectability the machinations of some of America's largest corporations and financial institutions, "entrepreneuring" was all the rage. This artful confusion of individual and organization was abetted by a resurgence of classical economic thought, which envisages the corporation as, in Adam Smith's phrase, "the shadow of one man." Similarly, a recrudescence of Social Darwinism, now psychologized, individualized, and never explicitly named, provided another popular framework for understanding the behavior of organizations and individuals. Instead of being viewed as insane and in need of humanizing, individualized corporations came to be seen as, inescapably, egoistic—artificial persons operating on the reality principle. In time, many of those who saw organizations that way would come to view themselves in the same light. As if this blurring of the distinction between individual and organization were not confusion enough, both the postsixties humanist image of the organization and the more recent egoistic image live on, sometimes separately, sometimes intertwined—in organizations and in individuals.

"Get used to being bought and sold."

Peter Hanson looks every inch the part he is playing. Wearing a dark-blue pinstriped suit, white shirt, and red tie, he is dressed for the success that seems like a birthright for this young, trim, and confident Manhattan marketing executive. It is early spring 1986, and Hanson has a toehold on a fast track. The merger-and-acquisition game has only just begun to build momentum on Wall Street, but the boyish-looking Hanson, age thirty-three, is already an accomplished player in the world of hardball business. The son of the CEO of a Chicago financial services company, Hanson talks candidly about the route to his current goals. Like many such stories, it contains numerous contradictions, as well as tantalizing hints about what motivates many of the members of Hanson's generation.

"I graduated from Brown in 1975," he says, "and I can remember it was a terrible job market." He decided that the prudent course would be to attend business school. "I don't know why business. I thought about law, about a profession. Now, I know that law is very uninteresting for ninety-nine percent of the practitioners. But I don't really know why business."

He applied to Harvard Business School, his father's alma mater. "I was immature enough when I got out of high school to worry that if I got into Harvard as an undergraduate, it would have been because of my father. But when I got out of Brown, I was pragmatic enough to say: 'Hey, I've got to have a job. I want to and have got to make a good living now. I want to get into the best place I can get into. I know I want to go into business, so it is really a matter of getting into the best place possible.'"

Judging from the average starting salary of graduates of the Harvard Business School then—more than thirty thousand dollars a year—employers certainly held it in high regard. Indeed, the *New York Times* had once called the Harvard MBA the "Golden Passport." But the school deferred Hanson's admission for two years, insisting that he gain some practical business experience first. So Hanson went to work for the Tribune Company in Chicago. He did not tell the company that he intended to leave eventually for business school.

"I was really afraid that if I told them they would have said, 'You will never get a job.' It was a good place to spend two years, but the Tribune is a sleepy American corporation involved in some pretty stable, albeit attractive, businesses. I really had no interest in returning there after Harvard.

"During my first year, I was a financial analyst," he says. "Then I had an experience the following year that changed me forever, from a business perspective. Someone said to me, 'You can't just be a financial guy; you've got to learn how a newspaper runs—advertising, production, editorial, circulation.' I didn't think I wanted to learn all those things, but I was getting bored with what I was doing. It had become so routine. So I said to myself *what the hell*."

He chose the highly unglamorous circulation department, where he began as night manager of a suburban circulation office. Eventually, he was rewarded with his own district.

"This district was a disaster. It was the winter of 1976–77 and it was real cold. About half the total circulation had no carriers because the weather had been so cold they just quit in droves. People weren't paying their bills because they weren't getting their newspaper and everything was in a state of chaos. It took me about four months to dig it out, but I did. And it gave me an enormous sense of satisfaction. I learned that I could run something. It was small. It wasn't grand. But it was mine, and I really enjoyed doing that."

He entered Harvard Business School in fall 1977, one of 720 in his class, chosen from more than 7,000 applicants. Devoted to the celebrated case method in which actual business situations are studied in minute detail, the Harvard curriculum stressed competition at every turn, not only among businesses but among the students themselves. Constantly pitted against each other in class, in simulated negotiations, and in competitive exercises, students learned to trust no one, to attack first, and to assume the worst of the adversary. The extracurricular competition that was stimulated among the students to replicate the competitive world of business offered as a model for human personality the purely self-interested behavior of corporations. As more and more people streamed into business schools in the seventies and eighties, this model, enjoying the imprimatur of America's most distinguished educational institutions, would become more widely diffused than ever.

"I hated it," Hanson says. "I just hated the sense of manipulation about the place. It is just astonishing. They set up the educational environment to manipulate and control students, and I have never liked that."

Nevertheless, he found it invaluable preparation for a business career.

"It was a real pressure cooker. I had a little bit of trouble with that, but I know it has made me a lot tougher. I think that in my past jobs in the past few years, when the pressure has gotten really bad, I realize that I am probably able to take it because of what happened at Harvard. I did very well there. I came through it and succeeded, but never enjoyed it. It's a psychological boot camp. That's what makes the place famous."

During the summer between his two years at Harvard Business School, Hanson worked for Bain & Company, a Boston-based management consulting firm, the company he would later sign on with after graduation and the kind of job most of his classmates were shooting for.

"I remember for the summer they paid seven hundred dollars a week. I thought that was more money than I would ever see in my life. That was amazing to me, absolutely amazing.

"While I think I may have joined for the wrong reasons, I learned a tremendous amount. I worked there for the summer and twenty hours per week during my second year. That made for a very tough year, but I made a fortune there, and I was not even out of business school yet. In the four years after I left Harvard, I learned an enormous amount with Bain—analytical techniques, how to manage, good analysis. I will never regret those years. I will never regret being around a bunch of bright, aggressive people either.

"The firm, however, was very strange. You have never seen anything stranger in your life—people working incredible hours, very competitive, very aggressive—and the homogeneity was absolutely astounding. It was every bit as bad as Wall Street, and perhaps worse. On Wall Street, people tend to dress alike; at Bain & Company, people started to *talk* alike. People became known as 'Bainees.' It was almost like a religion."

At Bain he routinely put in sixty-hour weeks, spending four years on the company's accounts with Firestone and with National Steel—"two sleepy, modest-growth American companies." It was no different, in effect, from working for those companies themselves. He soon tired of it. "There is a lot of consulting work to be done for such companies, but I didn't want to do it. I wanted something that was faster paced and growing and changing. The opportunity to make money is so much greater in a dynamic business than it is in a slow-growth business."

He chafed also at the steady but slow climb up the promotional ladder. "I realized that I would never be a top-ten vice president. I could have been a second- or third-tier VP, but I would never be in the top ten in the next twenty years. It would have been twenty years of sticking around—and *that* I just could not see."

His priorities changed.

"I would rather run something small and do something that I enjoy in the long run than do something where it would take forever to get to the top. What I wanted was a business that changed, so I could constantly relearn and manage. I like the day-to-day pulse of a business and I learned from just that little newspaper operation that it was wonderful. If I could put my imprint on something and make it better, make it grow and help others to grow, well, I got a lot of satisfaction out of that."

In 1983, he got his chance. Following a lead he found in the Harvard Business School placement bulletin, he applied for the job of vice president for corporate development with a small computer firm. He persuaded the firm's skeptical chairman to let him work on corporate planning and acquisitions, while aiming ultimately to take on line management.

"It worked out real well. For a time, my job was to evaluate, for possible purchase, microcomputer software companies. But after three or four months, we concluded that we would be better off going private, because our stock was undervalued, than we would be doing acquisitions. So we went private."

He got the opportunity he had been waiting for.

"I went into the mainframe systems software products business, first as vice president of sales, then I picked up marketing as well. I didn't know a thing about it. Nothing. I didn't know systems software. I didn't know mainframes. I didn't know selling and didn't know marketing. It was a hell of a lot of fun because all I could do was learn."

In the long run, however, the grandest lesson he learned had little to do with the nuts and bolts of running the company or of turning around an ailing department as he had done at the *Tribune*.

"The chairman taught me an important lesson," Hanson says. "First of all, he taught me that if I want to stay in this business, I had better get used to being bought and sold. And then he taught me the most important lesson: There is money to be made in that process.

"Here is how the process works. You take the company private and then sell off the various parts for more than they are worth. What he did in taking the company private is he boosted his share of ownership for half his initial investment. In other words, when he was a stockholder, he had fifteen percent of the stock. When we executed the LBO [leveraged buyout], when we bought out all the stockholders, we bought out him. He then, in a brilliant move, became a forty percent owner of the company. Now the company is about to be liquidated, and he will be worth about fifteen million dollars—his initial investment was two million—all in a year and a half. It was a brilliant move."

What happens to the dismembered company and its employees?

"The big software companies are looking for products. They have these big distribution arms, sales forces, marketing groups, and so on. The group that bought us out came and fired practically our entire marketing staff and administrative people. They kept the technical people and they are keeping the sales force for the time being and they are just pumping our product right through their entire system."

Such a result seems at odds with his professed determination to put his stamp on something and to help employees grow. The contradiction appears to make him uneasy.

"I don't like the fact that this kind of buying and selling, this volatile environment is out of my control," he says. "But as long as I want to work in a volatile situation, part of the fact of life of volatility is, by definition, you can't control it. Correct? So I just have to accept that. I have to shape it as best I can. It's not unlike surfing. There is this big goddamn wave coming over and the key to it is harnessing it and positioning it so that it doesn't clobber you. You can't control the thing, but you can harness it for your own ends."

And in an environment where companies themselves have become commodities, he intends to catch the wave: "Someday I hope to run a company where I get enough capital and I acquire products. Then I will pump them up and resell them to other companies. Or I get sold and start out all over again. In a cycle."

"You can't be emotionally bound."

What forces impelled people like Peter Hanson to go from the satisfaction of a job well done to the determination to grow and sell companies—and the lives of employees? How did we move in little more than a generation from team playing to looking out for number one? To a large extent the answer lies in an economy that went from the smooth sailing of the sixties to the "big goddamn wave" of today. A confluence of economic troubles—the Vietnam inflation, successive oil shocks, falling productivity, and the rise of global competition—changed dramatically the world of work and the way many organization offspring viewed their place in it.

After President Nixon closed the gold window in 1971, the mechanism was in place for inflation to become a way of life through the remainder of the decade. By the time he resigned in 1974, inflation had reached 12 percent, a figure it would reach again in the first half of 1979. And it remained at 11 percent the following year. A staggering increase in the price of raw materials exacerbated an already inflationary situation. Between October 1973 and January 1974, OPEC increased the price of oil 300 percent. By 1980, the barrel of the benchmark Saudi Arabian light oil that had cost $2.50 in 1972 cost $35. The resulting inflation was particularly pernicious because it came at a time when the economy was stagnant, an unprecedented condition succinctly, if ungracefully, captured in the neologism *stagflation*.

While prices rose, productivity fell. Because companies normally improve the quality and quantity of equipment they use, productivity (output per worker hour) normally increases every year; however, the *rate* of increase is a crucial element in determining the overall growth of the gross national product. For roughly the first half of this century, productivity grew by about 2–2.5 percent per year. But from 1947 through 1965, during the postwar boom, the growth rate was an unusually high 3.3 percent per year. After 1965, worker productivity fell back to a more usual 2.2 percent; after 1973, it suddenly stalled, growing at an average rate of only .8 percent per year for the next eight years. In 1979 and 1980, the rate of improvement in productivity was actually negative, and in 1985 and 1986, during a period of modest improvement, the rate averaged less than 1 percent per year. Overall, from 1973 to 1988, the growth in productivity averaged just 1 percent a year. In 1990, productivity gains outside manufacturing were zero.

While America grew less productive, much of the rest of the world grew more competitive. Countries whose economic capacity had been devastated by World War II finally recovered and challenged the American hegemony in world markets. (The Marshall Plan had worked.) Aided by rapid advances in communications technology and transportation, whoever could produce high-quality goods the cheapest, no matter where, could win significant shares of the world market. In 1960, America was responsible for 35 percent of the world's economic output, a figure that had fallen to 22 percent by 1980. Similarly, in 1960, America had shipped 22 percent of the world's exports; by 1980, the share had dropped by half, to 11 percent. Even those companies that avoided foreign markets increasingly found themselves competing in a global marketplace in the United States as more and more foreign-made products flooded the country. By 1980, 26 percent of the automobiles sold in the U.S. market came from abroad, as did 25 percent of the steel; 60 percent of the televisions, radios, tape recorders, and stereos; 43 percent of the calculators; 27 percent of the metal-forming machine tools; 35 percent of the textile machinery; and 53 percent of the numerically controlled machine tools. In 1960, imports had accounted for less than 10 percent of each of these products. By 1980, more than 70 percent of all American-made goods were competing directly with foreign-made goods.

For American companies stagflation, the low growth in productivity, and global competition meant shrinking profits, slowly growing markets, and an end to the days when they could sell almost anything they could make. To compete in this vastly changed business environment, corporations and the financial managers and institutions that increasingly came to dominate them tried various strategies. Some of America's older industries—steel being the most notorious example—bought time by seeking protectionist trade legislation and then, once they had secured it, merely using it to maintain profits instead of investing in capital equipment that would have allowed them to compete against the more modern industries of Germany and Japan. When the trade legislation lapsed, the industry petitioned the government for more. Other companies embarked on ambitious programs of cost cutting: they closed plants, shipped manufacturing offshore, fired hourly workers, eliminated layers of management, and sold unprofitable enterprises. A few of the more flexible companies came up with innovative products and processes that allowed them to compete with their foreign counterparts. Many more, however, were unwilling to make long-range investments in research and development (R & D) or in technology and instead elected to maintain profits or high stock prices through innovative financial and accounting maneuvers, mergers, acquisitions, leveraged buyouts, tax avoidance, and calculated bankruptcy.

The increased popularity of these purely financial strategies exacerbated the tension, inherent in the publicly held corporation, between the shareholders who own it and the managers who run it. Shareholders want enhanced stock values; managers want to use profits to enlarge the company and, not incidentally, their own power and prestige. During the twenty-five years of phenomenal growth following World War II, most companies were able to satisfy shareholders and managers without apparent strain. The imperatives of global competition and a bad domestic economy changed all that, putting immense pressure on managers to find near-term profits.

Moreover, as institutional portfolios came to dominate the stock market, their owners behaved far more like traders than like investors, thus severing shareholders from any long-term interest in a particular company. With the rise of conglomerates in the late 1960s, managers themselves, at least at parent companies, began to be similarly cut off from their subsidiaries, which they came to regard much as stock traders regarded their holdings—as sources of immediate return.

Into this pressurized situation stepped the investment banks and corporate raiders. Armed with junk bonds and other innovative credit instruments that allowed them to go after even the largest corporations, the raiders dazzled shareholders with higher stock values than they had ever dared dream of. There soon ensued a frenzy of mergers, acquisitions, and leveraged buyouts.

The trick for raiders and acquirers is to find companies whose stock understates the value of their assets, acquire the company, and redeploy those assets. Often redeployment means simply dismembering an acquired company and selling off its assets piecemeal. The profits can be enormous. For example, Kohlberg, Kravis, Roberts & Company, a Wall Street investment house and, during the 1980s, one of the country's largest industrial holding companies, bought out the Beatrice companies in 1986 for $6.2 billion, then broke them up and sold the parts, in the process realizing $2 billion in profits for its investors.

To resist the raiders, executives of target companies adopt a variety of tactics to keep stock prices high: layoffs, firings, divestitures, and stock buybacks at prices higher than the wildest-eyed raider's wildest calculation of the stock's true worth. And then there is the ultimate stock repurchase plan—management taking the company private through a leveraged buyout.

Called collectively, and euphemistically, *restructuring*, the tactics of the raiders and resisters have changed drastically the way corporations are run. Already notorious for managing for the short term only, wary American executives must now focus more narrowly than ever on immediate results as reflected in stock prices. They ignore R & D, discount return on investment, and live with dangerously high levels of corporate debt— interest costs now eat up 50 percent of pretax earnings, compared to 40 percent in the 1970s and less than 20 percent in the 1960s. Higher interest rates make it more expensive to raise money for basic research, and raiders look for target companies with big R & D budgets, which can be cut to produce immediate cash flow. As a result, by 1989 corporate spending on R & D did not even keep pace with inflation; more of the remaining R & D money was shifted from basic research to immediate product development.

In an environment in which a company's survival is threatened almost daily, CEOs must forget loyalty to employees, plants, products, communities, entire businesses, and even the nation. "You can't be emotionally bound to any particular asset," says Martin S. Davis, chief executive of Gulf and Western. And even if the widespread restructuring were to cease tomorrow, institutional investors and managers of pension funds would maintain intense pressure on executives to maintain high stock prices.

Through the eighties the pace of restructuring accelerated. As the decade opened, about $100 million was available to finance leveraged buyouts; by 1988, at least $250 billion was available. From 1985 through 1988, more than 500 companies were taken private. The total value of all these highly leveraged takeovers shot up from $244 billion in 1982 to $682 billion in 1987. By the end of the 1980s, more than $1.3 *trillion* had been spent on rearranging assets.

In dizzying succession, deals of gargantuan proportions were proposed only to be dwarfed days later by even bigger ones. In fall 1988, the British conglomerate Grand Metropolitan PLC offered $5.2 billion for the Pillsbury Company. A few weeks later Philip Morris offered $11.5 billion for Kraft. Three days later RJR-Nabisco said it was considering a $17.6 billion buyout proposal made by its top executives in partnership with Shearson Lehman Hutton. Within days, Kohlberg, Kravis, Roberts & Company offered $20.3 billion for the tobacco and food giant.

There were some spectacularly bad deals: LTV's acquisition of Republic Steel in 1984; Honeywell's acquisition of Sperry Aerospace; and Beatrice's disastrous purchase of Esmark, which subsequently led to the entire company's break-up in a Kohlberg, Kravis leveraged buyout. The crushing debt load that Campeau took on in 1986 and 1988 to acquire Allied Stores and Federated Department Stores, including such healthy retailers as Bloomingdale's, had driven the whole operation into bankruptcy by early 1990.

Critics of restructuring argue that today's buying and selling of companies—being almost entirely finance driven—bears little relation to the production of goods, the creation of new wealth, or the long-term health of the American economy or particular corporations. As Lee Iacocca, no enemy of capitalism, put it, "never before in history has so much capital produced so little of lasting value." And *Business Week*, surveying the best and worst deals of the decade, delicately concluded that "while most big corporate marriages don't result in complete failure, they rarely provide much decisive benefit."

Defenders of restructuring insist that it allocates capital more efficiently. They point out that assets have always been bought and sold as part of the process that Joseph Schumpeter called "creative destruction." But even good deals, such as UAL's acquisition of Pan Am's Pacific routes and Quaker Oats' acquisition of Stokeley–Van Camp, which increased earnings and enhanced shareholder value, did nothing to lessen the insecurity of managers caught in the crossfire. Whatever the merits of restructuring, it has undeniably abrogated the social contract once enjoyed by the organization man.

"Loyalty is the first casualty."

In the past, corporate giants kept longtime salaried employees on the payroll through the good times and the bad. That is no longer the case. Nor are staff reductions any longer confined to ailing companies, since restructuring has made massive cuts routine at even the healthiest concerns. During the 1980s, more than a million managers were fired or pushed out by companies that were fighting off hostile takeovers. During an eighteen-month period in 1985–86, nearly three hundred companies, including Apple, Bank of America, CBS, Dow, Du Pont, Eastman Kodak, Exxon, and Ford, cut their staffs by 10 to 20 percent. And nearly every time a company announces cutbacks, its stock price rises. All told, the number of managers discharged during the 1980s as a result of restructuring was estimated to be as high as 2 million.

Firings, layoffs, forced retirements, and job changing occur at an ever faster pace. Between 1976 and 1983, the rate of corporate firings doubled. During that same period, 15 to 25 percent of American executives left their jobs. After takeovers, nearly half the senior executives of the acquired firm depart. And personnel experts have calculated that at any given time today, 30 percent of managers and 34 percent of technical professionals have their résumés circulating.

For today's managers, creative destruction has become permanent revolution. Insecurity reigns from top to bottom in every organization: It is not only dismissed employees who are devastated, but those who remain, knowing that at any time they can wake up and discover that their job—or company—no longer exists. Little opportunity remains for a young manager to rise steadily through the ranks; job mobility must often be sought outside one's company in a constant game of musical chairs throughout entire industries and professions. Under such conditions, noted Paul M. Hirsch, "loyalty is the first casualty."

Genuine commitment to an institution, of the kind Dave Harrison felt for Chevrolet or Ray Myers felt for Continental Illinois, is a thing of the past. (And even Harrison and Myers had trouble, at the end, maintaining their commitment in the changed atmosphere.) A 1986 *Business Week*/Harris poll of middle managers found that 65 percent of corporate employees claim to be less loyal to their employers now than they were ten years ago.

Bill Thomas, a pilot for a major U.S. airline, has witnessed the steady erosion of loyalty in his industry, brought about by mergers and deregulation. Seeking the same sense of shared purpose he had known as a fighter pilot in the Korean War, he joined United Airlines in 1956. Five years later, when United acquired Capital Airways and thus regained its position as the nation's biggest airline, he got an early glimpse of what was to come in the airline industry and, subsequently, in many other American industries.

"It was pretty clear to everybody," he says, "that the surviving company, which was United, was sitting back enjoying the different employee groups [from the two airlines] fighting. The paternalism was over."

As if watching a fast-motion film, he witnessed, in the space of a few short years, the passage of his still-young industry from the age of the great aviator-entrepreneurs through the age of the organization man to today's paper entrepreneurs—from Lindbergh to Lorenzo, in effect.

"The idea that we were going to build a hell of a first-class air-transportation system was going out. The guys who thought that way—the Pat Pattersons, the C. R. Smiths, the Juan Turpeys, Eddie Rickenbacker—they were dying or retiring. The new breed was taking over that was going to show them a bottom line: 'I went to Harvard Business School, and I'm going to show you how to make profits and make 'em fast.' You don't build a big, beautiful operation by making a big profit next year. You may not make a big profit for twenty years, and if you are really motivated to build a big, beautiful operation you may not *ever* pull out of it the kind of money that a profiteer would want."

With the Airline Deregulation Act of 1978, there came a brief period of genuine competition among many large and small airlines, but the increasing popularity of mergers and acquisitions soon led to a shakeout. Of the twenty-two new airlines that began operating after deregulation, in 1979, only five were still operating independently ten years later, and many venerable airlines were merged or liquidated. For employees throughout the airline industry, the purely financial strategies of raiders like Carl Icahn and Frank Lorenzo, sometimes including calculated bankruptcy to bust unions, led to widespread job insecurity and, inevitably, loss of loyalty.

"It's very evident today that it's almost warfare," says Thomas of employer-employee relations in the industry. "It is no more perceived as an organization as it is a small group of money grubbers. It's all being cloaked in Harvard Business School rhetoric and a lot of philosophical theories that this is the way it should be; but the net result is that the human contact between the leadership running these organizations and the people in it [has been broken]."

To run its non-airline business, United created in 1968 a subsidiary called UAL, which soon became a holding company, with United becoming a subsidiary. In 1970 the holding company acquired Western—soon changed to Westin—International Hotels. The company continued to diversify, acquiring resort developments in Hawaii. United acquired Pan Am's Asian traffic rights as well as 2,700 Pan Am employees. An attempt to buy bankrupt Frontier Airlines from People Express in 1986 failed when the United pilots' union could not agree with management on a plan for absorbing the Frontier pilots. (Lorenzo's Texas Air Corporation bought Frontier instead and liquidated it.)

"The tendency is for [a company] to be bought by holding companies," says Thomas. "You lose any concept of being a part of it. It really belongs to some group of unknown men who own a lot of different things through a holding company. Who are they? I don't know. I don't know anybody who does know. Who is the ultimate policymaker for United Airlines? What do they want? A big airline? An asset?"

The effect on the morale of employees was immediate and palpable.

"When the holding company started preaching bottom line and profits to us, that's when the pilots lost interest. There was no more hangar talk. We were all into our outside investments, our little businesses on the side. There was no more interest in the airline."

In 1987 the name of the holding company was changed from UAL to Allegis, a full-service travel company that included not only the Hilton International and Westin hotel chains, the Hawaii resorts, and an airline, but Hertz Rent-A-Car, and a computerized reservation system. But this holding company soon attracted the attention of raiders, who noted that the subsidiaries would be worth more if they were sold off as separate businesses. To protect itself, the holding company sold off the car rental and hotel units and changed its name back to UAL. Nevertheless, the airline continued to attract raiders. In self-defense the management and the pilots tried, unsuccessfully, to buy the airline themselves.

For Bill Thomas, the descent from his heady days as part of a real team in Korea to the slow disillusionment he experienced with United brought two troubled marriages; estrangement from his children; and a long, ultimately successful struggle with alcoholism.

"I was just getting more and more furious the way life was just cramping me in," he says. "Just this narrow, long goddamned dark tube, getting smaller and smaller as I'm going down it. And all the hopes and plans of youth were just disappearing. I was becoming the organization man. And organizations were losing their appeal. The idea of loyalty to a corporation was getting the same treatment that the idea of patriotism to a nation got: 'Screw it, what's in it for me?' "

What was for Bill Thomas a lengthy process leading to bitter disillusionment is for many of the younger generation of organization people merely a given. The younger organization people neither give their loyalty to the organization nor expect any in return. And among the younger generation of managers, this lack of loyalty is no secret guiltily suppressed. Organization offspring express their lack of loyalty-for-loyalty's-sake openly and often. Their attitude may, like that of Scott Myers, outrage the older generation, but from their own perspective, the offspring are merely stating the obvious. In interview after interview in their homes, in their offices, and in their favorite restaurants and watering holes, the overwhelming majority of our subjects professed no allegiance to the organizations that employ them.

Nancy Caton, a foreign-exchange trader for CitiBank, San Francisco, told us she is ready to give herself to anything but her job. "I feel I'm ready to make some sort of commitment to something and I don't really want to make it to the company, to a corporate entity to which I feel no particular loyalty."

Laura Cory's far-from-straight career path illustrates the ease with which apostate organization offspring change jobs, even careers. She was graduated from the University of Connecticut with a degree in psychology. After several years of clerical work for a manufacturing company, she returned to school and earned an MBA from Stanford. She then studied to be a certified public accountant and went to work for an accounting firm for a couple of years. From there it was on to a consulting firm. Then she joined a small software company.

"I have basically changed jobs every two years," she says cheerfully.

At the time of her interview, she was a product-marketing manager for Hewlett-Packard, the computer giant widely respected for its humane personnel policies, especially its maternity policies. For a woman with small children, Hewlett-Packard is a good place to work. Already the mother of one child, Laura Cory plans to have two more and then move on. "I intend staying in my current job because it's a good environment for me to have children in. And then once I've got children that are a couple of years old, I will probably go off to a small company again."

Many organization offspring have also witnessed the sad spectacle of their fathers pushed out or otherwise betrayed at the end of their careers by companies to which they had given their lives and loyalty. The children vowed it would not happen to them.

Diane Cole, who has spent years working in nonprofit organizations devoted to prison issues, recalls watching helplessly as her father was forced into early retirement only two years after he had relocated. "I felt kind of bitter about that, how my dad was treated in that whole corporate world," she says. "And it's funny, because I remember saying back in high school that I would never marry someone who works for a corporation. I just can't do that, even though I've always had respect for my dad.

"I think I've always been resentful about how I think my dad was treated. I don't mean his just being singled out—but just the whole attitude that people are expendable. And I've never liked the image of the father leaving all day, the nine-to-five job, and then coming back from the cold, cruel world, briefcase in hand—the whole Park Forest image."

Carolyn Harrison recalls vividly the change in her father, just two years short of retirement, when General Motors gave him a choice of taking early retirement or transferring to Atlanta, half a continent away from his children who had begun to settle in the Bay Area.

"That was the first time I ever heard him complain about the company," she says. "He was very bitter about it. And it was upsetting to see my father so upset. I had never wanted to think he felt disappointed or unfulfilled, and it was clear that he did."

"Greed is good."

It was not only the behavior of organizations that created the contemporary view of organizations as necessarily egoistic and encouraged people to ape them. There were also powerful ideological currents running. For almost twenty years, American culture has been saturated with ideas and images that mutually reinforce the notion of the organization as an individual naturally pursuing its own best interests. Corporate apologetics, a resurgence of neoclassical economic thought, popularizations of organization theory, and media images of business have all done their part to create the egoistic pole of this generation's organizationalism. First, in time-honored fashion, many of these images and ideas confuse organizations with individuals. Second, in recent fashion, they psychologize them. And third, in even more recent fashion, they reduce psychology to egoism.

The third point is decisive for distinguishing the egoists from the humanists. Both the egoists and the humanists personify and psychologize the organization. But the attempt to cast the organization in the egoist mold entails a highly jaundiced view of human psychology. Where the humanist sees a hierarchy of needs, the egoist sees an anarchy of desires. According to the egoist position, all people at all times necessarily seek the gratification of their desires as mediated through the reality-oriented ego; even apparently altruistic acts are motivated solely by self-interest. By extension, corporations as artificial persons are seen to operate from the same logic and *it would be foolish to expect them to do otherwise*.

The time-honored confusion of individuals with organizations is rooted, of course, in classical economics, which treats corporations as if each were a single, individual entrepreneur. In the late 1970s and early 1980s, classical economics enjoyed a wide resurgence—and not only in academe. Milton and Rose Friedman's spectacularly successful bestseller *Free to Choose*, in conjunction with their ten-part, 1980 Public Broadcasting System series of the same name, trumpeted the virtues of laissez-faire capitalism to a wide audience. A diatribe against big government, regulatory agencies, and consumer groups, *Free to Choose* argues, as Adam Smith does, that in a society of individuals who are free to pursue their own self-interest in a system of voluntary exchange, the "invisible hand" of the marketplace regulates such competition for the good of all, though no individual intends such a consequence. Early in their book, the Friedmans make it clear that they see no appreciable difference between real individuals and corporations in such a system:

> The income each person gets through the market is determined . . . by the difference between his receipts from the sale of goods and services and the costs he incurs in producing those goods and services. . . . The case of the entrepreneur . . . is different in form but not in substance. . . . Similarly, the existence of the modern corporation does not alter matters.

The Friedmans believe that the corporation does not alter matters because, in the final analysis, the corporation consists of real individuals, each of whom derives his or her income from a system of exchange that works the same way at every level—from that of selling a product of one's craft to that of hiring out one's ability for a salary or to allowing one's capital or other productive resources to be used in a corporate enterprise. The corporation is merely an "intermediary" among such individuals and resources. By this intellectual sleight of hand, the corporation is more or less erased from the discussion, effectively collapsing the distinction between individuals and corporations back into the individual. Thereafter, the Friedmans' narrative proceeds smoothly as a tale of the struggle between big government and individuals whose freedom government almost invariably curtails.

American corporations have, of course, been staking their defense on various versions of the laissez-faire argument since the nineteenth century. In a world where the ability to administer and coordinate vast enterprises in oil, railroading, and steel counted for far more than the Horatio Alger virtues of luck and pluck, John D. Rockefeller, Cornelius Vanderbilt, and Andrew Carnegie, even though they knew better, had continued to offer themselves and their creations as examples of the self-made man. To attack the trusts was to attack the sacred notion of private property in which such individual freedom and social mobility were grounded. It was a straightforward, if decidedly anti-democratic and self-aggrandizing, identification of the company with the individual.

Apologists within corporations in the seventies found such reasoning to be as compelling as ever, and they, too, wrapped themselves in its rhetoric. But in the face of consumerism and environmentalism, they retreated from the swaggering position of the robber barons and essayed a slightly more subtle and democratic identification of the company with the individual. They did so by seizing on the idea of consumer sovereignty—the notion that unfettered competition is self-regulating because the consumer is "free to choose" among products and services. In this view, with consumer preference acting as the invisible hand, producers merely carry out the will of the people. To regulate corporations is to tamper with the natural mechanism of the marketplace, saddle producers and consumers with higher costs, and sometimes produce unintended consequences (as when manufacturers of children's clothing, required to make them fire retardant, did so with a chemical that turned out to be carcinogenic). To curtail the corporation is to deprive consumers of the benefits that accrue from freedom.

In an even stronger form (dearer to elegant theorists than to corporations) the argument maintains that individual freedom as an end in itself must never be diluted, though such freedom risks tainted meat, bogus pharmaceuticals, or lethal automobiles. But whether in this absolutist version beloved by theorists or in the more pragmatic version favored by corporations, the rhetoric of consumer sovereignty makes attacks on the corporation synonymous with attacks on the rights of individuals. Regulation imperils everybody's freedom, not just the freedom of a few plucky would-be Carnegies. Thus, the corporation is not merely identified with the individuals who own it, *but with the individuals who are its customers*.

Harold S. Geneen, the legendary chairman of International Telephone and Telegraph (ITT), which acquired more than 350 companies during his tenure, often invoked the consumer-is-king argument. In a 1970 speech about the role of business, Geneen said: "It is called the free

enterprise system. It could also be called the 'freedom of choice' system."
The operation of business is essentially benign, he said, because "the results of its pooled efforts are directed toward those values which *you* are
interested in, because *you* direct it." Using the homely example of the
wood-burning stove, which he saw threatened with extinction by antipollution laws, he pictured the consumer as the ultimate loser in governmental regulation. (In the illogic of Geneen's universe, only those people who
oppose governmental regulation qualify as individual consumer-citizens;
environmentalists and consumerists are presumably not citizens.)

But Geneen was after bigger game than antipollution laws. At the
time of his speech, ITT was facing an antitrust suit from the U.S. Justice
Department (later settled in ITT's favor after the company made a secret
"donation" of four hundred thousand dollars to help finance the 1972
Republican National Convention). "The original antitrust laws were
passed not against the power of business or commerce," he said; "they
were passed against the looming power of government. They are called
the Constitution and the Bill of Rights. This is what the founding fathers
were concerned about. They did not want the free enterprise system or
any other freedoms 'snuffed out.' They want it to remain a free choice
system, responsive to people." In implying that the attempt to prevent
ITT from acquiring Hartford Fire Insurance threatened the constitutional rights of every American citizen, Geneen was asserting that there
is no essential difference between individuals and companies.

Similar boilerplate issued from other corporate spokesmen of the
time. James M. Roche, the chairman of General Motors, in identifying
corporations with the individual, added a somewhat more sinister note:
"Much of the modern criticism of free enterprise is by no means idle, nor
is it intended to be. Many of the critics have the professed aim to alter
'the role and influence of corporations and corporate management in and
upon American society.' Their philosophy is antagonistic to our American ideas of private property and individual responsibility." Roche's artful *our*, like Geneen's blithe illogic, suggests that people who criticize
corporate behavior do not count as citizens, but Roche went Geneen one
better by implying that the critics are un-American.

John J. Riccardo, the president of Chrysler at the time, achieved the
blurring of individual and corporation by talking only about "businessmen," as if giant corporations like the automakers were merely enterprises
undertaken by lone, risk-taking entrepreneurs: "Business is a game of
risks and . . . the job of the businessman is to balance the risks. His function in a free enterprise system is to risk time, talent, energy, resources,
and capital in order to make gains." Riccardo did, however, recognize the
existence of corporations when he remarked: "I think it is . . . important

that we once again respond to the generalizations about the soulless corporations and,—by extension—about how the profit-motivated free enterprise system rejects basic human values and stifles cultural
achievement." But the response he developed conceded, in effect, the
truth of the criticism: "While I happen to believe that our economic system is fair and equitable, I don't think that the question of morality is
really essential to a discussion of any economic system." Issues like basic
human values are irrelevant because, for Riccardo, the important question
was the pragmatic one: Does the system work?

Though Riccardo's belief in the fairness of the system suggests at
least a vestigial faith in the rationalizing function of free markets, his
pragmatic brushing aside of values anticipates a turn in the popular understanding of free enterprise that, by the end of the 1970s, had developed into a fully egoistic image of corporations—and of individuals.
Indeed, the two went hand in hand. The injunctions to individuals to
"look out for number one" and to "win through intimidation" had their
counterparts in pictures of cutthroat corporate competition. In much
popular writing of the period, the watchword became not so much "rationalism" as "realism." In a world where everyone is maximizing his or
her own interests, individuals and corporations are said to be foolish to
behave any differently, whether or not selfish behavior yields any socially
desirable ends, like self-regulating markets or a humane social order.

"Greed is good," said Ivan Boesky in his commencement address
to the class of 1985 at the Graduate School of Business, University of
California at Berkeley. A spectacularly successful arbitrageur who was
later convicted of insider trading and banned for life from the securities
industry, Boesky declared expansively: "Greed is healthy. You can be
greedy and still feel good about yourself." His words, with their emphasis on mental health and feeling good, would come to stand as the credo
of the egoists.

A good deal of the decade's business writing presented a picture of
a jungle or of shark-infested waters, a confused and confusing world of
individual-corporate actors engaged in a grim struggle for survival. The
eighties began with *Life and Death on the Corporate Battlefield* and ended
with *The Alexander Complex* (self-described as "an unusual look at modern-
day Alexanders"), *Leadership Secrets of Attila the Hun*, and the best-seller
Swim with the Sharks Without Getting Eaten Alive.

Toilers in the relatively new disciplines of organizational behavior
and management theory unintentionally contributed to the confusion.
After the breakdown of the machine metaphor for organization, some
theorists, casting about for a new model, hit upon an old one—the biological comparison. These theorists argued that organizations are like

organisms; some "species" are better adapted to their "environment" than are others; organizations grow, evolve, and die. Taylorist concerns with efficiency were replaced by questions of organizational health and survival, and, ultimately, the survival of the fittest—high-tech industries versus big-volume mass production, say.

Other metaphors for organization vied with the biological—organizations as cultures, as political systems, and as brains, to name a few. (Based on highly speculative computer research in artificial intelligence, the brain metaphor, by bringing together the biological and the machine metaphors, achieved a highly specific form of the organization/individual confusion.) However, most of these models, like most of the humanist models, were addressed to the internal workings of the organization and bore little relevance to the highly unstable reality of takeovers and global competition that formed the backdrop for the far more widely disseminated Darwinian analogy.

One of those who was most responsible for disseminating the biological metaphor in the corporate world was Bruce Henderson, founder of the Boston Consulting Group, one of the country's preeminent dispensers of advice on corporate strategy. Henderson argued that every business has its ecological niche in the business environment: "You can find no species on earth which co-exists with another one, where both make their living in exactly the same fashion." He believed that if companies did not find their proper niche and then perpetually evolve to maintain it, they would become extinct like dinosaurs.

On first blush, organizational Darwinism, with its talk of "species," appears systemic and contextual. But just as in that other great crude application of Darwin to society—Social Darwinism—the popular imagination transformed a structural thesis about the survival of entire classes of entities into a moral prescription that was extended to include the survival of the fittest *individual*, in this case, the individual corporation. As if describing the famously indestructible sharks of evolutionary history, today's companies proclaim themselves "lean and mean," "all muscle and no fat," well adapted to today's predatory business environment. The theory, like Social Darwinism itself, had the added advantage of providing a justification in nature for the essentially social organization of power. This justification, too, was nothing new. "The growth of a large business," said John D. Rockefeller, "is merely a survival of the fittest, the working out of a law of nature and a law of God."

In movies and television, the realism of the business writers became the cynicism of the screenwriters. In thousands of fictional dramas, viewed by millions upon millions of people, totally unscrupulous businessmen engaged in every kind of iniquity. Images of corrupt and venal businessmen have long flourished in high and popular art in America. But in the seventies and eighties, films and television upped the ante considerably. Today's fictional businessmen not only pursue selfish ends, as they have done from the novels of Theodore Dreiser to the adventures of Scrooge McDuck, but they are now routinely shown brandishing guns, ordering rubouts, and masterminding drug cartels. Real corporate wrongdoing has been of the more familiar variety: insider trading, bribery, pollution, and defense-industry boondoggles. In only a few well-publicized instances did anyone go to jail—and without a harrowing car chase or a hail of bullets.

Though defenders of corporate honor decry these villainous media images (even producing for public television, in 1987, a documentary entitled "Hollywood's Favorite Heavy: Businessmen of Prime Time TV"), they should have been relieved. For melodramatic narrative, requiring an individual villain, tends to confirm Americans' traditional confusion of the organization with the individual. Leaving little room for penetrating analysis of systemic problems, such narrative deflects criticism from real issues to phony ones, from organizations to the individuals who represent them.

What measurable effect, if any, negative images of business have is impossible to judge. Television no doubt pandered to age-old populist views of "big business," but it certainly did not stem the tide of students toward business majors. And while the real crooks of Wall Street induced business schools to install an ethics course or two, the lives of such high rollers bore little resemblance to the reality in which most employees of organizations dwell. Besides, not a little glamour clung to some of the more spectacular malefactors, real and fictional. But media villains and real-life lawbreakers, representing the reductio ad absurdum of the individualist justification for corporate behavior, did help to solidify the contemporary view of organizations as necessarily egoistic.

"I love my job; . . . but that doesn't mean I don't have concerns."

Though the egoist pole of contemporary organizationalism may, for purposes of discussion, be distinguished from the humanist pole, both are often found side by side in a single individual, organizational theory, or organization. Peter Hanson can talk simultaneously about helping people to self-actualize and about erasing their jobs in the sell-offs he hopes to engineer. Similarly, the human-relations movement, with its instrumentalist advice on how to increase productivity, hopelessly intertwines the two views. AT&T, at least in two memorable series of ads that ran concurrently on television, also seems confused, though its confusion is of course highly calculated. One group of commercials, known in the advertising industry as "slice-of-death" ads, presents grim little dramas in which harried middle managers at unspecified companies make painfully obvious mistakes involving telecommunications. In a competitive world where there is no room for error, the managers earn rude comeuppances from their bosses, punctuated on the soundtrack by a metallic crescendo that clangs like a cell-block door. By contrast, another series of ads presents real AT&T employees, not actors, who appear to talk extemporaneously and earnestly about how much they care about what they do. Responsible, confident, articulate, empowered, and fulfilled, they seem sublimely unaware of the shark-infested waters pictured in the other ads. Thus, AT&T manages to have it both ways: The business world is a competitive, cutthroat place, populated by autocratic executives and insecure managers—and AT&T's bright, autonomous, well-adjusted people are ready to serve them.

But of all the images that crystallize the dual nature of the era's organizationalism, none was more ubiquitous—or confused—than that of the entrepreneur. In the first instance, the ideal of becoming an entrepreneur appears to be simply antiorganizational, a wish for pure self-expression. The creative and individualistic entrepreneur who is determined to transcend the petty limitations of corporate bureaucracy strikes out on his or her own. Against all odds, the entrepreneur produces valuable innovative services or products, creates new wealth, and achieves untold satisfaction and riches. As in Schumpeter's classic account of the entrepreneur, such a figure combines the self-actualizing needs of the humanist with the predatory instincts of the egoist. Where the former predominates, the image is of a creative, sensitive genius, which is to say Steve Jobs, co-founder of Apple Computer and founder of NeXT Computer. Where the latter predominates, the image is of an ambitious, insatiable power seeker, which is to say Donald Trump. What was overlooked in both cases was that these soaring individualists had to forge large organizations, even if they did have the luxury of creating those organizations in their own images.

In time, *entrepreneur* was stretched to cover the rapacious arbitrageurs and corporate raiders who enjoyed enormous profits by merely rearranging existing wealth. At the other end of the spectrum, it was stretched to cover managers charged with the responsibility of start-up businesses within giant corporations. Business writers dignified this confusion with the term *intrapreneuring*. Eventually, *entrepreneur* was stretched to cover even the most dronelike corporate functionary. So what if you push paper in the bowels of Engulf & Devour; find a slightly better way to do it; save the company a little money; and, according to contemporary mythology and much of today's gushy business writing, you are an entrepreneur.

The contradictory nature of the humanistic and egoistic organizational images, between which people like Peter Hanson may oscillate, reflects a profound ambivalence in the organization offspring. On the one hand, they desperately long to give themselves to something larger than themselves. On the other hand, they fear the power and indifference of purely self-interested organizations. What these two images embody, then, is a fully cultural response to the problem of authority and legitimacy. Forming the poles of the generation's organizationalism, they provide contradictory answers to the simple question: By what right does this organization rule my life?

Many who view organizations as egoistic simply concede authority to the organization and withhold legitimacy from it: The organization rules my life at my sufferance, but it has no legitimate right to do so. The egoist views individuals and individual organizations alike as self-interested actors doing what they must. Employment in an organization is merely a marriage of convenience. In such a grimly necessitarian world, the question of legitimacy is moot. Although this view has the dubious virtue of simplifying matters conceptually, it considerably complicates them psychologically. The concession of authority acknowledges the individual's dependence on the organization, while the denial of legitimacy seeks to alleviate the feelings of shame associated with dependence. The trick is to remain dependent without being vulnerable.

But this is an exceedingly difficult stance to maintain. The very act of rejecting the legitimacy of the organization tends to strengthen one's bond to it, if only negatively. It is for this reason that some of this generation's most vocal critics of organizational life have the greatest difficulty divorcing themselves from it. One young manager in a Fortune 500 company complained bitterly in an interview about the sexism and racism she felt existed in her organization, yet when she was asked how many hours a week she spent at her job, she replied proudly: "At least sixty-five to seventy." When it was suggested that her thorough denunciation of the company seemed at odds with her dedication, she explained, "I love my job; I would never choose to do something else. But that doesn't mean I don't have concerns."

By contrast, the humanistic image does not merely concede the authority of the organization, it seeks to legitimate that authority. To the question, "What right does the organization have to rule my life?" adherents of the humanist view respond: "Because it is responsible, caring, humane, and fair, or is potentially so." To understand the full significance of this view, it is helpful to turn to the work of Max Weber, the great theorist of bureaucracy.

According to Weber, authority may be legitimated in any of three ways, alone or in combination: on the basis of tradition, through the appeal of a charismatic leader, or on the basis of a rational-legal framework. Traditional organizations, such as patriarchal or feudal forms of order, justify authority by appealing to the sanctity of tradition usually embodied in bloodlines or divine right. The authority of charismatic organizations derives its legitimacy from the magnetism and will of a single, remarkable individual. (Weber was thinking of someone like Buddha or Christ, but subsequent events in Germany made it appear, falsely, that he was foreseeing and welcoming Hitler.) Rational-legal organizations, in ascendancy when Weber was writing, sought to legitimate authority through standardized rules and the separation of the powers of office from personal power. It was, of course, the rational-legal organization, with which Taylorism meshed so perfectly, that came to dominate the industrial democracies and continues to dominate them today.

To which of these three forms of legitimacy does the humanist image appeal? Obviously, given our democratic culture, the invoking of tradition plays no role. At first glance, then, the humanist view, which values fair treatment and the like, appears merely to imply the familiar rational-legal justification for the authority of the organization. But it was precisely this form of rationalism that attracted the withering scorn of the irrationalist critique that forms the backdrop for recent efforts to humanize the workplace. To think that organization offspring who cling to the humanist image merely want rule-governed organizations is to misread the depth of their longing for something to believe in. And despite the cult of Lee Iacocca and the occasional emergence of someone like Steve Jobs, it is not to charismatic leaders that the humanist view turns for legitimacy.

Where, then, in the current humanistic view of organization does legitimacy lie? It is in charismatic *organizations*, which is to say charismatic artificial persons. The missing link is provided by the initial personification of the organization. The humanist image, personifying and thoroughly psychologizing the organization, implies not a charismatic leader but a charismatic artificial person. Devotion is not to the Führer or the Christ, as the case may be, but to an idealized self that is seen to be distributed throughout the organization (a distribution that the images of democratic culture must perforce render as more or less equal). The organization itself is the charismatic figure.

Again, one need look no further than *In Search of Excellence* for evidence of the growing appeal of the charismatic organization. First published in 1982, it soon became the all-time best-selling book about business. Attacking rational models of corporations, the authors argued, as we noted, that successful big companies are "value-driven" organizations. Interestingly, they see the values of such innovative companies as deriving from a past charismatic leader whose spirit is diffused throughout the companies today: "We are fairly sure," they write, "that the culture of almost every excellent company that seems now to be meeting the needs of 'irrational man' . . . can be traced to transforming leadership somewhere in its history. While the cultures of these companies seem today to be so robust that the need for transforming leadership is not a continuing one, we doubt such cultures ever would have developed as they did without that kind of leadership somewhere in the past." Like so many who talk about corporate "culture," the authors isolate it from material culture and psychologize it, rendering culture merely the personality of a company's founder writ large. Thus, in the slippery medium of this highly idealist notion of culture, the charismatic organization does not so much replace the real charismatic individual as meld with it to produce the charismatic artificial person as the justification for the company's authority.

Needless to say, the ascendancy of the charismatic organization could be a potentially dangerous state of affairs for the society and for the individuals who thus lay themselves open to manipulation. On the other hand, it is possible that charismatic organizations could lay the groundwork for some badly needed institution building. The more important point for our purposes, however, is that the humanist image of organizations, like the egoist image, grows, in part, out of profound dissatisfaction with organizations. And like the egoist image, the humanist image individualizes and psychologizes the organization in an attempt to come to terms with the contemporary forms assumed by the problem of the individual and the group. Often existing side by side in the same person, both views provide imaginary solutions to real contradictions (solutions that, it should be clear by now, are none the less consequential for being imaginary). Together these two views encompass the entire range of this generation's ideology of organizations—its organizationalism.

Note what lies outside that range: any challenge to the ultimate authority of organizations. The question is no longer *whether* such organizations shall dominate our lives, but *how*. (The organization man, it should be said, rarely asked either question.) One may simply concede the authority of organizations and deny their legitimacy, or one may try to legitimate their already manifest authority. But in no case is there any genuine opposition to that authority, no reasonable expectation or hope that organizations will disappear.

Today about 90 percent of the working population in America labors for someone else. Following the Civil War, when the figure was only about 15 percent, many ordinary people were horrified by the wage system emerging with large organizations. The ever-growing legions of formerly self-employed citizens who became employees were routinely called "wage slaves." Only the comparison with slavery, so fresh in American memory then, was adequate to convey the depth of revulsion to such a loss of independence. But as the organizational revolution spread, the pejorative "wage slaves" steadily lost currency; today it is rarely heard.

And yet, as the personified form that organizationalism takes in our time shows, individualism colors everything we do. Independence dies hard. To keep it alive in an age of organization, this generation has evolved its own brand of individualism. Based on cultural experiences and changes in social organization that established the expressive self as the ground of value, this individualism provides a set of solutions related to but distinct from the solutions provided by organizationalism. It is to this individualism that we now turn.

6

Personal Artifice:
From the Self-Made Man
to the Man-Made Self

"I want to realize my creative potential."

Bob Cory's conversation is shot through with references to aesthetics, the arts, and creativity. A manager of business development for Apple, he hopes to combine his love of the arts with his knowledge of computers in a business he is forming with four partners.

"A short-term career goal," he says, "is to get into an area where I'm working directly with people in the creative arts and find some merger, some happy medium with people who are working creatively and using high technology."

Cory and his partners plan to produce laser video disks and develop software and computer graphics for them.

"It's computer animation," he explains, "not the kind of computer graphics you run on a microcomputer, but the computer graphics that were used in the motion picture *Tron*, for example. We'll be moving toward what I hope will be a new consumer product and an art form, which has been referred to as participatory cinema, or you can think of it as interactive software."

Cory envisions a future in which homes are equipped with large, flat-screen televisions connected to laser-disk players and computers capable of running his products. A variety of disks, software, and graphics will allow users to view movies, interact with recreational or educational disks, and create animation and graphics of cinematic quality. The risk is that if consumers in sufficient numbers do not buy the hardware—disk

226

players, computers, and television sets—then there will be no "installed base" to which to sell his company's products. "And that," he concedes, "would kill the company." Nevertheless, to reach his long-term goals, he's willing to take that risk.

One of those goals is to get out of Silicon Valley, where his current job and his entrepreneurial plans will keep him for several years to come. The reasons he and his wife Laura wish to leave, like his plans for his company, come down to matters of aesthetics.

"Silicon Valley has many of the characteristics of a suburban waste-land," he says. "The kinds of things we like to do are not the kinds of things that a lot of people in the Valley like to do. I can tell you some of the things they don't like to do—the performing arts, in particular, as well as the graphic arts. And we enjoy people who are creative in that sense and we enjoy discussing that kind of thing. The interests [of Silicon Valley people] tend to be more—well, to tell you the truth, I'm not really sure. I don't know what people do with their time."

Like many of his contemporaries who grew up in Park Forest, he recalls the suburb as isolated and unstimulating, but he admits, grudgingly, that he first acquired his taste for the arts there.

"Park Forest was very isolated. It was curious, because it was a rather intellectual environment. There were a fair number of Ph.D.s who lived there, certainly well educated; there were Great Books clubs, but a relative lack of culture. It was not common that somebody's parents would be going in to the [Chicago] symphony on a subscription series. They had very little awareness of ballet and theater and opera, for example."

"But it was a very intellectually and academically oriented community. I would say there was a very strong emphasis on literature and, to a lesser extent, on music. Even though they didn't do the symphony kinds of things, when I grew up I had some experience playing an instrument. My sister went to Interlochen Music Camp, so that was a value. It was just being out in the boondocks on the edge of the forest preserve—you were further removed from the major cultural institutions of the day, but many of the fundamental values were there."

His interest in the arts blossomed when he attended Stanford. A semester spent studying in France sealed it. "Now," he says, "a goal of my life is to get back to Paris to live."

Today aesthetic considerations are central to his life. "The value that I get the most pleasure from is the appreciation of aesthetics. It's a significant factor in my relationship with Laura."

It is also a significant factor in the raising of Laura's son from a previous marriage. But the widespread availability of drugs, a preteen subculture dominated by television and popular music, and the transient culture of California make child rearing difficult. Under those circumstances, says Cory, "I think it is very hard to inculcate classical values and classical aesthetics."

By "classical" aesthetics, he appears to mean high culture, as opposed to popular culture of the sort his stepson is exposed to in the family of his biological father, with whom Bob and Laura share custody of the boy.

"I would prefer that kids be exposed to art history and great composers and great literature, not some stupid TV series," Cory says. "It's very troubling to see him being exposed to values that you wouldn't want him exposed to, because the other family is quite different. They watch a lot of TV, and he picks up on that. Laura is very good at handling these kinds of issues. The way to do it is to explain it and talk over why you believe the things you do, including little things. Why it's important that certain shirts go with certain pants and not with others and why it's important to have nice art on the walls and why it's important to spend time in museums looking at things. All of those kinds of things. You try to point out the things you believe in and value and hope that some of it sticks."

It is tempting to dismiss his aestheticism as precious and self-congratulatory. And there is something disingenuous about sniffily dismissing popular culture while planning to market what are, in effect, sophisticated video games. Moreover, there is nothing new about the centrality of the arts to the self-improving culture of the middle class from which he springs or about their usefulness as a badge of rank in the upper middle class he has joined. (In fairness to Cory, it should be said that he also talked eloquently about his devotion to his family, many of whom live nearby.) Nevertheless, beyond these century-old social themes of self-improvement and rank, there is a new theme to be heard. That theme, voiced over and over in our interviews, is the astonishing degree to which the artist, however vaguely conceived, functions as the overriding occupational model for members of the generation, even for those whose work bears little resemblance to artistic endeavor.

For some, like Tom Harrison, who finds himself sucked farther and farther into the corporate world he has always detested, the figure of the artist stands in alluring contrast to the workaday world of work quotas and performance reviews. Though it has been several years since he attempted to write short stories and he now has little realistic expectation of pursuing such a calling, Harrison clings to the hope that he will find a career that embodies at least some of the features of the creative life.

"A lot of it is kind of idealistic," he says, "wanting to do something that helps the community or the world or something where I use myself more fully. A lot of it is kind of an artistic bent. Something that's—I don't know—that uses the creativeness in you."

Tom Harrison is by no means alone. Many of our interviewees, in the face of work they find meaningless and repetitive, cultivate artistic aspirations. A marketing executive in a multinational telecommunications company, weary of writing company puff pieces, takes a screenwriting course, reasoning that she can certainly write scripts that are superior to the ones that actually get produced. Film, an exalted art form for her generation, offers artistic respectability as well as financial payoffs that would allow her independence. She is dismayed, however, when she learns from her teacher, a former screenwriter, how infinitesimal is the possibility that an unsolicited, unagented script by a Hollywood outsider would get bought, much less produced.

A small number, like Julia Harrison, who has managed to eke out a living in modern dance while building her reputation as a choreographer, have actually made the arts their occupation. These lucky few are, in a sense, mirror images of the overwhelming majority of their contemporaries. While her contemporaries worry about being smothered in unfulfilling, uncreative, bureaucratic hackwork in exchange for a modicum of financial security, she worries about the financial security she is sacrificing to fulfill herself creatively—fulfillment that, as real artists like her know, comes only occasionally, if ever.

Some, like Dana Cole, have tried to arrange their lives so they might one day pursue their dreams. Says Cole, who grew up in Park Forest and now lives in California: "I really want to realize my creative potential. And for years I've been really suppressing that, in order to get a base from which to work."

After a period of transcontinental hitchhiking in his late teens and a stab at rock 'n' roll, Cole married, at age twenty-three, a woman eight years his senior who already had two children from a previous marriage. He returned to college, graduated, and soon thereafter plunged into community issues, helping set up voluntary child care service and securing a municipal playground for his neighborhood, largely, he says, for the sense of satisfaction it gave him to make a small civic contribution. "Now," he says, "I've turned inward with that same kind of commitment." In the late seventies, he took a job with the U.S. Forest Service as a forest ranger. He has been at it ever since, using it as a means to build the stable home life he feels he needs.

"Over a couple of years I began to really miss not feeling rooted. I really started working toward that and have been for the past ten years. Now I feel very satisfied with that. So those two priorities I feel comfortable with. My third priority is not my job—that's pretty far down. Not that I dislike my job, but it is more of a convenience. The third priority I have suppressed in pursuit of the other two is what I just call creative work.

"I'd like to be self-employed," he explains. "I would like to be able to work out of my house and do as much of any type of writing as I want to do."

Ideally, he says, he would like to articulate for his generation the experience of the late sixties and early seventies—no small ambition. In the meantime, however, the reality of a family and a full-time job has kept him from his typewriter.

"I really want to allow myself the time," he says. "I have the energy; it's just the talent that is the question. The desire is there; the talent is a question mark, but I just have to find the time to pursue it."

Asked if there might be some relationship between the strength of the desire and the finding of the time to satisfy it, he says vaguely, "I'm working on it, but it's not my number-one time commitment, and that's what I really need to make it eventually. I think I'm making progress; it's just going to take a little while longer."

Other organization offspring, like Randy Myers with his construction business, follow occupations that are connected, if sometimes tenuously, to artisanal traditions. While Randy's career in construction began accidentally, he has stayed in the unstable world of contracting precisely because it affords him a sense of artistry. Like so many of the organization offspring, Randy sees the artist in himself at the very center of what he does for a living.

"There is a part of me in everything I do," Randy explains. "Most of what I do—and what I am most proud of—involves design. It is more than just putting a bunch of wood together and having it work. It is something I designed. It is supposed to have a flow to it, a look to it; it is supposed to be pretty, and it is supposed to be usable."

Randy sees his work as expressing his creativity and as the means through which he might make a difference in the world.

"What I really want to do with my business is to build environments," he says. "To go beyond simply building boxes for people to live in. I want to build homes—environments—to fit people's life-styles. I want to build on a piece of property which will make a family feel like they are in their own sphere of protection."

In some cases, such occupations have turned out to be bitterly disappointing. Carpentry, for example, an "alternative" career once popular with the counterculture, often means uncertain seasonal work putting up drywall in the kinds of subdivisions one was trying to escape.

Many more of the organization offspring have tried to introduce creativity in the broadest sense into their jobs in organizations.

To some degree, of course, endless nattering about creativity is merely conventional, a reflex acknowledgment of a cultural value so pervasive as to be a cliché. Moreover, the notion of creativity is so broad as to encompass at one end of the spectrum the romantic, embattled artist and, at the other end, almost any kind of technological innovation or, indeed, almost any activity that is not done by rote. It is tempting, therefore, to dismiss creativity as an empty notion and these would-be artists as a generation of Walter Mittys. But their persistent emphasis on the creative and the artistic holds the key to their peculiar brand of individualism and their emerging social character. It is what unites the dropout dreaming in the garret of literary glory with the MBA "innovating" in the corporation. To understand who these people are, it is crucial to understand how this artistic myth functions for them, as well as why and how it arose when it did.

In part, the idea of creativity represents to them a means of adjusting their highest value—the private expressive self—to the demands of the public realm of work. Thus, creativity points in two directions at once. On the one hand, it is the mechanism for integration with the group through work; on the other hand, it is firmly rooted in the expressive self. Just as their organizationalism is inseparable from individualism, though not identical with it, their individualism is inseparable from considerations of collective life.

Says Randy Myers: "I don't think the kind of satisfaction I want and need—that I *really* need from my job—I could get from working for thirty years in a bank. What my dad wanted was achievement—pure achievement. He wanted to be held in high esteem by his colleagues. Of course, that is important to me, too. I want to be known around town as a good builder, but there is a real difference. There was a lack of personal creativity in his job. What he was doing may have been *his* image of creativity—not everybody paints or sculpts—but my father's satisfaction came from the programs he initiated."

The implication, of course, is that Randy's image of creativity, unlike his father's, is taken from the genuine artist and that what Randy does properly belongs in the realm of painting and sculpting. Thus, he hopes simultaneously to express himself and to win public esteem, to harmonize the private value of self-expression with the public world of work.

But that is only the beginning of the significance of creativity for this generation. Whether they are artists or merely dream about being artists; whether they set out as entrepreneurs or merely like to regard otherwise mundane jobs as somehow creative; whether they innovate in an organization, sublimate as teachers, or seek employment in "creative" professions like advertising, public relations, or the mass media, the organization offspring employ a myth of personal artistry to make sense of their lives in the widest senses. This myth harmonizes their values with their material reality, their lofty aspirations with their actual achievements, their individualism with their group life. It underpins their styles of consumption, their styles of personal relations, and their orientation to civic involvement. For many it functions as a democratic version of the religion of art propounded by the high modernists of the early twentieth century. Above all, it seeks to make sense of the two overriding imperatives of American individualism—happiness and success.

Finally, the myth of personal artistry leads us to the heart of the organization offspring's conception of the expressive self, where it confronts us with a paradox, raises an interesting historical question, and points to a problematical future for those who cling to it. That conception, rarely articulated, goes like this: In its inmost nature, the self is expressive; that is what it *is*. Its characteristic activity is creation; that is what it *does*. Its most typical creation is art, though it may be something else; those are its *results*. The paradox is this: Creativity may be exercised on the self, so that the self becomes one of its own creations, one of its own results. It is this paradox that is elided in cant terms like *self-actualization*, *fulfilling one's potential*, and *personal growth*. The self that emerges from this picture is one that appears to be simultaneously full and empty, richly originary and incompletely formed, unshakably authentic and infinitely malleable. And the creativity to which it is said to give rise ultimately must be understood in terms of this self, rather than in genuinely aesthetic terms. (That is why this particular social character is a chapter in the history of American individualism, rather than of American art. It also accounts for the appalling ignorance of the very arts that many of these would-be artists say they want to pursue.) The historical question it raises is simply, How did we get from the self-made man of the nineteenth century to this man-made self of today? And the problematic future to which it points is one in which such a notion of the self and such a myth of personal artistry will become increasingly difficult to sustain.

From character to personality to self. . . .

Since the 1830s, when Tocqueville first explored the subject, American social character could be said to have evolved from the self-made man of the nineteenth century to the organization man of the first three-quarters of the twentieth century to the man-made self of today. For the self-made man, the emphasis fell on *character*; for the organization man, it fell on *personality*; for the organization offspring, it falls on the *self*. Each distinctive type developed under the pressure of specific historical circumstances, especially changes in the social and occupational structure. For example, for the organization man, whose occupation put a premium on skills in personal relations, communication, and persuasion, it was more important to have a pleasing personality than to have the firm character of the nineteenth century's self-made man.

Each of these social types also embodies distinctive aspects of American ideology that still operate, often confusingly, in our contemporary understanding of individualism. In part, *self-made man* refers to an ideal of success in which an individual (almost always envisaged as a man), enjoying no privileges of inherited wealth or hereditary rank, rises from modest circumstances to prosperity and, sometimes, to unimaginable wealth, all through his own efforts. This is the familiar Horatio Alger story, though it is forgotten that Alger's heroes usually achieved their enviable position in the world through some marvelous piece of luck or marriage to the boss's daughter. The Horatio Alger myth also overlooks class, gender, and racial privilege and was largely untrue even in its own time. Only about 5 percent of the top corporation executives in the first decade of this century started out poor. For every Andrew Carnegie who rose from office boy to fabulous wealth, there were thousands of others who acquired their economic position the old-fashioned way—they were born into it. Many others took another traditional route to success that was open to the middle class—higher education. Nevertheless, within those not-inconsiderable advantages of white middle- and upper-middle-class origin, many nineteenth-century entrepreneurs and twentieth-century organization men made what to them seemed like a long and unassisted climb from modest, often rural, childhoods to the upper reaches of America's most powerful concerns. Thus, Dave Harrison, son of a carpenter-farmer and lacking a college education, can claim with some justification to be a self-made man.

But in the nineteenth century the idea of the self-made man meant far more than the lack of hereditary social status. More important, it pointed behind hard-won rewards to the firmly implanted qualities of character that were said to lead to such happy results: hard work, perseverance, sacrifice, frugality, self-denial, and honesty. In this more important sense of self-making, all these sterling qualities of character were seen to coalesce into a unitary individual. Such stable, productive, and self-denying individuals were necessary to confront—and exploit—the bewildering range of choices, opportunities, and changes presented by nineteenth-century America: a rapidly industrializing economy, a seemingly limitless physical setting, and an ever-more-egalitarian polity. Such a unitary character was required to concentrate capital, save for the future, seize opportunities, and undertake all the mammoth tasks that nation building required. And, less grandly, such a unitary, unswerving character was deemed more likely to navigate successfully the moral dangers thrown up by teeming urban life, individual economic competition, and slippery commercial values.

Though these productive and ascetic qualities of character were evoked and rewarded by the social structure, they were first implanted in childhood by parents. Indeed, it would almost be more accurate to call the self-made man the *parent*-made man. It was chiefly this internalization of parental authority that went into the making of character, which was to consist of general principles that could be applied to the nineteenth-century world of increased mobility, opportunity, and dynamism. In David Riesman's much-misunderstood phrase, it was this "inner direction" that guided people who were confronted with a bewildering and constantly changing choice of actions and opportunities. Numerous readers of *The Lonely Crowd* took the authors to be saying that the inner-directed character type was superior to the other-directed, conformist character type of midcentury America. Such misreadings took the inner-directed type to be the self-reliant, nonconformist individualist of American mythology. But the authors intended no such thing. In fact, the inner-directed type relied not on his own independent judgments, but on the severe strictures inculcated by his parents and the other adult authority figures of his youth. The result was a rigid, morally strenuous, often censorious character, albeit one who was capable of adapting those internalized principles to fluid social conditions.

In the beginning the occupational type that best embodied the character ethic of the self-made man was the yeoman farmer of Jacksonian democracy and later the banker and the tradesman. But as a largely agricultural society began to give way to industrialization, the entrepreneur came to dominate typologies of the self-made man. Indeed, as Weber observed, the accumulation of large amounts of capital to execute vast industrial projects became for many a paradigm of the visible operation of productive qualities of character. And in this secularized version of Calvinist election, worldly success counted as proof that one did possess such character.

The efficacy of the character ethic in exploiting seemingly limitless industrial opportunities eventually brought into being a social and occupational structure—the world of large organizations—to which the character ethic soon began to lose relevance. The new world of managers and administrators who presided over legions of wage earners required a different orientation and rewarded a different set of personal characteristics. The work of the new managerial class was increasingly abstract; it focused more on processes than on products, and it was set in a world of interdependence, rather than of unobstructed opportunity. These new managers were required to be adept at building consensus, manipulating people, and communicating with co-workers. To maintain the high levels of consumption necessary for expanding production, many managers had to master techniques of persuasion—advertising, sales promotion, public relations, and corporate communications. Increasingly, the manager's medium was people, not material.

The new order put a far greater premium on personality, eventually eclipsing considerations of character. However, vestiges of the character ethic did survive in many of these organization men; they still had to work hard, after all. But in a world of vast collectivities like corporations and suburbs, success required the ceaseless sending and receiving of social signals and depended on relations with other people, on what Erving Goffman called "impression management." The internalized authority of one's parents offered no guidance. Instead, one took one's cues from contemporaries or from the mass media, a mode of conformity Riesman called "other direction."

The occupational type in which the personality ethic reached its highest pitch was the salesman, sometimes derisively characterized in social criticism as the glad-hander, the fixer, and the huckster. The idea was to win friends and influence people. "Personality always wins the day," said Willy Loman, the most poignant representation of the type. But beyond the caricature, as Whyte argued, lay a real moral imperative for the organization man—a genuine belief that fulfillment lay in belongingness and cooperative effort.

Like the self-made man before him, the organization man as the dominant middle-class social character was doomed by his very effectiveness. Constantly increasing production required constantly increasing consumption. At some indeterminate point in our history—perhaps as early as the rise of national newspaper advertising for the first standardized department stores of the nineteenth century or as late as Henry Ford's five-dollar day—we began to change from a culture that emphasized the production side of capitalism to one that emphasized the consumption side. Thus was introduced what has been called the cultural contradiction of capitalism. As a producer, one is obliged to work hard, save for the future, and practice sobriety. As a consumer, one is obliged to play hard, spend today, and practice hedonism.

For the organization man, the personality ethic held the contradiction at bay. It was through personality—communication, persuasion, and "interpersonal" skills—that he succeeded at work, and it was through personality—symbolic consumption, the hail-fellow-well-met style of socializing, and nonauthoritarian child rearing—that he realized his life in the suburbs and in the family. Thus, he successfully assimilated the production themes of the character ethic to the consumption themes of the personality ethic. So successful was he in this assimilation that the themes of production would be invisible to his offspring and all but disappear in them, freeing the themes of consumption to be assimilated to their ethic of the self.

Isolated in suburbs and cut off from their fathers' already highly abstract work, the organization offspring had no contact with the productive qualities of character that had persisted in only attenuated form in their fathers anyway. Reared in the purely expressive arena of the family, educated in schools that emphasized self-expression, and exhorted to self-gratification by the media, they also encountered few contexts that required the skills and outlook of the personality ethic, no matter how much their parents bombarded them with truisms about the importance of getting along with others. Moreover, consumption was not tied in any way to production, as it had been for their fathers, which accounts for the often-remarked overweening sense of entitlement that many members of the younger generation exhibit. Their entry into the work force, delayed by ever-lengthening higher education, did nothing to make the connection clearer to them. When they did enter the work force, they found highly unstable organizations and institutions that only further severed the connection between work and any shared social purposes, a connection that had been prominent in the character ethic and paramount in the personality ethic. The organization offspring saw work as another arena for self-expression or as providing the financial means to pursue self-expression in private life. Thus, they completed the long transition from productivity to creativity, a transition the middle term of which was the sociability of the organization man.

The evolution in American social character from *character* to *personality* to *self* may be seen most readily in the literature on self-help and success. In much success literature of the nineteenth century one of the keys to success lay in having a good mother. It was the mother, as the guardian of moral life, who was to instruct and shape her children, to form in them a firm character for a lifetime. In the success literature of the personality ethic, the chief domestic requirement was a good wife. A man's success (and it was always men to whom such books were addressed) was no longer seen to depend on values descended from his parents, but on his behavior in the present, including the behavior of a wife who was adept at sending and receiving the right social signals; consuming correctly; and, in general, being the good corporate helpmate. In the recent success literature, however, the chief agent of assistance and guidance is oneself—you must learn "how to look out for number one" or, less viciously, "how to be your own best friend." Not only does this recent literature indicate a shift in the source of moral authority, but in its neutral application to men and women, it also indicates a shift away from the gender divisions of the character and personality ethics.

These evolutionary changes in American social character are often seen against the background of an overarching American individualism. (Indeed, some observers assert that individualism *is* American social character and that the changes described here are mere surface ripples on this much deeper, largely unchanged phenomenon.) Many people see the shift from the self-made man to the organization man as a disaster *for* individualism. The shift to the man-made self is seen as a disaster *of* individualism. Behind such laments there often lurks a nostalgia for the presumed sturdy individualist of the nineteenth century—independent and self-reliant, yet capable of building a nation. And behind the nostalgia there often lurks a great deal of confusion about the meaning and significance of *individualism* and its cognates.

Raymond Williams makes a useful semantic and historical distinction between *individualism* and *individuality*. Individualism, understood as a political and economic system that assumes the primacy and equality of each individual citizen's interests, emerged in the nineteenth century around the time Tocqueville was writing. Individuality, in the sense of qualitative personal uniqueness, is a much older concept, with roots in Renaissance humanism, the Protestant Reformation, and the Romantic movement.

In America *individualism*, in its political and economic senses, became a catchword for the celebration of natural rights, liberal democracy, and free enterprise. Unlike those who believed that the social contract entailed an exchange of natural rights for civil rights, Americans believed that they carried their natural rights intact into society, which was merely the spontaneous harmony of individuals, rather than a structure to which they submitted. Thus, individualism in this sense is by no means incompatible with conformity, as Tocqueville foresaw and the organization man confirmed. This uniquely American version of individualism refers neither to the sources of social dissolution nor to the cultivation of personal uniqueness, but, as Stephen Lukes put it, "to the actual or imminent realization of the final stage of human progress in a spontaneously cohesive society of equal individual rights, limited government, *laissez-faire*, natural justice and equal opportunity, and individual freedom, moral development and dignity."

Individuality, on the other hand, stresses individual self-development. In part, it grows out of the Reformation view that each believer has primary responsibility to work out his or her own spiritual destiny. In this universal priesthood of all believers, understanding was to come through the "inner light," rather than through the mediation of theology or priests. For the Romantics, self-development came to mean a cult of genius and originality of which the artist was the supreme exemplar. Stressing the values of solitude and subjectivity, romanticism portrayed the individual genius in conflict with society, cultivating his or her special talents and sensibility in defiance of convention. (The creative individual was also crucial to the ethical basis of Marx's thought, but his left-wing communitarian development of individuality had as little impact in America as individuality's right-wing communitarian development, fascism.) In our own time and place, self-development can mean hostility to society or it can mean the essentially asocial ideal of the individual pursuing his or her own independent path, the "road less traveled," a view that finds expression, for example, in the human potential movement.

Both *individualism* and *individuality* in their various senses are still very much with us today, and as a result we often talk at confusing cross-purposes. Classical economic and political individualism has become overlaid with romantic and psychological notions of individuality, so that when we look back at nineteenth-century individualism, we not only pine for its productive qualities but project onto it qualities of nonconformity and self-fulfillment with which it had little to do. Conversely, the rhetoric of individual self-fulfillment is often used to justify the most cutthroat forms of contemporary economic individualism.

The confusion of individualism with individuality also animates what we have called this generation's organizationalism. Its egoist pole depends on individualism in its economic and political senses, the context that provides the crucial metaphor of the artificial person. The humanist pole depends on individuality, the sense that invests the metaphor with a psychological dimension it wholly lacks in its original context. But this is not *merely* confusion, but an attempt to resolve felt contradictions of legitimacy and authority.

Similarly, this generation's individualism appears to be an often-confusing mixture of classical individualism with romantic individuality. But this mixture is not *merely* confusion, either. In fact, it is probably more accurate to say that individuality, understood as the expressive self, is the distinctive form of this generation's individualism. To put it another way, under the pressure of changing social and occupational structures, the evolution of American social character from the character ethic to the personality ethic to the self ethic accounts for the gradual shift in the meaning of individualism toward individuality. Though the contemporary notion of individualism still retains some of its political and economic connotations, for the organization offspring the idea is dominated by considerations of individuality. And it is within these highly psychologized considerations of individuality that the offspring have attempted to work out the dilemmas of individual and collective life that previously were assumed to have been solved by political and economic notions of individualism.

"We . . . need to live to the greatest potential of our lives."

It is no exaggeration to say that the organization offspring worship the self. Without a trace of irony, one young manager explained his rejection of Christian orthodoxy this way: "Christianity deals so much with who Christ is instead of who *you* are." Not for this generation is the selfless *imitatio Christi*. For them the watchwords have been self-development, self-fulfillment, and self-actualization. Daniel Yankelovich estimates that as many as 80 percent of Americans have, at one time or another, been actively engaged in the search for self-fulfillment. He found that 17 percent of all working Americans, or about 17 million people, place their personal self-fulfillment above all other concerns. Moreover, the majority of these "strong formers," as he calls them, are college-educated baby boomers who are either professionals or hold white-collar jobs, a profile that takes in most of the organization offspring.

The most conspicuous manifestations of the widespread search for self-fulfillment have been many: the appearance of cults; the growth of psychotherapy; the flood of psychological self-help literature; widespread interest in Eastern religions; the national obsessions with diet and exercise; and, most recently, the rise of the all-purpose codependency movement. To assist in the search, there have appeared innumerable therapists, prophets, messiahs, and plain old-fashioned charlatans offering a motley array of technologies of the self: transcendental meditation, *est*, transactional analysis, encounter groups, sensitivity training, bioenergetics, biofeedback, Rolfing, Lifespring, Arica, and on and on. None lacked eager customers. One researcher found that as of 1980 one in nine college-educated young adults in the San Francisco Bay Area, where *est* was based, had been through the training. But, as Yankelovich observes, the search for self-fulfillment has been far broader and deeper than have such highly visible and often foolish fads. The arena in which the average seekers of self-fulfillment struggled, Yankelovich wrote, was that of everyday life where their millions of life experiments engaged "the 'giving/getting compact'—the unwritten rules governing what we give in marriage, work, community and sacrifice for others, and what we expect in return."

As we have detailed, the way for this self ethic was paved by rising levels of education and affluence; by geographic and social mobility; by the economic shift from an emphasis on production to an emphasis on consumption; by a rigidly age-segregated society; by a changing occupational structure; by the fragmentation of institutional bases; and by the premium put on expressiveness by the schools, the family, and the mass media. All these things tell us much about the conditions that encourage the cultivation of the self. But they tell us little about the substantive content of the self ethic. How do worshipers of the self justify their faith? How do they conceive the object of their veneration, and how in practical terms is its fulfillment pursued?

The idea of the self as the highest reality has a long and complicated intellectual history that embraces thinkers as diverse as Rousseau, Nietzsche, Thoreau, and Emerson. It also takes in post-Freudians as different in social outlook as the psychologists Erich Fromm, Abraham Maslow, and Carl Rogers and their numerous epigones and popularizers to whom the contemporary popular conception of the self owes its greatest debt. That popular conception, rarely articulated by the organization offspring, nevertheless operates as a set of unspoken assumptions behind many of their attitudes and much of their behavior. For a clear and fairly representative statement of those assumptions, one need look no further than the work of Maslow. Among nine such assumptions that Maslow lists in the opening pages of *Toward a Psychology of Being,* three stand out: (1) each person possesses an essential and partly unique inner nature; (2) this inner nature is either morally neutral or positively good; (3) since this inner nature is either neutral or good, it is best to encourage it, rather than to suppress it. Though partly unique and partly "species wide," this authentic self is nevertheless conceived as ahistorical and acultural—a secular version of the soul, a timeless transcendent spirit neither shaped by culture nor formed by experience.

Maslow claims that if these assumptions about the self are true, they "promise a scientific ethics, a natural value system. . . . This amounts to automatic solution of the personality problems of the future. The thing to do seems to be to find out what one is *really* like inside, deep down, as a member of the human species and as a particular individual." In this view, cultivation of the self becomes one's moral *duty*, whereas in most of the great religious and ethical systems of former times, it was assumed that moral duty usually meant suppressing the self. But for Maslow, the model person is "the fully growing and self-fulfilling human being . . . the one whose inner nature expresses itself freely, rather than being warped, suppressed, or denied."

In speaking of this duty to the authentic self, which must in no way be denied, our interviewees often resorted to a rhetoric of *needs*. Ranging in tone from anxious to thoughtful to smug, this rhetoric sometimes implied the careful monitoring of interior states to identify genuine needs, sometimes the wrestling with moral dilemmas (within the narrowly circumscribed compass of the self), and sometimes merely the casual satisfying of whims.

One young woman, who in the course of an interview fell into a heated disagreement with her husband over the subject of divorce, is typical. Her husband, who did not grow up in an organization family as she had, said that people acquire and discard spouses much too lightly, like "changing toothpaste." She, on the other hand, sees divorce as an almost inevitable by-product of one's changing needs.

"I think people change," she said. "And I don't think you can ever predict how they're going to change and how you're going to change. And I don't think that means making light commitments or getting out of something lightly. But I also feel that we all need to live to the greatest potential of our lives.

"There *is* this authentic thing in us," she insisted. "But it is obscured by the forces that are shaping our lives daily as far as our age, how much we've experienced, what we know about, how it's shaping our perception of the world. And I feel that we fall in love with people for a lot of different reasons and at various times in our lives those reasons change and what we need or what our perception of our needs are also change. I think it's very hard to get to where we see clearly who our real authentic self is and stay with it."

To listeners who do not share this point of view, such people sound maddeningly self-centered. However, they see themselves as speaking from a deeply moral perspective. The young manager who rejects Christianity because it "doesn't deal with who *you* are" feels neither embarrassment nor any need to elaborate; he speaks comfortably from a position he regards as obviously ethical. Just as Whyte discerned a genuine moral imperative behind the social ethic of the organization man, it is possible to discern a genuine, if questionable, moral imperative here. To be healthy, to be "fully functioning" (in Carl Rogers's unfortunate machine metaphor), is to be someone who is able to love others because one loves oneself, to contribute more to the world by being the best one can be, and to transcend all the petty encumbrances of culture and history that oppress us all. Though each person pursues his or her self-fulfillment largely in private and alone, the aggregate result will be better people and hence a better collective life, a sane society instead of a sick one. To fail to fulfill one's self is to fail morally, to court the evils of guilt and conformity. In short, it is to deny one's individuality, and to deny one's individuality reduces the world's store of goodness by just that much. In effect, this argument for self-fulfillment constitutes a highly psychologized version of the old justification for political and economic individualism: Enlightened self-interest leads naturally to the greater social good.

But at the heart of this conception of the authentic self and its fulfillment lies a paradox. On the one hand, the authentic self is simply *uncovered*; on the other hand, it must be *expressed*. But the only possible realms in which it can come to expression are those of culture, history, and the particular circumstances of one's life—all the things that the self in its essential nature is said to be beyond, though it is still uniquely one's own. One might say that this authentic self is somehow unique without being specific. Looked at this way, the authentic self ultimately is without content, or at least none that could possibly be made manifest in the hopelessly compromised media of language and culture in which that self must find expression. The self that emerges from this picture is one that appears to be simultaneously full and empty, richly originary and incompletely formed. It is to be both excavated *and* created; it is authentic *and* invented; it is entirely self-sufficient *and* in need of constant nurture.

The solution to these contradictions is sought in the mysterious agency of creativity, that activity of the self that wells up from one's deepest being and yet creates something new. For Carl Rogers, it is creativity that functions as the opposite of conformity. His essay "Toward a Theory of Creativity" opens with a description of the regimented, stereotypical conformist against whom he counterposes the creative individual: "As a people we enjoy conformity rather than creativity," he writes. "To be original, or different, is felt to be 'dangerous.' " Thus Rogers, in the manner of Romantics everywhere, makes creativity synonymous with individuality (a move so familiar we rarely question it). Through creativity, you realize your authentic self *and* bring that self to expression.

It is immediately obvious that this is in fact no solution to the paradox of authentic self-expression at all, but merely the paradox in a slightly different guise. The paradox reappears in Rogers's circular claim that the mainspring of creativity is *"man's tendency to actualize himself, to become his potentialities."* We are still left with an essentially empty authentic self, though one that at least enjoys the possibility of being expressed. Thus, it is expression itself that comes to occupy—to fill up—the ultimately vacuous notion of the authentic self. The efficacy of creativity in this system lies not in any real agency that it possesses, but in a kind of elision or confusion: Creativity can be seen simultaneously to express the authentic self *and* to create it because expressiveness—creativity—is, by default, the authentic self's chief attribute.

As a practical matter, this creation-expression of the authentic self takes place in the everyday realm of choice, of making decisions about work, love, leisure, and consumption. And because it operates in this realm of action, choice occupies a central position in the value system of the self ethic. "You are the sum total of your choices," asserts one particularly popular self-help book. To choose is to express the self. And since expressing the self is a moral obligation and expressiveness is the essence of the authentic self, the very *act* of choosing is, in itself, moral, *regardless of what is chosen.* This value system is indeed—in Maslow's unintentionally revealing word—"automatic."

That the value system of many members of the generation has become automatic was vividly illustrated in an interview with an intelligent, young financial analyst. She talked easily about the various decisions she had made about her life: She was living happily with a man in the same business but had decided to defer marriage; she had decided to forgo childbearing because it would interfere with her beloved ski trips to Tahoe; she had decided not to pursue the corporate brass ring, so she could do consulting that would give her control of her time; and so on. Of all these things she spoke confidently. Asked, however, to place these decisions in some larger framework of values, she was stumped. At length, she laughed nervously and muttered: "Why have I never thought about these things?"

It was a pattern we encountered repeatedly: otherwise articulate people rendered speechless. Even allowing for the understandable consternation that blunt questions about values can cause, the confusion into which scores of interviewees like her were thrown contrasted markedly with their fluency about the decisions themselves. An unsympathetic observer simply sees amoral selfishness at work (especially faced with answers that calculate having children versus going skiing), but that is to miss the real point. The financial analyst had never thought about such things not because she lacked values, but because in choosing she was already enacting her highest value—choice itself—regardless of what was chosen, children or trips to Tahoe.

But what about the substantive contents of choices? Are they not what counts in assessing morality? Not really, because the only thing against which the substantive contents of the choices may be measured is the self, whose essence is expressiveness anyway; to measure them against anything else is to take the unlikely step of submitting them to some standard outside the authentic self. One can only, in circular fashion, anxiously scrutinize one's choices for their qualities of "expressiveness" and "authenticity," the feeling-tones that should accompany them. Thus, like the authentic self it is to express and like the creativity that is its agency, choice is both full and empty, deeply rooted and utterly baseless. On the one hand, one chooses out of the integrity of one's deepest being; on the other hand, one merely leaps in the dark, making a novel "commitment" that has no other ground than that one has made it. The financial analyst, talking of her reluctance to get married, stumbled instructively over the contradiction when she used "commitment" in two distinct senses: "I think both of us are real scared of that commitment; and yet I don't think there's any question that we have a commitment to one another."

It is tempting to see, as many commentators have, in this round of self-creativity-choice, a familiar moral relativism and perhaps even a casual, unreflective nihilism. But nihilist it is not, for it certainly champions choice and creativity as values in themselves, purely formal though they appear to be. It may not even be relativism, for the value of self-expression is seen by many of its proponents to be grounded in the "science" of psychology. Thus, far from being a kind of Nietzschean ethical individualism, this value system is regarded as a naturalistic ethics, based on demonstrable, if soft, scientific evidence. To put it another way, for the organization offspring, the claim that subjectivity is the highest reality is not a subjective judgment.

Nor should this self ethic be confused with existentialism, whose language of authenticity it borrows and whose dynamic of self-creation it appears to imitate. Unlike, say, the early Sartre, these organization offspring do not believe that existence precedes essence. Rather, they believe that essence—one's *essential* unique, authentic self—precedes the existential acts of choice that express the self. But because that essence turns out by default to be expressiveness itself, choice appears to be exercised in a vacuum of pure freedom, where the self must be newly created at every moment. To leave it at that, however, is to ignore the real hold the notion of a substantial authentic self has on these people, and their inextinguishable belief that they must "get in touch with it." Thus, moral deliberation for them appears to be far less like the existentialist's vertiginous suspension over the abyss than it does the ethical intuitionist's rapt listening to the dictates of an inner voice.

In fact, what this value system most resembles is homegrown American pragmatism, though of a distinctly new variety. Whereas the pragmatism of William James was a theory of truth based on the consequences of a belief—the idea's "cash value," as he put it—this new pragmatism is concerned not with beliefs (ideas, hypotheses, knowledge claims) and their consequences, but with feelings and their genuineness. For James, the truth of a belief in God or in a scientific or metaphysical theory or a course of ethical action was to be judged by the consequences of holding that belief. For example, according to James, if acting on a belief in God makes the world a better place, this consequence constitutes precisely the kind of evidence that validates the belief. Moreover, such validation takes place in a public realm, observable by all; truth is debatable, rather than merely subjective, and over time collective agreement about particular pragmatic truths is not only possible, but probable.

For self-fulfillers, however, the truth resides not in public consequences, but in private feelings. Confronted with a choice, self-fulfillers ask themselves how they *really* feel. Will the choice I make express my authentic self? But since my authentic self, to a large degree, *is* expressiveness, merely choosing validates my choice, at least to some extent. My belief in God is probably true because it was chosen. But, again, this is not quite the whole story. The qualifier "probably" suggests that I still sense the existence of some authentic self that remains elusive. I can be wrong about my true feelings; perhaps, deep down, submission to a supreme being is not really me. Nevertheless, for validation I am, for the most part, thrown back on the expressiveness inherent in choosing. This is, of course, an even more extreme, and not-at-all public, version of the self-validating nature of beliefs envisioned in Jamesian pragmatism.

To see how these two different versions of pragmatism play out in everyday life, compare the positive thinking so characteristic of the organization man's personality ethic with the authenticity of the organization offspring's self ethic. Positive thinking (called New Thought in James's day and sympathetically treated by him in *The Varieties of Religious Experience*) is an acting "as-if," in hopes that the reality will follow. If I tell myself I am successful (or friendly, or attractive, or whatever) and I act that way, then in time I may become that way. Acting on the belief leads to consequences that validate it. But self-fulfillers do not will a belief; they scan the inner horizon for a "true" feeling, not in hopes that the reality will follow, but that it is already there. I act friendly because I am genuinely friendly. And by virtue of the expressiveness inherent in *choosing* friendliness, I probably *am* friendly. It is the acting on the feeling that validates it, not the consequences of so acting. The positive thinker willfully engages in self-deception. The self-fulfiller affects to fear such delusions.

But even if the self ethic is a version of pragmatism rather than of nihilism, relativism, or existentialism, we still appear to be left with a thoroughly psychologized system of values, with the triumph of the therapeutic, and the narcissistic personality of our time. At the very least, the emergence of the self ethic supports the contention that we live in a psychological society, composed of atomized and isolated citizens, each pursuing his or her own individual journey of self-fulfillment and self-expression in private. But, as we have suggested, the high value this generation places on creativity—now expected to inform every area of experience—provides the key not only to their individualism but to the conception of collective life their individualism entails. For creativity is double-edged. It points inward to the expressive self and outward to the world of choice, action, and commitment, to the world where people (no matter how atomized they are imagined to be by distraught social critics) must necessarily live with one another.

The ubiquity of the artist as occupational ideal takes us a step further. A consequence of the veneration of creativity, the artist ideal embodies the expressive self's concessions to the realities of the world of work, concessions that may range from grudging to enthusiastic. It suggests a desire to adjust the inward realm of the expressive self with the demands of the public realm of work, creativity with productivity, the authentic self with the social role. Thus the artist ideal leads out of the private expressive world and into the larger world of work, where the issue of making a living has always been fraught with highly symbolic meanings, and there it engages the age-old American themes of success and happiness.

"It is not enough to succeed . . ."

Whether one is dressing for it, achieving it in business without really trying, or finding that nothing succeeds like it, success remains the dominant value of American culture. Since the Puritans tried, and failed, to establish their "shining city upon a hill" in the uncorrupted New World, Americans have agonized about the meaning of success and failure both for the nation and for the individuals who make it up. And we have produced, from the time of Benjamin Franklin's *Poor Richard's*

Almanac forward, an enormous number of manuals, books, and courses of study that purport to impart its secrets.

But what is success? As Richard Huber has reminded us, success is not synonymous with happiness. Happiness is how you feel, which is an internal matter; success is what you have *achieved*, which in America has always been a public, external matter. One may privately account oneself a success as a spouse, a parent, a friend, a faithful religious communicant, or a serene contemplative, but success in cultural terms has always been brutally objective and impersonal: one's rank in relation to others as represented by "the unequal distribution of money, power, prestige, and fame." As Gore Vidal acidly put it: "It is not enough to succeed. Others must fail."

Money alone is not success; cash must be converted to status. An improved economic position must be translated into an improved social position. High status may just as easily accrue to individuals who earn relatively little money. Whether one wins status through the business world, the nonprofit world, the arts, or government, the emphasis is on achievement.

That this should be so in a democratic culture is hardly surprising. In countries with rigid class systems and hereditary aristocracies, where status is said to be *ascribed*, the circumstances of one's birth determine one's status for life. In a democratic culture, with its less rigid class structure and its absence of a hereditary aristocracy, one's birth does not determine how high one may rise nor how far one may fall on the social scale—status is said to be *achieved*. In reality, the situation is somewhat more complicated. Class lines, not to mention racial lines, in America are less flexible than some apologists admit. Many people are guaranteed at birth a lifetime of ease; many more are consigned at birth to a lifetime of failure. And the advantages in educational, occupational, and social opportunity that middle-class origin confers over working-class origin have been well documented. Nevertheless, within the many social strata that run from the lower middle class to the upper middle class, there remains a great deal of status mobility. More important, Americans *believe* such mobility exists, and they act accordingly.

The price middle-class people pay for this status mobility is a pervasive anxiety, either about moving downward or, less frequently, about rising so high as to find themselves out of their depth socially. This anxiety is why status striving seems such a glum, even desperate, affair. In a society where status is ascribed, you at least know where you stand once and for all. In a society where status is achieved, you must worry constantly about your standing in a competitive situation that changes constantly but never concludes.

Status anxiety reproduces, at the level of individual psychology, the tensions of freedom versus equality that are at the heart of democracy. We fervently believe in the freedom to "better ourselves," and we just as fervently believe that no one is any better than anyone else. In the political arena the conflict of freedom versus equality plays out between the poles of libertarian and egalitarian social policy. In individuals it plays out as ambivalence—about our status and that of others—often producing social attitudes of comic perversity. We cling tenaciously to our own hard-won status, whatever it may be and however it may change, while regarding those of lesser status as mindless conformists and those of higher status as pretentious strivers. The former are seen as a travesty of equality, the latter as a travesty of freedom.

One way to allay status anxiety is to declare the whole system bogus, drop out, cultivate different values, and try to achieve some definition of "true" success. Another way is to overthrow the system. A few sainted and not a few demented individuals have tried both, but most Americans continue to realize their values within the larger framework of a capitalist, middle-class, democratic culture pervaded by an anxiety-inducing striving for success. Psychotherapy battens on this situation by offering models of mental health—"growth" and "change" are good; "rigidity" bad—that formally mimic the fluid structure of the economic and social systems.

Part of the anxiety arises from the difficulty of measuring success. If money were all that mattered, the depth gauge from Scrooge McDuck's money bin would do the job nicely. But, as we have noted, success can take many forms: fame, critical acclaim, a reputation for good works, occupational prestige, political power, and even money if rightly spent. Moreover, in democratic culture, measures of success are necessarily relative—to one's peers, to one's aspirations, to where one started out. As we noted in Chapter 3, Americans have typically measured their success against that of their fathers. It is still a relative measurement, but one that is ready at hand for most people and fairly easy to calculate, if not in strict monetary terms, certainly in status terms. But for the organization offspring, most of whom are adept at status striving, rising above one's father is not as easy as it was for previous generations. In addition, the high value the larger culture places on the largely external matters of success, status, and intergenerational mobility sooner or later comes in conflict with the supreme value the organization offspring place on the largely internal matter of the expressive self and its fulfillment. Success collides with happiness. To soften the impact, the organization offspring rely on the artist ideal, a myth whose utility and versatility can be most clearly seen in its application to the three traditional indexes of prestige: occupation, education, and income.

In a culture where making a living is freighted with so much significance, everyone dramatizes his or her occupation. Not surprisingly, we tend to frame what we do, whatever we do, in ways that heighten its significance. We may see our work as difficult or dangerous, as exciting, as uniquely valuable, or perhaps as patriotic, depending, in part, on the nature of the job, but largely depending on our underlying values, as, for example, the expressive self.

Since the romantic period, artists have been particularly adept at dramatizing the nature of their labor in terms of an individuality of self-expression. They struggle heroically, often in splendid isolation, to wrest difficult truths from their souls. Poets, wrote Shelley, "learn in suffering what they teach in song." They feel more deeply, suffer more intensely, and rejoice more fully than do ordinary mortals. "Writing is not a profession," said Georges Simenon, "but a vocation of unhappiness."

With the rise of bohemia, art came to be confused with the personal qualities of the artist. Sensitivity, eccentricity, and unconventionality of dress or behavior were cultivated as marks of the artistic temperament, as the "Bohemian project of living life in the name of art dissolved real artistic production in the life that was substituted for it." What was ultimately being dramatized was not the art objects produced but the self that produces them, not concrete creations but abstract creativity. It is this skill at *self*-dramatization that makes romantic artists and their bohemian imitators such a tempting occupational model for people who value the expressive self.

In accord with their faith in the expressive self, the organization offspring typically dramatize their jobs as creative and themselves as artists, broadly conceived, even when what they do all day long is traditional corporate drudgery. Or, if they dislike their jobs, they imagine a more creative alternative or simply assert that they are "really" poets, playwrights, novelists, songwriters, painters, actors, filmmakers, musicians, or, nonspecifically, artists. Moreover, if they not only dislike their job but have suffered a downward shift in occupation, either in absolute terms or in relation to their fathers, the artist ideal allows them to hope that simply by virtue of their sensitivity and temperament they are participating, if only prospectively, in a higher-status vocation. In a world of diminishing expectations, they may still cherish a kind of high status, even if they have not done much, for the status accrues from the devotion to self-expression, not from the works, though the works may help. Thus the artist ideal may offer consolation for occupational failure in traditional terms, or it may reinvigorate the status of occupations that were traditionally seen as high status until they began to be vilified as manifestations of the mindless conformity of the organization man.

The artist ideal does similar double duty with education, seemingly the most stable of the three prestige indicators. "Get your education because that's something they can never take away from you," depression-reared parents told their children, bitterly implying that you could be unceremoniously stripped of everything else, including your dignity. Most of the organization offspring heeded the advice, but when they entered the job market, many of them found their degrees devalued—everybody had one. The artist ideal, ever capacious, comprehends both sets of circumstances: superior education as well as its devaluation. On the one hand, one may, like Bob Cory, regard one's superior education as the source of one's aesthetic values, refined consumption practices, and superior taste. On the other hand, the artist ideal provides consolation for those who experienced the unexpected devaluation of their education, whether they attended the "wrong" schools or found themselves merely one among millions of degree holders. For like the personality ethic and the character ethic before it, the self ethic, including its artist ideal, is intensely anti-intellectual. Like the sentimental middle class from which their creativity is supposed to set them apart, these would-be artists equate art with feeling. Emotion is opposed to intellect, creativity to critical reason. Thus, if one possesses sufficient creativity, it is possible to succeed at any endeavor (including art), despite educational or intellectual deficiencies.

The artist ideal comprehends the vagaries of income in similar fashion. On the one hand, the artist's dedication to the vocation of art calls for a sublime indifference to money. Indeed, it is a powerful cultural belief that real artists starve nobly, while pretenders cynically reap fame and riches. On the other hand, the possibility exists that you can catch up in the income race by being suddenly and fabulously rewarded for your creativity. (Screenwriting exerts a particularly strong attraction in this regard.) In the event that you already enjoy a high income, the artist ideal allows you to claim your rewards on the basis of your creativity, even if they are earned in a job that is not usually associated with it. Or, no matter how high your income, you may still choose to believe yourself an artist apart from your job, thus appearing to disdain mere money.

To the conflict between the expressive self and the wider cultural value of success, the artist ideal, though flexible and even contradictory—perhaps *because* it is flexible and contradictory—brings coherence for a wide variety of organization offspring, though their circumstances differ markedly. Some find in the artist ideal warrant for their entrepreneurial enterprises. Others use the artist ideal to redefine their already abundant good fortune in the now high-status terms of creativity. Others, less traditionally successful, cling to the image of themselves as artists, hoping to compensate for the insufficient status conferred by their education, income, or occupation. Failure is held at bay, redefined as the "true" success of the artistic vocation. And failure at the artistic vocation is held to be a virtue. (At its worst, this ploy goes even further than the bohemian's substitution of the life for the work, substituting instead the *failure* for the work.) Of course, the virtue of artistic failure does not prevent anyone from simultaneously believing that lightning will strike, that they may suddenly and handsomely succeed. Finally, for almost all the organization offspring, no matter what their condition, the artist ideal helps process the problem of intergenerational status mobility by shifting the ground of measurement to creativity, the one quality the organization man was said so conspicuously to lack.

"One is an artist the way one used to be a property owner."

To the simple-minded ironist, the artist-ideal smacks of hypocrisy, not to mention rationalization and self-deception. "One is an artist," sneered Felix Pyat at nineteenth-century bohemians, "the way one used to be a property owner, it's the distinguishing mark of those people who don't have any." For the organization offspring, the artist ideal can justify great affluence, as well as cushion the blow of reduced expectations, and lend to both an aura of nobility. These would-be artists want self-expression, liberation, and happiness, but they also want creature comforts, acclaim, and high status. They simultaneously seem to reject success in traditional terms and to embrace it wholeheartedly. They take themselves to be sensitive souls who nevertheless want it *all*. The now tiresome Yippie-to-Yuppie narrative beloved by journalists in recent years trades on just such contradictions. But these contradictory attitudes, and the occupational ideal in which they are embodied, represent not so much hypocrisy as they do ambivalence. They express resistance *and* attraction to the middle-class identities for which the organization offspring have been destined since birth.

Ambivalence about middle-class identity is as old as middle-class life itself. The middle-class culture of individualism and equality that developed following the American and the French revolutions and that flowered in the mid-nineteenth century in France and the early twentieth century in America promised personal liberation, leisure, self-development, and limitless consumption, but it also required delayed gratification, self-abnegation, dedication to work, and unending production. The all-transforming engine of capitalism dissolved the hierarchy, tradition, and stability of the social order, opening it to the merit and ambition of the individual. But the result was so fluid that those same individuals longed for something to give structure to the moral anarchy of their lives and developed a way of life often caricatured as simultaneously priggish and purely commercial. Promising an existence of infinite possibilities and yet hedging it all around with instrumentalist imperatives, middle-class life issued in irresolvable contradictions for the culture and deep ambivalence for many of its members.

The character ethic, personality ethic, and the self ethic each inscribe the contradictions of middle-class life and attempt to resolve them in ways that are appropriate to the changing historical contours of the problem. The representative types of each ethic—the entrepreneur, the salesman, and the artist—reproduce those same contradictions at the level of identity. For the organization offspring, the artist ideal is the mechanism through which they simultaneously resist and embrace their middle-class identities. The artist is a figure for the liberation that a middle-class culture of freedom and individual self-development promises and a figure for the heroic dedication to work that same culture demands, an outsider whose internal dynamics reproduce the tensions found inside middle-class life. The artist ideal similarly concentrates the contradictions of freedom and equality. Creativity, seen to reside in everyone, is democratized; yet in that same insistently leveling culture of equality, the designation "genius" is one of the few titles that carries real distinction.

In Paris of the nineteenth century, bohemia offered a place that was geographically removed from middle-class life where one, usually in one's youth, might explore to the limit the moral ambiguities inherent in middle-class culture's promise of freedom. In America various bohemias have flourished at one time or another and have served a similar social function for their relatively small number of denizens and camp followers. But it was only with the ascendancy of the expressive self as the supreme value that the artist ideal, originating in bohemia, came to grip virtually an entire generation of middle-class Americans. And with this further difference: This new American version of bohemia is no longer geographically distinct from middle-class life nor confined to its younger members. It is found firmly within the organization offspring's upscale condominiums and cramped efficiencies, their refurbished row houses and suburban ranch homes, their exurban estates and their marginal neighborhoods. It is diluted, perhaps, and buttoned down in some cases, but nevertheless physically and spiritually at the heart of their middle-class lives.

In a world where almost no one, aside from religious fundamentalists and a handful of overpublicized neoconservatives, seriously defends authority and tradition anymore, virtually everything is permitted. Who among the organization offspring has not sampled drugs, indulged sexual fantasies, or lived openly out of wedlock? One up-and-coming young executive at a major U.S. corporation told us that if she decides to bear a child, she may then *consider* marrying the colleague with whom she lives. Homosexuality still encounters obstacles, but numerous gay and lesbian interviewees made no secret of their sexual orientation, sometimes asking only that they be disguised in print for the sake of their parents' feelings. Otherwise, the forbidden freedoms that young people formerly flirted with in bohemia are now givens of middle-class, middle-aged identity, the contradictions of which, far from being diminished by their new propinquity, are magnified by it, requiring the artist myth for their imaginary resolution.

It would be enough that middle-class identity is fraught with contradictions: It promises leisure and necessitates work, proffers happiness and mandates success, promotes liberation and requires repression. But there is an even deeper problem in that identity, in the sense of oneness, has been almost irretrievably fractured. Modernity dissolved not only older patterns of community and work, but the pattern of identity that went with them. Industrialization, rationalization, and bureaucratization created for each individual a wide variety of social roles that are not organically related to each other or to the individual. The dizzying variety of social roles that the individual is now called upon to fill in a lifetime— or even in a single day—requires the adoption of a multiplicity of identities. Geographic and social mobility further upset settled social scripts and the identity they conferred. In the absence of authority and tradition, each new stage of social mobility and each new site of geographic mobility present new roles and new choices of roles. The problem is especially acute for organization offspring, who cling most tenaciously to the authentic self at the same time that the diffusive processes of modernity accelerate. Thoroughly enmeshed in a middle-class culture of competitive individualism that fragments the very individuality they so prize, they long for some synthesis of their multiple social identities with what they feel to be their personal identity.

The organization man dealt with the dilemmas of identity in what appears to be a straightforwardly administrative fashion. Insofar as possible, he simply split his personal identity and his social identity, his expressive values from his instrumental values. On the one hand, he enthusiastically threw himself into his socially prescribed identities— employee, citizen, neighbor. Taking his cues from the people around him, he unself-consciously fulfilled the requirements of each new role that was thrust upon him in public and social life. On the other hand, he realized his personal identity through his connection to an expressive family life that was animated by the intense experience of loyalty he had known in his family of origin during the Great Depression. For the organization man, as we noted in Chapter 3, this meant an adult pattern of paradoxically expressing family loyalty through dedication to his work, thus consecrating the split in practice and bridging it psychologically. The term *breadwinner* nicely captures the way in which the multiple identities imposed by competitive commercial life are organized as personal identity around the family for whom they are undertaken. Thus, for the organization man, it was the family, even the family he neglected in favor of his career, that made sense of his many social roles and gave him his personal identity, his sense of continuity with the depression child and the American serviceman who had left his family behind because he loved them.

For his wife, the situation was more difficult, since the family she formed, which was to provide her sense of personal identity, came to have less and less continuity with her family of origin in which domestic labor had empowered her mother and given daughters a sense of vitally contributing to the family's material well-being. As an adult, she saw the personal identity conferred by domestic labor come to be more and more detached from potent social roles. As a result, this division of labor—husband working outside the home, wife working within it—tended more and more to gender the split: social identity as male, personal identity as female. (And this division consequently devalued personal identity by equating it with idiosyncrasy: The organization man's derisive jests about women turned on the supposed irrationality and individual unpredictability of females.) Just as her husband stood on one side of the divide between expressive and instrumental values, she stood on the other. The term "home*maker*" nicely captures the way in which her personal identity came to have purely expressive connotations (and, incidentally, why what she did was not thought to be work, but the natural expression of her identity—creation and procreation, not production). The social roles she assumed outside the home in charity work, civic affairs, and the like all took on the color of her domestic identity—nurturing, child centered, and local—and all entailed unpaid labor. For many women, the barriers to social identities came eventually to undermine their sense of personal identity, precipitating the "problem that has no name," chronicled by Betty Friedan in *The Feminine Mystique*.

For the organization man, social identities threatened to devour his personal identity. For his wife, personal identity threatened to subsume her social identities. For both of them, these contrarities were stabilized, if not entirely synthesized, around family—comfortably for him, sometimes uneasily for her. Each achieved an identity based on a continuity of self from the family of origin through the family of formation, a continuity that historical circumstances strengthened for the organization man and attenuated, but did not destroy, for his wife.

No such solution is available to their children. In part, changed conditions of work and family life preclude it. As more women now work, they inevitably find themselves assuming the multiple social identities their mothers were denied. Conversely, men must confront issues of personal identity presented by the change in women's roles. They can no longer simply displace personal identity onto work for a family that in today's two-earner household is no longer their exclusive financial responsibility. Moreover, in today's world of nervous "commitments," neither men nor women can stabilize personal and social identities around a family that is no longer reliably there. That is why divorce is a far less shattering—and far more frequent—occurrence for the organization offspring than it was for their parents, who did stabilize their identities around family.

Steeped in expressive values and unable to stabilize personal and social identities around a mediating institution like the family, the offspring find themselves thrown back upon the self to heal the breach. Thus, they attempt to carry personal identity into the public realm, to assimilate their various social identities to their personal identity, to fuse the world of expressive values acquired at home in childhood with the world of instrumental values encountered at work in adulthood. A tiny minority of the generation had earlier attempted this fusion through the political activism of the sixties. Today, a much larger number attempt it—or at least long for it—in their working lives. They may, in many cases, be more tentative than were their politicized siblings, and many may be self-deceived, but their far greater numbers give them a critical mass that is vastly changing occupational life in and outside organizations. As the artist ideal reveals, they want not merely a job or even a career, but a calling. (Robert Bellah and his colleagues succinctly defined a *job* as a way of making a living, while a *career* traces a lifetime of achievement in an occupation, and a *calling* is work that is morally inseparable from the person who is doing it). Sigmund Freud once said that the aim of psychoanalysis was to bring patients to a level of common unhappiness, enabling them to love and to work. But the organization offspring want far more than common unhappiness and the compartmentalization of expressive values and instrumental ones; they do not want merely to love and to work, but to *love their work*. If they cannot find a calling at their job in an organization, they can dream of having one apart from it. The latter course veers perilously close to the organization man's habit of separating the expressive and instrumental realms, but nevertheless preserves the desire for fusion.

In a larger sense, the artist ideal implies an all-embracing mastery. Artists are seen to harmonize the bewildering multiplicity of experiences by filtering them through the integral, originary self where order is brought out of chaos through the agency of creativity. The ubiquity of the ideal in no way indicates that such mastery has been achieved or even approached; rather, it indicates how keenly the need for such mastery is felt.

Thus, the adaptability of the artist ideal indicates neither hypocrisy nor cynicism, but the degree to which so many members of the generation, like millions of middle-class individuals before them, feel their identities to be problematic, and it specifies the way in which they try to resolve their particular historical experience of the problem. As with many of the myths explored in this book, the myth of personal artistry offers imaginary solutions to real contradictions—in this case, the contradictions of individualism—just as the myth of artificial persons offers imaginary solutions to the real contradictions of organizationalism. It is in the artist ideal that the personal identities and the social identities of the organization offspring meet—often uneasily and sometimes unhappily—on that middle ground where the question Who am I? shades over into How shall I live?, where, as we shall now see, the private myth of personal artistry translates into a public world of personal artifice.

"That isn't done here."

In the fluid world of middle-class striving, there is no framework that may unite who one is with how one lives—no cosmology, no religious imperative, no guild, no inherited status, no family tradition to make individuals feel unreflectively that they have been destined for the way of life that they find themselves living. To the question, How shall I live? there is no automatic answer because, as we have noted, the geographic and social mobility introduced by industrialization and bureaucratization put in doubt all answers to the question, Who am I? Moreover, not only is there nothing inevitable about the way people live at different status levels, but there is nothing natural about the progression from one level to another. As a result, mobility may be experienced as the constant learning of new ways of life, the flexible adaptation to highly arbitrary and artificial living patterns.

But this inherent artificiality of middle-class life is regarded differently by the generations. One need only compare the different tones of their lives. Unlike the organization man and his wife, the organization offspring live their lives with a high degree of irony, self-consciousness, and defensiveness. They make jokes at their own expense about the suburbs; they are defensive about their jobs; they seem self-conscious about almost everything they do, as if they were putting on a performance and ironically commenting on it at the same time. When describing themselves, they often seem to be speaking in quotation marks that disavow what they are saying. Indeed, they seem to be *living* in quotation marks, as if everything in their lives were provisional.

Their parents feel no such self-consciousness. They enthusiastically embraced the mobility of the organizational revolution and the identity diffusion it brought. But as creators of that revolution, they stood both inside it and outside it. They had deliberately abandoned the more stable identities of their small-town and rural childhoods, having "left home both physically and spiritually," as Whyte put it. But those abandoned identities remained in memory and provided a point of reference for the distance they had traveled, the choices they had made, the new identities they had eagerly adopted. And, as we have noted, the organization man and his wife managed to maintain some continuity of identity through their lifelong experience of family loyalty. Carried into the corporation, loyalty also helped unify their identities by narrowing the range of their mobility to one company. (The centrality of loyalty to their identities explains much about them—why, for example, McCarthyist loyalty oaths did not strike them as inherently nonsensical.) Thus, though they embraced the artificiality of middle-class life, more-or-less stable points of reference remained.

Their children possess no such points of reference. Reared entirely within the unsettled social scripts provided by their parents' geographic and social mobility, they know only the arbitrariness and artificiality of middle-class life, not any settled alternative. The children know their parents' revolution only from the inside as an accomplished fact, a state of affairs in which they have lived since birth. Moreover, as Joseph Bensman and Arthur J. Vidich observe, children of the mobile middle class, pressured to conform even more successfully than did their parents to the new way of life, grow up acutely aware of the artificiality of their own and their parents' lives. "This is not Park Forest," their parents might admonish them about some aspect of behavior now to be eschewed, "this is Bloomfield Hills, and that isn't done here."

If the children failed to perform successfully, there was ready recourse to tutors, reading specialists, psychologists, medical specialists, and speech therapists. "I think I wore corrective shoes because I had a slight pigeon toe," recalls one such now-adult child, "and I was in speech therapy to correct a little lisp. None of these were serious problems. I think I was constantly being polished and refined on the outside, and maybe that gave me an emptiness inside. Maybe everyone grows up with what I finally realized was a sense of emptiness." Thus, the children acquired an even stronger sense than their parents of the artificiality of their highly mobile middle-class lives.

But the experience of artificiality clashes painfully with the ideal of authenticity. In the bosom of the affluent family, the children had come to value self-expression above all and eventually to believe in an authentic self to be expressed. But their experience of mobility had taught them that there is no natural way to live. Hence, the questions Who am I? and How shall I live? appear to be even more disjunct for the children than for their parents.

As with work, however, the offspring in their way of life are unwilling to accept the disjunction between the private and the public, the expressive and the instrumental, the authentic and the artificial. Also as with work, the agency for integrating the two worlds is creativity, which, as we noted, operates as a practical matter in the everyday realm of choice, where to choose is to express the self. The offspring's choices of ways to live (even when these ways do not differ from those of their peers) are seen to go to the heart of who they are. Thus, the offspring live their lives as *life-styles*, as a kind of artistic shaping in which choices of leisure, consumption, domestic arrangements, and even personal relations are seen as expressions of the self. Choice is not merely the exercise of personal taste or of a democratic right; it is the means by which artificiality is to be supplanted by art. (The distinction between artificiality and art turns, of course, on their sentimental view of art as *honest* feeling.) To deride their obsession with life-style as merely trendy and superficial is to miss the real (if questionable) moral imperative behind it: the duty to express the authentic self. But because purely formal expressiveness—abstract "creativity"—comes to fill up the ultimately vacuous notion of the authentic self, the result is a life that is neither one thing nor the other, neither private artistry nor social artificiality, but a kind of semipublic world of personal artifice that lies somewhere in between.

Choosing versus having chosen correctly.

We may see concretely how a way of life that is characterized by personal artifice plays out in the world by looking briefly at three separate areas of life taken in ascending order of publicity—consumption, personal relations, and civic involvement—and by comparing how the meaning of each of these activities differs for the generations.

Where consumption is concerned, it is tempting merely to observe that the members of both generations buy the same things their peers buy. Styles change, of course—whereas the older generation preferred ranch houses, Ethan Allen furniture, gray flannel suits, and station wagons, the younger generation may prefer renovated Victorians, antiques, modern art, jogging shoes, and "precision driving machines"—but conformity we shall always have with us. To leave it at that, however, misses the point. We shall always have conformity with us precisely because that is what it means for people to share a culture. The difference between the generations lies not in a simple distinction between conformists and nonconformists, but between different modes of conformity: how each group collectively, even when its members imagine they are acting individually, fits itself into the social world. When the dominant mode of conformity changes, as is happening now, similar activities undertaken by different generations take on vastly changed meanings. No matter, then, that all organization offspring purchase jogging shoes, even the same brand of jogging shoes, or that all organization men bought suburban ranch houses; the issue is what these acts of consumption mean for each.

In the case of the offspring, what we said about the exemplary nature of choosing applies as well to consumption, a subcategory of choice. Like other choices, consumption expresses the self, the vacuousness of which comes by default to be expressiveness, the act of choosing (or of refusing to choose, of keeping "options" open). Like the irony, defensiveness, and self-consciousness that frequently accompany it, consumption for the offspring foregrounds the act of choosing, not the substance of the choices. And insofar as choosing is successfully foregrounded, self-conscious modes of detachment become inextricably and confusingly bound with the "authenticity" that inheres in choosing. That is why the offspring, as consumers, seem to exude naive enthusiasm and blatant hypocrisy at the same time, why their stereotypical choices feel authentic to them even though they know them to be stereotypical.

On the face of it, however, it often appears that it *is* substance that counts. In ways that bewilder their parents, the offspring can produce elaborate rationales, including ironic ones, for their choice of everything from audio equipment to wines to cuisine to personal computers. Such rationales may be based on virtually anything—value, beauty, utility, or even a self-conscious engagement with the social symbolism of particular purchases. But what this almost-compulsive rationalizing reveals is not a concern with substance, but a desire to be seen as *one who chooses*. Finally, it is not the rationale that counts, but having one, whatever it is.

Nor does it much matter whether one's purchase is like or unlike that of everyone else. Given marginal differentiation among goods and services, the substance of any one of them—one's car, say, so like everyone else's—says little. On the other hand, the widely divergent life-styles encompassed by the offspring's middle-class bohemianism—which is to say the notion of *life-style* itself—may lead to widely divergent purchases that place various purchasers at different points along the continuum of the acceptance-rejection of middle-class identity. What unites the person who self-consciously rejects three-piece suits in favor of flannel shirts with the person who ironically dons the suit is detachment from the substance of what they have chosen and ambivalence about the social meanings of their choices, which meanings they know to be artificial. Whatever discomfort ensues from such knowledge is assuaged by displacing social artificiality with personal artifice, by shifting attention from social expression to self-expression, available only as the exhibition of one's capacity to choose. Consumption for them is conspicuous all right, but in a sense never intended by Thorstein Veblen.

The organization man and his wife were straightforwardly interested in both the substance of their consumption and its social meanings. Taking their cues from the people around them, they consumed in a way that was meant to send reassuring social signals about class and status to others of like station. While their children are concerned to be seen *as choosing*, the organization parents are concerned to be seen *as having chosen correctly*. At each new stage of their mobility, they eagerly adopted the styles and tastes of the organizations and suburbs they joined, impressing on their children the artificiality of middle-class identity and earning from critics undying contempt for their conformity.

But their frank interest in conforming does not mean that they experienced no conflicts. The organization man and his wife often found their frugality to be at odds with conformity; second cars and bigger houses were not free. Uttered with contempt or resignation, the phrase "keeping up with the Joneses" pithily expressed the conflict between the pressure to conform and lingering anxiety from the Great Depression. In the larger sense, the conflict embodied the contradiction between the residual productive values of the character ethic and the consumption values of the personality ethic, a conflict that postwar affluence increasingly allowed them to resolve in favor of the latter.

The conflict lingers, as organization parents today express astonishment at the consumption practices of their now-adult children. In the fine wines, designer clothes, and expensive vacations of their children—especially those who seem unable to afford such things—the parents see extravagance and infantile impulsiveness. "Money to me is security," said a typical organization man; "money to my daughter is for making another purchase." In the voluntary simplicity of some of the less conventionally successful, they see a lack of ambition. Of one such son, another organization man says flatly, "He's complacent." Focusing on the social meanings of the *choices*, rather than on the social meaning of *choosing*, the parents are unable to understand why their children behave as they do.

The misunderstanding is mutual. The children, like many social critics, see as mindless conformism the parents' anxiety about what other people think. But the organization generation's eagerness to please is of a piece with their loyalty to the family, the organization, and the nation. The mutually reassuring way in which they consume is another kind of loyalty—to the group and the community in the form of respectability. Consumption symbolically links them to the other members of the groups to which they belong, providing tangible evidence that each of them is faithfully carrying out his or her socially prescribed roles as worker, spouse, parent, and citizen.

Despite the contempt our individualist age has heaped on respectability, it is worth remembering that respectability is a social bond. To the organization offspring, respectability means little, except as the extreme limiting case of middle-class life. The real difference between the meaning of consumption for the two generations is not between conformism and nonconformism, but between a mode of conformity that is social and a mode of conformity that is asocial, paradoxical as the latter may sound.

"My parents wanted me to be nice."

If there is little to prefer in the consumption practices of either group, the situation grows more complicated when we turn to a consideration of personal relations. Once again, we encounter an apparent contrast between the organization man's social ideal and the offspring's asocial one, but here the distinction soon breaks down. For the organization man, sincerity—aimed at greasing the wheels of social interaction—is paramount in personal relations, a social orientation that easily turned manipulative and exploitative in practice. For the offspring, honesty—aimed at establishing contact between authentic selves regardless of the social

consequences—is paramount, a personal orientation that ideally would reduce social alienation.

As Whyte and others have shown, the new work environment of
large organizations, in which success depended on communication and
persuasion, encouraged careful attention to the handling of people. So
did cooperative efforts like the building of new communities from the
ground up. The pervasive emphasis on human relations, team play, and
salesmanship yielded in the organization man a personal style characterized by sincerity. But sincerity meant not the honest expression of one's
feelings, but a "sincere" interest in other people. As far back as 1936,
Dale Carnegie formulated explicit rules for such behavior: smile, become
genuinely interested in other people, frequently repeat the other person's name, listen, get other people to talk about themselves, make the
other person feel important, avoid argument, and so on. The real aim,
however, in showering other people with such attention was to get something out of them: to make the sale, secure the promotion, win consensus, achieve popularity. In a straightforward and pragmatic way, personal
relations were to be exploited for practical ends.

And yet for all the manipulation such sincerity entailed, it was
rarely cynical. As Richard Huber notes, success writers like Carnegie
always advised against mere flattery, on the dubious moral ground that it
simply did not work. Instead, they urged *genuine* interest in other people,
failing, of course, to see the contradiction between this genuineness and
its utilitarian goal. Such writers, especially the positive thinkers who
succeeded Carnegie, urged people to believe in their own deceptions of
other people. Far from appearing cynical, the personal style of the organization man came more and more to fit David Riesman's characterization of the sincere man as someone who "may deceive himself and
others."

It was the unreality of their parents' style of personal relations that
constituted one of the chief experiences of artificiality for the organization offspring. "My parents wanted me to be nice," said one, "not smart
or good or kind—just nice." Another recalled how she sensed an essential
emptiness behind the hearty cordiality that marked her parents' relations
even with their closest friends: "These supposedly intimate friendships
seemed so repressed, so superficial. They would literally spend their
time talking about the weather, as if anything else might be too controversial. It was like they were all strangers to each other. I can't imagine
how they endured the boredom—and the loneliness."

For the offspring, it is honesty—as distinct from sincerity—that
they value in personal relations. "Honesty translates all the way down the
line," says Bob Alekno, a musical instrument repairman. "If I'm repair-

ing a musical instrument, it means doing an honest job. It means what I expect from other people and from myself in presenting myself to another person: to show them who I am and in turn show them who they are by responding to them honestly. If they are open and honest with me, that's how I'll be with them. I may go to bed at night with only a two-figure bank balance, but do I feel good about everything else I've done, the people I'm with, how I'm behaving and relating? That's what it comes down to. It really gets to honesty, just being true to whatever it is I'm doing."

Tom Harrison, who similarly puts honesty above all else, describes it this way: "It's kind. of how you relate to people. You can do other things, but if you're honest about it, you can make it better. You can be lecherous, but if you're honest about it, at least you're an honest lecher. There's less sin in Falstaff than in Iago."

Inge Stemmler, an IBMer, says: "The thing I most abhor in other people is when they are dishonest. I get very angry with people who don't allow me to trust them. I feel betrayed, but it's really their loss that I'm not going to trust them."

Honesty, openness, showing "who I am"—are all versions of the attempt to carry authenticity into the interpersonal world. But, as the interviewees' inevitable qualifications reveal, it is a project fraught with difficulty. Alekno says *if* people are open with him, he will reciprocate. Stemmler's hall-of-mirrors locution about "people who don't allow me to trust them" captures the fragile, uncertain, and multilayered nature of these "honest" interchanges. Such qualifications acknowledge the doubly difficult problem that authenticity presents in personal relations, when you have not only to achieve your own elusive authenticity but to judge its presence in other people. In face-to-face encounters, you can judge the other person's authenticity only on the basis of your own problematic experience of the simultaneous fullness and emptiness of the authentic self, the content of which turns out to be expressiveness itself. In practice, then, honesty in personal relations comes to mean the sending and receiving of signals about expressiveness, rather than the communication of what you authentically are. The best that can be hoped for is to sow the impression that you are, in fact, authentic, though authentically *what* is impossible to say.

Consequently, the organization offspring have developed sophisticated personal styles that, like their consumption practices, foreground expressiveness itself. At one end of the spectrum may be found *detached* modes of personal relations: the same kind of self-consciousness, irony, and defensiveness to be seen sometimes operating in consumption. At the other end may be found *engaged* modes: narcissism, openness, and candor. Though a given style may predominate in an individual, no one person may be a pure example of any of them. Indeed, the same person may employ different styles on different occasions or mix them in novel ways.

Detached personal styles indicate a conscious distancing from the artificiality of the social role one may be playing in any given encounter—even the roles of friend or lover. Such detachment may come in many forms. For example, a self-conscious style may, on the one hand, manifest itself as an open and coldly calculating manipulation of artificial social relations or, at the other extreme, as an almost neurotic self-criticism of one's inauthenticity in social relations. Similarly, an ironic personal style, whether cool or compulsive, in which everything is done as if in quotation marks, keeps social artificiality at arm's length and, like the other detached personal styles, points to a self that is seen to be authentic *in virtue of this act of pointing*. It is this act of pointing that constitutes personal artifice in these detached styles of personal relations. Such personal artifice is neither phony nor genuine, neither cynically deceitful nor substantively revealing. It merely calls attention to its own abstract expressiveness. Thus, personal artifice is an attempt to bridge the gulf between the personal artistry believed to characterize the authentic self and the social artificiality that infects public encounters.

Whereas detached styles of personal relations indicate a distancing from the artificiality of social roles, engaged styles suggest that one has infused those roles with one's authenticity. Like the sincere organization man who believes his own propaganda, some organization offspring, often after therapy or participation in some aspect of the human potential movement, believe themselves to have "gotten in touch" with their real selves and to be expressing those real selves in their personal relations. Such styles involve conscious attempts to overcome social artificiality, rather than to keep it at arm's length. For example, openness in personal relations may mean a compulsive (and sometimes thoughtless) candor, or it may mean a childlike vulnerability or a willingness to indulge and display feelings. A selfishly narcissistic style, on the other hand, overcomes social artificiality by trampling it: Authenticity in personal relations becomes synonymous with the satisfaction of one's desires.

It may appear that engaged personal styles—whether marked by candor, openness, or selfishness—do more than merely point to the authentic self the way that detached styles do. But that is to credit their pretensions to the direct tapping and substantive expression of an authentic self. In fact, engaged styles no less than detached ones emphasize expressiveness, for all these engaged styles entail, to a greater or lesser degree, a preening self-display that not only attempts to exhibit the self but expects that self to be appreciated as authentic *for having made the attempt*. It is just this expectation that informs the complacency of the honest style, the sullenness of narcissism, or the self-congratulation of openness. And it is this expectation that performs the pointing function, that points to a self that is seen to be authentic in virtue of this expressive act of pointing. Hence, engaged styles, though they assert a kind of self-identity on the part of their practitioners, nevertheless must resort to personal artifice—expressiveness itself—as the only accessible stand-in for the authentic self.

"It is a self-centered attitude."

When we turn from personal relations and consumption practices to civic involvement, the ambiguities in the life of personal artifice disappear. Civic involvement, which requires shared purposes, not individual self-expression, is largely shunned by the organization offspring. It is just such shared social purposes—beyond the vague hope for a sane rather than a sick society—that the self ethic rules out of court. Indeed, the value placed on authenticity renders the community, as the essence of social artificiality, unreal and at least morally neutral, if not malign. This not only explains why the organization offspring are less involved in community affairs than their parents were, but why they feel so little regret about it.

"I suppose I ought to be ashamed of it," says Peter Hanson, who obviously is not, "but I am realistic enough about myself to accept whatever judgment is made. The extent to which I get involved in the community is much more directly a function of what I think affects me directly. It is a self-centered attitude.

"My parents are much more idealistic about things," he cheerfully concedes. "My mother, for example, does a lot of work observing the county courts and the parole system. But I look at most of that stuff as sort of byzantine, arcane, and difficult to influence. I tend to pay attention to those things that directly affect me—local taxes, local zoning, that sort of thing—but not for any grand, humanitarian spirit that says 'I owe it to society because society has given me so very much.' "

Though he says his parents are more idealistic, it is doubtful whether he really believes it. He likely means that he and his parents have *different* ideals. For, like many of his contemporaries, he attempts somehow to stretch his generation's supreme value, individual self-expression, to cover now merely vestigial notions of social responsibility.

"I believe that my way of contributing to society is to help the people that work for me get more out of their lives and themselves," he says. "I really do believe that if you can help someone to self-actualize, to provide a work environment where people can grow and achieve things, well, I get a lot of satisfaction out of that."

Spreading a little self-actualization among a few middle-class, upwardly mobile employees hardly constitutes a stirring vision of human solidarity. Furthermore, the almost-unconscious reduction of society to a peer group of roughly the same age, values, and social class discloses how fundamentally unreal is the notion of material community for these children of the organization. Eschewing what they perceive to be social artificiality, they would substitute for it a more widely distributed personal artifice.

This is not to say that they are a bunch of hopelessly selfish and willfully atomized individualists. As we have noted, the ubiquity of the artist ideal, at least in its occupational form, demonstrates the depth of the generation's undoubtedly genuine desire to harmonize the private and the public, just as the life of personal artifice carried on in its name does. But the artist ideal as they conceive it in its more broadly social form—the artist's relation to the society—appears hopelessly inadequate to the requirements of collective life in the here and now. Harboring ambitions of doing work that brings about "the revolution in men's hearts," these would-be artists dispose of the problem of social involvement by yoking it to self-expression and then deferring it to some cloudy and almost certainly unrealizable personal future. As an attempt to stretch self-expression to cover social responsibility, the artist ideal differs from Hanson's only in being at once more feeble and more grandiose. Even granting them the best intentions, their lives of personal artifice finally bring them up against the limits of constructing a society on an ideal that, in practice, proves to be, at the least, asocial—and perhaps antisocial.

Less obvious to the organization offspring are the limits on constructing (or uncovering) an authentic self on the basis of an ideal that, in practice, proves to be merely expressiveness. The ambiguities and ambivalences encompassed by the artist ideal, no less than the doubleness embodied in detached and engaged personal styles, simultaneously expose the difficulty and prolong it. The doubleness of various modes of detachment and engagement, in betraying either uncertainty or smugness about particular choices, unwittingly acknowledges the contradictory nature of the generation's conception of choice and the authentic self it is to express: simultaneously full and empty, both deeply rooted and baseless. And yet, for all that, such attitudes contain a saving grace for those who hold them. In suggesting that no choice is final, the irony, defensiveness, and self-consciousness with which some organization offspring live their lives foreground choice itself—not choices, but choice, the act of choosing, "keeping your options open." Similarly, in betraying the willed quality of the authenticity of those who affect to be in touch with themselves, complacency, sullenness, and self-congratulation also foreground choice. And since it is purely formal expressiveness—choosing itself—that comes ultimately to fill up the vacuous notion of the authentic self and since self-expression is a moral obligation, the *act* of choosing is, in itself, moral. Hence, the doubleness of these modes of detachment and engagement may betray uneasiness, but they permit one to hold onto one's ethical integrity—indeed to display it—as someone who is always in the process of choosing, no matter what the substantive content of one's choices of the moment.

Thus limited on both sides, personal artifice—ambiguously pointing at personal artistry and less ambiguously recoiling from social artificiality—constitutes the generation's mode of conformity, their way of collectively fitting themselves into a social world. It is not surprising, then, that everybody should choose to be different in exactly the same way: by laying claim to the originality and individuality of the artist. Nor that the basis of resistance to middle-class identity should be a decidedly middle-class notion of art and creativity.

We should not, however, let the simple irony of this nonconformist conformity obscure the real issue. The question is not *whether* we conform—we do—but *how* we conform. As we observed earlier, the difference between generations, or epochs, lies not in a simple distinction between conformists or nonconformists, but between different modes of conformity. The problem with the personal artifice of the self ethic is not that it is conformity masquerading as individualism, but that it is so impoverished for individuals and for the culture they share. On the one hand, it courts a vacuous sense of the self and, on the other hand, it renders the social world unreal.

Why not adopt a more adequate mode of conformity? Because, despite our current veneration of choice, the question of how we collectively conform is not one we can simply choose an answer to. Rather, it is decided, as it has always been decided, by millions of life experiences that are both evoked by the social and occupational structure and help create it; that are channeled by the culture and change it; that are even, to some extent, chosen on an individual basis but have unforeseen consequences in the aggregate. Only by such large-scale movements and by almost-insensible degrees do new modes of conformity come into being. And when a new one is forming, we may misread it, mistake a partial version for the final one, or fail to see it altogether. But, in any case, we cannot simply choose it.

Now this generation's peculiar life course, intertwined with long-term changes in the social and occupational structure, is bringing the search for self-fulfillment to a close, undermining the generation's unique brand of individualism, and spelling the end of authenticity. Nowhere to be found except in the display of expressiveness in personal artifice, the authentic self was, in the eighties, everywhere in retreat. It was mooted by economic history, denied by a striking revolution in Western thought, and undermined by contemporary art and even popular entertainment (developments of special significance to people whose identities were based on the figure of the artist). Perhaps most important, self-fulfillment itself was found to be unfulfilling, a discovery that has come to the organization offspring in various ways and in various degrees—and to some of them not at all—but that nevertheless remains the real story of the decade just past.

7

The End of Authenticity

"I wouldn't do business with the Mafia."

The ideal of authenticity was thwarted at every turn in the eighties only to reappear in ever more desperate forms. One segment of the generation, small in number but able to attract enormous media attention, took a perilous turn away from the mainline of expressive individualism toward radical egoism—their reductive version of the authentic self. But in a remarkably short period, they moved on to an even more vicious, almost self-parodic, stance—that of radical materialism.

It is important and instructive to understand the distinction. Necessary psychological egoism, as the philosophers call it, maintains that any action, no matter how altruistic it may appear, is undertaken only to gratify the ego of the actor. Such an outlook is more sophomoric than selfish; it views the activity of Albert Schweitzer or Mother Teresa cynically, but it tacitly concedes that such activity can be gratifying. Radical materialism, though rooted in egoism, goes much further. Its proponents maintain that only money can supply such gratification.

Radical materialism may be called self-fulfillment with a chip on its shoulder or, in its most sinister incarnation, the get-rich-quick-at-any-price attitude. Cut from the same cloth as their more ethical, less ruthless colleagues, the radical materialists represented the vanguard of a potentially destructive force in this new generation—destructive to the society and to themselves. It was they who were most attracted to the egoist pole of organizationalism, who, not only like their more conventionally egoist peers, viewed corporations as merely self-interested money machines, but unlike most of those peers, adopted that model for their own personalities.

In the world of the radical materialists, money and status were straightforwardly equated, in a way that they had not been since the days of the robber barons. Even when the radical materialists were not unashamedly confessing to greed, their consumption practices gave them away. Unlike the overwhelming majority of their contemporaries, whose consumption practices were designed to foreground expressiveness, the radical materialists consumed in order to foreground money. They simply had to purchase the best, the biggest, and the most famously expensive goods and services. Connoisseurship, the display of taste, gave way to conspicuous consumption, the display of wealth.

Like many of their contemporaries, radical materialists looked for security from within themselves. At some fundamental level, they never learned how to trust—in friendship; in love; or, often with justification, in the religious, secular, or educational institutions of the organization man. As a result, they developed a profound fear of failure and fear of abandonment. At the heart of their fears lay their belief that the world is a casino, a mean-spirited zero-sum game made up of an infinite series of win-lose moves. In this life, everything is a deal; there are no ethical dilemmas, no limits. Winning is all there is; it is the only measure of success and failure, the only way to distinguish between right and wrong, and money is the only way to keep score.

The potential for ill in such an outlook has been aggravated by the information revolution that has overtaken the world's financial markets. Recent changes in technology make it possible for the market to amass, digest, and exploit information to the point where large computer systems, fast reflexes, and sheer luck have begun to replace skill, effort, determination, and a sense of ethical values. In this all-too-real casino environment, radical egoists, well on their way to becoming radical materialists, learned to press their advantage to the limit, believing that if they did not do so, they would find themselves replaced by others more ruthless than they.

There is no better place to see this game being played than in the investment-banking community. Talk to the deal makers of Wall Street and one gets the distinct sense that here is a world that nominally professes a code of ethics, but that is really driven by personal greed of a radical materialist kind. As Ken Auletta, author of *Greed and Glory on Wall Street*, observed: "It is quite an eye-opener to ask investment bankers what they wouldn't do—'what deal wouldn't you participate in?' While reporting a book on Wall Street, I regularly asked that question and was stunned at how little thought many senior Wall Street executives gave to it. Usually the question was greeted by a pained silence. And then you could hear the rusty parts clank like the Tin Man in *The Wizard of Oz* as they declared: 'I wouldn't do business with the mafia;' or, 'I wouldn't do business with a bad credit risk.' "

One finds in the personalities and life-styles of radical materialists the perfect fit for the potential treachery of Wall Street. On Wall Street in 1986, the prevailing cultural values of radical materialism, the character structure of the radical materialists, and the Reaganite doctrine of free enterprise ("every person in pursuing his own self-interest best promotes the general welfare") all came together to encourage an orgy of financial chicanery. "During this decade," suggested James A. Michener on New Year's Day 1987:

> the accumulation of wealth has been deified. Magazines keep score and glorify the latest adventurer to amass half a billion of other people's money. The 26-year-old lawyer who hauls down his first several million is applauded just before the tardy Feds toss him in the slammer for ignoring moral laws the average high school freshman would have honored.
>
> Ivan F. Boesky becomes the prototypical financier of this decade, and the takeover artist who can orchestrate a greenmail coup has become a more lauded hero than the manager of a corporation that is hiring people and making a usable product. The manipulation of money markets is seen as a more important function than the making of things.

In an environment where massive wealth had replaced all other measures of success, a small group of cocky, headstrong, and arrogant radical materialists played out the game of individual greed and glory to its very end. These radical materialists attracted attention because they were young (for the most part), because they commanded outrageous incomes (between 1979 and 1986 Dennis Levine's trading profits were over $11.5 million, and in a three-year period, from 1984 to 1987, Michael Milken made $1.1 billion trading junk bonds and companies), and because the magnitude of their crimes was staggering (in the billions of dollars). Here were men without shame, undeterred by moral precepts, social responsibilities, or the rules of Wall Street. This was where the most perilous incarnation of radical individualism led—to an amoral radical materialism.

Perhaps there is nothing new in this situation. Greed has always been a part of the world of high finance. There have always been operators who devoted themselves to circumventing the law in order to amass huge fortunes. What was different here, however, was that this new form of greed had become socially acceptable and, indeed, laudable. Such people, at least until they were unmasked, became culture heroes, and in some quarters remain so. Making lots of money by any means came to be considered an admirable career path.

These radical materialists were perhaps the most vicious and visible part of a national orgy of the denial of limits that took place in the eighties. "Your world should know no boundaries," declared Merrill Lynch in one of the most repellent advertising campaigns of the decade. In the face of a shrinking economy, Americans grew ever more willing to mortgage the future in order to sustain the illusion of affluence, as debt—personal, corporate, and federal—climbed to staggering levels. By the end of the decade, consumer borrowing as a fraction of income reached a postwar high, the debt of nonfarm businesses rose from 45 percent of the gross national product in 1981 to 61 percent of it in 1989, and the national debt run up during the Reagan years was greater than all previous federal deficits *combined*.

Attempting to ennoble some of the decade's worst features, apologists invoked the traditional rhetoric of the Protestant ethic. They talked of individual initiative, small government, and hard work. But it was mostly talk. The investment bankers, enriching themselves at everyone else's expense, bore in that respect, at least, some resemblance to the robber barons in whom the Protestant ethic reached its highest pitch. But the bankers created no new wealth, and their innovations consisted primarily of ever more creative ways to saddle an already overburdened economy with more debt. Social Darwinism, with its equation of economic status to personal character, enjoyed a particularly ugly recrudescence, allowing the well-to-do, under the cover of individualism, to effect through the tax code a redistribution of wealth in their favor and to let the devil take the presumably immoral hindmost.

In most other respects, the Reagan Era, as it came to be known, bore no resemblance to the heyday of the Protestant ethic. Reagan himself rarely worked hard; exhibited little religious fervor; and generally behaved like the genial, other-directed spokesman for General Electric he had once been. Far from exemplifying the ascetic character of the Protestant ethic, his government achieved stupefying levels of national indebtedness. Moreover, the cost to taxpayers of the savings and loan scandal that resulted from the deregulation of the industry—again under the guise of individual freedom—may go as high as $500 *billion*, or $5,000 for every taxpayer in the country. While corporations as artificial persons enjoyed an expansion of individual rights in the form of such deregulation, lax regulatory enforcement, and tax favors, real individuals, specifically millions of federal employees, became candidates for wholesale drug testing. At the same time, a massive arms buildup continued to steer much of America's diminishing manufacturing capacity into the notoriously inefficient and noncompetitive defense industry, which, contrary to the claims of its lobbyists, produces little in the way of manufacturing innovations or of products that have general applications. And the Strategic Defense Initiative threatened to take one of America's last remaining areas of industrial superiority—that of computers—down the same dead-end road as much of the rest of the country's productive capacity.

In fact, as the astonishing increase in debt suggests, the eighties emerged as a period that was far more concerned with consumption than with production, with *droits du seigneur* than with individual rights, and with acquisitiveness rather than with asceticism. It was an age of easy victories against not very great odds—the 1984 Olympics, the 1987 America's Cup, the invasion of Grenada, the raid on Libya—all celebrated as great triumphs. As the writer Roy Blount, Jr., pondering the discrepancy between rhetoric and reality, observed, "Americans don't like complexity; Americans like to yell 'We're Number One!' "

Early on there developed a backlash against the blatant materialism and breast beating of the period: Yuppie bashing. As marked by simple-mindedness and unreality as the phenomenon it attempted to combat, Yuppie bashing soon became the age's substitute for thought.

It began as a joke. Of uncertain origin, the term *Yuppie*—an acronym, as any ten year old now knows, for young, urban professional—had been cropping up with increasing frequency in the popular press when a group of editors at *Newsweek* sat down in 1984 to consider one of their perennial headaches: how to avoid the sales drubbing their year-end issue invariably suffered against *Time*'s Man-of-the-Year number. In a spirit of gleeful fatalism, they latched onto the idea of designating 1984 the Year of the Yuppie.

In the cover story that resulted, the editors gamely, if unrigorously, tried to make sense of the term. They attempted to identify Yuppies by income, by education and profession, and by political leanings. They essayed the Yippie-to-Yuppie argument. Unfortunately, the editors could not add and subtract. Their sidebars featured as typical Yuppies eight people who ranged in age from 32 down to 25 years old, which would have made the oldest 16 and the youngest all of 9 years old at the time of, say, the 1968 Democratic Convention. It didn't matter. The editors were hardly serious in the first place.

From these jocose beginnings as an imprecise demographic designation for a few grasping baby boomers who were highly visible in media centers like New York, *Yuppie*, as Hendrik Hertzberg observed in a laudable, if doomed, effort to inter the term forever, was transformed into a moral category. Soon it expanded into an all-purpose term of abuse, which members of the social class it was meant to encompass began using on each other. Eventually, it became the dominant generational figure for the decade.

But, as Hertzberg went on to argue persuasively, the currency of the term was based on some faulty premises. Chief among them was the idea that the economy of the eighties offered boundless opportunities and all anyone needed to do was reach out and grab some. But for most baby boomers, including most of the organization offspring, simply "going for it" did not suffice; much of their anger at Yuppies was actually anger at the lie that it did. Even if real income had not remained stagnant and even declined during the decade 1973 to 1984, the sheer size of the baby-boomer cohorts would have caused them to fall behind the older generation anyway.

Even some baby boomers in so-called Yuppie income brackets found themselves having difficulty buying a first house, forced to use a far greater percentage of their earnings to do so than their fathers had. Moreover, many family incomes in the top fifth (the mean average of which is about sixty-six thousand dollars) were being achieved only by dint of two paychecks and often at the cost of postponed or foregone childbearing. We need shed no tears for them, but what the situation of even the most advantaged suggests is that for the overwhelming majority of baby boomers reality was far more frustrating than was the effortless smash and grab presented in the media.

All these frustrations came to be focused on the brazen figure of the widely chronicled, if statistically insignificant, Yuppie. (Of the 74 million baby boomers in 1984, only 4 million earned $40,000 or more per year and only 1.2 million of that group lived in a city.) To be young and upwardly mobile in a stagnant economy and structural vise that had made youth and upward mobility mutually exclusive offended many people's sense of proportion, including upwardly mobile media types, who took the greatest offense.

Of course, another name for frustration at not getting what you want or expect is selfishness, the very sin of which the hated Yuppie stood accused. In a stagnant economy and demographic disaster that made it necessary to run twice as fast merely to stay in the same place, the projection of selfishness onto other people allowed one to pursue one's ever-more-pressing self-interest with a clearer conscience. In the ruthlessly competitive academic world of Carolyn Harrison, for example, baby-boomer junior professors, desperately strapped for time to write the books that might allow them to hang onto their jobs, reflexively trashed their undergraduate students as selfish Yuppie-wanna-bes, thus allowing themselves to feel less guilty about ignoring their teaching duties in favor of research. Thus, in one of those protean perversities of ideology, Yuppie bashing often served the very selfishness it affected to abhor.

In a similar vein, one's own privatization, masquerading as the inwardness of self-fulfillment, might compare favorably with the naked egoism of so-called Yuppies. The epithet Yuppie often rolled most easily off the tongues of those whose nobility consisted of little more than a conspicuous devotion to a vague personal spirituality, a program of self-improvement, or some soul-searching therapy. Next to grasping Yuppies, such sensitive creatures took themselves to be positively winsome.

Bad-faith Yuppie bashing was by no means confined to baby boomers, however. The assumption that significant numbers of the younger generation were hopelessly selfish allowed members of older generations to enjoy with a sense of moral superiority their numerous historical and structural economic advantages—everything from hundred-dollar monthly mortgage payments to uncrowded career ladders to a social security system that was amply supported by the huge number of younger workers.

Beyond the covert sanctimony of projecting selfishness onto other people, there sometimes lay an even uglier dimension to Yuppie bashing—antifeminism and misogyny. The mere mention of Yuppies conjured up pictures of not only men in red suspenders and yellow neckties, but of women in power suits hurrying to jobs that had formerly been exclusive male preserves. *Newsweek*'s "Year of the Yuppie" cover featured an illustration by Garry Trudeau that pictured Mike Doonesbury and Joanie Caucus on the way to work, she carrying a briefcase and wearing pearls, a skirt and a blazer, New Balance athletic shoes, and a Walkman. Behind bitter denunciations of such Yuppie hoards overrunning the streets lay not merely resentment of women working—they had been doing so in ever greater numbers since the Vietnam inflation began—but women working in the professions and in corporations, which is to say in positions of power. Moreover, the income women derived from good jobs made them less dependent on men, allowing them to choose prospective partners more carefully, to escape from unsatisfying marriages, or simply to remain independent.

Then on October 19, 1987, the party at which Yuppies had feasted and Yuppie bashers had carped came to an end. Without warning, the longest running bull market in postwar history collapsed. In a single day the Dow Jones average lost 508 points, or 22 percent of its value. Many of the young deal makers, lawyers, accountants, and brokers suddenly found themselves out of unimaginably remunerative jobs of a sort they were never likely to find again. Fifteen thousand people in the financial community of New York alone lost their jobs, most of them young hotshots. This is not to suggest that radical materialists were confined to the financial industry or that everyone who is employed in that industry is such a person, or that the collapse of the market, which slowly rebounded over the following two years, decisively killed radical materialism. But the market's 1987 collapse does mark symbolically the beginning of the end for radical materialism, which had engaged only a small minority of the generation in the first place.

Overlooking for a moment their considerable depradations, it is possible to see these radical materialists as having performed a useful public service. By living out the logic of their creed to the fullest, they exposed the folly of believing that every desire should be gratified and every itch scratched, that the unbridled indulgence of every drive of each individual somehow magically leads to the greater good—or even to individual good. They brutally ripped away illusions about the inherent goodness of the "authentic" inner nature. By putting their own inner natures on public display, they demonstrated that the inner nature could be ugly, indeed. Thus, in an indirect fashion, the cultural exorcism of the Yuppie that the market collapse represented also called into question the more subtle and complicated mixture of selfishness and frustration that characterized Yuppie bashing. If self-fulfillment with a chip on its shoulder was drawing to a close, so, too, were the more romantic and gentler forms of self-fulfillment.

"I've felt my values changing and I don't know what to make of it."

On the simplest pragmatic level, the economic disasters and demographic destinies that operated like a vise to squeeze the baby-boom generation have rendered the pursuit of self-fulfillment an almost unaffordable luxury. Even if the baby boomers had entered adulthood in a healthy economy, their sheer numbers would have slowed their economic progress relative to older workers, but at least they would have enjoyed absolute progress in their own earnings and against fixed reference points like their memories of their parents' standard of living. However, the combination of huge cohorts and a troubled economy was deadly. It is worth recalling here some of the more startling measures of the long-term decline of the generation's economic prospects as against the expectations that the postwar period of affluence had inculcated in them:

□ During Eisenhower's two terms of office, the average family's income, adjusted for inflation, rose by 30 percent; during the Kennedy-

Johnson years, it also rose 30 percent. But from 1973 to 1980, the prime years of the Me Decade and the search for self-fulfillment, the average family's income, adjusted for inflation, *declined* by 7 percent. During Ronald Reagan's first term, it grew by only 5 percent.

□ An average thirty-year-old man in 1956, when *The Organization Man* was published, could carry the mortgage on an average-price home for about 14 percent of his gross pay. By 1984 the figure was 44 percent.

□ Before 1973, a thirty-year-old man would have already been earning 15 percent more than his father was earning when the young man left home at age twenty. But by 1983, a young man who left his parents' home in 1973 was earning 25 percent less (rather than 15 percent more) than his father had earned in the early 1970s.

□ In 1975 the median income of forty-year-old men exceeded the median income of thirty-year-old men by 21 percent, but by 1984 that figure was 34 percent, which indicates that baby boomers were experiencing a wage gap relative to the generation that immediately preceded them, a generation that benefited from its small size, as well as from the head start that the postwar boom afforded them.

□ Wages stagnated in all occupations, including those in business and related fields, as formerly high-paying jobs became oversupplied. For example, the average thirty-year-old white male lawyer earned $39,304 in 1969, but only $34,821 in 1979.

Of course, the economic difficulties indicated by those figures were not distributed equally among all baby boomers. Hardest hit were hourly workers, people lacking higher education, female heads of households, and members of minorities. The suffering of all these groups was palpable, and the economic troubles of the well-educated and relatively privileged organization offspring pale in comparison. Nevertheless, if the long-term erosion of the economy did not put the organization offspring on the streets, it did clearly and cumulatively affect them, for incomes, as we have shown, take on meaning relative to other incomes. Thus, it was possible even for people in the upper half of the income distribution (above about $27,000) to feel, with justification, that they were not living as well as their parents, a comparison that is still the basis for most people's sense of their mobility. Even being in the top fifth of family income had lost some of its meaning. Prior to 1973 it had meant that you were doing better than most other families and that your goals were increasingly coming closer to being realized. After 1973, being in the top fifth still meant you were doing better than most other families, but it no longer meant that your goals might easily be reached. In 1973 the top fifth of families enjoyed a mean average income of $68,278 (in 1984 dollars), but by 1984 that figure had declined to $66,607.

The new reality was slow to dawn on people. As Frank Levy observed, "the dream expands in good times, and in bad times it is slow to contract." But as the American Dream receded from the grasp of people who had thought of it as their birthright, the new reality could be glimpsed not only in the complicated frustration that went into Yuppie bashing, but in the subtle changes that occurred in the meaning of the term *middle class* and in the significance of consumption.

In the day of the organization man, *middle class* was synonymous with the American Dream: home ownership, college educations for one's numerous children, and a comfortable retirement, all achieved on a single income. In those times of ever-rising purchasing power, the dream was within the reach of almost everyone whose income fell within the middle range of the overall income distribution. No distinction existed between a middle income and the ability to purchase a middle-class life-style. But after 1973, a middle income no longer guaranteed the ability to purchase what has been thought of as a middle-class life. As one of our interviewees astutely—and ruefully—observed: "To be middle class now means that your parents can afford to help you buy a house."

The significance of consumption underwent a similar modification. In the self-fulfillment ethic, consumption was designed to foreground expressiveness itself, to display—as a sign of the authentic self—one's capacity to choose. But as the American Dream grew more difficult to achieve, consumption took on an even more compensatory character. Fragments of the good life came to be substituted for the more substantial whole. Having children might not be economically feasible, but exotic vacations remained within reach. Rapid career advancement or high-status employment might be elusive, but you could assemble many of the accoutrements that often went with them—art prints, toney furniture, or meals at fine restaurants. Can't buy a house? Afford the car? Dress as if you could. Can't afford designer clothes? At least you could buy a fine wine to complement your gourmet cooking.

Lying somewhere between the pure expressiveness of self-fulfillment and the conspicuous consumption of radical materialism, these consumption practices took on a double fetish character: as a substitute for the vacuous authentic self and as compensation for the more difficult-to-attain features of the American Dream. It was easy to mistake these widespread consumption practices for the far-rarer conspicuous consumption of the handful of radical materialists. But these new practices, unlike conspicuous consumption, were not intended as a conscious display of wealth. In fact, they were carried on more or less unconsciously and had the effect of compensating their practitioners for a *lack* of wealth (relative to longstanding economic expectations). The result might even be a kind of self-delusion about one's real situation.

If the changes wrought by demographic destiny and economic decline no longer favored self-fulfillment, neither did changes in the world of organizations, where macroeconomic issues of takeovers, debt service, and the pressure to increase shareholder value overshadowed psychological concerns. More important, self-fulfillment itself turned out to be unfulfilling. Lives of nervous "commitments," the purely formal presentation of the vacuous authentic self, the endless exploration of feelings, and the exhausting pursuit of honest "communication" offered little of substance on which to build anything satisfying.

One native of Park Forest, after youthful wanderings that took him from New York to California and one hip scene after another, retreated in the late seventies to rural Oregon to "cleanse" himself and to gather material for a novel he planned to write. The scene he found there turned out to be even less fulfilling than the ones he had left behind. Gentle pastoralists who had gone there to seek self-fulfillment had degenerated into a collection of burnout cases. Their lives had dwindled to an aimless round of marginal jobs in the timber industry relieved only by bouts of drunkenness and heavy drug use.

"I hooked up with a whole different group of people when I moved there," he says. "While I was thinking my life was just starting, I got the impression that a lot of them were thinking that their lives had peaked and were now on the down side. The first few years I lived there, it was kind of interesting. But now that I step back, it's not as interesting anymore. There was no importance to it, to the people or what they were doing in this particular place. It was a lot of interesting people doing a lot of trivial things."

Asked what has changed from his point of view, he says simply: "I don't live there anymore."

For Randy and Debbie Myers harsh reality eventually intruded on their idyllic mountaintop. Nederland, even during the heyday of the Colorado oil boom, had never prospered. In fact, that had always been its appeal. It was a retreat, spiritually far, far away from the vapid materialism of nearby Boulder and Denver. It was a last refuge of flower power, a place of pastoral beauty and simple living. But as the oil boom turned into an oil bust and the recessionary gales of the early 1980s swept away all hope of an economic miracle on the front range, tiny Nederland settled into an economic funk. As the eighties wore on, Randy found it harder and harder to get work as a carpenter. The time between jobs grew longer. Debbie, who earlier in the decade had smoothed out the economic rough spots by working part time as a real estate agent, found it increasingly difficult to make a living in residential sales.

"There was no money," explains Debbie. "People had no money to spend to build homes. People had no money to buy homes. In my last job, the person I worked for had only so much money to pay me, and that meant that there were only so many hours per week that I could work that I could get paid for."

The Myerses' self-conscious pursuit of a simpler life turned into a struggle for mere subsistence. The search for self-fulfillment in the breathtaking beauty of the Rocky Mountains turned out, finally, to be unfulfilling.

"What was missing," says Randy, in a deadpan tone, "was an income. Our income had been so insufficient, unstable, and erratic that it was taking away from the environment we had created for ourselves."

Like Tom Harrison, the Myerses had gone searching for a simple life and found out that it is not so simple.

For Julia Harrison, the abandonment of self-fulfillment was more direct. Brought by cancer to face the unpleasant truth that the unbounded self is powerless against material reality, she nevertheless continued to hold on, albeit tenuously, to the expressive self as the ground of value. In the New Age hothouse of mideighties San Francisco, her wilting faith in such ideas enjoyed a brief second flowering. But another ubiquitous phenomenon of mideighties San Francisco—AIDS—helped extinguish that faith entirely. (The unforeseeable historical accident of AIDS has itself put a powerful brake on specifically sexual ideologies of self-fulfillment.) Weary of what she had begun to feel was her narcissism, Julia volunteered for a program devoted to counseling AIDS patients. She hoped her own brush with death might have provided her with some useful empathy for the dying. But before seeing patients, she was obliged to undergo bull sessions with other volunteers, informal encounter sessions in which they talked interminably about their feelings.

"It was absurd," she says. "They would sigh deeply and say things like, 'Well, my roommate's uncle's second cousin died recently, but I'm dealing with it.' Or 'my friend's cat ran away, but I think I can handle it now.' They treated everything, no matter how distant from themselves, as if it were a great personal tragedy for *them*."

From deep within her there welled up that one response to which earnest self-fulfillers are powerless to reply: amusement. She tried mightily to suppress it, but in those blithe solipsists weaving every event into the bathetic drama of their infinitely expressive selves, she recognized a caricature of herself. She stepped into the hall, where her furtive, nervous giggle exploded into hearty, cathartic laughter. Thenceforth she skipped the bull sessions and went straight to the patients.

As people awake from the dream of individual self-fulfillment, they are finding themselves drawn further from the dream by the issues of home and family that will increasingly dominate the 1990s. As the ticking of the biological clock forces, once and for all, the issue of childbearing, many women who did not have children in their twenties are now electing to have them. Since 1970 the number of women having their first baby after age 30 has quadrupled, as has the number for women age 35 to 39. (At the same time, rates for women in their teens and twenties have been declining.) In 1988 alone one-third of the children born had mothers aged 30 and over. In 1989, the U.S. Bureau of the Census found that among childless married women aged 25 to 29, 85 percent expected to have a child at some point (compared to 75 percent of that group in 1975). Among childless married women aged 30 to 34, almost 55 percent expected to have children someday, up from 33.5 percent among the same group in 1975.

Inge Stemmler, who gave birth to her first child at age thirty, illustrates the conflict between self-fulfillment and the daily dose of selflessness that parenthood requires, an experience that grows more common among the organization offspring when they finally have offspring of their own.

"My first thought," she says, speaking of her philosophy of life, "is to live life to the fullest, but to elaborate on that now is difficult to do. That's something that changes so much. There are so many things I'd like to do that I don't have enough hours in the day to do. I'd like to be a successful author, I'd like to go to school, I'd like to spend all my time with my son and have one more child."

Formerly, she had sought self-fulfillment in her work at IBM, where she rose rapidly from secretary—she is one of the small minority in our sample without a college degree—to program developer. Having a child changed her attitude about work.

"To be perfectly honest, programming products that belong to IBM is really not very important in life. The world would get by just fine without them, and in some respects would get by even better. I did something in nine months that no developer writing a program is going to be able to do. They can't program a baby. It brought me down to basics because he had to eat, he had to be changed, and he had to be clothed. Always. Continually. And if I didn't do it, who would do it? I thought a lot about that and how basic that really is: how dependent that little thing is on me and how that gave my life an importance, and it's one I'll never *not* have anymore."

The effects of these new family ties on self-fulfillment are by no means confined to women. A male bank executive who spent his younger days pursuing pleasure in Berkeley, California, is typical of many men of his generation. As he prepared to marry the woman he had been living with for several years and to start a family with her, he said, with a mixture of wonder and disbelief: "I have felt my values changing over the last couple of years and I don't know what to make of it. I've been pretty footloose and fancy free through the years. A lot of relationships never went anywhere. I used to fear that settling down and having a family and playing that traditional role—that was something that was terribly uncool. I look around me and see others going through the same thing. When the child enters the scene, there's an anchor there, a dependent. That makes, I suspect, a different situation."

Those traditionalists who see in these trends and attitudes a harbinger of women returning to the home while men become sole breadwinners are engaged in wishful thinking. Since 1987, more than half of all new mothers return to work within one year of giving birth. Inge Stemmler has no intention of giving up her career. Neither does the young banker's wife to be, a highly successful financial analyst. In fact, for most such couples, the arrival of children will more than ever require two incomes if they are to maintain anything like the increasingly expensive and elusive American middle-class life for themselves and to provide an education for their children.

The real issue arising from the baby boomers finally having babies will not be how to accommodate all the statistically small, if economically potent, new Ward and June Cleavers out there (already misleadingly and revoltingly labeled the New Traditionalists by marketers), but how to provide adequate day care for the majority of couples who are unwilling to forego one of their incomes. Thus, the turn toward family concerns in the nineties will not only introduce many members of the generation to the selflessness of parenthood, but will, through the problem of day care, push them into an arena of social interdependence far beyond "the small circle of family and friends" into which Americans have always withdrawn.

The issue of adequate child care has become central in the life of Randy and Debbie Myers. To have the kind of life they want for themselves and their children, they must both work. Now living in Santa Rosa, California, they find it a dramatic change from their carefree days in the Colorado mountains.

"Our lives," says Randy, "are heading in a direction that would be our parents' worst fears—being gone all the time, working too hard, not spending enough time with the kids—all those things our parents tried to avoid by having a single-income family."

"And there is not much we can do about it," adds Debbie. "We want our kids to be well fed and well clothed, and we want to give them the things they want and need—whether that is gymnastics or karate or whatever it is these days—but a lot of it is that *we* want to have a home. I want to have a flower garden, rose bushes, and I want to go on vacations—something we have not done in ten years."

For the present, however, not even the organization man's dream of middle-class servitude to mortgage payments is within the Myerses' grasp. Like many others of their generation, they find themselves on the verge of middle age wondering where they are going find the time to live the life they desire and where they are going to get the money to buy a house of their own.

"It's difficult, really difficult," says Debbie. "I took a day off three weeks ago, and that was the first time since I don't know when. Even so, I still had to spend three hours on the phone. So was that a day off? Not really. But that's as close as I ever get."

The Myerses are at least satisfied with their current child-care arrangement, though it leaves them little time with their children. "We have a day-care mom who considers herself available twenty-four hours a day," says Debbie. "She starts getting kids at five in the morning and is willing to keep them through the dinner hour. We are very lucky right now."

Still, they have not solved their financial and time-pressure problems, and they are not likely to do so in the immediate future. Yet, as their search for solutions continues, they will undoubtedly find themselves looking beyond their doorstep. Recognizing the limits of what they can do to solve their problems, they will likely turn more to the community for assistance. And when the local school board, local government, and the private sector cannot or will not help, the Myerses, like countless others of their generation, will no doubt create new institutions and new ways of working that take them far outside the immediate family in order to heed its call.

Family has reasserted itself in another way for the organization offspring, catching many of them by surprise and further undermining their belief in their own self-sufficiency. For despite their nearly lifelong devotion to a rhetoric of individual self-fulfillment and their experience of geographic and social mobility, they are discovering how strong are the bonds with their families of origin. For most people, of course, such awareness grows gradually and naturally with age. But for many of the organization offspring, adrift in a world of unstable and groundless "commitments," it has struck with the force of a revelation. The three Harrison children who live within minutes of each other and of their parents find themselves continually surprised by that fact.

There is a double irony in this realization. First, it was in the purely expressive arena of their families of origin that the organization offspring initially acquired their faith in the unencumbered self, and now it is the strength of those very bonds that are calling the premises of that faith into question. Second, that faith also led them to value choice, above all, as the sign for their expressiveness, but one's family of origin is by no means chosen.

Other equally powerful currents are undermining the ethic of self-fulfillment and its ideal of authenticity. The veneration of choice in general, which is the hallmark of the self ethic, will inevitably abate as more and more members of the generation pass into middle age, a time of life when one is less concerned with making new choices than with learning to live with the choices one has already made. Because of their distinctive life courses—late marriages, deferred childbearing, and unsettled career paths—the organization offspring have been able to hang onto choice, to the idea of keeping options open, far longer than have previous generations. But by the middle years, even those who have made a virtue of refusing to choose will find that such refusal is, itself, a choice with real consequences that are not easily reversed. As the realization dawns that one cannot undo one's education, professional training, career path, or marital history, the struggle for self-fulfillment gives way to the struggle for self-acceptance.

In the public realm, advocacy of the autonomous self contains the seeds of its own contradiction. In pursuing the fulfillment of their potential, many people have been brought up against social definitions of the self that they were powerless to control or affect. This is an old story for numerous ethnic and religious groups, gays and lesbians, handicapped people, and other groups. But it is a relatively new one for the organization offspring, reared with the kind of mainstream middle-class advantages that create the illusion of personal autonomy. And it is still a rare experience for the men among them. But for many of the women, it is a depressingly familiar experience as they still find themselves shut out at the top of organizations for reasons of gender, reasons that are purely cultural constructs.

The realization that the construction of gender is largely social and artificial brings women to a dramatic fork in the road. In one direction lies the familiar cry for the removal of impediments to the autonomous self, and in a world where the self is the ultimate ground of value, the logic and justice of such a demand appear self-evident. But in the other direction lies a far more subversive alternative. It is possible to understand not only that the construction of one's self as "female" is largely social and artificial, but that the autonomous self of one's more privileged male associates may also be merely a social construct (and one that happens to be highly advantageous to men). Thus, what begins as an insistence on individualism and autonomy may lead to a questioning of the very premises of individualism.

The organization offspring are, of course, not the first to experience limits to their self-fulfillment—economic limits, demographic constraints, changes in social organization, changes in the world of work, the closing down of choice in middle age, the unignorable call of family, and the unsatisfying nature of self-fulfillment itself. Previously, however, such experiences were always tempered by a pervasive ideology of individualism. But what is different about the organization offspring's practical experience of the problematical nature of self-fulfillment and the authentic self is that it is taking place in a context of what can only be called a fundamental paradigm shift in Western intellectual life and an accompanying upheaval in art and even in popular culture. Mounting a direct challenge to centuries-old pieties about the autonomous self, this broad and deep current of change makes explicit and articulate what is only vaguely expressed in the offspring's tentative questioning of the premises of their individualism: that perhaps as they have understood the authentic self there is, as Gertrude Stein said of Oakland, California, "no *there* there."

Identity . . . as difference.

The seismic shift in Western thinking that is currently under way travels under many names and in many guises—poststructuralism, postmodernism, semiotics, discourse theory, deconstruction, hermeneutics, interpretive anthropology, critical theory, and numerous others. Though such jargon suggests that these movements are confined to the ivory tower, that is far from the case: "Indeed, throughout the advanced capitalist world—and beyond—post-structuralism has achieved far more than a merely academic diffusion, and has helped to shape a broader political and cultural climate." Nor have these developments been confined to a single discipline. Cutting across virtually every area of the arts, humanities, and the social and behavioral sciences, they are profoundly altering the understanding of culture, society, language, and—most important—human beings. And they have provided a vocabulary for the social changes, especially the changes in social character, that are percolating just beneath the apparent calm of the past decade.

It is beyond the scope of this book to argue for or against the validity of this large and varied body of thought; we can merely record what is taking place and try to provide a brief account of the intellectual world that is emerging with the social changes we have been describing. But it is first worth recalling that the intellectual atmosphere does not *cause* social change. People do not check the *Zeitgeist* and then mold their social characters to fit it; neither do the proponents of the ascendant thought of a particular time decree social character. Social character is evoked by the social structure, of which the intellectual world is a part, but only a part. All these things—social structure, social character, intellectual paradigm—are inextricably bound up with each other in ways that talk of cause and effect is powerless to capture. Were such social changes as we are describing not actually taking place, it is unlikely that the intellectual paradigm and its attendant artistic expressions would emerge; were there not such a paradigm and such art emerging, it is unlikely that the social changes would actually take place. To put it another way, authenticity is coming to an end simultaneously in life, thought, and art.

Proponents of the many forms of what, for convenience, is now simply lumped together under the rubric "theory" would, of course, argue that their differences are at least as great as their similarities. Nevertheless, they share some overriding similarities, chief among them the perception that any meaningful reality, to *be* meaningful, must be constituted as a language. Such languagelike realities include not only language itself but all other social phenomena: games, social life, rituals, customs, economic life, and so on. In fact, language takes in virtually everything, including God, nature, and human beings—our understanding of which is enacted in discourse that simultaneously explains and creates such objects of understanding. Even science, for example, is not so much a transparent window onto hard reality as it is a set of discursive practices that create their own reality within which some things may be made to appear (quarks, for example), some to disappear (phlogiston, prime matter), and some not to appear at all (God, ghosts).

It should be clear, even from this brief description, that this view rests on a concept of language that is far different from the naive notion that words are merely the names for things. Rather, language is seen as a wholly conventional system of signs in which a signifier is arbitrarily linked to a signified. There is no intrinsic reason why speakers of English, say, should use the signifier represented by *dog* to talk about a certain kind of animal; any other set of marks or sounds would do just as well. But that does not mean that different languages merely use different signifiers to indicate universal concepts that exist prior to any language. If they did, translation from one language to another would be a simple matter of one-to-one correspondences. But as anyone who has had any experience in more than one language can attest, not only do the signifiers of different languages differ dramatically, but so do their concepts or signifieds. For example, what English identifies as "dark blue" and "light blue"—two shades of the same color—are treated in Russian as two distinct primary colors. Moreover, concepts attached to particular signifiers change meaning over time; *awesome* once meant "capable of inspiring religious terror," whereas now it means something closer to "impressive in scale or effect." The signified is as arbitrary as the signifier. Thus, languages do not give names to already existing concepts; they create the concepts as well.

To say that signifiers and signifieds are arbitrary is to say they are relational, not only in regard to each other, but among themselves. What formally distinguishes one linguistic sound from another is simply the fact that within the system they are distinguishable in relation to each other. They have no positive content; they simply have a differential function: the English sound *sh*, for example, is what it is because it is not the other sounds of the language. The noises we make when we say *bed*, for another example, need have no essential property; we have great latitude in pronouncing it just as long as our utterance is not confused with *bad, bud, bid, red, dead,* and so on. Paradoxically, then, the *identity* of linguistic units, whether signifiers or signifieds, lies in their *difference*, not in any positive content. The entirety of a language is the network of such differences.

The analogy of chess may help to make the notion of identity as difference clearer. The pieces in a chess game derive their meaning from their relations to the other pieces. As signifiers, it does not matter what they look like or what they are made of as long as rooks can be distinguished from pawns and pawns from knights and so forth. You could use bottle caps for pawns, stones for rooks, buttons for bishops, and so on. In fact, pieces of similar value, pawns say, do not even have to look like each other; they only have to be distinguishable from other pieces. Their identity derives from difference within a system.

Thus, the meaning of anything in a particular communicative or cognitive act is not fully present; it is also absent because meaning is differential. Meaning is derived from—is dispersed throughout—the entire network of oppositions and differences that make up the system. As the endless chain of significations among which we move, meaning always escapes; it is always elsewhere; it is always present as absence.

This is not to offer some piety about the richness or fullness of meaning. In fact, it is the opposite. Meaning is always disappearing around the next corner of our explanation; it is always deferred to the next link along the chain of signification. Moreover, the system constantly rearranges itself as it grows and changes. What we operate in is the endless and always unstable play of signs without a center, an origin, or an essence.

If this view of signification is not a piety about the fullness of meaning, neither is it the old existentialist claim that radically free individuals simply make meaning, that they choose it. We do not live among objects, concepts, and actions that we, in the fullness of our subjectivity, endow with meaning. Those objects, concepts, and actions come to us as already meaningful both within the specific system of language and within the larger symbolic system of culture, of which language is a part. The network of differences and oppositions within which those things are made to appear have already been endowed with meaning by the particular society. This does not mean that everyone understands everything the same way; it only means that any possible meaningful move within the system derives its meaning from the culturally created system itself, not from our fiat or from anything intrinsic in the object.

Again the analogy of chess helps to clarify the point. For something to count as a meaningful "chess move," regardless of the particular move, it must take place within the culturally agreed-upon relational system of chess. Further, the particular move is historically conditioned, though not determined, by the preceding moves that have yielded the current set of relations among the pieces. You might come up with an "original" move, within that evolving relational system, but you could not meaningfully move your rook diagonally or jump over an obstructing piece with your bishop.

So saturated are we in the culturally endowed system of oppositions and differences that make our world meaningful that we fail to notice it, just as we rarely take account of our breathing. It all seems so "natural" and effortless that we are deceived into thinking that we do endow things with meaning, rather than operate in a linguistic and cultural network in which we always already find ourselves. It is not so much that we speak language; language speaks us. We are always already in a language world and a set of discursive practices that form us, not in the sense of causality, but in the sense of giving us our identity—as difference.

In turning to the authentic self as an alternative to the artificial world of their parents, the organization offspring were seeking a center, a still point around which the turning world of signification might be organized. They sought a foundation that might stabilize the entire system, just as in former times the system was to be stabilized by God or nature or some other positive, transcendental signified standing outside history and culture. For the authentic self is no less a transcendental signified than is God. If there exists at least one such entity whose meaning and identity are fully present rather than present as absent, then the endless play of identity as difference might be halted. All the other signs in the system might acquire positive identities that ripple outward from this privileged center. Historically, as religious faith and a meta-physics of nature receded, the self came to occupy that central position in such "centered" systems.

The self has remained a prime candidate for such a privileged position because it seems so fully and immediately present—so self-identical—and because as "internal" and private, it appears to be of a different order than are "external" and public systems like language and culture. There is no doubt that we experience subjectivity—the cease-less inner monologue of thoughts, emotions, desires, and so forth. But contemporary theorists would say that these things are *products* of the differential system—of language, of the unconscious, of culture—not its center.

The point is not simply that the use of language, like chess, is governed by a set of culturally agreed-upon rules. The real import be-comes clear when signs like "I" and "self" are substituted for our chess pieces. If they, like all other signs, derive their identity from difference, which is to say from all the other signs that are absent and among which meaning darts in a movement of perpetual deferral, then there are pro-found implications for notions of personal identity. Chief among them is the conclusion that personal identity is paradoxically derived from and dispersed throughout the culture, not located deep "inside" the person at some "authentic" level beyond culture and history. The identity of an "I" is paradoxically composed of what is different from it, what is absent, what is not "I." What is absent, of course, is the perpetual play of signs that make up the culture in which that "I" is constituted as meaningful. The vacuity, which is to say the meaninglessness, of the authentic self, then, is not a personal failure but perhaps simply a consequence of signification.

Now we can say even more exactly what binds together the various, and in many ways divergent, strands of thought that make up the emerg-ing paradigm. Either starting from the premise, or arriving at the con-clusion, that any meaningful reality is structured like a language, each version of the paradigm in its fashion encourages us to see reality in a new way: as the convergence of self and culture in the play of signification. Thus, it is in the very artificial systems the self is supposed to flee that it finds its being, repugnant though such a thought may be to pursuers of the pure authentic self. It is so repugnant that pursuers of self-fulfillment may, in familiar American anti-intellectual fashion, wish to dismiss the emerging paradigm as the conclusions of a few out-of-it academics. But the intellectuals are not alone. Some of the most serious of American artists, as well as some of the most broadly popular purveyors of popular culture, are coming to the same conclusions.

"They put me in the mix."

Striking manifestations of this emerging paradigm may be found in many pop cultural forms, including much popular entertainment. Pop forms are a particularly fruitful place to look for concrete evidence of the paradigm shift because they are seemingly the most far removed from the rarefied world of theory. And none could be further removed than rap music, which is why we chose it to illustrate trends that may be found in many other popular forms, including television, videos, and dance pop. Moreover, rap is almost equally far removed from the everyday world of the organization offspring, which is also why we chose it, for if "deprived" people have already anticipated and assimilated these artistic and social changes, then it is certainly likely that a perception of those changes will eventually break in upon some of their putatively better-educated contemporaries.

Growing out of the house party scene of the South Bronx in the midseventies, rap-inflected music was, by the end of the eighties, the dominant commercial sound in American popular music. In the beginning, deejays at parties, working with multiple turntables, strung together particularly danceable instrumental breaks (hence the term *breakdancing*) from their favorite records. Eventually, verbally adroit emcees began rhyming to the beats, and the form was launched. As the music moved from the streets into the recording studios, all these techniques were greatly facilitated by the panoply of advanced recording technology: computers, electronic drum machines, and sampling devices that permit the reproduction of virtually any prerecorded sound at the touch of a button. The result is a highly rhythmic, machinelike sound, riddled with borrowings and musical cross-references that confound simple notions of musical authenticity and keep copyright lawyers hopping.

There are a number of things worth noting about rap music. By turning items that social critics associate with passive consumption—record players and pop records—into active constituents of their art, rappers challenge simpleminded notions about the central production of cultural commodities and their subsequent dissemination to helpless consumers. Rap's sampling and recombination of musical figures from other artists' records—bass lines, rhythms, snatches of melody or vocals—calls into question traditional notions of originality and authorship. The resulting works are somehow new but without being original in the romantic sense. The music does not originate in some anguished interior drama of the self; it is assembled out of the vast shared language of musical culture.

The form's dependence on pastiche (the mimicking of widely divergent styles) operates in a similar fashion. Deejays rifle soul, funk, rock, reggae, jazz, and even heavy metal for various styles that are used not merely as a seamless web of influences, as in more conventional music, but often as distinct elements in a collage of sound. Rap's verbal component often includes explicit commentary on the content of other records, and there is an unending stream of "answer" records and sequels that, taken together, constitute a vast ongoing social conversation. Thus, any given rap record may be seen as a highly conscious partial distillation of a constantly circulating and shifting system of verbal, musical, and sonic signs. Furthermore, it is clear that many rappers are conscious of what such an aesthetic implies about the constantly shifting ground of the self. "They put me in the mix," as one rapper wittily makes the point. Of course, he put himself in the mix—it's his record, after all; he mixed it. But he also understands that the mix is in a more profound sense not his: He is they.

This is by no means the whole story, nor is that story so unequivocal. Rap is artistically "revolutionary," in the sense just described, but it is also not unfamiliar. It often traffics in the rhetoric of artistic originality as rappers try to outdo each other. And the rhymes of the emcees—by turns moralistic, boastful, and salacious—are of a piece with black American oral traditions of the dozens, signifying, and toasts, a characteristic that could conceivably be pressed into the service of an argument for rap's "authenticity." Nevertheless, in this context, originality that largely consists of manipulating preexisting musical materials and operating in a verbal tradition that assumes the sociality of its discourse is a far cry from romantic notions of the isolated, originary artist.

Closer to home for the organization offspring is the world of so-called high culture: the gallery, the museum, and the concert hall. American anti-intellectualism reflexively identifies the arts—as well as universities, the feminist movement, and other threads of our story—as the exclusive concern of a small, out-of-touch elite, eggheads in ivory towers, or "sissies in tights," as one of our older interviewees put it. Such clichés notwithstanding, the arts, universities, and reform movements, like feminism, are all overwhelmingly middle-class institutions. The children of the organization man are also the children of such institutions: They were trained in them and they help maintain them today. And art—or at least certain conceptions of art—is, as we have argued, absolutely central to issues of identity for this generation.

Those conceptions of art on which the organization offspring draw did not occur in a vacuum. They grew out of artistic practices and polemics of real artists and eventually became common cultural coin. Thus, what transpires in the gallery and the performance space today is singularly relevant—as relevant as is the intellectual paradigm discussed earlier—to understanding the social character of this generation. For the *kind* of art to which new pop forms such as rap points—centerless, artificial, nonoriginal—indicates that the meaning of art itself is undergoing a fundamental shift, and this profound change in a cultural practice that is at the heart of the organization offspring's self-image has profound implications for them, whether they are conscious of it or not. If the particular view of art that supports their view of their own personalities collapses, then the integrity of those personalities is endangered. This integrity is endangered not because a changing idea of art *causes* an unsettling change in the idea of the self; rather, the point is that changes in artistic practices and in social character (as well as in the intellectual paradigm) are different aspects of the complicated cultural, social, and economic changes we have been attempting to describe.

The most significant thing going on in those galleries and performance spaces—as well as in much popular entertainment—travels under the name *postmodernism*, a trendy and hotly contested term, but the one we are stuck with for now as a preliminary characterization of our age. As the word *postmodernism* suggests, it must be seen against the background of the modernism that preceded it. The umbrella of early twentieth-century modernism covers many diverse artists—T. S. Eliot, Sergey Eisenstein, Arnold Schoenberg, and Antonin Artaud, to name but a few—and it encompassed many competing movements, some reactionary, some utopian, some determinedly avant-garde. But whatever their political and artistic differences, most of these artists and movements accepted the distinction between high culture and low culture and located the activity of the artist securely within the realm of the high. Even when the aim was a wider transformation of society, they venerated the artist as a kind of secular priest and the artwork as a cult object. By the midfifties, however, the modernism that emerged in America to become official culture had jettisoned utopianism and avant-gardism in favor of an adamantly apolitical aesthetic purity with pretensions to universality. It was out of this ahistorical, apolitical religion of art, practiced by romantic "geniuses," that the organization offspring first fashioned their artist ideal (later confusingly adding to it some of the elements of the sixties' revolt against such modernism). It is against this official and comfortable modernism that the most significant postmodernism arrays itself.

The road to postmodernism is a long one. It runs through the rebellion of artists like Jasper Johns against the abstract expressionism of the fifties, the Beats against literary modernism, John Cage against exalted notions of the composer. The sixties saw an attempt to revive the avant-garde along the Cage-Warhol axis. Alternatively, the decade also witnessed the championing of popular culture—folk music, popular film, and genre literature—against "elitist" high art. Crucial in this regard for this generation was the populist elevation of rock music to the status of art. But the populist position, which slides easily into philistinism, merely opposed popular culture to "elitist" high art. Postmodernism simply does away with the distinction. In the early seventies, when avant-gardism and populism were all but exhausted, there appeared in the visual and performing arts artistic practices that combined styles from many historical periods, often conflated high and popular culture in the same work, and tended to treat works of art as social "texts" to be read, rather than cult objects to be worshipped.

Postmodernism, as these artistic practices came to be known, soon developed along several lines that are not easily disentangled. Philip Johnson's AT&T building in New York, with its Roman colonnades, neoclassical midsection, and Chippendale pediment, has become a convenient marker for the affirmative eclecticism of an "anything goes" postmodernism. Today, this kind of cheerful pastiche surrounds us—in advertising, in music videos, and in clothing.

Another version of postmodernism attempts to turn the work of art into a "text" among many such texts in an endless chain of signifiers without origin, fixity of meaning, or authorship. "Picasso's Women," a 1988 exhibit by New York artist Mike Bidlo, consisted of 150 or so paintings that were painstakingly copied from all phases of Picasso's career, unified only by the presence of a female image in each and by the fact that each is recognizably, even famously, a "Picasso." The colors, however, appeared to be slightly off, as if the artist had copied from an art book rather than from the originals, thus suggesting another link in an endless chain of "texts" that has no center, no stable resting place, such as is traditionally supplied by notions of style, the integrity of the artwork, and the conventions governing intellectual property. Such a strategy attempts to disperse the illusions of individuality, originality, and subjectivity into the social codes that constitute them.

Yet another version of postmodernism is distinctly political. Pho-

tographer Cindy Sherman often photographs herself in various guises—
femme fatale, dumb blonde, movie star. The photographs invite the
viewer to supply a fantasy narrative, but they also undermine that narrative by suggesting that the photo is mere surface. The "feminine" is
made to appear not as if it existed in itself, but in its ongoing construction. Though Sherman's work is certainly textualized—to be "read," not
worshipped as formally beautiful—it also enacts a pointed cultural politics: The issue is how her identity and the identity of women generally
is socially constructed. This does not imply, however, that the artist and
art occupy some privileged role in social change. The photographs are
simply one highly problematic site where we enter into the drama of
cultural representation that is always going on around us.

The reinsertion of the artwork into the various discourses and "artificial" systems of which it is a part—social, historical, cultural,
linguistic—means the end of the religion of art, in which the artist as the
ultimate individualist is a high priest producing an isolated, one-of-a-kind
object to be worshipped. The generation's artist ideal will no longer have
the warrant of the genuine art world, just as their conception of individualism no longer has the warrant of an overarching intellectual paradigm.
Taken together, these currents in intellectual life, postmodern art, and
popular entertainment mean a wrenching reinsertion of the self into its
constitutive sign systems and thus an end to the worship of the self and
the ideal of authenticity. But any assessment of the ultimate significance
of these contemporary developments for inner life must start with that
earlier and still resonating experience of the centerless self captured in
the phrase *other direction*.

"Everything real is happening elsewhere."

In Riesman's famous formulation, other-directed individuals use
their peer group as the source of direction in their lives. Instead of relying
on sanctions based on tradition to mediate behavior ("tradition direction") or taking direction from an internalized set of parental principles
("inner direction"), the other-directed person "learns to respond to signals from a far wider circle than is constituted by his parents." As Riesman wrote: "What is common to all the other-directed people is that their
contemporaries are the source of direction for the individual—either
those known to him or those with whom he is indirectly acquainted,
through friends and through the mass media. This source is of course
'internalized' in the sense that dependence on it for guidance in life is
implanted early. The goals toward which the other-directed person
strives shift with that: it is only the process of striving itself and the

process of paying attention to the signals from others that remain unaltered throughout life."

The significance of the cultural shift from inner direction to other direction lay not so much in the change of focus, but rather in the riddle of other direction itself: If I turn to my contemporaries for guidance, where do my contemporaries turn for guidance? And if they turn to me for guidance, how can I turn to them for guidance? To the question Who am I? comes the answer: I am you. What is me is what is not me. Other direction is thus a striking example of identity as difference in action. And it is not merely static. The process of everyone looking at everyone else is continual, circular, and inconclusive—hence, the anxiety that accompanied participation in such an unfixed and uncentered system of meaning. In the absence of anything stable beneath this system of signs, the organization man gave his loyalty to the ever-shifting system itself, a value Whyte called "belongingness" and less generous critics called "conformism."

The centerless, ever-circulating character of this orientation was exacerbated by the growth and pervasiveness of the mass media—television, radio, movies, and the postwar explosion of paperback books. Into the ceaseless round of everyone looking to everyone else was inserted the media at which everyone was also looking and which were looking at everyone. Riesman explained: "The mass media are the wholesalers; the peer-groups, the retailers of the communications industry. But the flow is not all one way. Not only do the peers decide, to a large extent, which tastes, skills, and words, appearing for the first time within their circle, shall be given approval, but they also select some for wider publicity through contiguous groups and eventually back to the mass media for still wider distribution."

Ironically, however, the impact of other direction and the pervasiveness of television in an expanding consumer economy worked not to destroy individuality, as social critics of the time feared. Rather, these conditions led to an exaggeration and celebration of individuality. The children of the other-directed organization man grew up entirely within this new kind of world, a world where one's identity was fashioned from an ever-changing network of peer-group relationships and from projected images produced through the mass media. The effects have been ambiguous. In an attempt to find some meaning greater than the shifting images of the media and more elevating than the other-directed values of their parents, many of the children of the organization man turned inward, seeking in the authentic self some relief from such an alienating and artificial system. But they sought it in images that, again ironically, were found in media.

The primary source of those images was not television. That is why it is in many ways misleading to call baby boomers the "television generation." One of the oddest bits of evidence offered to characterize this generation as the television generation is the adroitness with which some young political radicals manipulated the medium, a circumstance that suggests not thrall to television but superiority to it. In fact, a strong case could be made that the organization parents, in their reception of television, have historically been far more naive than have their children. The relationship of the younger generation to television is important and complicated, but the notion that it has been the dominant shaper of their social character is simply false. An exclusive focus on television, aside from yielding a few unproved assertions about television's effects—that it encourages violence, shortens attention spans, "cheapens" political discourse, and so on—misses the far more important generational barometer of popular music. As we have suggested, it is through popular music, in which many members of the generation had a far greater emotional investment, that the generational story emerges more clearly. And that story is one of seeking some anchor for the uncentered system of meaning in which they grew up.

Recoiling against what they regarded as a pervasive artificiality, they turned in the mid- and late sixties to rock music and its accompanying ideology of authenticity. Certain sounds—folk, country, and blues-based music—were equated with various kinds of cultural authenticity: that of embattled underdogs, salt-of-the-earth rural people, and poor-but-noble blacks. This equation, as Simon Frith points out, embodies a supremely suburban idea: "Everything *real* is happening elsewhere." Moreover, such an ideology, in its conception of authentic others, veered perilously close to the myth of the noble savage. Not only was it patronizing, it was also, insofar as it was based in the media, merely a more self-deluded form of artificiality. Nevertheless, it expressed the depth of displeasure with the artificial world of the larger society and indicated a desire for community.

In practice, of course, the desire for community turned out to be merely an ideological community of youth, rather than a material way of life. In the early seventies, even this fragile version of community began to come apart. As it did so, the personalism that underlay it emerged as the ideology of individual self-fulfillment of which the artist was exemplar—the rock artist spectacularly so. There arose a host of "sensitive" singer-songwriters—self-involved, sentimental, middle-class artists par excellence singing heartfelt songs of personal confession, domestic pathos, and private anguish. Similarly, so-called progressive rock was dominated by guitar "geniuses" from whose souls were ripped anguished—and sometimes interminable—guitar solos. The singer-songwriters did represent an advance in that their ranks included female performers, suggesting that self-fulfillment was open to both sexes, while progressive rock remained aggressively male.

Consistent with their belief in the authentic self and the artist ideal, many of the older members of the generation remain locked into this "authentic" music of the late sixties and early seventies. They were put off by punk, which was partly an assault on the ideology of authenticity—"we're pretty vacant," sang the ill-fated Sex Pistols—and partly a revolt of the young against the not-so-young. They were only mildly interested in punk's more acceptable American repackaging as New Wave, and they were revolted by the rise of synth-pop and other "artificial" pop manifestations like music videos. They did, however, make up a significant part of the enormous audience for Bruce Springsteen, a vastly talented performer whose evident sincerity, songwriting ability, working-class subject matter, fondness for traditional rock licks, and inexhaustible energy on stage represented the quintessential expression of rock authenticity at a time when the most significant currents in popular music were running in the opposite direction. Apart from Springsteen, however, they largely remain loyal to older authentic music, hearing it as sonic wallpaper in restaurants and stores, repurchasing it on compact discs, shelling out for it at the endless reunion tours undertaken by aging bands, and listening to it on the two hottest formats in radio—"adult contemporary" and "classic rock" stations, which promise "no metal, no Manilow" but plenty of Beatles; Creedence Clearwater Revival; Eric Clapton; Crosby, Stills, Nash, and Young; and enough sensitive singer-songwriters to fill a creative writing seminar.

In sticking to the music of its youth, this generation differs not at all from millions of middle-aged people before them. As people take on adult responsibilities, they simply have far less time for popular music. But this generation's devotion to its old music is more than mere inattention to the present. Unlike their parents, for whom the sound of Glenn Miller evokes sweetly nostalgic memories of courtship, the offspring remain stuck in music that carries a far greater burden of psychological and social significance, as the advertisers who began using the music in the late eighties to sell virtually every product well know.

Advertisers have always used famous tunes to sell products, but in the eighties, as Frith observes, the sixties songs they chose were "those that were . . . the most 'meaningful,' in terms of youth culture, soul emotion, or 'art,' " employing "these anti-commercial icons to guarantee the 'authenticity' of the product they're being used to sell." The Beatles' "Revolution" was used to push athletic shoes; the Doors' "Riders of the

Storm," to move automobile tires, the Drifters' "There Goes My Baby," to flog a line of clothes. Eric Clapton, once a paragon of blues purism, turned up in person to sing "After Midnight" in a beer commercial. This nostalgic strategy worked, as its ever-widening use suggested, but the *way* in which it worked and its ultimate meaning are complicated:

> The advertisers don't just cynically manipulate the aging rock audi-
> ence; the aging rock audience already believes it has lost its hold on
> the rock secret, which is why the advertisers' smooth promises touch
> us. Nostalgia and authenticity provide salespeople with such effective
> patter because we do believe that rock's aim was once true, our desires
> once unequivocal. And the more our memories are corrupted . . . the
> more their account of the past becomes the measure against which we
> judge the value of the present.

The initial outrage upon hearing John Lennon's exemplary rock voice in a Nike commercial is quickly followed by wistful regret. *This* is what they've done to our song, ma. Such cavalier treatment of such authentic treasures only confirms the sad lack of authenticity in the present: You might as well buy the damn shoes. Thus, the older members of the generation are stuck at a kind of impasse: Their nostalgia and their discomfort are both a measure of how precious and yet how attenuated, how entrenched and yet how embattled, is the idea of authenticity.

To negotiate this impasse, they developed, as we noted, a style of personal artifice that pointed ambiguously at the authentic self and recoiled from the world of social artificiality. But as self-fulfillment has proved to be unfulfilling and authenticity elusive, even this compromise with reality has been strained. Furthermore, the emerging intellectual paradigm and changed assumptions about the nature of art no longer provide ideological support for the romantic individuality embodied in the generation's artist ideal.

Of course intellectual paradigms and artistic revolutions are explicitly recognized by a relatively small number of people and engage the full attention of an even smaller number. No matter. We are not suggesting some mechanism of intellectual trickle down. The explicit formulation of the paradigm in "theory" and in art is matched by its implicit operation throughout many diverse areas of ordinary experience. People now routinely operate within relational systems of endlessly circulating signs that lack center, origin, or essence, and they do so with increasing frequency, every day—systems that are forming us even as we are forming them. Perhaps none is more concrete than the postmetropolitan suburbs that first began appearing as the first wave of organization offspring was coming to adulthood. Neither center nor periphery, these postmetropolitan suburbs are a striking physical manifestation of the decentering that characterizes so much of contemporary life. Along with the changes that have been occurring in the rarefied worlds of intellectual and artistic life, there has also been occurring an almost unnoticed revolution in suburban living.

8

Nobody Home, Nobody Gone: The New "New" Suburbia

The urban village.

On a warm summer evening, in a newly constructed shopping center just off the San Diego freeway in the city of Irvine, California, a long line of adults and children waits patiently outside the doors of a large glass-and-stucco building. The line meanders into the parking lot, and the children, bored by the wait, race back and forth from the front of the building to their parents' place in line, reporting on how fast the line is moving. They are waiting to experience Southern California's latest restaurant craze—the cafeteria.

Michael Miller, age five, loves coming to the Soup Exchange, as this new-age cafeteria is called, because for him it is an event. He can ride in a chair on wheels that puts him at the same height as the food counters. He has his choice of a number of different desserts, and best of all, his parents do not give him a hard time.

The Soup Exchange is not one of those dreary, fifties-style cafeterias. There are no steam tables here, no smell of corned beef that has been cooking for days, no lime Jell-O cubes, soupy mashed potatoes, or meat loaf specials, and no employees in white smocks and hairnets standing behind a stainless steel counter. At the Soup Exchange the Jell-O cubes and cling peaches have been replaced by fresh vegetables, fruits, and different kinds of lettuce, all attractively displayed. Presentation is important here. Oak-trimmed tables have replaced the stainless steel counter, and at each of the tables a different variety of foods is available.

300

All are kept immaculately clean and fully stocked by young men and women who look like they just stepped out of a milk commercial. Instead of the familiar row-upon-row dining-hall atmosphere of the old-fashioned cafeteria, the Soup Exchange has created clusters of dining areas filled with natural light and huge vases of fresh-cut flowers.

This is the third time this week that Michael has been to the Soup Exchange. On Monday he came for lunch with his mother and three of her friends from her quilting circle and their pre-school-age children. On Wednesday, Michael's mother, Gretchen, decided she did not want to cook, and since her husband was working late, she decided it would be easier to go out for dinner. Gretchen likes coming here because the food is fresh, there is a wide variety of salads, it is a welcome change from the taste-alike fast-food chains, and it is one of the few places children are welcome.

On this day, a Thursday, Gretchen and Michael have been joined by Michael's father, Frank, who works as a financial analyst for an Irvine-based food company. This time they came here at Frank's suggestion because it would allow him to work a little longer.

Here in Irvine, a "new town" of ninety-five thousand people in the heart of southern California's booming Orange County, the scene outside the Soup Exchange provides a snapshot of how suburbia has changed and how it is evolving. It is here that we get the clearest picture of what life is like in postmetropolitan America.

The Millers are a typical Irvine family. Frank, born in 1948, and Gretchen, born in 1952, are the offspring of loyal organization men who raised their families in suburbia. Both Frank and Gretchen boast MBAs and both have worked full-time during most of their ten-year marriage. Much like the thousands of other organization offspring who live in Orange County, Frank and Gretchen have changed jobs often during the past decade. The Orange County Executive Survey reports that 54 percent of the county's "most important" executives (chief executive officers, managing partners, or executive vice presidents) have worked for their present employers for ten years or less (with 25 percent for five years or less). That is in sharp contrast to the single-employer careers of most organization men and a far cry from the average tenure of twenty-three years for CEOs in *Business Week*'s Top 1,000 (in 1989).

For the time being, Gretchen, with a five year old underfoot and another child on the way, has chosen to be a full-time mother. Frank works fewer than fifteen minutes from home in an "urban village" of commercial high rises adjacent to Interstate 405, the San Diego Freeway. His office is five minutes from Orange County's airport and only slightly farther from South Coast Plaza, one of the largest shopping malls in the world. Frank's job is demanding; he usually works at least one day each weekend and sometimes takes Michael with him to the office. The Millers own a three-bedroom house in Irvine that sits at the end of a long cul-de-sac. Across the street is a large, new elementary school where Michael plays soccer on a preschool team composed of boys and girls.

Baby boomers like the Millers dominate the housing market in Irvine and in Orange County. Sixty-five percent of the county's residents own their homes, and the median age in the county stands at thirty-eight. Forty-eight percent of the households have two or more incomes and fully 60 percent have no children. The size of the average household was 2.8 in 1987, slightly up from the recorded low of 2.7 in 1980, but it is still far below the 3.4 persons per dwelling recorded in 1960 at the height of the baby boom. Like the Millers, 57 percent of Orange County residents over age eighteen are married and 42 percent have college degrees, with 14 percent holding postgraduate degrees. And Frank Miller's short drive to work is also typical of the average Orange County commuter: the median commute one-way is twenty-two to twenty-four minutes, and 82 percent of executives who work in the county also live there.

As the demographics make clear, county residents do not fit the traditional model of the suburbanite. Like the Millers, most residents of the county live close to their place of work—few commute to Los Angeles. Most are young, with fewer children than their parents had. Most are more highly educated than their parents, and most are two-paycheck families. But perhaps most surprising of all, most do not work for big, organization man-style companies. Only 18 percent of the companies based in Orange County have more than five hundred employees. A large majority—68.5 percent—of county businesses have five or fewer employees. In fact, the median size of an Orange County company is 3.7 employees. That the economy is fueled by small, entrepreneurial businesses is astonishing when you consider how powerful an economy the county has—the twenty-seventh largest in the world. But is Irvine merely a refined form of Park Forest, differing only in the kinds of firms for which its denizens work?

In Part 7 of *The Organization Man*, entitled "The New Suburbia: Organization Man at Home," Whyte drew a detailed portrait of what he described as "the great package suburbs that have sprung up outside our cities since the war." These cookie-cutter communities were home to the organization man, and it was in them that Whyte made an important discovery. In Park Forest, Illinois; Levittown, Pennsylvania; and in many other communities and subdivisions developing on the outskirts of major American cities, the organization man was creating a way of life that reflected his changed values and, as Whyte put it, of the values "of the next generation to come."

In suburbs like Park Forest, Whyte suggested, the organization men were creating communities in their own images: "In suburbia, [they] can express themselves more clearly than in the organization itself. In such propinquity, they bring out in each other—and at times caricature—tendencies that are latent in organization life, and one sees in bold relief what might be almost invisible in more conventional environments." Whyte saw these tendencies everywhere: "everything they do carries a certain degree of exaggeration: the schools are a little more modern than elsewhere, the politics a little more intense, and most certainly the social life is a lot more social. Abnormal? Or the portent of a new normality? The values of Park Forest, one gets the feeling, are harbingers of the way it's going to be."

Thirty-five years later and half a continent away, the question is: Did it turn out that way? Is Irvine, California, the kind of future Park Forest foreshadowed? Is Irvine the inevitable result of what critic Dwight McDonald called "the tepid ooze of midcult spreading everywhere"? Or does Irvine represent genuinely new patterns of living and working? How, if at all, are the planned communities of Park Forest and Irvine connected? And what do they tell us about emerging social patterns and their implications for American social character?

From standard of living to quality of life.

In planning terms, Park Forest and Irvine are directly linked. Both were conceived as planned communities and both were created under the direction of a single, gifted private developer. Both are, in a way, spiritual descendants of the utopian settlements of the Oneida community and the Fourier settlements. And both can trace their origins back to London's garden cities, the world's first suburbs, and forward through Frederick Law Olmstead's 1868 plan for Riverside, Illinois, to Clarence Stein's and Henry Wright's "new town" of Radburn, New Jersey, in 1928.

Planning traditions aside, however, Park Forest and Irvine are different places indeed. The nature of the differences cannot be explained by their locations on the map or the span of years that separates their development. To understand how their destinies are tied together and to explain why they are such different places requires a look back at the multiple forces that conspired to create the suburbanization of the United States.

In a landmark study of suburbia, *Crabgrass Frontier*, urban historian Kenneth T. Jackson argues that the suburbanization of the United States is largely the result of the interaction of market dynamics and governmental policies. Moreover, inexpensive housing, racial prejudice, and "a pervasive fondness for grass and solitude" worked together to create the urban and suburban patterns that exist today.

Jackson identifies six key factors that encouraged the growth of postwar suburbia:

1. Americans, enjoying one of the highest standards of living in the world and possessing unprecedented per capita wealth, could afford the relative wastefulness of suburban sprawl.

2. Cheap and plentiful land around American cities encouraged large-scale speculative development.

3. Inexpensive transportation, most notably automobiles, enabled Americans to commute between their place of work and their "dream houses" in the suburbs.

4. Balloon-frame construction of houses dramatically lowered the material and labor costs of home building.

5. Mortgage insurance programs of the Veterans Administration and Federal Housing Administration; federal tax policy (allowing home owners to deduct mortgage interest and property taxes from their total taxable income); federal financing of public works projects, such as sewers and water systems; the placement of federal housing projects in central city locations; and the development of the interstate highway system all contributed to the promotion and expansion of suburban development.

6. The capitalistic system itself, in which land speculators, real estate firms, mortgage bankers, developers, and the housing industry were able to take advantage of the unique market conditions created by postwar prosperity and pent-up demand for housing, also was a major factor in the growth of suburbia.

Combined with pervasive racial discrimination, the deep-seated American distrust of city life, and the American dream of owning a parcel of land and a home to go with it, these six economic factors are responsible for what America had become by the 1980s: a largely suburban nation. In 1950, as the postwar building boom was beginning, only 24 percent of the population lived in the suburbs; by 1960, the figure had risen to 33 percent, and by 1970 38 percent of the population called suburbia home. In 1980, 40 percent of Americans lived in suburbia. By 1987 that percentage had risen to 45, and there were 109 million suburbanites, 76 million central-city dwellers, and 56 million nonmetropolitan residents. Thus, even at a time of renewed interest in downtown redevelopment and, for the first time in decades, something of a revival in small-town America, suburbia continued to grow.

However, the market forces and government policies that gave rise to postwar America as it exists today are no longer operating in the way they once did. What looks the same no longer acts the same. Park Forest appears much as it did in the late sixties, but the lives of Park Foresters have changed dramatically. The social, political, and economic structure that emerged after World War II and helped create America's suburban society has been slowly changing. As early as 1960, there were signs that the affluent society of the organization man was beginning to fade, even though the growth of suburbia continued unabated. In the mass-production economy, at the center of which stood the organization man, the emphasis was on the production of goods; manufacturing was the key economic sector. Yet manufacturing, which had accounted for 30 percent of the labor force, had shrunk to 27 percent by 1960, beginning a slide that continues today. Though no one noticed at the time, the nation had already begun to move from an industrial to a postindustrial society. The mass-production society of the organization man was beginning to give way to a new and fundamentally different social and economic order.

In corresponding fashion, suburbia had also begun to change. As the oldest members of the successor generation were reaching adulthood in the late sixties and early seventies, the way of life they had grown up with was being quietly transformed. Between 1960 and 1970, what demographers refer to as "nonadjacent, nonmetropolitan" growth roughly equaled "adjacent, nonmetropolitan" growth. That is, the population growth taking place independent of metropolitan population centers was roughly equal to the growth taking place on the outskirts of major metropolitan areas. For the first time in a century and a half, the concentric-ring pattern of urban growth had been broken. New, low-density settlements were growing far from urban areas and in many cases were developing beyond the economic and social reach of the large, metropolitan centers.

When this phenomenon of new, low-density growth beyond cities and suburbs was first identified, it baffled geographers and urban planners, who could not explain why this new type of growth—which could not be classified as urban, suburban, or rural—was occurring. Some argued that the new pattern of growth was merely another wave of suburbanization; but because these settlements were sixty to one hundred miles beyond central cities, it was hard to make a case that these were merely the newest commuter suburbs. Others argued that a small-town renaissance was under way as Americans rediscovered their lost heritage and their love of wide, open spaces. Yet, on closer inspection, it was found that small towns were not growing. The growth that was taking place was happening almost independently of small-town America. Still others believed that this new growth was an aberration—an anomalous blip in the larger pattern of suburbanization that had begun in 1950. These experts expected that the larger pattern would reemerge once the economy grew stronger. They waited in vain.

No explanation was satisfactory. Clearly, this form of growth was something new. The thoroughgoing changes occurring in the American economy—and in the American family—were becoming visible, embodied in a new pattern of residential development. This new pattern was a harbinger of many of the dramatic changes taking place in American life—the physical embodiment of a remarkable wave of social and economic transformations.

As the 1980s dawned it was unclear how this new pattern would evolve. Yet one fact stood out: The simple oppositions urban/rural and central city/suburb were being dramatically altered by the dynamics of a fast-developing postindustrial economy. The spectacular postwar period of suburbanization was coming to an end. In its place there was developing something strikingly different—the postmetropolitan world of the successor generation.

These massive changes have gone largely unnoticed, in part, because making sense of such change is never easy, except in retrospect. But the invisibility of these changes can also be traced to the twenty-five- to thirty-year period of uncommon stability after World War II. The Cold War, Americanization, industrialization, the rise of an economy based on mass production and mass consumption—each of these defining forces of that period was based on a particular form of simplicity, namely, uniformity. There was uniformity in goods, uniformity in services, uniformity in production methods, and uniformity in persons. There was only one telephone company, two superpowers, three television networks, and four automobile manufacturers. Moreover, there was uniformity in the way that uniformity was promoted: It was imposed from the top down through large institutions.

To a far greater extent than most of us realize, we carry around in our heads today a stereotypical picture of ourselves and our society that was developed during that period. While Americans have always had a kind of national portrait that helped them to define who they were and what they wanted, the picture that emerged during the postwar period of uniformity and stability has itself proved to be remarkably stable, as it remains the chief means by which Americans understand their lives— either as living up to the picture or as deviating from it.

In the picture there is a house, vaguely colonial in design. The house is located in suburbia and is surrounded by a lush, green lawn and shaded by large oak trees. There is a two-car garage filled with bikes, toys, and sports equipment. The house has three bedrooms and a den; the shutters are painted green, the rest of the house—and the picket fence around the property—are white. In the house there is a wife, a husband, three children, and a family pet or two. On weekday mornings the husband goes to work and the school-age children go to school. The woman stays home with the younger children, washing, ironing, cleaning, and preparing meals. In the evening, after she has done the dishes, she may go to a PTA meeting or a church meeting. On Saturdays the husband mows the lawn and barbeques hamburgers and steaks in the evening. On Sundays the family goes to church. Everyday life has a rhythm to it, a regularity and uniformity that brings a sense of balance, a feeling of continuity, and a measure of perceived control.

It is the America of Ozzie and Harriet and the Cleaver family—and America as lived by most organization men's families. It was based on a clear system of rules and roles and institutional structures that were easy to understand and conform to. Not everyone liked the system and for many it was racist, sexist, and boring. But it possessed a certain clarity that worked for the middle class. And it continues to color our perception of who we are and what we are.

Yet, today, most Americans' lives bear little resemblance to the picture-perfect, look-alike model of life fashioned in the fifties. In most families, both the husband and the wife now work full-time. Many children come home from school to an empty house, a house that is, in many cases, rented because home buying is out of reach for many families, even many middle-class ones. Nevertheless, no new picture of model American life has taken hold in the public mind. Therefore, many Americans, including many of the organization offspring, continue to view their current life-styles as departures, more or less, from the suburban model of the fifties. To a much greater extent than they realize, they continue to judge themselves by an organization-man family standard that simply no longer exists.

Yet, we know it does not exist anymore if we look closely at places like Irvine. We can see the changes in people standing in line outside the

Soup Exchange. We know something has changed when we notice that the traffic on Interstate 405 running through Irvine never seems to let up. There are slowdowns all day long and traffic comes to a standstill in *both* directions during the morning and evening rush hours. And grocery stores are open far into the night, and some stay open twenty-four hours a day.

But we have difficulty understanding what we are looking at. How are the daytime traffic tie-ups and all-night supermarkets related? What is the connection between short commutes to work and long lines at a cafeteria? Entrepreneurial firms and new residential patterns? Weak job loyalty and a powerful local economy?

To get a better grasp on this new reality, one can begin by walking the terrain. Walk down any residential street in Irvine or any similar suburb on a weekday morning or afternoon. What do you see? Probably not much. No one is out walking a dog. No children play in the yards. No mothers are hanging laundry. No Fuller Brush men are going door to door. No milkmen are delivering milk. Occasionally, you see an elderly woman out strolling or a nanny pushing a baby carriage. But with the exception of mail carriers delivering mail and overnight delivery trucks moving up and down the streets, the sidewalks are quiet and the streets empty.

There are no door-to-door salesmen, no Avon ladies ringing doorbells, because no one is home to answer the door. The woman in our fifties picture of suburbia has gone to work. There are no children playing in the yard because with their mothers working, the children are in day care or preschools. The elderly woman out strolling is probably a widow living independently of her children. As anthropologist Barbara Whitehead said, "suburbia has become a childless landscape."

Jonathan Schell is among the few who have recognized what is happening. In a 1985 book about how the residents of one community responded to the 1984 election, he observed: "The service economy was the household turned inside out. The empty neighborhood street and the busy shopping mall went together. Seen from the vantage point of today's economy, the households of the 1950s were like cottage industries, with payment for the wife-worker coming out of the husband's paycheck." As the mass-production economy gave way to a service economy, urban areas "exploded." "As if a cake had been unbaked and returned to its original ingredients," cities began to separate all the elements of urban life that formerly had existed together. Downtown offices, retail stores, theaters, restaurants, and apartments, all of which had once happily coexisted, began to separate into specialized districts. Retailers escaped to regional shopping malls, offices were clustered in low-density office parks far from the central city, and restaurants and fast-food outlets lined up along major thoroughfares leading away from the city.

There were many reasons why the pattern of urban workplace/ suburban residence of the organization man came unraveled. Not only was the economy shifting from an industrial to a postindustrial base, but women in ever increasing numbers left the home for the workplace. The number of working women aged 25–54 more than doubled from 1948 to 1987, climbing from 35.1 percent to 71.9 percent. Furthermore, taking into account that women enter and leave the labor force more frequently than do men—and therefore should be counted differently—the percentage of working women is perhaps as high as 90 percent. What is most striking is the number of mothers who have gone to work. In 1950 only 28 percent of married women with children under six worked, a figure that had climbed to 54 percent by 1986; today two-thirds of *all* mothers are in the labor force.

With the number of working women, especially working mothers, skyrocketing, the need for services jumped dramatically. Everything that had once been done in the "cottage industry" of the suburban home was increasingly given over to outsiders to provide. Thus women, asserting their rights in the economy (often out of pressing economic need) and in the home, changed not only their own lives but the prevailing pattern of urbanization.

As the two-earner household became more and more common, time became the most precious commodity in the lives of families—hence, the importance of short commutes and the appearance of long lines at family restaurants. Instead of having mom fix dinner, the family eats out. The Soup Exchange in Irvine is popular because it caters to the needs of busy families, offering fast service, healthful food, and affordable prices. It also fills another market niche—serving the needs of families who might otherwise rarely eat meals together because their busy schedules usually conflict. A study done for the National Restaurant Association found that the increase of restaurant traffic for children between 1982 and 1986 was more than double that for the population as a whole. While overall restaurant traffic during that period increased by 10.8 percent, traffic for children under age 6 increased 27.4 percent and for children 6 to 17, 20.8 percent.

Similarly, most other household services that had traditionally been provided by wives have become booming businesses. Housecleaning companies, for example, more than doubled in the short span of three years, increasing from 669 in 1985 to 1,621 in 1988. Nationwide, revenues for such companies tripled in that same three-year period, going from $41 million in 1985 to $127 million in 1988. The number of companies providing live-in child care or nannies went from *zero* in 1984 to more than 200 by 1988. And the demand for day care outside the home far outstripped the number of day-care spaces that were available. In 1988 alone, working parents spent $11 billion on outside day care. One child-care provider, founded in 1969 with a single center, had grown to over 1,150 centers by 1988. (Such statistics, especially the huge dollar volumes they represent, make it clear just how valuable the services of housewives really are, and yet homemaking is still classified as unpaid labor.)

It begins to make sense that the streets of Irvine seem deserted on weekdays. But what about the constant traffic on Interstate 405, the San Diego Freeway? What is the relationship between the deserted residential streets and the crowded freeways? Where are the men and women going when they leave their Irvine homes every weekday morning?

Again, the answer lies in the service economy. Instead of making steel, building cars, making clothes, or growing food, many Americans are now making their living by distributing parcels, writing computer software, conducting medical procedures, distributing fast food, moving data from one place to another, creating and exchanging information—in short, using manufactured goods and information to create better ways of doing work. In 1970, the service sector accounted for $1,015.5 billion in revenues of the gross national product. By 1985, that figure had risen to $3,998.1 billion, or over two-thirds of the gross national product. The service sector is growing so fast that the Bureau of Labor Statistics estimates that by 1995 as many as 90 percent of all new jobs will be created in that sector.

This shift to a service economy has had a profound effect on patterns of recent suburbanization. In large measure, the phenomenal growth that has taken place in Orange County in the past decade and the corresponding slow growth that has plagued Park Forest are both results of this emerging service- and information-based economy. Stated simply, service industries and the people they employ have different needs and make different demands on an area than do goods-producing industries and their work forces. What Park Forest was to the organization man, Irvine is to the successor generation. This generation is part of America's first postindustrial work force, part of a growing service-based work force that wants far more from their communities than postwar suburbia was designed to deliver.

Service industries require different kinds of locations, have different kinds of transportation needs, require different kinds of government services, have different energy needs, and use capital differently. And just as service firms require a different kind of employee, service employees seek a different kind of work environment and a different kind of leisure. For the organization man, with his personality ethic, "standard of living" was paramount, that is, the quantity of consumer goods—a new car every two or three years, a boat, a recreational vehicle, a riding lawnmower. For his children, with their self ethic, it is "quality of life" that counts, that is, the quality of goods, services, and amenities—health care, education, recreation, environment, and the arts.

Success in a mass-production economy required low-cost labor, cheap raw materials, and ready access to transportation and markets. In a service economy, the formula for success differs sharply. First, service industries need intelligent workers and office space to house them. In the age of the knowledge and information worker, the raw material of work is ideas. Labor costs are relative and usually high. And access to transportation and markets is more a function of high technology than of location. Indeed, the workplace of the knowledge worker is not a "place" at all in the usual sense. Work takes "place" whenever and wherever information is circulated, processed, manipulated, assimilated, interpreted, or otherwise acted upon. Productivity is measured not by quantity or the creation of goods that can be counted, inventoried, and stockpiled, but by the value that has been added to the information, which is another way of saying that it is the quality of the work that counts most.

Thus, work, like so many other experiences of postmodern life, entails operating in relational systems of endlessly circulating signs. And the requirements of this kind of work have helped create a physical manifestation of such systems not only in the communications technologies that compose them, but in the suburban landscape where they are located. While a manufacturing economy needs large tracts of land for the manufacturing and warehousing of goods, a service economy requires high-quality office space. As the service economy has grown, the demand for office space has grown with it. Between 1978 and 1986 the United States added 1.1 billion square feet of office space—the equivalent of forty new downtowns the size of downtown San Francisco. But unlike urban development in the past, many of these new office structures were built not in big-city downtowns, but in the suburbs, thus creating an entirely new form of urbanization. Since the early 1970s, and at an accelerating pace in the 1980s, these suburban developments have evolved into what have variously been called "urban villages," "edge cities," and "technoburbs."

These office parks now coexist with huge regional shopping malls, condominium developments, restaurants, theaters, and residential areas—all far distant from the central city and beyond its reach socially and economically. Whereas suburbanites formerly headed to the city to work, hear a symphony, eat in a good restaurant, or see a lawyer, today they may drive a short distance from home in almost any direction to do those things. And whereas every morning the organization man left a house teeming with children and tended by his wife, the houses of the successor generation stand empty in the daytime: The wives work, couples have fewer children, and those few are in day care. And yet most of these men and women are not working far away in some central business district, but nearby in low-density office parks. Nobody is home, but nobody is really gone, either. It is a curious landscape: busy, but not bustling with the life of the city; apart, but not standing isolated as reservations for women and children. Neither center nor periphery, these postmetropolitan suburbs are knitting new patterns across the landscape.

Good-bye central.

The forces that are creating these new patterns may be observed at work on the southeastern edge of the San Francisco Bay area. Forty miles east-southeast of San Francisco, where Interstate 680 crosses Interstate 580, two massive postindustrial office parks are taking shape within eight miles of each other. The larger of the two is being built on 876 acres, and when it is completed, sometime around the turn of the century, it will contain 11.75 million square feet of mixed-use space, at a cost of $1.86 billion. It will employ thirty-six thousand people. The other park is nearly as large—585 acres, 6.5 million square feet of leased space, and a $2 billion price tag. Both are already phenomenal successes.

Such parks are indicative of how the emergence of an information and service economy is changing the face of the suburbs. In the late seventies and early eighties, when both developments were on the drawing boards, there was no development within miles of the two sites. There was only the intersection of the two interstates surrounded by miles and miles of ranch land. Only the far reaches of the Bay area's bedroom suburbs were within a ten-to-fifteen minute drive. By the standards of an industrial economy, it seemed an improbable location for the next major business hub of the region. There were no raw materials, no rail access, and no industrial infrastructure. However, the area did have all the ingredients needed to create a postindustrial boom town: high-speed highways, low-to-moderate land and development costs, and—most important—close proximity to a high-quality work force. And almost as important, a beautiful setting and an ideal climate.

Highway transportation plays a key role in such development. The interstate highway system and its interlocking network of expressways and high-speed arterials form the skeleton on which posturbia grows. Information and service industries locate close to the intersections of major freeways or interstates because service industries need to be near their base of employees and the fastest and most efficient transportation systems available—trucking and air transport. In many service industries, time has become just as important as quality, productivity, or innovation. In the industrial past, companies paid attention to costs, quality, and inventory as measures of competitive advantage, but time was rarely taken into account. Today, however, leading service companies recognize that managing time—in the development of new products, production, sales, marketing, and distribution—means perhaps the ultimate competitive advantage. The research and development department needs to be close to a high-quality, research-oriented university, the production department needs to be close to its suppliers, the sales force needs easy access to its potential customers, and shipments must move door to door in the shortest possible time.

In addition, for the two Bay area parks, land and development costs were far lower than in downtown San Francisco, Oakland, or San Jose. And just as important, there is room to grow. While service industries can locate in downtown areas—and most downtowns have benefited from the growth of the service economy—space is limited and the cost of expansion can be prohibitive. Downtowns also suffer from transportation problems, and parking is expensive and in short supply. Parking in suburban office parks is usually in surface lots or above-ground structures that are inexpensive and easy to maintain. As a result, posturban office rents are substantially lower than are rents for comparable space in downtown areas—in some locales, as much as 50 percent lower.

However, lower rents and easy access to highways could not, in and of themselves, have attracted companies from downtown locations. The key ingredient was people. Both the office parks are within easy commuting distance of the high-quality work force that service industries require. When Pacific Bell decided to relocate 7,000 of its employees to a 2-million-square-foot facility it built in one of the parks, it did so because 40 percent of its employees were already living within the county where the park is located. The same dynamics convinced such major service employers as Chevron, Toyota, Beckman Instruments, Westinghouse Electric, and Pacific Gas & Electric to locate in this beautiful but "remote" corner of the Bay Area.

Good location is a relative term. When viewed from the top of San Francisco's highest office building, the Bank of America Tower, the intersection of Interstates 580 and 680 looks to be a world away. If you were to take a compass and center it on the Bank of America building and then draw concentric circles so each successive ring was five miles farther out, you would have to go to the thirty-five-mile radius point before you would include both business parks. And you would find that the newest suburban housing developments were included in only the last two rings—between twenty-five and thirty-five miles. And that distance is as the crow flies; by car, of course, most of those suburban communities are much farther from San Francisco.

However, if you were to center your compass on the intersection of Interstates 580 and 680 and construct a similar series of concentric circles, the perspective would change dramatically. Suddenly, a majority of the newest homes, as well as some of the most affluent communities in suburbia, would be within ten miles of your center point. Thus, if there is a match between the kind of work force an organization needs and the skills and experience of people living in these outlying communities, then you have an almost irresistible location—at least in a postindustrial context. But the city-to-suburb commute pattern is broken, perhaps forever.

In the industrial metropolis, the central business district was the commercial heart of the region and it dictated the pattern of growth. Growth of the area was stimulated first by the railroads and then by the construction of networks of radial highways. Both transportation systems were designed to increase the attractiveness and accessibility of the central business district. As growth moved outward from the center, through successive zones of urbanization, the typical pattern was for inner rings to be progressively downgraded in their perceived value and the farthest ring to be populated by the most affluent residents. Downtown businesses orchestrated this pattern of development, and "social class characteristically varied with distance away from the center."

In the postindustrial metropolis, the pattern of urbanization is turned inside out. Unlike urban-suburban development, which is the result of dynamics set in motion by a central business district, postmetropolitan development has no central focus, but multiple centers and multiple foci. In a word, it is decentered. In many instances, available housing, recreational opportunities, and choices of life-styles are the prime motivators—not available jobs. As if a city had been subjected to a giant egg beater, posturban development looks at first like a wild scattering of buildings in all directions. There seems to be no rhyme or reason for the placement of these buildings, no ordering principle at work, merely an ugly, random, chaotic sprawl across the landscape.

There is, however, a powerful pattern at work here, but it is invisible to the industrial eye. This pattern moves to the beat of the service economy and to the needs of a generation that makes different demands on its environment than the organization man did. Postmetropolitan development can—and inevitably will—take place almost anywhere the magic ingredients coexist: good highway transportation, low-to-moderate land and development costs, access to a high-quality labor pool, high-quality governmental services (or the potential for them), good telecommunications, strong educational resources—particularly at the university level—and an attractive setting with many leisure and cultural opportunities.

Irvine is one of America's first postmetropolitan "cities." It has its roots in the urban-planning utopias of the industrial age, but its residents and the surrounding region are pure postmetro. Irvine was begun in the early 1970s, when Orange County was mostly orange groves, tomato and sugar-beet fields, and vast stretches of mesquite-covered range land. Today, fewer than 20 years after Irvine's founding, the Costa Mesa–Irvine–Newport Beach complex (as this instant postmetropolis has come to be called) boasts California's third largest "downtown"—or, more accurately, postmetropolitan center—with more than 21.1 million square feet of office and business park space. But, of course, it is not a center (or a periphery), but something more akin to a network with many nodes, none more central than any other. And leading this massive growth is Irvine, the largest planned community on the West Coast. It is here that one glimpses America's postmetropolitan future. For the pattern emerging in Orange County is one that much of America is sure to follow—for better or for worse.

"Roots and Wings."

By eastern standards, the scale of Irvine is overwhelming. There are twelve residential neighborhoods, each with a distinct identity. Each has its own schools, parks, recreational facilities, and shopping centers. The city is laid out on what planners call a "supergrid." Major highways crisscross the city, as if it were an enormous ticktacktoe board, with the boundaries of each neighborhood marked by the major arterials. The high-speed arterials make it possible to travel from one end of the city to the other in under ten minutes. This gives Irvine a quality rarely achieved in other cities and towns—the usually contradictory features of accessibility and privacy. Each of the neighborhoods is like a village unto itself. With most of the basic necessities available from the nearby neighborhood center, residents can choose to stay close to home, or they can jump in their cars and be across town in no time.

Irvine is an excellent example of what David Birch called a "high-innovation" city, possessing all the elements—educational resources, high-quality labor, high-quality government, good telecommunications, and high quality of life—to attract the kind of businesses that are driving an entrepreneurial revolution. Irvine is the home of the University of California at Irvine, the newest campus in the prestigious University of California system. Irvine also sits within the largest concentration of high-technology companies in the United States, boasting more than Silicon Valley or Massachusetts' Route 128 corridor. In fewer than twenty years, from 1965 to 1984, Orange County experienced a phenomenal six-hundred-fold increase in the number of its businesses, making the county one of the fastest-growing economies in the world.

Orange County and Irvine have grown at such extraordinary rates because they have created the kind of environment that information and service-based industries need, and the area has developed the quality of life a successor-generation population seeks. As Ever Jaques, executive vice president of the Del Taco restaurant chain, observes, "Not only in Irvine, but elsewhere in the area, a great deal of attention has been paid to the quality of life." The man-made lakes, golf courses, gourmet restaurants, tennis clubs, and olympic-size neighborhood swimming complexes were not afterthoughts in Irvine, but an integral part of the overall design to attract business and industry and their successor-generation work force. The Irvine Company, developers of the city, likes to promote it as a "Roots and Wings" community. According to them, the city's attraction lies in "roots"—the traditional values of family, neighborhood, and community—and in "wings"—the civic, cultural, educational, and business opportunities that exist in the city and the region.

The developers have proved right. Irvine has become one of the most sought-after addresses in southern California—and in the nation. In summer 1988, the median price of a single-family detached home in Orange County stood at $224,828 (with 17 percent of all households qualifying), the highest in the nation. (By comparison, the U.S. median home price was $91,300, with fully 46 percent of all households qualifying; the median for California was $172,406, 24 percent of households qualifying; and the median for the New York metropolitan region was $191,900.) Meanwhile, the median household income in Orange County (in 1986) was $41,000, more than 80 percent higher than the median for the nation then.

Not long ago, residents of Los Angeles liked to say of their neighbors to the south that Orange County's highest cultural peak was the Matterhorn, a fake mountain and roller-coaster ride at Disneyland. But that is no longer the case. In fall 1986, the $65 million Orange County

Performing Arts Center opened, and it has quickly become one of the required stops on tours by the world's most celebrated orchestras and dance companies. The center's three-thousand-seat theater and three-hundred-seat companion stage are among the finest in the nation. For some, it is incredible to think of a suburban wasteland having a world-class symphony hall, but to the postmetropolitan dwellers of the Costa Mesa–Irvine–Newport Beach complex, it is a natural addition to an environment they already consider one of the most desirable in the country.

As the region has grown, attracting more and more successor-generation families and more and more high-tech companies, the area has become more sophisticated. Near Orange County's John Wayne Airport, a postmetropolitan commercial hub has developed that includes a Westin, a Meridien, and a Four Seasons hotel. And South Coast Plaza, which in 1987 exceeded $700 million in sales—surpassing downtown San Francisco and Beverly Hills' famous "Golden Triangle" shopping district—boasts many of the most high-end retail stores in the country, including Saks Fifth Avenue, Jaeger, Abercrombie & Fitch, Bally of Switzerland, Cartier, Mark Cross, Charles Jourdan, and the only California branch of the respected Rizzoli book store.

Upscale shops and hotels are, of course, only minor ingredients in defining a high quality of life. Other desirable features, many of which are rooted in values that the organization offspring learned in their childhood homes, are even more important. Among them are good schools for their children, a good local government, and good planning. Irvine is also attractive because of its location at the foot of a majestic mountain range, its closeness to Pacific Ocean beaches, its nearly ideal climate—267 days of sunshine annually, temperatures from the sixties to the seventies in summer and from the forties to the sixties in winter, and fewer than fifteen inches of rain per year—and the quality and design of its housing. However, its greatest distinction lies in its character as a planned community.

With the same boldness and vision as the developers of Park Forest, the Irvine Company set out to meet the needs of a new generation of suburban dwellers. Its aim was to provide a diversity of housing types; recreational facilities; educational facilities, from day care through university training; retail shopping; and hassle-free transportation, all within a planned environment. It sought to create a community in which residents could live *and* work, do their shopping, play, practice their religion, and be entertained as well as enlightened. It wanted to create more than a sophisticated subdivision. It wanted to create, insofar as is possible in today's centerless pattern of suburbanization, a sense of place, something rarely found in tract developments.

This is not to suggest that Irvine has somehow rejoined what industrialism sundered. Home and work have not been physically combined, only moved closer together. And though many amenities that were formerly found close together only in small towns are now found across the postmetropolitan landscape, these new communities are far from organic, formed as they are, for all their careful planning, by the dynamics of highway construction, housing prices, and the movement of capital.

Nevertheless, to a great degree, Irvine has succeeded in a way that Park Forest never did. For all its careful planning and slowly phased-in development, Park Forest never became a community in which residents could both live and work. Its industrial park never attracted the industries it had hoped to draw, and to this day most residents work at jobs outside the boundaries of the village.

Park Forest was, in many ways, ahead of its time, but it could not rise above the prevailing wisdom of the day. Postwar suburbia was built on the assumption that the man of the house would commute to work each day, leaving his wife at home to cook the meals, clean the house, and care for the children. As Dolores Hayden observed: "Most American housing is based on Levitt's model of the home as a haven for the male worker's family. Americans chose the Levittown model for housing in the late 1940s; we have mass-produced the home as haven and transformed our cities to fit this model and its particular social, economic, and environmental shortcomings." Indeed, nearly three-quarters of the nation's housing has been built since 1940, and nearly two-thirds of that housing stock consists of single-family detached homes.

In the late 1940s and early 1950s, Americans wanted a separation between their homes and their jobs. They wanted to continue a pattern of living and working that had begun with the rise of streetcar suburbs and expanded dramatically with the dawning of the automobile age. As Robert Fishman pointed out in *Bourgeois Utopias: The Rise and Fall of Suburbia,* "every true suburb is the outcome of two opposing forces, an attraction toward the opportunities of the great city and a simultaneous repulsion against urban life." Suburbia originated as a place to escape the perils of the city, to provide a crime- and disease-free environment for women and children. Such a haven was seen as a necessity. And in the view of postwar planners—and citizens—all the traditional functions in a community, such as living, shopping, and working, should be separated. And so cities and suburbs across the nation enacted comprehensive plans and zoning ordinances that were designed to legalize and ensure the separation.

The fact that the separation of basic functions encouraged urban sprawl and a massively inefficient land-use pattern was seen as a side effect the public was willing to tolerate and the planners were unable to stop. Public officials turned a blind eye to the downside of urban sprawl because they recognized, perhaps unconsciously, that suburbia represented something more important than a nice house and a patch of grass. Suburbia, in the form of the single-family, detached house, was the embodiment of the American dream.

It is one of the ironies of history that one of the most fervent dreams of twentieth-century urban planners—to rejoin the home and the workplace, a bond that was severed by the industrial revolution—would occur in a community whose master plan was inspired by the great planners of the industrial age. Irvine, as one of America's first postmetropolitan cities, has been able to achieve what what all other postwar planned developments could only hope for—a place where it is actually possible to work as well as to live.

This century-old dream became a reality not because planners finally succeeded in convincing citizens of the reasonableness of their comprehensive plans but because of the sweeping economic, social, and cultural changes that have moved the nation from an industrial and manufacturing economy to a service- and information-based society. Postindustrialization, globalization, spreading levels of education, the emergence of a multipolar world order, and the rise of an economy based on customized production and niche consumption have all undermined more familiar hierarchies—hierarchies that appeared in the landscape as city-center/suburban-periphery. The centripetal forces that once flowed inward to give shape and texture to communities—physically, socially, and politically—have reversed and now surge outward, resulting in a deconcentrated pattern of urbanization. Such patterns can now be observed in such unfamiliar places as Tyson's Corner, Virginia; City Post Oak–Galleria (on Houston's west side), and the King of Prussia–Route 202 complex northwest of Philadelphia. And with the growth of the service economy expected to continue, we can anticipate a continuation of this new form well into the next century.

All these social forces entail a particular form of complexity, namely, diversity—of people, locations, methods, and loci of power. Moreover, diversity emerges in various ways, often in the movement of new conditions or new initiatives from the margins to the middle—or, more precisely, what is left of the middle, since the rise of diversity eats away at the middle itself. Consequently, the number of centers of initiative is far greater. And there are many ways for such initiatives to be structured.

The task for communities, as well as for individuals, in a postmetropolitan world is to navigate diversity, for the effects of such powerful social forces are not limited to wide-open western spaces that are ripe for development. They are already being felt in many older communities and suburbs that also find themselves swept up in—and in some cases left behind by—the emerging postmetropolitan environment. Aging Park Forest, no less than much younger Sunbelt suburbs, is daily confronted with challenges to its very survival by these new realities. Nowhere do these new realities—and the potential for misunderstanding them—show up more clearly than in the rapidly changing world of suburban retailing.

A tale of two towers.

Twenty minutes north of the Golden Gate Bridge off U.S. Highway 101, the main artery linking San Francisco to affluent suburban Marin County, sits Town Center Corte Madera. Completed in 1988 at a cost of $58 million, it is a 456,000-square-foot complex of department stores, specialty shops, restaurants, and financial institutions. But with its red-tile roofs, fountains, tan stucco exteriors, and open-air courtyards filled with large terra-cotta pots spilling over with bright flowers, it is vaguely reminiscent of a Mediterranean fishing village. The developers and the architect consciously scaled the center to draw shoppers into and through its numerous plazas and courtyards. Many of the restaurants have outdoor seating; storefronts are set back at various angles and placed on different levels to reinforce the imagery of a small, European town. Expensive architectural details abound: cornices, parapets, tile trim, brass-and-copper light fixtures, brick-and-tile walkways, European-style granite paving.

With its neotraditional (Mediterranean) design, Town Center Corte Madera is one of a number of new commercial centers built in the late 1980s that seek to revive the vernacular architecture of bygone eras. The goal is to recapture the human scale that made small towns so appealing. Town Center is worthy of note because of its unique design—it has won numerous awards—but what makes it really distinctive is that it is a renovation of Marin County's oldest retail center (built in 1958). Designed originally to meet the needs of organization men's families, it now seeks to re-create itself in an image that is more in tune with the needs of the successor generation. But there is serious question whether its developers have read correctly the postmetropolitan realities.

The giveaway is a structure rarely seen these days in shopping developments—a clock tower. Viewed through the fog that tumbles over the west Marin hills and into the complex, the sixty-foot tower is meant to evoke the famous tower in the center of Venice's San Marco Piazza.

And like the tower from which it takes its inspiration, the Town Center's tower stands as a symbol of what the development would like to be—the heart of the community, the gathering place where friends meet and lovers stroll, the vibrant town square. In the decentered postmetropolitan world, it seeks—as its name proclaims—to become a town center. As the too-insistent literature of its developers puts it:

> Corte Madera Town Center's tenant mix has been carefully developed to support and enhance the architectural design of a small town village square. The feeling and synergy of a downtown has [*sic*] been created with financial institutions, restaurants, a variety of services, department stores, specialty stores, a drugstore, and a supermarket. Prominently tagged in advertising as "The Main Street of Marin," Town Center is Marin's one-stop, family-oriented shopping center. As Corte Madera's only "downtown," Town Center has a unique role as a community focal point.

But the developers protest too much. This is not a village, a downtown, a main street, or a center, no matter what its name and its prospectus say. It is, rather, the latest incarnation of a postwar American classic—the suburban shopping mall. And its vaunted tenant mix resembles that of the dreary, older, unfocused malls that have recently been failing all over the country in ever greater numbers. There are, among other things, a McDonald's, a Payless shoe store, a Woolworth's, a J. C. Penney's, an eyewear shop, a nail-care store, a Safeway, a Thrifty drugstore, a hot dog stand, a B. Dalton bookstore, a savings and loan association, and—incongruously—a fine Italian restaurant.

Despite the old-world facade, Town Center is not unlike the places Americans flocked to in the fifties and sixties and now do not. Most supermarkets and many drug stores moved out of malls long ago. The components of "one-stop" malls, like the downtown centers that preceded them, have been dispersed all across the postmetropolitan landscape. And newer malls are not targeted at the great mass middle of the market anymore, but at particular niches: Recent upscale malls feature two or more flagship department stores like Macy's, Nieman-Marcus, and Lord & Taylor and offer specialty stores of similar appeal, while the low end is dominated by discount factory-outlet malls. Meanwhile the vast middle market is taken care of largely by easily accessible strip malls featuring drugstores, hair salons, fast-food places, and other small stores designed to serve everyday needs. None of these types of malls pretends to be anything other than what it is—and certainly not a town center.

Whether one can turn back the clock—symbolized, in Corte Madera's case, by *bringing* back the clock—is a question that is yet to be answered by Town Center. The attempt to re-create the liveliness of a small-town business district by providing space for some of the functions that once populated main-street America is perhaps a worthy goal. But the odds against it succeeding are overwhelming.

Meanwhile, 2,100 miles to the east, another retail mall is undergoing extensive renovation. And while its goal may be similar, its approach is altogether different.

On a cold winter day in January 1987, a large crane equipped with a wrecking ball moved to the middle of what was once one of the most successful shopping centers in the nation. The heavy cast-iron ball slammed into the side of a three-sided, white, brick clock tower. With little resistance, the tower, at the heart of one of America's first shopping centers—the Park Forest Plaza—came tumbling down. The Plaza had been the centerpiece of Park Forest, America's first postwar planned community, and the clock tower stood as a proud symbol of what was to become one of the most celebrated suburbs in the world.

Although the concept of planned shopping centers with free off-street parking had been around since the early 1920s (most observers trace the modern shopping center back to Kansas City's Spanish-Moorish style Country Club Plaza), no private developer had ever designed a community with a shopping center at its heart. Around the time ground was being broken for Park Forest, many developers had begun to build shopping centers—the first major planned shopping center was built in Raleigh, North Carolina, in 1949. And other developers were building large suburban residential projects—the Levitts were building Levittown at a rate that peaked at one house every fifteen minutes. But no one had put the two elements together, along with schools, church sites, public utilities, municipal services, and open space, to create a planned community. Thus, when American Community Builders broke ground on the Park Forest Plaza in 1948, they were making planning and real-estate-development history.

As the village of Park Forest grew, the Plaza grew with it, and by 1968, twenty years after its founding, the Plaza ranked fourth in retail sales among forty-eight Chicago suburbs. Because the shopping center was designed to serve as the village center—not merely as the community's shopping district—the center's first phase included an ultra-modern grocery store, a pub, a bowling alley, a theater, a bank, and second-story offices for doctors, dentists, lawyers, accountants, and other service providers. On the periphery of the parking lot that encircled the mall, the developers set aside land for the police and fire departments, the village hall, a public utilities building, the public library, and churches. All the elements that might be found within three blocks of the town square in a small town were included.

But as the village grew, the needs of the residents changed. In response, the retail environment began to change. First, the most popular retailer, the grocery store, at the center of the mall, wanted to expand and provide additional parking. So it abandoned the shopping center and moved across the street as the anchor of a strip development that included a full-service drug store and a hardware store. Later, as the demand for medical and dental services grew, the doctors and dentists who had occupied many of the second-story offices in the Plaza moved out of town and developed a "professional arts building," as they called it. Many of the lawyers and accountants also left in favor of their own buildings, also out of the village. The bank left the center in search of more space because its officers believed they needed an auto drive-up facility to remain competitive. The bakery and the meat market both closed because they could no longer compete with the "bake shop" and the meat counters of the newly expanded supermarket.

Even with the loss of some major tenants, the shopping center continued to thrive, largely because of the drawing power of its three largest tenants—Sears, Goldblatt's, and Marshall Field. These department stores, each catering to slightly different but overlapping clienteles, acted as powerful magnets drawing customers from a large geographic area. However, with the completion of two interstate highways within a few miles of the center, the retail dynamics of the entire region changed. Interstate 57, built in the midsixties to connect Chicago to St. Louis; Memphis; and, eventually, New Orleans, passes fewer than five miles to the west of the shopping center. Just to the north and west of Park Forest, Interstate 57 crosses one of America's most historic highways, U.S. 30, or the Lincoln Highway, as it was known to millions of Americans during its heyday in the 1930s.

It was at the intersection of Interstate 57 and U.S. 30, where the work of the first generation of great American highway builders met the master work of the second generation of highway builders, that the area's first regional shopping center was developed. Appropriately, the center was named the Lincoln Mall. Unlike the Park Forest Plaza, which had been designed to operate as a town center, Lincoln Mall, like most regional centers of its type, unashamedly catered to the automobile and eliminated any pretense of serving as a town center. It was designed to take full advantage of its easily accessible location on the interstate within a trading area estimated at more than eighty square miles.

The impact of Lincoln Mall on its much smaller predecessor, the

Park Forest Plaza—1.2 million square feet of retail space versus 695,101 square feet—was immediate and devastating. By 1987, the Plaza's roster of eighty retailers had dwindled to twelve. The Plaza could not compete with the variety, convenience, and diversity of Lincoln Mall. Even Park Foresters turned their backs on the Plaza.

Park Forest officials were faced with the prospect that the Plaza would soon die, leaving a gaping hole at the center of the community. They were also faced with the even grimmer thought that without retail sales, tax revenues would plummet, thus threatening the ability of the village to provide needed services. The officials decided to take matters into their own hands. If the retailers could not turn the situation around, perhaps the town could. Anyway, they thought it was worth a try.

In the best tradition of Park Forest–style activism—in 1956 Whyte wrote, "Park Forest probably swallows up more civic energy per hundred people than any other community in the country"—the village's elected officials went to the citizens for help. Residents turned out in force at a series of town meetings to weigh their options. Eventually, they settled on a unique—and risky—solution: The village decided to become partners with a private developer to save the shopping center.

The redevelopment package included several interesting features. First, Park Forest induced the state of Illinois to issue $13 million in low-interest bonds, guaranteed by the developer, to pay remodeling expenses. Second, the developer put up several million dollars. Then, to demonstrate the village's faith in the project, Park Forest backed $5 million in tax-increment financing. If the project succeeded, "then increases in real estate tax valuation and sales revenues would pay for the project." If it failed, the villagers would have to pay.

The redesign and reconstruction of the Park Forest Plaza began in summer 1986. One year later, on Saturday, August 29, 1987, the plaza—renamed "The Centre"—officially reopened. A headline in the local paper proclaimed: "Centre geared to community versus mega-mall mentality."

"I think we've seen it come full circle," said William Carpenter, vice president of leasing for the center, explaining the philosophy behind the redevelopment. "There are so many malls in this country, all with dozens of smaller malls built around them—it's only a matter of time before each market becomes over-saturated. Stores begin turning over, traffic and crime become a problem. It creates a kind of hustle-and-bustle atmosphere where shoppers are treated like cattle—but shoppers aren't cattle, and they get fed up."

Here was the community-center idea again. The Park Forest Centre would become what it had once been—the center of community life.

What had become its most damaging feature—that it was landlocked in the center of the community, surrounded by municipal buildings, schools, the public library, a civic center, churches, and inaccessible by freeways—would be turned into its most appealing asset. Declared the local newspaper: "With a stage for entertainment, and space for public access and recreation built into the main park area, the project represents a return to the old-fashioned town center concept, and a radical departure from what the developers call the 'mega-mall' trend. It is this aspect that first attracted [the developer] and later became an integral part of the redevelopment plan. Space for community groups to meet and hold events was included, along with benches and game tables for the interior park."

The appeal of the Centre was much the same as that of Town Center Corte Madera. The developers and their Park Forest partners were betting that the desire to turn back the clock to a time when people strolled from shop to shop, exchanging greetings and gazing in store windows, when friends lingered over coffee and watched the world go by, would prove irresistible. So they jackhammered the concrete of the old Plaza and replaced it with fountains, ponds, and streams crossed by wooden footbridges and complemented by large beds of flowers, trees, and shrubs. Carved redwood signs replaced chrome and neon store signs; large canopies of wooden beams replaced the cold, steel overhangs.

By mid-1990, the shopping center had begun to rebound. Its two anchor stores, Marshall Field and Sears, had been extensively renovated—a strong indication of the retailers' faith in the viability of the Centre. The movie theater, long idle, had reopened as a three-screen complex, and the roster of tenants had grown to almost forty. That was still far short of the seventy-five stores the developer had promised on "reopening day," but it was a good start.

Even at that, it had not been smooth sailing. On January 13, 1987, with the massive redevelopment well under way, the corporate parent of Marshall Field, the center's most important tenant, filed a lawsuit seeking permission to break its lease, which still had ten years to run. Only intense community pressure, a six-thousand-signature petition to Field's CEO, picketing of the firm's flagship store in Chicago's Loop, and extensive media coverage persuaded the company to reconsider. Marshall Field stayed, and the redevelopment continued. Thirty-one years after Whyte had heralded the community's high level of civic involvement, Park Foresters still possessed the spirit to mount a grass-roots citizens' protest and to win the day.

In suburban San Francisco, a clock tower rises symbolizing a new day. In suburban Chicago, a clock tower is demolished and the same message is proclaimed. But difficult questions remain. Is Park Forest swimming against the tide of history, attempting to turn a fervent wish into reality? Can civic activism and innovative public-private commercial partnerships successfully oppose the powerful forces that are creating postmetropolitan America? Is the emergence of more intimately scaled, more community-oriented town "centers" like Corte Madera evidence of something more than the latest wave of slick marketing copy or the dreams of retired organization men? Or are these centers merely poorly conceived retail concepts, out of touch with new realities?

Whatever the answers, this much is certain: The dynamics driving postmetropolitan development also drive those communities that ostensibly lie outside it—whether trendy enclaves in Marin County or almost anachronistic bedroom communities in the heartland. Willingly or not, these communities, too, must confront the disorienting implications of postmetropolitan geography, where the pattern of urban center/ concentric suburbs is being replaced by a decentric landscape that includes home and work, leisure and commerce, privacy and public life. No less than the residents of Irvine, the residents of every community live in the postmetropolitan world, even if they do not physically reside there.

Postmetropolitan paradoxes.

Although the requirements of the service economy are fundamentally altering the suburban landscape and establishing a new relationship between the workplace and the home—lateral commuting now exceeds the suburb-to-city pattern that dominated in the fifties and sixties—this pattern of growth is fueled by economic and political forces that simultaneously sustain it and undermine it. Housing prices, highway construction, and the location of businesses, when they are all in sync, encourage postmetropolitan development, but when the resulting development destroys that delicate balance, housing development, highways, and businesses may then leapfrog each other in ways that recall old-fashioned urban sprawl. This is the postmetropolitan paradox: The dynamics that are producing seemingly more stable arrangements are prey to constraints that, in the manner of all the other centerless systems in which we increasingly live, continually defer stability.

One of the chief constraints on postmetropolitan areas is rising energy costs. When energy costs rise, the price of land and housing near available employment and other services also rises. The better the location, the higher the costs. That has always been a truism in real estate, but it takes on added significance in a world of scarce energy and political instability in the Middle East. Although economists and politicians differ about what increased energy costs will mean, there is widespread agreement that the cost of fossil fuels will continue to rise. Perhaps even more important, the real cost of energy in relation to disposable income is expected to increase, which suggests that rising energy costs will force Americans into a series of tough choices. We can

□ remain essentially automobile dependent, but accept higher density and less privacy;
□ continue to allow low-density sprawl, but accept longer, slower commutes and much higher infrastructure costs;
□ allow a dispersed pattern of development to continue, but accept an increased reliance on more hazardous energy sources, such as liquid natural gas and nuclear energy;
□ move toward a greater use of mass transit or risk the imminent danger of the greenhouse effect.

It is not surprising that there is a great deal of resistance to the notion that such hard choices are inevitable. Many Americans, especially those who live in postmetropolitan areas, continue to want it both ways: They want inexpensive housing *and* a short commute; they want good highways, adequate sewer systems, good schools, *and* low taxes; they want to be close to shopping and recreational facilities *and* to have a great deal of privacy. They want clean air, clean water, *and* less governmental intrusion into their lives. The list is almost endless. In effect, they want the best of suburbia, organization-man style, and the best of postmetro, successor-generation style.

Out of this dilemma arises what may well become the second most important limiting factor to postmetropolitan growth: the growth-control movement. It is the first important cause to develop in postmetropolitan society and it is significant because it illustrates how the successor generation—these children of the suburbs—acts on the beliefs they were taught by their suburban-dwelling parents. It also exposes the paradoxical nature of postmetropolitan dynamics and raises for the organization offspring—once again—the specter of limits.

The explosive growth of the service economy created postmetropolitan areas almost overnight and in the process made multimillionaires out of the developers of commercial and residential property. But with the boom came the unwanted reality of overloaded sewer systems, inadequate water systems, clogged highways, and overburdened public schools. For example, while the standard of living in Orange County rose to among the highest in the country, the county has also become home to some of the most horrendous traffic jams in the nation. The area is also creating two jobs for every housing unit it puts up, resulting in a severe housing shortage. Residents who moved to the area to enjoy its beautiful climate and laid-back life-style now find themselves sitting in traffic jams and breathing polluted air. In other words, Irvine is sliding from a "quality-of-life" community into a "standard-of-living" one.

Although such a story of paradise lost is hardly new, having occurred repeatedly in postwar suburbia, the scenario this time has a decidedly different twist—a postmetropolitan spin. The growth-control movement, while in its infancy nationwide, is already well established in California, especially in the postmetropolitan areas of the vast Los Angeles basin. In 1987, twenty California communities voted on growth-control initiatives, and fourteen such measures passed. By 1988, fifty-seven California cities and eight counties had voted to limit growth. In the paradoxical fashion of the emerging age, the growth-control movement brings together individuals and groups that were usually bitter enemies in the industrial past. Environmentalists, business executives, chamber-of-commerce officials, politicians from both the left and right, urban planners, and citizens of all social classes have joined in an attempt to slow and, in some cases, halt further growth.

Such diverse groups are unified by the view that local governments have lost control of the development process. Local municipalities that are eager to gain additional tax revenues encourage the development of office buildings and commercial structures but discourage the development of new homes, which would require the addition of new municipal services. Developers gravitate to outlying areas where planning and controls on growth are not yet in place. Without comprehensive planning and restrictive controls on growth, developers can offer housing at prices that are below those prevailing in surrounding communities. All this sets up a vicious dynamic. High-rise offices go up in one community, and the jobs follow. But no housing is available. Farther out, affordable homes are built, but without adequate infrastructures to support them. The new home owners from the affordable homes flood an inadequate road system, and huge traffic jams result.

The way out of the dilemma, say the growth-control advocates, is to place severe restrictions on the developers. Make all developers pay for all the improvements necessary to support their projects. Stop new development altogether until improvements in the highway, sewer, and other infrastructure improvements are in place or impose inflexible limits on new construction.

Unfortunately, this approach sets in motion another vicious dynamic—only this time in the other direction. Limiting growth in a community may well create a housing shortage. If the demand for housing does not decrease, housing costs will tend to escalate rapidly, thus forcing many of those who wish to buy in the area to look farther out. As these people move farther out, highways become even more congested. Eventually, if the highway problem goes unsolved, business expansion slows, the cost of doing business rises, and businesses relocate out of the area. Unlike the dynamics of the metropolis, where workers followed jobs, in a postmetropolitan world it is just as likely that employers will move to where the employees are located. And if the right mix of affordable housing, good climate, recreational facilities, and the like exist somewhere else, employers will flee the high cost of growth-controlled communities.

This double whammy is further complicated by what appears to be an obvious solution but turns out to be part of the problem: the building of new roads or the widening of existing freeways to meet current and projected traffic demand. This solution is so alluring that when the Orange County Executive Survey asked senior executives of the county's largest employers what the county's most serious problem was, more than 75 percent of them identified transportation, and the most popular solution offered was the construction of more freeways and roads. But the almost inevitable result of building more roads is to encourage further growth. The more roads, the more growth that can be accommodated. The more growth, the more roads that are needed.

As planners, some governmental officials, and urban experts have pointed out, the only way out of such a double bind is to widen the frame of reference for the problem. Taken in isolation, there is no solution to the traffic problem, or the housing problem, or any other postmetropolitan problem of this sort. Planning, they say, must be done on a regional basis; transportation, housing needs, and the creation of jobs must be coordinated; and local governments and regional and state authorities must work together. Public officials and private developers must be willing to work cooperatively. There must be agreement about what kind of a community residents want. There must be a more unified sense about what the region should look like as far as twenty-five to fifty years in the future. There must be region-wide consensus about when a community can limit its growth and when it cannot.

The difficulty, of course, with such reasonable positions is that they require mass action and the subordination of individual advantages to some concept of the greater good. Historically, however, Americans have tended to reject greater-good arguments, especially in the realm of urban affairs. As a nation of private decision makers, Americans hold most dear the freedom to travel, to live wherever they choose, and to associate with whomever they wish. While the workings of the marketplace may be inadequate and inefficient or may contain largely hidden forms of compulsion, most Americans are more willing to put their faith in the market than in the solutions offered by experts.

Out of these postmetropolitan paradoxes there is developing yet another, perhaps more promising, paradox. It can be seen operating in what are called "neotraditional developments"—places like Mashpee Commons, Massachusetts; Grand Harbor, Florida; and RiverPlace in Portland, Oregon. Mashpee Commons, on Cape Cod, is modeled after the old New England town with clapboard buildings, mansard-roof stores, and brick-edged sidewalks. It even has a village green. Grand Harbor, in Vero Beach, Florida, is a large, stucco-and-tile development on the Intracoastal Waterway. It is designed to look and feel like a Mediterranean village. Across the county, in Portland, is RiverPlace, a modern, ten-acre, mixed-use development along the Willamette River at the edge of downtown.

What distinguishes these projects is not only their distinctive design, but their combining of housing, shopping, services, and entertainment. RiverPlace even includes a marina. These developments are among the first in what may become a major trend in American planning—moving forward by going back. By returning to the town-planning traditions of the early twentieth century and before, they seek to create places where it is possible—and enjoyable—to walk to shops and services, where housing and day care are located close to jobs, where children can walk to school, and where public spaces are inviting and friendly. They seek nothing less than to restore residents' sense of place and to reverse the centrifugal forces of postmetropolitan America.

The paradox is that without the continuing evolution of the decentered society, this attempt to recapture the magic of small-town America would be impossible. It would be impossible because the developing market for neotraditional development is the result of two postmetro forces that are working against each other.

On the one hand, the postmetropolitan pattern of housing, stores, public facilities, services, and work sites has become so scattered, separated, and inefficient that Americans now spend an inordinate amount of time just trying to get from here to there. In 1989, Americans lost an estimated 2 billion hours sitting in traffic jams. As frustrations have risen and the quality of life has dropped, Americans have begun to search for alternatives to postmetro living.

On the other hand, the rise of new technologies, such as fax machines, local area networks, and computer workstations, and the development of new organizational forms, including project-based and team-oriented work designs, are enabling more Americans to work wherever they wish. The technological revolution that created the information age triggered the development of the scattered, cluttered postmetro landscape. Now in their second stage, the new technologies make it possible to reverse the patterns created in the first stage. Workers can work from home and employers can locate closer to their work force. The technology takes the place of cars and freeways, creating the opportunity for more compact, human-scale development.

In architect Robert A. M. Stern's Harbor Center in Vero Beach, Florida, it is once again possible to live above the store. One hundred sixteen apartments with terraces and balconies sit above the ground-level stores of the arcade overlooking the Intracoastal Waterway. Chances are, however, that the residents will not be the shop owners, as in the nineteenth and early twentieth centuries. They will likely be executives who are connected to their work through networked computer systems. Some days they will leave home and drive to visit colleagues or customers. But on most days they will walk to nearby shops, restaurants, and services, and they will spend more time with their families and friends and far less time in their cars.

In a world of two-earner families, where time is precious, where rising land values prohibit the excesses of suburban sprawl, where the desire to escape the frustrations of endless commutes is rising and where the technology has the power to free workers from the patterns of the industrial past, there stands a good chance that the neotraditional models of today could become the standards of tomorrow. But until that time, postmetropolitan development, as well as the forces operating against it, will go right on raising the question of limits and generating physical manifestations of artificial, relational systems in which stability is continually deferred. Pleasant as life may be for people like the Millers, these postmetropolitan suburbs are concrete instances of the unsettling nature of the postmodern condition, more likely to exaggerate than to eradicate the social artificiality of such a world.

9

Networks and Niches: Emerging Organizational Life

From hierarchies to networks.

Of all the manifestations of the emerging social structure and its antiparadigmatic paradigm, perhaps the most striking and far reaching is the accelerating transformation taking place in organizations. Under the pressure of global competition and advances in communication technology, there have appeared almost overnight new organizational forms that are the antithesis of the centered, functional hierarchies elaborated during the era of the organization man. Like postmetropolitan suburbs, these new-style organizations offer yet another concrete experience of the decentering that is taking place in every area of life—including personal identity—for the organization offspring.

In a sense, the decentering of organizations, especially corporate ones, seems almost inevitable, for after language itself the most general and pervasive centerless system is capitalism. Located everywhere and nowhere, this economic system endlessly circulates capital and power. And it is also the most notoriously unsettling: It uproots communities, it eradicates essentialist values, and it fragments the identity of individuals. Just as language operates on the principle of identity as difference, capitalism depends on the exchange relations of commodities, rather than on anything intrinsic to them. Much as any signifier derives its significance from all the signifiers that are not present, the value of any commodity, including one's labor, is found not in what it *is*, but in its relation to all the other absent commodities for which it may be exchanged, including money.

Money, however, is not merely a convenient "symbol," standing in for things in a kind of one-to-one relationship anymore than words are in a one-to-one relationship with things. Rather, money concentrates a whole system of social relations to which people, whose labor is converted into commodities, are extrinsic. Whether production workers, white-collar employees, or managers, they see their labor commodified and dispersed into a centerless and unstable system of never-ending exchange. Commentators across the board, from the Marxist Left to the high-Tory Right, have noted—and usually deplored—this alienating effect of capitalism. Individualist ideals of authenticity, as well as communitarian ideals of organicism, also implicitly criticize such alienation of human beings from their creations and from each other.

Though not nearly as old as language, this particular economic system has been with us for some time, and it has grown more centerless as it has evolved from the monopoly capitalism of the nineteenth century, located in centers of imperial might, to the finance capitalism of the late twentieth century, dispersed throughout the developed world. With the advent of new transportation systems, instantaneous communications, computer technology, and global financial markets, the system's effects have been rapidly accelerated and its reach vastly extended. Huge tanker ships, jet air-cargo systems, and containerized shipping have made it possible to move goods easily and cheaply anywhere in the world, abetted by developing countries that have improved their internal transportation networks and built seaports and central airports.

Meanwhile, new computer and satellite-communications technology have made it possible for businesses to break up their operations and disperse different steps in the production process to sites around the world. While this dispersal has led to the "export" of American jobs, it has also allowed formerly third-world countries to move boldly and quickly into global industries. Instead of the grinding, inexorable march of nineteenth-century industrialism outward from centers of colonialist empire, there now are former client states—South Korea, for example—rising almost overnight to prominence in industries that were formerly dominated by a few Western giants. Instead of a world economy dominated by one or two players, there now are many participants in a single, highly competitive global market. Instead of one financial center—New York—there are now many, moving capital from country to country at the touch of a computer key.

Moreover, in a world economy, where competitive advantage often lies in the quick and unimpeded flow of information across national boundaries, some of the most repressive regimes in the world, including the Soviet Union and its formerly Stalinist satellites, have been forced to loosen their control over what their people may see, hear, read, and say. These imperatives are shifting the framework of international politics from a bipolar world consisting of the United States versus the Soviet Union to a world of rapidly shifting and confusing allegiances. In Eastern Europe, the collapse of communism and the rise of mixed economies that will inevitably enter the global economy promise even more international players, more competition, and more shifting nodes of power. And it is not too fanciful to suggest that one day many of the impoverished nations of Africa will duplicate the miracle of the Pacific rim.

To cope with these new realities, many organizations now more closely resemble the decentered networks of which the organizations are a part than they do the centered hierarchical models out of which they grew. Organizational life often means flatter structures, the dissolving of departments in favor of teams across functions, and the ad hoc creation of small, flexible groups to accomplish specific tasks. Increasingly, the model of organization is coming to be that of the network, with constantly shifting nodes of power and influence, often geographically distant from each other, but tightly linked by communications.

To understand how and why the network organization emerged and what, as another decentered system that is molding us as we are molding it, this new form means for social character, we have to look first at the revolution in information technology. Though the triumph of this revolution has been loudly proclaimed many times before, its second and far more complicated stage is just getting under way and its implications are far from clear. Second, we have to look at the nature of information itself, which has become the chief resource of the postindustrial economy. The convergence of all these forces—the globalization of enterprise, the ubiquity of new information technologies, and the peculiar characteristics of information—has not only given rise to network organizations but has reversed the relationship between employer and employee, obliterated the distinction between "inside" and "outside" in organizations, and made space for niche companies that similarly blur the distinction between large and small organizations. For the organization offspring, these developments mean another step toward the artificiality they have always resisted.

"The more you change, the more you have to change."

In the 1950s, the rise of other direction—the ceaseless round of everyone looking to everyone else for guidance—was abetted by the appearance of an apposite new technology, television. Inserted into the distinctive pattern of other direction, television provided a national and instantaneous loop in the social feedback system, reflecting and, in part, helping to create the dominant social character of the period. Four decades later, the emergence of a group of new technologies, helping to create new organizational forms, as well as the new patterns of postmetropolitan suburbs, is similarly encouraging a new social character.

The technological side of this phenomenon has, for some time, been routinely referred to as the information revolution. In actuality, however, the technological changes taking place today are the beginning of the second stage in the evolution of information technologies. The first stage of the information revolution began with the invention of the computer in the late 1940s. However, until the invention of the personal computer, the information age was more of a skirmish than a revolution.

From the sixties through the eighties, computers were used primarily for relatively simple tasks. They were designed to capture information and speed up the process by which work was transacted. Computers helped people work more efficiently, but they had little impact on the nature of work itself. Consider the use of personal computers. The vast majority of them have been used for only two purposes: word processing and data analysis. Accountants and financial managers found that financial software packages dramatically shortened the time it took them to do financial analyses, and administrative assistants moved from electric typewriters to word-processing packages because such programs made their work easier. But the jobs themselves did not change, and neither did organizational processes and organizational structures. Computers were used merely as high-speed extenders; they made it possible for people to do more of what they were already doing. The quantity of work grew, but the quality was left unchanged. The much-heralded "office of the future" did not materialize.

In manufacturing, where the greatest hopes had been held for the technological revolution, the disappointment was greatest. Robert H. Hayes and Ramchandran Jaikumar explained why the hoped-for changes did not come about in that sector:

> For years, manufacturers have acquired new equipment much in the way a family buys a new car. Drive out the old, drive in the new, enjoy the faster, smoother more economical ride—and go on with life as before. [However] executives are discovering that acquiring FMS [flexible manufacturing systems] or any of the other advanced manufacturing systems is more like replacing an old car with a helicopter. . . . Buy a helicopter and you can engage in new professional and recreational activities, live in some remote place, develop new work methods, get a new perspective on the lay of the land. If you

don't do these things, you waste the small fortune you paid for the machine and for acquiring new skills and logistical support.

But in the second stage of the revolution, information technologies are evolving into a seamless integration of hardware, software, and tele-communications—electronic-information networks (local, regional, and global) from which individuals will be able to get whatever information they need whenever they need it. From 1985 to 1990—fewer than five years—we have witnessed the development and widespread adoption of electronic mail, voice mail, desktop publishing, computer workstations, fiber optics, CD/ROM storage devices, relational data bases, local area networks, expert systems, and videotext. And the list will grow as newer technologies appear in the nineties: parallel-processing computer archi-tectures; artificial intelligence systems; imaging technology; optical me-dia; virtual-reality systems; neurocomputers that emulate the pattern-recognition processes of the brain; and multimedia computing and interactive video in which audio, text, graphics, and interactive video are combined in one machine orchestrated by a computer.

What the personal computer was to the 1980s, interconnectivity and global-communications networks will be to the 1990s. As we move closer to the turn of the century, interconnected computer systems and the sophisticated communications networks carrying video, voice, and data will become commonplace.

"The PC, as it will evolve, will be your window on the world," says Bill Gates, chairman and CEO of Microsoft. "Take the work place. When you walk in you'll have this screen that will know the types of things you're interested in. That is how you find about things. Any document less than five pages long will be electronic." Mitch Kapor, founder of Lotus and now chairman of On Technology, adds: "The standard desktop [computer] will be 20 to 50 times faster than people typically have on their desks. . . . You'll have the integration of full motion video freely intermixed with computer graphics." And as the late Robert Noyce, one of the pioneers of the semiconductor industry, ob-served: "I would guess there will be a continuing trend to get everyone wired up. I think that can be pretty explosive."

The growth of interconnected communication-computer systems will follow a pattern much like that of the personal computer. In the late 1970s, research organizations optimistically predicted that personal com-puter sales might grow to $2 billion by the mid-1980s; actual sales by 1985 exceeded $25 billion.

It is impossible to predict how long it will take for this new world of interconnected computer systems to evolve, what direction it will take, or how large the market may become. However, as Bill Joy, vice president of research and design at Sun Microsystems, explains, we can say with some certainty *how* it will develop: "High technology obeys what a recent issue of *The Economist* called the Iron Law of Revolution, which is, the more you change, the more you have to change. There's no getting off this train. You sign up for the program. You must be willing to accept that the rules keep changing."

One begins to get a feel for what the future might hold by considering the recent history of communications technology. "If you look back to the very first electronic computer built around 1945 in Philadelphia," says John Hennessy, a professor of computer science at Stanford and a founder of MIPS Computer, "and you compare that to a machine today, the time to do basic primitives—like add two numbers together—has [decreased] by 10,000 times. Put that in perspective. If cars had improved as well as computers, you could drive from the East Coast to the West Coast in 20 seconds and your car would cost fifty cents." Will such a remarkable rate of change continue in the 1990s? Hennessy has no doubts: "Certainly, I expect to see performance increase by 50 percent or more a year for the next five years."

More change in the computer industry occurred in the five-year period 1985–90 than in the entire decade that preceded it. Such extraordinary rates of change result from the unique way information- and technology-based change tends to feed on itself. This phenomenon holds the key to understanding the coming explosion in network computing or, as it is variously called, interpersonal computing, social networking, co-ordination technology, cooperative processing—all terms that attempt to encompass the trend toward using digital data for text, graphics, sound, and video through interconnected computer systems.

There is something nearly magical about the way this process works—"magical" because it violates all the rules of innovation in a mass-production society as we have come to understand them. Apple's experience with the development of desktop publishing on the Macintosh personal computer illustrates how this process of change feeding upon change works. And it explains what we can expect to see in spades as the network society evolves.

As Regis McKenna explains, Apple entered the personal computing field with the Macintosh, which was easy to use and featured good graphics. "But desktop publishing didn't even exist then," writes McKenna; "it wasn't on anyone's pie chart as a defined market niche, and no one had predicted its emergence. Apple's customers made it happen; newspapers and research organizations simply started using Macintosh's unique graphics capability to create charts and graphs. . . . As customers explored the possibilities presented by the technology, the technology, in turn, developed to fit the customers' needs. The improved software evolved from a dynamic working relationship between company and customers, not from a rigid, bureaucratic headquarters determination of where Apple could find extra slices of the marketing pie."

This pattern of users and technology driving the evolution of new markets and new products will be duplicated with the growth of interconnected systems. As in the case of desktop publishing, the nature of this process precludes predicting what innovations will come next, but we can say where they will come from. Explains Bill Joy: "The odds-on thing to happen will be some breakthrough we can't imagine today. You have to have a philosophy about this. Instead of trying to imagine what the next breakthrough might be, think of where it will come from. The truly great products of the 21st century will come from people and companies whose names we don't know. Take that as a theorem." However the pattern evolves, this much is virtually certain, according to technology analyst Mel Phelps: "The worldwide electronics industry will not only be the largest industry on planet Earth sometime this decade, but it will make a difference in our standard of living that ranks with the beginnings of the Machine Age."

Supporting the continual creation of new organizational forms and processes—in short, permanent adhocracy—these new information technologies are the enemy of industrial-age organizational charts, functions, and job descriptions. The new technologies are inherently antiorganization, but not antiorganizational. They act relentlessly to destabilize the status quo in organizations, but they are not, it is interesting to note, anti-institutional. In large part, their destabilizing influence comes from the peculiar nature of information itself and its increasing importance to enterprises of all kinds.

"The more we have the more we use and the more useful it becomes."

Information has become the raw material of work, the postindustrial equivalent of what iron ore was to the industrial age. In less than a decade, information has become the key resource for nearly every kind of organization. So quickly is this change occurring that some experts predict that within twenty years only 5 to 10 percent of all workers in the industrialized world will be engaged in manufacturing. Though that may be stretching things a bit, the information age is upon us and its impact is being felt throughout the industrialized world.

Information as a resource—or, as economists would say, as a factor of production—differs greatly from other resources. Unlike natural resources, such as minerals, food, fuel, or land, information is shareable. That is, although information can be transferred from one organization to another, it cannot be taken away from the organization that initiated the transfer. There is no exchange transaction in the form normally associated with natural resources. If you buy a piece of property from someone, you have it and he does not. But if you buy information, you have it, but so does the organization from which you got it.

Information as a resource has other unique properties. Among the most prominent are those listed by management theorist and statesman Harlan Cleveland in *The Knowledge Executive:*

1. *Information is expandable.* Quoting Anne Wells Branscomb, Cleveland explains: information is a "synergistic resource . . . the more we have the more we use and the more useful it becomes." And the more we have, the more it must be managed and manipulated if it is to be useful and form the base for the expansion of knowledge.

2. *Information is compressible.* It can be summarized, combined, and recombined in various ways to create new insights; it can be integrated and concentrated.

3. *Information is substitutable.* It can replace capital goods, labor, and physical materials. For example, companies using computer-assisted design and manufacturing can actually replace physical materials and people with information.

4. *Information is instantaneously transportable.* It can travel at the speed of light and it can defy the attempts of authorities to prevent its dissemination. The tragic events in China's Tiananmen Square on June 4, 1989, were witnessed by the entire world. The attempt by Chinese authorities to cover up the government's massacre of unarmed demonstrators did not work because, try as they might, the officials could not completely control the flow of information into and out of Beijing. Chinese students studying abroad used fax machines to get the truth to Chinese citizens. When the government broadcast photographs of demonstrators and asked citizens to inform on them, the broadcast was relayed around the world and individuals who were sympathetic to the demonstrators called from all over the world and jammed the government's hotlines.

5. *Information is diffuse.* It has an almost inherent tendency to leak. As Cleveland puts it: "Information is aggressive, even imperialistic, in

striving to break out of the unnatural bonds of secrecy in which thing-minded people try to imprison it . . . monopolizing information is very nearly a contradiction in terms that can be done only in more and more specialized fields, for shorter and shorter periods of time."

Power based on control and influence based on secrecy are tactics of the preindustrial and industrial ages. As the Chinese government discovered, the tendency of the new information technology to push power and control down to individuals and away from the top can be halted only by massive military repression and even then only temporarily, a reality that the Soviets and their former client states have already recognized. Whether carried on satellites, fax machines, computers, or television, information does not obey the rules that govern other resources. It makes far different demands on its users, and its very use transforms individuals, organizations, economies, and governments.

As information has become the most important resource in the economy, the second stage of the information revolution has proceeded apace. In this second stage, two circumstances have changed. First, organizations have learned from their experience of the first stage. They now recognize that when you buy "helicopters," you are also buying social and organizational change. They have begun to understand that the promise of technological advances comes from the manner in which the technology is used, not from the technology itself. Second, they have begun to recognize that the nature of information as a factor of production does not operate the way land, labor, capital, or raw materials do. As organizations adopt the new information technologies and confront the peculiarities of information, they are bringing about the first major change in organizational structure since the development of the matrix form in the early 1960s. In some respects, the new organizational form—the network—is the first important change in organizational design since the creation of functional hierarchies.

Corporate executives did not greet this second stage of the information revolution with enthusiastic cheers. In fact, the second stage arrived unheralded; uninvited; and, for the most part, unwelcome. Corporations did not embrace the new technologies or their possibilities. Instead, in one of the great ironies of the eighties, they were pushed into accepting the changes. They had little choice. The economic havoc created by corporate restructuring, hostile takeovers, mergers, acquisitions, and global competition led corporations to seek innovative solutions to their problems wherever they could find them.

"From things to thinking."

In the mid- to late eighties, as companies attempted to respond to increasingly volatile business conditions, they began to experience severe strains in their organizational structures. Under the threat of takeovers, they downsized and reduced their middle-management ranks. Or, once acquired by another company, they were shrunk to help service the debt incurred in the takeover or to push up the value of the stock. Heavily leveraged and faced with a highly competitive global economy, companies came under enormous pressure to shorten the time it took to develop products, improve customer service, respond more quickly to threats from competitors, and reduce operating expenses. As a result of these diverse pressures, new informal communication and decision-making systems began to evolve. These far more fluid, more horizontal, and more cross-functional patterns of communications and decision making were needed to provide more efficient, timely, and cost-effective solutions to organizational problems. The development of these informal systems was largely unplanned, and it often resulted in many unintended consequences.

Sometimes companies brought in new technologies almost out of desperation. For example, in an effort to decrease costs, many companies abandoned expensive printing operations in favor of desktop publishing; other companies laid off support staff and gave their executives computers and instructed them to do their own data analysis and word processing. Still others cut back on expensive air travel and learned to use the telephone for conference calls and fax services.

In and of themselves, the installation and use of the new technologies did not constitute the beginning of the new organizational form—the network. Much as in the first stage of the information revolution, the first uses of the new technologies did little more than automate previously manual functions. They had little impact on improving the overall efficiency of organizations or the quality of the goods and services produced.

However, companies soon realized that harnessing the power of information and the new technologies to reduce the cost of doing business and increase operational efficiency meant thinking about the organization and its members differently. Instead of trying to use the new technologies to increase the effectiveness of departments, organizations needed first to reexamine their business processes, organizational structure, and workflow patterns. Instead of focusing on departmental needs, company planners needed to examine broader cross-organizational functions.

Consider the case of a large midwestern bank that found itself losing its market share to more aggressive competitors. At first, in an effort to decrease its overhead and increase its responsiveness to customers, it built a massive data-base system and gave each officer a personal computer tied to the mainframe data base. The bank's officers could use the system to get up-to-the-moment information on any of the bank's financial products. However, as with most computer systems, the bank's new system was designed to support the bank's existing organizational structure—product-based divisions, each of which marketed a different financial product. As a result, bank officers could get comprehensive information about products within their divisions, but they could not get a comprehensive profile of a customer.

Resourceful bank officers, however, began to share their divisional information with other officers in other divisions. Although they could not use their new computer system to get comprehensive information on customers directly, they could use the system to tally information in return for the same kind of information from other divisions. And they could use their fax machines to transmit the data from one part of the bank to another. It was a clumsy, inefficient way to achieve efficiency, but it was far better than what had previously existed. These innovative officers had created an informal network to meet their customers' needs better. What they created, however, was not what the bank's system designers had intended.

Similar stories unfolded in many organizations, large and small, in the late 1980s. The new systems, however, did not conform to the rules and regulations of industrial bureaucracies. They stood outside the formal organizational systems. They were unsanctioned; compensation and benefits systems were not tied to them; they did not follow the prescribed chain of command, and their structure, such as it was, did not show up on anyone's organization chart. They were, in effect, shadow organizations operating alongside the older formal structures.

Unquestionably, the shadow systems worked. As in the case of the bank, they solved problems and met needs. In other cases, they proved that organizations could, indeed, function without multiple layers of middle management. And, in still others, they proved that product-development time could be cut dramatically and costs could be contained without jeopardizing quality.

But their success proved to be a major problem, even something of an embarrassment. No organization could operate two parallel and usually competing systems indefinitely. Moreover, the employees who created the new systems and made them work wanted the recognition they believed they deserved. They had produced results and they wanted to be compensated accordingly. Somehow companies had to find a way to sanction the shadow systems, to support the new successes. They needed to institutionalize what had been seen as informal, temporary solutions to pressing problems.

Eventually, the midwestern bank recognized what was happening across departmental lines and moved to change its approach. A company-wide information strategy was applied to the bank's data-base design that focused on customers' use of bank services, not merely on the bank's market penetration. The change converted an informal network into a formal one, and it led to a dramatic change in the bank's performance. The bank could now identify cross-selling opportunities, and it was able to meet customers' needs on a more timely and far more individual basis.

Some companies went further: They began to abandon the time-honored industrial-age concept of vertical integration (controlling all aspects of a given market, from raw materials through finished product with the objective of market dominance) and moved to outsourcing as much of the entire process as possible, using computer networks to monitor and control the process. For example, Toyota, one of the leaders in the development of network structures, outsources more than 70 percent of its parts (compared to a figure of 30 percent for General Motors) and has a profit per car that is 36 percent higher than that for General Motors. Companies learned they could gain much-needed flexibility and higher profits (without lowering quality) by creating networks of vendors, material suppliers, and technical services in place of vertically integrated bureaucracies.

The midwestern bank's cross-organizational network and Toyota's outsourcing network illustrate how companies are being redesigned both internally and externally to achieve new levels of responsiveness and efficiency as they try to take full advantage of the new information technologies. While network organizations will take many forms, all of them will share a common attitude and approach: Organizational success depends on using technology to put information and decision-making power into the hands of the right people at the right time. The trend toward decentralized decision making and organizational structures designed to harness the power (and idiosyncrasies) of information as a vital resource mark the beginning of the second stage of the information revolution—the rise of the network organization.

It is here that the changed business environment and the new technologies came together to trigger the second stage of the information revolution. Pressed into service by a new generation of managers who were less fearful of organizational change and more interested in the potential of technology, the new systems were used to solve more and more business problems, eventually evolving into a new organizational form—the network.

The emergence of the network organization is the second distinguishing mark of the second stage of the information revolution. The first true structural innovation since the appearance of the matrix form in the 1960s, network organizations formalized the informal networks that began to develop in the 1980s. They are "global networks of knowledge workers linked together with electronic communications and individually supported by powerful processing and communications technologies." The chief characteristics of this new form include "rich electronic communication, permeable boundaries, coordination through communication, few levels, interdependent responsibilities, interdisciplinary teams, organic form and extended integration through strategic alliances." As the vice president of research at Bell Labs, Arno A. Penzias, puts it, this change is a movement from "things to thinking."

Evidence of the change is everywhere. Vast computer networks now link employees worldwide. Commodities and stock traders operate in real time on every exchange in the world, trading electronically an astonishing half *trillion* dollars every day on the world's foreign exchange markets. Closer to home for most people, the rapid growth of fax machines, voice-mail systems, automatic teller machines, cellular phones, video games, and videocassette recorders attests not only to the fast pace of technological innovation, but to the eagerness of the public to embrace the latest advances.

Because the second stage of the information revolution is just beginning, there are no fully mature network organizations. Apple Computer is perhaps the most advanced example in the United States. Under the leadership of John Sculley, Apple has consciously sought to develop as a network organization. Sculley explains how his company's structure differs from those of older, industrial organizations: "We are built on a different model," he says. "Our model goes back to the network of interdependencies. We don't want vertical integration. We try to off-load things that we aren't expert in. Instead of trying to do everything ourselves, we focus on what we feel we can be very good at; that is how we can get the very best quality."

Apple is building a network organization not only because the new technologies make such a structure possible, but because a network makes the best use of the highly specialized and high-priced talent Apple relies on. Moreover, in a knowledge-based network organization like Apple, information is *the* strategic resource. The ability to create, retain, reformulate, and communicate knowledge is the critical competence such a company needs, and the ability to attract, support, and retain knowledge-based workers who direct and monitor their own performance is the critical factor for ensuring sustained success.

Network forms also differ fundamentally from hierarchical and entrepreneurial forms. For example, in a network, the relationship between organizational structure and the design of information systems is reversed. John Sculley explains how this has changed the way Apple operates.

"The old way of doing things," says Sculley, "was to look at the organization and say, 'Here is the structure.' You would talk to the leaders of the different divisions or departments and say, 'What do you want to know?' Then you would map the information systems onto that organizational structure. . . . We have completely reversed the traditional process at Apple. We've said: 'Let's look first at what we are trying to do systematically. . . . What is the information we need. What is the base of data that we need to know throughout the systemic process?' Then we build that same process as we expect to do it in five years, or seven years, or even ten years, if we can think that far out. Then, regardless of what the current organization structure is, we will map the organization structure on top of the information system. That way we have the flexibility to change the organization structure every year if we choose to—and we usually choose to."

Such procedures dramatically change the focus of the organization. As Sculley notes: "The focus shifts from the institution to the individuals in the organization, and they are empowered as part of the network. There is a shift from a structured to a flexible management style as we realize that *change* is the very essence of the Information Economy. From the lens of the Industrial Age, change is threatening because change threatens stability; and stability has usually meant strength. In the Information Economy, change is the source of opportunity. Flexibility in an organizational design is very important because that is the way to take advantage of new opportunities."

If there is one characteristic, above all, that distinguishes the network organization from every other organizational form, it is this: Network organizations are specifically designed for the *management of knowledge as a resource*. The network form uses the capabilities of the new technologies to turn an organization's knowledge into a "distinctive competence." Representatives of Nolan, Norton, & Company, the information-technology subsidiary of the consulting firm Peat Marwick, explain how this works: "The computer offers an opportunity for executives to leverage their company's knowledge in ways that previously were impossible. The creators and user of knowledge (i.e., knowledge workers) can be networked with computers through time and space, their

knowledge stored electronically for future use and applied quickly anywhere in the world. All the information and knowledge within a company
can, in theory, be accessible to any individual or group, at anytime,
anywhere."

Crucial to understanding these network organizations are the distinctions among data, information, and knowledge. Harlan Cleveland
sees them as a hierarchy: Data are "undigested observations, unvar-
nished facts"; information is "organized data—organized by others, not
by me"; and knowledge is "organized information, internalized by me,
integrated with everything else I know from experience or study or in-
tuition, and therefore useful in guiding my life and work."

"The ultimate effect of knowledge," says Cleveland, "is to organize things or people, arrange them in ways that make them different
from the way they were before. . . . There is no such thing as useless
knowledge, only people who haven't yet learned how to use it." Lewis
Branscomb, when he was chief scientist at IBM, made the same point
slightly differently: "The yawning chasm is between what is already
known by some but not yet put to use by others." It is the purpose of a
network organization, whether it is a bank, a computer company, a law
firm, or an automobile manufacturer, to take data, turn it into information, and then transform it into knowledge that can give the organization
a distinctive competence, which is to say a competitive advantage.

Bill Joy, the founder of Sun Microsystems and a software genius,
offers examples of the process at work: "The two great [computer] plat-
forms of the 1990s will be the evolutions of UNIX and the Mac, for two
different reasons. The Mac because Apple figured something out about
computing a long time ago that the rest of us only figured out recently.
And UNIX because it's incredibly open. It's really the only system that
everyone has the code for. UNIX is permeable to innovation; it doesn't
have an immune system."

Both Apple, with the Macintosh, and Sun, with its UNIX-based
workstations, used their network organizations to create new ways of
understanding the world—and in so doing, gained a significant competitive advantage in their markets. In the 1990s, building a better mouse-
trap means building an information-based network organization that is
capable of turning information into knowledge. Thus, what began in
high-technology companies, which naturally experienced the information revolution first, will soon spread to all organizations, regardless of the
kind of products and services they provide.

Network organizations, as centerless systems, are as different in
their form and function from hierarchical organizations as postmetropol-

itan suburbs are from their postwar suburban predecessors. Like post-metro suburbs, networks are webs of interrelationships having no form other than that created and continually re-created by the dynamics of direct communication among organization members. Unlike the pyramid design of functional hierarchies, in which concepts like organizational level or rank (upper, middle, and supervisory management) and span of control define power relationships (who can talk to whom and under what circumstances), networks encourage the flow of information in many directions that are unregulated by a formal command structure. Information is controlled by the demands of the situation—the nature and urgency of the problem, the persons who need to be involved, and the like. In network organizations, information crosses departmental boundaries and organizational levels freely, going wherever it is needed to get the job done.

As Peter F. Drucker suggests, in the information-based organization, the concept of span of control—the idea that a manager can effectively manage no more than seven plus-or-minus-one subordinates—is replaced with the concept of span of communication. In a network organization, it is the kinds of communications and the relationship among teams and team members working together to solve problems that must be "managed." The key to adding value, to turning knowledge into a distinctive competence, involves the flexible development of a multitude of relationships. Such relationships determine how well the organization runs and whether value is added. It is the job of the network manager to manage the quantity and quality of the relationships within his or her span of communication. The only difference between one network manager and another is the complexity, urgency, sensitivity, and quantity of information under the span of communication of each.

The move from a span-of-control mentality to a span-of-communication mentality is a major—perhaps revolutionary—change. It involves far more than installing the latest technologies; it demands that companies change the way they think and act. Companies must attend to relationships, not to raw information; to knowledge, not to technology. They must emphasize horizontal communication across functions, not vertical communication through departments. They must fit information systems to people and jobs, not the other way around. They must let go of rigid organizational hierarchies and embrace ever-shifting networks. And when they do, what will emerge is not only a fluid and perhaps unsettling change *within* organizations, but an equally revolutionary change *among* organizations.

"We cultivate relationships."

One of the most striking differences between network organizations and either hierarchical or entrepreneurial organizations is the nature of what is "inside" and what is "outside" the organization. In bureaucracies or entrepreneurial firms, you are either inside or outside. You either work for the organization or you are an outside contractor or vendor. The boundaries are clear and the relationship is defined in contractual terms. In network organizations, the boundaries are still contractually defined, but the definition is less rigid. "Insiders" and "outsiders" see their destinies as tied together and their businesses as relying on one another. Electronic communication systems link "outsiders" in the same way they link "insiders" to one another. Thus, for almost all intents and purposes, they look more like partners than like contracting parties. As Ken Haven, a mechanical engineer at NeXT computer, one of the new network organizations, says, "One thing we do is to cultivate relationships with our suppliers. We don't just go with the lowest bid."

As network organizations grow in prominence and the new information technologies link more and more firms, new types of strategic alliances are being forged and new kinds of managerial and legal challenges are developing. For example, what if the Kremlin orders ten thousand workstations from NeXT by electronic mail and NeXT then translates that order into electronic-order requests for disk drives from a Japanese supplier (which is also a part-owner of NeXT), software manufactured in Singapore, and printer components from China—all via electronic transactions that require less than a minute to complete? Since all the companies are on the same communication network, they then coordinate their production schedules and ship all the components on a just-in-time basis to a Hungarian subsidiary of a Western European computer maker for final assembly. What, then, are the legal implications, the import-export and taxation issues, and the political ramifications of this far-flung and fast-acting network? Not only will people working in such networks have to be supple, but so will the people who must deal with them—governmental officials, professional service personnel, and small-business people. Just as people who do not physically live in postmetropolitan suburbs nevertheless live in a postmetropolitan world, so do people who do not toil in network organizations live in a networked world.

This does not mean that some people will be shut out of giant networks and forced into marginal small businesses. In fact, what it means to be big and what it means to be small will change dramatically. The existence of internally linked network organizations and externally linked networked organizations will make it possible for legions of small, responsive companies to join forces and produce products and services that meet market needs no matter how fast the market changes or the technology evolves.

The trend toward increased outsourcing, as is done by Toyota, is an example of how externally linked networked organizations (large with small) will work together on a worldwide basis. Charles R. Morris calls this trend "horizontal globalism." "Instead of large, integrated companies on the Morgan-Rockefeller model dominating a global industry," Morris explains, "the trend is toward global specialists supplying their specialties to end-product manufacturers in all the industrialized countries. Along with global scale and the advent of high-productivity, flexible manufacturing systems, the disintegration of the old industrial monolithic structures into sharply focused worldwide specialty producers is a powerful force driving a radical re-ordering of world manufacturing."

Morris uses the automotive industry as an example: "The process of global specialization is being carried forward so rapidly that the day is not far off when most cars will be assembled from virtually identical parts supplied by the same worldwide suppliers. . . . Virtually all the European and American subsystem specialists have entered into joint ventures with the Japanese majors to supply the new overseas Japanese factories and are beginning to compete for business in the Japanese homeland. . . . The far-reaching alliances between the major vehicle manufacturers mean that cars are getting increasingly similar under the hood."

Taken to its extreme, as some analysts predict, cars could become almost design-it-yourself vehicles. "As final product manufacturers more and more become assemblers of mixed-and-matched subcomponent modules purchased from global specialist suppliers, the variety of potential final products will be nearly infinite," says Morris. "Stan Feldman predicts that in the near future the turnaround time from ordering a car to producing the finished product in a factory will be just a few days."

It is therefore possible, in fact probable, that in the near future the ultimate paradox could occur: Worldwide manufacturers, such as Honda, IBM, or Sony, will be creating totally custom-designed products for the ultimate niche market—the individual consumer. They will run production "batches" of one, instead of the hundreds of thousands that have been the standard batch run of the industrial-age, organization-man era.

The merger of small, internally linked network organizations, using flexible manufacturing techniques to manufacture high-quality modular subcomponents, with externally linked networked global companies that assemble the subcomponents into final products of an infinite variety represents an extraordinary breakthrough in the manufacturing process. Some believe it means the beginning of the third industrial revolution.

Although this "third industrial revolution" is just beginning, the experience of the automotive industry suggests that it is a revolution that will not be stopped. The 1990s will be a time when global network organizations drive further and further into local niche markets. To survive, local companies will have to meet global standards, and global companies will have to adapt to the tastes and trends of local markets. The ultimate result is likely to be "relentless global competition on price and quality, a steady, even startling, worldwide increase in manufacturing productivity, and sharp increases in real world output." Decentered organizations will abound—and eventually dominate—as networks and niches become the order of the day.

The decentering of organizations in which distinctions like large-small, inside-outside, and even manager-worker are effaced is, like post-metropolitan suburbs, providing for the organization offspring yet another experience of permeable boundaries, shifting nodes of power, and relational systems in which stability is continually deferred. In such organizations, one's identity is defined less by a job description, as in the old bureaucratic ideal, than by one's relation at any given moment to groups and people inside and outside the organization whose identities are similarly shifting. Thus, the remark of NeXT's Ken Haven about cultivating relationships resonates more profoundly than perhaps he intended.

The effect on individuals, even those who reap significant advantages from these emerging networks, can be dizzying. Historically, of course, the middle-class operatives who staffed and ran the competitive system were shielded from its most damaging psychological effects by the illusion of personal autonomy it conferred (especially as the marketplace became a metaphor for the freely choosing self). But in today's accelerated and globalized version, which has nullified space and time, that illusion of autonomy becomes harder to sustain, as is made clear by the increasingly acrobatic uses to which the artist ideal must be put to maintain it. Now, however, employees of all kinds—production workers, clerical and service personnel, and managers alike—watch as their labor, which is to say their identities as active human subjects, is dispersed into a system of relationships and exchange that is not only centerless, unstable, and never ending, but that is instantaneous and global.

Thus, the accelerating penetration of the organization offspring's lives by these highly mobile and decentered systems—showing up in everything from art to popular entertainment to residential patterns to organizational structures—ineluctably draws personal artifice closer to social artificiality, rendering ever more irrelevant and unsatisfying the generation's highly psychologized brand of individualism. Moreover, as long-term changes in the social and occupational structure, long-term economic stagnation, and the closing down of choice bring the search for self-fulfillment to a close, authenticity and the life of personal artifice lived in its name are being transformed. This unmooring of the generation's individualism, coupled with the proliferation of concrete social phenomena in which identity is difference, is bringing into being among the organization offspring a new American social character: the artificial person.

We have already encountered the artificial person in embryo in the offspring's organizationalism, which envisions the many contending elements of a complex organization as one entity, not only personified as an individual but endowed with a psyche. Just beginning to be reimported into their individualism, the notion of the artificial person, applied to real individuals, could, in this altered context, paradoxically produce a more satisfying sense of self and a more accessible social world. On the other hand, like any new social type, artificial persons also present a terrifying prospect. But benign or malign, the real successors to the organization man will be these organization offspring who are just beginning to make the slow and, in many ways, painful transition from personal artifice to artificial person.

10

Artificial Persons: The Rise of the Enterprise Ethic

"I was afraid of open windows, afraid of everything."

It is difficult to date precisely the beginnings of such a glacial and subtle transition as that from personal artifice to artificial persons. In fact, it is the argument of this book that the newly emerging social character of the organization offspring has roots that stretch back not only to their own childhoods but to the childhoods of their parents. But if there is a year that may stand as a decisive turning point, it is 1982, though the ensuing years of the eighties would simultaneously hasten and forestall the change. Glimpsed as a kind of cross-section of the period, the experiences of the Harrison children are typical.

Like many of the organization offspring, the Harrisons were more or less starting over at the beginning of the 1980s. But to start over was not necessarily to succeed. The economy, the culture, and personal life still had prices to exact, shocks to deliver, and pain to inflict. Applied to the seventies, the game of dating the end of the decade yields the conclusion that the miscalled "Me Decade" ended (or culminated) not with the election of Ronald Reagan, but with the severe recession of 1982, the deepest since the Great Depression. The oil embargo of 1973, perceived when it occurred as merely a temporary interruption of the long postwar party, had proved to be the inaugural event of many similar economic catastrophes that, by 1982, had done long-term damage to the American economy and greatly restricted the opportunity and outlook of a rising generation that had grown up with such limitless expectations. It is more than coincidental that the Harrison children's period of greatest personal difficulty was to coincide with the nadir of the postwar American economy.

Joann, after her disillusioning experiences in Vietnam and Iran, began her consulting business in 1979 with high hopes and even higher ideals, including respect for herself and her employees. The 1982 recession would nearly kill the business—and her.

Joann found the early going rough, but the prospects for computer consulting were good. During the seventies many companies had adopted the philosophy that any expertise that was not directly related to producing the company's product was to be hired from outside on a temporary basis. The recession drastically changed that practice. To save money, companies decided to grow their own expertise. They were no longer willing to be billed at seventy-five dollars per hour for the contract workers supplied by companies like Joann's. The consulting business dried up. In one year her company's billings dropped from two hundred thousand dollars to just over fifty thousand dollars. Joann had to lay off programmers, permanently it turned out, a grim necessity no amount of respect for employees could forestall. Apart from the financial problems, she found the unpredictability of the business unsettling.

"There was a vast insecurity because of clients that would come and go, projects that would be up and down, contracts that would suddenly be canceled," she says. "One of the things that resulted from this constant change was fear. I didn't know what was happening tomorrow, and I *wanted* to know."

A failed love affair, after two unsuccessful marriages, coincided with the business reversals. She descended into a harrowing depression.

"I was suicidal," she says matter-of-factly, "seriously suicidal, thinking of ways to do it. I had terrifying experiences where I felt like there were two of me and one of them was out here observing and the other was going through terrors that I could only associate with things I'd read about hell, but I was experiencing them—terror to the point where I was afraid of open windows, afraid of everything."

For Joann's sister Carolyn, it was in 1982 that her father's open heart surgery brought her face to face with mortality. It was also the year she completed her doctorate and first went on an academic job market that had been depressed for nearly a decade. Of the twenty people with whom she had begun her doctoral program, she was one of only two who finished.

"Most of the other students decided to do other things," she says, "because it was such an unpromising field and the kinds of hurdles that were put before you did not seem worth leaping when there was nothing on the other side. Continuing with graduate school seemed foolhardy in the seventies.

"I didn't know what else to do. And my experience with the job outside academe was so bad that I feared that's the way every corporate job would be. And I suppose I thought I might be able to do something academically. I guess it's always in your mind that you'll be able to beat the odds."

In the heady days of academic expansion in the sixties, doctoral candidates who had not completed their dissertations were often deluged with job offers. They picked the most appealing schools, completed their dissertations during the first several years of employment in them, and then easily won tenure on the strength of a scholarly article or two. Later, publication of a book, written in maturity and at leisure, yielded a full professorship. For prospective academics of Carolyn's generation, those days were long gone. Nowhere were the Darwinian effects of baby-boom demographics and a bruising economy more apparent than in the job market for liberal arts scholars in the seventies and early eighties. Scholarly publication while still in graduate school was required merely to obtain a job interview. Even then, there were no guarantees. Though figures are hard to come by, thousands of liberal arts scholars who completed doctorates in the seventies and eighties and often published scholarly material never found jobs and are now lost to the profession forever, despite their superior qualifications and promise. With little publication, Carolyn secured only two job interviews, neither of which panned out.

Younger sister Julia, like Carolyn, ventured into the academic job market in 1982 and, like Joann, went into a deep depression. When Julia first moved to San Francisco, where she had family and a few contacts in the dance world, she was, she says, "a nonfunctioning human being." The plan was to teach dance in college. It would solve her long-standing problems of self-support and self-esteem, allow her to remain in the dance world, and release her from the rigors of performing during her slow recovery from cancer. But her brief, stormy graduate career had taught her to hate academe. Relieved when her halfhearted applications for teaching jobs in the area were rejected, she worked sporadically at word processing and retail sales. To make ends meet, she even painted Joann's apartment. Eventually she found a tolerable job at an art gallery, but the gallery soon folded. She was thirty-two, jobless, and out of dance.

For Tom, the consequences of the sheer number of baby boomers and a constricting economy were to push him, by 1982, into service jobs he did not like in locales he had always disdained. In part, it broke up his marriage. He seized the occasion of his marital breakup to try to find out what he really wanted to do.

"Originally, we agreed on joint custody of the children," he says. "She was going to stay in the house and I was going to move someplace and have them on weekends. I kind of saw it as an opportunity to try something different with my life, to get into a career I might be happier with."

Tom planned to find a small apartment and retain half custody of his children, which he would fully exercise when he got on his feet in a new career. But as soon as Tom moved out, his wife moved another man in and decided to seek full child custody. Now, for purposes of the legal battle, Tom needed a residence large enough to accommodate the children. To give up his job to pursue his dreams would be to give up his children forever.

Tom, like his sisters, found himself at a point where historical trends and personal circumstances converged to overwhelm the self ethic. Though a small minority of the generation, especially the radical materialists, engaged in an orgy of denial, many more, like the Harrisons, found themselves struggling through a difficult period for which the self ethic and its ideal of authenticity had left them ill-prepared.

To people who were less advantaged than the organization offspring—poor members of minorities, the uneducated, and many industrial workers—the performance of the economy during that period brought even greater pain and suffering. Of the 11.5 million American workers who lost their jobs between 1979 and 1984, only 60 percent were able to find new jobs and almost half the new jobs paid less than the old ones. The real income of men aged twenty to twenty-four with less than a high school education dropped an astonishing 42 percent between 1973 and 1986. From 1975 to 1983 the number of black citizens living below the poverty line went up by almost one-third, from 7.5 million to 9.9 million.

Some politicians tried to put the best face on things. In 1984 Ronald Reagan, instinctively understanding that Americans prefer a Madison Avenue sunrise to a Niebuhrian malaise, simply declared it "morning in America." As the vote totals show, he was by no means alone in his optimism. Many organization offspring, like the Harrison children (though none of them ever voted for Reagan), often exude what would appear to be an unwarranted confidence in themselves and their futures. But such irrepressible optimism, as both an enduring feature of the American character and a particularly prominent feature of a generation reared in affluence, is only one component of the personal sorting out that took place in the mideighties and whose results are only just becoming clear.

Though many organization offspring maintain an element of the optimism encapsulated in the Reagan campaign slogan, Reagan should have added that the mid- to late eighties were also a period of *mourning* in America. For many organization offspring lived and continue to live in what may be called—relative to their great expectations and the immense store they placed on expressive individualism—a culture of loss. Despite their optimism, many members of the generation have been forced by the economy, by personal problems, by the imperatives of the life course, and by hard demographic reality to lower their expectations, face disappointment, and postpone or forgo dreams. In short, they have had to acknowledge limits, many for the first time in their lives. Portentous though it sounds, one can see in the story of the Harrison children that the ultimate limit, the horizon within which other limits, other losses, occur is none other than death. The fragile mortality of a parent on the operating table, suicidal tendencies, cancer—these are the final terms in a line of losses the near terms of which include divorce, loss of child custody, death of a cherished self-image, narrowed opportunity, and personal failure.

The invoking of finitude, though it echoes familiar themes in existentialism, does not augur its revival, for it was popularizations of existentialism that had underlain the self ethic in the first place. In European existentialism, the radical freedom of the individual was a consequence of finitude, the recognition of which was said to require one to live authentically. But the American rewriting of existentialism in ego psychology and pop philosophy dispensed with the recognition of finitude while retaining the emphasis on the radical freedom of the individual, turning it into a highly psychologized version of time-honored American optimism, a belief not in the finitude of the self but in its unlimited possibility. Far from being a consequence of finitude, the ideal of authenticity in its American guise became a denial of such limits. Thus, for the organization offspring, the recognition of limits has meant not a confrontation with authenticity but the end of authenticity as they have conceived it.

The transition from authentic self to artificial person will not be easy, since the authentic self gives way to a sense of self that owes more to social artificiality than to personal artifice. Of all their experiences of loss and limits, none has been more painful (or is potentially more liberating) for the organization offspring than is the slow and agonizing death of the authentic self.

Loss, especially of the cherished authentic self, is inevitably accompanied by mourning. Indeed, mourning usually accompanies any momentous life change, but in the lives of the organization offspring mourning will play as central a role in their social character as anxiety did in that of their parents or guilt did in that of their nineteenth-century forebears. And this sense of loss, of great things behind them, of diminished expectations, may paradoxically open up great things before them as they bury the vacuous notion of the authentic self and acquire a new sense of themselves as individuals who are more intricately connected to social life—and thus to other individuals—than is allowed by the lonely imperatives of the self ethic. In fact, it will be mourning, especially mourning of the authentic self, that keeps them on course, that continually reorients them to their status as artificial persons, rather than as authentic selves, and hence that drives them back to a kind of optimism, though one tempered by a diminished sense of their formerly grandiose expectations.

Pushed more and more by personal, historical, and economic circumstances to confront realities they have always derided as *merely* artificial, some of them are making the difficult transition from personal artifice, floating uneasily between authenticity and artificiality, to an individualism of the artificial person in which the self is seen as derived from and dispersed throughout the culture in "artificial" systems of significance. As they do so, they are finding that similar forms of such individualism have been serviceably at work in America for centuries, are becoming increasingly prominent, and may be found right under their noses.

"Men will have to learn that whole way of operating."

All cultures draw a line between what is considered intrinsic to the self and what is considered extrinsic, but where the line is drawn varies greatly from culture to culture. In complex cultures like ours there may be variations from subculture to subculture. However, the dominant "indigenous psychology of the self" in America has always maintained a sharp distinction between what is "inner" and what is "outer." The self is assumed to end at one's skin, and in confronting a social world that is wholly external, this self-contained, self-determining agent must exercise personal responsibility and self-control to guarantee freedom and achievement.

In some other cultures, including a number of subcultures in America, the boundary is less sharply drawn. In these cultures and subcultures, the indigenous psychology of the self is more fluid, more inclusive, and recognizes that the self exists as part of various social networks, rather than as an independent entity somehow apart. In such "ensembled individualism," as Edward Sampson calls it, the self is viewed not as autonomous, but as an ensemble of social relations; the line between "inner" and "outer" is blurred; the self does not stop at the skin.

These two psychologies of the self are ultimately incompatible. The one does not offer a little healthy balance to the other, though the more inclusive form of individualism is now evolving out of the historical exhaustion of the self-contained form. The signs of this exhaustion are to be found in the personal artifice that is reduced to a kind of desperately hopeful pointing to an authentic self that is systematically elusive. With the contemporary notion of the authentic self—the most extreme, narrowly circumscribed version of self-contained individualism to date and perhaps the most extreme that is conceivable—the organization offspring have already gone as far inward as it is possible to go. Thus, stuck in a foundationless expressiveness, they are being drawn ineluctably outward to the world of social artificiality in which their expressiveness and their selves are actually constituted.

As they move outward (for the variety of historical reasons we have been describing), they may find that they are hardly the first in America to do so. There are models of a more ensembled individualism ready at hand. Such models have been at work in American culture for centuries, and although they have been recessive under previous historical circumstances, they are likely to become dominant under today's changed conditions. Most prominent among these alternative indigenous psychologies of the self are those to be found in much African-American culture and in the culture of many American women.

Obviously, these two cultures overlap—not all blacks are men and not all women are white—something that must be borne in mind throughout the discussion that follows. Just as obviously, black culture and female culture are not free of self-contained individualism. The notion of an inviolable self has been indispensable in pressing claims for racial justice, just as calls for autonomy and authenticity informed early feminism. Furthermore, many of our female interviewees are among the most confirmed seekers of the authentic self, which is not surprising, given their position in the middle class from which such ideology originates. Nevertheless, they also have one foot in female culture (which includes black females and may cut across class lines) and its alternative way of envisioning the self. As these women have risen in the world of work, the conflict between the two kinds of individualism has been acute for them and they are, in general, moving toward an individualism of artificial persons more rapidly than are their male counterparts.

Though the African-American indigenous psychology of self ingeniously engages self-contained individualism, it differs markedly from the white, middle-class sense of self in being far less dogmatic about where to draw the line between the inner and the outer, the individual and the other. The individual speaking through the group and the group affirming the individual are central to a wide variety of black cultural practices, from sermons and oratory to the procedures of musical ensembles. One may see it, for example, in the call-and-response pattern of much African-American music, which, in contexts of communal performance, allows the individual simultaneously to preserve his or her voice as a distinct entity and to blend it with those of other members of the community.

Even in the most individualistic American art form, the autobiography, black autobiographers often manage to convey a far more inclusive sense of the self. The mere act of writing an autobiography is an assertion of selfhood in a society that has denied that black people are individuals. But the successful assertion of a self in black autobiography, by enacting a refutation of pervasive racist discourse, paradoxically subverts Anglo-American self-contained individualism by opening up a social space for an entire people. By seizing and then subverting the discourse of selfhood, black autobiographers, from Frederick Douglass to Malcolm X, have managed to show it up *as* discourse. On a superficial level, they challenge the hypocrisy of self-contained individualism but, more fundamentally, they demonstrate the extraordinary degree to which selfhood and nonselfhood alike are socially constructed.

It is toward something more closely resembling this black sense of ensembled individualism than self-contained individualism that the organization offspring are moving. Christopher Lasch perceived the first stirrings of such a movement among disaffected, middle-class whites during the hard times of the late seventies:

> In some ways middle-class society has become a pale copy of the black ghetto, as the appropriation of its language would lead us to believe. We do not need to minimize the poverty of the ghetto or the suffering inflicted by whites on blacks in order to see that the increasingly dangerous and unpredictable conditions of middle-class life have given rise to similar strategies of survival. Indeed the attraction of black culture for disaffected whites suggests that black culture now speaks to a general condition, the most important feature of which is a widespread loss of confidence in the future. The poor have always had to live for the present, but now a desperate concern for personal survival, sometimes disguised as hedonism, engulfs the middle class as well.

But because of his patronizing view of black culture, Lasch regarded this development with alarm. The foregoing passage is rife with racial stereotypes: "Black" and "poor" are used interchangeably, black people are pleasure-seeking victims who live only for the present, and black people have no historical traditions that are recognizable even to a historian (which Lasch is) and few cultural or psychic resources. Lasch ignores the resilience of black cultural patterns, most apparent in towering artistic accomplishments: a vast and growing autobiographical literature, spirituals, blues, gospel, jazz, funk, and most recently—from the cruelly impoverished South Bronx—the remarkable phenomenon of rap and hip hop. Many whites often view these black artistic accomplishments incorrectly and sentimentally as pitiful laments or primitive effusions, rather than as internally consistent and complex cultural expressions created out of a far more inclusive sense of individualism than that which informs the romantic notion of the individual artist. In failing to appreciate black culture, Lasch fails to understand its psychology of self and, therefore, cannot imagine that a move toward that psychology of self by the dominant culture may not be such a bad thing.

The point, however, is not that these lily-white organization offspring are consciously taking on the black psychology of the self. The point is that alternatives to abstract individualism and to the self ethic already exist, and have existed, right here for a long time. An alternative that lies even nearer to hand for these middle-class children than the often subterranean and heavily denied and repressed influence of black culture is that found among women.

In a celebrated study of the way people talk about morality, Carol Gilligan discovered that males and females employ two different modes of "describing the relationship between other and self." Gilligan found that when asked to resolve moral dilemmas, men tend to think in terms of competing rights that require a resolution that is formal or abstract and often decide conflicts between duty and desire by reference to a hierarchical ordering of such rights. Furthermore, men see morality as a question of fairness and justice—everyone is to be treated the same, regardless of the consequences.

Women, on the other hand, tend to see moral problems as conflicts of responsibilities that require a resolution that is narrative or contextual. Rather than look to abstract rules in a moral dilemma, women are more apt to explore the concrete situation in all its human complexity, recognizing that people have different needs. Where a man sees a hierarchy of rights, a woman sees a network of relationships. Thus, women view morality as a question of care—no one is to be hurt.

A classic case of the conflict between these two different conceptions of morality occurred in the widely chronicled Baby M trial. A surrogate mother, who had been paid ten thousand dollars by another couple to allow herself to be inseminated with the man's sperm and produce a baby for them, subsequently refused to surrender the child. She had been unprepared for the emotional attachment she developed during pregnancy and delivery. For her, the concrete narrative of that attachment, unfolding over time, overrode the abstract and "timeless" rules of the contract into which she had entered.

Male talk about morality assumes a world made up of isolated selves locked in competition and regulated by abstract contractual hierarchies. Female talk about morality assumes a world of interdependent selves joined in cooperation and adjusted in connective networks. "Rules are rules," the absolutist male emphatically states; "a contract is a contract." The contextualist female replies: "But look at the situation; consider how each person is affected." The male conception accepts no encroachment on the isolated self from "outside"; the female conception sees the self as far more constrained: "Since the reality of connection is experienced by women as given rather than as freely contracted, they arrive at an understanding of life that reflects the limits of autonomy." Interconnection is part of identity.

Though it may be true that women are likely to move more easily toward an individualism of artificial persons, is there any reason to think that men will budge at all? The answer is yes, once it is understood that this transition has nothing to do with men "getting in touch with" some idealized "feminine" part of the self, but with adopting a way of doing things that will grow increasingly prominent. Amnesiac talk of the post-feminist era and of New Traditionalism is the wishful thinking of reactionaries: Women are in the work force in greater numbers than ever and they will continue to be. In organizations where they have achieved some critical mass in management, the influence of a more inclusive sense of self is already being felt.

"I believe that we're going to see the mode of operation [of organizations] as totally different," says a male manager at a *Fortune* 500 company (and the son of an organization man). "The way things get done is going to be wholly different. And, interestingly enough, I see the women spearheading the job."

No feminist, he speaks in tones of genuine bemusement about the different work styles of men and women in the corporation: "Men will come together and work and they can acknowledge not liking one another but still go forward and get the job done. But I know that a number of the women we work with day to day spend an awful lot of time working with one another over personal issues and so forth in order to *set the stage* for getting the job done properly. That's part of a networking process, and I'd say it's a bunch of hooey if it weren't for the fact that it gets results. It's clearly getting results, and I think maybe setting the standard for the future. Men will have to learn that whole way of operating."

This does not mean that as the organization offspring evolve from personal artifice to artificial persons they will necessarily adopt wholesale either the indigenous psychology of the self characterized as female or that characterized as African-American, only that alternatives to abstract individualism are not nearly so foreign as all of our invoking of European "theory" suggests. On the other hand, as the organization offspring move closer to an individualism of artificial persons, they will not simply replicate their parents' anxious participation in the world of other-direction. For the offspring's experience of artificiality is marked by suspicion and disdain. It is this suspicion of the world of social artificiality that marks them off decisively from their parents. They will see the social world as a play of voices, interests, and discourses to be explicated, not a standard of behavior to be anxiously checked. They enter this world of social artificiality reluctantly, driven there by historical circumstances and their peculiar life courses. To the shifting, confusing, and complicated world of the artificial person, they would much prefer the simple, comforting, unitary authentic self, the death of which will always stand behind their embrace of artificiality.

Mourning in America.

At the heart of the embrace of artificiality lies the recognition that the self is as much a creature of the play of signification as are all the other cultural-sign systems that converge in it. This symbolic self, as it may be called, will increasingly be understood to be composed out of the play of the very sign systems that were previously disdained as mere social artificiality: personal history, gender, race, class, family, region, occupation, media, language, and culture. The belief in the authentic self is itself such a construct, the cultural roots of which we hope we have made abundantly clear by now. This *imaginary* authentic self is thus part of the symbolic self and enjoys no other existence except as imagined out of those cultural materials. To put it another way, the longed-for, substantial, authentic self—the imaginary self—will be, if not abandoned, at least recognized for what it is in favor of the symbolic self.

This does not mean that artificial persons have no agency, no freedom, and no subjectivity. Nor does it imply a rigidly deterministic world in which people are the mere epiphenomena of historical and social forces, something which few Americans are capable of crediting. People are artificial yes, but they are nonetheless *persons*. Possessed of their singular personal histories and crisscrossed by unique and ever-shifting combinations of social artificiality of every variety, artificial persons paradoxically partake far more of particularity—which is to say individuality—than do vacuous authentic selves.

In feeling themselves constituted by the convergence of self and culture in the symbolic self, artificial persons are *more* real, *more* particular, and *more* idiomatic and individual than are abstract and imaginary authentic selves. They are *subjected* by cultural systems, but as the site of a unique convergence, they are also *subjects*, in the sense of subjectivity. Thus, as individuals, they are more fully characterized and individuated, not by the empty expression of choices but by the particular impression of voices. Instead of all people being different in exactly the same way (by declaring themselves artists, for example), everyone is the same in a different way. *That* is individualism.

But various individualisms, as we have shown, are not merely opposed to conformity; they are themselves different modes of conformity. So, to Riesman's three historical modes of conformity—tradition direction, inner direction, and other direction—we add a fourth: subject direction. (All are ideal types, in Weber's sense, useful for analysis even if no pure example of the type can be found. As Riesman says, "the inwardness of individuals is only awkwardly if at all captured by a typology designed for the understanding of large-scale social change.") Artificial persons—influenced by the search for self-fulfillment, but feeling their identity to be partly constituted by the play of "artificial" cultural systems—may be said to be subject directed. The culture is always present in the sign system that constitutes the self: One is subjected. But as a subject one acts—either highly consciously, in simplified concepts of relativism, or more or less unconsciously through vague feelings of absence and loss—with an understanding of the arbitrariness and variousness of those sign systems. Thus, the term *subject-direction* is ambiguous, referring simultaneously to subjection and subjectivity, but it is worth retaining for precisely that reason.

A way to see the differences among the various modes of conformity, says Riesman, is to examine the differences in the sanctions or emotional control in each type. What guidance system keeps each type on course? For the tradition directed, it is shame. For the inner directed, it is guilt. For the other directed, it is anxiety. Shame ensures that one acts as members of the culture have always acted. Guilt ensures that one acts as one's parents may. Anxiety ensures that one acts as one's peers may.

But what sort of culture do subject-directed individuals inhabit? As we have been arguing, it may be called a loss culture (or a limits culture or, in theoretical terms, a world in which absence lies at the heart of presence). To reiterate their losses, limits, and absences: Subject-directed individuals have been conditioned by a history of childhood affluence and a maturity of diminishing expectations. They have been repeatedly frustrated by the untenable search for the authentic self. Whether they know it or not, they are surrounded by an intellectual paradigm, artistic practices, and a popular culture that deny the very possibility of the paradigmatic. They function in a society constituted by networks and media that formally and vividly enact the antiparadigmatic paradigm. And they are confronted daily with the loss of community, social cohesion, and institutional integrity.

Though it seems faintly absurd to speak of loss and these privileged people in the same breath, the point is to understand their social character, however much or little sympathy any one of them may deserve. Their relative losses and their experiences of limits must be understood in the context of their life courses, and so understood, our invoking of "loss" is meant to be morally neutral. The aim is not to moralize but to get at the emotional control that holds the key to this emerging social character. In a world where loss and absence have become paramount, the emotional control that makes sense of loss comes to the fore. Thus, for the subject-directed type in this loss-culture, the emotional control is mourning.

In "Mourning and Melancholia," a metapsychological paper written in 1915, Sigmund Freud describes mourning as "the reaction to the loss of a loved person, or to the loss of some abstraction which has taken the place of one, such as one's country, liberty, an ideal, and so on." The distinguishing marks of mourning are loss of interest in the world, the incapacity to adopt any new object of love, and the turning away from any activity that is not connected to thoughts of the lost object. Depression (melancholia) entails the same characteristics, but includes a lowering of self-esteem, which is absent in mourning. Moreover, mourning is not a pathological state. When its work is done, the erstwhile mourner is restored to an interest in the outside world.

In Freud's formulation, mourning works in the following way: "Reality-testing has shown that the loved object no longer exists, and it proceeds to demand that all libido shall be withdrawn from its attachments to that object. This demand arouses understandable opposition—it is a matter of general observation that people never willingly abandon a libidinal position, not even, indeed, when a substitute is beckoning to them. . . . Normally, respect for reality gains the day. Nevertheless, its orders cannot be obeyed at once. They are carried out bit by bit, at great expense of time and cathectic energy, and in the meantime *the existence of the lost object is psychically prolonged*. . . . when the work of mourning is completed the ego becomes free and uninhibited again."

One of the central losses in the loss culture we have been describing is the authentic self, at least in its substantial form. The authentic self is one of those abstractions, like freedom or the idea of one's country, mentioned by Freud, that may be mourned like a lost loved one and thus have its existence prolonged until the mourning is completed. During the work of mourning, the subject-directed person, having failed to find the substantial self, psychically prolongs its existence by mourning that failure. The self-conscious pointing of engaged and detached personal styles is an incipient version of this substitution of signs for a nonexistent authentic self. The work of mourning substitutes for an authentic self that nowhere exists—that has died, so to speak—a set of signs that psychically establishes its existence, though in a form that is different from the form that is conceived as substantial.

What Freud's essay teaches us is that it is possible to establish a relationship to a "lost archaic object"—whether a dead person or a dead ideal like the authentic self—that is not merely a repetition of the original relationship. The authentic self, nowhere to be found and therefore mourned, is thereby psychically established, but not as the original lost archaic object. Mourning, then, establishes the authentic self in the only form in which it could possibly be said to exist—presence in absence. Hence, the authentic self of our imagination and longing—conceived as a substantial entity believed to reside beneath all the layers of history and experience—has been converted by mourning into a sign system.

Of course, the authentic self has always been a set of signs within a culturally generated discourse of expressive individualism and authenticity, though it was not generally recognized as such. The point is that the dynamics of mourning will hold artificial persons to such a recognition. Eventually, the work of mourning, by establishing the presence in absence of the "dead" authentic self, allows for its dispersal into the play of the symbolic self, made up of the convergence of self and culture.

Thus, mourning replicates the play of presence and absence that characterizes the very cultural phenomena it confronts. That it should do so comes as no surprise. The dynamics of shame, guilt, and anxiety are similarly consonant with the worlds in which they became the paramount emotional controls. Shame, enforcing solidarity with the endless generations living and unliving, accomplishes the same thing that ritual accomplishes in a traditional culture: access to the timeless. Guilt, implanted historically by one's parents and watching unseen over all one's actions and lending those actions a teleology that one only imperfectly understands, operates like Providence in a providential world. Anxiety, enforcing an assimilation of and an adjustment to a diffuse and ever-shifting set of variables, reflects a relativistic universe. Mourning, with its substitution of signs for what is lost, enforces participation in a world that is constituted by the play of presence in absence.

To what degree would our subject-directed social character be aware of the dynamics of mourning? Perhaps not at all, or at least no more explicitly than the other-directed person is of the source and operation of anxiety or the inner-directed person is of the source and operation of guilt. Nor would mourning, even mourning the authentic self, be a process that one somehow completes for all time, any more than guilt or anxiety are ever completed for the inner-directed and other-directed character types. American notions of acultural individualism and Western notions of the substantial soul die hard. They are likely to be with us for a long time to come. Without them, the dynamic of mourning, in the sense intended here, would be unnecessary anyway.

Despite all this talk of loss and absence, subject direction echoes familiar American themes of optimism. Insofar as the sanction of mourning succeeds, it restores the mourner to the world. Far from appearing glum, the subject-directed character type ordinarily appears to participate purposively, even energetically, in the play of cultural systems. But such behavior, tempered as it is by a simultaneously chastened and expanded sense of identity, resembles neither the mindless optimism of the booster nor the self-congratulation of authenticity.

Out of this unquantifiable mix of optimism and mourning, there is growing an accompanying enterprise ethic. Supplanting the self ethic but by no means harking back to the social ethic of the organization man, the enterprise ethic embodies the marching orders for this new social character.

"You shouldn't be this age and just be starting out."

Not to be confused with Margaret Thatcher's odious "Enterprise Society" or the laissez-faire swindles of the Reagan years, the enterprise ethic belongs to the realm of social character, not to economics. It is the yardstick to which the organization offspring increasingly refer, consciously or unconsciously, their behavior, just as the behavior of their parents took place against the background of the pervasive social ethic chronicled by Whyte.

Numerous commentators on organizations have detected glimmerings of a new ethic in today's young managers. In books that are widely divergent in seriousness and scope, such writers as Robert E. Kelly, Michael Maccoby, Daniel Yankelovich, D. Quinn Mills, Robert Naisbitt, and Daniel Yankelovich and Sidney Harmon agree that these young managers differ dramatically from the organization man. In tabular form, a summary of the differences would look like this:

The Organization Man	The "New" Manager
loyal	"disloyal"
prudent	adventurous
caring	self-interested
averse to taking risks	takes risks
homogeneous	diverse
autocratic	participative
takes orders	demands explanations
security conscious	change oriented
status quo oriented	seeks innovation
team player	self-developing
rigid, rule oriented	flexible, tolerant
tradition bound	imaginative

Such lists portray a brave new world of hardy entrepreneurs, fiercely independent iconoclasts, and self-seeking hard chargers. But the enterprise ethic, out of which this new social character operates, is far more complicated than such simple lists suggest. And having been forged in the crucible of the organization family, the enterprise ethic neither takes in all young managers nor is confined to them.

Growing out of mourning and the peculiar optimism in which it issues, the enterprise ethic appears ambiguous, perhaps even contradictory. To keep that ambiguity in view, it is helpful to recall that the etymology of *enterprise* leads us back to *undertaking*, a word that has funereal as well as entrepreneurial connotations. Thus, the enterprise ethic suggests a far more complicated set of motives than a simple desire to take risks.

Compared to the organization man's generation, this generation certainly *appears* to include far more people who are willing to take risks. A precious few, no doubt, court risk for the same reasons that all such bold people have. Others, operating out of a lifelong sense of entitlement gained from having never known failure, exhibit a blithe unconcern that may be indistinguishable from risk taking. Others behave boldly under the banner of self-fulfillment. But even these ostensibly enterprising people take actions that look more like leaps in the dark than like the ambitious schemes of visionaries.

When thirty-six-year-old Mike Lieberman left his secure job as a social worker to set up T. L. Computing to manufacture and market IBM-compatible personal computers, he was declaring his allegiance to this new and evolving ethic. Lieberman, along with his partner, an elementary school teacher and basketball coach, started his company because he was driven by the desire to do something he loved. "I'm addicted to working with computers," he says, "and I needed a way to make a living at it."

A similar declaration can be heard in the words of Mitch Kapor, founder of Lotus Development Corporation, one of the world's leading software companies, when he explained his decision to leave the company he started and built into a 1,350 person, $275 million operation: "The subject here is my life and I'm passionate about it. Fundamentally, my leaving was a function of the company's growth and of my growth. I will always be somebody who is highly motivated by things I regard as challenges, and I tend to be terribly unmotivated by—if not downright resistant to—anything else. And because Lotus grew so large so fast, it rapidly ceased to play that central role in helping give meaning to my life. And therefore, the honorable and responsible thing for me and for 1,350 employees and for several million customers and all that was to remove myself from the company sooner rather than later."

He is not seeking new entrepreneurial heights to scale so much as he is looking for something that is challenging enough to hold his interest and on a scale that is human enough to connect him meaningfully to a network of people. The sheer size of Lotus turns him off, but he is by no means antiorganizational. It is as easy to imagine him founding another powerhouse company as it is to see him toiling away quite happily among a small group of like-minded colleagues. Neither a riverboat gambler nor a cautious caretaker, he seems almost driven to courses of action that cannot be encompassed by mere entrepreneurialism. Whatever he does in the future may involve risk, but it will come as a by-product, not as the origin, of his restless undertakings.

Many of the organization offspring are reluctant risk takers, often motivated as much by a sense of having nothing to lose as by a positive desire for achievement. Frequent job changing—and members of this generation change not only jobs but *careers* far more often than their fathers did—may appear to Pollyannas as a sign of resurgent boldness. But viewed in light of the instability of organizations, a constricting economy, and structural economic imbalances, this enterprising spirit is often as much a matter of self-preservation as of self-assertion. Thus *enterprise*, with its mortal undertow, is meant to capture the ambiguity in behavior that may look, alternately, like boldness, dissatisfaction, or desperation and to suggest that whatever risks artificial persons take will spring as much from their mourning as from the apparent optimism in which it issues.

Joann Harrison illustrates the ambiguities of the enterprise ethic. Her striking combination of discipline, flexibility, and equanimity in the face of unrelenting difficulties with her business and an unsatisfying love life came only after her deep depression and brush with suicide.

"Because my life had changed so much as I was getting older, I found the changes more disruptive," she says. "I know it sounds like somebody reprogrammed me, but it was more a matter of me taking away a lot of the fears. And what was left after I got rid of all this shit was: *I find this fun*. I thought: 'My God, if all this happened to me in forty or so years, what are the next forty going to be like now that I'm so primed.' "

Her new attitude did not magically bring on a happy ending. If anything, her experiences as the decade of the eighties closed confirmed her view that there are no guarantees, as adversity continued to dog her business. The major computer manufacturer to which her software in- novations are tied was beset by bad management. The manufacturer was sinking fast and taking her down, too. To switch her products to another computer platform, she needed a million dollars in new capital. Mean- while, a fifty-thousand-dollar loan was falling due, and the bank refused to extend her line of credit. And though she enjoyed record revenues in 1989, she also suffered from rising expenses as she expanded her payroll. Unable to attract venture capital, she contemplated selling her home to keep her company afloat.

The earthquake that struck the Bay area on October 17, 1989, dealt Joann the final blow. She was alone in her office, talking on the phone to her sister Julia, when the temblor, at 7.1 on the Richter scale, first hit, sending her computers, valued at fifty thousand dollars each and unpro- tected by prohibitively expensive earthquake insurance, crashing to the floor.

"Before I realized what I was doing, I had dived under the desk, still clutching the phone," she says. "The jolt was so powerful that I knew immediately it was a major earthquake. The lights went out, and I heard this tremendous roar. I felt like a feather being shaken in a box—the desk was banging me up—and I was thinking, *I'm going to die*. When the aftershocks started, I said into the phone, 'Julia, if this is the end, I want you to know I really love you.' "

She eventually stumbled from the building and made her way home to her darkened apartment. The next morning she returned to the office building, waiting for permission from a building inspector to enter it and retrieve any valuables. "The streets were full of broken glass, the building was roped off with yellow tape, and nobody could be sure it wouldn't fall down. I thought: Whatever's in there is not worth it." She turned away and, without so much as a toothbrush, drove to her parents' house in the East Bay to collapse for a few days. A telephone conversation with a ferociously accomplished friend who had decided, before the quake, to give up pursuing the brass ring helped bring things into focus.

"Only when my friend, at the peak of her career, said she was letting go was I able to conceive of walking away from my business. Until then, I could not see that it wasn't giving me what I wanted—recognition, creation, success. And I began to realize that as I get older, my need for fortune and recognition is decreasing. I will no longer make the sacrifices for them I did when I was younger. I'm very much aware of being on the downside of life; once you hit your midforties, the likelihood of making it is far less. And you have less time left for the things you really enjoy, which I want to do before I die."

Painfully, she decided to close her ten-year-old business. By selling her software products to competitors, she managed to cover her debt and have enough left over to pay off her employees and provide a cushion for herself while she sorted out her future and came to terms with her experience. The process was a slow one.

"Only now can I look back and see it for what it was—failure," she says. "But I accept it as failure. And that's something I've never had to confront much in my life. I think the 1980s were a coming to a realization of my capacities and limitations. I never accepted failure before, even though my marriages were failures. But I always refused to call them that."

She found in her failure instructive differences from the bout of depression that had almost killed her in 1982.

"When I closed my business," she says, "there was no depression, just tremendous feelings of loss. In 1982 my depression came from my anger over my inability to get what I wanted out of life. After the earthquake I wasn't angry, I was just very sad. I saw myself as being unable to achieve what I wanted because of my own limitations *and* the limitations of the world around me, but without blaming myself or the external situation."

Without her being consciously aware of it, the process of mourning—for her failure and for her formerly inflated sense of self—restored her to the world.

"My sense of joy comes from being able to own up to the failure—to look at my business and say, 'That's not what I had in mind' and walk away from it," she says. "It's been very liberating. I haven't obsessed about it. I think about the failure as I've described, then I'm happy and I don't think about it."

Much like Joann Harrison, Randy and Debbie Myers were led by an experience of failure—their inability to make it in Nederland, Colorado—to a calm acceptance of whatever the future holds. As the Rocky Mountains was displacing the southeast as the region with the lowest per capita income in the nation, Randy and Debbie relinquished their live-for-today philosophy and moved to the more robust economy of Santa Rosa, California.

"We made a value shift in coming here," says Randy of the move today. "I no longer think that living just one day at a time is what I thought it was. Twenty years of that attitude has gotten me where I am today, which is obviously not where I want to be or else I would not have moved. I wouldn't be trying to change my life so radically."

Where they used to drift, they now plan, setting goals for Randy's contracting business and for Debbie's work in real estate.

"I think that setting goals is critical to being a successful entrepreneur," says Randy. "This is something I am just beginning to realize. If you don't make goals, there is no way you are ever going to get ahead."

Realizing that he sounds like his father, Randy takes pains to clarify the difference between them.

"I am becoming more of my father than I ever would have admitted in my younger days. I think planning has an important part to play in one's life and, of course, my dad was a master of planning. But I don't think it is necessary for me to go into corporate life to have the kind of life I want. It was, however, necessary for him. I don't think he could have been an entrepreneur. He would not have been happy—too much worry, too much insecurity involved, too much risk.

"As I get older," Randy says, "I see that the world is a balance. You can't have all of everything. Life is a balance."

Instead of continuing their search for the elusive authentic self, they see their future as involving the world beyond their doorstep. Though they still disdain large organizations, they have come to believe that their sense of self and place will be found in seeking alliances and forming networks outside the small circle of family and friends.

"I have this need to feel a part of a community," says Debbie. "It is not that I want to be a member of this or that group but to be a part of a larger 'family.' That is important to me."

As with many members of their generation, the fact that they survived the rough economic times of the eighties has actually served to embolden them, bringing them to view the future with more confidence than fear.

"There are opportunities that were not evident in Colorado," says Debbie. "The possibilities are endless."

"We are optimistic about our lives," insists Randy. "We are going to make it out here."

Carolyn Harrison, over the course of the eighties, developed a similar mixture of fatalism, acceptance, and optimism that drives her today. After completing her course work in 1982 and failing to find a full-time teaching position in the disastrous job market for liberal arts scholars, she took a part-time lectureship at her old school while she completed her dissertation. With little prospect of ever getting a job, she realized it did not really matter what her dissertation committee thought, so she wrote as she pleased, avoiding the stodgy dissertation form and its compulsory genuflections to authority.

"I just wrote about what interested me," she says, "in a way that you never can when you have an eye on a career. My committee let it pass because they probably didn't think it mattered, either. Since they were engaging in a kind of consumer fraud by continuing to accept doctoral students in a nonexistent job market, they probably figured I might as well at least be allowed the consolation of a degree."

A casual conversation with an editor at an academic publisher led to an invitation to submit the manuscript for consideration. The publisher, delighted that it was not in standard dissertation form, quickly accepted it. Job offers followed, and Carolyn took her present position in Boston, where she now tries feverishly to write a second book in order to keep her job. In the five years she has been there, she has watched the qualifications for tenure rise ever higher as successive waves of her ferociously qualified contemporaries reach the next bottleneck in their life courses.

Compared to the large numbers of her baby-boomer contemporaries who did not make it in the brutally competitive academic world, she is a success. But as she approached forty, she began to realize the personal consequences of a long-stagnant economy, coupled with her youthful refusal to acknowledge it. Thus, despite the real satisfaction her achievements bring her, she sees her lifelong prospects as paltry compared to her earlier expectations.

"I was aware of the bad economy in the eighties," she says, "but it was not brought home to me until I got a good job, a prestigious job, and found that it was financially a kind of dead end—a marginal house in a marginal neighborhood and little prospect of ever catching up with my older colleagues in real terms. I now know it will never give me the kind of life that I always thought I would have. So then you feel like you've been wasting your time and that you shouldn't be this age and just be starting out and only just realizing what you have to do."

Nevertheless, her experience of limits has brought her a kind of freedom to do the best work she can, just as her earlier experience of her father's heart surgery had impelled her to hang on in her impossible profession.

"There's no reason not to do the best, most adventurous work I can," she says. "Doing less than that won't do me any good anyway in terms of keeping my job. And economics aside, you still have to hope to do something as a teacher or as a scholar that will make a real difference— not some earthshaking difference—but those almost imperceptible differences that cumulatively add up to a life well lived."

Julia Harrison, like her sister Carolyn, was also determined to stay in a field in which she saw little future. In 1982, finding herself out of dance, out of a job, and only partially recovered from cancer, she swallowed her pride and auditioned for a dance company run by a former acquaintance.

"She was really surprised that I would come in and audition for the company," says Julia. "It was the kind of thing where I felt myself to be her peer as far as being a choreographer and having run my own company—I wasn't only a dancer. I just laid myself on the line and said, 'I really want a job—any job—with the company.' "

She was appointed associate artistic director. But within two years, her friend, exhausted by the company's financial problems and poor reviews, resigned. The general manager and the dancers followed. As the board of directors was preparing to fold the company for good, Julia stepped reluctantly forward. She persuaded them to let her try to make a go of it.

Julia threw herself into fund-raising, auditioned a newer and far less experienced set of dancers, and choreographed and rehearsed them tirelessly for the company's make or break concert, its first under her direction. She publicized the concert as a new start for the company and saw to it that potential patrons attended. The concert was neither a smashing success nor a flop, but her all-out effort on all fronts paid off. Reviews, crucial to winning ever tighter grant money, were marginally better, and survival was assured at least until the next concert.

In the concerts that followed she introduced ever stronger work, garnering excellent reviews and attracting more financial support. Her choreography began to win awards and earned a grant from the National Endowment for the Arts, a key to opening up other sources of philanthropy. In the space of three years, she had brought the company back from near-extinction to a position of regional prominence and was poised to push for national recognition.

Viewed from a distance, her experience, like that of her sister Carolyn, appears to be a conventional success story—a triumph of will and talent. But on closer inspection, her apparent boldness and persistence issue not from an indomitable spirit as much as from an almost broken one—cancer, depression, failure, and the limits they placed on her for virtually the first time in her life.

As the first concert under her direction approached, she could say, entirely without drama, "If things don't go well, it will probably be the end of my career in dance. My whole adult career in dance has been failure after failure in that I've had no support for my work. I've always created my own situation to do my work—no one has hired me to do it. And then I was in the right place at the right time to become director of the company and continue to produce my work. But if the company folds, it would be hard for me to take that step backward of not having money to produce my work with, of having to ask dancers to work for free again. If I can't make it work now, then I'm not going to make it work. And with my résumé no one would hire me, except maybe a small school to teach, and I'm not interested in that situation. I would rather go into something new."

Having gradually relinquished her more grandiose visions of her self, she had been able to audition as a mere dancer and, in time, to take over the struggling company without illusions. And when she did, something surprising happened. Her habit of blithely creating her own situation, a characteristic that had always been of a piece with her sense of entitlement and had always held her back because of the spotty résumé it yielded, now stood her in good stead. That lifelong indifference to standard career paths in dance (and in dance, such paths are as clearly marked as those in, say, banking) had perfectly prepared her to weather the uncertainty and precariousness of the company's crisis. From the time she founded her own upstart company in Utah on a shoestring to the time she begged, borrowed, and stole most of the resources of the dance department in graduate school to put on a concert, she was accustomed to improvising, making do, and bucking the odds. But now she did it on a much larger scale, with a much chastened sense of self and a more acute sense of the reality of failure. Her former blitheness had been replaced by something more akin to a cheerful fatalism—the enterprise ethic in its manifold senses of undertaking.

Julia's case is all the more interesting because as a genuine artist, she constitutes a kind of early warning system for her many peers whose identities, no less than hers, have been informed by the artist ideal. We may surmise that many artists are sustained by the purely self-expressive form of the artist ideal, and many, like Julia, were enticed by it into genuine artistic vocations in the first place. But many now actively reject it, in some cases preferring, like artists for centuries before them, to locate value not in the private expressive self but in the public standards and achievements of their art form, which is to say in communal values widely shared in time and place. Others frontally attack the cult status of the art object and the privileged notion of the artist and the expressive self, critically dissolving them back into the cultural processes that produced them. As Philip Rieff presciently put it in 1966: "Confronted . . . with a picture gallery as the new center of self-worship, civilized men [*sic*] must become again anti-art, in the hope of shifting attention toward modalities of worship wholly other than that of self." Other artists, like Julia, have shifted the emphasis in their work from the symbol to the sign, from the representation of "inner" states to the reproduction of public meaning.

Her new work, the crucial element in the company's turnaround, represents a real departure from her earlier efforts. It not only reveals the change in her thinking about her vocation but inadvertently illustrates the kind of changes she and many people like her, artists and dreamers alike, were undergoing in the eighties.

The turning point came in a highly theatrical, mixed-media piece based on her postcancer depression. Where her earlier work had sometimes tended toward the sentimental, this work dispersed her harrowing personal experience into a collage of textual fragments, multiple characters, and overlapping monologues without center or anchor. Her experience was not so much universalized as externalized in those discursive fragments, the very fragmentariness of which are seen to constitute the conditions of depression. Yet, like much postmodern work, her choreography remains highly accessible; it is less rooted in classical ballet than is much modern dance, and the chief influence on her movement is Fred Astaire. Subsequent work moved even more boldly into explorations of reality as competing discourses marked by gaps, silences, and absences. She began to incorporate foreign languages into her work, fracturing them and reassembling them with various dance idioms in surprising ways, shifting from an emphasis on "inner" expressiveness to a focus on signification. In effect, one can see in her work (at the risk of doing violence to her intentions) the interplay of mourning and meaning, the move from personal artifice to a tentative embrace of social artificiality.

For Tom Harrison, the near-bankruptcy of the company for which he worked when he was first interviewed for this book was merely a fortuitous circumstance that gave him many free days to fulfill his obligations as a single parent and to contemplate his options.

"I want to keep living the way I am as far as keeping up a certain income level," he said then. "But the longer I go on, it's not that great. I'm making around twenty-five thousand dollars a year now, and I can get by living where I do and supporting two children and have a bit of money to spend on myself, but that's about it." Nevertheless, he says, "there are a lot of things I can do to rearrange that."

It was rearranged for him when the company finally went under in 1989. Unworried, he collected his severance pay and did not begin to look seriously for another job for two months. With his technical skills, he easily hooked on with another computer company and quickly rose to manager. Having come to management late, in his midthirties, he still finds himself unsatisfied, casting about for ways to "rearrange" things.

In the behavior of all these people—from Tom, serenely looking for one more option even as the options he has always kept open begin to close down; to sisters Julia and Carolyn, maintaining difficult careers against long odds; to Joann, calmly facing down disaster; to Randy and Debbie Myers, discovering a new optimism as a result of their chastened sense of self; to Mike Lieberman and Mitch Kapor, unpredictably deserting secure situations—can be seen the operation of the enterprise ethic. The enterprise ethic impels them to take bold risks, but it also allows them to drift. It is outwardly optimistic, but based on a gnawing pessimism to which the work of mourning addresses itself. It is ostensibly individualistic, but, in effect, throws one back onto the socially artificial in which the individual is constituted.

Instead of persisting in some private search for an authentic self, these new individualists are seeking to realize their selves in public realms of meaning, but in a world where meaning is never fixed. In chasing those meanings, they show a great willingness to form, to join, and to leave ever-shifting networks and a great unwillingness to seek niches in immortal hierarchies. Antiorganization but not antiorganizational, they are uncommitted to any particular institution, but understand the necessity of collective effort. Simultaneously subjective and subjected, they are artificial persons all, and their bold leaps in the dark, as well as their resigned rolls of the dice; their persistence, as well as their lack of it; their undertakings and their leave-takings are all equally manifestations of their emerging enterprise ethic.

From choices to voices.

Though knowledge of the dominant social character and its accompanying ethic cannot predict the behavior of particular individuals, such knowledge can make that behavior intelligible. Any of the people we have used as examples of the enterprise ethic in action might have acted differently, but those actions would be nonetheless explicable in terms of the enterprise ethic. Similarly, Dave Harrison might have gone along with the schemes of John DeLorean instead of blowing the whistle on him, but, either way, he would be adhering to the organization man's social ethic with its values of loyalty and team play. As we have said, social character is a framework, not a calculus. Nevertheless, we can speculate on what these momentous changes portend for large areas of life. Just as we looked at the way in which personal artifice and its self ethic played out in everyday life, we turn now to what subject-directed artificial persons and the enterprise ethic might mean for interpersonal relations and the problem of community. (What it might mean for this generation's organizationalism is reserved for a separate section.) Most important, we ask what it might mean for ethical-religious values, whether the enterprise ethic, arising from a diffuse and unstable context, is an ethic that denies the very possibility of ethics.

Of course, none of the proponents of authenticity experience the life lived in its name as purely abstract and empty. They have complicated inner lives, and their days are filled with concrete activity. Nevertheless, their answers to the questions Who am I? and How shall I live? produce a vastly different (and no less complicated) world from what is likely to be produced by the answers embodied in the enterprise ethic. In practice, the ideal of authenticity yields a world of personal artifice in which personal relations are marked by a kind of hopeful pointing—a purely formal expressiveness—as the only accessible stand-in for the authentic self. Community, as the essence of artificiality, is rendered unreal, and ethics becomes a matter of fulfilling the moral obligation to self-expression, largely, again, through a formal expressiveness in which the act of choosing is seen as moral in itself.

The enterprise ethic carries no guarantee of superior virtue. It provides no answers that are necessarily better than those provided by the self ethic. But it certainly does provide *different* answers. Under its sway, personal relations, the understanding of community, and ethical principles are likely not only to be altered but to be sources of considerable confusion and misunderstanding until the transition from personal artifice to artificial persons is completed.

Taking personal relations first, it is obvious that their texture largely depends on one's concept of what it is to be a person. As we have noted, the concept that persons have absolutely free, acultural authentic selves yields interpersonal styles, whether engaged or detached, that remain hopelessly ensnared in purely formal expressiveness, a kind of hopeful pointing at something that is otherwise inaccessible. But if the individual does not end at the skin, if—as with artificial persons—the individual is seen as the convergence of self and culture in the play of signification, then interpersonal relations are likely to be greatly different. In a world of artificial persons, individuals will no longer be regarded as the sum of their choices; rather, they will be *read* as the peculiar mix of voices—of all the "artificial" social discourses—that speak through each individual. In personal encounters, then, we confront not the choosing self, but a speaking subject, one that is both subjected and subjective.

This reading of people is a trick we all partially perform, for the most part badly, almost every day—from reflexively stereotyping other people to suspecting that their motivation is determined by interests of class, gender, or race. But there is a great difference between seeing such things as gender or race as substantial entities with real immutable characteristics, as we do when we stereotype, and seeing them as largely culturally generated discourses that are intertwined with other culturally generated discourses. When we stereotype, we not only assign positive identities to signs that have identity only as difference, but we overlook the individual as a unique site of a unique and ever-shifting matrix of discourses.

We come closer to assuming the model of the artificial person on those occasions of ordinary suspicion. For example, when a woman challenges her husband's seignorial assertion of authority, she may be asking not *who* is speaking but *what* is speaking through him. She hears not *the* voice, but *voices*. And they may be many: biblical, contractual, the language of brute strength, or whatever. She hears not the authentic self of her husband with whom she must communicate, but a speaking subject whose voices she must explicate.

Hearing those voices clearly—in oneself or in other people—is by no means easy. The voices may be confused, contradictory, cacophonous. And they can never be definitively untangled—meaning is always deferred along endless and shifting chains of signification. Nevertheless, the task is not to get beyond or below this speaking subject to a more authentic self by simply dismissing its voices as artificial. The task is to engage this particular matrix of voices—this particular idiom—the very artificiality of which makes such engagement possible in the first place.

This is not to suggest that the explication of another person's voices is merely a technique of suspicion. The point is that artificial persons are not isolated in their particularity. Through the public, conventional, and artificial systems that converge in them, they are connected to other people and to social life in a way that the authentic self, adrift in its solipsism and desperate to "communicate," is not.

One of those forms of connection is love—love between persons whose individuality consists not in their abstract authenticity but in their particular artificiality. In the self ethic, by contrast, these artificial particulars are seen to be tainted. They are distractions that must be transcended, mere barnacles that must be scraped off the pristine authentic self. The possibility of love is replaced by an impossible ideal of communication between abstract authentic selves, yielding in practice a world of empty "commitments."

It is also possible that the emerging sense of the artificial person may signal an easing of the chief gender-related difficulties in personal relations—that of intimacy for men and of individuation for women. The roots of these problems, and their difference from each other, lie in our culture's assigning the primary responsibility for child rearing to women. Because the primary caregiver for girls is the same-sex parent, maturation for them is a process of identification. As adults operating in culturally prescribed roles of cooperative caring (like child rearing or charity work), women may have difficulty establishing any strong sense of self. For boys, the primary caregiver is the opposite-sex parent, so maturation for them is a process of differentiation. As adults operating in culturally prescribed roles of competitive individualism, men may have difficulty developing intimate ties to other people. The rise of the artificial person as a dominant social character suggests that men will move toward a more female sense of self, one that assumes connection to other people and eases problems of intimacy. And the ascendancy of such a model of individuality helps women with the problem of individuation by mooting it: To be connected is to be an individual.

Again, this does not mean that men will get in touch with some essential "feminine" side of their psyches, any more than women will tap some essential "masculine" side of theirs. Rather, it means that in moving toward ensembled individualism for all the economic and historical reasons we have detailed, men are adopting a sense of self that has historically been gendered "female" by the culture, but in the future will be less so, a future that has already been prepared, to a small extent, by the relatively gender-neutral imperatives of the self ethic.

Turning to the issue of community, we find that no one is quite sure what it is, though everyone agrees we have lost it and need to get it back. As Raymond Williams observed, community "unlike all the other terms of social organization (*state*, *nation*, *society*, etc.) . . . never seems to be used unfavorably, and never to be given any positive opposing or distinguishing term." It does, however, have a *negative* opposing term: the atomized individual. Cut off from direct and immediate social relations with each other by the forces of capitalism, the mass media, geographic mobility, and ideologies of competitive individualism, atomized individuals are seen to lack shared purposes, mutual care, and social responsibility. They are, indeed, a lonely crowd.

In such criticism, *community* refers both to the quality of social relations and to the material context in which they may be realized. In current calls for a "return" to community, these two senses are often glibly or carelessly conflated, producing visions of great emotional appeal that bear little scrutiny when dissected. Currently, such calls for community take several broad forms: the nostalgic, the hortative, the committed, and the idealist-historical.

Nostalgic talk about community focuses on the material context of communities past. It often evokes images of small-town America—the village square and the Fourth of July picnic. Or, for those Americans who grew up in urban areas, the idea of community harks back to neighborhood block meetings or sitting on the stoop during sweltering summer evenings. These concepts of community rarely evoke images of suburbia. Yet for many in this generation of Americans, suburbia is the only kind of material community they have ever known, and all other images they might have of community, from Mayberry R.F.D. to the Woodstock Nation, are just that—images.

They are powerful images nonetheless. Forgetting the repressiveness, narrowness, parochialism, and real difficulty of life in earlier times, such simple nostalgia offers an attractive alternative to anxiety about the complicated present. Nostalgia for small-town America may also veil resentment about the social mobility of newly enfranchised (and generally non–Anglo-Saxon) groups—blacks, Asians, Jews—or about the demands of women, including middle-class ones. In traditional communities, such people knew their place, in both the geographic and the hierarchical sense.

Nevertheless, calls for a "return" to such community are often warmly received even by people who have no intention of moving to small towns or taking to their stoops. It should go without saying, but apparently does not, that such idyllic communities, if they ever existed, are gone with the wind; no amount of wistfulness will bring them back. In an age of increasingly mobile capital and global communications, the obliteration of such self-contained social units is likely to accelerate, not to decrease. Nor are the children of the middle class going to give up the geographic mobility that, in America, has always gone hand in hand with social mobility. Essentially frivolous and deluded, when not meanly reactionary, the evocation of irretrievable material contexts of community suggests, in the end, that improving the quality of social relations is impossible.

Other champions of community, recognizing the delusions of nostalgia for what they are, promote an "ethic of commitment" to heal the breach between the alienated individual and the society. This ethic can quickly degenerate into the merely hortatory: The talismanic word *community* is pronounced, and we are all enjoined to pull up our socks and pitch in, regardless of what *community* may concretely mean or whether personal, historical, or economic circumstances make such commitment on a broad scale likely or possible. There is the further question of whether *any* highly self-conscious commitment to an ideal of community may not be a contradiction along the lines of "trying to relax" or "acting naturally." And the question remains: Is it possible for the shared purpose of a community to be merely each individual's determination to have shared purposes?

More empirical observers, like Daniel Yankelovich, see an ethic of commitment growing out of the search for self-fulfillment itself. In an age of diminishing expectations, they say, the pursuit of fulfillment is being redirected to include more satisfying communal endeavors. Commitment, argues Yankelovich, emphasizes the needs and reality of other people and expels the Maslovian self. Nevertheless, because of its roots in the expressive self, out of which Yankelovich sees it evolving, such commitment still retains an air of the willed, the worked up, the existential choice having no other grounds than that one has chosen it.

In the widely read *Habits of the Heart*, Robert Bellah and his colleagues, on the other hand, offer a prescription for achieving community that specifically excludes expressive individualism. They call for "reappropriating tradition" by applying to present realities the still living, if attenuated, elements of America's biblical and republican heritage. They see vestiges of these traditions still alive in "communities of memory"— institutions like churches, universities, the family, and voluntary associations. But they add that there would also have to develop out of these existing groups and organizations a social movement, like the earlier civil rights movement, dedicated to achieving a transition to a new level of social cohesion.

Laudable as these goals may be, there are several reasons why this prescription, though rooted in a highly sophisticated understanding of the problem, seems misguided and highly unlikely of fulfillment. The example of the civil rights movement reveals the difficulty. There is simply no comparison between the black church, which produced the movement, and the institutions of the overwhelmingly white, middle-class people who are the subjects of Bellah's (and our) investigation. The black church did not have first to be revived to produce the civil rights movement; it was already the central institution of social cohesion and transformation for an embattled people whose unceasing travails had only made the black church stronger and more necessary. The active creation and protection of a community were already at the heart of its meaning; it was not a "community of memory," but a community of current practice; not a repository of abstract ideas to be "applied," but a material way of life. Bellah's resort to this example is a tacit admission that many of the white, middle-class institutions in which they place their hopes for transformation are socially moribund, and it begs the question of whether the revival of these institutions is likely.

Given the pervasive distrust of large, hierarchical organizations, the likelihood of such a revival seems remote. As we have noted, members of this generation have little loyalty to such institutions *even when they work in them*. The awakening of the church, or at least of the white, middle-class, mainline Protestant church, appears the least likely. Such churches, never strong as an *institutional* force in American life, are deader than ever among the successor generation. The middle-class suburban churches with which the organization offspring are thoroughly familiar have been objects of their indifference and even quiet contempt for so long that it is unlikely they will seek to make them socially meaningful. Even those who attend church do so largely in the same perfunctory spirit as do their parents, vaguely desiring some religious education for their children, though orthodox religion is not central in their homes. Universities offer little more hope than churches. Significant numbers of students sink ever deeper into racism and careerism, financially strapped administrators increasingly depend on corporate financing to fund academic programs that have little to do with humane values, and superstar professors flit from job to job like baseball's free agents while their less eminent colleagues chafe under structural inequities in salaries that their institutions cannot correct.

There is an even larger sense in which pleas like Bellah's for reappropriating tradition are likely to fall on deaf ears. For the idealist conception of history—the notion that ideas in the abstract are the motors of history—is precisely what a conception of reality as competing discourses and circulating power denies. In a society that is growing more multi-ethnic and more multicultural with each passing day, the question is increasingly: *Whose* memory, *whose* community? The belief that we can and should simply select the best ideas from "our" tradition and put them to work, regardless of concrete history, economics, and social character, is finally merely a more sophisticated version of exhortations to commitment.

The historical emergence of the artificial person does not mean an end to the dream of community. But neither does it augur its achievement. The nature of this new social character does, however, promise to shift debates about community onto new ground. Currently, those debates proceed on an assumption of a simple contrast between isolated individuals and the human solidarity for which they thirst. But this simple dualism of self/community, which we are repeatedly urged to overcome, conceals numerous hierarchies—of class, gender, ethnicity, and so on. For the artificial person, with a more accessible self that already includes the social, this simple opposition gives way, however. The self is not a free-standing entity "inside" confronted by an alien world "outside." Its identity is identity as difference; its place is among constantly shifting differential systems of significance. As the unique site where any number of these social systems crisscross in peculiar mixes, the individuality of the artificial person is not absolute and abstract, but concrete and particular. From this perspective, community is not the overcoming of a simple opposition, but the embrace of differences—of the *not I* from which the *I* derives its identity. The possibility and hope for community lie not in some worked-up commitment or idealist revival of selected traditions but in the everyday working assumption that one is far more profoundly (and mysteriously) connected to other people than merely as one of millions of isolated actors outside time and culture.

It is impossible to say specifically what kind of community this everyday assumption may bring into being and, therefore, whether the outcome will even be desirable. But the kind of community that artificial persons pursue will be unrecognizable to the nostalgists and the exhorters alike. It is likely to arise out of ad hoc associations and far-flung networks, not out of more traditional hierarchical institutions or narrowly circumscribed areas. And what it is likely to produce in the way of community is an "assertion, not of centralized sameness, but of decentralized community—another postmodern paradox."

There are as many problems as promises in such a prospect. On the one hand, the understanding that social life is power circulating in signs and discourses creates at least the possibility of seeing social problems systemically or understanding social life in terms of narratives of care instead of hierarchies of rights. On the other hand, decentered networks, which may not be tied to any particular place, can simply ignore, lose, or efface whatever lies in the interstices of the network: individuals as well as entire social classes. (The "centralized sameness" of traditional community achieves a similar result by forcing people into their place in hierarchies.) We have already noted the disturbing tendency of many of the organization offspring to regard community as a group of people who are roughly the same age, hold similar values, and come from the same social class. It is, of course, partially their acultural individualism that makes them blind to such social matters. But even if, as artificial persons, they leave behind the idea that the individual ends at the skin, it is perfectly possible that they will create middle- and upper-middle-class networks that form a simulacrum of decentralized community while everyone and everything outside those networks falls by the wayside, further aggravating the two-Americas syndrome of the 1980s.

Though it would be nice to think that the emergence of the artificial person as the predominant social character would result in narratives of care, it remains only a possibility, for Americans have a fluid character that foreign as well as homegrown commentators have often remarked on. As a site of the ever-shifting play of culture, the artificial person may appear to be the most fluid to date and, ethically, the most frightening. Having rid ourselves of the bane of radical individualism, have we wound up with something far worse—a radical nominalism that undermines any coherent notion of reality and an ethical nihilism that renders action morally unintelligible? If so, the enterprise ethic would appear to be an ethic that denies the possibility of ethics.

But consider, once again, the moral sanction of mourning. Generated by the historical and cultural experiences we described earlier, mourning enforces the mode of conformity we call subject direction. In a world where identity is difference, mourning holds subject-directed persons on course, helping them negotiate the tricky terrain of subjectivity and subjection. Looking neither "inside" nor "outside" for guidance, mourning precludes the exclusive pursuit of subjectivity, idealized by many of the organization offspring as the authentic self, and the exclusive surrender to subjection, realized by the organization man in belongingness. Instead, mourning promotes the participation, playful or resigned, in one's own idiom—socially artificial but nonetheless personally unique. The ethical import of an action is no longer to be found in what it *means* (the pointing behind itself to an abstract entity like the authentic self) but in what it *says* (the putting into play of the discourses enveloping it, including those that make up the actor). In ethics, as in personal relations, the choosing self gives way to the speaking subject. Thus, conflicts of values are not glossed over as mere differences of personal preference; they are explored as competing narratives, each linked internally and to each other along complicated and elusive chains of discourses.

But a larger question remains: What informs the sort of world implied by mourning? Substituting signs for what is lost, mourning replicates in its operation the languagelike universe to which it enforces allegiance, just as anxiety imitates a relativist universe in its operation and guilt, a providential one. These correspondences suggest coherent worlds in which moral sanctions are seen as grounded in the nature of those worlds. Beyond guilt lay God, brooding over the providential world. Beyond anxiety lay nothingness, haunting the relativist world (and driving the organization men to huddle together in belongingness and their children to retreat into the autonomous self as the sole source of value.) But what lies beyond or, more precisely, *within* the world invoked by mourning?

Retrospectively imposing a later formulation of Freud's on the concept of mourning, we would say that within the work of mourning lie Eros and Thanatos, the life instinct and the death instinct. Given the human and cultural wreckage left in the wake of the headlong search for self-fulfillment, Daniel Yankelovich has written that the future depends on what ethical status we assign desire. Mourning, enacting the problematic of desire and death, ensures that the subject-directed character type hews to precisely that question, although, given the character of play operating in sign systems, the bewildering variety of answers at which the subject-directed arrive may appear to traditionalists as indistinguishable from radical nominalism and moral nihilism. Nevertheless, the sanction of mourning ensures that such a character and such a culture and its ideology are not likely to be without a profoundly ethical dimension, however repugnant or unfamiliar it may appear to people who do not share it.

In a practical fashion, seemingly far removed from esoteric psychoanalytic notions, we are all being forced to face, with increasing urgency, the question of desire and death raised by two tragic contemporary phenomena: addiction and AIDS. Indeed, the two meet in intravenous drug use. Just as concretely, economics, especially the economics of limits that has replaced the economics of affluence so widely touted in the fifties, raises questions of desire and death. In the final analysis, economics is the study of who eats and who does not, whose desires are fulfilled and who dies. And it is economies and economic policy that decide how desire and death are to be circulated in society. The growing numbers of homeless people in the streets of our cities provide ample evidence of the way these questions have been answered in the recent past when the ultimate moral obligation was the duty to express the self. Ultimately, Eros and Thanatos, along with economics, grounded in an analogous dynamic of desire and death, form the material base for the culture we have been describing and locates the crux of its ethics. How the rising generation responds to its own diminished economic expectations and to the plight of those who never had any expectations will be the great test, as well as a significant determinant of, the enterprise ethic.

None of the foregoing necessarily means that people will behave any better or that moral reasoning will be any less controversial, only that such behavior and reasoning will be framed differently. Nevertheless, the difference is real. It is a move from an experiential to a consequential ethics, from a justification of actions in terms of self-expression to an explanation in terms of context. It also represents something of a return to a more traditional pragmatism, away from a theory about the self-validating nature of private feelings and toward a theory of truth based on public results.

Because of the pervasiveness of the ideology of authenticity, we are not accustomed to welcoming the artificial calmly. The notion of artificial persons sounds repugnant, robotic, and conformist. But consider how the ideology of authenticity permits a far more thorough domination of individuals than does the frank acknowledgment of artificiality. Devotees of Abraham Maslow, Carl Rogers, and the like assume that the substantial, culture-free, ahistorical self, once uncovered, provides a place to stand, an Archimedean point from which to move the world. Ironically, in many therapies that are carried on in the name of finding this real self, the befuddled customer accepts uncritically a managerial model of the self that is, in conception, deeply beholden to the bureaucratic organization of twentieth-century industry. The beleaguered learn stress *management*, the shy practice *techniques* of assertiveness, and the ambivalent assess emotional *trade-offs* with the skill of cost accountants. Still, some therapists hold out the chimerical hope that a substantial, authentic self exists; is accessible; and waits to be pressed into service if only we can "get in touch with it." Yet this substantial self is simultaneously conceived of as free and contentless, and what the therapy inadvertently fills it with is the dominant culture in the form of adjustment. This process of domination is not exclusive to therapy (or present in every therapy); it is only more clearly visible there.

This is not to say that the understanding of people as artificial persons will do away with domination. To be able to explicate various discourses is not necessarily to create a possibility of freedom. The application of such understanding can turn scientific and technological, manipulative and exploitative. It is perhaps not so fanciful to imagine that there will arise a new kind of success literature—one that purports to show people how they are constituted in discourses and social texts and how they can attempt to manipulate and circumvent, insofar as possible, their positions in such webs of significance. The titles may be easily imagined: *Changing the Subject, Signing On, Contexts for Success*. Such an instrumentalist approach does not yield one's own idiom (or anyone else's). One remains solely artificial, the alternative to which is not, as the self-fulfillers think, authenticity (whether created or uncovered), but particularity, artificial to be sure, but nevertheless individual.

Our argument for the emergence of the artificial person, then, is an assertion not of progress but of change, an attempt not to bring it into being but to track it. But even if it is wrong in the particulars, one thing is clear: There will be no going back. This is the lesson that social critics of all stripes refuse to admit, yet it is the one thing that should go without saying. There will be no going back: to God, to the substantial self, or to pastoral community. Perhaps the social character now emerging will not fit exactly our model in all particulars. But whatever model emerges, it will not be something that looks backward, though it will not be entirely disjunctive with previous American character, either. As T. S. Eliot observed, in a different context, if something is not new, then it is not in the tradition.

11

In the Spirit of the Enterprise Ethic: Organizational Life Reconsidered

"Our big job is to hasten obsolescence."

The dual imperatives of the global economy and the emergence of the rising generation's enterprise ethic place new, and largely unknown, demands on organizations. The globalization of almost every industry and the development of new information technologies will, as we discussed in Chapter 9, force dramatic changes in organizational structure. The rise of the enterprise ethic will challenge organizations to adapt to a work force that regards organizations differently than did the loyal organization man. In effect, everything we have ever known about what management is and how it should be practiced is now open to question. That is why the 1990s will be the most challenging economic decade since the beginning of the automobile age.

Though network organizations and the ubiquity of information technologies, like so much else in postmodern life, provide experiences of decentered systems that undermine the authentic self, they neither guarantee the emergence of artificial persons nor necessarily promise hospitable work environments. As we have said repeatedly, and in a variety of ways, social structure and social character do not merely reflect each other. They may be wildly out of phase, or there may be aspects of each that are complementary and other aspects that are antagonistic. The day-by-day churning of all these aspects, in varying proportions, produces all kinds of unforeseeable consequences and contradictions. For example, many of these network structures and technologies have been crudely grafted onto older organization-man structures. Thus, it is certainly possible that network structures may be simultaneously hastening the end of authenticity and forestalling the emergence of the artificial person, for Americans change faster than do their institutions. And while the social character of the organization offspring has been changing steadily over the past two decades, the assumptions that underlie American management have not. If anything, those assumptions have become more widespread, elaborate, and entrenched than ever. Hence, far from reflecting the social character of the organization offspring, the social structure, especially as it is embodied in the management of large corporations, remains largely disjunctive with it. Though long-term stability of organizations and the loyalty they evoked may be long gone, the management philosophy of the organization-man era endures. It is the one legacy of the organization man that is indeed still with us—and that grows more costly, in human and economic terms, each day.

As William H. Whyte, Jr., observed more than three decades ago, at the heart of the practice of professional management, as it evolved after World War II, lay a belief in method. Modern managers directed their attention to questions of organizational structure, role definition, and control. The practice of management revolved around how things got done, not what things meant. Method took precedence over vision or purpose.

Managers were taught that organizational success was primarily a function of controlled rationality. They were trained to put their faith in logic, objectivity, analysis, and evaluation. They learned to think of themselves as rational problem solvers. They were conditioned to deal with problems as they arose—one at a time. And the difference between success and failure was seen to be a function of the methods that were employed. Correct methods produced good results. Wise decisions flowed from orderly processes and appropriate decision-making procedures. Problem solving was a dispassionate discipline. It was emotionally neutral, detached, and, above all, professional—and the more verifiable, quantifiable, and replicable, the better.

The best decision-making processes were those that employed the most sophisticated quantitative methods. Formal techniques, such as decision analysis, linear programming, and cost-benefit analysis, were useful and powerful because they provided the manager with politically neutral data. Furthermore, "clean" data could be used for the measurement of performance. The manager would not have to rely on subjective data from other managers or employees. All individuals and, indeed, the problem-solving process itself could be measured against the same objective standard.

The area that was most susceptible to quantitative analysis was, of course, finance. Thus, over time, good management came to be equated with good financial planning and analysis. The formal budgeting process, yearly financial plans, quarterly budget reviews, capital expenditure reports, and the accounting system became the most important aspects of management. Financial techniques and procedures became more than a set of tools; they became the vehicle through which the manager understood and controlled reality.

Since financial methods were among the most valued in decision making by management, it followed that those managers who were most adept at understanding and using sophisticated financial tools (such as capital-markets theory, which was the rage of Wall Street in the late 1980s) would inevitably be considered among the very best managers. Over time, this form of reasoning became institutionalized. By the 1980s, it was a given that the best business schools would concentrate on teaching financial analysis and analytical methods and that the best jobs would go to graduates with the strongest financial and analytic skills.

Professionalism, control, rationality, teamwork, and efficiency became the hallmarks of the professional manager. And indisputable logic, verifiable data, objective analysis, and solid financial strategy were the keys to successful management. In the evolution of this concept of the professional manager, there was little place for the idea of leadership or vision. In the world of the modern organization inhabited by the organization man and his immediate successors, everything was method masquerading as substance. It took more than two decades for this worldview to mature, but by the 1970s it dominated corporate America. What had begun in the 1950s as little more than organizational pragmatism—the "art of muddling through," as it was then known—developed into a form of elitism, in which structure, order, and reliability came to mean more than substance, content, and vision.

Managers came to believe that a smoothly functioning organization and an organization making money on a quarter-by-quarter basis were synonymous with a successful organization. In their commitment to coordination, cooperation, and control, professional managers lost sight of their organization's purpose. They came to believe that the manipulation of data—and, most important, financial data—was the substance of their work. Producing high-quality products or providing superior service became secondary issues.

This perspective produced some curious definitions of success. For example, in the 1950s and 1960s, many manufacturers purposely designed their products to become obsolete either by going out of style or actually failing. Called "planned obsolescence," this strategy was the brainchild of marketing and finance managers who shamelessly figured that the faster the product broke down, the more you could sell. What counted, after all, was how many you sold, not whether the product was any good. Success was a function of the quantity that was sold and the per-unit cost, not quality. Harley Earl, the head of General Motors' styling department in the midfifties, spoke for corporate America when he explained: "Design these days *means taking a bigger step every year*. Our big job is to hasten obsolescence. In 1934 the average car ownership span was five years; now it is two years. When it is one year, we will have a perfect score."

In manufacturing facilities, the measure of success was that the assembly line was kept running at all times. Supervisors were typically evaluated on the basis of "downtime"—the amount of time the line was shut down on a given shift. The more downtime, the less productivity. The fact that there might have been good reasons for stopping the line—such as problems with quality—never occurred to the rational, measure-everything-that-can-be-measured manager.

In the 1980s, American manufacturers began to recognize the limitations of this "method-and-measurement" perspective. Nevertheless, its influence remained strong, as, for example, in the way American companies undertook "Just-in-Time" (JIT) inventory-control systems. The idea is simple. Instead of warehousing parts needed in an assembly process, a JIT system brings the purchased parts to the factory floor at the precise moment they are needed, no sooner and no later. But the real value of JIT was lost on managers who were accustomed to thinking in purely financial and quantitative terms. As Charles Morris points out, American executives who are steeped in finance assume that the advantage of JIT systems is that they save working capital by reducing the time that parts lie uselessly in warehouses. Though JIT systems do save working capital, that is not their point. "The reason for pushing toward zero inventory," explains Morris, "is that it forces you to squeeze out production-line inefficiencies relentlessly." But professional managers are so enamored of financial analysis that they find it almost impossible to grasp a meaning beyond the immediate bottom line.

To the professional manager, the reason for automating an assembly line is simple. Automation saves labor costs. However, once again, the reasoning is spurious: "In many industries, labor costs have already fallen to only about 10 percent of sales costs anyway; in high technology industries, direct labor costs are often 5 percent of sales or less," argues Morris. "Cutting out a few more workers here or there isn't going to make much difference. The reason to automate is *quality*." When a part that does not fit comes down the line, the automated line will shut down until the problem is corrected. The quality of the product is not compromised in favor of speed or efficiency, as measured by the number of units per hour.

The professional manager's one-dimensional view of reality could not have survived had it not been for one important historical circumstance: American companies had no real competition. During the time this managerial ethos was forming, Western Europe and Japan were on their knees, still recovering from World War II. American companies had the luxury of almost unlimited time to develop products, bring them to market, and build their market share before they had to begin thinking about foreign competitors. American managers came to believe that their overwhelming success was a result of their superior management techniques. American corporations fooled themselves into believing that their industrial dominance was their manifest destiny.

Success bred complacency. Instead of promoting individuals of vision and leadership into the top executive positions, American corporations tended to select men (and they were all men) who were good controllers or strong general managers. In 1979, when the executive placement firm Korn/Ferry International asked senior executives to name the fastest route to the top in the corporate world, a plurality said finance and accounting. Almost a decade later, things had changed little. Forty-nine percent of the senior executives polled still believed that the fastest way to the top was through finance or general management. America's drubbing at the hands of the Japanese had chastened few senior executives.

In 1989, when *Business Week* asked the chief executive officers (CEOs) of the top 1,000 American corporations to describe their career paths, the largest number (264) said finance and financial control. Only 11 checked off "entrepreneur"—at a time when Peter F. Drucker was proclaiming "the new entrepreneurial economy."

As recently as 1988, America's premier executive recruiter, Lester Korn, advised aspiring young executives: "Most successful careers in American corporations are built by staying put, not moving. Eighty percent of all job promotions are made from within. Earning big money is often a function of longevity." According to Korn/Ferry's survey of senior executives that year, most senior executives had worked for only two employers, and a remarkable 24 percent of them had stayed with the same company for their entire careers. The average tenure with their current employers was seventeen years. Korn's counsel was confirmed by *Business Week*'s finding that the CEOs of the Top 1,000 had been with their firms an average of twenty-three years.

Thus, *Business Week*'s 1988 composite description of the CEOs of the Top 1,000 read like a casting call for the organization man: "He's a fair representative of America's affluent executive class: middle-aged, middling rich, and resolutely middle class in his tastes and avocations. Overwhelmingly, the CEOs of the nation's most valuable corporations are men—all but four, in fact. And that's twice as many women as last year. Beyond maleness and whiteness . . . the composite CEO is 56. . . . He's a college graduate, and he has worked for his company for about a quarter-century, as CEO for nine of them." And, adhering to the ethos of the professional manager, only seventy-seven of the CEOs of the Top 1,000 owned 10 percent or more of their company's stock, directly or indirectly.

William H. Whyte, Jr.'s prophecy of a nation of organization men had come to pass. The American CEO was a man—a white man. He was a manager, not an owner. He was a company man, not an entrepreneur. And he had learned to play the corporate game, and learned to play it well.

"It is mostly anonymous people . . . that make the engines run."

In 1976 Michael Maccoby became the first of many social commentators and business writers to declare the demise of the organization man. He wrote: "As a description of corporate reality, the other-directed organization man is too narrow and time-bound. The modern technology-creating corporation needs more than one type of person, and those who reach the top in the seventies are more active and adventurous than the stereotypes of the fifties." Maccoby sensed a change in the air, but the organization man and his brand of professional management were far from extinct. In fact, the organization man was still at the top of his game.

It was to take a decade longer, and an extraordinary series of social, political, and economic events, to bring him down. The massive flood of mergers, acquisitions, and leveraged buyouts in the late 1980s made a mockery of the concept of corporate loyalty. Takeover firms rarely took into account the years of dedicated service an organization man had put in—except negatively. Foreign competition and diminishing profits battered many an organization man's corporate duchy, and when cost-cutting corporate raiders went looking for places to trim the budget, the big salaries of upper middle-level organization men usually turned out to be a great place to begin. What the organization man had willingly given the organization—his loyalty—the organization began unceremoniously to take away.

However, even the pressure of massive social and economic change was not enough to dislodge the organization man from his exalted position in American business. Early in 1989, thirty-three years after the publication of Whyte's book, *U.S. News & World Report* declared, in a cover story: "Reports of the death of the organization man are premature." The magazine based its conclusion on a survey of middle-level executives from twenty of America's largest and best-known corporations, including American Express, AT&T, Du Pont, Ford, General Motors, Hewlett-Packard, Honeywell, Mobil, 3M, and Westinghouse. "Just as such large companies still dominate the American landscape, it is the mostly anonymous people in their middle ranks who remain the willing cogs that make the engines run." The magazine found strong evidence that the organization man's way of seeing the world endured: Seventy-six percent of the men who were interviewed expected to end their careers with their current employers (compared with half the women), 80 percent declared their deep commitment to their companies, and 65 percent said they would choose the same career path again.

It should have come as no surprise that in a time of such significant economic upheaval, many people would seek refuge in the great corporations. To those seeking a safe harbor, the appeal of life with a secure corporate giant might well have appeared even more attractive than it had to the organization man in the early 1950s. Certainly, the rewards and satisfactions seemed much the same: collegiality, steady promotions, the implied promise of secure employment, and a career that mattered.

For Don Pippins, one of the Du Pont employees profiled by *U.S. News & World Report*, the well-trodden path of the organization man was very appealing. Pippins began his career with Du Pont right out of engineering school and he had been with the company ever since—eighteen years. In the manner of the true organization man, he had done whatever the company asked. He had been a shift supervisor, a marketing representative, a public relations staffer, and a business strategist on a new business venture.

The long hours and many moves were not pleasant for Pippins or his family, but he persevered for the same reason the organization man had—he thought his loyalty would be rewarded. "A little suffering was O.K.," Pippins told the magazine, "if there was a reward at the end of the road." And like the organization man, Don Pippins wants to believe that someone upstairs in the corporate hierarchy is looking out for him. "I know I'm on a list somewhere," he said. "I know how long the list is, and I know I'm not at the bottom." However, unlike the organization man, who felt little reason to worry about his future prospects, Pippins adds anxiously, "But how far am I from the top?"

For Pippins, life in the corporate middle is full of uncertainties, but much like his organization-man predecessors, he would rather live with familiar uncertainties than with unfamiliar ones. He wonders what he will do if he does not get the next promotion to marketing manager. "You either go along with lowered expectations, or you leave," he says. "I honestly don't know what I'll do if I'm forced to choose."

So the melody lingers on. Don Pippins exemplifies today's organization man (and, as the magazine's figures regarding the commitment of female managers reveal, today's version is, like yesteryear's, likely to be male). The new organization man's faith in the beneficence of the organization is, in some ways, every bit as strong as that of the junior executives of the 1950s. But his faith in the organization is tempered by the knowledge that these are difficult times; he knows that even a corporate powerhouse like Du Pont may face unexpected challenges that threaten his career. Still, behind such doubts there remains a staunch belief in the system. The new organization man does not question the fundamental assumptions of life in the organization. He sees no reason to buck the system. Unlike his predecessors, he may well decide to leave his current organization in search of greener pastures, but his leaving will not signal his disillusionment with corporate life or suggest some deeper level of questioning about the compact he made with the system. As William H. Whyte, Jr., put it in late 1986: "Despite the current mythology of the entrepreneur, most people still work in organizations. When I wrote the book, we were a nation run by organization people, and they still are dominant. I don't see the Organization Man's death. He's very much alive."

These new organization men and women, though more fearful in today's volatile business environment, nevertheless continue to put their faith in the power of professional management. To them, the men at the top of corporate America are living proof of how the game must be played. To them, getting along means going along. In many respects, Whyte remains correct. The system that nurtured the organization man endures, even in the face of the devastating success of its foreign competition.

But as the eighties faded, neither organizational loyalists nor their more entrepreneurial colleagues had much to cheer about. "In 1975, America's machine-tool manufacturers were among the world's leaders; by 1985, machine-tool exports were virtually nonexistent, and German and Japanese machine tools were standard throughout American industry. In just a few years the American share of world semiconductor fabrication dropped from 60 percent to 35 percent. America's share of memory chips plunged even more—from 85 percent to about 15 percent.

For all practical purposes, America simply exited the consumer electronics industry. *No* home radios, black-and-white television sets, phonographs, or cassette players are made in the United States any longer. . . . No American company makes VCRs or CD players. Industry after industry told the same story."

The federal government, despite rhetoric to the contrary, was bankrupting the nation. For the six years from 1982 through 1987, the federal deficit totaled $1.1 *trillion*. When Ronald Reagan assumed the presidency, the nation had a $914 billion debt. By the time he left office, the national debt had risen to an astonishing $2.6 trillion.

The public schools were graduating seven hundred thousand functional illiterates every year. Forty-eight percent of the patents granted (in 1988) were issued to foreign investors. Real hourly wages for workers were at approximately the same level as in 1973. And basic industries were overwhelmed by low-priced, high-quality products from Hong Kong, Japan, Korea, Singapore, Taiwan, and West Germany.

Under the stewardship of the organization man, America had gone into an economic free-fall. American companies had grown complacent and sleepy. American managers no longer understood their marketplace; they had lost sight of their competitors, and they found themselves at odds with their workers and ambivalent about their own loyalty to their companies. The result was a deepening economic disaster. By the end of the 1980s, there was plenty of blame to go around. But excuses and finger pointing aside, the reality remained: America, far from "standing tall," as Reagan had it, headed into the 1990s with its head bowed in humiliation.

While we may not yet know what we need to do, we have learned what does not—and will not—work. It is now clear that professional management is at the heart of America's continuing economic difficulties. The very revolution that helped create America's robust economic health—the command-and-control mentality of the organization man—has worked to bring about its decline. William H. Whyte, Jr., was correct in his diagnosis. The social ethic of the organization man turned business leadership into financial strategy, and the consequences were devastating.

"The managerial orientation," concludes Abraham Zaleznik, of the Harvard Business School, "with its emphasis on form over substance, on structure over people, and on power relationships over work, is at the heart of the disability of modern business in the United States and probably in other countries as well." Charles Morris goes further: "The dominant intellectual error in the United States in the 1960s and 1970s . . . was a faith in our ability to rationalize and measure everything. If you couldn't measure it, it wasn't worth talking about. The insistence on measurement often meant overlooking everything that was important." Means and ends became confused. Short-term methods of correlating prediction with performance became more important than having a clear vision of the future. And a mentality of calculation and compliance replaced individual responsibility and creativity.

It is often said these days that what American management needs— and has not yet even approached—is sophisticated leadership. Organizations need leaders, not professional managers. But understanding what leadership is and developing it have always been a challenge. While we know a great deal about management—for which we can thank the organization man and the business schools—we know little about leadership. As difficult as it is to understand changes in market forces, effectively track demographic and social trends, manage fast-track product cycles, and incorporate the latest in technological advances, it is far more difficult to inspire commitment, create a sustainable vision, and encourage self-management and autonomous work teams. We know how to train managers; we are far less certain how to train leaders—or whether it can even be done.

Moreover, as the outlook for professional management has become clouded in recent years, *leadership* has become something of a mere buzzword—promising to become for the nineties what *bottom line* was to the eighties or *accountability* was to the seventies—talismanic words to be pronounced reverently regardless of what they may concretely mean in particular historical circumstances. It is difficult to understand what leadership would even mean in the world of the information-based, network organizations and the new social character of the successor generation. Clearly, it does not mean leaders on the model of, say, Winston Churchill, the supremely confident colossus; Franklin Delano Roosevelt, the patrician populist; Dwight D. Eisenhower, the general as self-effacing administrator; or Douglas MacArthur, the misunderstood megalomaniac general—four of the organization man's formative images of leaders. Nor is it leadership on the model of the charismatic John F. Kennedy, the bullying Lyndon B. Johnson, or the devious Richard M. Nixon—three leaders who were the generation's own. And certainly it does not mean Ronald Reagan, whose empty-headed sloganeering, while America went into receivership and its businesses lost competitiveness, exemplified the ultimate bankruptcy of the genial, positive-thinking style of the organization man's personality ethic.

In fact, searching for models has it backwards to begin with. The idea is not to look for historical examples of leadership—whether Attila the Hun or Mahatma Gandhi—and then to extrapolate from them some Platonic ideal of leadership. On the basis of romantic-heroic theories of history and unexamined assumptions about rugged individualism, the reliance on models leads to little more than lists of personal characteristics of dubious relevance. Better to look at the nature of what and who is to be led—and where. And doing so means looking at knowledge-based organizations that are peopled by artificial persons whose enterprise ethic makes them difficult, if not impossible, to lead at all.

"Their knowledge made them free."

As organizations become more knowledge based—as almost all organizations in America will—they become increasingly less amenable to the techniques and methods of the "measure-and-control" mentality. In fact, the locus of control tends to shift away from the organization and toward the individual knowledge worker. Ever since the beginning of the Industrial Revolution, the contract between the individual worker and the organization has been controlled by the employer. All rights and privileges that the individual employee possessed were granted by the employer. However, in a knowledge-based organization, that relationship is effectively reversed. Legally, the power may continue to reside with the organization, but in a practical sense, knowledge workers hold many of the cards. They have the skills that the information society needs. Those skills give them mobility; they are no longer tied to one job or one employer: "Knowledge workers know that their knowledge, even if not very advanced, gives them the freedom to move. . . . Their knowledge made them free. It is a lesson knowledge people in America—and especially the young ones—have learned and will never forget. All of them—the geologist, the mathematician, the industrial engineer, the computer programmer, the secretary at the word processor, the personnel trainer, the accountant, the nurse, the salesperson—now know that they are not dependent on any one employer. Practically every institution needs them one way or another." Moreover, "only in a genuine and long-lasting depression does the knowledge worker need a job more than the employer needs the knowledge worker."

Knowledge workers identify with their work, not with the organization where the work is performed. They identify with their profession or their craft. They are specialists who realize that they know more about their own area of expertise than does perhaps anyone else in the organization. Thus, their loyalty tends to be to themselves and to their profession, not to the organization.

What matters to them is that they have an opportunity to advance their knowledge, to continue to grow in their profession. They seek work assignments that are professionally challenging, assignments where they can work with state-of-the-art technology or with specialists in their own field. Knowledge workers can be—and usually are—highly committed workers, but they tend not to be loyal in the manner of the organization man. As the thirty-three-year old director of marketing at a supercomputer firm told us: "Getting another job is never the issue. There will always be jobs out there. The only real issue is finding an opportunity—the kind of breakthrough opportunity where I can really learn something or really make a difference."

In an information economy, workers cannot be managed by the principles of professional management, which is to say the organization-man model. It is not possible to supervise knowledge workers. They do not work on assembly lines and they cannot be managed as if they did. Since their work involves the formulation, interpretation, and manipulation of information—all of which are mental functions not open to supervision from the outside—knowledge workers cannot be managed in the traditional sense. As Peter F. Drucker puts it: "Now we are managing people paid for their knowledge. We have never done that, and we don't know how to do it."

Perhaps the key to learning how to manage knowledge workers lies in understanding the operating principle that information obeys. The most distinctive characteristic of information is that it cannot be managed like other resources. It must be focussed, narrowed, and directed toward a clearly defined goal. In much the same way that a laser focuses and concentrates many smaller light sources into one, high-intensity beam of light, information can be compressed, clarified, and focused for maximum impact. In an information-based organization, the focusing is achieved through a clearly defined mission and set of objectives that follow from that mission. Of course, since the days of "management by objectives," it has been assumed that organizations and their employees must have clear goals. Nevertheless, many organizations stumble along without clear direction and their employees lack any shared vision of the future. Organizational momentum, outside market forces, and the sheer staying power of ingrained rules, procedures, and structures keep many organizations alive long after their mission and objectives have been effectively forgotten.

In an information-based organization that employs knowledge workers and successor-generation workers who cannot be traditionally supervised and who have little loyalty for loyalty's sake, it is essential to have a mission that these employees find desirable. Knowledge workers cannot be told what to do. They must want to go where the organization is going and they must be allowed to develop their role in helping it get there. If they believe the mission is worthy of their effort, then—and only then—will they exercise self-control and find ways to get the job done. Otherwise, they are likely to be bored, unhappy, and eager to leave.

To an increasing number of members of the successor generation, driven by the enterprise ethic, it is what they do that is important, not necessarily where they do it. They want the freedom to innovate, the power to control their own destinies—inside and outside organizations—and the respect of being measured against their achievements, not against their company's norms. They want to be known for what they have accomplished, not for their positions in a hierarchy.

"Key employees don't care about things like pensions," says Kenneth Oshman, former president and CEO of Rolm. Oshman, who went on to become CEO of Echelon, a computer company specializing in local operating networks, is talking about Rolm's largely successor-generation work force. "Things like guaranteed pension programs and unusual medical programs are not very important. They really are not worried about paternalistic or egalitarian kinds of rewards or compensation. They are very happy not to get a reward if they fail, but if they succeed, they want a very significant, tangible, and unusual reward. People here believe in entrepreneurial rewards, and they want a shot at them."

On June 16, 1989, the *New York Times* reported: "In an unusual case of musical chairs in Silicon Valley, Joseph A. Graziano, chief financial officer at Sun Microsystems Inc., has left to take the same job at its rival, Apple Computer Inc. More unusual is that Mr. Graziano was chief financial officer at Apple until 1985 before turning up at Sun." The article also noted that Graziano, age forty-five, had taken two years off before joining Sun.

While it may have appeared unusual to the reporter, Graziano's behavior is rather ordinary in Silicon Valley, where Apple and Sun are located. Taking time off between jobs, moving from one company to another and then back again, and job-hopping in general are a way of life in California's most famous valley. Silicon Valley's labor force is dominated by successor-generation employees, and what is happening there is likely to become standard practice in the 1990s.

Unlike organization-man companies, which have always viewed defections to competitors as treason, companies in Silicon Valley make no attempt to punish talented employees who leave their organizations. They recognize that part of the vitality of their industry comes from a continual turnover of talent. Senior managers expect dedication from employees, but few such managers have any illusions about keeping those employees for the duration of their careers.

"One of the realities of Silicon Valley," says Echelon's Oshman, "is

that you can walk right next door and get a new job. There are continuous job offers for anybody at any level who is any good. There is the
added competition from venture capital ready to finance new ventures.
There is a great deal of money available at all times to finance any
reasonable idea. As a result, if you don't recognize innovation in your
own organization, a venture capitalist will."

The flow of venture capital through Silicon Valley depends a great
deal on the strength of the economy, and at the turn of the decade the
flow had dramatically slowed. Nevertheless, rates of turnover remained
high, especially against traditional standards. Instead of fighting this
trend, many companies institutionalized it by offering bounties for the
successful recruitment of key employees from other companies. Depending on the position to be filled, it was not uncommon for companies
to pay bonuses of ten thousand dollars or more to an employee who
successfully recruited another key person.

Walk among the cars in the parking lot at Sun and you will see
Apple, NeXT, DEC, and IBM decals on car windows and bumpers. The
same holds true at almost any successful company in Silicon Valley.
Those tiny artifacts of the past business lives of Sun employees are a
measure of accomplishment. And they testify to Sun's ability to lure away
from its competitors the most valuable asset the Valley offers: its talented
employees. Those decals do not look like much, but they are tracer
bullets in a revolution, tiny markers of the far-reaching realignment taking place between employers and employees.

Though knowledge workers are the most visible candidates for
changing the compact between the organization and the employee, they
are by no means alone. Most of the other organization offspring in our
sample—both inside and outside large organizations—also value their
professions over their employers. On the face of it, this suggests a continuing devotion to the figure of the artist as their occupational ideal, and
many do remain devoted to a personal myth of artistry. But as they make
the difficult, and largely unconscious, transition from personal artifice to
artificial person, their occupational ideal is also undergoing a subtle, but
significant, transformation.

From artist to artist manqué.

It is in the artist ideal of the self ethic that the personal identity and
social identities of organization offspring meet on that middle ground
where the question Who am I? shades over into How shall I live? The
organization offspring, as we explained, employ the myth of personal

artistry to help them process their ambivalence about their middle-class identities, to help them resolve anxieties about status and success, and to help them fuse their personal and social selves. As an occupational ideal, the artist myth attempts to integrate the world of expressive values acquired at home in childhood with the instrumental values acquired at work in adulthood.

But with the inexorable pressure toward accepting all that was previously disdained as artificial has come a different answer to the question, Who am I? Identity, paradoxically derived from and dispersed throughout the culture, rather than located "inside" the person, is composed of what is different from it, what is absent. To the question Who am I? comes the answer: "I" am composed of what is not "I." In keeping with this notion of identity as difference, the ideal type for the enterprise ethic ceases to be a positive, self-identical entity like the yeoman farmer, the salesman, or the artist. Rather, it means a simultaneous negation and affirmation of the ideal figure for identity, a kind of anti-ideal. Instead of imagining themselves artists, artificial persons will, with different degrees of consciousness, see themselves as artists manqué.

(Having historically been used as a term of abuse for failed artists and pretenders, the term *artist manqué* has always carried a stigma. But in the world of artificial persons, it is, of course, the term *artist*, insofar as it means the originary, authentic genius, that should be a term of abuse because the artist myth represents such a feeble and ultimately empty gesture. Nevertheless, because of the stigma attached to *artist manqué* and because the change is largely unself-conscious, the term, which we use because it best conveys our argument, is unlikely to gain currency. Rather, the meaning of the term *artist* is likely to undergo a gradual and subtle evolution toward what we wish to convey by *artist manqué*.)

This reorientation away from the artist myth and toward the anti-ideal of the artist manqué is achieved through the process of mourning. Mourning the "death" of the authentic self is tantamount to accepting the unreality of the private myth of artistry. But the artist ideal, having played such a crucial role in the self-understanding of the organization offspring, cannot be given up once and for all any more than the authentic self can; the work of mourning is forever unfinished. Like the imaginary authentic self that mourning continually reintegrates into the symbolic self, the artist ideal is reinterpreted as part of the system of differences that form the subject. This process is not a matter of the artist ideal giving way in a dialectical fashion to its opposite, but a matter of recognizing identity as difference: I am not an artist; therefore, my identity is largely structured by the artist I am not.

Nor is the stance of the artist manqué a matter of simply seeing reality more clearly and then moving on. Rather, for artificial persons, it is a working assumption that helps make sense of day-to-day life, just as the artist ideal does for the life of personal artifice. To assume the identity of the artist manqué, whether consciously or unconsciously, means to turn away from the notion of creativity as the agency of authentic self-expression. Just as, in a more general way, the artificial person abandons authenticity for particularity, the artist manqué abandons creativity for creations. It means redirecting effort and attention toward concrete activity in its context, not the abstract qualities of "creativity" and "originality" that stand behind or above activity. (As we have shown, the privileging of creativity over creations can justify virtually any activity—from greenmail to indolence—as long as it is said to be sufficiently creative, regardless of its context or concrete results. Thus, a mundane real-estate sharpster like Donald Trump drew few snickers when he titled his autobiography *The Art of the Deal*. Similarly, people who use abstract claims to creativity to deny their middle-class identities regard the pretense as inspired, rather than as a contemporary feature of middle-class identity itself.) Instead of regarding actual endeavors—whether in personal relations, occupation, or social life—as the mere epiphenomena of some internal, private, and more fundamental world, the artist manqué turns for significance from the empty inner drama of authenticity to the play of particular social reality.

The anti-ideal of the artist manqué carries no guarantee of superior virtue. It provides no answers that are necessarily better than those provided by the artist ideal. But it certainly does provide *different* answers. Under its sway, personal relations, the understanding of community, and ethical principles are likely not only to be altered, as we have noted, but to be sources of considerable confusion and misunderstanding until the transition from personal artifice to artificial persons is completed. The same holds for the world of work. For what the successor generation is doing, without consciously realizing it, is seeking to re-create a way of working that dates back to the preindustrial age, when there was less separation between art and craft, creativity and creations, personal identity and public identity. It may or may not be a better answer to the question, How shall I live? but the giving up of creativity as an abstract psychological category in favor of concrete creations in the public world is certainly a different answer. Such workers are not morally superior, any more than subject-directed artificial persons are morally superior to searchers for the authentic self (though they may be). Superior or not, the point is that whatever work they do will be performed in the artisanal style of the artist manqué. And the appearance of large numbers of such workers, professing neither the organization man's occupational ideal of the salesman nor their brothers' and sisters' occupational ideal of the artist, will frame the problems of work—and management—in a new way.

Since *artisanal* carries connotations of handicrafts and the like, it seems strange to claim its reappearance when the nature of work, in an age of information, grows more abstract each day. But one can see the force of the claim even in the creation of the shadow information systems described earlier. As we detailed, these shadow systems were obviously not formed in accordance with a hierarchical, organization-man model, which, in any case, has little to do with art *or* craft. But neither were they fashioned from an abstract technological aesthetic (driven by considerations of elegance, simplicity, complexity, or whatever, assumed to be built into the technology itself). No information systems "geniuses," consumed by a vision of technological beauty and convinced of their personal creativity, fashioned these ad hoc and, in some ways, home-made information systems. Rather, these systems were created cooperatively by people who were under pressure to deal with reality as they found it. If the creators of these systems were indifferent to the pecking order of the hierarchy, they were equally uninterested in making grandiose claims for their own creativity. True, they wanted rewards and recognition for their success, but only for their success, not because they possessed some inner and invisible quality of creativity that hovered above or beyond their actions. (The infantile desire to be rewarded for one's inner, and largely unproved, good qualities is more widespread in business than many people assume.) In effect, the creators of these highly successful shadow information systems were practicing a familiar American pragmatism—a pragmatism of the sort that the organization man, dazzled by financial analysis, had lost sight of and that his children, deluded by "true feelings," always disdained.

What these new artisanal-style workers seek is work that allows a large measure of individual responsibility, where attention to detail is rewarded, and where satisfaction comes from producing a high-quality product or providing a high-quality service. But even that is not enough. For it is in this artisanal way of working that the anti-ideal of the artist manqué fuses personal identity and artificiality in the instrumental world of work. It is therefore critical to their sense of well-being and identity that these new-style workers know why they are working. They want what they do to matter; they want their work to have meaning and purpose beyond facile ascriptions of abstract creativity and certainly beyond a status that is derived from their position in a hierarchy. In short, they seek meaning.

But meaning is in short supply. "Every age has a critical shortage," says Paul Hawken, an entrepreneur and author. "In the industrial age, it was money. People in industrial society were willing to give up time for money, and in many areas of the country that's still true. But . . . many people will no longer give up their time for money. In a postindustrial age, the critical shortages are time and meaning. And people will only give up their time for meaning. If they don't find it, money won't substitute."

But how does one impart meaning to an organization? Meaning is not implicit in an organization's structure or design or even its history. Selling a product or providing a service (including governmental services or education), no matter how good the product or useful the service, is not good enough. It would appear then that the job of the leader—as opposed to the professional manager—is to create meaning (the key reality in a languagelike universe). But because meaning is elusive, always disappearing along endless chains of significance, both in general and for the personal identities of employees, it is difficult to see a role for any type of leadership we would recognize as such. Where, then, is meaning to be found in an organization? What does the artificial person, as the generation's new form of individualism—imported from its organizationalism in the first place—portend for the generation's organizationalism in the future? That question brings us to the most basic issue of all in a world of organizations: authority and legitimacy.

From the legible to the audible.

Indifferent to organizational hierarchy but needing no grandiose conviction of their own artistry, artisanal workers respond neither to traditional command-and-control methods of the organization-man-style management nor to the manipulative, touchy-feely methods of the neo-human-relations movement. In effect, they reject both the egoist and the humanist poles of their generation's organizationalism, neither conceding authority to the organization and denying its legitimacy, as the egoists do, nor seeking to legitimate the organization by humanizing it, as the humanists do. To put it another way, real artificial persons no longer see organizational entities as artificial persons.

This rejection of the central premise of their generation's organizationalism is the latest twist in the continuing interpenetration of individual and organization that has marked American social development. To recapitulate: Nineteenth-century abstract individualism, applied to the giant corporations then emerging, led to a personification of the organization as an artificial person that had the same legal rights as individuals. Eventually, the successor generation, applying its own highly psychologized version of individualism to organizations, refined the metaphor by endowing that personification with a psyche, either egoistic or humane. Both versions of their organizationalism managed to view the many as the one, conceiving the various competing voices, forces, and elements of the organization as a single, psychologized artificial person. But when this organizationalism, in its turn, redounded upon their individualism at a time when historical, economic, and demographic pressures were bringing an end to the reign of the unitary, authentic self, the image was reversed: Instead of seeing the many concentrated into the one, they began to see the one as dispersed in the many, thus producing an individualism of artificial persons whose identity is constituted by all the cultural systems previously disdained as "artificial."

Now this new version of individualism is being taken back into their organizationalism, transforming the unitary artificial person of their current organizationalism into something more closely resembling the dispersed artificial persons of their individualism, but with a crucial difference between the two. In their individualism they see identity as culture; in their organizationalism they see culture as identity. For individuals, the unique convergence of artificial systems in the person yields personal identity. For organizations, corporate identity is dispersed in artificial systems that converge nowhere. Thus, the organization is no longer endowed with a psyche, but is seen as a culture in which the identities of its members are dispersed and out of which those identities are partially constructed.

To find where legitimacy resides in the successor generation's emerging organizationalism, it helps to look at the switch from choices to voices in their individualism—their move from a concept of the unitary, choosing self to a concept of the person as a multivoiced, speaking subject. Rather than being regarded as the sum of their choices, individuals are read as the peculiar mix of voices—all the artificial social and cultural discourses—that speak through each person. Those voices, as we have said, are not easily disentangled; many competing and contradictory voices converge in the particular idiom of any given individual. As they reimport this view into their organizationalism, the artificial person that is the organization will be seen in a similar way—as a cacophony of competing voices, discourses, and interests. But, having given up the idea of a unitary self in their individualism, they will, in their organizationalism, no longer hear these voices unified in a self that is distributed throughout the organization. Instead, they will hear the voices of the organization as dispersed, competing, sometimes cohering, sometimes clashing, but always in daily flux.

Moreover, given their sense of identity as difference—as made up of what is not "me"—they see their very identities as deeply implicated in and formed by these organizational voices. Therefore, just as they explicate the mix of voices with which an individual confronts them in personal relations, they will similarly explicate the voices of the organization in organizational life. Out of that mix of voices they will construct and have constructed for them narratives in which their identity is bound up. And it is in those narratives that they will discover—or fail to discover—the legitimacy of the organization.

This reading of institutions, as well as of people, in terms of the voices that compose them suggests that authority will, in the postmodern society now emerging, have to find new ways to legitimate itself. As Peter Clecak points out, in traditional societies the source of authority was *visible* in the person of the king. In bureaucratic societies like ours, authority is *legible* in laws, regulations, and standard operating procedures. Clecak says he is being somewhat fanciful, but his observation is worth pursuing for what it can tell us about the changing nature of authority and legitimacy. We may say that legible authority seeks to legitimate itself through "self-evident" rational-legal propositions ("self-evident" because they are more or less obviously measurable against universal notions of truth, logic, and rights). The ideal of the authentic self, though it implicitly criticized rational-legal discourse in many ways, is ultimately compatible with universal truths and natural rights legible in such discourse because like them, the authentic self is believed to stand beyond history and culture.

However, with the emergence of the artificial person as the dominant social character among the organization offspring, the break with legibility is likely to be complete. To a much greater extent than ever before, they will no longer see the rational as unproblematically legible in self-evident laws or rules. Rather, they will attend to the discourses that surround those laws and rules, interpenetrate them, and render them ambiguous and almost instantly dated artifacts of the never-ending play of power and signification. Rational-legal discourse thus becomes just one more highly problematical discourse among many (as any woman or black person who has been consistently shut out of job advancement by the supposedly impersonal operation of the rules can testify). Legitimacy, then, will be conceived not as legible and univocal but as *audible* (even when written down) and equivocal. The notion of the audible should not, however, suggest the presence of some transcendant speaking voice. What is "heard" is not some real or authentic voice, but various discourses intertwined in utterances *or in documents*.

This is a radically new way to conceive legitimacy and it portends a genuine crisis. Of course, we often hear that we face a crisis of legitimacy—that no one any longer believes that *any* authority is legitimate. And then we go through all kinds of empirical investigations to see if statistically this is true. But the real crisis of legitimacy that is shaping up in this country has less to do with disillusionment than it does with the *way* in which legitimacy is recognized. The real crisis will occur not in some massive loss of legitimacy, but in the clash between the old and the new ways of approaching legitimacy. The conflict is not so much about whether any institution is legitimate, but about the very way in which we interpret legitimacy. Is legitimacy legible in rules, regulations, laws, and standard operating procedures? Or is it audible amid all the discourses that are competing and combining in the play of power and signification?

One way of seeing the huge upsurge in litigation, legislation, judicial activism, and special-interest politics that has overtaken American life in recent years is as a harried and always belated attempt to adjust our predominantly rational-legal society to our changing concept of legitimacy. Similarly, the grinding, state-by-state battles over abortion that are now taking place, turning on a religious and scientific-rational argument about when life essentially begins versus a critique of the hidden agendas of power in such fixed discourses, promises to heighten the tension between the two competing concepts of how one recognizes legitimacy.

This way of recognizing legitimacy is not merely a technique of suspicion—though at times it can be—any more than attending to the voices of individuals is solely suspicious. It may also entail the positive construction of narratives from the welter of voices and discourses, the active pursuit of (always elusive) meaning, and a process of recovery to complement techniques of suspicion.

One may conclude from all this that the task of the leader in organizations is to produce meaningful narratives in the form of manifestos, programmatic statements, and inspired visions that everyone then signs onto. But to come to that conclusion is to misunderstand that narratives are constructed daily in the real events that take place throughout the organization. Inspirational manifestos and the like are just one among many competing discourses. A discourse, it should be remembered, refers not merely to utterances and documents, but to any meaningful activity—from a market strategy to the distribution of washroom keys—whether it is explicitly verbalized or not. For example, the style of personal behavior in an organization, implicitly followed though never stated, constitutes a discourse. So does the layout of offices, the pattern of vacations, or the types and frequency of informal contact among employees. Among all these competing and overlapping discourses, a formal corporate philosophy may be of little real significance, or it may, as a result of its relation to other activities in the organization, take on unintended connotations. "Bullshit is bullshit," as one of our interviewees put it about such a document, contradicted daily at his company by reality.

Meaning cannot simply be decreed to these new workers, and certainly not from the top down. Nor can it be forever fixed or even easily controlled, for it is changing, coalescing, and dispersing constantly in many competing narratives throughout organizations. Only as long as these new workers believe they are shaping the narrative, either of the organization or of their own lives in relation to the organization, will they concede any kind of legitimacy to the organization. (This version of legitimacy is another instance of moving toward a form of moral reasoning—tracing narratives of care—that has been traditionally seen as female. And it is a move away from the male form of moral reasoning—constructing hierarchies of rights.) When the narrative turns unpalatable, they are likely to leave, for it is in these public and artificial narratives that they see their identities taking shape. When they were under the sway of authenticity, they tried to distance their "real," inviolate, abstract selves from such social discourses, which they saw as irrelevant to identity. But as artificial persons, they recognize that those discourses *are* their identity.

For example, one of these artisanal-style workers might find herself in an organization where inherently good work was increasingly discouraged by the company's growing obsession with short-term profit or, for that matter, with long-term aesthetics. The narrative, as she "heard" it in the daily unfolding of events at the company, might well contradict other narratives, other discourses (including some others that the company also generated, as well as some she generated) in which she felt more comfortable. Feeling herself compromised by the change in her identity entailed by the new narrative, she might well leave. In effect, the artificial person resembles a character in a story, who has no other identity apart from that story. But there is this crucial difference: This character, being subjective as well as subjected, can change the story, walk out of it, or reinterpret it.

It is partially because issues of identity for the artificial person are directly engaged by social narratives that behavior under the banner of the enterprise ethic appears so ambiguous. On the one hand, these leaps into new narratives, new meanings—Mitch Kapor giving up Lotus—appear bold; on the other hand, they often appear to be accompanied by weary resignation—what else could he do? By contrast, acolytes of authenticity, under the sway of the self ethic, simply separated themselves from the implications of social narratives by clinging to an identity seen to be apart and unsullied by events as long as one's actions were formally expressive or abstractly "creative."

None of this is meant to suggest that the artisanal worker who resigns is somehow more noble than is an employee who stays. (After all, the artisan might have simply reinterpreted the narrative in a way that could be seen as rationalizing.) The employee who stays might well take the rational-legal view of legitimacy and require of the company only that it treat him fairly in accordance with well-established rules. From his perspective, the actions of the artisan make little sense. The point is that the two employees take *different* views of legitimacy, not that one view is necessarily superior to the other.

Given the influx of employees who do take a new view of legitimacy, organizations will increasingly find themselves faced with a paradox. As we have seen, the old techniques of professional management, once so effective, no longer suffice. What is needed, it has been repeatedly suggested, is leadership. Therein lies the paradox: *Would-be leaders must lead people who will not follow.* All a manager or anyone else can do by way of leadership is to become a sort of narrator, joining his or her voice to the other voices in the organization. This does not mean simply cooking up some high-sounding mission or corporate philosophy (most of which are laundry lists of "values" subordinated to the ultimate, statutory aim: increasing shareholder value). It means telling an ongoing story, through word and deed, while recognizing that co-workers will see the story, in part, as forming part of their identity and, therefore, are likely to scrutinize it closely.

The kind of leadership required does not mean, in the manner of the human-relations movement, manipulating employees by manufacturing the appearance of their involvement or paying lip service to glittering generalities like "respect for the individual." Nor does it mean the power of positive thinking or some other strenuous inspirational style. Primarily, it means leading by example. The best you can do is to live your own narrative; leave room for others' narratives of professional growth, challenge, recognition, or whatever; and try to orchestrate all these competing narratives into a mutually satisfactory web of relationships for as long as it can be sustained. *Everything else—motivational programs, corporate philosophies, manipulation—is a waste of time.* Such a style of leadership is, in the manner of the enterprise ethic, simultaneously fatalistic and optimistic. It recognizes unblinkingly that these employees have no reason to give long-term loyalty to the organization (and that the organization could not provide a reason for them to do so if it wanted to) and that there is nothing the leader can do about it. On the other hand, such a leader fully expects that from this constantly shifting cast of characters, the best work such employees are capable of doing is likely to flow.

Bill Campbell, former president and CEO of Claris, Apple Computer's software subsidiary, was able to attract to Claris many of the best and brightest minds in the software industry. The relationship of these employees to him, to each other, and to their work illustrated the form that leadership must take in the future. Said a regional manager of the company: "I took a substantial pay cut to come here. But I came because of Bill Campbell. Campbell is a real leader. He is a person you can believe in; he brings out the best in others." This quote reads, of course, like a statement that might be true of any kind of leader, but it is what the regional manager added that is indicative of the new requirements for leadership. "Life is too short," he said, "to work someplace where you don't like the people and can't learn anything. Campbell knows where he wants to go, and it's a joy to help him get there."

Campbell, leading by example, helped provide that most elusive and scarce commodity—meaning. And meaning arose because Campbell's narrative by example was capacious enough to accommodate the narratives of his co-workers—their desire to learn and to like each other (the latter, an unsurprising desire if one's identity does not end at the skin). They helped Campbell get where he wanted to go because he helped them get where they wanted to go.

Such leadership and such opportunity for forging a meaningful identity have heretofore been available in small organizations or in entrepreneurship. As Donald Povesjil, vice president of corporate planning at Westinghouse, explained to *Inc.* magazine: "At a small company, you very seldom saw anything like a comprehensive market analysis—or any of the things that big companies like to do—just the feeling that this ought to work. The founder believed that this was the way the world worked. You could see the way that type of vision . . . affected the decisions, performance, and motivation of an entire organization. You saw people making day-to-day decisions guided by that vision."

It is an old lesson, but one with particular relevance for the 1990s, when the dominant social character is likely to be of a sort that will neither meekly obey nor mindlessly follow. That is the lesson that the would-be leader must not only learn but fully accept, as some of the people in Silicon Valley have learned about these new kinds of employees. Neither this new social character nor the kind of leadership it calls for is a panacea. While this style of leadership may elicit the best work such employees are capable of, it does not mean that their best work is the best possible—or even that it is necessarily *good* work. Perhaps some other kind of employee may perform better. But the point is that these artificial persons are likely to be the kind of employees who are available in increasingly large numbers in all kinds of organizations, and whether those organizations and these kinds of employees will be up to the formidable tasks facing them remains to be answered.

"Many have begun to question the strength of American character."

So the stage is set. A new generation of workers, inside and outside large organizations, with a different view of organizational life, is about to confront the realities of doing business in a new America. The new America is an environment of economic uncertainty, global competition, and managerial myopia. In the new America, old answers no longer suffice. In the new America, the economy remains at risk; the false gods of management still stalk the landscape, and foreign competitors continue to outperform and outsmart us.

Whatever the problems of the nation and whatever their causes, they will not be solved by the organization man. The organization man's watch is about to end. By 1995, all the organization men will have left the stage, and by 2010, all members of the Silent Generation will have reached retirement age. Twenty years from now, the transition to the successor generation will be complete. In 1988, only thirty-eight members of the baby-boom generation were among the leaders of the *Business Week* Top 1,000, and most of them headed high-technology firms. However, by 2010, they will dominate the ranks of American CEOs. If the federal-deficit crisis is going to be solved, the successor generation will have to solve it. If the nation's decline in competitiveness is to be reversed, the successor generation will have to reverse it. If the crisis in management is to be weathered, the successor generation will have to do it. If the erosion in real wages is to be stopped, they will have to stop it.

Through the sheer force of numbers, their movement into the work force represents the most important change in American organizations since the end of World War II. Of equal importance is the fact that women make up a large proportion of this work force, since more than two-thirds of the female baby boomers are either working at paid jobs or looking for work. As the most educated work force in the history of the world—46 percent have completed at least one year of college, compared to about 29 percent of those born before 1946, and more than five million members of the generation are still in school—their influence will undoubtedly be disproportionate to their numbers, and those numbers are already large.

What the large numbers of baby boomers mean is that for American organizations in the 1990s demography will be destiny. Organizations of all kinds will increasingly be faced with employees—as well as outside vendors, service providers, and many customers—who operate from the ambiguous dictates of an enterprise ethic that arises from an unquantifiable mix of optimism and fatalism, risk taking and resignation, meaning and mourning.

For a great many companies, the emergence of this new social character, operating from the enterprise ethic and working in the artisanal style of the artist manqué, is not necessarily good news because it does not inevitably mean higher profits or increased shareholder value, especially in the short term. Moreover, competing on the basis of quality is only one among many possible business strategies. And regardless of whether inherently good work pays off, it is certainly true that many American companies turn a tidy profit despite the relatively poor quality of their products. General Motors continues to enjoy huge earnings, though no one would accuse it of producing high-quality automobiles. In such companies, individuals who are interested primarily in quality are not only unlikely to thrive but are likely to be considered eccentric, at best, and obstructionist, at worst. Besides, says the hard-eyed realist, the primary purpose of General Motors is not to make cars anyway; it is to make money. But the question for the long run is whether General Motors will be making either.

Thus, in deciding whether to accommodate or resist this new social character, organizations—whether they know it or not—will be making perhaps the most fateful business decision they are likely to face in the decade to come. It is possible that some organizations would be better off without artificial persons, at least in the short term. But it is also possible that such companies cannot survive over the long term without them. Most cruelly, it is possible that some old-style organization-man companies can neither get along with them nor get along without them: They need such employees to survive in the new environment of global competition and an information-based economy, but the sudden influx of such employees would be so disruptive that the company could not survive anyway. Consequently, in the years to come, we are just as likely to see some of these venerable companies slowly expire attempting to resist the new reality as we are to see others of them go down in flames attempting to embrace those realities.

On the whole, it is probably wiser to risk going down in flames than to risk slow death, for to ignore or resist this new social character is apt to be fatal in the long run anyway. It is conceivable that an organization, exercising vigilance and tight control, could screen out such employees, bypass the important market segment represented by such a social character, and still survive for a while. Positioning or repositioning to ignore this market segment, or any market segment, is relatively easy. But screening out this kind of employee will be fraught with danger. First, it will mean lowering the educational level of the organization relative to competing organizations. Second, it will mean spurning the kind of personalities—autonomous, self-starting, antihierarchical—who are best suited to performing knowledge work. Third, it will mean a growing inability to understand and deal with the increasing number of outside vendors, service providers, and other organizations that are dominated by such employees. Fourth, those other organizations, vendors, and service providers will increasingly avoid doing business with such dinosaurs or, as one software vendor described them to us, "old-fart companies that are getting everything in triplicate while an opportunity disappears." Fifth, the more established such an organization's reputation for intransigence becomes in the 1990s, when companies that are not that way will be plentiful, the more difficult it will be for the intransigent company to attract such employees should the day come when the need for them is obvious.

Organizations that choose to hire or, as is much more likely, merely stumble into hiring exemplars of this new social character should, like some of the high-tech companies in Silicon Valley, understand clearly what they are getting and not getting. A comparison of the submissiveness and flexibility of the organization man, the organization offspring, and the artificial persons who are now emerging among the organization offspring helps, at the risk of oversimplification, to make it clear.

The organization man was malleable, but not adaptable (in the sense of being adept at seizing opportunities when conditions change). He made a great follower and a poor leader. He functioned best in noncompetitive situations requiring consensus and team play, such as the building of new communities and the running of mass-production-based, hierarchical organizations. Loyal to a fault, he worried little about authority or legitimacy, in effect regarding authority *as* legitimacy.

The organization offspring, living lives of personal artifice under the spell of the self ethic, are neither malleable nor adaptable. They make poor followers and poor leaders. They function best in solitary situations, competitive and noncompetitive alike, and when they find themselves in organizations, they tend to behave in ways that are purely self-interested, whether by single-mindedly pursuing their careers or by reserving their best energies for private life. Because they do not like being followers, they make good entrepreneurs in the start-up phase of an enterprise, but bad CEOs in the consolidation phase, when adaptability is called for.

Lacking loyalty in the conventional sense and wanting something to believe in as fervently as they believe in the authentic self, they either concede authority to the organization and withhold recognition of its legitimacy or seek to make the organization legitimate by conceiving it in their own image.

Artificial persons are not malleable, but they are adaptable. They make poor followers and poor leaders in command-and-control organizations. But in organizations with flat structures and permeable boundaries across functions, their adaptability allows them to perform in self-starting ways that are neither following nor leading, in the conventional sense. Because they are at home in networks and shifting relationships and because they value what they do over where they do it, they see any particular organization as only a temporary node in a larger network or as a subplot in a larger narrative—and they are always prepared to change positions in the network or find another subplot they feel more comfortable in. For them, legitimacy is an ongoing daily construction, and they are ever ready to heed its siren call—from whatever source.

Obviously, none of these social types is ideal for every situation. Artificial persons work well in network organizations—and the rise of such organizations is, in part, helping create this social character—but they also present problems even for such organizations. They are, as we have noted, difficult to lead, requiring for their care and feeding an optimistic/fatalistic style of leadership that few executives are capable of providing. Moreover, such organizations are, for all their permeability and lack of center, still carefully defined concentrations of resources and investment that require accountability in some form. If the ultimate goal is to increase shareholder value from quarter to quarter—and given the legacy of the organization man and the requirements of the securities laws, such is likely to remain the goal of many companies for the foreseeable future—then artificial persons may not be the best employees to accomplish it. On the other hand, in an environment of global competition, they may be ideal for adding value over the long run, but executives have a hard time seeing how they can do so when any such employee is unlikely to *be* there for the long run. It is another of the paradoxes that new-style employees present to leaders of organizations: As a leader, not only must you lead people who will not follow, but you must also depend for the long run on individuals who do not believe in the long run. It is difficult for shortsighted executives, steeped in the methods of professional management, to see how the only possibility for long-term survival could lie in such an inherently unstable work force.

For organizations, learning how to use these new kinds of workers effectively means taking seriously not only their valuing of their profession over their employer, but their desire to bring their work lives and their private lives into better balance. Having abandoned the lonely imperatives of the self ethic and recognized that their identities reside in connections to other people, they are increasingly less willing to immolate their families or other loved ones on the altar of work. They want and need more flexibility in their work lives, for two-job families make up 58 percent of all married couples with children, two-thirds of all mothers are in the work force, and more than half the mothers with children under age six work. While most members of the generation still stumble toward new roles for men and women, much of the burden of parents' overextended lives continues to fall on women. (Arlie Hochschild and Anne Machung calculate that women work "an extra month of twenty-four hour days a year" doing housework and providing child care.) How much longer these families can—or will—tolerate the resulting strains can already be seen in the alacrity with which many of our interviewees left for more flexible jobs or, like Scott Myers, simply created their own work situations.

Organizations could do a great deal to help parents integrate work and family life, but for the most part they continue to ignore the revolution sweeping over them. Ignoring such change might have been possible during the heyday of the organization man, for he dutifully obeyed the dictates of the organization, but his children will not. Both men and women of the successor generation are no longer willing to make a separate peace with their family or companionate life. They want a new balance in their compact with the organization—and they will walk if they don't get it.

But even if particular organizations and individuals in the decades to come reach some mutually satisfactory modus vivendi—the organizations making an acceptable profit, the ever-changing cast of individual employees finding satisfaction in their work—the larger question remains. Can this new American social character restore American competitiveness? If, as it is often said, innovation and creativity hold the keys to economic success in the new global marketplace, then the answer to that question may be found, again, by comparing the attributes of the organization man, the organization offspring, and the artificial persons who are now emerging among the offspring.

The organization man neither valued creativity nor was ever accused of possessing it. Indeed, a major thrust of Whyte's attack on the social ethic was directed at the assumption that the group is the source of creativity. In practice, argued Whyte, that assumption stifled individual achievement and resulted in a gray consensus that was inimical to creativity. So uncreative was the organization man seen to be in everything—from his philistine view of the arts to his conformist behavior—that his children would solve the age-old American status problem of intergenerational mobility by using creativity to measure the distance by which they had surpassed their parents.

For the children, creativity came to lie at the heart of their highly psychologized version of individualism. That is why clarion calls to greater creativity find such an enthusiastic audience, regardless of what creativity may concretely mean. For the offspring, creativity, as the agency of authentic self-expression, simultaneously creates and expresses the authentic self. Its real function in the psychic economy of the organization offspring is not to produce creative works, but to produce the self. Thus, the works matter far less than one's abstract sense of one's creativity. Moreover, the ideal of total originality—of the never-before-seen, one-of-a-kind creation—requires for its fulfillment in the public world the achievement of Nobel-quality scientific breakthroughs, Edison-like inventions, and genius-level works of art, things of which few people are capable. The only thing within easy reach that can fill such a tall order is the private self, easily the most complicated thing personally known to most people.

Given such a lofty notion of creativity, it is no wonder that most of the offspring, when it comes to the production of actual artworks, are paralyzed into inactivity or that in the more mundane world of everyday endeavor it is the abstract quality of one's inner, unknowable, and mysterious personal creativity that counts above all. It matters not what you do, as long as you do it with what amounts to a kind of smug mysticism about your self. These are two sides of the same coin: The inability to create in any real artistic sense and the necessity to live in the real world of mundane activity both tend to drive "creativity" further inward and further apart from what one actually does.

It is precisely this version of creativity that has been disastrous for American competitiveness. Disdaining the Japanese as mere imitators, Americans confidently expect to come up with something totally original that will leapfrog us ahead in the competitive race. Meanwhile, we go about our business as usual, each of us secure in our own sense of our creativity, the proof of which is our manifestly unique and complicated selves. The Japanese, by contrast, unapologetically imitate *and adapt* Western technology, and by a process of incremental, but steady, improvement in products, arrive at pioneering innovations. Testifying before the House of Representatives' Committee on Science, Research, and Technology, Harvey Brooks, of Harvard University, compared these two competing versions of creativity:

Successful imitation, far from being symptomatic of lack of originality, as used to be thought, is the first step of learning to be creative.
This is probably true of nations, as it seems to be of individuals,
something which Americans may have forgotten in our almost obsessive belief in originality and individual creativity. It may be only
those who try continually to reinvent the wheel that will lose out in
the innovative race. In my opinion, the United States, so long accustomed to leading the world, may have lost the art of creative
imitation, and is deficient in scanning the world's science and technology for potential commercial opportunities relative to what is done
by its competitors, particularly Japan.

For artificial persons, with their occupational anti-ideal of the artist
manqué and their artisanal style of working in which that anti-ideal is
realized, creativity means an attention to concrete creations, not to some
abstract quality of the self that hovers above such creations. This concrete and public sense of creativity not only frees them to do innovative
imitation, but liberates them from an isolated individualism that, by
definition, excludes creativity from collective endeavors. It does not,
however, represent a return to the organization man's faith in the group
as the source of creativity. The point is not that innovation arises from
the group but that in focusing on what is actually done, rather than on the
inner attributes of the doers, individuals are more likely to come up with
useful ideas and good work. Furthermore, artisanal workers' relative
indifference to where they practice their profession means that their
loyalty and commitment is not to any group for its own sake, but to what
that group can concretely accomplish. This attention to concrete accomplishments suggests not only that American companies will likely become more competitive in the world, but that their own intramural
competition for these "disloyal" employees will help make them so.

Thus, a strong possibility exists that this new American social character is the right one at the right time, though this is not the type of social
character envisioned by those who call for a return to American "greatness." This new social character—ambiguously enterprising, abandoning
a vacuous authenticity for a particular artificiality, held on course between subjection and subjectivity by mourning, and operating on a model
of the individual traditionally gendered as female—hardly fits the picture
of the hardy, self-reliant individualist of pre-organization-man days or of
the inviolable, creative authentic self that arose in reaction to him. So
strong, in fact, is the cultural legacy of isolated individualism, whether of
the rugged or the highly psychologized variety, that its value for the
purposes of economic competition goes almost unquestioned. As Edward
Sampson observes:

The core cultural values of freedom, responsibility, and achievement are all assumed to require self-contained individualism for their realization. In the current climate of worldwide economic competition, many have begun to question the strength of American character and to advocate firming up its individualistic base in order to make America more competitive in global markets. In other words, people have not challenged the centrality of self-contained individualism, but rather its failure to have been properly nurtured. The ensembled type of individualism is either not mentioned in these discussions about restoring American greatness or . . . is criticized for undermining those very qualities said to be central to our national success.

But prescriptive calls for self-contained individualism notwithstanding, the artificial person is, for better or worse, the kind of dominant social character we are likely to get. The real challenge of the coming decades will not lie in trying to whip such people back into shape, but in understanding them; not in trying to protect organizations from them, but in accommodating organizations to them; not in bemoaning the loss of authentic community, but in seeing how narratives of care may be humanely elaborated in a mobile and fragmented society that is likely to become more so. Then we may begin to restore American competitiveness as well as American compassion.

Notes

INTRODUCTION *The New Individualists: Authentic Selves and Artificial Persons*

2 *The Organization Man:* William H. Whyte, Jr., *The Organization Man* (New York: Simon & Schuster, 1956).

2 **"The corporation man":** Ibid., 3.

5 **when industrialism forced:** Michael Maccoby, *The Gamesman: The New Corporate Leaders* (New York: Simon & Schuster, 1976), 44.

6 **work in many fields:** The perspective of the present book is heavily indebted to John Demos and Elaine Spence Boocock, eds. "Turning Points: Historical and Sociological Essays on the Family, Supplement to *American Journal of Sociology* 84 (1978); Richard Easterlin, *Birth and Fortune: The Impact of Numbers on Personal Welfare* (New York: Basic Books, 1980); Glen H. Elder, Jr., *Children of the Great Depression: Social Change in Life Experience* (Chicago: University of Chicago Press, 1974); Frank Levy, *Dollars and Dreams: The Changing American Income Distribution* (New York: Russell Sage Foundation, 1987); and *Daedalus*, special issue devoted to the problem of generations (Fall 1978).

7 **concept of the life cycle:** Gail Sheehy, *Passages: Predictable Crises of Adult Life* (New York: E. P. Dutton, 1976).

10 **"contemporary body of thought":** Whyte, *The Organization Man*, 7.

10 **"a belief in":** Ibid.

11 **"our worship":** Ibid., 13.

11 **"If America ever":** Ibid., 396.

12 **Recognized in law:** The most cogent discussion of the metaphor of artificial persons may be found in James Oliver Robertson, *American Myth, American Reality* (New York: Hill & Wang, 1980), 183 and passim.

13 **"created a class":** Charles Francis Adams, "A Chapter of Erie," *North American Review* 109, no. 224 (July 1869):104.

13 **machines or predatory animals:** Robertson, *American Myth, American Reality*, 171–74.

13 **single individual intelligence:** Ibid., 177–78.

13 **"It is precisely":** Ibid., 178.

17 **Three historical character types:** David Riesman, with Nathan Glazer and Reuel Denney, *The Lonely Crowd* (1950; abridged ed. with 1969 preface, New Haven, Conn.: Yale University Press, 1969), 3–36.

19 **the other family:** *Harrison* is not their real name. In addition, a few minor details of their lives have been changed to disguise their identities.

CHAPTER 1 *The Passing of Organization Man*

29 **Liquid assets:** William H. Chafe, *The Unfinished Journey: America Since World War II* (New York: Oxford University Press, 1986), 112.

30 **cars increased 133:** Ibid., 118.

30 **1.5 million new homes . . . 1.4 million power lawn mowers:** Thomas Hine, *Populuxe* (New York: Alfred A. Knopf, 1986), 11.

30 **In 1957 the fertility rate:** Chafe, *The Unfinished Journey*, 123.

30 **13 million homes . . . 11 million:** Ibid., 117.

30 **"It was built":** "They Built Themselves a Hometown," *Pageant*, January 1952, 26.

32 **"one great and genuinely benevolent":** Quoted in Chafe, *The Unfinished Journey*, 142.

32 **"tenant agrees":** Philip S. Gutis, "Levittown, L.I., at 40: Once a Solution, Now a Problem," *New York Times*, September 21, 1987, B-6.

33–34 **"In studying an organization":** William H. Whyte, Jr., *The Organization Man* (New York: Simon & Schuster, 1956), 53.

36–39 **"On the one hand, suburbanites":** Ibid., 312.

44 **era of innovation:** Peter F. Drucker, *Innovation and Entrepreneurship: Practice and Principles* (New York: Harper & Row, 1985).

46 **only 15 percent of American families:** Figures are from an analysis of data from the U.S. Bureau of the Census by University of Connecticut sociologist Jane Riblett Wilkie cited in Alan L. Otten, "The Job Scene Drives Men From Families," *Wall Street Journal*, May 16, 1990, B-1. According to the *Journal*, "her analysis of Census Bureau data shows that in 1988 only 75% of working-age men were actually in the labor force, compared with 83% in 1960, and that the proportion of families with men as the sole wage earners had dropped to 15% from 42%."

46 **"One reason women take a deeper interest":** Arlie Hochschild with Anne Machung, *The Second Shift: Working Parents and the Revolution at Home* (New York: Viking Press, 1989), 7. Italics in original.

47 **he landed on a story:** Paul Leinberger, " 'Organization Man' Revisited," *New York Times Magazine*, Part 2, *The Business World*, December 7, 1986, 46–48, 96, 98.

48 **"people are fearful of saying"**: John Sculley with John A. Byrne, *Odyssey: Pepsi to Apple . . . A Journey of Adventure, Ideas, and the Future* (New York: Harper & Row, 1987), 125.

49 **"Be loyal to the company"**: Whyte, *The Organization Man*, 129.

49 **"the goals of the individual"**: Ibid., 129.

52 **"When you grow up"**: Harry Levinson, personal communication with Paul Leinberger, August 29, 1986.

52 **"There is a self-perpetuating mediocrity"**: John Kenneth Galbraith, personal communication with Paul Leinberger, August 29, 1986.

52 **"seen its standard"**: Steven Schlossstein, *The End of the American Century* (New York: Congdon & Weed, 1989), ix.

53 **"From the beginning of 1980"**: Amanda Bennett, *The Death of the Organization Man* (New York: William Morrow), 15.

53 **Firestone shrank**: Figures for all companies are from ibid., 165, 115, 136, 122, 118.

53 **25,000 mergers**: Ibid., 131.

53 **More than 100**: Calculation by Paul Leinberger.

53 **59 percent of all companies with 50,000**: Bennett, *The Death of the Organization Man*, 15.

53 **35 percent of all middle-management jobs**: Ibid., 15.

53 **"the corporate world is a cold, hostile war zone"**: Ibid., from the dust jacket.

54 **"entrepreneurial economy"**: "What is happening in the United States is something quite different: a profound shift from a 'managerial' to an 'entrepreneurial' economy." Drucker, *Innovation and Entrepreneurship*, 1.

54 **"small companies were the source"**: Cited in Bennett, *The Death of the Organization Man*, 232.

54 **more than two-thirds of jobs eliminated**: David L. Birch, "Here Comes the Neighborhood," *Inc.*, March 1990, 52.

54 **The Bureau of Labor Statistics reported**: Timothy D. Schellhardt, "Small Business Monitors Statehouses, Lobbies Harder," *Wall Street Journal*, May 9, 1990, B-2.

Chapter 2 *The Harrisons: Displaced Persons*

66 **capitalism's mechanism for converting**: This is a recasting, with a different emphasis, of Christopher Lasch's observation: "Bureaucracy transforms collective grievances into personal problems amenable to therapeutic intervention." Christopher Lasch, *The Culture of Narcissism: American Life in an Age of Diminishing Expectations* (New York: W. W. Norton & Co., 1979), 13–14.

67 **His children . . . came to be seen as "priceless"**: See Viviana A. Zelizer, *Pricing the Priceless Child: The Changing Social Value of Children* (New York: Basic Books, 1985).

74 **"The children"**: William H. Whyte, Jr., *The Organization Man* (New York: Simon & Schuster, 1956), 383.

90 **"DeLorean used Chevrolet's":** Ivan Fallon and James Srodes, *Dream Maker: The Rise and Fall of John Z. DeLorean* (New York: G. P. Putnam's Sons, 1983), 68.

92 *On A Clear Day:* John Z. DeLorean and J. Patrick Wright, *On a Clear Day You Can See General Motors* (Grosse Pointe, Mich.: Wright Enterprises, 1979), 32–48.

115 **domestic market share dropped:** John Holusha, " 'Cannibal' Peril for GM Sales," *New York Times*, October 9, 1987, D-1.

CHAPTER 3 *The Wealth of Generations*

119 **his annual cash compensation:** *Korn/Ferry International's Executive Profile: A Survey of Corporate Leaders in the Eighties* (New York: Korn/Ferry International, 1986), 19.

119 **55 to 65 enjoyed ... 65 to 75 possessed. ... 65 or older outstripped:** Anthony M. Casale with Philip Lerman, *USA Today: Tracking Tomorrow's Trends* (Kansas City, Mo.: Andrews, McMeel, & Parker, 1986), 157.

120 **72.4 million babies:** Exactly how big is the baby boom? In 1983, when *People* magazine did a detailed study of baby boomers' attitudes, values, and life-styles, it pegged the size of the generation at 75.9 million. Paul C. Light, in *Baby Boomers* (New York: W. W. Norton & Co., 1988), uses the figure 75 million. Phillip Longman, research director of Americans for Generational Equity, speaking in June 1986 ("Richer or Poorer: Will the Baby Boom Live Better Than Their Parents?" *Demographic Outlook '86* [New York: American Demographics Institute, June 4–5, 1986]), used the number 78 million. According to the U.S. Bureau of Census, the number of baby boomers has been growing since 1965 and will peak in 1993: "By 1965, all the baby boomers were born. But they weren't all here yet. That year, the generation was aged 1 to 19 and numbered 72.4 million. But immigration plays a part in population growth, especially among the young, and the baby boom grew to 76.4 million by 1980, when it was aged 16 to 34. The Census Bureau's new population projections show that the baby boom is still growing, and will peak at 78 million in 1993" ("The Boom is Still Booming . . .", *The Numbers News*, no. 3 (March 1989): 2; boldface in original deleted). In 1990, when baby boomers were aged twenty-six to forty-four, they made up 32 percent of the population (77.7 million).

120 **Landon Y. Jones:** *Great Expectations: America and the Babyboom Generation* (1st ed., 1980; New York: Ballantine Books, 1986), 180.

120 **relative earnings of college graduates:** Ibid., 179.

120 **labor force increased:** Both figures are from Denis F. Johnston cited in Richard Easterlin, *Birth and Fortune: The Impact of Numbers on Personal Welfare* (New York: Basic Books, 1980), 17.

120 **the younger fall farther behind:** Easterlin, *Birth and Fortune*, 22–23.

120–121 **A 1970s worker:** Frank Levy, *Dollars and Dreams: The Changing American Income Distribution* (New York: Russell Sage Foundation, 1987), 124–25.

121 **clearly in incomes:** figures on family income from Jones, *Great Expectations*, 3.

121 From 1968, . . . the median price: National Association of Realtors, personal communication with Bruce Tucker, September 1990.

121 $600 billion . . . inflation: Charles R. Morris, *The Coming Global Boom: How to Benefit Now from Tomorrow's Dynamic World Economy* (New York: Bantam Books, 1990), 107. Italics in original.

121 average down payment: "Home Ownership Found to Decline," *New York Times*, October 8, 1989, 32.

121 a 1990 report: "The American Dream is Becoming a Nightmare for Some," *The Numbers News*, 10, no. 9 (September 1990):1.

122 40 percent of young renters: Ibid., 1.

122 the average interest rate: All figures on interest costs and monthly payments are from "Home Ownership Found to Decline."

122 home ownership declined: All figures on the decline are from ibid.

122 a typical thirty-year-old man: Frank Levy and Richard C. Michel, "An Economic Bust for the Baby Boom," *Challenge*, March–April 1986, 33–39.

123 Intergenerational mobility: John Demos, *Past, Present, Personal: The Family and the Life Course in American History* (New York: Oxford University Press, 1986), 62; Glen H. Elder, Jr., *Children of the Great Depression: Social Change in Life Experience* (Chicago: University of Chicago Press, 1974), 172; Richard M. Huber, *The American Idea of Success* (New York: McGraw-Hill Book Co., 1971), 1.

123 As Richard Easterlin: Easterlin, *Birth and Fortune*, 39–44.

124 "an optimistic outlook": Ibid., 40.

125 Per capita income . . . 30 percent: J. Ronald Oakley, *God's Country: America in the Fifties* (New York: Dembner Books, 1986), 228.

125 10 million more home owners: Ibid., 236.

125 than rented them: Ibid., 236.

125 Ninety-eight . . . air conditioner: Ibid., 236.

125 Eighty percent: Ibid., 239.

125 20 percent owned: Richard Polenberg, *One Nation Divisible: Class, Race, and Ethnicity in the United States Since 1938* (New York: Viking Press, 1980), 130.

125 $6,500, as against $3,800: Jones, *Great Expectations*, 44.

125 real purchasing power: Ibid., 53.

125 nearly 60 percent: William Manchester, *The Glory and the Dream: A Narrative History of America 1932–1972* (Boston: Little, Brown & Co., 1974), 773.

125 55 percent rise: Ibid., 774.

125 abundance would wipe out: For a thorough discussion of the elaborate (and bankrupt) social thought that lay behind this belief, see Godfrey Hodgson, "The Ideology of the Liberal Consensus," in Hodgson, *America In Our Time* (Garden City, N.Y.: Doubleday & Co., 1976), 67–98.

125 The number of salaried white-collar workers: Chafe, *The Unfinished Journey*, 115.

125 During the same period: Ibid., 114.

125 The greatest growth: Ibid.

125 The number of scientists: Ibid.

426 □ Notes

125–126 The white-collar workforce in the chemical industry: Ibid., 116.

126 middle-class occupations surpassed: Manchester, *The Glory and the Dream*, 778.

127 41 percent of all nonfarm mortgages: Polenberg, *One Nation Divisible*, 131.

127 urban areas were redlined: Ibid., 132. See also Kenneth T. Jackson, *Crabgrass Frontier: The Suburbanization of the United States* (New York: Oxford University Press, 1985), 197–218.

128 $10 billion: Oakley, *God's Country*, 286.

128 $25 billion: Manchester, *The Glory and the Dream*, 724.

128 Between 1929 and 1933: Ibid., 33.

128 $2,300 in 1929 to $1,500 in 1933: Elder, *Children of the Great Depression*, 20.

128 the nonrural population: Manchester, *The Glory and the Dream*, 36.

128 Manchester recalls: personal interview with Paul Leinberger, August 29, 1986.

129 Using his work: Our own research, coupled with Elder's study (*Children of the Great Depression*), has led us to draw from his work conclusions about the long-term effects of the depression and postwar prosperity that do not agree in all particulars with those Elder draws himself. Elder is, of course, in no way responsible for the use we have made of his invaluable study.

130 strategies to cope: Elder, *Children of the Great Depression*, 25 ff.

130 studies of affluent children: Ibid., 71.

131 views of children: See Viviana A. Zelizer, *Pricing the Priceless Child: The Changing Social Value of Children* (New York: Basic Books, 1985), 5–6.

131 going to work with serious intent: Elder, *Children of the Great Depression*, 172.

132 family adaptations . . . explain: Ibid., 202–39.

133 happiest in marriage: Ibid., 237.

134 increase in the spiritual: Carl Degler, *At Odds: Women and the Family from the Revolution to the Present* (New York: Oxford University Press, 1980), 73–74, as cited in Zelizer, *Pricing the Priceless Child*, 9.

134–135 "But much as one must praise": "Women, Love, and God," *Life*, December 24, 1956, 36.

136 "point to a plowed field": Jerome Kagan, "The Child in the Family," *Daedalus* (Spring 1977), 43; as quoted in Zelizer, *Pricing the Priceless Child*, 220.

137 By 1950, . . . ten times faster than were central cities: Jackson, *Crabgrass Frontier*, 238.

137 For the entire decade . . . forty times as fast: Polenberg, *One Nation Divisible*, 129.

137 21 million: Thomas Hine, *Populuxe* (New York: Alfred A. Knopf, Inc., 1986), 23.

137 37 million: Chafe, *The Unfinished Journey*, 117.

137–138 Westerns on network television: All figures are from Alex McNeil, *Total Television: A Comprehensive Guide to Programming from 1948 to the Present*, 2d ed. (New York: Penguin Books, 1984).

138 **Titles:** John Keats, *The Crack in the Picture Window* (Boston: Houghton Mifflin Co., 1956); Richard Gordon et al., *The Split-Level Trap* (New York: B. Geis Associates, 1960); and David Riesman, "The Suburban Sadness," in William Dobriner, ed., *The Suburban Community* (New York: G. P. Putnam's Sons, 1958), 375–402.

138 **But the more sociologists studied suburbia:** See, for example, Herbert J. Gans, *The Levittowners: Ways of Life and Politics in a New Suburban Community* (New York: Alfred A. Knopf, 1967).

138 **Of the 21 million suburbanites:** William L. O'Neill, *American High: The Years of Confidence, 1945–1960* (New York: Free Press, 1986), 19.

138 **Of the 37 million suburbanites:** Polenberg, *One Nation Divisible*, 150.

140 **Initially progressive education:** The discussion of progressive education is heavily indebted to Diane Ravitch, "The Rise and Fall of Progressive Education," in Ravitch, *The Troubled Crusade: American Education, 1945–1980* (New York: Basic Books, 1983), 43–80; to Richard Hofstadter, *Anti-Intellectualism in American Life* (New York: Alfred A. Knopf, 1963); and, of course, to William H. Whyte, Jr., *The Organization Man* (New York: Simon & Schuster, 1956).

141 **"Everything the children learn":** Quoted in Whyte, *The Organization Man*, 386.

141 **"Ours is an age":** Quoted in ibid., 388.

141 **Dewey himself:** John Dewey, *Experience and Education* (New York: Macmillan Co., 1938).

141 **By 1953 . . . four books:** Arthur Bestor, *Educational Wastelands: The Retreat from Learning in Our Public Schools* (Urbana: University of Illinois Press, 1953); Robert M. Hutchins, *The Conflict in Education in a Democratic Society* (New York: Harper & Bros., 1953); Albert Lynd, *Quackery in the Public Schools* (Boston: Little, Brown & Co., 1953); and Paul Woodring, *Let's Talk Sense About Our Schools* (New York: McGraw-Hill Book Co., 1953).

142 **"The new school":** Ravitch, "The Rise and Fall of Progressive Education," 50.

143 **1940 to 1958, church membership:** *Yearbook of American and Canadian Churches 1988*, Constant H. Jacquet, Jr., ed. (Nashville, Tenn.: Abingdon Press, 1988), 262.

144 **In 1800:** Will Herberg, *Protestant—Catholic—Jew: An Essay in American Religious Sociology*, rev. ed. (New York: Anchor Books, 1960), 48.

144 **In 1990 . . . between 35 and 40:** Edwin S. Gaustaud, "America's Institutions of Faith: A Statistical Postscript," in William G. McLoughlin and Robert N. Bellah, eds., *Religion in America* (Boston: Houghton Mifflin Co., 1968), 123, fig. 3.

144 **The figures for 1989:** *1989 Yearbook of American and Canadian Churches* (Nashville, Tenn.: Abingdon Press).

144 **Church attendance:** Oakley, *God's Country*, 327.

144 **The value of such new buildings:** Herberg, *Protestant—Catholic—Jew*, 50.

144 **The Bible . . . 140 percent:** Ibid., 2.

144 **in 1954, only the Bible outsold:** Oakley, *God's Country*, 323.

144 **"context of self-identification":** Herberg, *Protestant—Catholic—Jew*, 23.

145 fundamental American values: Ibid., 72–98.

146 fifty-three percent . . . 1951 Gallup Poll: Ibid., 2.

146 A survey of Park Foresters: Whyte, *The Organization Man*, 367–68.

146 "Our government": Cited in Herberg, *Protestant—Catholic—Jew*, 84.

146 "The American believes": Ibid., 89.

146–147 "commandments for": Joshua Loth Liebman, *Peace of Mind* (New York: Simon & Schuster, 1946), 202.

147 proportion of young Americans: Wade Clark Roof and William McKinney, *American Mainline Religion: Its Changing Shape and Future* (New Brunswick, N.J.: Rutgers University Press, 1987), 69.

147 The scale of these defections: Ibid., 20.

147 10 percent per decade: Ibid., 21.

147 Though Catholicism . . . attendance at mass: Ibid., 21.

148 And studies showed: Ibid., 17.

148 Frances Fitzgerald: "Liberty Baptist," *Cities on a Hill: A Journey Through Contemporary American Cultures* (New York: Simon & Schuster, 1986), 121–201.

148 Tom Howell: not his real name.

149 seven thousand television sets: Oakley, *God's Country*, 97.

149 two hundred thousand per month: Manchester, *The Glory and the Dream*, 584.

149 By 1955, 88 percent: Ibid., 586.

150 And network broadcasts . . . "from nowhere": The phrase is from Edward J. Epstein, *News from Nowhere: Television and the News* (New York: Random House, 1973).

151–152 Thenceforth . . . ideological community . . . material community: The distinction is from Simon Frith, *Sound Effects: Youth, Leisure, and the Politics of Rock 'n' Roll* (New York: Pantheon, 1981), 50.

152 Much of its latent significance: See Bruce Tucker, "Tell Tchaikovsky the News: Postmodernism, Popular Culture, and the Emergence of Rock 'n' Roll," *Black Music Research Journal* 9, no. 2 (Fall 1989): 271–95.

CHAPTER 4 *The Nervous System: From Cybernetics to Psytopia*

154 "Sure, I can ground Orr": Joseph Heller, *Catch-22* (1st ed., 1961; New York: Dell Publishing Co., 1970), 47.

155 "exact scientific investigation": "Taylor's Testimony Before the Special House Committee" (January 25, 1912), in Frederick Winslow Taylor, *Scientific Management: Comprising Shop Management, The Principles of Scientific Management, Testimony Before the Special House Committee* (New York: Harper & Bros., 1946), 31. Taylor, who disliked the term *Taylorism*, denied that the activities of the efficiency expert were the "essence" of scientific management, though he did say "I believe in them" ("Testimony," 26).

155 "In the past": Frederick Winslow Taylor, "The Principles of Scientific Management," in Taylor, *Scientific Management*, 7.

156 "These specialized thinkers": Robert B. Reich, *The Next American Frontier* (New York: Times Books, 1983), 68.

157 "specialization by simplification": Ibid., 67.

157 As large organizations . . . implicit in this view of rationality: The discussion of these values is heavily indebted to Robert Weibe, *The Search for Order: 1877–1920* (New York: Hill & Wang, 1967), 133–63.

158 Managing the process . . . as Robert Weibe observed: Ibid., 154.

158 "The application . . . society of organizations": Peter F. Drucker, *Innovation and Entrepreneurship: Practice and Principles* (New York: Harper & Row, 1985), 15.

158 By 1962 . . . 169 of the 200: Robert J. Larner, "Ownership and Control in the 200 Largest Non-Financial Corporations, 1929 and 1963," *American Economic Review* 56 (September 1966), cited in Reich, *The Next American Frontier*, 71.

159 Wrote Wiener . . . "thus a field": Norbert Wiener, "Cybernetics," *Encyclopedia Americana*, international ed., vol. 8. (Danbury, Conn.: Grolier, 1988), 364.

160 "a society can be viewed": Jerome B. Wiesner, "Society as a Learning Machine," *New York Times*, April 24, 1966, advertising supplement "The Computer and Society," 15.

160 "What is at stake": John F. Kennedy, "Yale Commencement Address," *New York Times*, June 12, 1962, 20.

161 Between 1961 and 1966 corporate profits doubled: Godfrey Hodgson, *America in Our Time* (Garden City, N.Y.: Doubleday & Co., 1976), 248.

161 Bolstered . . . by 24 percent: Ronald Lora, ed., *America in the 60s: Cultural Authorities in Transition* (New York: John Wiley & Sons, 1974), 141.

161 In contrast, from 1950 to 1955, corporate profits: U.S. Bureau of the Census, *Statistical Abstract of the United States: 1968* (Washington, D.C.: U.S. Government Printing Office, 1968), 481.

161 But by the end of the 1960s: Lora, *America in the 60s*, 15.

161 "the biggest increase in economic concentration": Peter F. Drucker, quoted in ibid., 15.

161 The government grew: Statistics throughout this paragraph are from *Historical Statistics of the United States, Colonial Times to 1970* (Washington, D.C.: U.S. Bureau of the Census, 1976), 1100.

161 In 1966, 42 percent of Americans surveyed: Robert B. Reich, *Tales of a New America* (New York: Times Books, 1987), 202.

161 It was an era of good feeling: All statistics on confidence in business as expressed in ORC surveys are from Seymour Martin Lipset and William Schneider, *The Confidence Gap: Business, Labor, and Government in the Public Mind* (New York: Free Press, 1983), 35–39.

162 *"Not a single industry":* Ibid., 39. Italics in original.

162 Confidence in government . . . twenty percentage points between 1966 and 1981: Ibid., 78–85.

162 "Trust in government declined": Daniel Yankelovich, quoted in ibid., 15.

163 "A rising tide": John F. Kennedy, address in Frankfurt, Germany, June 25, 1963.

163 Hart found: William Greider, "Portrait of a Generation," *Rolling Stone*, no. 523, April 7, 1988, 35.

430 □ Notes

163–164 **"We are people ... social responsibility"**: Port Huron Statement, reprinted in James Miller, *Democracy Is in the Streets: From Port Huron to the Siege of Chicago* (New York: Simon & Schuster, 1987), 329–74.

164 **"There is a time"**: Mario Savio, quoted in Walt Anderson, ed., *The Age of Protest* (Pacific Palisades, Calif.: Goodyear Publishing Co., 1969), 61–62.

165 **"The most advanced areas"**: Herbert Marcuse, *One Dimensional Man: Studies in the Ideology of Advanced Industrial Society* (Boston: Beacon Press, 1964), 17.

165 **"virtually all the techniques"**: Charles Morris, *A Time of Passion: America, 1960–1980* (New York: Harper & Row, 1984), 29.

166 **this superrationalist**: David Halberstam, *The Best and the Brightest* (New York: Random House, 1972).

166 **"the data reveal"**: Lipset and Schneider, *The Confidence Gap*, 3.

166 **By 1968, more than two thousand high-ranking, retired military officers**: William Issel, *Social Change in the United States, 1945–1983* (New York: Schocken Books, 1985), 23.

167 **"Ordinarily I would be ashamed"**: Paul Goodman, quoted in Anderson, ed., *The Age of Protest*, 11.

167 **"We took it"**: Quoted in Myra MacPherson, *Long Time Passing* (Garden City, N.Y.: Doubleday & Co., 1984), 51.

169 **"The trouble with Eichmann"**: Hannah Arendt, *Eichmann in Jerusalem: A Report on the Banality of Evil* (New York: Viking Press, 1963), 253.

169 **"You have disrupted"**: Paul Goodman, quoted in Anderson, ed., *The Age of Protest*, 16.

169 **"We have learned lessons"**: Quoted in William Manchester, *The Glory and the Dream: A Narrative History of America 1932–1972* (Boston: Little, Brown & Co., 1974), 1055.

169 **"No doubt there are"**: Theodore Roszak, quoted in Anderson, ed., *The Age of Protest*, 19–20.

171 **By 1969 ... 50 percent**: Hodgson, *America in Our Time*, 330.

171 **The U.S. Public Health Service**: Manchester, *The Glory and the Dream*, 1114.

171 **by 1975 ... "angel dust"**: National Institute on Drug Abuse/University of Michigan Institute for Social Research, cited in *World Almanac and Book of Facts 1988* (New York: Pharos Books, 1987), 774.

171 **In 1970 less than 1 percent**: *Licit and Illicit Drugs*, (Mount Vernon, N.Y.: Consumers Union, 1972), 480.

172 **"disillusionment with the universalist"**: Michael Novak, quoted in Peter N. Carroll, *It Seemed Like Nothing Happened: The Tragedy and Promise of America in the 1970s* (New York: Holt, Rinehart, & Winston, 1982), 68.

173 **"For over a half century"**: Ralph Nader, *Unsafe at Any Speed: The Designed-In Dangers of the American Automobile* (New York: Grossman, 1965), vii.

173 **Calling the Corvair "one of the greatest acts"**: Ibid., 4–5.

176 **"We rely on quantification"**: Ralph Nader, quoted in William Greider, "Ralph Nader," *Rolling Stone*, no. 512, November 5–December 10, 1987, 118.

184 **"Who knows what women":** Betty Friedan, *The Feminine Mystique* (1st ed., 1963; New York: Dell Publishing Co., 1970), 364.

185 **the percentage of working married women with children under age 6:** "Mothers with Babies—and Jobs," *New York Times*, June 19, 1988, E-26.

185 **By 1965 . . . by 1970:** Ibid., E-26.

185 **In 1976 . . . *within one year* of giving birth:** "Working Mother Is Now Norm," *New York Times*, June 16, 1988, A-19.

185 **1,362 . . . 143 percent:** Sarah Hardesty and Nehama Jacobs, *Success and Betrayal: The Crisis of Women in Corporate America* (New York: Franklin Watts, 1986), 11.

189 **"These . . . are the needs":** Douglas McGregor, *The Human Side of Enterprise* (New York: McGraw-Hill Book Co., 1960), 39.

189 **"achieve their own":** Ibid., 49.

189 **Writing in 1981:** William Ouchi, *Theory Z: How American Business Can Meet the Japanese Challenge* (Boston: Addison-Wesley, 1981).

190 **"scientism":** William H. Whyte, Jr., *The Organization Man* (New York: Simon & Schuster, 1956), 23.

192 **"Man's desires":** Ibid., 35. Our account of the Hawthorne experiment draws heavily on Whyte's analysis (pp. 34–36) and Reich's insightful analysis in *The Next American Frontier*, pp. 73–74. As Reich observed: "Mayo did not draw the inference that production workers should actually be given more responsibility. . . . Instead, Mayo urged that professional managers and their staffs be trained in 'human-social' skills" (p. 74). See also, F. S. Roethlisberger and William J. Dickson, *Management and the Worker* (Cambridge, Mass.: Harvard University Press, 1939), for a full account of the Hawthorne experiment.

194 **"the clear starting point":** Thomas J. Peters and Robert H. Waterman, Jr., *In Search of Excellence: Lessons from America's Best-Run Companies* (New York: Harper & Row, 1982), 102.

195 **An early anticipation:** Eric Berne, *The Structure and Dynamics of Organizations and Groups* (New York: Ballantine Books, 1973), 7.

195 **A full-blown recent view:** F. R. Kets deVries and Danny Miller, *Unstable at the Top: Inside the Troubled Organization* (New York: New American Library, 1987).

CHAPTER 5 *The I of the Beholder: Organizations as Egos*

197 **The numbers are staggering:** Statistics on education throughout are taken from U.S. Bureau of the Census, *Statistical Abstract of the United States: 1990* (Washington, D.C.: U.S. Government Printing Office, 1990), 162. Percentage changes were calculated by Bruce Tucker.

198 **In the fifties and sixties . . . a pattern not starkly reflected:** Statistics and reasoning here are indebted to Frank Levy and Richard C. Michel, "Are Baby Boomers Selfish?" *American Demographics*, vol. 7, no. 4 (April 1985), 39–41.

199 **Adjusted for inflation . . . young families with incomes of thirty-five thousand dollars:** Ibid., 41.

199 **According to surveys:** Deirdre Carmody, "To Freshmen, A Big Goal Is Wealth," *New York Times*, January 14, 1988, A-4.

205–206 **inflation to become a way of life:** Inflation figures for 1974, 1979, and 1980 are from Frank Levy, *Dollars and Dreams: The Changing American Income Distribution* (New York: Russell Sage Foundation, 1987), 62, 65.

206 **OPEC increased:** Peter N. Carroll, *It Seemed Like Nothing Happened: The Tragedy and Promise of America in the 1970s* (New York: Holt, Rinehart & Winston, 1982), 131.

206 **the *rate* of increase is a crucial element:** Robert Heilbroner, "Hard Times," *The New Yorker*, September 14, 1987, 103.

206 **But from 1947:** Productivity figures for 1947 through the seventies are from Frank Levy, *Dollars and Dreams*, 48, 84.

206 **In 1979 . . . 1 percent per year:** Heilbroner, "Hard Times," 103.

206 **In 1990 . . . :** James C. Cooper and Kathleen Madigan, "The Consumer Has Seen the Future—And Gotten Depressed," *Business Week*, December 10, 1990, 22.

206 **In 1960, America was responsible . . . to 11 percent:** Robert B. Reich, *Tales of a New America* (New York: Times Books, 1987), 44.

206–207 **By 1980, 26 percent . . . less than 10 percent of each of these products:** Ibid., 121–22.

207 **By 1980, more than 70 percent of all American-made goods:** Ibid., 121.

207 **tension, inherent in the publicly held corporation:** For the classic statement of this tension, see Adolf A. Berle and Gardner Means, *The Modern Corporation and Private Property* (1st ed. 1932, rev. ed.; New York: Harcourt Brace Jovanovich, 1968).

208 **They ignore . . . interest costs now eat up:** "Deal Mania," *Business Week*, November 24, 1986, 93.

208 **As a result, by 1989 corporate spending on R&D:** John Markoff, "A Corporate Lag in Research Funds Is Causing Worry," *New York Times*, January 23, 1990, 1.

208 **"You can't be":** "Remaking the American C.E.O.," *New York Times*, January 25, 1987, sec. 3, 6.

209 **As the decade opened, about $100 million . . . $250 billion available:** Rick Gladstone, Associated Press, October 1988.

209 **500 companies:** Sarah Bartlett, "One Year After, The Market Lives But Matters Less," *New York Times*, October 2, 1988, sec. 3, 10.

209 **total value of all:** IDD Information Services, cited in Michael M. Lewis, "Japanese Takeout," *New Republic*, October 3, 1988, 19.

209 **$1.3 *trillion:*** "The Best and Worst Deals of the '80s," *Business Week*, January 15, 1990, 52.

209 **"never before":** Lee Iacocca with William Novak, *Iacocca, An Autobiography* (New York: Bantam Books, 1984), 327.

209 **"while most big":** "The Best and Worst Deals of the '80s," 53.

210 **During the 1980s, more than a million managers were fired:** Paul M. Hirsch, "So Much for Managers' Loyalty," *New York Times*, February 27, 1987, 27.

210 **nearly three hundred companies:** "The End of Corporate Loyalty?" *Business Week*, August 4, 1986, 43.

210 **All told, the number of managers discharged:** Claudia M. Deutsch, "Why Being Fired Is Losing Its Taint," *New York Times*, January 24, 1988, sec. 3, 1.

210 **Between 1976 and 1983 . . . firings doubled:** Robert B. Reich, *The Next American Frontier* (New York: Times Books, 1983), 162.

210 **During the same period, 15 to 25 percent of American executives:** Reich, *Tales of a New America*, 142.

210 **personnel experts:** Reich, *Next American Frontier*, 161.

210 **"loyalty is":** Hirsch, "So Much for Managers' Loyalty," 27.

210 **1986 *Business Week*/Harris poll:** "The End of Corporate Loyalty?" 42.

210–211 **Bill Thomas:** Not his real name.

211 **Of the twenty two new airlines, only 5:** Darryl J. Jayson, *The Structural Effects of the Airline Industry After Deregulation*, M.A. Thesis (New Brunswick, N.J.: Rutgers University, 1989), 25.

215 **"The income each person":** Milton and Rose Friedman, *Free to Choose: A Personal Statement* (New York: Harcourt Brace Jovanovich, 1979), 20.

216 **manufacturers of children's clothing:** The example is in ibid.

216–217 **"It is called the free enterprise":** Harold S. Geneen, "Free Association, Free Enterprise and Free Choice." Speech delivered before the Greater Hartford Chamber of Commerce, November 24, 1970. Reprinted in *Vital Speeches of the Day*, Vol. 37, no. 7, January 15, 1971, 221–24.

217 **"the results of its pooled efforts":** Ibid., 223. Italics in original.

217 **"The original antitrust laws":** Ibid., 224.

217 **"Much of the modern criticism":** James M. Roche, "The Competitive System: To Work, To Preserve, To Protect." Speech delivered to the Executive Club, Chicago, Illinois, March 25, 1971. Reprinted in *Vital Speeches of the Day*, Vol. 37, no. 14, May 1, 1971, 446.

217 **"Business is a game of risks":** John J. Riccardo, "The American Businessman: Agents of Social Change." Speech delivered to the Adcraft Club, Detroit, Michigan, March 12, 1971. Reprinted in *Vital Speeches of the Day*, Vol. 37, no. 14, May 1, 1971, 435.

218 **"I think it is":** Ibid., 435.

218 **"While I happen to believe":** Ibid., 435.

218 **The eighties began with:** Paul Solman and Thomas Friedman, *Life and Death on the Corporate Battlefield: How Companies Win, Lose, Survive* (New York: Simon & Schuster, 1982); Michael Meyer, *The Alexander Complex* (New York: Times Books, 1989); Wess Roberts, *Leadership Secrets of Attila the Hun* (New York: Warner Books, 1989); and Harvey Mackay, *Swim With the Sharks Without Getting Eaten Alive* (New York: William Morrow, 1989).

219 **"You can find no species":** Bruce Henderson, quoted in Solman and Friedman, *Life and Death on the Corporate Battlefield*, 37.

219 **"The growth of a large business":** John D. Rockefeller, quoted in Alan Trachtenberg, *The Incorporation of America: Culture & Society in the Gilded Age* (New York: Hill & Wang, 1982), 84–85.

221 **Schumpeter's classic account of the entrepreneur:** Joseph A. Schum-

peter, *The Theory of Economic Development* (Cambridge, Mass.: Harvard University Press, 1949).

221 *intrapreneuring:* Gifford Pinchott III coined the term and published a book by the same name, *Intrapreneuring* (New York: Harper & Row, 1985).

222 **Many who view . . . concede authority . . . and withhold legitimacy:** It could be argued that in a classic Weberian sense there is no such thing as authority—as distinct from coercive power—without some accompanying form of legitimacy. But as a practical matter, there are certainly degrees of legitimacy that individuals accord to organizations, and the *felt* legitimacy involved in the simple exchange of work for pay or experience or whatever can be extremely attenuated if not altogether nonexistent.

223 **the work of Max Weber:** H. H. Gerth and C. Wright Mills, translators and editors, *From Max Weber: Essays in Sociology* (New York: Oxford University Press, 1946), 196–264.

224 **"We are fairly sure":** Thomas J. Peters and Robert H. Waterman, Jr., *In Search of Excellence: Lessons from America's Best-Run Companies* (New York: Harper & Row, 1982), 82.

CHAPTER 6 *Personal Artifice: From the Self-Made Man to the Man-Made Self*

233 **For the self-made man, the emphasis:** Richard M. Huber, *The American Idea of Success* (New York: McGraw Hill Book Co., 1971), 93–106.

233 **Only about 5 percent:** William Miller, cited in Irvin G. Wyllie, *The Self-Made Man in America: The Myth of Rags to Riches* (New York: Free Press, 1954), 145–46.

234 **the bewildering range of choices:** On the "revolution in choices," see Robert Wiebe, *The Opening of American Society: From the Adoption of the Constitution to the Eve of Disunion* (New York: Alfred A. Knopf, 1984), 143–67.

234 **"impression management":** Erving Goffman, *The Presentation of Self in Everyday Life* (Garden City, N.Y.: Doubleday Anchor Books, 1959), 208–37.

234 **Instead, one took one's cues from:** David Riesman, with Nathan Glazer and Reuel Denney, *The Lonely Crowd* (1950; abridged ed. with 1969 preface, New Haven, Conn.: Yale University Press, 1969).

235 **Thus was introduced . . . called the cultural contradiction of capitalism:** Most notably in Daniel Bell, *The Cultural Contradictions of Capitalism* (New York: Basic Books, 1976).

236 **The evolution in American social character:** The discussion of self-help literature and the literature on success is indebted throughout to Huber, *The American Idea of Success*.

237 **Raymond Williams makes a useful:** Raymond Williams, *Keywords: A Vocabulary of Culture and Society* (New York: Oxford University Press, 1976), 136.

237 **Americans believed that they carried their natural rights intact:** Yehoshua Arieli, *Individualism and Nationalism in American Ideology* (Cambridge, Mass.: Harvard University Press, 1964), 90–180.

237–238 **"to the actual or imminent":** Stephen Lukes, *Individualism* (Oxford, England: Basil Blackwell, 1973), 26.

239 **Yankelovich estimates:** Daniel Yankelovich, *New Rules: Searching for Self-Fulfillment in a World Turned Upside Down* (New York: Random House, 1981), 3.

239 **One researcher found:** Stephen Tipton, *Getting Saved from the Sixties: Moral Meaning in Conversion and Cultural Change* (Berkeley: University of California Press, 1982), 176.

240 **"the 'giving/getting compact' ":** Yankelovich, *New Rules*, 8.

240 **Among nine such assumptions:** Abraham Maslow, *Toward a Psychology of Being*, 2d. ed. (New York: Van Nostrand Reinhold, 1968), 3–4.

240–241 **"promise a scientific ethics":** Ibid., 5. Italics in original.

241 **"the fully growing":** Ibid., 5.

242 **"As a people":** Carl Rogers, "Toward a Theory of Creativity," *On Becoming a Person: A Therapist's View of Psychotherapy* (Boston: Houghton Mifflin Co., 1961), 348.

243 ***"man's tendency to actualize":*** Ibid., 351. Italics in original.

243 **"You are the sum total":** Wayne Dyer, *Your Erroneous Zones* (New York: Funk & Wagnalls, 1976), 4.

246 **the triumph of the therapeutic:** See Philip Rieff, *The Triumph of the Therapeutic: Uses of Faith After Freud* (New York: Harper & Row, 1966); and Christopher Lasch, *The Culture of Narcissism: American Life in an Age of Diminishing Expectations* (New York: W. W. Norton & Co., 1979).

246 **the psychological society:** Martin L. Gross, *The Psychological Society: A Critical Analysis of Psychiatry, Psychotherapy, Psychoanalysis and the Psychological Revolution* (New York: Random House, 1978).

247 **As Richard Huber has reminded us:** Huber, *The American Idea of Success.*

247 **"the unequal distribution":** Ibid., 1.

247 **"It is not enough":** Gore Vidal quoted in *The Oxford Dictionary of Quotations,* 3rd ed. (New York: Oxford University Press, 1979), 556.

249 **"Learn in suffering what they teach in song":** Percy Bysshe Shelly, "Julian and Madalo," *The Poetical Works of Percy Bysshe Shelly*, ed. by Harry Buxton Foreman (London: Reeves and Turner, 1882), vol. 3, 127, 546.

249 **"writing . . . a vocation of unhappiness":** Georges Simenon, quoted in *The Writer's Quotation Book*, ed. James Charlton (New York: Penguin Books, 1981), 31.

249 **"Bohemian project":** Jerrold Seigel, *Bohemian Paris: Culture, Politics, and the Boundaries of Bourgeois Life, 1830–1930* (New York: Viking Press, 1986), 120.

251 **"One is an artist":** Felix Pyat, quoted in ibid., 17.

255 **Robert Bellah and his colleagues:** *Habits of the Heart: Individualism and Commitment in American Life* (Berkeley: University of California Press, 1985), 66.

256 **In the fluid world . . . to make individuals feel unreflectively:** Joseph Bensman and Arthur J. Vidich, *The New American Society: The Revolution of the Middle Class* (Chicago: Quadrangle Books, 1971), 121. The discussion of the

artificiality of middle-class life is indebted throughout to Bensman and Vidich, esp. pp. 119–57.

256 **there is nothing inevitable:** Ibid., 121.

256 **But this inherent artificiality:** Ibid., 137.

257 **irony, self-consciousness, and defensiveness:** Bensman and Vidich, *The New American Society,* 121–22, make this point about the middle class generally, but in the context of the larger argument here it is applied more particularly to the organization offspring.

257 **As Joseph Bensman and Arthur J. Vidich observed:** Ibid.

261 **respectability is a social bond:** Yankelovich, *New Rules,* 115–23.

262 **Dale Carnegie formulated explicit rules:** Cited in Huber, *The American Idea of Success,* 239–40.

262 **"may deceive himself and others":** David Riesman, with Nathan Glazer and Reuel Denney, *The Lonely Crowd* (1950; abridged ed. with 1969 preface, New Haven, Conn.: Yale University Press, 1969), 197.

263 **Consequently, the organization offspring have developed sophisticated personal styles:** These seemingly airy conclusions are based on hundreds of interviews, the cultural and historical evidence we have already adduced, and our own far-from-perfect self-knowledge as members of the generation under discussion. Of course, interviews of the kind we conducted encourage self-consciousness and self-absorption by the subjects. But the parents, when similarly interviewed, exhibited few of these traits, which suggests differences in personal style that cannot be accounted for merely by the form of the interview.

CHAPTER 7 *The End of Authenticity*

270–271 **"It is quite an eye-opener":** Ken Auletta, "The Bad Barrel," *Washington Monthly* 18, no. 11 (December 1986), 31.

271 **"During this decade":** James A. Michener, "You Can Call the 1980's 'The Ugly Decade,' " *New York Times,* January 1, 1987, A-27.

271 **Between 1979 and 1986, Dennis Levine's:** Dennis B. Levine, "The Inside Story of an Inside Trader," *Fortune,* May 21, 1990, 88.

271 **And in a three-year period:** James Kaplan, "Thy Brother's Keeper," *Investment Vision,* November–December, 1990, 31.

272 **By the end of the decade, consumer borrowing:** Robert Kuttner, "The Abyss," *New Republic,* October 29, 1990, 23.

272 **debt of nonfarm business:** Benjamin Friedman, cited in ibid., 23.

272 **the cost to taxpayers:** Sarah Bartlett, "Getting a Mental Grip on the Dimensions of the Savings Disaster," *New York Times,* June 10, 1990, sec. 4, p. 1.

273 **"Americans don't like":** Roy Blount, Jr., statement on the "Larry King Live" television program, Cable News Network, December 30, 1985.

273 **In the cover story:** "The Year of the Yuppie," *Newsweek,* December 31, 1984, 14–31.

273 **Hendrik Hertzberg observed:** "The Short Happy Life of the American Yuppie," *Esquire,* February 1988, 101.

274 **only 4 million earned $40,000:** "The Year of the Yuppie," 16.

275 **Beyond the covert sanctimony . . . an even uglier dimension:** That misogyny lay behind much Yuppie bashing was first suggested by Suzanne Westphal, private communication with Bruce Tucker, February 9, 1985.

275 **Fifteen thousand:** Christopher Ward, *Boom & Bust: The Rise and Fall of the World's Financial Markets* (New York: Atheneum, 1989), ix.

276 **Even if the baby-boomers:** Frank Levy, *Dollars and Dreams: The Changing American Income Distribution* (New York: Russell Sage Foundation, 1987), 25.

276–277 **During Eisenhower's two terms:** Ibid., 4.

277 **An average thirty-year-old man in 1956:** Ibid., 68.

277 **Before 1973, a thirty-year-old man:** Ibid., 80–81.

277 **In 1975 the median income:** Ibid., 9.

277 **average thirty-year-old white male lawyer:** Ibid., 127.

278 **In 1973 the top fifth:** Ibid., 22.

278 **"the dream expands":** Ibid., 6.

278 **"middle class":** Ibid., 206.

281 **Since 1970 the number of women having their first baby:** National Center for Health Statistics report July 5, 1989. Stephanie J. Ventura, "Trends and Variations in First Births to Older Women," *U.S. Public Health Service Vital and Health Statistics*, Series 21, No. 47 (Washington, D.C.: U.S. Government Printing Office, 1989).

281 **In 1988 alone:** Richard L. Berke, "Plans for Births Are Seen to Shift," *New York Times*, June 22, 1989, A16.

281 **the U.S. Bureau of the Census found . . . same group in 1975:** Ibid.

285 **"Indeed, throughout the advanced":** Peter Dews, *Logics of Disintegration: Post-structuralist Thought and the Claims of Critical Theory* (New York: Verso, 1987), xii.

287 **what English identifies as "dark blue" and "light blue":** Jonathan Culler, *Ferdinand Saussure* (New York: Penguin Books, 1977), 13.

287 **when we say *bed:*** Ibid., 19.

291 **"They put me":** M. C. Hammer, "They Put Me In The Mix," *Let's Get It Started*, Capitol Records, C1-90924, 1988.

293 **The road to postmodernism:** This account of postmodernism is indebted to Andreas Huyssen, "Mapping the Postmodern," *New German Critique* 33 (1984): 5–52.

294 **"learn to respond":** David Riesman, with Nathan Glazer and Reuel Denney, *The Lonely Crowd* (1950; abridged ed. with 1969 preface, New Haven, Conn.: Yale University Press, 1969), 25.

294–295 **"What is common":** Ibid., 21. Italics in original omitted.

295 **"The mass media":** Ibid., 84.

296 **"everything *real*":** Simon Frith, *Music for Pleasure: Essays in the Sociology of Pop* (New York: Routledge, 1988), 61. Italics in original.

297 **"pretty vacant":** The Sex Pistols, "Pretty Vacant," *Never Mind the Bollocks Here's the Sex Pistols*, Warner Brothers BSK 3147, 1977.

297–298 **"those that were . . . the most meaningful":** Simon Frith, "Video Pop:

Picking Up the Pieces," in Frith, ed., *Facing the Music* (New York: Pantheon, 1988), 90.

298 **"The advertisers don't":** Ibid., 90–91.

CHAPTER 8 *Nobody Home, Nobody Gone: The New "New" Suburbia*

301 **The Orange County Executive survey:** Jone L. Pearce, Director, Orange County Business and Economic Studies, Public Policy Research Organization, University of California, Irvine, *Orange County 1988: Executive Survey and Employment Forecast,* February 11, 1988. Reporting on the results of the *1988 Orange County Employment Analysis,* Professor Ralph Catalano, Program in Social Ecology, and *1988 Orange County Executive Survey,* June 22, 1988, Addendum, p. 1 and figs. 1 and 2.

301 **twenty-three years for CEO's:** Robert Mims and Ephraim Lewis, "A Portrait of the Boss," *Business Week,* October 20, 1989, 23.

302 **Sixty-five percent ... holding postgraduate degrees:** "Market Focus: Central Orange County," *Southern California Real Estate Journal,* June 6–19, 1988, 22.

302 **median commute:** Orange County Chamber of Commerce, *Fact Sheet,* 1988, unpaginated.

302 **82 percent of executives:** *1988 Orange County Executive Survey,* iii.

302 **Only 18 percent of the companies:** January 22, 1988 press release, *1988 Orange County Executive Survey,* 5.

302 **A large majority ... 3.7 employees:** "Market Focus," 22.

302 **twenty-seventh largest:** *Orange County 1988,* iii.

303 **"of the next generation":** William H. Whyte, Jr., *The Organization Man* (New York: Simon & Schuster, 1956), 267.

303 **"In suburbia":** Ibid., 267.

303 **"everything they do":** Ibid., 281.

303 **"tepid ooze":** Dwight McDonald, quoted in William H. Chafe, *The Unfinished Journey: America Since World War II* (New York: Oxford University Press, 1986), 142.

304 **six key factors:** Kenneth T. Jackson, *Crabgrass Frontier: The Suburbanization of the United States* (New York: Oxford University Press, 1985), 290–96.

304–305 **In 1950 ... 38 percent:** David Clark, *Post-Industrial America: A Geographical Perspective* (New York: Methuen, 1985), 59.

305 **In 1980, 40 percent:** Jackson, *Crabgrass Frontier,* 4.

305 **By 1987 ... 45:** "Patterns of Metropolitan Area and County Population Growth: 1980–1987," U.S. Bureau of the Census, *Current Population Reports,* Series P-25, No. 1039, cited in *Numbers News* 9, no. 9 (September 1989), 3.

305 **Yet manufacturing ... 30 percent ... 27 percent:** Clark, *Post-Industrial America,* 6–7.

308 **"Suburbia has become a childless landscape":** Barbara Defoe Whitehead, "Harder and Lonelier: A Working Paper on Young Parents" (unpublished, undated manuscript), 4.

308 "The service economy": Jonathan Schell, *History in Sherman Park: An American Family and the Reagan-Mondale Election* (New York: Alfred A. Knopf, 1987), 123.

308 "As if a cake": Ibid., 121–22.

309 The number of working women: Horst H. Stipp, "What Is a Working Woman?" *American Demographics* 10, no. 7 (July 1988.): 24–27.

309 as high as 90 percent: Ibid., 24.

309 28 percent of married women . . . 54 percent by 1986 . . . two-thirds of *all* mothers: Arlie Hochschild with Anne Machung, *The Second Shift: Working Parents and the Revolution at Home* (New York: Viking Press, 1989), 2.

309 National Restaurant Association: Peter Applebome, "Setting the Table for Kids' Cuisine," *New York Times*, March 19, 1989, F-4.

309–310 Similarly, most other household services . . . 1,150 centers by 1988: All statistics are from Francis Huffman, "Service Boom—No End in Sight," *Entrepreneur*, September 1988, 82–87.

310 In 1970, the service sector . . . by 1995 as many as 90 percent: Ibid. See also, James L. Heskett, *Managing in the Service Economy* (Boston: Harvard Business School Press, 1986), 1–4, 179–84.

311 Between 1978 and 1986 . . . 1.1 billion square feet: Christopher B. Leinberger and Charles Lockwood, "How Business Is Reshaping America," *Atlantic Monthly*, October 1986, 45.

311 "urban villages": Ibid., 44.

311 "edge cities": Joel Garreau, "Edge Cities,' *Landscape Architecture* 78, no. 8 (December 1988): 48–55.

311 "technoburbs": Robert Fishman, *Bourgeois Utopias: The Rise and Fall of Suburbia* (New York: Basic Books, 1987), 17.

313 managing time: See, for example, Roy Merrills, "How Northern Telecom Competes on Time," *Harvard Business Review* 67, no. 4 (July–August, 1989): 108–14.

314 "social class characteristically": Clark, *Post-Industrial America*, 19.

315 "high-innovation" city: David Birch, *Job Creation in America: How Our Smallest Companies Put the Most People to Work* (New York: Free Press, 1987), 135–65.

316 six-hundred-fold increase: Jone L. Pearce, *Orange County 1988*, iii.

316 "Not only in Irvine": Ever Jaques, quoted in Charles Lockwood, "California's Instant Metropolis," *America West Airlines Magazine* 1, no. 12 (February 1987): 20.

316 the median price for a single-family detached home: Orange County data from August 1988, California Association of Realtors. New York data from June 1988, National Association of Realtors.

317 $700 million in sales: Lockwood, "California's Instant Metropolis," 18.

318 "Most American housing is based on Levitt's model": Dolores Hayden, *Re-designing the American Dream: The Future of Housing, Work, Family Life* (New York: W. W. Norton & Co., 1984), 12.

318 three-quarters . . . two-thirds of that housing: Jackson, *Crabgrass Frontier*, 326.

318 "every true suburb": Fishman, *Bourgeois Utopias*, 5–6. See also, p. 117.

324 **"Park Forest probably":** Whyte, *The Organization Man*, 287.

324 **"then increases in real estate tax valuation":** Jane Steinmetz, ed., "All-American City Award" entry form, March 15, 1988. Submitted to National Civic League by the Village of Park Forest, Illinois.

324 **"Centre geared":** "Centre Geared to Community versus Mega-mall Mentality," *Park Forest Star*, August 30, 1987, C-1.

324 **"I think we've seen it come full circle":** Ibid..

325 **"With a stage for entertainment":** Ibid.

326 **lateral commuting now exceeds:** John Herbers, *The New Heartland: America's Flight Beyond the Suburbs and How It Is Changing Our Future* (New York: Times Books, 1986), 86.

329 **75 percent of them identified transportation:** Pearce, *Orange County 1988*; and *1988 Orange County Executive Survey*, fig. 6.

330 **2 billion hours:** Address by Elaine Chao, deputy secretary of transportation, to the Commonwealth Club of California, National Public Radio live broadcast, June 22, 1990.

CHAPTER 9 *Networks and Niches: Emerging Organizational Life*

335–336 **"For years, manufacturers":** Robert H. Hayes and Ramchandran Jaikumar, "Manufacturing's Crisis: New Technologies, Obsolete Organizations," *Harvard Business Review*, vol. 66, no. 5 (September–October, 1988): 77–78.

336 **"The PC, as it will evolve":** Quoted in William M. Buckley, "Computer Gurus Cast Their Eyes Toward Tomorrow's Hot Machines," *Wall Street Journal* centennial ed., July 23, 1989, A-15.

336 **"The standard desktop":** Mitch Kapor, quoted in ibid.

336 **"I would guess there will be":** Robert Noyce, quoted in ibid.

336 **research organizations optimistically predicted:** Regis McKenna, "Marketing in an Age of Diversity," *Harvard Business Review* 66, no. 5 (September–October, 1988): 91.

337 **"High technology obeys":** "Computing in the 1990s: With Bill Joy, John Hennessy, and Larry Tesler," *Upside* 2, no. 5, (July 1990): 21.

337 **"If you look back":** Ibid., 24. The original reads "has increased by 10,000" times, but he clearly means that the *speed* has increased and thus that the time it takes to perform functions like adding two numbers has *decreased*.

337 **"Certainly, I expect":** Ibid., 24.

337–338 **"But desktop publishing":** McKenna, "Marketing in an Age of Diversity," 93.

338 **"The odds-on thing":** "Computing in the 1990s: With Bill Joy, John Hennessy, and Larry Tesler," 18.

338 **"worldwide electronics industry":** Mel Phelps, "How Integrated Can You Get?" *Upside*, July 1990, 14.

338 **only 5 to 10 percent of all workers:** Peter F. Drucker, *The New Realities* (New York: Harper & Row, 1989), 188.

339 **those listed by . . . Harlan Cleveland:** *The Knowledge Executive: Leadership in an Information Society* (New York: E. P. Dutton, 1985), 19–144.

339 **"synergistic resource":** Ibid., 30.

339–340 **"Information is aggressive"**: Ibid., 32.

343 **Toyota . . . higher than that of General Motors**: *Fortune*, February 15, 1988, cited in Richard L. Nolan, Alex J. Pollack, and James P. Ware, "Creating the 21st Century Organization," *Stage by Stage* 8, no. 4 (1988): 8.

344 **"global networks of knowledge workers"**: Ibid., 5.

344 **"rich electronic communication"**: Richard L. Norton, Alex J. Pollack, and James P. Ware, "Toward the Design of Network Organizations," *Stage by Stage* 9, no. 1 (1989): 3.

344 **"things to thinking"**: Arno A. Penzias, quoted in Karen Wright, "The Road to the Global Village," *Scientific American: Readings for Managers* 3 (1990): 8.

344 **half *trillion:*** Charles R. Morris, *The Coming Global Boom: How to Benefit Now from Tomorrow's Dynamic World Economy* (New York: Bantam Books, 1990), 95. Italics in original.

344 **"We are built"**: John Sculley, "Building a Third Wave Organization," *Stage by Stage* 9, no. 1 (1989): 21.

345 **"The old way"**: Ibid., 23.

345 **"The focus shifts"**: Ibid., 19.

345–346 **"The computer offers"**: Nolan, Pollack, and Ware, "Toward the Design of Network Organizations," 3.

346 **Harlan Cleveland sees them**: Cleveland, *The Knowledge Executive*, 22–23.

346 **"The ultimate effect"**: Ibid., 25.

346 **"the yawning chasm"**: Lewis Branscomb, "Information: The Ultimate Frontier," *Science*, January 12, 1979, 143–47, cited in ibid., 25.

346 **"The two great"**: "Computing in the 1990s," 21.

347 **As Peter F. Drucker suggests**: "Playing the Information-Based Orchestra," *Wall Street Journal*, May 22, 1986, cited in Nolan, Pollack, and Ware, "Creating the 21st Century Organization," 6.

348 **As Ken Haven**: Personal communication with Paul Leinberger, August 10, 1989.

349 **"Instead of large, integrated companies"**: Morris, *The Coming Global Boom*, 62–63.

349 **"The process of global specialization"**: Ibid., 68–69.

349 **"As final product manufacturers"**: Ibid., 69–70.

350 **"relentless global competition"**: Ibid., xvi.

CHAPTER 10 *Artificial Persons: The Rise of the Enterprise Ethic*

355 **11.5 million American workers**: Barbara Ehrenreich, *Fear of Falling* (New York: Pantheon Books, 1989), 207.

355 **The real income of men**: Blayne Cutler, "Up the Down Staircase," *American Demographics* 11, no. 4 (April 1989): 41. Cutler cites "The Forgotten Half: Pathways to Success for America's Youth and Young Families," a report of the William T. Grant Foundation.

355 **black citizens living below the poverty line**: *Economic Report of the President* (Washington, D.C.: U.S. Government Printing Office, February 1985), 264.

357 **All cultures draw:** Edward Sampson, "The Debate on Individualism: Indigenous Psychologies of the Individual and Their Role in Personal and Societal Functioning," *American Psychologist* 43, no. 1 (January 1988): 15.

357–358 **In such "ensembled individualism":** Ibid..

358 **Most prominent among these alternative indigenous psychologies of self:** It cannot be emphasized enough that these psychologies of self are cultural, not genetic or biological.

359 **In some ways "middle-class society has become":** Christopher Lasch, *The Culture of Narcissism: American Life in an Age of Diminishing Expectations* (New York: W. W. Norton & Co., 1979), 67–68.

360 **different modes of "describing the relationship between other and self":** Carol Gilligan, *In a Different Voice: Psychological Theory and Women's Development* (Cambridge, Mass.: Harvard University Press, 1982), 1.

361 **"since the reality of connection":** Ibid., 172.

363 **artificial persons are *more* real:** The concept of persons being developed here—as subjected and subjective, as more particular and individual because they are located in a historical and cultural matrix—is deeply indebted to Harriet Davidson, *The Located Self,* in progress.

363 **"the inwardness of individuals":** David Riesman, with Nathan Glazer and Reuel Denney (1950; abridged ed. with 1969 preface, New Haven, Conn.: Yale University Press, 1969), xxviii.

364 **"the reaction to the loss":** Sigmund Freud, "Mourning and Melancholia," *The Standard Edition of the Complete Psychological Works of Sigmund Freud,* trans. James Strachey, Anna Freud, Alix Strachey and Alan Tyson, vol. 14 (1914–16) (London: Hogarth Press, 1957), 243.

364–365 **"Reality-testing has shown":** Ibid., 244. Italics added.

365 **"lost archaic object":** What is that lost archaic object? Were we dealing with actual personality here, instead of social character, we might suggest that it is the self of primary narcissism, when the infant, as Freud succinctly put it, "is his own ideal." Given the importance of narcissism in mourning, as described by Freud in his paper, a case could be made that the so-called narcissistic personality of our time might evolve into the mourning personality of our future.

367 The tabular list of characteristics ascribed to this generation is the authors' summary and interpretation of the following works: Michael Maccoby, *Why Work: Leading the New Generation* (New York: Simon & Schuster, 1988); D. Quinn Mills, *The New Competitors: A Report on American Managers from D. Quinn Mills of the Harvard Business School* (New York: John Wiley & Sons, 1985); Paul C. Light, *Baby Boomers* (New York: W. W. Norton & Co., 1988); Daniel Yankelovich and Sidney Harmon, *Starting with the People* (Boston: Houghton Mifflin Co., 1988); Cheryl Moser, *Grown-Ups: A Generation in Search of Adulthood* (New York: G. P. Putnam's Sons, 1987); Robert E. Kelly, *The Gold Collar Worker: Harnessing the Brainpower of the New Work Force* (Reading, Mass.: Addison-Wesley, 1985); Teresa Carson, John A. Bryne, and bureau reports, "Fast Track Kids: They're Smart, Impatient for Authority, and Willing to Take Risks," *Business Week,* November 10, 1986, 90–104; Walter Kiechel, III, "The Workaholic Generation," *Fortune,* April

10, 1989, 50–62; John Naisbitt and Patricia Aburdene, *Re-Inventing the Corporation* (New York: Warner Books, 1985).

368 **thirty-six-year-old Mike Lieberman:** Quoted in Tom Richman, "The Hottest Entrepreneur in America," *Inc.*, February 1987, 52–53.

368 **A similar declaration:** Quoted in Robert A. Mamis and Steven Pearlstein, "Walking Away From It All: Lotus's Mitch Kapor on Calling It Quits," *Inc.*, January 1987, 36.

371 **As the Rocky Mountains was displacing:** "The Gap in Regional Income Is Widening," *The Numbers News* 9, no. 7 (July 1989): 3.

375 **"Confronted . . . with a picture gallery":** Philip Rieff, *The Triumph of the Therapeutic: Uses of Faith After Freud* (New York: Harper & Row, 1966), 10.

379 **The roots of these problems:** Nancy Chodorow, quoted in Gilligan, *In a Different Voice*, 7–8.

379 **"unlike all the other terms of social organization":** Raymond Williams, *Keywords: A Vocabulary of Culture and Society* (New York: Oxford University Press, 1976), 76.

381 **Daniel Yankelovich:** *New Rules: Searching for Self-Fulfillment in a World Turned Upside Down* (New York: Random House, 1981), 244–64.

381 **a social movement:** Robert Bellah et al., *Habits of the Heart: Individualism and Commitment in American Life* (Berkeley: University of California Press, 1985), 286.

383 **"assertion, not of centralized sameness":** Linda Hutcheon, *A Poetics of Postmodernism: History, Theory, Fiction* (New York: Routledge, 1988), 12.

385 **ethical status we assign desire:** Yankelovich, *New Rules*, 247.

CHAPTER 11 *In the Spirit of the Enterprise Ethic: Organizational Life Reconsidered*

391 **"Design these days":** Quoted in Jane Fiske Mitarachi, "Harley Earl and His Product," *Industrial Design* 2 (October 1955): 52. Italics in original.

391 **"The reason for pushing":** Charles R. Morris, *The Coming Global Boom: How to Benefit Now from Tomorrow's Dynamic World Economy* (New York: Bantam Books, 1990), 34.

391 **"Cutting out a few":** Ibid., 33. Italics in original.

392 **Korn/Ferry . . . asked:** "Korn/Ferry International's Executive Profile: A Survey of Corporate Leaders," cited in *Korn/Ferry International's Executive Profile: A Survey of Corporate Leaders in the Eighties* (New York: Korn/Ferry International, 1986), 13.

392 **Forty-nine percent of the senior executives:** Lester Korn, *The Success Profile: A Leading Headhunter Tells You How to Get to the Top* (New York: Simon & Schuster, 1988), 46.

392 *Business Week* **asked the chief executive officers:** Robert Mims and Ephraim Lewis, "A Portrait of the Boss," *Business Week*, October 20, 1989, 25.

392 **"new entrepreneurial economy":** Peter F. Drucker, *Innovation and Entrepreneurship: Practice and Principles* (New York: Harper & Row, 1985), 7.

392 **"Most successful careers":** Korn, *The Success Profile*, 70.

392 **Korn/Ferry's survey:** Korn, *The Success Profile*, 71.

392 **average tenure . . . seventeen:** Ibid., 70–71.

392 **an average of twenty-three years:** Mims and Lewis, "A Portrait of the Boss," 23.

393 **"He's a fair representative":** "The Business Week Corporate Elite," *Business Week*, October 21, 1988, 27–28.

393 **"As a description":** Michael Maccoby, *The Gamesman: The New Corporate Leaders* (New York: Simon & Schuster, 1976), 35. William H. Whyte, Jr., immediately responded to Maccoby: "Your description of *The Organization Man* and the outlook of its author leaves me incredulous. . . . You say I didn't recognize 'the jungle fighter' in the entrepreneur. No I didn't. Your book had not been written yet so your typology was not available to me. With other words, however, I did say a good bit about entrepreneurs and aggressors. I wrote a whole chapter about a school for aggressors—the Vicks School for Applied Merchandising—for it was a classic expression of the old dog-eat-dog approach. If you think I wrote the chapter in praise of such rugged individualism, you are impervious to irony." Private correspondence from William H. Whyte, Jr., to Michael Maccoby, September 2, 1976.

394 **"Reports of the death":** Jerry Buckley, "The New Organization Man," *U.S. News & World Report,* January 16, 1989, 42.

394 **"Just as such large companies":** Ibid., 42.

394 **The magazine found strong evidence:** Ibid., 42–43.

394 **"A little suffering":** Quoted in ibid., 45.

395 **"You either go along":** Quoted in ibid., 46.

395 **"Despite the current mythology":** Quoted in "Organization Man: Very Much Alive," *Business Week*, November 10, 1986, 92.

395–396 **"In 1975, America's machine":** Morris, *The Coming Global Boom*, 7–8.

396 **federal deficit totaled:** Benjamin M. Friedman, *Day of Reckoning: The Consequences of American Economic Policy Under Reagan and After* (New York: Random House, 1988), 132.

396 **When Ronald Reagan . . . 2.6 trillion:** Ibid., 19.

396 **seven hundred thousand functional illiterates:** David T. Kearns, "Business, Economics and the Oval Office," *Harvard Business Review* 66, no. 6 (November–December, 1988): 70.

396 **Forty-eight percent of the patents:** Edmund L. Andrews, "A Foreign Push for U.S. Patents," *New York Times*, June 4, 1989, 4-F.

396 **real hourly wages:** Max Holland, *When the Machine Stopped: A Cautionary Tale from Industrial America* (Boston: Harvard Business School Press, 1989), uncorrected proof, p. 263.

396 **"The managerial orientation":** Abraham Zaleznik, *The Managerial Mystique: Restoring Leadership in Business* (New York: Harper & Row, 1989), 29.

396–397 **"The dominant intellectual error":** Morris, *The Coming Global Boom*, 58.

398 **"Knowledge workers know":** Peter F. Drucker, *The New Realities* (New York: Harper & Row, 1989), 181.

398 **"only in a genuine":** Ibid., 95.

399 **"Now we are managing people":** Peter F. Drucker, "The Coming of the New Organization," *Harvard Business Review* 66, no. 1 (January–February 1988): 50. See also Drucker, *The New Realities*.

400 **"Key employees don't care":** Kenneth Oshman, quoted in Andre L. Desbecq and Joseph Weiss, "The Business Culture of Silicon Valley: Is It a Model for the Future?" in Jerald Hage, ed., *Futures of Organizations: Innovating to Adapt Strategy and Human Resources to Rapid Technological Change* (Lexington, Mass.: Lexington Books, 1988), 136.

400 **"In an unusual case":** Andrew Pollack, "From Apple to Sun, and Now Back Again," *New York Times*, June 16, 1989, C-5.

400–401 **"One of the realities":** Kenneth Oshman, quoted in Desbecq and Weiss, "The Business Culture of Silicon Valley," 135.

404–405 **"Every age":** Paul Hawken, "Coming of Age," *Inc.*, April, 1989, 60.

407 **As Peter Clecak points out:** In *America's Quest for the Ideal Self: Dissent and Fulfillment in the 60s and 70s* (New York: Oxford University Press, 1983), 283.

408 **a process of recovery to complement techniques of suspicion:** Paul Ricoeur distinguishes between a hermeneutics of suspicion and a hermeneutics of recovery in *Freud and Philosophy: An Essay on Interpretation*, trans. Denis Savage (New Haven: Yale University Press, 1970), 27–36.

411 **"At a small company":** Donald Povesjil, quoted in Hawken, "Coming of Age," 42.

412 **two-thirds of the female baby boomers:** "The Baby Boom Generation" (Washington, D.C.: American Council of Life Insurance and Health Insurance Association of America, 1983), 17, cited in Daniel Yankelovich and Sidney Harman, *Starting with the People* (Boston: Houghton Mifflin Co., 1988), 238.

416 **two-job families:** all statistics from Arlie Hochschild with Anne Machung, *The Second Shift: Working Parents and the Revolution at Home* (New York: Viking Press, 1989), 2.

416 **Arlie Hochschild calculated:** Ibid., 3.

418 **"Successful imitation":** Harvey Brooks, quoted in James C. Abegglen and George Stalk, Jr., *Kaisha: The Japanese Corporation* (New York: Basic Books, 1985), 146.

419 **"The core cultural values":** Edward E. Sampson, "The Debate on Individualism: Indigenous Psychologies of the Individual and their Role in Personal and Societal Functioning," *American Psychologist*, vol. 43, no. 1 (January 1988), 19.

Index

447